SCIENCE IN THE KITCHEN
AND THE ART OF EATING WELL

Pellegrino Artusi
With a new introduction by Luigi Ballerini

First published in 1891, Pellegrino Artusi's *La scienza in cucina e l'arte di mangiar bene* has come to be recognized as the most significant Italian cookbook of modern times. It was reprinted thirteen times and had sold more than 52,000 copies in the years before Artusi's death in 1910, with the number of recipes growing from 475 to 790. And while this figure has not changed, the book has consistently remained in print.

Although Artusi was himself of the upper classes and it was doubtful he had ever touched a kitchen utensil or lit a fire under a pot, he wrote the book not for professional chefs, as was the nineteenth-century custom, but for middle-class family cooks: housewives and their domestic helpers. His tone is that of a friendly advisor – humorous and nonchalant. He indulges in witty anecdotes about many of the recipes, describing his experiences and the historical relevance of particular dishes.

Artusi's masterpiece is not merely a popular cookbook; it is a landmark work in Italian culture. This English edition features a delightful introduction by Luigi Ballerini that traces the fascinating history of the book and explains its importance in the context of Italian history and politics. The illustrations are by the noted Italian artist Giuliano Della Casa.

(The Lorenzo Da Ponte Italian Library)

LUIGI BALLERINI is a professor in the Department of Italian at the University of California, Los Angeles.

PELLEGRINO ARTUSI

Science in the Kitchen
and the Art of Eating Well

Foreword by Michele Scicolone
Introduction by Luigi Ballerini
Translated by Murtha Baca and Stephen Sartarelli

UNIVERSITY OF TORONTO PRESS
Toronto Buffalo London

The Lorenzo Da Ponte Italian Library
©University of Toronto Press 2003
Introduction ©Luigi Ballerini
Toronto Buffalo London
Printed in the U.S.A.

Reprinted 2004, 2006, 2007, 2009, 2011, 2014

ISBN 0-8020-8704-3 (cloth)
ISBN 0-8020-8657-8 (paper)
First published in Italian as *La scienza in cucina e l'arte di mangiar bene*

This English translation first published by Marsilio Publishers in 1997 as *Science in the Kitchen and the Art of Eating Well*

Printed on acid-free paper

The Lorenzo Da Ponte Italian Library

National Library of Canada Cataloguing in Publication

Artusi, Pellegrino
Science in the kitchen and the art of eating well / Pellegrino
Artusi ; translated by Murtha Baca and Stephen Sartarelli ; foreword
by Michele Scicolone ; introduction by Luigi Ballerini.

Translation of: La scienza in cucina e l'arte di mangiar bene.
ISBN 0-8020-8704-3 (bound). ISBN 0-8020-8657-8 (pbk.)

1. Cookery, Italian.   I. Baca, Murtha   II. Sartarelli, Stephen, 1954–
III. Title.

TX723.A7713 2004   641.5945   C2003-906316-X

This volume is published under the aegis and with the financial assistance of:
Fondazione Cassamarca, Treviso; Ministero degli Affari Esteri, Direzione Generale per
la Promozione e la Cooperazione Culturale; Ministero per i Beni e le Attività
Culturali, Direzione Generale per i Beni Librari e gli Istituti Culturali, Servizio
per la promozione del libro e della lettura.

Publication of this volume is assisted by the Istituto Italiano di Cultura, Toronto.

University of Toronto Press acknowledges the financial assistance to its
publishing program of the Canada Council for the Arts and the
Ontario Arts Council.

University of Toronto Press acknowledges the financial support for its
publishing activities of the Government of Canada through the
Book Publishing Industry Development Program (BPIDP).

For *Teresa Santi,* who made an unsurpassable minestrone,
and *Cesare Santi,* who always ate it cold in the middle of the night.

TABLE OF CONTENTS

Illustrations by Guiliano Della Casa following pages 116, 180, 212, 308, 340, 468, and 532

viii

FOREWORD

La scienza in cucina e l'arte di mangiar bene is 110 years old, yet around the world Pellegrino Artusi's cookbook is as popular as ever. In Italy, the book is revered, and few home are without at least one stained and tattered copy, passed down like a family heirloom from mother to daughter. With hundreds of new cookbooks published every year, it is remarkable that one more than a century old has survived. Yet, there are many reasons for its longevity.

At the time it was published in 1891, *Scienza in cucina* was the first cookbook written in Italian for the home cook. Other cookbooks of the era typically were written by French-trained chefs who either wrote in French or focused on French cooking. Their works were geared towards other professionals employed in wealthy homes.

Scienza in cucina was the first book accessible to those who could read only Italian. It especially appealed to the newly emerging middle class. Wives and mothers ran the household and prepared the family meals, sometimes with the assistance of a cook or another servant or two. Neither the housewives nor their cooks were highly trained, and their families were accustomed to simple, uncomplicated meals, as opposed to formal and elaborate French fare. Artusi's book helped them to expand their repertoire of recipes and further educated them about topics as varied as manners, nutrition, and culinary technique. He made the book pleasing to his unique audience, dedicating one recipe to the "ladies with delicate and sophisticated tastes" and at times flattering them with compliments on their beauty and good sense.

In the century since its publication, *Scienza in cucina* has been copied and interpreted by many other authors. It was not until the 1960s and 1970s, when Italy became a vacation and study destination for millions of travellers, especially from North America, that food writers began to delve more deeply into Italian regional cuisines and elaborate on recipes and ideas first proposed by Artusi. Despite the wealth of information about Italian food available today, Artusi's work remains vital.

Leafing through the book, the reader is both entertained and informed. It is the culinary equivalent of browsing the internet or leafing through an encyclopedia – the reader discovers something new and fascinating every time. Artusi shares titbits of information, such as the fact that certain fish, including red mullets, makes noises by expelling air as they swim. There are intriguing recipes to try, such as egg yolks canapé style, in which the yolks are tucked into slices of toast, sauced, and finally baked, and inspiring stories to read and enjoy, such as the one describing how chicken Marengo was invented by Napoleon's desperate chef.

The recipes in *Scienza in cucina* have withstood the test of time and rarely seem dated or outmoded. Ricotta cake, saltimbocca, and frittatas are as familiar and as easily prepared and enjoyed today as they were 100 years ago. Few restaurants that claim to be Italian would be without Bolognese-style ragu, ravioli filled with meat or cheese, pasta with beans, risotto, and roasted and stewed meats on the menu, all of which can be found in *Scienza in cucina*. Though Artusi would never have imagined it, his recipes continue to be used by cooks the world over who appreciate Italian home cooking.

In his introduction, Artusi states that he is an amateur who has collected these recipes over the course of the years, and that his readers, with a little practice, can achieve impressive results if they heed his advice. Throughout the book, Artusi reassures the reader and boosts his or her confidence. With regard to apple strudel, Artusi declares: "Do not be alarmed if this dessert looks like some ugly creature such as a giant leech or a shapeless snake after you cook it; you will like the way it tastes" (p. 388 below).

His writing style is relaxed and never pedantic. The recipes, together with the headnotes and commentary, are more like a conversation with a favorite uncle, who happens to be a knowledgeable cook, rather than a mere listing of ingredients and instructions.

At several points, he states that his recipes are easy to do, even when they really are not. For a jelly roll cake, which Artusi dubs "sweet English salami," he writes: "This cake, which could more properly be called sponge cake with filling, makes a handsome sight in the windows of confectioners' shops. To those untrained in the art of baking, it might seem to be a very fancy dish, but it really isn't at all difficult to make" (p. 434). His confident, casual tone is infectious, and the reader feels encouraged to proceed. Regarding meatballs, Artusi says: "Do not think for a moment that I would be so pretentious as to tell you how to make meatballs. This is a dish that everybody knows how to make, beginning with the jackass" (p. 238). His cooking techniques are sound, and the book is full of helpful hints: how to use a rosemary branch to baste roasting lamb, and how to cook garlic properly so that it does not turn bitter.

Though the author is often vague in stating exact quantities of ingredients, pan sizes, cooking times, and temperatures, he teaches readers to think and reason out what they are doing as opposed to slavishly following overly precise instructions. By contrast, many of today's cookbook authors are so exacting as to tell their readers to expect utter failure if they use the wrong shape of pasta, the wrong kind of pot or even – heaven forbid – stir their ingredients in the wrong direction. Their dear Uncle Pellegrino makes no such demands. For anyone with a modicum of experience in the kitchen, Artusi's way can expand the readers' creativity by making them think about what and how they are cooking.

This technique is not always successful, however. A truly novice cook will occasionally need more directions than Artusi offers. For example, Artusi assumes the reader knows how to make fresh pasta. In recipes for tortellini, tagliatelle, cappelletti, and the like, he simply calls for a "dough."

No matter how serious his subject, Artusi writes with personality, charm, warmth, humor, and wit. Indeed, if Artusi were alive today, he would surely be the star of a popular cooking show on television. He laced *Scienza in cucina* with anecdotes about people who, while largely unknown to readers a hundred years later, inevitably resemble someone they know. Some of these stories are downright gossipy, like the tale of the miserly Romagnan count who stuffed himself every other day at a hotel's buffet table and fasted on alternate days to save a few pennies. Others are simply amusing, like that of the nosey priest known as "Don Pomodoro" because, like the tomato, he gets into everything. These characters are timeless and we might recognize some of the same traits in a neighbor or acquaintance. Who among us cannot relate to Artusi's story wherein a cook is faced with the dilemma of planning a menu for an assemblage of very fussy guests? His employer informs him that one guest does not eat fish and cannot even abide its odor nearby, while another despises vanilla. Spices, almonds, lamb, prosciutto and other pork products, beef, cabbage, and potatoes are also banned. The perplexed cook walks away shaking his head with no idea what to do. If he had consulted *Scienza in cucina* he would have found that the author suggests menus for just about every occasion.

Artusi's readers have changed in many significant ways, but the book remains timely because the author focuses on simple things that do not change. He offers recipes for both economical meals and celebrations, dishes to please children, and others to nurture someone who is not feeling well. He worries frequently about his digestion and recommends and condemns certain foods based on whether or not they are "windy."

Artusi engages his readers personally. He often writes in the second person, directly addressing the reader. He asks questions as if he expects an answer: "What trick do you suppose he [the aforementioned Romagnan count] found to maintain such a façade while spending little?" asks Artusi before revealing the end of his story (83). Of course, the reader has no idea of the answer, and can't help but be drawn in and read on.

Over the years critics have attacked *Scienza in cucina* for including recipes as typical of French cuisine as of Italian. Artusi was a native of Emilia-Romagna in northern Italy and was accustomed to a cooking style that was closer to the French – especially with regard to its use of butter, meat, and cream – than southern Italian cooking, which is more reliant on vegetables, fish, and olive oil. Any cookbook, no matter how scrupulous the author is about authenticity, reflects his or her personal taste. Furthermore, the worldly Giuseppe Garibaldi, who led his thousand "Red Shirt" troops across Italy to bring about its unification, is often quoted as saying, "It will be spaghetti, I swear to you, that unifies Italy." If he was correct that the acceptance in the northern regions of this staple food of the South helped to bring a common thread to the twenty disparate regions that became one nation, then we must credit Pellegrino Artusi for having provided the recipe.

Italian cooking has never been more popular than it is today. While chefs in high-priced restaurants experiment with fusion food and exotic ingredients from around the globe, *Scienza in cucina* can be relied upon for the kind of classic Italian fare that needs no explanation and is always pleasing. People today have less time to spend in the kitchen and fewer skills to devote to preparing meals: they need a guide that they can trust.

With the publication *La scienza in cucina e l'arte di mangiar bene* in its complete form in English, Artusi's masterpiece will become accessible to a whole new audience.

MICHELE SCICOLONE

INTRODUCTION: *A* as in Artusi, *G* as in Gentleman and Gastronome

Luigi Ballerini

In love, the *beforehand* is either an itch that hurts or a hurricane that topples trees and ruins crops. The *meanwhile* is ever so sweet, but, alas, it does not last very long. I am not one to agree with the French Epicurean who say that *it lasts only for the time it takes to swallow an egg*, but I must confess, nonetheless, that the meanwhile can be measured not in days, nor in hours, but in seconds on the hands of a watch.

Afterwards is at times tart, at other times bitter: in the most fortunate cases it is a wearisome state, in other words, a kind of tiredness. In the most unhappy cases, which are rather frequent, it is like pain or regret, or both.

With food instead, the *beforehand* is delicious, the *meanwhile* more delicious, and the *afterwards* more delicious still.

Paolo Mantegazza, *In Praise of Old Age*

In 1910, upon reaching its fourteenth edition (the last to be printed under the author's direct supervision), Pellegrino Artusi's *La scienza in cucina e l'arte di mangiar bene* began to be recognized as the most significant Italian cookbook of modern times. Since its first appearance in 1891, it had sold 46,000 copies. The first run of the fourteenth edition would bring the total number of books printed and sold to the surprising figure of 52,000.[1]

A success of this magnitude – or any success at all, for that matter – could not be anticipated from either the dismissive early assessment of the manuscript by a friend of the author's, or the rejection by the "well known" Florentine publishing house to which Artusi, "dismayed but not entirely convinced" by his friend's opinion, had turned in the hope of seeing his book in print. Rebuffed, Artusi printed and marketed the book at his own expense, but initial sales were discouragingly slow.

In a new item added to the 1902 edition, and revealingly entitled "The Story of a Book That Is a Bit Like the Story of Cinderella," Artusi himself provides a fairly amusing chronicle of the early difficulties the book encountered.[2] We learn that, after turning down the offer of a second publisher – who had asked for a monetary contribution of "two hundred lire ... and the surrender of all royalties" – and being dismissed by a Milanese publisher, who sniffed that "We do not deal in cookbooks," Artusi engaged the services of the Florentine typographer Salvatore Landi and proceeded to print the work at his "own risk and peril."

In addition to the rather effervescent and somewhat self-indulgent assertions of Artusi, the early life of the book has been carefully reconstructed by Gian Enrico Venturini in his essay "Storia (del successo) di un libro."[3] The documents he examined (and made public) in the Municipal Archives of Forlimpopoli (Artusi's hometown) reveal, among other things, that while Landi continued to print *Scienza in cucina*,[4] the Florence-based publisher R. Bemporad & Figlio took charge of its national distribution beginning with the fifth edition.[5] It was due largely to this company's efforts that the book's impact turned from a snowball into an avalanche. Artusi was quick to recognize Bemporad's contribution. The concluding paragraph of his 1902 note on the book's fortunes reads as follows: "Let me close, then, with a well-deserved tribute and expression of thanks to the publishing house of R. Bemporad & Son of Florence, who made every effort to bring this manual of mine to the knowledge of the public and to disseminate it."[6]

Eventually Bemporad became the official publisher of the book,[7] and from that moment the kitchen bookshelves of a vast and ever increasing number of Italian families – no matter how limited their holdings might be – would include a copy of *Scienza in cucina,* with its unmistakable cover featuring the heading "Hygiene – Economy – Good Taste" right above the title and the author's name. The numbers of printings and copies sold appeared at the bottom.[8] The book became so popular that, to this day, most people refer to it simply as "Artusi." Widespread use of the author's name had resulted in a small but extremely significant antonomastic triumph: in his 1931 edition of *Dizionario moderno delle parole che non si trovano negli altri dizionari* (Modern dictionary of words not found in other dictionaries), Alfredo Panzini included the term *artusi* and defined it thus: "Cookery book. How glorious! The book has become a noun. How many writers are there who could boast a similar destiny?"[9]

Ever since the book "fell" into the public domain, dozens of editions have been issued by a variety of publishers besides Bemporad (now Bemporad-Marzocco). They include Giunti, Rizzoli, Garzanti, and other less prominent presses. Fourteen of these editions are currently available. Among those who printed the book, Casa Editrice Salani should not go unnoted: its early (1907) and unauthorized printing of the tenth edition of *Scienza in cucina* shook the Florentine publishing world and persuaded the concerned parties to turn to legal action.[10] Most of the current editions take pride in reproducing the "canonic" fourteenth edition; occasionally, however, Artusi's recipes have been revisited and reshaped so as to make them compatible with today's dietetic requirements and trends.[11]

It would be both difficult and unproductive to give a full account, or even a rough estimate, of the relevance and accuracy of each of these editions. It would be a crime, however, not to issue a few words of praise about one of them. Although all other editions testify to the high esteem in which *Scienza in cucina* has been held among chefs, gourmets, and anyone intrigued by culinary tales, legends, and dreams, the edition first published by Einaudi in 1970 has, to say the least, widened Artusi's readership to include scholars, cultural historians, artists, and intellectuals of all persuasions. The carefully documented introduction – easily a book in its own right – authored by the late Piero Camporesi[12] of the University of Bologna, identifies Artusi's masterpiece as an essential document in the history of Italian literature and society. It is not merely a peculiar and much-acclaimed cookbook, but a veritable quarry from which to extract facts and values that are crucial to a serious understanding of the long and contradictory political travail that ferried Italy from the battlefields of the *Risorgimento* to the drawing (and dining) rooms where an incipient bourgeoisie could, at the beginning of the new century, reap some of the material benefits once reserved for the nobility and the clergy.

One more thing should be said about the company Artusi has been keeping, for over thirty years, with Camporesi and Einaudi. Recently, a fourth boon-fellow joined in, and a new edition was brought out that doubles, or even triples, the pleasure of reading, consulting, or simply leafing through the book. In this new edition, the author's text is once again served with Camporesi's exhaustive introduction,[13] but it is also seasoned with the watercolors of Giuliano Della Casa, the most exciting visualizations ever attempted of Artusi's sense of taste and smell. As Pablo Echaurren has written in his affectionate description of the miraculous encounter between the gastronome and the artist:

> Giuliano Della Casa's painting is anti-conceptual, free-flowing, and instinctive; the artist himself is a force of nature, and, at the same time, the cultural product of his region, of the tradition dating back to a time when Pellegrino Artusi's instructions were carried out religiously and no attention would have been paid to the abstruse officiants and devotees of *nouvelle cuisine* ... In the same way that no second thoughts, no dawdling, no hesitation are allowed in the creation of a watercolor, the art of eating was based on authenticity ... Giuliano Della Casa's specialty lies in the binomial figure of color/flavor. His mark is rapid yet pregnant like a *tortello* [dumpling],

incisive yet delicate like *culatello* [salt-cured pork rump], ephemeral yet permanent like truffles in a *timballo* [savory pie].[14]

We are grateful to Giuliano Della Casa for having accepted the invitation to illustrate the present edition of *Science in the Kitchen*, which resurrects (with revisions) the only adequate English translation of the book.[15]

The many incarnations of Artusi's book are another sign of the role it has played in the history of modern Italy, both as an incentive to retrieve its centuries-old gastronomic tradition and as a binding factor in the shaping of a culturally grounded national unity. While the two issues are tightly connected, the former comes equipped with a curious corollary: the ancient *diaphorà* between France and Italy in their quest for gastronomic primacy. Coming as it did at a time "of transition, listlessness, and decadence in Italian cuisine, which was on one hand entirely regional, and on the other entirely French (the menus at court, the menus at official banquets ... were French in both form and substance), the linguistic and culinary purism endorsed by this book filled a void in the Italian national consciousness that a reawakening of rancor and animosity toward 'our scantily benevolent neighbors,' the French, had rendered more acute."[16]

Victor Emmanuel II, Italy's first king, was himself a great lover of French food, and when Florence became the temporary capital of the nation and he took up residence there (1865–71), Florentines immediately noticed how he much preferred "French" butter to their "superior" Tuscan oil. Artusi's pages, written in Florence during those years and printed there some twenty years later, showed not only that French and Italian culinary traditions ought to be viewed as parallel experiences, but that the common Renaissance denominator they shared, thanks to Catherine de' Medici, patron saint of both Italian and French cuisine, was perhaps more "common" on the southern side of the Alps than in the land of the Sun King.

Florence was indeed a good spot from which to observe the curious reentry into Italy of recipes (with French names) that Catherine herself, granddaughter of Lorenzo il Magnifico, had first exported to Paris in 1533, when she was married off by her uncle, Pope Clement VII, to Henry of Orléans, who would eventually be crowned king of France. Thus *crespelle*, a quintessential Tuscan dish, returned as *crêpes suzette*; *colletta*, which dates back to the times of ancient Rome, came back as *béchamel* (after Monsieur de Béchamel, who claimed it as his own invention).

When on 10 November 1878 King Umberto I (son of Victor Emmanuel) and his queen Margherita paid an official visit to Florence – the pope had finally relinquished his grip on Rome, which in 1871 had become the latest capital of the new nation – the mayor offered a banquet that did not include a single Florentine dish. The menu read as follows: "*Potage à la regence – Croutades à la Saint Cloud – Crêpes Villeroy – Ombrine garnie sauce normande – Filet de boeuf à la diplomate – Poulardes à l'impératrice – Domenicains de bécasses à l'ancienne – Artichauts et haricots verts à l'hollandaise – Punch au Kirschwasser – Rot de dindes et de perdreaux – Salade trouffée – Suprème de profiteroles à l'écossaise – Dessert de glace crème et chocolat – Abricot à l'Allemande*" And not a drop of Chianti or Trebbiano. In their stead: "*Chateau d'Yquem, Chateau Larose,*" and "*Johannisberg.*"[17] It was enough to make Artusi turn green.

Centuries of domination by various foreign powers and the precipitous series of military campaigns and annexations that made up the *Risorgimento* had resulted in the imposition of a set of national tasks and responsibilities on people who did not even share a language (excluding the literary Italian written and read, and not necessarily spoken, by the small number of citizens who had access to books).[18] From this perspective, the reclaiming of recipes, and the gastronomic ingenuity to which they bear witness, had to be motivated, at least in part, by the desire to see the newly established nation "off to a good start" in an area where the settling of disputes, and the implementation of historical justice, required, for a change, no shedding of human blood. An unprejudiced application of gastronomic philology was a prerequisite to transforming the game of claiming and reclaiming into the infinitely more rewarding intellectual pursuit of testing the validity of paradigms connecting individuals in adjacent or partially overlapping societies. This meant not simply transcending shortsighted nationalistic politics, which all too often concealed malevolent exploits with self-aggrandizing eloquence, but enabling local cultures to play an international role, both real and symbolic, without having to be first subsumed by a national, often stultifying and frequently artificial, configuration. The incipient habit of eating out, adopted by many fin-de-siècle gentlemen (and a few daring ladies), and the curiosity elicited by the multi-regional menus of many restaurants, also helped bring about whatever cohesiveness Italy could boast in the second half of the nineteenth century.

It has also been observed that Artusi's book, read over and over again at home,[19] was much more effective in bringing about a modicum of social harmony than were the heavily ideological and frequently high-brow novels – chief among them Alessandro Manzoni's *I promessi sposi* (The betrothed) – that thousands of young men and women were forced to read in school, in the vain hope that this exercise would transform them from the young Sicilians, Venetians, or Romans that they and their forebears had been into young Italians. Unlike those novels, which emphasized uniformity, Artusi showed how the preservation of diversity does not contradict collective interests. It is perhaps this validation of diversity operating within the boundaries of a nation both ancient and newly established that gave the book its most genuine political value.

In his article "Artusi," Folco Portinari cautions against this assumption, first suggested by Camporesi, arguing that well over half a century of Manzonian "popularity" had preceded even the first glimpse of *Scienza in cucina*. Portinari does recognize, however, that the comparison of Manzoni and Artusi promoted an interest in Artusi's project "to elaborate a national culinary koine with which all Italians could specifically identify, from the Po River to Mount Aetna."[20] Whether such a project ought to be considered absurd, as Portinari seems inclined to believe, given the fundamental vernacular quality of Italian cooking, or whether Artusi's stubbornness in pursuing it wins out in the end, the gastronome's contribution to the devolpment of the recipe as a literary genre is generally acknowledged. We shall return to this topic later.

Let us just add here that even Artusi's much celebrated sense of humor falls far short of Manzoni's superbly euphemistic style. Nor would Artusi have presumed to make any claim to the contrary. As an example of the distance separating the two, compare his musings on the dishonesty of Florentine butchers (who "call both yearlings and any bovine animal about two years old a 'calf.' But if these animals could speak they would tell you not only that they are no longer calves, but that they have already had a mate and a few offspring as well")[21] with Manzoni's reflections on the great prestige the town of Lecco derives from the mere fact of housing "a garrison commander, and ... a permanent force of Spanish soldiers, who gave lessons in modest deportment to the girls and women of the area, and who tickled the back of the odd husband of father with a stick from time to time. They also never failed, at the end of summer, to spread out across the vineyards and thin out the grapes, so as to lighten the labours of the peasants at harvest-time."[22]

Doubtless the claims of gastronomic originality surfacing here and there in Artusi's text are to be taken with a grain of salt and measured against the backdrop of a political unification that, contrary to the tranquilizing reassurances of official propaganda, seemed ensnared in complications so severe that the wisdom of the venture itself was being seriously called into question. Significantly, in *Scienza in cucina*, the philological, and archaeological, reconfiguration of the Italian (and, consequently, the European) culinary map was masterfully accompanied by the tribute Artusi paid to topical peculiarities: while it is true that Emilia-Romagna and Tuscany emerge from these pages as areas of gastronomic excellence, all of the regions of Italy are given their due.

At the end of the nineteenth century, debate raged between proponents of regional autonomy and those who claimed the necessity of a centralized bureaucracy no matter how detrimental to thriving cities such as Milan, Trieste, and Naples. Furthermore, rightist governments endorsed socio-economic policies inspired by the principle that capital had to be protected at all costs, even when it meant using public money to bail out private entrepreneurial incompetence. If the forces for increasing centralization of state administration appeared to be winning the day, Artusi's book, with its embrace of local diversity, seemed to be some sort of consolation prize for the proponents of regionalism. No one could seriously argue against the fairness of the author's selections and preferences, and most felt gratified to find in the table of contents a sufficient number of dishes from cultures whose peculiarity (often deeply rooted in childhood memories) did not constitute an impediment to the solution of national political and social issues.

Although perhaps less evident than the claim of originality and the preservation of topical differences, a third factor ought be considered in attempting to explain the book's slow but unfaltering success: the presence, in this guide to "Italian" cooking, of a fair number of "foreign" recipes, mostly English, French, and German.[23] Given the historical time-frame, this "contamination" may be read as a sign of self-assurance, the relevance of which should not be underestimated. A propos of *piccioni all'inglese* (squabs English style, or squab pie; recipe 277) Artusi proclaims: "I would like to make it clear once and for all that names do not mean much in my kitchen, and that I give no importance to high-sounding titles. If an Englishman should tell me that I have not made this dish, which also goes by the odd name of 'piccion paio,' according to the customs of his country, I do not care a fig."[24]

Such boldness seems consistent with a lexicological observation made by Niccolò Machiavelli, at a much earlier date, in his *Dialogo intorno alla nostra lingua* (Dialogue on the Italian language): "Languages cannot be pure. They must be mixed with other languages. A language will be called national that can turn to its own use terms gleaned from other languages. And those terms will not disrupt it, because it is so powerful that it will disrupt them. Such a language garners these terms in such a way that they will appear to have belonged to it all along."[25] Inviting the allogeneous to penetrate the indigeneous without fearing any loss of identity – and actually presuming that, in the process of assimilation, the latter will metabolize the former to become stronger – bespeaks a confidence that only a solid, fertile tradition can foster. Indeed, this was the case with Machiavelli, who could look back at a linguistic development sustained by an amazingly powerful and uninterrupted literary flowering: Stil Nuovo, Dante, Petrarch, Boccaccio, Lorenzo, Politian, Sannazzaro, and so on. In Artusi's field, finding predecessors and forebears may have seemed a considerably more laborious task. But a solid, fertile Italian gastronomic tradition had existed, and it was still available to anyone with enough patience and curiosity to look for it. And these were two qualities Pellegrino Artusi possessed in the highest degree.

Furthermore, in this quest for Italy's gastronomic roots and traditions, Artusi was not alone. Four years prior to the publication of *Scienza in cucina*, his Bolognese friend, the noted poet Olindo Guerrini,[26] had unearthed and published with Zanichelli *Frammento di un libro di cucina del sec. XIV* (Fragment of a fourteenth-century cookery book). In 1890, the same publisher had brought forth *Ricette di cucina del buon secolo della lingua* (Recipes from the golden century of the language), edited by Salomone Morpurgo. One year earlier, in Livorno, Ludovico Frati had produced *Libro di cucina del secolo XIV* (A fourteenth-century cookery book), and back in 1863 – Artusi was in his forties – G. Romagnoli, another Bolognese press, had issued Francesco Zambrini's edition of *Libro della cucina del secolo XIV*. These texts, long buried on the shelves of inaccessible libraries, brought to light for the first time the early tangible signs of a gastronomic culture that would peak in the mature decades of the Renaissance. They, and others older still, are, in the words of Massimo Montanari, "the point of arrival of the long evolution by which, little by little, medieval cuisine had become distinct from the Roman-based cuisine of antiquity. In great part, it was an international cuisine," but it was already "possible to identify in it national and even regional characteristics ... To begin with, 'southern' cuisine seemed to be clearly definable by the use of oil, 'northern' cuisine by the prevalence of animal fats."[27]

The task of mapping in detail the gastronomic literature of the fifteenth, sixteenth, and ensuing centuries leading up to Artusi exceeds both my aspiration and the scope of this essay. As the identification of a few stepping stones cannot be avoided, however, let us begin by underlining the enormous influence exercised by the humanist Bartolomeo Sacchi, better known as Plàtina, whose *De honesta voluptate atque valetudine* (On right pleasure and good health) was not simply the first cookbook ever printed (Rome, 1474), but also the first to be translated from the Latin original into French and German (and Italian, in 1487), facilitating a vast, unprecedented understanding of the dignity of both the culinary art and the writerly discipline focusing on it.

In the years when Artusi was cultivating his gastronomic vocation, Plàtina's enormous indebtedness to Maestro Martino's *Libro de arte coquinaria* (Book on the art of cooking) had not yet been discovered. We owe this precious acquisition to Joseph Dommers Vehling (1879–1950), the Chicago-based author of *Plàtina and the Rebirth of Man*.[28] In 1927, Vehling acquired one of the five extant scribal manuscripts of Maestro Martino's work and proceeded to compare the cook's manual with the erudite volume of the humanist. Maestro Martino's is, arguably, an epochal text, one in which old culinary traditions (Catalan, Arab, etc.) are subsumed in a formerly unimaginable perspective, and new practices are enacted that no longer depend on the spice trade (effectively blocked by the Turkish occupation of the Eastern basin of the Mediterranean). With Martino, the use of garden herbs and the filling of ravioli with minced meats ceases to be an oddity and becomes the hallmark of modern Italian cuisine.

Other gastronomes further developed Martino's legacy: Cristoforo Messisbugo's *Libro novo nel qual s'insegna a far d'ogni sorte di vivanda* (A new book that teaches how to make every sort of victual; Ferrara, 1549) aimed to teach "the method for preparing banquets, setting tables, furnishing palaces, and decorating chambers for every great Prince." Bartolomeo Scappi, the private cook of Pope Pius V, published his *Opera* (Works) in Venice in 1570. Vincenzo Cervio's *Il Trinciante* (The carver; Ferrara, 1581) delves into the art "of carving victuals (especially meats) in the same hall where the banquet was taking place, in front of the table set with foods. In a culture that attributed great importance to the serving of the meats and to the distribution of the parts in accordance with the prestige and the power of each single guest, the centrality and signficance of this ancient custom speaks for itself, not just from a technical point of view, but from the social and, if you will, political as well."[29]

Moving rapidly through the centuries, we cannot leave unremarked curious texts such as the *Brieve racconto di tutte le radici di tutte l'erbe e di tutti i frutti che crudi o cotti in Italia si mangiano* (A short account of all the roots and all the herbs and all the fruits eaten in Italy raw or cooked; 1614), by Giacomo Castelvetro. In the first years of the seventeenth century, when the impetus of the Italian gastronomic adventure was beginning to slacken, he taught his stupefied mutton-eating English hosts that salads and fruits are edible and, in fact, excellent nutrients.

Of singular importance, from our Artusian point of view, is the second edition of Bartolomeo Stefani's *L'arte di ben cucinare* (The art of cooking well; Venice, 1666), with an appendix devoted to meals prepared for limited numbers of people.[30] A second feature of this work, one that would seem to anticipate Artusi, is the concern shown for "money matters" (Stefani doesn't hesitate to offer estimates of what a given set of courses might cost), showing that gastronomy is moving away from the unconstrained *otium* of the aristocracy towards the much less glamorous, but no less fastidious, *negotium* of the bourgeoisie.

As a token of his esteem, Artusi included one of Stefani's recipes for soup in *Scienza in cucina*, calling it *Zuppa alla Stefani*. In his exhaustive introduction to the Einardi edition of *Scienza in cucina*, Professor Camporesi has given us a whole list of the recipes borrowed from the ancient masters, and yet, he rightly points out, Stefani's is the only case in which the name of the source is unequivocally brought forth.[31] Typically, the compliment paid does not go unaccompanied by some good-humored criticism, the illustration of which we shall leave to Artusi's own pen: "At [Stefani's] time, much use and abuse was made of all manner of seasonings and spices, and sugar and cinnamon were used in broth, as well as in making boiled or roasted meat. Omitting some of his instructions for this soup, I shall limit myself, aromatically speaking, to a bit of parsley and basil. And if the ancient Bolognese cook, meeting me in the afterworld, scolds me for it, I shall defend myself by explaining that tastes have changed *for the better*. As with all things, however, we go from one extreme to the other, and we are now beginning to exaggerate in the opposite direction, going as far as to exclude herbs and spices from dishes that require them."[32]

A fair summary of the Italian gastronomic tradition was offered, just before its waning from the stage upon which it had trodden for so long, by Antonio Latini's *Scalco alla moderna* (Modern carving; Naples, 1694). Indeed, Artusi's recipe 334 (*polpette di trippa* [tripe meatballs]) comes straight from its pages and is introduced by the following words: "This dish, taken, from a treatise on cooking dating from 1694, might seem strange to you, and the mere mention of tripe will probably make you reluctant to try it. But in spite of its homely character, when prepared with the proper seasonings it turns out quite pleasant and does not lie heavy on the stomach."[33]

During the last decades of the seventeenth century and throughout the eighteenth, French cultural supremacy permeated every aspect of Italian life, particularly gastronomy. From an Italo-centric point of view, the phenomenon can be viewed as a kind of abdication, political as well as ethical. The transalpine challenge met with no resistance whatsoever: the only perceivable reaction was perhaps a diffused sense of inferiority, eloquently borne out either by the habit of marketing manuals as if they were translations from the French, or by the unashamed use of titles in which inferiority is openly admitted, as with the anonymous *Il cuoco piemontese perfezionato a Parigi* (A Piedmontese cook perfected in Paris), published in Turin in 1766.[34]

The much quoted Massimo Montanari, writing about this re-trenchment of Italian gastronomy from positions of dominance to pockets of regional resistance (I assume full responsibility for the military intonation of the metaphor), has remarked that "This phe-nomenon should not necessarily be read as an involution: we can also see in it the discovery of a repressed vocation, of a submerged cultural reality in the early stages of appreciation ... Perhaps the very political weakness of Italy and its distance from the true centers of power allowed it to free up local gastronomical culture from the frills of ostentation that had concealed its character and content for so long. Perhaps it was this that kept local peculiarities alive and accentuated them by denying Italy a true national cuisine and by reinforcing the connections between gastronomy and territory."[35]

Many, indeed, are the manuals published in Italy from the age of Vico to the time of Artusi that offer their readers samples of localized competence couched in decidedly modest linguistic performance.[36] Yet, a small number of treatises attempt to recover a national dimen-sion, such as Francesco Leonardi's *Apicio moderno, ossia l'arte di apprestare ogni sorta di vivande* (The modern Apicius, or the art of preparing every sort of victual; Rome, 1807), a six-volume gastro-nomic encyclopedia introduced by what is likely to be the first historical profile of Italian cuisine,[37] and Giovanni Nelli's *Il re dei cuochi* (The king of cooks; Milan, 1868), an ample culinary disserta-tion whose shaky claims of universality are shored up by "lessons" in hygiene, food preservation, table setting for both intimate and deluxe meals, and a special section of recipes for children and conva-lescents.

Artusi knew both Nelli's and Leonardi's books well (he borrows substantially from the latter), as he did many of the "regional" trea-tises. Furthermore, he had a keen eye for yet another kind of cooking manual: those that were no longer aimed at professional chefs but at middle-class family cooks, housewives, and their domestic helpers.

Throughout the nineteenth century, in the north as well as in the southern regions of the nation, such manuals compulsively recommended that the pleasures of the table be seasoned with the principles of temperance and, above all, thriftiness. Such is the case with Vincenzo Agnoletti's *La nuovissima cucina economica* (New economical cooking; Rome, 1814), from which Artusi borrows "his" *zuppa di visciole* (sour cherry delight).[38]

The author is so much aware of this new middle-class audience – and so in agreement with their economic and ethical values – that he worries about his ability to communicate to them. At times his recipes read like answers to queries gleaned from the columns of a daily paper: "My fear of not being understood by everyone leads me to provide too many details, which I would gladly spare the reader. Still, some people never seem to be satisfied. For instance, a cook from a town in Romagna wrote to me: 'I prepared the blood pudding described in your highly esteemed cookbook for my employers. It was very well liked, except that I didn't quite understand how to pass the almond and the candied fruit through the sieve. Would you be good enough to tell me how to do this?' Delighted by the question, I answered her: 'I am not sure if you know that you can find sieves made especially for this purpose. One type is strong and widely spaced, and is made with horsehair. Another is made of very fine wire. With these, a good mortar and *elbow-grease*, you can purée even the most difficult things.'"[39]

Artusi's voice may be that of the well-meaning schoolteacher with a sense of humor as preposterous as the nonchalance with which it is proffered, yet his style is never obscure and ridiculous (or ridiculously obscure), as was often the case in the history of culinary writing.[40] One never knows whether Artusi's mixture of "sacred and profane" is a deliberate stylistic statement, or simply the outcome of a prodigiously active inertia. Of this critical incertitude, the entry with the recipe for minestrone is a sublime example. It opens with the story of a cholera outbreak that struck Tuscany in 1855 and showed no special concern for Artusi:

I had taken lodgings in the Piazza del Voltone, in a whitewashed villa run by a certain Mr. Domenici. That night, I felt the onset of a frightening disturbance in my body ... "Damned minestrone! You will never fool me again!" ...

Morning came, and feeling myself totally drained, I caught the first train and escaped to Florence, where I immediately felt much better. Monday the sad news reached me that cholera had broken out in Livorno, and the first to be struck dead was no other than Domenici himself.

And to think that I had blamed the minestrone!

After three attempts, improving upon the dish each time, this is how I like to make it ...[41]

And so on, without batting an eyelash. Indeed, Artusi seems to be as unaware of any impropriety in the juxtaposition of essentially incompatible materials as Peter Sellers, in the guise of Chief Inspector Clouseau, is of the equally unmitigated dangers he is constantly going through, and emerging from, unscathed.

Sitting atop this double patrimony of classical Italian gastronomy and its regional diversity – which for centuries had been the exclusive domain of technicians, and the singular privilege of the upper classes who employed them – and faced with the task of redeeming it from French dominance and disseminating it among bourgeois readers whose economic values and ethical expectations he fully shared, Artusi may seem more like a pop orchestra conductor than an avant-garde musician. In fact, he is an inspired synthesizer: while the substance of traditional recipes is only minimally altered (a few wrinkles are merely smoothed away), the idea of turning loose so many anecdotes, historical references, scientific condensations, cameos profiling Italian everyday life, and so much more, upon pages earmarked for measurements and cooking times, proved to be a major step forward in the evolution of the cookbook as a literary genre.

Typically, his recipe for *spaghetti alla rustica* (country-style spaghetti) opens with two cases of aversion to garlic: the ancient Roman aristocracy and Alfonso King of Castile, who "hated it so much he would punish anyone who appeared at his court with even a hint of it in his breath." Artusi then switches to the esteem in which it was held by ancient Egyptians, who "worshipped garlic as a divinity, perhaps because they had experienced its medicinal properties." Next he describes these healthful properties, ranging from the beneficial effects on hysteria to garlic's immunizing power "against epidemic and pestilential diseases." Finally he warns against banning garlic from cooking on account of its problematic smell (when poorly cooked) and encourages his readers not to deprive themselves "of healthy, tasty dishes," such as the one he is presenting, "which has often comforted my stomach when upset."[42] Alfredo Roncuzzi, who first drew my attention to the unsurpassable quality of this small but exemplary jewel, has counted the lines and remarked on the perfect balance of the whole: "19 lines in the preface [17 of them in translation], 11 lines of instruction, but the text in its entirety is simply flawless."[43]

To introduce *tartufi alla bolognese* (truffles Bolognese style),[44] Artusi does not hesitate to compare the colors of truffles to the Whites and the Blacks, political factions that, during their struggle for power, caused the citizens of medieval Florence great suffering. When calling attention to a particularly inappropriate usage of gastronomic terminology, he goes so far as to lift an example from the most sacred of texts: "The Holy Scriptures say that Joshua stopped the sun and not the earth. *Well, we do the same when we talk about chickens*, because the hip should be called the thigh, the thigh should be called the leg, and the leg should be called the tarsus."[45]

Stunned by the preposterous quality of the display, we might not even stop to ask what kind of subliminal connection could possibly justify the linkage of such distant realities. Indeed, Artusi's blasé attitude results in some extraordinary detours: Focusing on peacocks, whose meat, Artusi assures us, is "excellent for young people," the opportunity to impress his readers with the marvels of this bird's history engrosses him to such a degree that he ends up retaining the secret of how to prepare them for a meal.[46] Southeast Asia is their native home, he informs us, and Alexander the Great introduced them to Greece. Struck by their loveliness, the great military leader issued an edict protecting peacocks from the appetites of less sensitive souls. In Rome, things were dramatically different. A rival of Cicero in the Forum, Quintus Ortensius, found them rather delicious and dined on them with no pangs of conscience. In the end the peacock lore in Artusi's pages may whet our curiosity, but hardly our appetite. These days it may be hard to appreciate the bravery it took to disregard Alexander's decree, as peacock-meat fanciers are likely to find their favorite fowl (plucked, of course) frustratingly elusive in supermarket poultry departments. Thus we might be better off leaving the stuff such culinary dreams (nightmares?) are made of to the estimable Petronius Arbiter or to Federico Fellini's visual repagination of his *Satyricon*. Artusi alternately teases and flaunts in *Science in the Kitchen*.

Whatever else they may be, his pages read like a humorous collection of practical, naive, and sometimes blasphemous, remarks. They are a meticulous compilation of culinary rules, means, and advice, tickled and bedazzled by a panoply of anecdotes and commentaries drawn from history and myth as well as mildly encyclopedic samples of zoological and botanical information. If not a perfect admixture, they form a decidedly irresistible cocktail.

Failing all else, significant episodes from the author's life, or the lives of his friends, are conjured up and elevated to the rank of indispensable digressions. In the early 1840s,[47] some seventy years before *Scienza in cucina* reached its apotheosis, the gastronome, as he himself recounts, met with a law student from the University of Bologna, whose name would soon become notorious for reasons unrelated to food history. The meeting, actually no more than a casual encounter, took place at the Trattoria Tre Re (The Three Kings), one of the oldest eating and sleeping establishments in town.[48]

Felice Orsini, whom Artusi describes as a "congenial young man, of middling height, lean build, pale and round face, refined features, the blackest eyes, crinkly locks, who lisped slightly when he spoke," attempted to assassinate Emperor Napoleon III in Paris in 1858. To no one's surprise, the student was subsequently executed. Artusi acknowledges the tragic nature of the event, but goes on to suggest that the assassination attempt may have played a significant role in the French monarch's decision to aid the Piedmontese in their war with the Austrians. These and other details can be gleaned from the recipe for *maccheroni col pangrattato* (macaroni with bread crumbs).[49]

Somewhat longer (though some are longer still)[50] and a great deal more political than the average Artusian digression, such a rambling introduction to the preparation of a dish is, as we have indicated, not unusual. It is nontheless astonishing to encounter Artusi's highly inappropriate adoption of an expression commonly used to return to a primary subject after a digression: "Ritorniamo a bomba" (literally, "And now, let's go back to the bomb"). Given that Orsini's was the first known act of terrorism to be carried out by means of an explosive, would it not have been advisable, on the part of Artusi, to avoid that expression altogether?

Although Artusi is sometimes inadvertently outrageous in his choice of metaphors and more than slightly irreverent in his similes and historical anecdotes, his syntax and lexicon seem to conform to the widespread notion that the Florentine dialect was ideally suited to become the national linguistic standard. This opinion, which still holds sway in some remote North American colleges and even among a select group of Florentine loafers, fueled many a heated discussion, especially during the post-unification era. In fact, it had received the endorsement of none other than the Milanese Alessandro Manzoni, who made a point of taking up residence in Florence in order to "Tuscanize" his otherwise "Lombardian" novel. Tuscans were generally pleased, though some snobs among them suggested that Count Manzoni's newly acquired language was as good as his French,[51] too good, that is, to be in harmony with the content of a seventeenth-century story having as its background Milan and the lesser branch of Lake Como.

Artusi was not a Florentine either, and had moved to that city for reasons that were not at all linguistically motivated. Yet he followed

Manzoni's example and became himself *plus royaliste que le roi* (*parfois*). Yet in his case, the notion of "rinsing one's linguistic clothes in the waters of the Arno River" (God forbid!) did not become an onomasiological theorem, as it did with Manzoni. Also, let us not forget that, unlike Manzoni, who spent just enough time in Florence to do the rinsing, Artusi lived there from 1851 till the day of his death sixty years later.

From a normative point of view, the so-called *questione della lingua* (that is, the quest for lexical and stylistic standards of expression), which dates back to the *Rinascimento*, has been, by and large, a sterile or marginal affair. (Not infrequently, in their creative practice, authors contradict or disregard their own most cherished linguistic beliefs.) Rekindled, for obvious political reasons, during the *Risorgimento,* it has resurfaced at almost regular intervals, as the manifestation of a misguided, when not decidedly undesired quest for national identity. As a yardstick to measure what should be used, kept, or dismissed by modern Italian speakers, strict Florentine observance has proven to be a rather ridiculous affair. Artusi himself more than once assumed his readers to be familiar with Florentine terms that were in fact far more obscure to them (and maybe even to the Florentines) than the regional variations he was determined to extirpate.

While there can be no doubt of his appreciation of Bologna and its food, as well as the jovial character and the longevity of its inhabitants – so many are the praises he lavishes on them in *Scienza in cucina*[52] – the vernacular and, above all, the gastronomic jargon used in that city is clearly not Artusi's favorite *modus loquendi*. "What a strange language they speak in the learned Bologna!" he writes:

> They call carpets rags; wine flasks gourds; sweetbreads milks. They say "zigàre" for "piangere" (to weep), and they call an unsavory, ugly, annoying woman, who would normally be termed a "calia" or a "scamonea" a "sagoma" (Italian for silhouette and, figuratively speaking, a funny person). In their restaurants you find "trefoils" (instead of truffles), Florentine style "chops" (instead of "steaks"),

and other similar expressions that would drive anybody mad ...
When I first heard the Bolognese mention a crescent, I though they
were talking about the moon. Instead they were discussing the
schiacciata or focaccia, the ordinary fried dough cake that everybody recognizes and all know how to make. The only difference is
that the Bolognese, to make theirs more tender and digestible, add a
little lard when mixing the flour with cool water and salt.[53]

To fully appreciate Artusi's idiosyncratic attitude, one should add
that while "sagoma" enjoyed, as it does today for that matter, a wide
currency in a number of northern Italian regions (including Artusi's
native Romagna), who has ever heard of "calia" and "scamonea"
(yes, they can be looked up in a very good dictionary), apart from
Artusi, of course, who wants to be more Florentine than his Florentine
interlocutors? As a result, in *Scienza in cucina,* many lexical items
remain whose origin, carefully tagged by phrases such as "in the
language of," "as they say in," and so on, have no significant ties to
the "language" of Florence.[54]

Even on the "Western front", not all things were quiet. Artusi's
relentless campaign to "purify" gastronomic language of unwarranted
francophonic infiltrations looks more like the symptomatic displace-
ment of some discomfort than a legitimate linguistic concern: "How
strange is the nomenclature associated with cuisine! Why white mountain," writes Artusi to introduce the recipe for salted codfish Mont
Blanc style (no. 118), "and not yellow mountain, as one would think
from the color this dish takes when made? And how could the French,
demonstrating their usual boldness when it comes to metaphors, have
stretched their name for this dish into *Brandade de morue? Brandade,*
they say derives from *brandir,* to move, strike, wave a sword, halberd,
lance and similar weapons. In fact, what is being brandished except a
paltry wooden mixing spoon?"[55]

At time his insistence verges on the ludicrous. With a verse of
dubious literary merit ("What the French call soufflé / And use as an
entremet / By your leave I name 'sgonfiotto' / And serve as a

'tramesso'"),[56] he tries to teach his fellow citizens (who, I am afraid, turned a deaf ear) to discontinue the use of the terms *soufflé* and *entremets*. Internationally successful as they had been for so long, these terms were not about to make way for homespun equivalents. Ironically, here too the proof is in the pudding: to this day, in Sicily, a chef is referred to as a *Monsu*, from the French *Monsieur*.[57]

While Artusi's were certainly not easy times for the *questione della lingua*, graver problems besieged the incipient nation, chief among them poverty and hunger. For an idea of how serious these problems were, we can look at one of the many food-related episodes to be found in Carlo Collodi's *Pinocchio*,[58] first published in book form in 1883, and thus a mere eight years older than *Scienza in cucina*. In the following episode, the wooden puppet is taught a lesson in, let us say, frugality. Extracting from the jumble of words with which Pinocchio greets him upon returning from jail the very simple truth that Pinocchio is dying of hunger, Geppetto, Pinocchio's "father," takes three pears, which he had intended for himself, and offers them to his starving son: "'If you want me to eat them, kindly peel them for me.' 'Peel them for you?' cried Geppetto, astonished. 'I would never have thought, my lad, that you were so refined and fastidious. That's too bad! We should get used, from childhood, to eating everything, and liking it; for one never knows what might happen in this curious world.'" Not only will Pinocchio end up eating the parings for which he had shown such disdain, but, being still vexed with a problem that the pulp (and the peels) of three little pears can hardly solve, he will proceed to eat the cores as well. Having gobbled down everything, Pinocchio can finally tap on his stomach and announce cheerfully, "Now I feel better."[59]

In another famous episode, that of the meal taken by Cat and Fox at the Inn of the Red Lobster, the idea of poverty filters through the voracious appetites of the eaters: "The poor cat had bad indigestion, and could eat no more than thirty-five mullets with tomato sauce and four helpings of tripe with parmesan cheese; and because she thought the tripe was not well seasoned, she asked three times for extra butter and grated cheese. The fox too would gladly have nibbled at something, but since the doctor had put him on a strict diet, he had to be content with a hare in sweet and sour sauce, garnished with fat spring chickens and young pullets. After the hare, he ordered a special dish of partridges, rabbits, frogs, lizards and other tidbits, but he would not touch anything more."[60]

This comic intermezzo hearkens back to a centuries-old literary topos, referred to as poor man's paradise, the land of plenty, or the land of Cockaigne, according to a thirteenth-century *fabliau* whose anonymous author swore to have visited it on strict orders from the pope for the highly credible purpose of doing penance. In this land "qui plus i dort, plus i gaigne" and "Cil qui dort jusqu'a miedi, / gaigne cinq sols et demi."[61] In the *Decameron*, Bocaccio turned the narrative into a comic masterpiece: Calandrino, whose gullibility knows no bounds, is told of a country called Bengodi where "vines are tied up with sausages and a goose can be had for a farthing, with a gosling thrown into the bargain." Around these parts there is a mountain made entirely of Parmesan cheese; its inhabitants spend their days preparing ravioli and macaroni, which they cook in capon broth. When these doughy delights are thrown down the slopes, the lucky individual who retrieves "the most of them, the most he eats." Nearby flows a stream of Vernaccia wine, "the best that ever was drunk."[62] The gallery of characters seeking free food would not be complete without at least a passing mention of such Commedia dell'Arte masks as Harlequin and Pulcinella, whose stage life is dominated by the grumblings of their empty stomachs and the need to secure food by outwitting masters and innkeepers alike.

These examples bespeak a long-standing preoccupation or fear that had marked peasant life since the Renaissance days of Ruzante,[63] and had by Artusi's time become the daily experience of the urban working classes as well. It was a tragedy of vast proportions that the very limited strength of incipient workers' movements seemed incapable of taming. Hunger, poverty, and injustice were everywhere in the streets of Italy, as well as in Italian literature, of the end of the nineteenth century: in Pirandello's *I vecchi e giovani*,[64] a novel of epic dimensions, significantly poised between Roman political corruption and the brutal military crushing of a miners' rebellion known as the *Fasci siciliani* (1894); in Giovanni Verga's *Per le vie*, a collection of short stories focusing on the life of the Milanese working class;[65] and in books such as Edmondo De Amicis's *Cuore* (1886), another work whose popular appeal survived various political transformisms, two world wars, and a depression.[66]

Structured as the personal diary of a boy attending the last year of elementary school (and thus compulsory education), *Cuore* focuses on episodes involving children from different social classes: some will continue to study and become doctors, lawyers, politicians, professors; others will learn a trade and disappear from the protagonist's horizon. All of them, however, are summoned to gestures of exceptional abnegation, in defense of motherland, family, and other "peculiar" values such as honesty and unselfishness. In recent years, the tales of these little heroes of the bourgeoisie, working class, and urban subpoletariat have been frightfully castigated by "smart" critics who have chosen to show how impudently paternalistic and pathetic the author really was, not realizing, perhaps, that De Amicis had already ravaged his own writing, describing it as a kind of "watered-down Manzonianism, bereft of any courageous statements; a perpetual see-sawing between I believe and I don't believe; a desire to make something heard without compromising it with words; a double-edged fear of making misbelievers laugh and upsetting the pious people; a constant catching of the heart by surprise, when it is the head that should be surprised instead."[67]

Quite revealing, of course, is the distinction between heart and head, and the deliberate and, judging from his other works, reluctant choice De Amicis made in favor of the former: "Show me you are good-hearted boys; our class will be like a family," implores schoolteacher Perboni upon meeting his class on the first day of school. Whatever our take on the book, there is enough poverty in it to convince readers of all persuasions that, even when not explicitly referred to, hunger must be close by.

Distressing signs of penury are certainly not the exclusive legacy of fictional narratives. In accounting for the dissemination of Artusi's book, which was "especially brisk among the bourgeoisie," Professor Camporesi reminds us that the success of the book "could be called class-oriented" and that "Venetian farmers continued to eat their polenta and southern workmen continued to eat olives, fava beans, and tomatoes unaware that things were changing at the tables of other Italians."[68]

The scarcity of food and the poor nutritional value of the staples consumed day in and day out by the lower classes were indeed the talk of the nation. Ideas were conceived, proposals examined, projects debated. They ranged from the bizarre to the tragic, and none was found that could resolve the problem. Professor Paolo Mantegazza, a pathologist and Darwinian whose lectures in anthropology and ethnology at the Istituto di Studi Superiori of Florence (where he began to teach in 1870) were assiduously attended by his good friend Pellegrino Artusi, suggested a truly astonishing way out of the predicament. Mantegazza joined in the widespread condemnation of the nutritional poverty of the food habitually consumed by the lower classes ("Of all his dishes, the poor city dweller prizes most of all his soup which is meager nourishment even if consumed in large volumes; the poor country dweller lives but for polenta and yellow bread ... , a barely digestible and niggardly food that makes his blood listless and ill"). Having traveled extensively in Latin America, and having noticed the prodigious effects of coca leaves chewed by Andean peasants, he declared that their diffusion among the working classes would stymie the onslaught of hunger from which they perpetually suffered. Mantegazza, who wrote extensively on the subject, beginning with "Sulle virtù igieniche e medicinali della coca" (On the medicinal and hygenic virtues of coca; Milan, 1859), and who is likely to have been the first to advocate the introduction of the plant to Europe, made his point with a "symptomatically reassuring" stylistic levity: "A pinch of leaves chewed slowly and gently during the day helps us to smoke fewer cigars, it warms our hearts and lungs, and it sustains us above all during hard physical labor and especially during long marches."[69] His "revolutionary" line of thinking met, apparently, with little enthusiasm.

A second, much more persuasive strategy would be adopted by agencies of the Italian government with the unconditional approval of the reigning monarch. Four years after the despicable handling of the Sicilian Fasci, thousands of people took to the streets of Milan to protest economic policies that had reduced them to utter destitution: they were brutally mowed down by the soldiers of General Fiorenzo Bava Beccaris.[70] Fifty years earlier the Milanese had rebelled against the Austrian rulers of their city in an attempt, officially celebrated as "The Five Days of Milan," to join the Piedmontese in the creation of a unified nation. God only knows how many of those who defied the Italian army with stones and sticks had reason to regret the patriotism of their forebears. After four days of fighting, one hundred people (two of them soldiers) lay dead in the streets. Four hundred and fifty people were wounded and eight hundred arrested. A month later King Umberto awarded Bava Beccaris the prestigious Cross of "Grande Ufficiale" for "the great service rendered to civilization and its institutions." Two years later anarchist Gaetano Bresci assassinated the king.

There were other "solutions" to the problem of hunger: emigration and colonial expansion. Italy did not refrain from trying either. Between 1891 and 1911 millions of Italians resettled in North or South America, referred to respectively – on the basis of the time it took to get there – as *America corta* (Short America) and *America longa* (Long America). Central to the narrative of *Sull'oceano*, the theme of emigration, with depictions of the pains and lacerations caused by this massive uprooting, recurs in many other works by De Amicis, including *Cuore*. Significantly, one of the "monthly tales" punctuating *Cuore* bears the title "Dagli Appennini alle Ande" (From the Appennines to the Andes) and tells the story of a child who, all by himself, travels by sea and by land, searching for his mother (naturally!).

As for colonial expansion, Italy's determination to find riches on the African continent proved to be costly both in term of human lives and international prestige. Not only did efforts to conquer Ethiopia, for instance, bring nothing but pain to thousands of people in both nations, but the crushing defeat inflicted by the troops of Emperor Menelik upon the army of General Barattieri at the battle of Adwa (1896) caused the downfall of the Italian government and increasing political confusion while creating new economic difficulties for many Italian families. The only good to come of it was the myth it dispelled, that Africa was there for the taking by European powers. More important, it marked the entry of Ethiopia into the modern community of sovereign and independent nations.

A deplorable state of domestic affairs, no doubt. Yet we would have to look very hard to find any trace of it in Pellegrino Artusi's book, which was first printed during a year that saw the official birth of the Italian Socialist Party and the publication of Pope Leo XIII's encyclical *Rerum novarum*, a document of rare significance, focusing on the relation between capital and labor. While condemning socialism as a measure falling short of the mark and depriving humanity of some "indisputable" rights (such as a right to retain private property, no matter how achieved), *Rerum novarum* calls attention to the "spirit of revolutionary change, which has long been disturbing the nations of the world, [and which] should have passed beyond the sphere of politics and made its influence felt in the cognate sphere of practical economics." It is quite explicit, about the "changed relations between masters and workmen" as well as "the enormous fortunes of some few individuals, and the utter poverty of the masses." Its concluding words encourage the creation of representative bodies to mediate between the employers and the employed. When "either a master or a workman believes himself injured, nothing would be more desirable than that a committee should be appointed, composed of reliable and capable members of the association, whose duty would be, conformably with the rules of the association, to settle the dispute. Among the several purposes of a society, one should be to try to arrange for a continuous supply of work at all times and seasons; as well as to create a fund out of which the members may be effectually helped in their needs, not only in the cases of accident, but also in sickness, old age, and distress."[71] The document is a major step forward, if not in the history of social doctrines, then certainly in that of the Catholic Church, which for centuries had sided almost exclusively with the masters.

Rich as it is in historical and scientific information, *Scienza in cucina* scrupulously avoids any mention of strife and unrest. One could point to temporal and spatial circumstances to justify this avoidance. First, by the year 1897, when the book was undergoing revisions and enlargements, and its dissemination was getting under way, the increase in prices that would drive Milanese workers to despair as well as an increase in real estate values had begun to act as economic boosters as well. The following decade and a half turned out to be (surprisingly enough) a period of relative prosperity, which came to a halt with the unfortunate decision to enter the First World War. Second, Artusi conceived and wrote his book in Florence, a well-governed and fairly peaceful town, especially when compared to Forlimpopoli and the continuous troubles caused there and throughout Emilia-Romagna by the combined presence of a reactionary Vatican administration and Austrian troops charged with the task of making sure that the equilibrium between church privileges and popular ignorance would not be disturbed.

Artusi's descriptions of Florence are not incongruous with those typically found in the literature of the Grand Tour; nor is his criticism much different from the words of annoyance we occasionally find in E.M. Forster's *A Room with a View* and, earlier, in the letters, diaries, and recollections of proven admirers such as William Wetmore Story[72] and his fellow Anglo-American expatriates such as Elizabeth and Robert Browning and Margaret Fuller, to mention but a few. "Surrounded by a smiling, picturesque sky ... and magnificent promenades," writes Artusi, "its citizens are born with artistic genius. Here there are museums, galleries, institutes for divulgement of the sciences, letters, and art, a beautiful language – the cradle of the Italian language – all things to make your sojourn exquisite, were it not for the continuous nightmare of being preyed upon by degenerate plebs ... ,"[73] plebs towards whom Artusi – and here he parts with at least some of the foreign visitors and expatriates – felt not at all attracted, even unconsciously. All in all, however, the gastronome and the city, at that particular point in time, were made for each other.

There is a third and possibly more profound explanation for the absence of Italy's immediate and bloodstained history from the pages of *Scienza in cucina*. It lies within the boundaries of Artusi's psychological persona, within his ability to smooth away any obstacle, to avoid contradictions and aporias. It is a "perverse" disposition and it makes an absolute winner of the person who can endure it (or to whom it comes naturally). As Artusi's life clearly exemplifies, many advantages result from a deposition that represses even the slightest temptation to admit defeat. In a city with a great (and well-sedimented) past such as Florence, a *laudator temporis acti* like Artusi could easily ward off the dangers of a curiosity aimed at the radically new. His principal project was the enjoyment of results that could be achieved by exploiting rationally what was already known or foreseeable, given the "scientific" premises of the materialistic culture he subscribed to. "You can be sure," he writes, "that the moral world is made up of combinations and fortuitous cases; the supernatural has no part whatsoever in human events."[74]

Accustomed as we are to frowning upon bourgeois values, identifying them with hypocrisy and double standards, we forget that liberalism and lay thinking are part of the same package. In a country where culture had too often been confused with the dogmatic voice of Catholic clericalism, the convictions of a moderate "free-thinker" such as Artusi had a chance, if not to win, at least to place or show. In 1870, the Piedmontese, *manu militari*, took over the eternal city, and for fifty years afterward the reigning popes considered themselves prisoners of the Italian state.[75] To get a sense of the tension that ravaged the Catholic world, caught between the devil of its nascent allegiance to a sovereign nation and the deep blue sea of mighty papal condemnation, let us resuscitate the old anecdote of a priest who, for the benefit of some ignoramus (*un mangiapreti?*),[76] translates the acronym D.O.M. (*Deo Optimo Maximo*) carved above the façade of many churches, as *Demanio Omnia Manducavit* (Crown property office gobbled up everything), with *omnia* standing for the recently confiscated church possessions. Against this kind of background, consider how bold the following statement by Artusi must have sounded: "Indissoluble vows [such as the marital vows towards which he feels nothing but aversion and repugnance] are Medieval dogmas, obligations *contra natura* which have no more reason to be in the world of rationality and progress in which we live, therefore ... for the good of humanity I call for a well-elaborated divorce law, a law that the most civilized nations of the world have implemented a long time ago."[77]

Prior to the annexation to Italy,[78] and after the relatively short but quite intense Napoleonic intermezzo, Florence and the whole of Tuscany had been ruled by members of the Hapsburg-Lorena dynasty. Under their "englighted despotism," tolerated, if not loved, by Florentines, the city had become a refuge for the Romagnoli who had managed to escape the oppressive clerical rule under which they were born. Artusi had moved to Florence in 1852, together with his mother and father, "to deal in fabrics and silk and make himself a Florentine ... who knew how to appreciate the services of the banks and the advantages of the first railroads."[79] A well-to-do member of society from birth, he confesses in his surprisingly dull *Autobiografia* to having nourished feelings of gratitude for his parents, "not for giving birth to me, which I consider a misfortune, but for leaving me the legacy of a good name and the means to lead a comfortable life."[80]

The son of Agostino, a prominent merchant whom friends called "Buratel,"[81] and of Teresa Giunchi, Pellegrino Artusi was born on 4 August 1820. In 1831, his father had participated in the insurrectionary movements of Forlimpopoli, which at the time was one of the Legazioni Pontificie, a territory governed by the church. In March of that year Buratel was among the signatories of a proclamation extolling "Liberty, Union, and Fatherland." In later years, his patriotism would abate considerably. To get a taste of the lukewarm national sentiments that afflicted old Buratel and the parallel insurgence, in him, of a "sound" one-never-knows philosophy, let us pay heed to an episode narrated by Pellegrino himself: "A public subscription was opened in order to aid the State Treasury in paying for war expenses. At that time my father had given me the key to the [family] coffer and I could rummage around in it just as he did. I opened the box with him there and said: 'I have not been able to offer Italy my arm, when She asked for it ... Let me now give a sign, at least, of my love for her liberty and independence' ... I took 300 liras and rushed them over, asking the clerk to register them in my father's name. Caught unnaware by my sudden action, he could not keep himself from exclaiming: 'What are you doing? What are you doing? Who knows if things will last like this?' 'They will,' I said, 'this time they will,' and I fled."[82]

Couched in language that could not be more pietistic and is, nowadays, slightly repulsive, the passage also sheds light on the shifting of power from father to son within a fairly representative upper-middle-class family. Most of all, it alerts us to the kind of rhetoric to which an accomplished bourgeois would unashamedly resort, in order to disguise as an act of patriotism what in reality is nothing but a crude (and very profitable) financial investment.

A male child among seven sisters, Pellegrino grew up in comfort, thanks to his father's successful business as a textile merchant and drug store owner. Of his early education, Pellegrino writes: "When I was big enough, it was decided that I'd be sent to school ... And what an awful school it was! ... What awful teachers, especially for the lower classes! Real slave drivers. On top of everything else, the one I'm talking about was an acrimonious man whom they called *Strapianton* [the Well-Rooted]. A rabid papist, he used to make us read the Office of the Virgin every Saturday in Latin even though he himself didn't understand a word of it. Every so often when a student didn't know his lessons, he would say, 'put your hands out'... and whack with the rod."[83] Later Artusi studied at the episcopal seminary schools of Bertinoro and for a time sojourned in Bologna, without, however, attending the Pontifical University, as many of his more creative biographers contend.[84]

As a young man, he helped with his father's business and traveled as far as Trieste, Milan, Ancona, Rome, Naples, and many other places where he acquainted himself with much of the gastronomic lore he would later whip into the cauldron of *Scienza in cucina*. The immediate cause of the family's move from Romagna to Florence was the brutal assault to which they, and the entire town of Forlimpopoli, had been subjected by the a band of brigands led by the notorious (and controversially romantic) Stefano Pelloni, better known as the *Passatore* (Ferryman), a nickname he inherited from his father, who was a real *passatore* on the River Lamone.[85]

It was in Florence that Artusi found the world he had always been looking for. Having become an investment banker, and a very wise investor,[86] in less than thirteen years, he had earned enough money to be able to dedicate himself more freely to intellectual pursuits and to attending university lectures, which were then public. Above all, his prosperity and changed family situation (having buried his parents and overcome "the nightmare" of his sisters[87]) enabled him to be inducted into what we might call a self-styled club of permanent bachelorhood, characterized, as the editors of his autobiography have not failed to notice, by "a modest hedonism, an elegant wardrobe, and a real passion for food."[88] Perfectly harmonious with the "philosophical" premises in which it was grounded, the third of Artusi's predilections would become a very special labor of love, leading to a pot of gold at the end of a savory rainbow.

Whatever reticence may have hindered him at the beginning, the insistence of the many gentlemen and ladies "of my acquaintance, who honored me with their friendship" led to his resolve to proceed with the project of publishing *Scienza in cucina*. The "materials had long been prepared," he writes in a paragraph of the preface, "and served only for my personal use. I thus present it to you now as the simple amateur that I am, certain that I shall not disappoint you, having tried and retried these dishes many times myself."[89] These modest and yet highly informative lines shed light on both Artusi's social life and the specific environment within which he cultivated his culinary talents.

A bachelor who enjoyed the covenient intimacy of a fair number of female friends, as he somberly but unequivocally declares in his *Autobiografia*, Artusi basked in the reflected light of acquaintances whom he could admire without losing his own balance, and in the trust he inspired in people seeking either gastronomic advice or ways to improve their assets. Nothing illustrates his notion of "covenient familiarity" better than his "strategic" retreat from the proximity of a "good oil and fresco painter, judged to be among the best in Florence," whom Artusi had befriended for the purpose of "forming an idea of artistic beauty." "I used to visit his studio to admire his work and, to make sure that I would be tolerated, I wasn't negligent in using those courtesies practiced among friends."[90] When, however, the painter suggests that Artusi consider buying a painting the *gradus ad amicitiam* is rudely interrupted. Clearly Artusi did not care to include this gentleman artist in the cohort to which Mantegazza and many other members of the upper bourgeoisie and Anglo-Florentine aristocracy contributed social lustre and intellectual vitality.[91] Numbered among the luminaries were Enrico Hillyer Giglioli[92] and Adolfo Targioni Tozzetti, both of them colleagues of Mantegazza's at the Regio Istituto di Studi Superioiri,[93] poet Renato Fucini,[94] critic Alessandro D'Ancona,[95] marquis and marchioness Almerici, and even the controversial English writer Walter Savage Landor.[96]

If the marrige of friendship and patronage was not meant to be, that of friendship and free professional service encountered no obstacle whatsoever. It is again Artusi who informs us of how well-disposed he could be towards people whom he hardly knew, as in the case of Domenico P., better known as Mengone, from Faenza. On moving to Florence, "he came over to my bank and introduced himself, imploring me to invest a sum of money, the fruit of his savings. I could see that he was a gentleman and that he had promise, and what's more, he was proving to be a fellow patriot. So I was happy to help him without charging him anything."[97]

As for the specifics of Artusi's culinary environment, many clues indicate that he used his modest kitchen as a laboratory equipped with an affordable coal-burning stove and well stocked with implements and utensils. Unfortunately, unlike more modern books, Artusi does not include a section describing the kitchen equipment he considered essential. An inventory is possible nonetheless. A paragraph in his recipe for *stufatino di petto di vitella di latte coi finocchi* (stewed breast of milk-fed veal with fennel) is, in this respect, quite illuminating: "When I say 'saucepans'," Artusi expounds, "I mean copper pans, well coated inside with a layer of tin. People can say what they like, but copper, when kept clean, is always preferable to iron or earthenware, which get too hot and tend to burn the food cooking in them. Earthenware cracks and absorbs grease, and after some use starts to give off a bad smell."[98]

Other ubiquitous utensils are the wooden mixing spoon and, above all, the *mezzaluna*, to whose versatility *Scienza in cucina* could be considered a monumental ode. Then, of course, there are the sieves. Sooner or later, not merely vegetables but also fish and meat are pounded in a mortar and passed through a sieve. Bizarre as it may sound, a strainer can also do as well as a baking dish. "To bake," Artusi writes in the first recipe for *bocca di dama* (lady cake, recipe 584), "pour into a copper baking pan greased with butter and dusted with confectioners' sugar and flour. Or you can use a strainer with a wooden ring, and cover the bottom with a sheet of paper."[99]

The most colorful testimony of Artusi's painstaking involvement in the actual testing of his recipes – and of the strenuous efforts of his two kitchen aides to make the most of the master's verbal explications – comes perhaps from Domenico Amaducci, a young fellow citizen from Forlimpopoli who, during his military service in Florence, visited repeatedly with the white-haired gastronome. Artusi, for his part, used Amaducci as a guinea pig: "finally I was asked to sit at the table," recounted Amaducci of one such visit, "or more precisely, a small little round table where there was room for two persons, and I was forced to sit there observing all rules of etiquette. 'The meal is served!' said Artusi who paced restlessly between the dining room and the kitchen, which had been transformed (as I would later see) into a well-equipped laboratory with two earthenware stoves ... Before taking leave, I wanted to meet the two 'martyrs' of the stoves ... 'Did you enjoy the meal?' they asked me. I answered with a military expression: 'I'll sign off on that!' 'Lucky you. We're here almost all day long working on these stoves and our master drives us crazy with his continuous experiments."[100]

It is doubtful that Artusi ever touched a kitchen utensil, that he ever lit a fire under a pot or finely chopped or gently stirred anything. These tasks, as can be gathered from the Amaducci story, were entrusted to his housekeeper and cook, Francesco Ruffilli and Marietta Sabbatini. Artusi's role was exclusively that of a taster, a pronouncer of verdicts, approving or disapproving the domestically re-created gustatory experiences he had been exposed or alerted to in the outside world. His debt of gratitude for the cares of his two "semper fideles" would neither go unacknowledged nor remain unpaid. In his will, Artusi bequeathed to Marietta "5,000 lire, free of inheritance tax, the complete bed from my bedroom, including my yellow silk bedcover, and, as a memento, my long gold chain and watch," and to Francesco, "3,000 lire, likewise free of any inheritance tax or withholding, and, as a memento, my gold watch, which you wind with a little key." For Marietta, he actually goes a significant step further and enters a *Panettone Marietta* among the recipes in *Scienza in cucina*. In the introduction to that recipe (no. 604), Artusi credits her as "a good cook, and such a good-hearted, honest woman that she deserves to have this cake named after her, especially since she taught me how to make it." Further praises are added at the end: "This panettone is worth trying, because it's much better than the Milanese-style panettone that's sold commercially, and isn't much trouble to make."[101]

This comment brings us back to the issue of provenance. Centuries of exchanges and debates brought about by colliding gastronomic cultures have revealed the symptomatically idealistic nature of the quest and turned it into a "consummation to be wished," perhaps, but not "devoutly." At best, it can be gauged in terms of insistence on and/ or variation in the selection of ingredients and condiments, and in the manner of amalgamating them in mediocre, plausible, or even excellent dishes. In this respect Artusi is as original as the next person, actually a little more, since he aggressively campaigned in favor of vegetables, upon which the majority of food-minded contemporaries looked with a great deal of suspicion. Take potatoes, for instance, which had been imported into Europe at the end of the sixteenth century, and for which Italian cooks would not find any systematic use until the nineteenth century was well under way. Indeed, it is only after the validation they receive in *Scienza in cucina,* Professor Camporesi informs us, that *"Gnocchi di papata* (potato dumplings) attain full and stable national citizenship."[102]

The same, Camporesi goes on to remark, can be said of tomatoes, which literally counterinvade the Italian peninsula from the south, after Garibaldi's red-shirted troops "delivered" those regions from the Bourbons and turned them over to the Piedmontese. Tomatoes give "new fleshy texture and flavor to eclectic, anonymous Romantic cuisine, which was largely an offshoot of French cooking, and had doggedly survived the restoration, without any effort at originality. Much more than the potato, the tomato is a new disruptive and revolutionary element in 19th-century Italian cuisine. Long neglected in culinary practice and looked upon with suspicion, it had been relegated, at best, to negligible services."[103]

Artusi can also be called a fighter of gastronomic prejudice, which he finds dietarily unacceptable. He even points out the subtle manifestation of racism inherent in some such prejudices: "Forty years ago," he writes in his recipe for *petonciani* (eggplant; recipe 399), "one hardly saw eggplant or fennel in the markets of Florence; they were considered to be vile because they were foods eaten by Jews. As in other matters of greater moment, here again the Jews show how they have always had a better nose than the Christians."[104]

Much simpler aetiological questions (where did Artusi get his inspiration, whence did he transcribe the treatments for his full-fledged scripts?) can be answered in a variety of ways. Apart from the recipes he drew from the classic cookery books that, contrary to common opinion, did not feature prominently in his not entirely impressive library,[105] he borrowed from friends who shared his gastronomic proclivity and, above all, from their wives.

As late as April 1909, Marchioness Blandina Almerici sends him the recipe for the *ciambelline* (little rings) she had eaten at the Albergo Tre Re di Bologna, the same establishment where Artusi ate his *maccheroni* next to an overly vociferous (according to Artusi, anyway) Felice Orsini (see above, page xxxii). Other feminine presences can be sensed in *Scienza in cucina*, but protected by a veil of anonymity. Who is the "young, charming Bolognese woman known as la Rondinella [the little swallow]" we are invited to thank for having taught Artusi how to make *strichetti alla Bolognese* (strichetti noodles Bolognese style; recipe 51),[106] or "the lovely and most gracious Signora Adele [who] wishes me to tell you how to make" *sformato della Signora Adele* (Signora Adele's Gruyère Mold; recipe 346)?[107] And are such epithets as "charming," "lovely," and "most gracious" reason enough to believe, as someone has suggested, at least in the case of la Rondinella, an actual, and perhaps food-related, love affair?

What he did not learn from his paramours or his friends and their wives, Artusi drew from anonymous or vaguely identified sources (such as the family from Santa Maria Capua Vetere who gave him the recipe for *maccheroni alla napoletana* (macaroni Neapolitan style I; recipe 85) or borrowed from the chefs, the innkeepers, the *maîtres d'hôtel* with whom he became acquainted at the many prestigious eateries and spas he could easily afford to frequent. He also lent a favourable ear to his correspondents, housewives and housekeepers who, upon buying *Scienza in cucina*, would write the author with variations and/or suggestions of their own. A diligent interlocutor, Artusi never forgets to acknowledge the contributions of his readers, unless of course the adopted recipe has been substantially altered. Such is the case of *rossi d'uovo al canapè* (egg-yolk canapés; recipe 142), which offers Artusi one more opportunity to rail against "stupid and often ridiculous names," but not to thank Adelina Galasso from Breganze, in the county of Vicenza, from whom he may have received the original input.[108]

There are two basic culinary traditions that find a home in Artusi's book: the then unpopular and now highly fashionable simple cooking of the *contadini*, and the complex cooking of courtly chefs smartly adapted to modern needs and tastes. In both cases he was ahead of his time: the pains he took to rehabilitate country-style cooking paved the way to its current widespread acceptance as a sign of sapience and refinement. He also brought together the culinary tradition prevailing in his native Emilia-Romagna with the dishes he learned to appreciate in Florence, where he pitched his tent for the longest time.

The people of Romagna use butter and animal fat for frying and are partial to pasta dishes and meats, reflecting a tradition that has Celtic origins. Tuscans, on the other hand, use oil for frying and favor soups and vegetables, preferences considered "quintessentially Mediterranean," as we have fallen into the somewhat mysterious habit of saying. The alloy Artusi created from the two formative elements of Italian culture – the unbridled energy of the Gothic and the delicate "design" of the Renaissance – was unprecedented. Romagna and Tuscany are adjoining regions. Forlimpopoli and Florence are fewer than a hundred miles apart, and the portion of the Appenine range separating them is not particularly impervious. Yet their basic gastronomic (as well as phonetic) physiognomies diverge significantly. No one was more conscious of the divergence than Artusi himself, who felt the need to alert anyone interested in his *minestra di due colori* (two-color soup; recipe 31) that "this is a light and delicate soup which in Tuscany is most likely to be appreciated by the ladies. However, it should not be served in Romagna, that homeland of tagliatelle, where softness to the bite is not to the locals' taste. Even less would they appreciate the pasty texture of tapioca, the very sight of which would, with few exceptions, turn their stomachs."[109]

Whichever way you slice it, one conviction remains intact in Artusi's pages from beginning to end. He creates his recipes for those who can afford them, those who have the means not just of feeding themselves, but of doing so pleasantly and, above all, intelligently. He does not believe in wasting money (he was a banker, after all) and instructs his readers to be frugal (not stingy). By the same token, he affirms, in no uncertain terms, that top-quality ingredients and produce are to be obtained or else the art of eating well will go down the drain. "If you do not aspire to become a premier cook," writes Artusi, "you need not have been born with a pan on your head to become a good one. Passion, care, and precision of method will certainly suffice; then, of course, you must choose the finest ingredients as your raw materials, for these will make you shine."[110]

It is not merely a question of affordability, however. Appealing to upper-middle-class taste requires a strategy that transcends the identification of expensive or neglected ingredients. While the encoding of gastronomic concerns in the rubric of bourgeois values is inevitable, Artusi's readers may simply be aspiring members of that social class. Reading *Scienza in cucina,* in other words, can become an effective enticement to upward mobility. As to those who could exhibit an old membership card, they too had to feel justified in spending, or paying people to spend, so much time in the kitchen. Domestic dinner parties had to become, or pass for, a cultural event, as well as a statement of prosperity.

There are several clues in the text that makes these statements plausible, if not final. The large number of digressions have already been observed. Let me just add here a particularly poignant example, as it brings together scientific competence and Artusi's beloved *religio oeconomica*: "The angel shark (*Rhina squatina*)," he writes in the recipe for *pesce squadro in umido* (stewed angel shark; recipe 462), "has a flat body similar to the ray. The skin, which is rough and hard, is used to polish wood and ivory, and to line sheaths for knives, swords and the like. The flesh of this fish is rather ordinary, but when prepared in the following manner it makes a family dish that is not only edible, but more than passingly good. And it is economical, because it is easy to find, at least in Italy."[111]

The juxtaposition of "culture" and culinary instructions is a shrewd rhetorical device to reassure readers who otherwise may have felt embarrassed by their own familiarity with a book of recipes. In this way they could not only consult it as frequently as they pleased, but leave it around the house and even show it to their friends (which does wonders for sales). Similar sentiments, in our day and age, may be elicited by "serious" men's magazines, such as *Playboy*, where the enjoyment of female nudity is made acceptable by the presence of sophisticated literature. There are also lexical clues: when a dish is ready, it is never *brought* to the table: it is *sent* there by someone who actually slaved away to make it for you in your kitchen, or by a figment of your wishful imagination. Which means, let me say one more time, that the reader must be a bourgeois or have bourgeois aspirations.[112]

Another prominent indicator of the audience "targeted" by Artusi is the concern he shows for hygienic norms, which prompted him to equip his book with sections entitled "A Few Health Guidelines" and "The Nutritional Value of Meats." While *all* of his notions hearken back to the idea connecting health with intelligent food intake – an idea from which sprung Hippocratic medicine itself – *some* specifically link good health to the observance of the "seasonal principle," implying the exclusive consumption of what nature produces at any given time during the year. The seasonal principle also entails the necessity of eating more when the "natural body heat" is stronger, which happens during the winter months, according to medieval doctor Ugo Benzi's *Regole della sanità e della natura dei cibi* (Principles of health and the nature of foods). This view – the backbone of a centuries-old tradition, profusely exemplified in the *Theatrum* and *Regimen Sanitatis* of the Salernitan school – has been totally demolished by modern systems of refrigerated transportation. In Artusi's times, however, this kind of wisdom was on every body's lips, as attested by dozens of adages and popular rhymes:

> Slender in Spring thy diet be, and spare
> Disease, in Summer, springs from surplus fare.
> From Autumn fruits be careful to abstain,
> Lest by mischance they should occasion pain.
> But when rapacious winter has come on,
> Then freely eat till appetite is gone.[113]

Health concerns extend to food variety – no single food item is so necessary that it cannot be replaced, nor can it possibly constitute a complete diet by itself – as well as clothing, physical exercise, and, above all, ambience.[114] This last issue offers Artusi yet another opportunity to exercise his wit:

> Try to live in healthy houses, full of light and well ventilated: illness flees where the sun shines in. Pity those ladies who receive guests in semi-darkness, and in whose homes you stumble into the furniture and know not where to put your hat. Because of this custom of living in dimly lit rooms, of not moving their feet or getting out into the open air, and because their sex tends by nature to drink little wine and rarely eats meat, preferring vegetables and sweets, such ladies are seldom seen with red cheeks, the sign of prosperous health, or with fine complexions all blood and milk. Their flesh is not firm but flaccid, their faces like vetches that one grows in the dark to adorn tombs on Holy Thursday. Is it any wonder, then, that among women one finds so many hysterics, neurotics and anemics?[115]

How far and wide we have traveled from the Romantic idolization of the *mansarde* or the much-below-standard dwellings of the proletarian and sub-proletarian families that populate Edmondo De Amicis' pages.

It is not just the dining room that undergoes radical changes during the last decades of the nineteenth century. Even more radical innovations take place in the kitchen, where meat grinders make their first appearance and the old wood-burning oven is replaced by the cast iron stove, a modern cooking unit that enables domestic chefs to determine precise cooking times at fairly exact temperatures, and boil, roast, and bake different dishes all at once.[116] Cooking leaves the world of alchemy and crossed fingers to enter the arena of precision, with no unpleasant surprises.

From the time of Artusi to the present, Italy has become a country and, by and a large, a culture where the scientific adventure of cooking and the artistic experience of eating have once again sidestepped the emotions surrounding technology and intuition to achieve the status of a religious initiation. In and of itself, this is not necessarily an indication of progress, yet I would challenge anyone to label the rediscovery of gastronomic rituals as regressive. It would be enough to remember that the great-grandparents of those Italians who, in our own time, are subjecting themselves to one or more dietetic treatments, were likely to have eaten far less than was required for their daily sustenance. In spite of such major catastrophes as two world wars and the widespread irresponsibility that has characterized the last half century of their political and economic history, vast numbers of Italians have left behind poverty and malnutrition (as well as illiteracy) to live in a world where the immediate satisfaction of material needs has become not simply a birthright, but an opportunity to reconnect to a legacy of luxury and sophistication dating back to the Renaissance, when Swiss guards wore, as they do now, uniforms designed by none other than Michelangelo.

On this evolutionary trajectory, the figure of Pellegrino Artusi occupies a pivotal place, not too remote from that of Maestro Martino in the late fifteenth century. Both of them, each in his own cultural and political environment, twisted into a cogent and organic whole threads of intuitions and habits that might have appeared unreconcilable on first sight. Each leaned on the past to usher in the new, reacting positively to difficult circumstances and turning "necessary conditions into desirable qualities," as the old Italian adage goes. As for the inevitable temptation to suggest that Artusi is to Italian gastronomy what Escoffier is to French, heeding it is by far less heretical than many culinary theologians are prepared to admit. It is true, however, that the analogy is not proportional and, consequently, neither specular nor infinitely reassuring. It may, however, offer some help, if only by way of contrast. The role played in Italy by Artusi's historic persona and the symbolic values attached to it is likely to differ in kind, not just degree, from the role played in France by the celebrated author of *La guide culinaire*. To appreciate the difference within the analogy, all we have to do is turn to some edifying examples of "European" gastronomic literature. Following in the footsteps of the *Larousse gastronomique* (where Escoffier is treated with all the respect he deserves), *The Oxford Companion to Food* wholly ignores the name of Pellegrino Artusi and assumes "assafoetida" to be the first possible entry after "artichoke." (It is worth noting, by contrast that all Italian gastronomic dictionaries honor the name and the talent of the French virtuoso.)

A much nobler attitude transpires from the behavior of the good people of Forlimpopoli and those of Villeneuve-Loubet (in the south of France, where Escoffier first saw light, in 1847), who agreed to "twin" their townships and, to make sure that even the most distracted traveler would not miss the significance of their gesture, set up road signs, each acknowledging the existence of the other. Whether real or merely wished for, the seductive energy of this "egotisme à deux" in which *here* and *there* merge into one aspiration, at a time when public attention seems to be monopolized by a resurgence of inflated patriotism and embarrassing episodes of pseudoheroic behavioral patterns, may be read as an auspicious sign that difference and equanimity can still go hand in hand.[117]

Escoffier was a professional cook who, in 1859, as a mere thirteen-year-old boy, began to apprentice in his uncle's Restaurant Français, in Nice on the French Riviera. From such humble beginnings, he moved on to supervise the kitchens of the most famous eating establishments of his time, ranging from the Petit Moulin Rouge restaurant in Paris to the Grand Hotel in Monte Carlo, the Savoy and the Carlton in London, and, of course, the Ritz in Paris. He blossomed into a larger-than-life personality – "le roi des cuisiniers … le cuisinier des rois," as he was called. He was a celebrity who often overshadowed the celebrities he served and after whom he occasionally named his dishes: Kaiser Wilhelm II, Marcel Proust, Frederic VIII of Denmark, Emperor Franz Joseph of Austria, actress Sarah Bernhardt, singers Adelina Patti and Nellie Melba,[118] and dozens of Sagans, Vanderbilts, and Radziwills – in a word, anybody who, before, during, and after la Belle Epoque, was a bona fide regular of the *beau monde* or resembled one.

As Chef Gualtiero Marchesi, one of the earliest and most gifted exponents of *nouvelle cuisine*, has recently remarked: "Artusi's recipes should be read in the context of the era in which they were written and the audience to whom they were addressed. We are at the end of the nineteenth century, when there was no codified Italian cuisine. We are not in France, where at the end of the 1920s August Escoffier published his *Guide culinaire*, which delved not only into the ambit of French cuisine but international cuisine as well. In his rigorous exposition, he leaves nothing to chance. Artusi, instead *'gives complete freedom to the cook in his recipe book, and by doing so he foresaw the current tendency of the present era which runs against the orthodoxy of classic cuisine.'*"[119]

But that's just it: Is the time not yet ripe to hail freedom and even individual whims as signs of a much needed and long-awaited culinary emancipation? In other words, does this newly conceived latitude, of which many "Artusian" recipes are a testimony, not encourage the very assumption and display of responsibilities that strict obedience to blueprints (no matter how perfect) would in fact discourage? In the recipe for *pasticcio di maccheroni* (meat and macaroni pie; recipe 349) the ultimate implications of Artusi's softer, less obsessive, and, in this case, mirthful approach cannot go underestimated: playing on the the word *pasticcio*, which of course means *pie*, but also, *pastiche, hotchpotch, jumble, mess,* and so on, he concludes his invitation to "modify the recipe as you please" with the remark that "a pasticcio always comes out well no matter how it is prepared."[120]

Progress does not stand in the way: quite the contrary. The more precisely cooks can control their equipment, the freer they will be to improvise, to add personal touches, and to rely on established and codified experience merely as an inspiring point of departure. When basic procedures can be repeated with a minimal margin of error, even culinary "transgressions" are welcomed as the sign of a need to explore the realm of the possible, that kingdom of temerity and risk, situated just opposite the land of the plausible. In this inspirational territory ideologies and manifestos do not qualify as devices to shore up knowledge: observance of premises are profoundly shaken by an alternative and deliriously provocative logic. The implication in *Scienza in cucina* is that, while a rather mediocre kind of pleasure can be derived by confining oneself to the laws of calculability, real fulfillment implies a ravaging of the certainties that have enabled the process in the first place. Sapience and savoring are once again connected in Artusi's book.

Much has been written about a title that would seem to imply that the cognitive advantages of *scienza* belong with the making of food, while those of *arte* refer to its appreciation and consumption. In reality their coming together is a marriage of convenience. While Artusi may not have the confident air of superiority of a true man of science or the divine inspiration of the artistic genius, he shares with the first the dominant ideology that reason and science can provide certain and lasting answers to any problem, physical or metaphysical, and with the second the reliance on techniques and the training of the imagination.

Citizen of a century filled with books singing the praises of "physiology" (dozens by Mantegazza alone), dating back to Jean-Anthelme Brillat-Savarin's trail-blazing *Physiologie du goût* (1825), Artusi was in no position to ignore the temptation to secure his culinary edifice on a clearly marked positivist foundation. The debt *Scienza in cucina* owes to this philosophical school, however, does not extend much beyond lip service, except perhaps in the area of social problems, where a modicum of rationality has never done any harm anyway.

The Artusian notion of *art*, on the other hand, while not antagonistic to that of *science*, is akin to that of *technè* – of ability, or skill obtained (and surpassed) by observing masters at work. It conjures up the atmosphere of a Renaissance *bottega*[121] or any other ergonomic environment in which the original semantics of *Ars* have not been altered or betrayed. They can be encapsulated as follows: "any productive activity of man (as opposed to nature), disciplined by a group of specific, technical knowledge (by means of norms and rules) and founded as much on experience as on ability and the personal geniality of the person who is executing it."[122]

While seemingly swarming with "mothers, sisters and servant girls"[123] whose "culinary wisdom" the author neither shuns nor ridicules, Artusi's kitchen is in fact the ideal training ground of those sorcerer's apprentices who, having studied statistics, prefer to be guided by the empirical wisdom of their palates, and by the notion that while taste is doubtless one of the senses nature bestows upon all her children, a taste for food is a "knowledge" one develops through a strategy of instinctual perceptions. It is safe to assume that, in Artusi's title, *science* and *art* are to be entered as chiastic members of same basic linguistic register. In our times, *Art in the Kitchen and the Science of Eating Well* would be equally satisfactory; in nineteenth-century rhetoric, this would not have been the case.

Beyond these semasiological explorations, two major achievements have remained unchallenged from Artusi's times to our own: the reaffirmation of a direct link between health and a sensible diet[124] and the definitive defeat of those "medically proven theories" that assigned different digestive and assimilative powers to stomachs belonging to people of different social origin. Clearly these theories did not hold taste to be a matter of culture, and anchored metabolism to a set on non-physiological observations. While gentlemen and ladies[125] would be harmed by the ingestion of popular and rustic food, feeding "delicate food" to bean-eating peasants would result in sickness and death.[126] Variously manipulated, this rather convenient assumption became a powerful political tool in the hands of the privileged classes and an occasion for self-defeating vainglorious declarations on the part of their subjects.[127]

Now that gastronomic democracy seems to be solidly entrenched in certain regions of the West (not necessarily those that glitter most: just look at the millions of Americans who poison themselves daily with fast-food products and turn their bodies into walking garbage bins), poor parents may renounce their cruel tease of promising to reward the good behavior of their ice cream–craving children by showing them other more fortunate children *actually* eating ice cream in the main piazza of an Italian or French city. The repercussions of this type of "grey" humor may still be traced in the darker psychic recesses and ostensible lifestyle of many a Rolex-flaunting adult.

A caveat to conclude: The Artusian predilection for excessive quantities of butter and lard is a myth. As is the idea that the recipes liberally deploy spices: neither Tuscan nor Romagnan cuisine is particularly spicy; and Artusi recommends using modest amounts of salt and pepper. Exaggeration, even if judged by our standards, is not really Artusi's game. Indeed, a revealing *excusatio* concludes the brief preface to the book: "I should not like my interest in gastronomy to give me the reputation of a gourmand or glutton. I object to any such dishonorable imputation, for I am neither. I love the good and the beautiful wherever I find them, and hate to see anyone squander, as they say, God's bounty. Amen."[128]

In their *Artusi 2000*,[129] Giuseppe Sangiorgi and Annamaria Tosi have rearranged 775 Artusian recipes in order to construct a rational model of food consumption, on a day-to-day basis. They show beyond any doubt that consulting *Scienza in cucina* does not automatically mean preparing for a royal banquet. On the other hand, Claudio Moras, president of the Associazione Cuochi Romagnoli (the Romagna Chefs' Association) and editor of *L'Artusi cent'anni dopo, 1891–1991*[130] argues, with good reason, that the classification of *pagnottelle ripiene* (stuffed rolls; recipe 239) under the heading "entremets" – that is, minor dishes to be served between main courses – may contradict eating habits on any rung of the social ladder. The caloric content of the stuffing itself, which consists in Artusi's words, "of chickpea-size chunks ... [of] chicken livers, white chicken meat, sweetbreads and the like ... cooked in brown stock and bound with a pinch of flour ... [and], to make the mixture tastier, ... truffles,"[131] is enough to discourage the modern chef from treating *pagnottelle* as a dependent clause in an already rich edible sentence. But, if that is the case, why not trim it and treat it as a main course?

To balance these two assessments, we may wish to turn to the endorsement of Artusi's recommendations that Emanuela Djalma Vitali proffers in her review of the celebrated Einaudi 2001 edition of

Scienza in cucina, whose author she notes, "prematurely died at the age of 91" due to an overdose of good food. "There is no great cuisine (or health) wherever there is room for margarine, seed, palm, or coconut oil, processed fats and 'light' cheeses, or other disgusting abominations. This is sensorial squalor ... It occurs when butter (a great deity among foods), lard, rendered pig cheek, and rendered lard (why not?) are ostracized. You cannot live to be almost one hundred if you allow yourself to be ground up by nutritional whims, by fears of lipids and cholesterol. These are diseases of the soul."[132]

Whatever you yourself choose to do, I sincerely hope you will not pronounce the same malevolent (but largely justified) verdict that Artusi reached with regard to his competitors: "Beware of books that deal with this art: most of them are inaccurate or incomprehensible, especially the Italian ones. The French are a little better. But from either, the very most you will glean are a few notions, useful only if you already know the art".[133]

Of course, much more can be said about the "gastronomic father of us all" and his epochal book, and we would gladly oblige anyone kind (or hungry) enough to advance a request for further information, had we not been taught by schoolteachers and parents, at a time and in a country where many children did not have enough to eat, to chew each morsel thirty-three times, regardless of its consistency, and to leave the dinner table with a little bit of appetite.

NOTES

1 The number of recipes had also grown prodigiously: from 475 to 790. The second edition (1895) brought the number to 575, the third (1899) added 19 new recipes, the fifth (1900) 35, the sixth (1902) 25, the eighth (1905) 15, the tenth (1906) 15, the eleventh (1907) 8, the twelfth (1908) 88, the thirteenth (1909) 10. Artusi's death, which occurred on 30 March 1910, ensured that this figure would not increase further.

2 This section was added to the sixth edition and reprinted in all subsequent editions.

3 "Story (of the Success) of a Book" appears in *La cucina bricconcella* (Cooking is a troublesome sprite), a precious collection of essays edited by Andrea Pollarini and published in 1991 by the Region Emilia Romagna (Grafis Edizioni) to celebrate the one hundredth anniversary of *Scienza in cucina*.

4 Landi and/or his heirs reissued *Scienza in cucina* thirty-one times, until 1928.

5 Or, rather, international distribution: in 1901, an unidentified American customer placed an order for 100 copies. In the beginning books were sold directly by the author. As late as 1932 they were sold by R. Bemporad e Figlio as well as by the estate of Pellegrino Artusi.

6 See p. 5.

7 Bemporad began its own printing in 1924, creating a four-year overlap with Landi.

8 Displaying on the front cover the number of copies sold in the hope of enhancing sales was a widespread practice, not merely a promotional device introduced by Bemporad. In fact, the same kind of information was avialable on the front cover of the editions issued by Landi. It would also seem to bear the "imprint" of the author's churlish style.

9 Not too many Italians (literati or otherwise) can claim to have achieved a similar station in their lifetime or after. The few exceptions include Machiavelli, whose name stands, quite mistakenly, for political cunning and even treachery; and Casanova, of course, whose name now has a mildly obscene connotation. Unless otherwise noted, all translations from the Italian are mine.

10 In 1908 Salani "retrenched" to the third edition, which featured a much reduced number of recipes. This edition, to which they had legal rights, was then reissued for a good number of years.

11 See *La scienza in cucina etc.*, ed. Davide Paolini (Milan: Sperling & Kupfer Editori, 1991). The title page informs us that this "most famous cookbook" has been "revisited by five great chefs: Gianfranco Bolognesi, Arrigo Cipriani, Gualtiero Marchesi, Fulvio Pierangelini, Gianfranco Vissani." That same year, under the auspices of the Comitato Segavecchia (a club, in Forlimpopoli, created to preserve a folklore tradition that dates back to 1547), the Association of Chefs from Emilia-Romagna celebrated the one hundredth anniversary of the book by "slimming down" Artusian recipes and reformulating Artusian menus. See *L'Artusi cent'anni dopo* (Artusi, one hundred years later) (Bertinoro: Tipolitografia Ge.Graf, 1991). Prior to these centennial "reformulations," in 1962 Luigi Volpicelli had authored a much quoted preface to a luxury edition of *Scienza in cucina*, featuring a valuable "panorama della cucina italiana nei secoli" (panorama of Italian cooking through the centuries), while in 1968 a dietetically conscientious Irene Bosco brought forth a "selected and reduced" *Nuovo Artusi*.

12 An anthropologist and literary historian, Piero Camporesi (Forli, 1926–Bologna, 1997) taught Italian literature and cultural history at the University of Bologna. In the early 1960s he published the vernacular writings of Giulio Cesare Croce, a sixteenth-century Bolognese author. This was a prelude to a series of original studies dealing with topics such as blood, milk, sex, hunger, and the Italian landscape. Some of his titles are *La carne impassibile* (1986), *La via del latte* (1993), and *Le belle contrade* (1995).

13 It is also sprinkled with the witty prefatory remarks of the prominent writer/ painter Emilio Tadini.

14 The complete text, penned for the exhibition of Della Casa's watercolors at the Biblioteca civica Luigi Poletti in Modena (March–June 2002), is now available at: *http://www.comune.modena.it/biblioteche/artusi/artusi.htm*.

15 Issued by Marsilio Publishers in 1997. Prior American editions of *Science in*

the Kitchen are plagued with grave faults. Some are abridged, and many have simply misunderstood the original (Artusi, who was not a Tuscan, chose to flavor his Italian with expressions from that a true Tuscan would have perhaps avoided, ultimately complicating a translator's task). Worst of all, they have not paid due attention to the things that make this book exceptional: anecdotes, literary references, personal reminiscences. In editing out most of these jewels, they have, regrettably, transformed a classic into a poorly translated cookbook. Needless to say, ours is not a perfect edition either. We apologize for any mistakes on our part, and would be very grateful to any readers who can bring them to our attention. In the true spirit of Artusi, we will incorporate plausible suggestions in all future editions.

16 Piero Camporesi, introduction to *La scienza in cucina e l' arte di mangiar bene* (Turin: Einaudi, 1970), lix.

17 See *La cucina italiana*: *www.emmeti.it/Food/Toscana/Storia/Firenze7.it.html*.

18 In his *Storia linguistica dell'Italia unita* (Rome-Bari: Laterza, 1970), Tullio De Mauro writes that in 1861 a meager 2.5 percent of the Italian population could read and write standard Italian. Although this figure increased dramatically in the following decades – thanks, primarily, to the enforcement of compulsory (elementary) education – results were not as encouraging as they could have been. Writing in 1910, Camillo Corradini, reported that the structure for the dissemination of literacy resembled more closely that of a chain for the distribution of "luxury items," depending as it did on the revenues of individual municipal administration that were, by and large, indirectly proportional to the seriousness of the problem. See, in particular, De Mauro, *Storia linguistica*, 92–5.

19 "For many ... this book represented the only reading of their lives, the singular excursion in the garden of science and literature, the unique and tentative contact with that which burns beyond the oven in the great universe of knowledge" Camporesi, introduction to *La scienza in cucina*, lv.

20 See, Folco Portinari, "Artusi," in Pollarini, ed. *Cucina bricconcella*, 100.

21 See p. 386 below.

22 *The Betrothed*, trans. Bruce Penman (London: Penguin Books, 1972), 26.

23 The recipe for *Bue alla California* (beef California style; recipe 300), is not, however, an indication of origin: "Whoever concocted this dish," writes Artusi, "probably did not know what to call it, so he gave it this strange name. But for that matter, almost all culinary terms are either strange or ridiculous" (p. 230).

24 See p. 215. The active presence of *pie*, at the root of *paio*, should not go unnoted. It may give us a hint of the Anglo-Tuscan language spoken in Florence in the late nineteenth century.

25 A critical edition of Machiavelli's text has been published by Ornella Castellani Polidori in her *Niccolò Machiavelli e il "Dialogo intorno alla nostra lingua"* (Florence: Olschky, 1978). The passage quoted here is on page 243. Some scholars, first among them Pio Rajna in 1893, have doubted the paternity of this essay. Their arguments are carefully summarized by Castellani Polidori in the first chapter of the book (13–29).

26 Guerrini was also a librarian and a gastronomer in his own right. As a poet, he wrote under the pseudonym Lorenzo Stecchetti. "Artusi's legacy was not lost on a learned countryman of his. Capricious to the point of eccentricity, [Guerrini] was indeed Artusi's kindred spirit, and his personal friend. In a time when everyone could feel the

economic hardship of the First World War ... Olindo Guerrini fashioned a work that could also be read as a completion of Artusi. *L'arte di utilizzare gli avanzi della mensa* (The art of using table leftovers) covers average to below-average, middle-class, economical, and frugal cuisine. Much attention is paid to techniques for savings, which, certainly not overlooked by Artusi, found in Stecchetti's pages their most suitable dwelling." See Camporesi, introduction, lxi–lxii.

27 Massimo Montanari, "Leggere il cibo: un viaggio nella letteratura gastronomica" (How to read food: a journey through gastronomic literature," in *La cucina bricconcella,* 23.

28 Chicago: W.M. Hill, 1941.

29 Montanari, "Leggere il cibo," 28.

30 It may not be possible, here, to invoke the "philosophical" lesson of Plàtina (and Maestro Martino), whose food-related permissible pleasure (*honesta voluptas*), obfuscating the notion of sin that was inherent in the activity of eating well or for reasons not strictly connected with one's own sustenance, goes hand in hand with the idea of dining for the sake of being with friends and kindred spirits. Nevertheless it is in that cultural environment that the notion of "dinner party" takes shape. In Martino's manual, next to the measurements (a great novelty in and of themselves), the cook always indicates the number of people (varying from 8 to 12) for whom a given recipe has been conceived.

31 Camporesi, introduction, xliv–xlvi. He writes: "Artusi used multiple and often times unpredictable sources. The formulas and titles were often modified, revised or changed by the author. As a result they blossomed once again thanks to the skillful manipulation of the author who exhorted his readers not to trust 'the books that deal with the subject' because 'they are for the most part fallacious or incomprehensible, especially the Italian books.' But Artusi, a man of letters, had read and studied them during the long years of his seemingly interminable life."

32 See below, p. 69. Emphasis added.

33 See below, p. 251. For Artusi, the lightness of food was a constant concern. A year before his demise, he added the appendix "Foods for Weak Stomachs" to the text of the fourteenth edition.

34 In 1809, in Milan, probably under the "democratic" influence of the French Revolution exported to Italy by Napoleon Bonaparte, the amphibious *Il cuoco moderno ridotto a perfezione secondo il gusto francese e italiano* (A modern cook elevated to perfection in accordance with Italian and French tastes) saw the light. The author, identified only as L.O.G., is unknown.

35 Montanari, "Leggere il cibo," 30.

36 Among others: *La cuciniera piemontese* (The Piedmontese female chef; Vercelli, 1771); *La cuoca cremonese* (The Cremonese female cook; Cremona, 1794); Antonio Nebbia's *Il cuoco maceratese* (The cook from Macerata; Macerata, 1781); Ippolito Cavalcanti's *La cucina teorico-pratica* (Theoretical-practical cooking; Naples, 1837, with an appendix written in Neapolitan dialect); Giambattista Ratto's *La cuciniera genovese (The Genoan female chef*; Genoa, 1867), etc.

37 Leonardi was possibly the first chef who thought of seasoning pasta with tomato sauce. He was once employed by Catherine II of Russia, and was "fluent" in Polish, Turkish, French, and German gastronomy as well.

38 See recipe 678, p. 490 below. Giancarlo Roversi ("Pellegrino Artusi a Bologna", in *Cucina bricconcella,* 135–7) emphasizes the familiarity Artusi must have had with such Bolognese annual publications as *La serva ammaestrata dal cuoco piemontese* (A maidservant trained by the Piedmontese cook) and *La cuciniera* (The female cook), aimed explicitly at teaching housekeepers and domestic cooks how to please their masters and mistresses "and to avoid extravagant expenses."

39 See p. 510 below; emphasis in original. Artusi is jovial and patient most but not all of the time. He can even be rather curt, as he undoubtedly is in the opening lines of his recipe for *ciambelline* (little rings; recipe 190): "This dish, too, is difficult to make well if you have not seen it prepared. I will try to describe it, but I cannot guarantee you will understand me" (p. 162).

40 In a pamphlet, published in Florence in 1972, celebrating Artusi's gastronomic importance, and appropriately entitled "Il re dei cuochi" (The king of cooks), author Giovanni Celati transcribes, directly from *Scienza in cucina,* a parody Olindo Guerrini made of a recipe by Giovanni Vialardi, whose *Trattato di cucina, pasticceria moderna, credenza e relativa confetteria* (Treatise on cooking, modern pastries, buffets, and appropriate desserts; Turin, 1854), he regarded as a supreme example of the pompous style that blemished so many cookbooks of the time, and next to which Artusi's prose must have seemed a veritable antidote.

41 See pp. 65–6 below.

42 See pp. 107–8 below.

43 See his *Profilo di Pellegrino Artusi* (Forlimpopoli: Cassa Rurale e Artigiana, 1990), 39. To the endearing formal traits that characterize many of his recipes, we should add the "lighter touch" Artusi exhibited in the description of actual, often brutal, culinary actions. In the words of Piero Camporesi, "drawing upon an *humeur culinaire* unknown to professional cooks ..., [Artusi allayed] the most intimidating aspects inherent in culinary operations. Naturally he could not abolish them completely because they are an integral part of this 'science' that falls back daily into an unredeemable orignal sin." Camporesi, introduction, lxi.

44 See p. 299 below.

45 See p. 379 below; emphasis added.

46 "Scientific" digressions take prevalence over purely culinary instructions in the turkey, duck, and guinea hen related recipes. Artusi was perhaps satisfied with his expostulations about chicken and capon and in all likelihood felt that his readers could draw from there the guidance they would need to cook those birds.

47 According to the rather convincing computations of Giancarlo Roversi (cit., pp. 125–8), and not in 1850 as stated by Artusi himself in the fourteenth edition of *Scienza in cucina.*

48 Listed by Giuseppe Maria Mitelli in his *Gioco delle osterie* printed in 1712 and highly recommended by Claude Pasquin, the director of the Royal Library of Versailles, who visited in Bologna in 1826 and wrote about it in *L'Italie confortable* (printed 1842): a book that, writes Roversi (132), "could not have escaped the attention of that devourer of books that was Artusi."

49 See p. 186 below.

50 The recipe for *budino di farina di riso* (rice flour pudding) includes a dissertation on medieval delicacies that required colouring roasted peacock with a dark red clay, the description of a very bad meal inflicted on Messer Goro (courtier to Pope Pius

II) by a totally incompetent cook, a quotation from Homer, and the recipe itself. See pp. 473–6 below.

51 He was educated in Paris.

52 "When you hear someone speak of Bolognese cooking, salute it, because this cooking deserves it. It is somewhat heavy perhaps because the climate requires it, but it also succulent, tasty and healthy. This may explain why in Bologna a life span of 80 or 90 is more common than elsewhere" (p. 40 below). It is in Bologna, furthermore, that Artusi dreamed of founding an institute "to train young women to be cooks, for they are naturally more economical and less wasteful than men. These women would then be easy to employ, and would possess an art which, when brought into middleclass households, would serve as a medecine against the frequent quarrels that occur in families as a result of bad dining" (p. 42). All this, and more, in the recipe for *tortellini alla Bolognese* (tortellini Bolognése style; recipe 9).

53 See p. 164 below.

54 Artusian "Florencentricy" is epitomized in the literary writings the author dabbled in prior to his gastronomical conversion. Two of them – *Vita di Ugo Foscolo* (Life of Ugo Foscolo, 1878) *Osservazioni in appendice a trenta lettere di Giuseppe Giusti* (Marginal remarks on 30 letters by Giuseppe Giusti, 1881) – met with no success whatsoever but are occasionally mentioned by his biographers.

55 See p. 115 below.

56 See p. 493 below.

57 In English, a language whose gastronomic lexicon is greatly indebted to French, Artusi's titanic efforts to re-Italianize culinary jargon will necessarily go undetected.

58 Carlo Collodi (Carlo Lorenzini's *nom de plume*) lived from 1826 to 1890. At the end of the book, Pinocchio turns into a "normal boy" of flesh and bone. During his puppet years, he had many opportunities to be embarrassed by his nose that grew larger and longer whenever he told a lie. The story inspired many filmmakers, among them Walt Disney, whose animation 'Americanized' Pinocchio beyond recognition. A.M. Murray first translated the story into English in 1892.

59 *Pinocchio* (London: Puffin Books, 1996), 33.

60 Ibid., 66–7.

61 See "C'est li fabliaus de coquaigne," in Etienne Barbazan, ed., *Fabliaux et Contes des Poètes François tirésa des meilleurs auteurs,* vol. 4 (Paris: Chez B. Warée oncle, 1808), 176. "Those who sleep longer hours / Make more money" and "Those who sleep until noon / Earn five farthings and a half."

62 Giovanni Boccaccio, *Decameron*, trans. G.H. McWilliam (London: Penguin Books, 1972). See VIII Day, 3rd story, pp. 560–75. It has been more than plausibly shown that Boccaccio's *maccaroni* are, in reality, *gnocchi* (made with cheese and flour).

63 See in particular his "Bilora" (*Teatro*, ed. Ludovico Zorzi [Turin: Einaudi, 1967]), a "dialogue" in which indigence drives its "victim" to moral dejection and murder. In the late nineteenth and early twentieth centuries, the peasant condition had improved in Piedmont and Lombardy (then under Austrian Rule), thanks especially to the agricultural success of the mulberry tree and the development of a silk industry.

64 Written in 1909 and published in 1913.

65 Published in 1883. Verga had already denounced the horror of a poverty-driven rebellion, which actually took place in Sicily, during the *Risorgimento*. See "Libertà" in *Novelle rusticane* (Turin: F. Casanova, 1883).

66 Edmondo De Amicis (1846–1908) was a progressive intellectual open to socialist ideas. Besides *Cuore* (Heart), he wrote travel books like *Spagna* (Spain, 1873) and novels like *Amore e ginnastica* (Love and gymnastics, 1892). *Sull'oceano* (On the ocean, 1899) is an account of the terrible conditions in which Italian immigrants traveled by sea to America. *Primo maggio* (May day), one of his most significant accomplishments as a writer of "socially minded" literature, was published only in 1980.

67 *Pagine sparse* (Milan: Treves, 1911), 22.

68 Camporesi, introduction, xi–xx.

69 See *Igiene di epicuro* (Epicurean Hygene [Naples: Società editrice partenopea, 1910], 72). The subject is treated at length in Mantegazza's earlier book, *Igiene della cucina* (Hygiene in the kitchen [Milan: Brigola, 1867]) from which the preceding quote is derived (36–7). A a bon vivant who personally shopped for his food, and who happily recognized Artusi's competence in selecting cooks ("the new cook Orsolina is the best I've had in all my life. Every day she prepares a new a dish and they are all, or almost all, excellent. Every day I praise my friend Artusi who recommended her to me"). See his *Giornale*, 10 Dec. 1894, quoted by Capatti and Pollarini. See their edition of Artusi, *Autobiografia* (Milan: Il Saggiatore, 1993, 136). Paolo Mantegazza was born in Monza in 1831 and died in La Spezia in 1910, one year before his esculent friend. He is a perfect example of Italian neo-positivistic thinking. In his book *The Physiology of Pleasure* (1854), pleasure is divided into three very neat categories: senses, emotions, intellect. Mantegazza's passion for taxonomy leads him to some revealing subdivisions. For example, the first category is broken down into three classes of tactile experiences (plastic, epidermic, sexual), followed by taste, smell, music, sight, and three kinds of inebriation (from coffee, alcohol, and drugs). These types of pleasure are then "measured" on various, and somewhat undefined, ethnic groups ranging from Greeks, to Bolivians, Chinese, Guaranis. Each group is graded with a scale of signs of descending value: 2, 1, +, –. Indians, for instance, pull a 2 in plastic tactilism, together with the Belgians, while Italians, Germans, Chinese, Dutch, and French people have to content themselves with a 1. Worse still fare the Brazilians and "Northamericans" (+), while Argentines, Spaniards, and Arabs flunk altogether (–). Other books by Mantegazza (a truly "impressive" list of publications) include: *Fisiologia dell'amore* (Physiology of love, 1873); *Fisiologia del bello* (Physiology of beauty, 1891); *Fisiologia della donna* (Physiology of woman, 1893), *Elogio della vecchiaia* (In praise of old age, 1895), etc. In 1887 he published *Testa* (Head), a novel written "in response" to De Amici's *Cuore*. A pioneer in numerous scientific endeavors, he was among the first to experiment with artificial insemination. Flattered by the interest shown for his book by such an illustrious personage, Artusi thanks him profusely in his "Story of a Book That Is a Bit Like the Story of Cinderella":

> after so many setbacks, a man of genius suddenly appeared and took up my cause. Professor Paolo Mantegazza, with that quick and ready wit that is his trademark, immediately recognized that my work indeed had some merit ... He said: "With this book you have done a good deed; may it have a thousand editions."
>
> "Too many," said I. "I would be happy with two." Later, to my great astonishment and surprise, he praised the book and recommended it to the audience at two of his lectures."

Mrs Mantegazza was also an admirer. A letter of praise she sent to Artusi on 14 November, 1897, complements the one he cites from Olindo Guerrini at the conclusion of "A Few Health Guidelines." See pp. 21–3 below.

70 The straw that broke the camel's back was the reduction of workers' wages, which had been decreed concomitantly with the increase in the cost of flour and therefore of bread: a kilogram of bread cost 40 cents of a lira, a full hour of work was compensated with 18 cents.

71 See the complete text on line: *www.vatican.va/holy*_father/leo_xiii_enc_1505891 rerum novarum_en.html.

72 See the Florentine pages of this American sculptor's biography penned "From Letters, Diaries and Recollections" by Henry James (*William Wetmore Story and His Friends* [Boston: Houghton, Mifflin & Co., 1903]).

73 Pellegrino Artusi, *Autobiografia,* ed. Alberto Capatti and Andrea Pollarini (Milan: Il Saggiatore, 1993), 96. No one in his right mind, apart from food history *aficionados,* would bother to read this document, which its own editors do not hesitate to describe as lacking "an essential quality: appetite and food ... Parties and banquets are carefully avoided, and when it would highly desirable to expect something about the culinary experiments that made Artusi famous, the manuscript comes to an end." Luckily, what the *Autobiografia* holds back, Capatti's and Pollarini accompanying text provides with doubled interest.

74 Ibid., 85.

75 On 11 February, 1929, during Pius XI's pontificate, a historic agreement was reached between the Italian government and the Vatican, re-establishing the political power and diplomatic standing of the Catholic Chuch. Prime Minister Mussolini signed for Italy, Cardinal Gasparri for the Holy See. Newspapers all over the world proclaimed that the "wound" inflicted on the Vatican had been healed.

76 Literally, a "priest-eater."

77 Artusi, *Autobiografia*, 94.

78 On 27 April 1859, "at six o clock p.m., the prince and his family, accompanied by members of the diplomatic body all the way to the State border, took leave of the silent crowd and made way towards Bologna." Thus the *Monitore Toscano,* of 28 April. And this too is a sample of bourgeois culture: taking down a regime without shedding a single drop of blood.

79 Capatti and Pollarini, eds., *Autobiografia,* 15.

80 Ibid., 47.

81 In the dialect of Emilia-Romagna, a small and very swift eel.

82 Artusi, *Autobiografia,* 101.

83 Cit. p. 43.

84 See Giancarlo Roversi, "Pellegrino Artusi a Bologna," 129–30. Artusi himself makes no mention of it in his *Autobiografia.* Whatever private school he may have attended, he writes proudly as a self-taught gentleman. At the same time, he is intimidated by those (like his friend Mantegazza) whose sophistication and knowledge were officially recognized.

85 The Pelloni gang's legendary invasion of Forlimpopoli is one of the most celebrated episodes of nineteenth-century Italian history (in fact, there are at least seventeen novelized versions of the bandit's life, and countless folk songs, poems, plays, and "historical" accounts, which continued to be brought forth by Italian writers and

publishers with great frequency and success through the 1970s). Born in 1824, he lived to be only twenty-six: betrayed by one of his own men, he was killed by the pontifical gendarmes in March of 1851. Most famous is the mention poet Giovanni Pascoli makes of him in his "Romagna" (see *Myricae*, also published for the first time in 1891), where the bandit is described as "courteous" and lauded as "king of the forest, king of the highway." And while many tall tales have been derived from the events of 25 January, 1851, perhaps the most reliable source is the report filed on the following day by the commander of the gendarmes of the Forlì Station: "Purporting to be Public Forces, the robbers took possession of [one of] the city gates [facing Forlì] ... Then they headed toward the theater where a comic performance [*La morte di Sisara*, a tragedy, according to Artusi and others] was under way and they disarmed the guards there. Three of the robbers mounted the stage, and when the curtain rose for the second act, they pointed their guns at the audience. Dumbfounded by the way in which and by the place where they were being threatened with death if any one of them moved, and horrified and convinced that a great number of men blocked their exit from the theater and the city, none of them dared to flee for home. The list [of town dignitaries, previously obtained by Pelloni's Gang] was read and those listed were forced to make a pecuniary contribution ... The robbers then entered the homes of those tallied and those of other noblemen as well. Without any regard to age or condition, the robbers made enormous abuses and they did not even spare those who were ill. In vain, they attempted to force open the doors to the Bank of the Monte di Pietà. They violated a woman." Transcribed from Leonida, Costa, *Il rovescio della medaglia: storia inedita del brigante Stefano Pelloni detto il Passatore* (Faenza: Fratelli Lega Editori, 1976), 379–81. For a more detailed report of the events of that day, see Francesco Serantini, *Fatti memorabili della Banda del Passatore in terra di Romagna* (Faenza: Fratelli Lega Editori, 1929). Max David (*Il Romanzo del "Passatore"* [Milan: Rusconi, 1977], 66) wrote that Artusi's father was in attendance and that despite his efforts not to reveal the location of his home, he was accompanied there by some of Pelloni's men: "However well informed they may have been, Stuanè's (vernacular for Stefano) men had labored greatly trying to find the address of the [Artusi] family. But in Forlimpopoli everyone knew everyone and it only took a few slaps to make one of the victims talk. When the robbers arrived at the home, the old Artusi managed in time to hide. But his son Pellegrino and his three sisters, who had sought refuge on the roof, remained there. One of the sisters, Gertrude, paid dearly as a result of her fear: she went mad and died in an asylum." In his *Autobiografia* (82) Artusi objects, rather elegantly, I must add, to the rendition of the event authored by another poet: "[Arnaldo] Fusinato was poorly inspired in my opinion, when he thought he could narrate the worthy enterprise of the Ferryman in playful verse." Considering that of the "50,000 singing *scudi*" pocketed by the gang, many had to be contributed directly by his family, and that, above all, the violated woman was more than likely Artusi's own sister Gertrude, the idea of defining Fusinato as a victim of poor inspiration is a stroke of genius as well as a rare, and not easily forgettable, touch of class.

86 For himself as well as for others. He regarded railroad stocks and treasury bonds as the most secure investments. See Artusi, *Autobiografia,*106. Illustrated by a slightly misinformed biographical profile, Artusi's name actually appears in the *Dizionario storico dei banchieri italiani* (Historical dictionary of Italian bankers; Florence, 1951).

87 They all married, except for Gertrude, who spent the rest of her life in mental institutions.

88 Capatti and Pollarini, eds., *Autobiografia*, 15. They go on to add that "Epicureanism is a duty in lay society" (22).

89 See his preface, p. 7, below.

90 Artusi, *Autobiografia*, 115.

91 Another colorful member of the gang was the Brazilian Francesco Mosquera de Magalhaes, "a learned man, a free-thinking man whose goodness knew now bounds. He suffered from chronic pneumonia, which would lead him to his grave after 25 years of constant friendship. It hurt me that I was not able to assist him in his last moments of life because his wife thought that I would perhaps disapprove of the nuns to whom she had entrusted his care ... I knew that I was not desired at my dear friend's bedside" (*Autobiografia*, 97).

92 In 1875 (Milan: V. Maisner e Compagnia, Editori), Giglioli published his *Viaggio intorno al globo della Regia Pirocorvetta Italiana Magenta negli anni 1865–1866, 1867, 1868,* one of the earliest scientific (and tragicomic) scientific explorations commissioned by the Italian government and financed with public money.

93 A precious glimpse of the life of this institution of truly higher learning can be garnered from the pages of Artusi's *Autobiografia*: "I myself can bear witness that the Natural Sciences were entirely neglected even though there were excellent professors. Apart from the botany class, which was taught magisterially by Prof. Parlatore, a great number of people gathered, and in particular, ladies from the foreign colony." And, just a few lines further down: "I can always remember the singular case of the illustrious professor of zoology, invertebrates, and comparative anatomy [Targioni Tozzetti]. One year, when he was teaching the highly important subject of spontaneous generation, my classmates began to disappear a few at a time, and I alone remained with the professor" (97).

94 Prose writer and poet, Fucini was born at Monterotondo (Massa Marittima) in 1843. He worked in Florence as an assistant in engineering projects. Later he turned to teaching. He died in 1921 at Empoli: the local library is named after him. In his short story "Scampagnata" (An outing) included in his *Le veglie di Neri* (Neri's vigils, 1884), we find the exemplary description of a lunch where "The well-to-do, prosperous bourgeoisie devour mountains of food without any orderliness, taste, or elegance ... Following the soup, the fruit, and the boiled meats, no less than seven stews will appear on a given table: two made with chicken, one with milk-fed veal, one with beef, one with sweatbreads, and one with turkey and noodles" (Camporesi, introduction, lxiv).

95 A philologist and literary historian, D'Ancona taught Italian literature at the university in Pisa, where he was born in 1835. His books include *Origini del teatro in Italia* (1877), *Poesia popolare italiana* (1878), *Studi di critica e storia letteraria* (1880), *Studi sulla letteratura italiana dei primi secoli* (1884). He died in Florence in 1914.

96 English poet and prose writer, Landor was born at Ipsley Court, Warwick in 1775. He was expelled from rugby and Trinity College (Oxford) for firing a shotgun in his rooms. In 1808 he fought as a volunteer in the Spanish War of liberation against the French. Having been sued for libel, he and his wife went into exile in Italy. He was also threatened with expulsion from Florence for being abusive to the local police and for writing condemnatory material about Italy in his *Imaginary Conversations* (1824–29). He died in Florence in 1864.

97 Artusi, *Aurobiografia,*106.

98 See p. 245 below.

99 See p. 408, below. In Artusi's time and for a much longer while, baking was an expensive proposition, and families that lacked the proper stove (they may have owned a *forno da campagna*, or Dutch oven) or that simply wanted to save on fuel brought their cakes to the local bakery. There, a large wood-burning oven would serve the whole neighborhood.

100 "Incontro con Pellegrino Artusi" (Encounter with Pellegrino Artusi, Forum Popili, 1961), as reported by Andrea Pollarini in "Storia di una mostra che assomiglia a una Cenerentola" (Story of a show that resembles Cinderella). See *Cucina Bricconcella*, 14. In fact, the same Pollarini, in an appendix to Artusi, *Autobiografia* (149–50) re-edits the story of the event from a somewhat different perspective. The young soldier "felt bewildered from the very beginning: no soup but rather 'bananas with ham.' Even today the pairing is suspect ... The dinner began in a rather shrill fashion and then it continued with an indecipherable quince-stuffed guinea hen and concluded with a traditional cake. Before the end, as if for a lark, gorgonzola was served. In the face of such a peculiar tableau, nearly any hypothesis could be valid. Is it a portrait of a peculiar and senile Artusi?"

101 See pp. 422–3 below. Such language is particularly significant if pitched against the expression of chagrin and contempt employed by Artusi to flesh out the long catalog of the domestic crooks he had had in his service prior to the "encounter" with Francesco and Marietta. See *Autobiografia*, 109–14.

102 Camporesi, introduction, xxxix.

103 Ibid., xlii.

104 See p. 296 below. The term *petonciano* is fairly rare in contemporary Italian. Most people would hardly recognize it as a synonym for *melanzana*.

105 "We possess a handwritten catalogue of Artusi's library ... There are 578 volumes for a total of 300 works ... Few of them pertain to cuisine ... Artusi was not a bibliophile, nor did he collect valuable rare books." Capatti and Pollarini, eds., *Autobiografia*, 128. A *zibaldone*, a scrapbook filled with hand-copied excerpts from books or lectures, and letters, proverbs, quotations, reminiscences (but no photos and, strangely enough, no recipes), is more in harmony with his idea of culture as reference. It is part of the Fondo Artusi of the Muncipal Archives of Forlimpopoli.

106 See p. 68 below.

107 See p. 258 below.

108 See p. 130 below. In his "Story of a show etc." Andrea Pollarini has published her letter to Artusi, See *Cucina Bricconcella*, 19. Artusi replaces Galasso's "good sauce or leftover stew with a little bit of spleen" with béchamel and Parmesan cheese.

109 See p. 54 below. Artusi's awareness of this divergence shows even in the choice of his kitchen helpers: Francesco Ruffilli hailed from Artusi's hometown, while Marietta Sabatini hailed from Massa e Cozzile, in Tuscany.

110 See Artusi's preface, p. 7 below.

111 See p. 331 below. Compare Artusi's language with that of the brief he received from his friend and teacher Giglioli (see also note 95), clearly in response to a request for elucidation: "A family unto itself, the *Rhinidae* [skate] are called *Rhina squatina* in science. They are common [in Italy] and while their skin is useful, their meat is very bad." From Camporesi, introduction, lviii.

112 Exactly forty years prior to the first edition of *Scienza in cucina*, Dr Giovanni

Rajberti had published an *Arte del convitare spiegata al popolo* (The art of entertaining made simple for the masses), where the notion of "popolo" must be approached with caution. Bear in mind the small number of people who then knew how to read an write, and who had money to invest in a cookbook, and the notion of "the masses" becomes questionable.

113 *Regimen Sanitatis, XIX, Code of Health of the school of Salerno*, trans. John Ordronaux, (Philadelphia, 1870), p. 00. "Artusi revives this tradition ... in a last-ditch attept to anchor man's diet to the cycle of days and months. He was perhaps the last *philosophe de table* to believe in nature. After him, cuisine would no longer acknowledge the seasons and their rhythms." Camporesi, introduction, liii.

114 "Get in the habit of eating everything, if you don't wish to become a burden to your family," he reminds his reader, resuscitating, I am sure, his mother's appeals to frugality. "Those who refuse to eat many things offend the others and the head of the family, who are forced to conform to their whims, to avoid making twice the number of dishes" (pp. 15–16 below). As to clothes:

In April stay appareled,
In May just go halfway,
In June discard your pantaloon,
But give it not away,
For it may serve another day (p. 15).

115 Ibid., 15.

116 And if some of the burners remain idle, they can be used to heat up irons.

117 Sunday, 27 June 1999, the second day of the traditional Festa Artusiana, which yearly celebrates the achievements of Forlimpopoli's most famous citizen, and during which even some street are named after gastronomic products, was dedicated to August Escoffier and featured an exhibition organized in direct cooperation with the Cooking Museum of Villeneuve Loubet. A tasting of peach Melba was offered to all participants. These celebrations are a fairly recent affair and have come about after long neglect, which actually began from the day Artusi, at the request of a friend, contributed two copies of *Scienza in the cucina* to a charity raffle held in Forlimpopoli. "Those who won the books, he tells us in his "Cinderella Story," "instead of appreciating them, held them up to ridicule and then went off and sold them to the tobacconist" (p. 3 below). Thus the contemporary "fuss" is not free from suspicions of guilt and the desire to make amends. Artusi's birthplace, which was in the main square, was demolished and has been replaced with a cheap, modern building. There is no museum of Artusiana in Forlimpopoli. A few pieces of furniture that belonged to the culinary wizard now adorn the mayor's office.

118 For the celebrated soprano, whom he had admired in *Lohengrin* at Covent Garden in 1894, Escoffier created the dessert *Pêche au cigne* (renamed peach Melba in 1889, at the inauguration of the Carlton Hotel). A legend in her own time, the Australian-born soprano began her career when she was already twenty-seven years old, under the auspices of Mathilde Marchesi. By age thirty she was a star in both London and Paris. On the lighter side, she became famous also for her peformance in Britain's first advertised public broadcast, when she sang into a telephone microphone with a horn made of a cigar box a rendering of "Home Sweet Home" and the "Addio"

from Puccini's *la Boheme*. It was 7:10 on the evening of June 15, 1920. Escoffier's recipe calls for two peach halves that have been poached in syrup and cooled. Each half is placed, hollow side down, on a scoop of vanilla ice cream, then topped with puréed and strained fresh raspberries, red currant jelly, sugar, and corn starch, and sometimes whipped cream and sliced almonds.

119 See *La scienza in cucina etc.*, ed. Davide Paolini (Milan: Sperling & Kupfer Editori, 1991), p. 21. Emphasis added.

120 See p. 261 below.

121 In an imaginary (and then again not so imaginary) list of books whose existence should have spurred him to write his own tract *Physiologie du marriage* (1829), Honoré de Balzac had also employed the word "art" (*L'art de conserver les substance alimentaires, L'art d'empêcher les cheminées de fumer,* etc.) not so much to mark its difference from *physiologie*, as to rather to underline their proximity.

122 Salvatore Battaglia, *Grande dizionario della lingua italiana* (Turin: Utet, 1961), *ad vocem*. This technologically conscious definition is available in English as well: just think of the expression "state of the art."

123 As suggested in Capatti and Pollarini, ed., *Autobiografia*, 132.

124 The opening words of "A Few Health Guidelines" confirm this assertion: ("Emperor Tiberius used to say that man, after the age of thirty-five, should no longer have any need of doctors ... The ... maxim is true inasmuch as man, by the time he has reached the halfway point of his life, ought to have gained enough experience about himself to know what things are harmful and beneficial to him. By means of a good diet he should be able to govern himself ...").

125 The notion that women's stomachs are weaker than men's obtains in Artusi as well. See p. 15.

126 Which is exactly what happens to the hero of *Le sottilissime astuzie di Bertoldo*, a very successful example of popular literature, authored by G.C. Croce and first published in 1608.

127 Dating back hundreds of years, this theory found a particular insidious champion in Dr Giacomo Albini, author of *De Sanitatis Custodia* (On guarding one's own health), probably written between 1341 and 1342.

128 This preface remained part and parcel of the project from the very first edition of the book which, by the way, was dedicated to two of Artusi's best friends: Sibillone and Biancani, his cats.

129 Florence: Giunti, 1998.

130 Recipes from *Le scienza in cucina et l'arte di mangiare bene*, revised with a modern twist with the aide of the Association of Chefs of Romagna, published by the Comitato Segavecchia, Forlimpopoli, 1991.

131 See p. 190 below.

132 See *L'Espresso*, 12 July 2001.

133 See Artusi's preface, p. 7 below.

SCIENCE
IN THE KITCHEN
AND THE ART
OF EATING WELL

THE STORY OF A BOOK
THAT IS A BIT LIKE
THE STORY OF CINDERELLA

See how often human judgment errs.

I had just put the finishing touches on my book, *Science in the Kitchen and the Art of Eating Well,* when my learned friend Francesco Trevisan, professor of Literature at the Scipione Maffei Secondary School in Verona, happened to come to Florence. A passionate scholar of Ugo Foscolo, he had been chosen to serve as a member of the committee to oversee the construction of a monument to the Bard of the Sepulchers in the church of Santa Croce.[1] Having had the pleasure, on that occasion, of hosting him at my home, it seemed to me an opportune moment to ask him his refined opinion of my culinary work. Alas! After examining the work, and with it my humble efforts of many years, he passed the terrible sentence: *This book will have little success.*

Dismayed but not entirely convinced by his opinion, I was pricked by the desire to appeal to the public, and thus decided to turn, for publication, to a well-known Florentine publishing house. I enjoyed what could be described as friendly relations with the proprietors of this house since the time, some years back, when I had spent a considerable sum of money on various publications of mine. I thus hoped that they might be willing to indulge me. Indeed, to encourage these gentlemen, I proposed that we make the undertaking a partnership;

---

1 One of Ugo Foscolo's most famous poems is entitled "Dei Sepolcri" ("On Sepulchers"). Many illustrious Italian artists and men of letters are either buried or honored by a monument in the church of Santa Croce in Florence (unless otherwise specified the notes to the text are the editors').

and so that they might give the matter due consideration, after having shown them the manuscript, I also wished them to have a real sampling of my cooking. Thus I invited them one day to dinner, the results of which appeared satisfying both to them and to the fellow-guests I had invited to keep them good company.

My enticements were in vain, however, for after much thought and shilly-shallying on the matter, one of them said to me: "I'm terribly sorry, but only if your work had been written by Doney[2] could we talk about it seriously."

"If it had been written by Doney," I replied, "probably no one would understand a thing in it, which was precisely the case with that large tome, *The King of Cooks*. With my Manual, on the other hand, one need only know how to hold a wooden spoon to work something out."

It should be noted here that publishers generally care not a whit whether a book is good or bad, useful or harmful. For them it need only bear a well-known name on the cover, so that they might sell it with ease; a famous name serves to give it a push, and on the wings of its guidance it may then soar to great heights.

Thus having to start all over again, I went in search of a less demanding entrepreneur. Knowing by reputation an important Milanese publishing house, I turned to them, since, as they claimed to print *omnia generis musicorum*, I thought that amidst that hodgepodge they might find a small place for my modest work. Before long came the humiliating and ever so brusque reply: We do not deal in cookbooks.

Let us have done, I told myself, with begging others for help, and publish the book at our own risk and peril. And so I hired the Florentine typographer Salvadore Landi (proprietor of "The Art of Printing") to print the book. Yet as I was negotiating the terms of our agreement, I had the idea to offer the book to yet another large publisher, better

2 Owner of a famous restaurant in Florence at the time.

suited to publications of this sort. Truth be told, I found him better disposed than any of the others; but on what conditions, alas! Two hundred lire for the work, and the surrender of all royalties! May this, and the others' reluctance, stand as proof of the discredit into which cookbooks had fallen in Italy.

At this humiliating proposal I exploded in a fit of rage, which I need not repeat here, and decided to take my chances and publish entirely at my own expense. Discouraged as I was, however, and to prevent an utter fiasco, I had only a thousand copies printed.

Shortly thereafter, it just so happened that a great charity fair was to be held at Forlimpopoli, the town of my birth. A friend of mine wrote to me asking to contribute two copies of my *Life of Foscolo*. But as I had none of these left, I compensated with two copies of *Science in the Kitchen and the Art of Eating Well*. I should never have done so, since I later learned that those who had won the books, instead of appreciating them, held them up to ridicule and then went off and sold them to the tobacconist.

Yet even this was not to be my last humiliation. Having sent a copy of my work to a Rome magazine to which I subscribed, not only was it not accorded the few words of praise and criticism promised in a notice for all books sent to said magazine as gifts; it was actually listed in the rubric of books received, with a mistake in the title!

Finally, after so many setbacks, a man of genius suddenly appeared and took up my cause. Professor Paolo Mantegazza, with that quick and ready wit that is his trademark, immediately recognized that my work indeed had some merit and might be of use to families. Congratulating me for my work, he said: "With this book you have done a good deed; may it have a thousand editions."

"Too many," said I. "I would be happy with two." Later, to my great astonishment and surprise, he praised the book and recommended it to the audience at two of his lectures.

At this point I began to take heart and, seeing that the book was beginning to have a measure of success, however limited at first, I wrote to my friend at Forlimpopoli, to complain about the offense his town folk had given to a book that would one day bring honor to *their* town. Anger prevented me from saying *my* town.

When the first edition sold out, with some hesitation—since I still could scarcely believe my good fortune—I began the second printing, also of only a thousand copies. As this sold more quickly than the previous one, it gave me the courage to undertake a third one, of two thousand copies, and then a fourth and fifth, of three thousand each. These were then followed, at relatively brief intervals, by six other editions of four thousand copies each. Finally, seeing that as my manual aged, it only seemed to gain favor, and the demand for it only became greater and greater, I decided to increase the print runs of the next three editions to six thousand copies each. 52,000 copies have thus far seen the light of day, many of them supplemented with new recipes (for cooking is an inexhaustible art). All of which is very reassuring to me, especially as the book's buyers also include learned and illustrious people.

With my pride tickled by these happy results, I was anxious to oblige the public with editions of increasing elegance and accuracy. When, one day, it seemed to me that those overseeing the printing were less than fully committed to this purpose, I said to them in jest: "So just because my book smells of stew, I suppose that you, too, disdain to take it seriously? But let me tell you, and I say this reluctantly, that with our century tending towards materialism and life's enjoyments, the day shall soon come when writings of this sort, which delight the mind and nourish the body, will be more widely sought and read than the works of great scientists, which are of much greater value to humanity."

Blind is the man who cannot see this! The days of seductive, flattering ideals, the days of the hermits, are coming to an end. With greater eagerness than it ought to, the world is rushing to the wellsprings

of pleasure, and those who know how to temper this dangerous inclina-
tion with healthy morals shall take the palm.

And so I conclude my opening peroration. Let me close, then,
with a well-deserved tribute and expression of thanks to the publishing house of R. Bemporad & Son of Florence, who made every effort
to bring this manual of mine to the knowledge of the public and to
disseminate it.

PREFACE

Cooking is a troublesome sprite. Often it may drive you to despair. Yet it also very rewarding, for when you do succeed, or overcome a difficulty in doing so, you feel the satisfaction of a great triumph.

Beware of books that deal with this art: most of them are inaccurate or incomprehensible, especially the Italian ones. The French are a little better. But from either, the very most you will glean are a few notions, useful only if you already know the art.

If you do not aspire to become a premier cook, you need not have been born with a pan on your head to become a good one. Passion, care, and precision of method will certainly suffice; then, of course, you must choose the finest ingredients as your raw materials, for these will make you shine.

The best teacher is experience, under an adept's watchful eye. Yet even lacking this, with a guide such as mine, and devotion to your labors, you should be able, I hope, to put something decent together.

It was at the insistence of many gentlemen and ladies of my acquaintance, who honor me with their friendship, that I finally decided to publish the present volume. Its materials had long been prepared, and served only for my personal use. I thus present it to you now as the simple amateur that I am, certain that I shall not disappoint you, having tried and retried these dishes many times myself. If at first you do not succeed, do not despair; with good will and persistence, you shall manage to make them one day, I guarantee it, and perhaps even to improve them. For I, after all, cannot presume to have reached the acme of perfection.

Yet seeing that this volume marks the 14th edition and a total print run of 52,000 copies, I may discreetly assume that my dishes have been generally well received, and that to my great fortune few people, thus far, have cursed me for stomach aches or other phenomena that decency forbids me to mention.

Finally, I should not like my interest in gastronomy to give me the reputation of a gourmand or glutton. I object to any such dishonorable imputation, for I am neither. I love the good and the beautiful wherever I find them, and hate to see anyone squander, as they say, God's bounty. Amen.

FROM THE AUTHOR TO THE READER

Life has two principal functions: nourishment and the propagation of the species. Those who turn their minds to these two needs of existence, who study them and suggest practices whereby they might best be satisfied, make life less gloomy and benefit humanity. They may therefore be allowed to hope that, while humanity may not appreciate their efforts, it will at least show them generous and benevolent indulgence.

The meaning contained in these few lines, which preface the third edition of this book, was better expressed in a letter to me by the celebrated poet, Lorenzo Stecchetti. It is my pleasure to transcribe them here:

> The human race survives only because man possesses the instincts of self-preservation and reproduction, and keenly feels the need to satisfy both. The satisfaction of a need is always accompanied by pleasure. The pleasure of self-preservation lies in the sense of taste, and that of reproduction in the sense of touch. If man did not find food appetizing, or experience sexual desire, the human race would quickly come to an end.
>
> Taste and touch are therefore the senses most necessary, indeed indispensable to the life of the individual and the species. The other senses are only there to help, and one can, after all, live life blind and deaf, but not without the functional activity of the organs of taste.

How is it, then, that on the scale of the senses, the two most necessary to life and its continuance are considered the basest? Why are those things that satisfy the other senses—painting, music, etc.—called art and deemed noble, while those that satisfy the sense of taste are considered ignoble? Why is a person who enjoys gazing at a lovely painting or listening to a beautiful symphony held in higher esteem than one who enjoys eating an excellent dish? Is the equality among the senses perhaps comparable to that among humans, whereby those who work may be well off, but those who do not are even better off?

The blame, no doubt, must lie with the tyrannical sway the brain now holds over all the organs of the body. In the time of Menenius Agrippa, the stomach ruled; nowadays it no longer even serves, or, if so, serves badly. Of all those who overwork their brains, is there a single one who can boast of good digestion? They are all nerves, neuroses, and neurasthenia. The height, chest-size, strength and reproductive powers of this ingenious, rachitic breed of sages and artists, all refinement and glands, are in daily decline. Indeed they do not even eat, but rather overstimulate themselves and keep going by dint of coffee, alcohol and morphine. Thus are the senses that direct the brain's functions deemed nobler than those that preside over self-preservation—and the time has come to right this unjust verdict.

God bless the bicycle, which lets us know the joys of a hearty appetite, notwithstanding all the decadent and decayed who dream of chlorosis, consumption and boils in the name of the ideal art! Let us go out, out into the open air, into the free-flowing, healthy air! It reddens the blood and strengthens the muscles! Let us not be ashamed, therefore, to eat the best we can and return gastronomy to its rightful place. In the end, even the tyrannical brain will be the better for it, and this nerve-wracked society will finally understand that, even in art, a discussion on how to cook eel is every bit as worthy as a disquisition on the smile of Beatrice.

It is true that man does not live by bread alone; he must eat something with it. And the art of making this something as economical, savory and healthy as possible is, I insist, a true art. Let us rehabilitate the sense of taste and not be ashamed to satisfy it honestly, and as best we can, according to its own dictates.[3]

It is not for money, nor the pursuit of honor in an art that the unjust world wishes to appear to revile, but in the conviction that I am doing something useful for the public, that I now reprint, with corrections and a supplement of 100 new recipes, this gastronomical treatise of mine, having also been encouraged by the reception given the first edition of 1,000 copies, which has now sold out.

I beg the kind Ladies and good Housewives, for whom this work of great effort and expense is intended, to study it with love, for they will derive great advantage from it. May they continue to bestow their much-desired favor on me, and I shall be a happy man.

3 The paragraphs that follow were added by the author under this heading in the second edition of the work.

A FEW HEALTH GUIDELINES

The emperor Tiberius used to say that man, after the age of thirty-five, should no longer have any need of doctors. While this aphorism, in a broad sense, may be true, it is no less true that if called in time, a doctor can nip an illness in the bud and even save you from a premature death. Moreover, even if a doctor does not cure you, he often provides relief, and always gives comfort.

The emperor Tiberius's maxim is true inasmuch as man, by the time he has reached the halfway point in his life, ought to have gained enough experience about himself to know what things are harmful and beneficial to him. By means of a good diet, he should be able to govern himself in such a way as to keep his health in perfect balance. This is not difficult to do so long as his condition is not threatened by innate defects or internal injuries. Moreover, having reached that age, any man should also have acquired the conviction that the best care is prophylactic, or preventive, that one should expect very little from medicines, and that the cleverest physician is the one who prescribes few and simple things.

Nervous and oversensitive persons, especially if idle and apprehensive, imagine themselves as having a thousand ills that in fact exist only in their imaginations. One such person, speaking of himself, said to his doctor one day: "I don't know how a man with so many ailments can survive." Not only did he survive, with a few small inconveniences shared by many; he actually lived to a ripe old age.

These unhappy hypochondriacs—for that is exactly what they are—deserve all our sympathy, for they are unable to free themselves from the fetters of an exaggerated, constant fear, and there is no way to convince them otherwise, since they feel suspicious of the zeal of those who seek to comfort them. You often see them with a sullen look in their eyes, clasping their wrists and sighing audibly as they gaze with horror into the mirror to look at their tongues; at night they will leap from their beds, frightened by the throbbing of their startled hearts. Food, for them, is an ordeal, and not only because of the quality of the ingredients; fearing they have eaten too much, they will worry about some impending disaster, or else, wishing to correct this with excessive abstinence, they will lose sleep at night or have unpleasant dreams. Always thinking of themselves, they live in fear of catching a cold or cough, and go outside so wrapped up they look like pig-livers in cheesecloth. With each new hint of cold, they add layer upon layer, to the point of discrediting the very layers, I say, of an onion. For such persons as these, no form of medicine is valid. A conscientious doctor would say to them: have fun, amuse yourselves, take frequent walks in the open air, as much as your strength will allow, travel, and in good company, if you can afford it, and you will feel better.

It goes without saying that I am speaking here of the privileged classes, since those not favored by fortune are forced, in spite of themselves, to make a virtue of necessity and to seek consolation in the belief that an active, frugal life leads to a sound body and lasting health.

Passing now from these preliminaries to some general considerations of good health, let me recall for you a few precepts that have long enjoyed the endorsement of science, but which are never repeated enough. First of all, as concerns wardrobe, I turn my attentions to those of you Ladies who may be mothers, and I say to you: Start by dressing your children lightly, from infancy, for with this method, when they are grown up they will be less sensitive to sudden changes in atmospheric temperature and less subject to colds and bronchitis. And if in winter you do not let the stove raise the heat in your apartment above 12 or 14 degrees Centigrade (about 60 degrees Fahrenheit), you will probably be safe from pneumonia, which has become so prevalent these days.

With the arrival of the first cool days, do not weigh yourself down all at once with too many clothes. One outer garment should suffice, one that can be easily taken off or put back on with the frequent alternations of the season, until the cold has definitively settled in. Later, when spring is approaching, remember the following proverb, which I find to be unquestionably true:

In April stay appareled,
In May go just halfway,
In June discard your pantaloon,
But give it not away,
For it may serve another day.

Try to live in healthy houses, full of light and well ventilated: illness flees where the sun shines in. Pity those ladies who receive guests in semi-darkness, and in whose homes you stumble into the furniture and know not where to put your hat. Because of this custom of living in dimly lit rooms, of not moving their feet or getting out into the open air, and because their sex tends by nature to drink little wine and rarely eats meat, preferring vegetables and sweets, such ladies are seldom seen with red cheeks, the sign of prosperous health, or with fine complexions all blood and milk. Their flesh is not firm but flaccid, their faces like vetches that one grows in the dark to adorn tombs on Holy Thursday. Is it any wonder, then, that among women one finds so many hysterics, neurotics and anemics?

Get in the habit of eating everything, if you don't wish to become a burden to your family. Those who refuse many things offend the others and the head of the family, who are forced to conform to their caprices to avoid making twice the number of dishes. Do not become a slave to your stomach: this whimsical entrail, so easily annoyed, apparently takes special delight in tormenting those who eat more than they need, a common vice of those not constrained by necessity to eat frugally. If you were to pay heed to it—now with its nausea, now with its upchucks of flavors of foods already eaten, now with its unpleasant acidities—it would reduce you to the diet of a convalescent. Thus, if you are innocent of all excess or overindulgence, then wage war on it. Fight it head-to-head and conquer it. Yet if your nature should decidedly rebel against a given food, then and only then should you concede defeat and desist.

Anyone who does not engage in physical activity must live more moderately than others. In this regard, Agnolo Pandolfini, in his *Treatise on the Care of the Family,* says: "I find that sobriety, not eating and not drinking when you do not feel hungry or thirsty, are integral parts of a healthy diet. And however raw or hard to digest a thing might be, I find that, old as I am, from one sunrise to the next, I shall have digested it. My children, take to heart this simple, general, and perfect rule. Take care to learn what things are harmful to you, and stay away from them; and find and keep doing the things that are beneficial and good for you."

Upon awaking in the morning, find out what best agrees with your stomach. If it does not feel entirely empty, limit yourself to a cup of black coffee; and if you precede this with half a glass of water mixed with coffee, it will better help to rid you of any residues of an incomplete digestion. If, then, you find yourself in perfect form and (taking care not to be deceived, for there is also such a thing as false hunger) you immediately feel the need for food—a definite sign of good health and presage of a long life—this is a most suitable moment, depending on your taste, to complement your black coffee with a piece of buttered toast, or to take some milk in your coffee, or to have a cup of hot chocolate. After some four hours, the time needed to digest even a scant and liquid breakfast, one moves on, in accordance with the modern custom, to a solid repast at around 11 or 12 o'clock. This meal, being the first of the day, is always the most appetizing, and therefore it is better not to slake your hunger entirely, if you wish to enjoy your dinner later on. And unless you lead an active life and engage in physical labor, it is not a good idea to drink wine with your morning meals, since red wine is not easily digested, and white, being alcoholic, clouds the mind when one needs to concentrate.

It is better, in the morning, to take one's meals with pure water and, at the end, to drink a small glass or two of bottled wine. Another custom is to have tea, plain or with milk, which I find a very fine complement; it does not weigh on the stomach and, as a warm tonic for the nerves, it aids digestion.

At dinner, which is the principal meal of the day and, I would say, a kind of family celebration, one can truly indulge oneself, though more in winter than in summer, for in the heat one needs light and easily digestible foods. A broad, diverse range of foods from the animal and vegetable kingdoms, with meat predominating, best contribute to good digestion, especially if washed down with aged, dry wine. Take care, however, not to overeat, and beware of those foods that tend to stimulate evacuation. And do not wash out your stomach with excessive drinking. In this regard, some health experts advise drinking only water even during dinner, and saving the wine for the end. You may try this if you have the nerve for it; to me it seems a bit too much to ask.

Here is a good rule to follow: at dinner you should stop eating at the first bite that seems to turn your stomach, and move on immediately to the dessert. Another good practice for avoiding indigestion while partaking of copious meals is to eat lightly the day after you have eaten heavy foods.

Ice cream at the end of dinner does no harm; indeed, it does good, since it draws back to the stomach the warmth necessary for good digestion. Unless your thirst demands it, always abstain from drinking between meals, so as not to interfere with digestion, since this labor of nature's highest chemistry must not be disturbed.

Between lunch and dinner, you should allow an interval of seven hours, for that is how much time is needed for full digestion. In fact, for those with slower systems, even that is not enough. Thus, if one has lunch at eleven, it is best to wait until seven for dinner. In truth, however, one should only go back to eating when the stomach demands relief, and this need will make itself all the more pressing if you stimulate it with a walk outdoors or with some moderate, pleasurable exercise.

"Exercise," writes the aforementioned Agnolo Pandolfini, "preserves life, kindles the body's natural warmth and vigor, skims off excess and harmful materials and humors, fortifies every faculty of the body and the nerves. It is necessary for the young, useful for the old. He who does not exercise, does not wish to live in health and happiness. We read that Socrates used to dance at home and jump for exercise. The simple, restful and happy life has always been the best medicine for health."

Temperance and physical exercise are thus the two factors on which good health depends. Be advised, however, that "when overdone, virtue is as vice become"—since the constant discharges of the organism need to be replenished. You should beware of falling from one excess, overabundant eating, into the contrary one: scant and insufficient nourishment, which weakens the body.

During adolescence, during growth, that is, man needs a great deal of nourishment. In adulthood, on the other hand, and especially in old age, moderation in eating is a virtue indispensable to prolonging one's life.

To those who have preserved our fathers' blessed custom of eating dinner at midday or at one o'clock, I should like to recall the ancient maxim: *Post prandium stabis et post cenam ambulabis* (After dinner you stand, after supper you walk). And I should like to remind everyone that digestion first takes place in the mouth; therefore I could never recommend too strongly that you preserve your teeth, for suitably chopping and grinding your food. For with the help of saliva, well-chewed food is much more easily digested than foods chopped and pounded in the kitchen, which require little mastication and sit heavy on the stomach, as though the organ took offense at having had part of its task taken away. Indeed, many foods considered difficult to digest can actually be better digested and enjoyed by vigorous chewing.

If, with these rules as your guide, you are able to regulate your stomach well, you shall make it strong, if it was weak; and if it was strong by nature, you shall keep it so without recourse to medicines. Stay away from laxatives, which are disastrous if used frequently; they should be taken very rarely, and only when absolutely necessary. Oftentimes animals, with their natural instincts, and perhaps even with their powers of reasoning, teach us how to behave: whenever my very dear friend Sibillone[4] used to suffer from indigestion, he would go a day or two without eating and work it off on the rooftops. We should therefore deplore those pitiful mothers who, in an excess of maternal sentiment, keep a forever watchful eye over the health of their little ones, and the instant they see them a bit listless or not evacuating with regularity—obsessed as they are with the silly notion of worms, which most often are only in their imagination—immediately resort to medications, to enemas, instead of letting nature take her course, since at that florid, exuberant stage of life, nature, when left to herself, can work miracles.

The use of liquors, if one is not careful, can quickly turn to abuse. All health experts disapprove of them, for the irreparable damage they wreak in the human organism. The only exception might be made for a light punch of cognac (even with a hint of rum) on cold winter evenings. This helps you to digest at night, and you wake up the following morning with a freer stomach and a fresher mouth.

4 This was the name of Artusi's cat.

Those who give themselves over to wine also do a very, very bad thing. Little by little, they begin to feel nauseated by food and nourish themselves on wine alone. After which they deteriorate before the eyes of the world, becoming ridiculous, dangerous, and beastly. There was once a merchant who, upon arriving in a city, used to stop at a street corner and observe the people passing by; when at last he saw one with a red nose, he would ask him where he could buy some good wine. Even if we overlook the mark of intemperance that this vice stamps on the human face, and certain scenes that inspire only hilarity—such as the story of the cook who, as his masters were waiting at the dinner table, held the frying pan over the sink, furiously blowing below it—still there is no doubt that whenever you see such heavy drinkers, who with their glassy eyes and their slurred r's often say and do embarrassing things, you feel your heart sink in the fear that it might come to blows, and then someone might even draw a knife, as often happens. And if one persists in this brutish vice, whose demands grow greater with each day, one becomes an incorrigible drunkard, all of whom come to wretched ends.

Neither should we praise those who seek to spur their appetites with stimulants, for if you accustom your stomach to needing external agents to help it digest, you will end up sapping its vitality, and the production of gastric juices will become defective. As for sleep and rest, these functions are entirely relative and should conform to the needs of the individual, since we are not all made the same way. It sometimes happens that someone will feel a general, undefinable malaise without knowing the cause, when in fact it derives from nothing more than a lack of restorative repose.

I now close this series of precepts—jotted down as they came to me, simply and without pretensions—with the following two proverbs, drawn from foreign literatures:

ENGLISH PROVERB

Early to bed, early to rise
Makes a man healthy, wealthy and wise.

French Proverb

Se lever à six, déjeuner à dix,
Dîner à six, se coucher à dix,
Fait vivre l'homme dix fois dix.

(Up at six, lunch at ten,
Dinner at six, in bed at ten,
Makes a man live ten times ten.)

And with this I wish my readers happiness and a long life.

*   *   *

A letter from the poet Lorenzo Stecchetti (Olindo Guerrini) to whom I sent a copy of the third edition of my cookbook as a gift:[5]

Bologna
December 19, 1896

My dear Sir,

You cannot imagine what a pleasant surprise it was to receive your volume, in which you were good enough to remember me! I have long been, and forever remain, one of the most fervent followers of your work, which I find to be the finest, most practical and best, not only of all such works in Italian, which are a real disgrace, but even of foreign ones. Do you remember Vialardi,[6] considered the standard in Piedmont?

5 Later editions of Artusi's book included, in a kind of appendix to the introductory chapters, the following letters from enthusiastic readers and the stories associated with them.
6 Giovanni Vialardi, head chef of Charles Albert and Victor Emmanuel II (House of Savoy, royal family of Italy from 1861–1946), wrote a *Treatise on Cuisine*, published in 1854. Like the imaginary quote that follows, it was full of Gallicisms typical of the Piedmontese dialect.

"GRILL BRAISÉ—The poultry should be singed, not pour boiled, while the filet, piqué with truffles and jambon, should be rouladed like a little valise in a brazier with butter. Humect often with graisse, then degorge and blanch some sweetbreads, making a farci as for quenelles the thickness of a cork, to be placed beside the filet. When cooked, degustate for salt, paint with tomato sauce cooked down to a glaze, and make as garniture a macedonia of chopped melonette and courgette and serve hot en terrine."

You won't find that in the book, but the terminology is all there.

As for other Kings and Queens of Cooks and other culinary majesties, all we have are translations from the French and incoherent compilations. To find a sensible recipe fit for a family one had to grope about, try to guess, and blunder. Thank God for Artusi!

This chorus of tribute hails from Romagna, where I have preached your volume with true enthusiasm. Praises are coming from every quarter. One dear relation of mine wrote to me: "At last we have a cookbook without the usual cannibalism, for the others always tell you: Take your liver, cut it into slices, and so on," and expressed heartfelt thanks.

I myself had been thinking about writing a cookbook for the Hoepli's series of manuals. I would have liked to write a book of vulgarization, as such works are sometime called; but lack of time as well as budget considerations[7] made the experimental part of it very difficult. Then your book came along, and this discouraged me utterly. I stopped thinking about it, but I was left with a pretty good collection of cookbooks that makes a handsome display in the dining-room bookcase. The first edition of your book, newly bound, interleaved and augmented by many recipes, has the place of honor there. The second edition is for everyday consultation, while the third will now steal the place of honor from the first because it boasts the Author's autograph.

So as you can see, I have long known, admired and recommended your work. You can now appreciate how keen was my delight at receiving the copy you so kindly sent to me. At first only my stomach

7 This is a lie (Artusi's note).

felt due gratitude toward you, but it is now joined by my whole spirit. For this reason, most distinguished Sir, in expressing my heartfelt thanks for your gift and courtesy, I am honored to humble myself with due recognition and esteem.

Your devoted admirer,
O. Guerrini

* * *

To my great surprise, the contessa Maria Fantoni, wife of the illustrious professor Paolo Mantegazza, honored me with the following letter, which I cherish as a welcome reward for my humble efforts:

San Terenzo (Golfo della Spezia)
November 14, 1897

Dear Mr. Artusi,

Please excuse my boldness, but I truly have to tell you how useful and precious your book has been to me. Yes, precious, for not a single one of the dishes I have made has turned out *not so well* and, indeed, some have been so perfect as to win high praise. Since the credit is *yours*, I wish to tell you this as a way of expressing my heartfelt thanks.

I have made *your* quince jelly, and it is now on its way to America: I sent it to my stepson in Buenos Aires, and I am sure it will be appreciated as it deserves. You write and describe things so clearly that executing your recipes is a true pleasure and brings me real satisfaction.

I wanted to tell you all this, and thus I took the liberty of writing you this letter.

My husband sends his affectionate regards.

And I shake your hand with sincere gratitude.

Maria Mantegazza

*   *   *

The dramas of the kitchen, or the despair of poor cooks when their employers invite friends to dinner (a true story; only the names have been changed):

The master says to his cook:

"Mind you, Francesco, Signora Carli doesn't eat fish, be it fresh or cured, and won't tolerate even the smell of its derivatives. And you already know that the Marquis Gandi cannot stand the smell of vanilla. Take care to avoid nutmeg and spices, since Judge Cesari hates them. In the desserts, be sure not to put in any bitter almonds, because Donna Matilde d'Alcantara won't eat them. You already know that my good friend Moscardi never uses ham, lard, bacon or salt pork in his kitchen, since those things give him gas; so don't put any in this dinner, or he might get sick."

Francesco, who has been listening to the master with his mouth agape, finally exclaims:

"Anything else you would like to leave out, *my lord*?"

"Actually, knowing my guests' tastes as I do, there are a few other things I ought to warn you about. I know that a few of them take exception to mutton and say it tastes like tallow, and others find lamb difficult to digest. A number of them have also maintained, speaking of these matters in theory, that when they eat cabbage or potatoes they suffer from tympanitis, that is, their bodies swell up in the night and they have bad dreams. But these last ones we need not worry about."

"All right, I know what to do," adds the cook, muttering to himself as he leaves. "To satisfy all these people and ward off tympanitis, I think I'll go see Marco (the house donkey) and ask him for his learned opinion and a platter of his products, without the related condiments!"

THE NUTRITIONAL VALUE OF MEATS

Before beginning this book, it seems appropriate to list here—without pretensions of scientific exactitude—the meat of different animals in diminishing order of nutritional value.

1. *feathered game*
2. *beef*
3. *veal*
4. *poultry*
5. *milk-fed veal*
6. *mutton*
7. *furred game*
8. *lamb*
9. *pork*
10. *fish*

This ordering could give rise to many objections, given that the animals' age, the environment in which they live, and their diet, can all appreciably alter the quality of the meat among individuals of the same species, and even invalidate the distinctions drawn between the various species themselves.

A mature hen, for example, makes a better broth than beef does. And the ram, which grazes on the aromatic herbs found in high mountain valleys, can yield a meat more flavorful and nourishing than that of milk-fed veal. Among fish there are several species—including the Lake Garda carp (a relative of the trout)—which are more nourishing to eat than four-footed animals.

ADMONITION

The hypocritical world gives scant importance to eating. Nevertheless, we can never celebrate a religious or civil holiday without unfurling the tablecloth, the better to gorge ourselves.

In the words of the poet Pananti:

Tutte le società, tutte le feste
Cominciano e finiscono in pappate
E prima che s'accomodin le teste
Voglion essere le pance accomodate.

I preti che non son dei meno accorti,
Fan dieci miglia per un desinare.
O che si faccia l'uffizio dei morti,
O la festa del santo titolare,
Se non v'è dopo la sua pappatoria
Il salmo non finisce con la gloria.

(Every social gathering and holiday
is with a feast begun and terminated;
and before our heads can have their say
our bellies must be fully sated.

Priests, who are said to know a thing or two,
will walk ten miles for a meal.
Whether giving last rites with little ado
or calling on the local saint to heal,
if food and drink don't close the story,
they cannot end the psalm in glory.)

THE RECIPES

BROTHS, ASPIC, AND SAUCES

1. BRODO (BROTH)

As common folk know, to make a good broth you must put the meat
in cold water, and bring the pan to a very slow boil, never letting it
boil over. If, instead of a good broth, you prefer a good boiled beef,
then put the meat in boiling water without any special care. Everyone
knows that spongy bones add flavor and fragrance to broth; but a
broth of bones is not especially nutritious.

In Tuscany, the custom is to give fragrance to the broth by adding
a little bunch of aromatic herbs or *bouquet garni*. The bunch is not
made of the leaves, which would quickly fall apart, but with the stalks
of celery, carrots, parsley and basil—all of them in small proportions.
Some add a little grilled onion; but since onions make wind they are
not for all stomachs. If you like to color the broth in the French manner, you need only burn some sugar, and when it has sufficiently
browned, dilute it with cold water. Boil this liquid until the sugar is
completely dissolved, and then store it in a bottle.

To preserve the broth from day to day during the summer heat,
bring it to a boil each morning and evening.

The foam that forms on the pot is the product of two substances:
albumin from the surface of the meat which coagulates with the heat
and combines with hematin, a blood coloring substance.

Earthenware pots, being slow conductors of heat, are preferable to steel or copper, because they are easier to control on the fire. The only exception might be those English-made cast-iron pots, which have a valve in the center of the lid.

It has always been believed that broth was excellent food, nutritious and invigorating, but doctors now say that broth does not nourish at all, and in fact its main function is to stimulate the production of gastric juices in the stomach. Not being a competent judge in such matters, I will leave responsibility for this new theory, which seems to fly in the face of common sense, to those selfsame doctors.

2. BRODO PER GLI AMMALATI (BROTH FOR THE SICK)

An eminent specialist, who was attending a very ill woman of my acquaintance, ordered a broth for her prepared in the following manner.

> Cut thin slices of veal or beef and layer them one atop the other in a wide pan. Salt them well, and cover them with cold water. Cover the pan with a plate, on which you will place a little water, and cook the meat at a gentle simmer for six hours. When the meat is nearly done, increase the heat to a rolling boil for ten minutes, and then pass the broth through a linen cloth.
>
> With 2 kilograms of meat (about 4-1/2 pounds), you will thus obtain between 2/3 and 3/4 of a liter (almost a quart) of broth of fine color and rich in substance.

3. GELATINA (ASPIC)

500 grams (about 1 pound) of lean veal, boned (see recipe 323)
1 calf's foot, or 150 grams (about 5 1/4 ounces) of meat from
*   a calf's foot*
2 or 3 chicken legs
2 chicken heads, with necks

Brown the chicken legs and cut them into pieces. Put everything on the fire in two liters (about two quarts) of water. Add salt and bring to a boil, skimming the surface from time to time. Simmer for seven or eight hours until half the liquid has boiled off. Pour the broth into a bowl and, when it has cooled, skim off the fat which will have congealed on the surface. If the broth has not thickened, return it to the fire and reduce it further, alternatively add two sheets of isinglass to it. Now the gelatin is done, but it must be clarified and given its amber color.

To do this, first mince as finely as you can 70 grams (about 2-1/2 ounces) of lean veal with a knife and then grind it in a mortar; then place it in a saucepan with an egg and a little water (a few tablespoons), mix it well and pour the cold gelatin over it. Place it on the heat and whisk it until it comes to a boil; then simmer it for about twenty minutes, tasting for salt.

This is also the time to color the aspic. Place two pinches of sugar and a few drops of water in a metal spoon (do not use tin-coated spoons). Hold it over the flame until the sugar has become nearly black, then pour it bit by bit into the simmering gelatin, until you have the right color. Some like to add a small glass of Marsala wine.

Now, take a cheesecloth, wet it, wring it out well, and strain the hot gelatin through it, being careful not to squeeze it. Then immediately pour the gelatin into molds. In the summer, if the aspic does not to thicken well, place it on ice. When you want to remove it from the mold, pass a cloth dipped in boiling water around the sides. A beautiful aspic is clear, soft, transparent and the color of topaz. It is ordinarily served with a galantine of capon or other cold dishes. It is also an ideal dish for the sick. If it turns bitter from not having been eaten soon enough, simply put it back on the fire and bring it to a boil. Common broth or even simple meat broth, can be clarified in the same manner.

4. SUGO DI CARNE (BROWN STOCK)[8]

In Romagna, which is a stone's throw from Tuscany, they do not much care for dictionaries, and so they call meat sauce "brown stock," perhaps because of its brown color.

8 The "meat sauce" described here is not what we have come to understand by that name, i.e., the "ragù" or "bolognese" sauce often served with pasta. It is, in fact, more like a "dark broth," and is used as a base or flavoring for many other dishes. Artusi makes frequent mention of it in the recipes that follow.

Watching a good cook do it would be the best way to learn how to make this stock. But I hope that with my directions you will be able to make, if not an exquisite stock, then at least a reasonable one.

Cover the bottom of a saucepan with thin slices of lardoon, or preferably, bacon, and on top of them dice a large onion, a carrot, and one stalk of celery. Add to this a few pieces of butter, and then place some lean beef, either chopped or thinly sliced, on top. Any beef at all will do, and, to save money, you can use the bloody neck parts, or other inferior cuts which the Florentine butchers call *parature* (trimmings). Add any meat scraps you might have, bacon rind or anything else, as long as it is clean. Flavor only with salt and two cloves, and place the pot on the fire, without stirring.

When you can smell the aroma of burning onions, turn the meat, and when you see it well-browned all over—indeed, nearly black— pour a small dipper of cold water over it, repeating this three times as the water is gradually absorbed. Finally, if the amount of meat is roughly 500 grams (about 1 pound), pour 1-1/2 liters (about 1-1/2 quarts) of hot water in the saucepan or, better yet, a broth made of spongy bones, and bring it to a slow boil. Let it simmer for five or six hours to reduce the liquid, and extract the essence of the meat. Then strain, and when the fat forms a thick film on top, skim it off to make the sauce lighter for the stomach. This sauce may be kept for several days, is versatile in its applications, and can even be used to make good macaroni pies.

Chopped necks and heads of chickens, when mixed with the beef, will give the sauce a better flavor. The leftover meat may be used to make meatballs.

5. SUGO DI CARNE CHE I FRANCESI CHIAMANO SALSA SPAGNUOLA (THE MEAT SAUCE THE FRENCH CALL SPANISH SAUCE)

This culinary find, which yields boiled beef and a good thick sauce, seems to me both felicitously constructed and economical, given that nothing used for it goes to waste, and the sauce is a good accompaniment to any number of dishes.

Take one kilogram (about 2 pounds) of lean beef—including the bone and joint—and from it cut 400 grams (about 14 ounces, i.e., not much less than a pound) in small slices. With the rest, make a broth in the usual fashion with a good 1-1/2 liters (about 1-1/2 quarters) of water.

Cover the bottom of a saucepan with slices of lardoon and prosciutto and a few pieces of butter. Dice an onion, and lay the meat slices on top. Apply a high flame, and when the underside of the meat begins to brown, baste it with a small ladle of broth. Turn it over to brown on the other side, and then pour another ladleful of broth over it. Season with salt, one clove or nine to ten crushed peppercorns, and a teaspoon of sugar. Now add the rest of the broth, adding to it a sliced carrot and a *bouquet garni* composed of parsley, celery, and other aromatic herbs. Simmer gently for about two hours, then remove the meat slices, strain the liquid and skim the fat. With this you can make the base for the soup described in recipe 38. You can also use it to add flavor to vegetables or, thickening the sauce with a mixture of potato flour and butter, serve it on pasta.

Potato flour is better than wheat flour for binding sauces.

6. SUGO DI POMODORO (TOMATO SAUCE)[9]

Later I shall speak about another kind of tomato sauce that we call "salsa," as opposed to "sugo." Sugo must be simple and therefore composed only of cooked, puréed tomatoes. At the most you can add a few chunks of celery or some parsley or basil leaves, when you think these flavors will suit your needs.

9 As Artusi points out, there is an important difference between "sugo di pomodoro" (which is described here) and "salsa di pomodoro" (which will be described in recipe 125). Unfortunately, English does not allow for this distinction and both dishes are therefore called tomato sauce. To avoid confusion, whenever the "sugo" (rather than the "salsa") appears in a recipe the text will include a parenthetical reference to this recipe.

FIRST COURSES

It used to be said that pasta was the forage of man. Today doctors advise us to eat it sparingly, lest it overly dilate the stomach and reduce our consumption of meat. Meat strengthens the body's fibers, while starches, which pastas are usually made of, create fatty tissue, which cause flabbiness. To this theory I raise no objection; but if I may be permitted, I would like to make the following suggestions. Small amounts of pasta are for anyone who, not being in his prime or in perfect health, must be treated with special care. Small amounts of pasta are also for those who tend to put on weight and would like to keep such gains in check. Finally, small portions of pasta with a light sauce should be served at banquets, if the guests are to do justice to the various dishes that follow. But aside from these cases, a good and generous helping of pasta will always be welcome at humbler dinners, so go ahead and enjoy it. Governed by this principle, I shall make a point of listing every kind of pasta and soup that experience suggests to me.

Peas as prepared in recipe 427 can give flavor and charm, as we all know, to soups made with rice, pastina and malfattini.[10] But if you have no broth, they are better used in the risotto described in recipe 75.

---

10 "Pastina" simply means "small pasta," such as is often used in soups; "malfattini" are a kind of irregularly shaped pasta, also small and used in soups.

Soups and Pastas with Broth

7. CAPPELLETTI ALL'USO DI ROMAGNA
(CAPPELLETTI ROMAGNA STYLE)

They are called cappelletti (or "little hats") because of their hat-like shape. This is the easiest way to make them so that they are less heavy on the stomach.

180 grams (about 6-1/3 ounces) of ricotta, or half ricotta and half
    "raviggiolo" (a soft cheese made from goat or sheep milk)
1/2 capon breast cooked in butter, seasoned with salt and pepper
    and finely chopped with a "mezzaluna"[11]
30 grams (about 1 ounce) of grated Parmesan cheese
1 whole egg
1 egg yolk
a dash of nutmeg, a few spices, some lemon zest (if desired), and a
    pinch of salt

Mix all the ingredients and then taste, checking for seasonings and flavor. If you do not have a breast of capon, use 100 grams (about 3 1/2 ounces) of lean pork loin instead, cooked and seasoned as above.

If the ricotta or raviggiolo is too soft, leave out an egg white, or if the mixture comes out too firm, add another yolk. Enclose this stuffing in a soft dough made with flour and eggs only, using some of the leftover whites. Roll out the dough in a thin sheet and then cut it into disks the size of the one shown on the following page.

Place the stuffing in the center of the disk and fold, so as to form half-moon shapes. Then take the two ends, press them together and you will have a "cappelletto."

If the dough dries out as you are working with it, then dip a finger in water and wet the disks along the edges. For best results, this pasta calls for a broth made with capon, that silly animal that every year out of the goodness of its heart offers itself to be sacrificed to mankind during the solemnities of Christmas. Cook the cappelletti in the capon broth, as they do in Romagna, where, on

---

11 A knife with a curved, crescent-like blade and handles at both ends, used for chopping; also called "lunetta."

DISK FOR CAPPELLETTI

Christmas day, you will find braggarts claiming to have eaten a hundred of them. This can also suffice to kill you, however, as happened to a friend of mine. For a moderate eater, a couple of dozen cappelletti will be quite enough.

Apropos of this pasta, I will tell you a little story, which, though it may be of little importance, may yet give pause to reflect.

You should know that the gentlemen of Romagna are not in the least interested in racking their brains over some tome, perhaps because from infancy children are accustomed to seeing their parents doing anything but turning the pages of books. Another factor may be that, being in a place where one can lead a happy and pleasurable life with little, the Romagnoli do not believe much instruction in life is necessary. For this reason, after they finish grammar school, a good ninety per cent of them takes up a life of leisure, and then no matter how hard you prod or pull, they will not budge. This was the situation a husband and wife living in a village of lower Romagna found themselves in with their teenage son Carlino. The father, however, believed in progress and, though he had the means to leave his son well provided for, would have liked the boy to become a lawyer, or possibly even a member of Parliament, since it is but a short step from one to the other. After many conversations, deliberations, and squabbles within the family over the great separation, the decision was made to send Carlino to continue his studies in a big city. Ferrara was chosen, being the nearest. Carlino's father accompanied him there, but did so with a heavy heart, having had to tear him from the arms of his loving mother, who had drenched him with tears.

Less than a week had passed. The parents were sitting down at table for a dish of cappelletti. After a long silence and several sighs, the mother exclaimed:

"Oh, if only Carlino were here! He so loves cappelletti!" No sooner were these words spoken than they heard a knock at the front door, and into the room sprang a cheerful Carlino.

"Oh, you are back!" exclaimed the father. "What happened?"

"What happened," replied Carlino, "is that wasting away over books is not for me. I would rather be drawn and quartered than return to that jail." Overjoyed, the mother ran to embrace her son, and turned to her husband.

"Let him do as he wishes," she said. "Better a healthy fool than a sickly scholar. He will be busy enough looking after his interests here." Indeed, from that moment on, Carlino's interests revolved around a rifle, a hunting dog, a frisky horse hitched to a fine little racing gig, and continual assaults on the young country girls.

8. TORTELLINI ALL'ITALIANA
(TORTELLINI ITALIAN STYLE)[12]

300 grams (about 10 ounces) of pork loin chops
1 calf's brain or 1/2 a brain of a larger animal
50 grams (about 1-2/3 ounces) of ox marrow
50 grams (about 1-2/3 ounces) of grated Parmesan cheese

12 Artusi mentions that these can also be called "agnellotti." Today a more common variation is "agnolotti."

3 yolks and, if necessary, the white of 1 egg
a dash of nutmeg

Bone and trim the fat from the pork chops, and then cook them in a saucepan with butter, salt and a dash of pepper. In case you cannot find pork, you may use 200 grams (about 7 ounces) of lean turkey breast, cooked in the same way. Pound or finely chop the meat with a mezzaluna (see note 8); then boil and skin the brain and add this to the pork (or turkey) along with the uncooked marrow and all the other ingredients, mixing thoroughly. Then wrap the tortellini in a sheet of dough much as you did the cappelletti, and fold them in the same manner. The tortellini, however, will be much smaller and here is the size of the disk you will normally need:

DISK FOR
TORTELLINI

9. TORTELLINI ALLA BOLOGNESE
(TORTELLINI BOLOGNESE STYLE)

When you hear someone speak of Bolognese cooking, salute it, because this cooking deserves it. It is somewhat heavy perhaps because the climate requires it, but it is also succulent, tasty and healthy. This may explain why in Bologna a life span of 80 or 90 years is more common than elsewhere.

The following tortellini, though simpler and less costly than the preceding ones, are just as good—as you will learn when you taste them.

30 grams (about 1 ounce) of untrimmed prosciutto
20 grams (about 2/3 of an ounce) of Bolognese mortadella

60 grams (about 2 ounces) of ox marrow
60 grams (about 2 ounces) of grated Parmesan cheese
1 egg
a dash of nutmeg
no salt or pepper

Finely chop the prosciutto and mortadella with the mezzaluna. Chop the marrow equally fine, but don't melt it over the fire. Add the other ingredients, and knead it all together with an egg, mixing well. Enclose this paste in a disk of the same dough used for the previous recipes cut to the size shown in recipe 8. These tortellini will keep for days and even for a few weeks, and if you want them to turn a nice yellow color, place them to dry in a warming oven as soon as they are made. With this amount, you will make about 300 tortellini. And you will need a dough made with three eggs.

"Bologna is a big old town where the feasting never stops," said a fellow who went there now and then to dine with friends. The hyperbole in this sentence is based on a truth, one that might well be put to advantage by a philanthropist wishing to link his name to a new public work for the glory of Italy. I am speaking of the need for a culinary institute, or cooking school, to which Bologna would lend itself better than other city, given its excellent cuisine and its citizens' passion for eating well. No one, apparently, wants to pay to much attention to eating, and the reason is easy to understand. But then, leaving hypocrisy aside, everybody readily complains about a bad dinner or about indigestion due to badly prepared food. Nourishment being life's primary need, it is certainly reasonable to take care of this need and satisfy it in the best manner possible.

A foreign writer says, "The health, morale and joy of a family are dependent on its cooking. Therefore, it would be a wonderful thing if every woman, whether of common or high birth, knew an art that brings well-being, wealth and peace to the family." Our own Lorenzo Stecchetti (Olindo Guerrini) in a conference held at the Exposition of Turin on June 21, 1884, said: "We must be rid of the prejudice that deems cooking vulgar, for what nurtures an intelligent and elegant pleasure is not vulgar. A producer of wines who manipulates the grapes and occasionally the ground itself to create a pleasant drink, is coddled, envied, and granted public honors.[13] A cook who likewise manipulates his raw materials to obtain a pleasing food, is neither honored nor esteemed—he is not even let into the waiting room. And yet the wise man says: "tell me what you eat, and I will tell you who you are." And yet the very nations of the world derive their natures, strong or weak, great or wretched, in large part from the food they eat. There is therefore no just distribution of praise. Cooking must be rehabilitated."

I say therefore that my institute should serve to train young women to be cooks, for they are naturally more economical and less wasteful than men. These women would then be easy to employ, and would possess an art which, when brought into middleclass households, would serve as a medicine against the frequent quarrels that occur in families as a result of bad dining. Indeed, I have heard talk of a sensible woman from a Tuscan city, who, to avoid such quarrels, enlarged her too-small kitchen to make it into a more comfortable place in which she can enjoy using my book.

I mention this idea in its embryonic state, as a suggestion that others may pick up, develop, and use to their benefit if they find it has merit. I am of the opinion that a well-managed institution of this sort—accepting private orders and selling already cooked meals—could be established, grow and prosper with relatively small initial capital and expense.

If you want even nicer tortellini, you can improve this recipe by adding a half-breast of capon cooked in butter and an egg yolk to the other ingredients.

13. Lorenzo Stecchetti, *La tavola e la cucina nei secoli* XV and XVI, Florence, Barbera, p. 4.

10. TORTELLINI DI CARNE DI PICCIONE
(TORTELLINI STUFFED WITH SQUAB)

These tortellini truly deserve to be described here, for they are excellent in their simplicity. Take a squab (i.e., a young pigeon bred for meat) of about 1/2 a kilogram (about a pound) and, having plucked it, combine it with:

80 grams (about 2-2/3 ounces) of grated Parmesan cheese
70 grams (about 2-1/3 ounces) of untrimmed prosciutto
a dash of nutmeg

Clean and gut the squab (the liver and gizzard will not be used in this recipe), and then boil it in salted water for a half hour (it must not be fully cooked). Then remove the squab from the fire, bone it, and chop the meat and prosciutto very fine, first using a knife, and then the mezzaluna. Add the Parmesan and the nutmeg, working and blending the mixture with the blade of a knife until it has the consistency of a smooth paste.

To make the tortellini use the disk in recipe 8. Making the dough with three eggs you should get enough disks for 260 tortellini.

You can serve them in broth, as a soup, or plain with just cheese and butter. They work even better in a giblet sauce.

11. PANATA (BREAD SOUP)

The people of Romagna solemnly celebrate Easter with this soup and call it "tridura," a word whose meaning has been lost in the Tuscan dialect, but which was in use in the early 14th century. We know this because the word appears in an ancient manuscript, which mentions a ceremonial gift to the friars of Settimo at Cafaggiolo (Florence) which involved sending every year to the monastery a newly made wooden bowl full of tridura and covered by sticks that supported ten pounds of pork decked with laurel. Everything in the world grows old and changes, even languages and words, but not the ingredients of which dishes are made. For this soup, they are:

130 grams (about 4-1/2 ounces) of day-old bread, grated, not crushed
4 eggs
50 grams (about 1-2/3 ounces) of grated Parmesan cheese
a dash of nutmeg
a pinch of salt

Place the ingredients in a large saucepan and mix them together, but do not let the mixture thicken too much. However, if the mixture is too loose, add more bread crumbs. Dilute with hot but not boiling broth, setting some aside to add later. Cook with embers around the pot, but with little or no heat directly under it. When it begins to boil, try to gather it gently with a wooden spoon in the center of the saucepan by pushing it inwards from the sides of the pan, but without breaking it apart. When it has thickened and set, pour it into the soup tureen and send it to the table. These amounts are enough for six people.

If the panata has turned out well, you will see it gathered in small bunches, with the clear broth around it. If you like it with herbs and peas, cook these separately, and stir them into the mixture before you pour broth over it.

12. MINESTRA DI PANGRATTATO
(BREAD CRUMB SOUP)

Dried out leftover bread pieces are called "seccherelli" in Tuscany. Crushed and sifted, they are used as bread crumbs in cooking, and can also be used to make a soup. Pour the bread crumbs into boiling broth, in the same proportions you would use when making soup with semolina. Depending on the quantity desired, break two or more eggs into the soup tureen, mix with one heaping spoonful of grated Parmesan cheese for each egg, and pour the boiling soup over it a little bit at a time.

13. TAGLIERINI DI SEMOLINO
(THIN SEMOLINA NOODLES)

These are not much different from those made with flour, though they bear up better when cooked—firmness being a virtue in this dish. In addition, they leave the broth clear, and are apparently lighter on the stomach.

A fine-grain semolina is required. It must be mixed with egg several hours before you are ready to roll it out. If, when you are about to roll it, it is still too soft, add a few pinches of dry semolina to obtain a dough of the right consistency, so that it does not stick to the rolling pin. Neither salt nor other ingredients are necessary.

14. GNOCCHI (DUMPLINGS)

This is a dish to be proud of. But if you do not wish to use up a chicken or capon just to use the breast, then wait until you have some breast meat left over from another meal.

Cook in water, or better yet, steam 200 grams (about 7 ounces) of large, floury potatoes, and pass them through a sieve. To this add the breast of chicken, boiled and chopped very finely with a mezzaluna, along with 40 grams (about 1-1/3 ounces) of grated Parmesan cheese, two egg yolks, salt to taste and a hint of nutmeg. Mix and pour the mixture onto a pastry board evenly sprinkled with 30 or 40 grams (between 1 and 1-1/3 ounces) of flour, which should be enough to bind it and allow you to roll it out in small cylinders about the size of your little finger. Cut these in sections which you will throw in boiling broth and cook for five to six minutes.

These amounts serve seven to eight people.

If the breast of chicken is large, two egg yolks alone will not be enough.

15. MINESTRA DI SEMOLINO COMPOSTA I
(SEMOLINA SOUP I)

Cook enough fine-grain semolina in milk to obtain a firm mixture. When you take it from the heat, season it with salt, grated Parmesan cheese, a dollop of butter and a hint of nutmeg. Allow it to cool. Then moisten the mixture with enough eggs to turn it into a creamy liquid. Take a smooth tin mold, butter the bottom of it well, and then place a sheet of paper (also buttered) inside it. Pour the mixture into the mold, and then thicken it by cooking in *bain-marie*.[14] When it is cooked and has cooled, run the blade of a knife around the inside of the mold. The paper at the bottom will help you unmold it. Cut the mixture into little bricks or cakes as thick as a heavy coin and between 1 or 2 centimeters wide (about 1/2 inch), which you will cook in broth for a few minutes.

Two eggs and a glass of milk make enough soup for four or five people. With a glass and a half of milk and three eggs, I made soup for eight people.

16. MINESTRA DI SEMOLINO COMPOSTA II
(SEMOLINA SOUP II)

I like this semolina soup even more than the preceding one. But this is a question of taste.

For each egg:
30 grams (about 1 ounce) of semolina
20 grams (about 2/3 of an ounce) of grated Parmesan cheese
20 grams (about 2/3 of an ounce) of butter
a pinch of salt
a dash of nutmeg

Melt the butter over the fire and, having removed it from the hearth,

14. Cooking in "bain-marie" is often translated as cooking in a double boiler. However, this is not what Artusi means. Rather, the process he is describing involves the following: you pour the mixture that needs to be cooked into a pan or mold, then you put this pan or mold into a much larger pan in which you have poured enough water to surround and come about 3/4 of the way up the sides (on the outside) of the smaller pan. The water in the larger pan should be hot but never boil. This type of cooking is usually done in the oven.

pour the semolina and cheese over it. Then mix in the eggs, stirring well. To thicken the mixture, pour it into a pan lined with a buttered sheet of paper. Put the pan in the oven with embers on both sides, taking care not to roast it. When cooled and removed from the mold, cut the semolina into small cubes or similar shapes, which you will boil in broth for ten minutes.

With three eggs you will make enough soup for five people.

17. MINESTRA DI *KRAPFEN* (SOUP WITH FRITTERS)

Except for the sugar, the ingredients are the same as for recipe 182. Here are the amounts for a soup for seven or eight people.

100 grams (about 3-1/2 ounces) of Hungarian flour
20 grams (about 2/3 of an ounce) of butter
a walnut-size dollop of yeast
1 egg
a pinch of salt

Roll out the dough to a thickness of a little less than half a finger; cut it with a tin cookie cutter of the diameter shown here

to make as many disks as possible. Set aside to rise. You will see them swell into little balls, after which you must fry them in fine oil, or alternatively in lard or butter. When ready to bring the fritters to the table, place them in the soup tureen and pour boiling broth over them.

18. MINESTRA DEL PARADISO
(PARADISE SOUP)

This is a substantial and delicate soup. But paradise, even Mohammed's paradise, has nothing to do with it.

Beat four egg whites until stiff, then blend in the yolks. Add four not very full tablespoons of fine bread crumbs made from dry bread, an equal amount of Parmesan cheese, and a hint of nutmeg.

Stir the mixture gently so that it remains fluffy, and drop it by small spoonfuls into boiling broth. Allow it to boil for seven or eight minutes and send it to the table.

These amounts serve six people.

19. MINESTRA DI CARNE PASSATA
(PURÉED MEAT SOUP)

150 grams (about 5-1/4 ounces) of milk-fed lean veal
25 grams (about 4/5 of an ounce) of untrimmed prosciutto
25 grams (about 4/5 of an ounce) of grated Parmesan cheese
2 tablespoons of a paste made with crustless fine bread, water, and a little butter
1 egg
a dash of nutmeg
salt to taste

First chop the meat and the prosciutto with a knife, and then dice more finely with a mezzaluna. Pound it in a mortar and pass through a sieve. Mix with the egg and the other ingredients. When the broth is boiling, drop the mixture in by small spoonfuls or squeeze it through a pastry tube to give it a more pleasing form. When the dumplings are cooked, send the soup to the table.

This amount is enough for four or five people, but it can serve as many as twelve if you make the following bread soup. Take very good, dry, day-old bread, dice it small, brown it in a saucepan with a generous amount of fat. When you are ready to serve, place the bread in the soup tureen and pour the puréed meat soup over it.

20. MINESTRA DI PASSATELLI
(PASSATELLI NOODLE SOUP)

Here are two recipes which, apart from quantity, differ very little from one another.

First, to serve four people:
100 grams (about 3-1/2 ounces) of bread crumbs
20 grams (about 2/3 of an ounce) of beef marrow
40 grams (about 1-1/3 ounces) of grated Parmesan cheese
2 eggs
a dash of nutmeg, or lemon zest, or both

Second, to serve seven to eight people:
170 grams (about 6 ounces) of bread crumbs
30 grams (about 1 once) of beef marrow
70 grams (about 2-1/2 ounces) of Parmesan cheese
3 whole eggs
1 egg yolk
nutmeg or lemon zest as above

The marrow makes the dumplings more tender. It is not necessary to soften it over the heat, you just need to chop it finely with the blade of a knife. Mix everything together to form a rather firm loaf—but leave aside some bread crumbs to add later, if necessary.

These noodles are called passatelli because they take their form by being passed through the holes of a metal device made especially for the purpose, and few are the families in Romagna that do not possess the implement. This dish is prized there, as indeed, for climatic reasons, are all kinds of egg noodles, which are eaten nearly on a daily basis. The noodles can also be squeezed through a pastry tube.

21. MINESTRA DI PASSATELLI DI CARNE
(SOUP WITH MEAT NOODLES)

150 grams (about 5-1/4 ounces) of beef fillet
50 grams (about 1-2/3 ounces) of bread crumbs
30 grams (about 1 ounce) of grated Parmesan cheese
15 grams (about 1/2 an ounce) of beef marrow

15 grams (about 1/2 an ounce) of butter
2 eggs yolks
salt to taste
a dash of nutmeg

Pound the fillet in a mortar and pass it through a sieve. Chop the marrow finely and mix it with the butter, using the blade of a knife. Add this to the ground meat. Then, add the rest of the ingredients making a loaf firm enough to pass through the same tool described in the previous recipe.

Boil it in broth for ten minutes. It serves six people.

You may replace the beef fillet with chicken or turkey breast, boiled or raw.

22. MINESTRA A BASE DI RICOTTA
(RICOTTA SOUP)

Take the stuffing for cappelletti in recipe 7, but instead of enclosing it in a pasta sheet, drop it by small spoonfuls into boiling broth. As soon as it firms up, pour the soup in a tureen and send it to the table.

23. MINESTRA DI NOCCIUOLE DI SEMOLINO
(SOUP WITH SEMOLINA DUMPLINGS)

1 glass of milk
100 grams (about 3-1/2 ounces) of semolina
20 grams (about 2/3 of an ounce) of grated Parmesan cheese
1 whole egg
1 egg yolk
a walnut-size dollop of butter
salt to taste
flour as needed
a dash of nutmeg

Heat the milk with the butter, and when it begins to boil, add the semolina little by little. Sprinkle with salt; when it is cooked and still hot, though no longer boiling, add the eggs, along with the Parmesan and nutmeg, and mix well. Let it cool and spread it out onto a floured pastry board. Roll it gently into a thin cylinder which you will cut into equal pieces to be made into little balls the size of hazelnuts. Throw them into broiling broth, and soon after pour them into the soup tureen, and send to the table. Normally, they will absorb about 25 to 30 grams (about 4/5 to 1 ounce) of flour; but this can be less or more, depending on how the mixture turns out.

These amounts serve five to six people.

24. MINESTRA DI BOMBOLINE DI FARINA
(SOUP WITH FLOUR FRITTERS)

These are the same fritters as in recipe 184, but without the mortadella; to make them, therefore, see that recipe. The quantities given there should suffice for eight to ten people, because the fritters swell in the broth, even if you make them as small as hazelnuts. To throw them in the pot, scoop the mixture in a wooden spoon, and with the point of a kitchen knife dipped in simmering fat, shape it into round pieces. Fry them in pure lard or butter, place them in the soup tureen, and pour the hot broth over them. Send immediately to the table.

To make your life easier, if you are giving a dinner, you can make the mixture the day before and fry the fritters the next morning. In winter they will not suffer even if fried several days in advance.

25. MINESTRA DI MATTONCINI DI RICOTTA
(SOUP WITH LITTLE RICOTTA "BRICKS")

200 grams (about 7 ounces) of ricotta cheese
30 grams (about 1 ounce) of grated Parmesan cheese
2 eggs
salt to taste
lemon zest and a dash of nutmeg

Pass the ricotta through a sieve. Add the other ingredients—the eggs one at a time. Mix well and pour the mixture into a buttered mold, with buttered paper lining the bottom. Cook in *bain-marie*. When cool, remove it from the mold, discard the paper, and cut it into cubes approximately one centimeter (about 2/5 of an inch) wide. Place them in a soup tureen, add boiling broth, and send to the table.

These amounts serve five to six people.

26. MINESTRA DI MILLE FANTI
(THOUSAND FOOT SOLDIERS SOUP)

A half egg per person is more than enough for this soup, when it is made for a large company.

At the bottom of a pot, place as many heaping teaspoonfuls of flour as you have eggs. Add grated Parmesan cheese, a hint of nutmeg, a pinch of salt and finally the eggs. Blend together well, and pour the mixture into boiling broth through a strainer with a wide mesh, while stirring the broth at the same time. Let boil a while, and then send it to the table.

27. MINESTRA DI LATTE COMPOSTA
(MILK-DUMPLING SOUP)

60 grams (about 2 ounces) of flour
40 grams (about 1-1/3 ounces) of butter
30 grams (about 1 ounce) of Parmesan cheese
4 deciliters (about 1-2/3 cups) of milk
4 eggs
salt to taste
a dash of nutmeg, if desired

Melt the butter and as, soon as it is liquefied, pour in the flour. Stir, and when it begins to brown, add the milk a little at a time. Bring it to a boil, and after a while remove it from the fire. Season it and, when it has cooled, add the eggs. Cook it in *bain-marie* like the semolina described in recipe 15.

These amounts serve eight to ten people.

28. MINESTRA DI PANE ANGELICO
(ANGEL BREAD SOUP)

150 grams (about 5-1/4 ounces) of crustless fine bread
50 grams (about 1-2/3 ounces) of untrimmed prosciutto
40 grams (about 1-1/3 ounces) of beef marrow
40 grams (about 1-1/3 ounces) of grated Parmesan cheese
flour as needed
1 whole egg
1 egg yolk
a dash of nutmeg

Moisten the bread with hot broth and then squeeze out the broth using a cheesecloth. Finely chop the prosciutto. Pound the beef marrow with the flat part of the knife and then use the knife to knead it until it is reduced to a paste. Combine these three ingredients with the Parmesan, and then add the eggs.

Spread the mixture on a pastry board sprinkled with flour. Then cover with more flour—about 100 grams (about 1 cup) should do—so that you can shape the mixture into soft balls about the size of hazelnuts. Throw them into the boiling broth and, after letting them cook for ten minutes, send to the table.

These amounts serve ten to twelve people.

29. MINESTRA DI BOMBOLINE DI PATATE
(SOUP WITH POTATO FRITTERS)

500 grams (about 1 pound) of potatoes
40 grams (about 1-1/3 ounces) of butter
40 grams (about 1-1/3 ounces) of grated Parmesan cheese
3 egg yolks
a dash of nutmeg

Cook the potatoes in water, or better yet, steam them. Then peel them, pass them hot through a sieve, and salt them. Then work in well all the other ingredients. Pour the mixture on a pastry board sprinkled with flour so that you can roll it into long, thin cylinders without letting the flour get inside. Use these cylinders to form little balls the size of hazelnuts. Fry them in a generous amount of oil or lard. Place them in a soup tureen, pouring boiling broth over them, then send to the table.

These amounts serve eight to ten people.

30. MINESTRA CON BOMBOLINE DI RISO
(SOUP WITH RICE FRITTERS)

100 grams (about 3-1/2 ounces) rice
40 grams (about 1-1/3 ounces) of butter
40 grams (about 1-1/3 ounces) of grated Parmesan cheese
1 egg yolk
a dash of nutmeg
salt to taste

Cook the rice in the milk until it is very thick (1/2 a liter or about 1/2 a quart of milk should do). Before removing it from the fire, add the butter and salt, and when it has stopped boiling, add the egg yolks, Parmesan cheese and nutmeg. To complete the preparation, follow the directions in the preceding recipe. These fritters are more flavorful than those made with potatoes.

These amounts serve six people.

31. MINESTRA DI DUE COLORI (TWO-COLOR SOUP)

This is a light and delicate soup which in Tuscany is most likely to be appreciated by the ladies. However, it should not be served in Romagna, that homeland of tagliatelle, where softness to the bite is not to the locals' taste. Even less would they appreciate the pasty texture of tapioca, the very sight of which would, with few exceptions, turn their stomachs.

180 grams (about 6-1/3 ounces) of flour
60 grams (about 2 ounces) of butter
40 grams (about 1-1/3 ounces) of Parmesan cheese

4 deciliters (about 1-2/3 cups) of milk
2 whole eggs
2 egg yolks
salt to taste
a handful of spinach
a dash of nutmeg

Boil the spinach, squeeze it dry and pass it through a sieve. Heat the butter and when it has melted, add the flour, stirring well. Then add the milk, a little at a time. Salt it and, while it is cooking, work the mixture with a wooden spoon, turning it into a smooth paste.

Remove it from the heat, and when it is lukewarm add the eggs, grated Parmesan and nutmeg. Then divide the mixture into two equal parts. Use one part to blend in just enough spinach to make the mixture turn green.

Place the mixture in a pastry-tube using the attachment that has rather wide round holes. Squeeze the dough into boiling broth in the same manner as for the passatelli in recipe 48. This procedure must be repeated twice, once with the yellow mixture and once with the green one.

These amounts serve eight to ten people.

32. ZUPPA RIPIENA (SOUP WITH MEAT STUFFING)

Take a half breast of capon or of a large chicken, a slice of untrimmed prosciutto, and a small piece of marrow. Work these into forcemeat, season with grated Parmesan cheese, add a dash of nutmeg, and bind it with an egg. Since you are using the prosciutto, salt is not necessary.

Take a long thin loaf of stale bread, slice it into round, half-finger-thick pieces and then trim off the crust. Spread the meat mixture on half of the pieces you have and then cover them with the remaining pieces, pressing firmly so that they will remain attached. Cut these paired slices into small cubes and fry them in pure lard, olive oil or butter, depending on personal or regional taste.

When it is time to send the soup to the table, place the fried cubes in a soup tureen, and pour the boiling broth over them.

33. ZUPPA DI OVOLI
(ROYAL AGARIC MUSHROOM SOUP)

During mushroom season, you can serve this soup even at an elegant dinner, and it will not embarrass you.

"Ovoli" are the orange mushrooms described in recipe 396. Take 600 grams (about 1-1/3 pounds) of these mushrooms—after cleaning and peeling them, you will be left with about 500 grams (about 1 pound). Wash them and then cut them into thin slices or small pieces.

Make a paste out of 50 grams (about 1-2/3 ounces) of lardoon and a pinch of parsley, and place it on the fire with 50 grams (about 1-2/3 ounces) ounces of butter and three spoonfuls of oil. When this begins to brown, add the mushrooms, salt lightly, and wait until they are half-cooked. Then pour them with all the rest into a hot broth and allow them to boil for another ten minutes. Before removing them from the stove, break one whole egg and one yolk into the pan, and add a handful of grated Parmesan cheese. Then pour in the broth little by little, stirring constantly. Add cubes of toasted bread—but make sure that the soup stays very watery.

These amounts serve six to seven people.

If you make only half the portion, one whole egg will be enough.

34. ZUPPA DI ZUCCA GIALLA
(PUMPKIN SOUP)

Peel and thinly slice 1 kilogram (about 2 pounds) of yellow pumpkin. Cook it with two ladlefuls of broth and pass it through a sieve.

Over the fire make a paste with 60 grams (about 2 ounces) of butter and two level tablespoons of flour. When it begins to color, add broth and simmer. Then add the puréed pumpkin and enough broth to feed six people. Pour the boiling soup over cubes of fried bread and send it to the table with grated Parmesan cheese on the side.

If you make this soup properly and with a good broth, it can be served at any table, and will have the added merit of being refreshing.

35. ZUPPA DI PURÈ DI PISELLI, DI GRASSO
(PEA SOUP WITH MEAT BROTH)

Since the peas for this dish are to be puréed, they need not be the most tender. 400 grams (about 14 ounces) of shelled peas should suffice for six people to dine fashionably—that is, with little soup. Cook the shelled peas in broth with a *bouquet garni*, which you will later discard, made with parsley, celery, carrot and a few basil leaves. When the peas are cooked add to their broth two pieces of bread fried in butter. When the bread has become soggy pass the mixture through a sieve. Dilute the result with broth as needed. You may add a little brown stock (recipe 4) if you have it, pouring it over the soup. This soup must be made with fine stale bread, diced and fried in butter.

36. ZUPPA SANTÉ (HEALTHY SOUP)

A variety of garden vegetables can provide the ingredients for this soup. If you serve, for example, carrots, sorrel, celery and white cabbage, cut the cabbage like taglierini, squeeze firmly, and then place in a pan on the fire to get the water out. Cut the carrots and the celery into strips about three centimeters long (about 1-1/5 inches), and place them on the fire, together with the cabbage and the washed sorrel stalks, adding a little salt, a pinch of pepper and a piece of butter. When the vegetables have absorbed the butter, add broth and finish cooking.

In the meantime prepare the bread, which should be of good quality and at least a day old. Cut it into small cubes and fry it in butter, virgin olive oil or lard. To keep the bread from becoming too greasy, use a good deal of fat but wait until it is sizzling before tossing in the bread. Alternatively, roast the bread in slices half a finger thick, and then cut them into cubes. Place the bread in a soup tureen, pour the boiling broth and the vegetables over it, and send to the table immediately.

With professional paring utensils you can cut the vegetables into charming and elegant shapes.

37. ZUPPA DI ACETOSA (SORREL SOUP)

200 grams (about 7 ounces) of sorrel
1 head of lettuce

After having soaked the vegetables, drain them well, cut them into strips, and place them on the fire. When they are cooked, flavor with a pinch of salt and 30 grams (about 1 ounce) of butter. In the soup tureen place two egg yolks with a little lukewarm broth. Add the vegetables and then, a little bit at a time, enough boiling broth as needed for soup, stirring constantly. Add diced, fried bread, and send to the table with Parmesan cheese on the side.

Prepared in this way, this soup serves five people.

38. ZUPPA SUL SUGO DI CARNE
(SOUP WITH MEAT SAUCE)

Certain cooks, to give themselves airs, mangle the phrases of our less than benevolent neighbors, using names that resound mightily and say nothing. According to them, the soup I am describing should be called soup *mitonnée*. And if I had stuffed my book with these exotic and disagreeable names, to please the many who grovel before foreign customs, who knows how much prestige I would have enjoyed! But, for the sake of our national dignity, I have made every effort to use our own beautiful and harmonious language, and so it pleases me to call the soup by its simple and natural name.

To succeed with this soup one must know how to make a good meat sauce (see recipe 5), something of which not everyone is capable.

To serve four, you will need about 500 grams (about 1 pound) of beef for stewing, with some chicken necks and kitchen scraps, if you have them. In addition to its sauce, this soup requires plenty of garden vegetables. Depending on the season, you can use a combination of celery, carrot, Savoy cabbage, sorrel, zucchini, peas, and even a potato. Dice the potato and the zucchini, slice all the rest.

Boil all the vegetables together, and then sauté them in butter, moistening them with the sauce. Slice the bread a half-finger thick, brown the slices and cut into cubes. Take a pan, or better yet, a pot—something presentable, since it must be brought to the table—

and assemble the soup in it as follows: a layer of bread, one of vegetables, and then a sprinkling of Parmesan cheese. Continue in this fashion. Finally, pour the sauce over it, cover with a plate and a napkin, and keep it near the fire for a half hour before serving it.

I warn you that this soup is supposed to be nearly dry. Therefore it is well-advised to keep a little sauce on the side, to add to the soup when you send it to the table, in case it is too dry.

39. ZUPPA REGINA (THE QUEEN OF SOUPS)

From the name alone, one would have to judge this the best of all soups. Certainly it belongs among the most distinguished. The name, however, is a bit exaggerated.

The soup is made with the white meat of a roasted chicken, skinned and stripped of tendons. Chop it fine with the mezzaluna, and then pound it in a mortar with five or six sweet, blanched almonds and crustless bread soaked in milk or broth. The amount of bread should be between a fifth and a sixth of that of the meat. When the mixture is well mashed, pass it through a sieve, place it in a soup tureen, and then pour in a ladleful of hot broth.

Take some dry bread, cube it, fry it in butter and add this to the sauce in the tureen. Then add very hot broth, stir and send to the table with Parmesan cheese on the side.

This soup will serve you well when, after a dinner, you have leftovers of roasted or boiled chicken, although the best results are obtained using only roasted chicken.

Almonds serve to add a milkiness to the broth, but the resulting liquid should not be overly dense. Some people dissolve the yolk of a hard-boiled egg in the broth.

40. ZUPPA ALLA SPAGNUOLA (SPANISH-STYLE SOUP)

Take the breast of a young hen or capon, cut it into small pieces and cook it in butter over a low flame, seasoning it with salt and pepper. If the butter does not provide enough moisture, add a little broth. Remove the chicken breast from the pot, and throw in a handful of crustless bread. Add broth to make a firm paste. Place this paste and the chicken breast in a mortar. Add two egg yolks and a dash of nutmeg. Crush it into a fine mash, and leave it in a cool place to firm up. When you are ready to use it—which may even be the next day—place the mixture on a pastry board sprinkled with flour and roll it out in a small cylinder (no wider than a finger) which you will cut with a floured knife into many identical small pieces.

Use your hands (also dusted with flour) to roll the pieces into balls about the size of hazelnuts or smaller. Throw the little balls in boiling broth, and after five or six minutes pour them into a soup tureen, where you will have already placed some cubed bits of bread sautéed in butter or in pure lard. Better still, instead of bread you can serve the meat stuffing described in recipe 32.

This is an elegant soup that serves ten to twelve people.

41. ZUPPA DI PANE D'UOVO (EGG-BREAD SOUP)

This soup has not much flavor, but having seen it frequently served at foreign-style tables, I will describe it to you.

3 eggs
30 grams (about 1 ounce) of flour
a walnut-size pat of butter

First blend the three egg yolks with the flour and butter. Whip the three egg whites and add them to the mixture. Pour it all into a smooth mold, lining the bottom with buttered paper. Cook in the oven or in a Dutch oven.

After the loaf has cooked and cooled, cut it into cubes or into small lozenges, pour the boiling broth over it, and send to the table with Parmesan cheese on the side.

These amounts serve six to seven people.

42. RISI E LUGANIGHE (RICE WITH SAUSAGE)

One might say that the people of Veneto know of no other first course than rice, and therefore they cook it well and in many different ways. One way is rice in broth with sausage—but there the sausage is left whole, while I prefer to crumble it into the broth when I add the rice. Rice should not be washed, but only cleaned and rubbed in cloth to remove the dust. To my rice and sausage, I like to add either turnips or cabbage. Both must first be "blanched," or, in other words, parboiled. Cut the turnip into cubes, the cabbage into strips the size of fettuccine, and sauté them in butter. Just before removing the rice from the fire, add a good pinch of Parmesan cheese to bind it and give it additional flavor.

43. RISO ALLA CACCIATORA (RICE HUNTER'S STYLE)

Once, when I was a young man, a horse dealer and I set out on what was in those days a long trip to a fair in Rovigo. On the evening of the second day, a Saturday, after many hours of long travel with a horse which, under the very able hands of my companion, made short work of the road, we arrived, hungry and tired, at Polesella. Naturally, our first attentions were for our valiant animal. Then, upon entering the ground-floor room which in many inns serves as both kitchen and dining hall, my friend asked the innkeeper, "Have you anything to eat?"

"No, I do not," she replied. And then reconsidering, she suggested, "I wrung the necks of several chickens for tomorrow, and I could make some rice."

"Make the rice and make it at once!" came the answer, "We are starving!"

The innkeeper set to work, and I stood there watching carefully how she would put together this rice dish.

Cutting a chicken into pieces, she removed the head and feet, and placed the rest in a pan in which a "soffritto"[15] of lardoon, garlic and parsley were browning. She added a small piece of butter, and seasoned with salt and pepper. When the chicken was browned, she put it in a pot of simmering water, then threw in the rice, and before removing it from the fire added a good handful of Parmesan cheese to flavor it. You should have seen what an enormous plate of rice she set before us. But we got to the bottom of it, because it had to serve as first course, main course, and side dish.

15. See the note on "battuto" in the next recipe.

Now, to embroider upon the rice of the Polesella innkeeper, I would say that, instead of salt pork—unless it is of the exquisite pink variety—it is better to use finely chopped bacon. Tomato sauce (recipe 6) or tomato paste is also quite good with this dish. Also, for it to bind well with the chicken, the rice should neither be too cooked, nor too watery.

44. QUAGLIE COL RISO (QUAIL IN RICE)

Make a "battuto"[16] of prosciutto and a quarter of an onion; place it on the fire with butter and, when the onion begins to brown, add the quails, plucked and cleaned. Season the birds with salt and pepper, and, when browned, cook them in broth. When they are half done, add the rice and as much broth as may be needed to cook the rice and quail together. When the rice is ready, flavor it with Parmesan cheese, and then serve the rice and the quails, either dry or with broth, as you prefer.

Four quails and 400 grams (about 14 ounces) of rice will serve four people.

45. MALFATTINI (EASY EGG NOODLE SOUP)

In those parts of the country where homemade egg pasta is eaten almost daily, every housemaid has mastered the art of making it, and especially this dish, which is the essence of simplicity. Thus I speak about it not for them, but for the inhabitants of those provinces who know of no other soups than those made with bread, rice or store-bought pasta.

The most simple malfattini are made with flour. Fold the eggs into the flour and knead the mixture on the pastry board until you obtain a firm loaf. Cut this into large slices a half finger thick, and leave them a while to dry in the air. Then chop them with the mezzaluna into tiny bits about half the size of a grain of rice. You can achieve consistency of size by passing them through a strainer, or by grating them from the whole loaf. But do not do as those who leave them large as sparrow's beaks, for this will make them difficult to digest. Indeed, for even easier digestion, rather than with flour,

---

16 "Battuto" provides the foundation for numberless dishes. It usually consists of finely chopped prosciutto or "pancetta," onion and/or garlic, and other ingredients; once sautéed, it is called "soffritto."

you can make them with bread crumbs, either plain or with a pinch of grated Parmesan cheese and a dash of spices.

However you make them, you can serve them with peas as in recipe 427, when peas are in season, or use finely diced beet, or both. *À propos* of beet, I have noticed that in Florence, where they make a great use of aromatic herbs in cooking, dill is unknown. Mixed with beet, as is done in other towns, dill graces the palate. Indeed, I have tried to introduce this fragrant herb to Florence, but with little success. Perhaps this is because in that city beets are sold in bunches, whereas in Romagna they are carried loose to the market or already mixed with dill.

46. CUSCUSSÙ (COUSCOUS)

Couscous is a dish of Arab origin, which the descendants of Moses and Jacob, in their peregrinations, have carried around the world. But who knows how many and what kind of modifications it has undergone in its travels. Nowadays it is used as a first course by the Jews of Italy, two of whom were kind enough to let me taste it and see how it is done. I then made it again in my own kitchen as a test, and can therefore guarantee its legitimacy. However, I cannot guarantee I shall make you understand it:

> *For it is no simple thing to seek*
> *this odd concoction fully to describe,*
> *for a tongue that human words can speak*[17]

The following amount will be enough for six or seven people.

750 grams (about 1-2/3 pounds) of veal brisket
150 grams (about 5-1/4 ounces) of lean boneless veal
300 grams (about 10-1/2 ounces) of coarse-grained semolina
1 chicken liver
1 hard-boiled egg
1 egg yolk
a variety of vegetables, including onion, cabbage, celery, carrot,
*   spinach, beet and others*

---

17 A facetious revision of Dante's declaration (Inferno xxxii, 7-9) of his difficulty in describing "the bottom of the universe," i.e. the lowest circle of Hell.

Put the semolina in a wide, flat earthenware dish, or in a copper saucepan. Season with a bit of salt and a dash of pepper, and sprinkle with a few tablespoons of water, a little at a time, kneading it with the palm of your hand so that the flour swells, and becomes loose and granular. When you have finished adding the water, slowly pour a tablespoon of oil over it, while kneading it in the same manner as before. The whole process should take about half an hour. After working the semolina in this fashion, place it in a soup bowl and cover it with a cloth, the ends of which, gathered together beneath the dish, you will tie firmly with string.

To make the broth, put on the fire the veal brisket with 3 liters (about 3 quarts) of water. When the broth begins to simmer, skim it and then place the soup bowl with the semolina on top of the pot. Make sure that the broth does not touch the bottom of the bowl, which must fit as tightly as a lid so that no steam escapes. Cook the semolina over steam in this way for an hour and fifteen minutes. Halfway through the cooking process, open up the cloth to stir the semolina and then put everything back together as before.

With a knife mince the lean veal, add a piece of finely chopped crustless white bread and season with salt and pepper. With the mixture make little meatballs not much larger than hazelnuts and fry them in oil.

Chop the vegetables well and begin by sautéing the onion in oil. When the onion turns a golden brown, add the other vegetables. Season with salt and pepper, stirring constantly. Let the vegetables cook until they have reabsorbed their own water. When they are nearly dry, moisten them with brown stock, or with broth and tomato sauce (recipe 6) or tomato paste. Cook them together with the sliced chicken liver and the meatballs.

Remove the semolina from the bowl, place it on the fire in a saucepan and without bringing it to a boil, fold one egg yolk into it. Add some of the sauce, mix, and place on a large platter. The semolina should be almost dry so that you can decorate the top with the hard-boiled egg diced in small crescent shapes. Mix the rest of the sauce into the broth and serve it into as many bowls as there are people at the table—accompanied, of course, by the platter of semolina. Each person takes a portion of semolina onto his or her plate, and has a spoonful of broth with each mouthful.

The brisket can be served later as boiled meat.

Having given this long description, it seems to me that two questions will spontaneously arise in the reader's mind:

1. Why all that oil, and why always oil as seasoning?

2. Is this dish worth all the maddening effort it requires?

The response to the first question, this being a Jewish dish, is given in Deuteronomy, 14:21: "Thou shalt not seethe a kid in his mother's milk." The less scrupulous however, add a bit of Parmesan to the meatballs to give them more flavor. The second I can answer myself. To me, it is not a dish to make a great fuss over, but if prepared with great care, it can please even those whose palates are not used to such dishes.

47. MINESTRONE
(MIXED VEGETABLE AND RICE SOUP)

Minestrone brings back memories of a year marked by collective anxiety and a singular personal experience.

In the year of Our Lord 1855, I found myself at Livorno during the bathing season. Cholera was then making its way through several provinces of Italy, gripping everyone with the fear of a major epidemic, which, in fact, was not long in coming. One Saturday evening I entered a trattoria, and asked: "What's today's soup?"

"Minestrone," was the answer.

"Fine, bring the minestrone," I replied. I ate, took a stroll, and then went to bed. I had taken lodgings in the Piazza del Voltone, in a whitewashed new villa run by a certain Mr. Domenici. That night, I felt the onset of a frightening disturbance in my body that had me running regularly back and forth to the rest rooms—which in Italy should rather be called an *unrest* room. "Damned minestrone! You will never fool me again," I cried out, raging against something which was perhaps quite innocent.

Morning came, and feeling myself totally drained, I caught the first train and escaped to Florence, where I immediately felt much better. Monday the sad news reached me that cholera had broken out in Livorno, and the first to be struck dead was none other than Domenici himself.

And to think I had blamed the minestrone!

After three attempts, improving upon the dish each time, this is how I like to make it. Feel free to modify it to suit the tastes of your part of the world, and the vegetables locally available.

Start by making the usual meat broth, and cooking in it a handful of shelled fresh beans. If the beans are dry, then simmer them in water until they soften. Then cut some Savoy cabbage, spinach and a little chard into thin slices, and soak them in cold water. Then, to get the water out of the vegetables, place them on the fire in a dry saucepan. Drain the contents well, pressing them firmly with a wooden spoon to get rid of excess water. For a minestrone that serves four to five people, finely chop 40 grams (about 1-1/3 ounces) of fatty prosciutto, a clove of garlic, and a sprig of parsley, and sauté them together. Add this to the saucepan, along with some celery and carrots, one potato, one zucchini, and very little onion, all cut into short, thin slices. Add the beans, and if you wish, some pork rind (as some people like to do), and a bit of tomato sauce (recipe 6) or tomato paste. Season with salt and pepper and cook in the broth. As a last ingredient add enough rice to absorb most of the liquid, and before removing the minestrone from the fire throw in a good pinch of Parmesan cheese.

I should warn you that this is not a soup for weak stomachs.

48. PASSATELLI DI SEMOLINA
(PASSATELLI NOODLES MADE WITH SEMOLINA)

150 grams (about 1/3 of a pound) of fine-grain semolina
30 grams (about 1 ounce) of grated Parmesan cheese
6 deciliters (about 2-2/3 cups) of milk
2 whole eggs
2 yolks
salt, a dash of nutmeg and lemon zest

Cook the semolina in milk, adding a bit more dry semolina if you think the mixture is not firm enough. Salt it when it is done, and wait for it to cool before you add the eggs and the remaining ingredients.

Place the mixture in a pastry tube with an attachment that has fairly large holes. Press the mixture into boiling broth, holding the pastry tube perpendicular to the surface of the liquid. Let the passatelli cook until they are firm.

These amounts serve six to seven people.

49. RISO CON ZUCCHINI
(RICE WITH ZUCCHINI)

Take some small zucchini equal in weight to the amount of rice you wish to cook, and cut them into chunks the size of hazelnuts. Sauté them in butter, seasoning with salt and pepper. As soon as they begin to brown but are still rather firm, throw them in the half-cooked rice, so that they will finish cooking together.

The rice should be fairly dry, and the zucchini should not lose their shape. You may cook this dish in water instead of broth, and serve it quite dry. But in this case, add tomato sauce (recipe 125) to give it character, likewise pouring the sauce into the rice when it is half cooked. Also add some Parmesan cheese.

50. ZUPPA CON LE CIPOLLE ALLA FRANCESE
(FRENCH ONION SOUP)

This soup can be made with either broth or milk, and the following amounts serve five people.

250 grams (about 8-3/4 ounces) of white bread
80 grams (about 2-3/4 ounces) of grated Gruyère cheese
50 grams (about 1-2/3 ounces) of butter
40 grams (about 1-1/3 ounces) of grated Parmesan cheese
3 eggs, beaten
2 large white onions
1-1/2 liters (about 1-1/2 quarts) of milk or broth

Slice the onions very thinly and sauté them in butter. When they begin to brown, add the broth or milk (depending on what you are using). Cook well so that the onions are soft enough to be passed through a sieve. Mix the puréed onions with the remaining liquid. Cut the bread into slices or cubes, toast it, and then arrange it in layers in a soup tureen. Garnish the bread with the beaten eggs, the Gruyère and the Parmesan cheese. Lastly, pour in the boiling broth or milk and send to the table.

If you make this dish with milk, you should salt the eggs well. Given the amount of onion used in this soup, it is not recommended for those suffering from loose bowels.

51. STRICHETTI ALLA BOLOGNESE (STRICHETTI NOODLES BOLOGNESE STYLE)

Make a dough with flour, two eggs, 40 grams (about 1-1/3 ounces) of finely grated Parmesan cheese, and a dash of nutmeg. Roll out the dough, not too thin, and cut it with a pastry wheel with a scalloped edge into strips a finger and a half wide. Then, with the same pastry wheel, cut the strips at an angle, at intervals as wide as the strips, to obtain lozenge-shaped pieces. Take a piece at a time and with your fingers squeeze the four corners—two above and two below—in such a way as to form two attached rings. Cook briefly in broth. With two eggs you should be able to make enough strichetti for five people.

If you like this soup, you can thank a young, charming Bolognese woman known as la Rondinella, who was so good as to teach it to me.

52. ZUPPA DI GAMBERI COL SUGO DI CARNE (PRAWN SOUP WITH BROWN STOCK)

If we take a soup for four people as the norm, 150 grams (about 5-1/4 ounces) of shrimp should do. Wash the shrimp and place them on the fire in two ladles of broth. When they are cooked, scoop them out, and dissolve in the broth 30 grams (about 1 ounce) of crustless white bread sautéed in butter. Shell the shrimp, mash them in a mortar and pass them through a sieve, moistening them with the mixture of broth and bread. Add the resulting mixture to a brown stock like that in recipe 4. If you do not have brown stock handy, you can make one with about 100 grams (about 3-1/2 ounces) of meat. Finally, stir the mixture into the broth you have set aside for the soup, and pour the liquid over the roasted bread, or bread cubes fried in lard or oil.

Serve with grated Parmesan cheese.

53. ZUPPA ALLA STEFANI (STEFANI SOUP)

The distinguished poet Olindo Guerrini, librarian of the University of Bologna, has a taste for learning so developed that he enjoys digging up the bones of the culinary paladins of old, and drawing astonishing inferences from them that make modern cooks laugh out loud. He was good enough to favor me with the following recipe, taken from a little book, *The Art of Cooking Well,* by Signor Bartolomeo Stefani of Bologna, who was the cook of His Serene Highness the Duke of Mantua in the mid-1600s. At that time, much use and abuse was made of all manner of seasonings and spices, and sugar and cinnamon were used in broth, as well as in making boiled or roasted meat. Omitting some of his instructions for this soup, I shall limit myself, aromatically speaking, to a bit of parsley and basil. And if the ancient Bolognese cook, meeting me in the afterworld, scolds me for it, I shall defend myself by explaining that tastes have changed for the better. As with all things, however, we go from one extreme to the other, and we are now beginning to exaggerate in the opposite direction, going as far as to exclude herbs and spices from dishes that require them. And I shall tell him as well of the ladies who, at my table, have made gruesome faces when confronted with a bit of nutmeg. Here is the recipe for the soup (serves six):

120 grams (about 4-1/4 ounces) of veal or lamb brains (or brains of a similar animal)
3 chicken livers

3 eggs
1 sprig of basil and 1 of parsley, chopped
the juice of 1/4 lemon

Scald the brain so as to be able to skin it, and then sauté with the chicken livers in butter. Finish cooking them in brown stock, adding salt and pepper for seasoning.

Put the eggs in a pot and beat them with the basil and parsley, as well as the lemon juice and a bit of salt and pepper. Add cold broth a little at a time, to dilute the mixture. Then dice the brain and the livers and add to the pot. Put this on a low flame to thicken, stirring constantly with a wooden spoon. Take care not to bring it to a boil. After it has thickened, pour into a soup tureen over some diced bread sautéed in butter or oil and sprinkled with a handful of grated Parmesan cheese.

This is a delicate, substantial soup. However, if you, like me, are not particularly fond of foods with such a soft texture, then you may want to substitute sweetbreads for brains. And this reminds me to mention—and I know whereof I speak—that in some regions where, because of the climate, one must be careful about what one eats, the inhabitants have so enfeebled their stomachs by eating light and preferably soft, liquid dishes, that they can no longer withstand food of any weight.

54. ANOLINI ALLA PARMIGIANA
(ANOLINI DUMPLINGS PARMA STYLE)

A woman from Parma, whom I have not the pleasure of meeting, wrote me from Milan, where she lives with her husband, as follows: "I take the liberty of sending you a recipe for a dish which in Parma, beloved city of my birth, is a tradition at family holiday gatherings. Indeed I do not believe there is a single household where the traditional 'Anolini' are not made at Christmas and Easter time."

I declare myself indebted to this woman, because, having put her soup to the test, the result delighted not only myself but all my guests. To serve for four to five people:

500 grams (about 1 pound) of lean, boneless beef loin
20 grams (about 2/3 of an ounce) of lardoon
50 grams (about 1-2/3 ounces) of butter
1/4 of a medium-sized onion, chopped

Lard the piece of meat with the lardoon, tie it and then season with salt, pepper and spices. Then place it on the fire to brown in an earthenware bowl or other saucepan with butter and the roughly diced onion. When the meat has browned, add two ladlefuls of broth, and then cover with several sheets of paper held firmly in place by a soup plate containing some red wine. As to why wine and not water, I cannot explain it, and neither could the lady.

Now let the meat boil gently for eight or nine hours, to obtain some four or five spoonfuls of flavorful, concentrated sauce, which you will then strain, pressing firmly against the mesh. Set it aside for use the next day. Make the filling for the anolini with:

100 grams (about 3-1/2 ounces) of grated day-old bread, lightly
*   toasted*
50 grams (about 1-2/3 ounces) of grated Parmesan cheese
a dash of nutmeg
1 egg
the meat sauce you prepared the previous day

Blend this all together into a smooth mixture. Then make a dough with flower and three eggs, keeping it fairly soft. Roll it out and cut it into scalloped disks as in recipe 162. Fill the disks with the stuffing, then fold them in half to obtain small half-moon shapes.

These amounts should yield about 100 anolini. They are good in broth or with a sauce like tortellini, although they are lighter on the stomach than the latter. You can eat the leftover meat as stew by itself or with a side dish of vegetables.

Pasta Dishes and Soups in Vegetable Stock

55. TORTELLI (STUFFED DUMPLINGS)

200 grams (about 7 ounces) of ricotta or raviggiuolo (soft white
cheese), or both mixed together
40 grams (about 1-1/3 ounces) of Parmesan cheese
1 whole egg
1 egg yolk
a dash of nutmeg and spices
a pinch of salt
a little parsley, chopped

The stuffing is enclosed in dough like cappelletti but the pasta is cut
with a somewhat larger round disk. I use the disk described in recipe
195. You can leave the dumplings in the half-moon shape obtain-
able after the first fold, but the cappelletti shape is preferable. Cook
them in sufficiently salted water, drain and garnish with cheese and
butter. These amounts will yield 24 or 25 tortelli, and being large,
they will serve three people.

56. ZUPPA DI PURÈ DI PISELLI, DI MAGRO
(MEATLESS PEA SOUP)

400 grams (about 14 ounces) of shelled fresh peas
40 grams (about 1 1/3 ounces) of untrimmed prosciutto
40 grams (about 1 1/3 ounces) of butter
1 new onion, no larger than an egg
1 small carrot
a pinch of parsley, celery and a few of basil leaves

Dice the prosciutto finely with a knife, and then mix it with the
other ingredients, also finely chopped. Place on the fire with butter,
a little salt and a pinch of pepper. When it begins to brown, pour in
as much water as you judge sufficient for the soup, and when it
comes to a boil, throw in the peas together with two slices of bread
fried in butter. Then pass it all through a sieve. This will yield a
purée sufficient for six people. Pour this over some additional bread,
prepared as in the recipe for pea soup with meat broth (35).

57. ZUPPA DI FAGIOLI (BEAN SOUP)

It is said, and rightly so, that beans are the meat of the poor. And when the manual laborer going through his pockets sees with a sad eye that he is unable to buy a piece of meat large enough to make soup for his little family, he often finds in beans a healthy, nourishing and cheap alternative. Moreover, beans take some time to leave the body, quelling hunger pangs for a good while. But . . . and even here there is a but, as there so often is in the matters of this world—and I think you get my point. For partial protection, choose thin-shelled beans, or pass them through a sieve. Black-eyed beans partake of this drawback less than other varieties.

To make the bean soup more pleasant and tasty, and sufficient for four to five people, make a soffritto as follows: take a quarter of an onion, a clove of garlic, a bit of parsley and a nice piece of white celery; chop these finely with a mezzaluna and place them on the fire with a good amount of oil—and be generous with the pepper. When the soffritto has begun to brown, add two ladlesful of bean broth, add a bit of tomato sauce (recipe 6) or tomato paste, bring to a boil, and then pour it into the pot containing the beans.

For those who like some vegetables in their soup, they can add a bit of red cabbage, first washed and then boiled in the liquid of the soffritto.

Now the only thing left is to pour the soup over some bread already roasted in slices one finger thick and then diced.

58. ZUPPA TOSCANA DI MAGRO ALLA CONTADINA (MEATLESS TUSCAN PEASANT SOUP)

Prepared with the necessary care, this "modest" soup—whence the epithet "peasant"—will, I am certain, be enjoyed by all, including the not so modest.

400 grams (about 14 ounces) of stale, soft brown bread
300 grams (about 10-1/2 ounces) of white beans
150 grams (about 5-1/4 ounces) of oil
2 liters (about 2 quarts) of water
1 head of a medium-sized Savoy or regular cabbage
1 red cabbage, about the same size and perhaps more

1 bunch of beet greens and a little thyme
1 potato
some rinds of bacon or prosciutto cut into strips

Put the beans on the fire in a pot with the water and bacon rinds. Beans, as you already know, are placed in cold water and if they absorb it all, you may add some hot water. While they are boiling, finely chop and mix one quarter of a large onion, two garlic cloves, two celery stalks the length of the palm of your hand, and a good pinch of parsley. Sauté all of this in oil, and when it begins to brown, pour into the same pan the vegetables, starting with the coarsely chopped cabbages, then the beet greens or chard, and finally the potato (cut into chunks). Season with salt and pepper, and then add tomato sauce (recipe 6) or tomato paste. If the vegetables are too dry, moisten them with the bean broth. When the beans are cooked, toss one quarter of them, whole, into the vegetables, adding the bacon rinds. Pass the other beans through a sieve and dissolve them in the broth, which you will then pour into the pot with the vegetables. Stir, allow to a boil for a moment, and then pour everything into a soup tureen in which you have already placed some thinly sliced bread. Cover for twenty minutes and then send to the table.

These amounts serve six people. It is good warm and even better cold.

59. FARINATA GIALLA DI MAGRO
(YELLOW CORNMEAL PORRIDGE)

Among ordinary soups, this ranks with the best.

To serve four people, place 4 deciliters (about 1-2/3 cups) of white beans on the fire with a suitable amount of water. Once cooked, strain them, pass them through a sieve and then stir the purée into the bean broth, adding half a head of chopped white or Savoy cabbage and seasoning with salt, pepper, and thyme leaves. Boil for about two hours.

In a pot on the fire put a generous amount of oil and two whole cloves of peeled garlic. When the garlic cloves have begun to brown, discard them, and add to the oil some tomato sauce (recipe 6) or tomato paste diluted with water. Season once more with a pinch of salt and pepper. After it has boiled for a while, pour this sauce into the pot containing the broth and the cabbage. Finally, when the cabbage has finished cooking, pour in the cornmeal a little bit at a time with one hand, while mixing well with the other hand to prevent lumps from forming. When the mixture is of the desired consistency, that is still rather liquid, boil a little longer, and then send to the table.

60. SEMOLINO DI MAGRO (SEMOLINA SOUP)

Strictly speaking, this soup cannot be termed "lean," since it contains eggs, butter, and Parmesan cheese. But it can come in very handy when you have no meat broth.

Cook the semolina in water. Before taking it off the stove, salt it, melt in a piece of butter proportionate to the amount of semolina, and flavor it with a little tomato sauce (recipe 6) or tomato paste. Break two or three eggs into a soup tureen, mix them with grated Parmesan cheese, and pour the semolina over them. If making soup for only one person, one egg yolk and two tablespoons of Parmesan cheese will suffice.

61. ZUPPA DI LENTICCHIE (LENTIL SOUP)

If Esau indeed sold his birthright for a plate of lentils, then it must be admitted that their use as food is ancient, and that Esau either had a great passion for them or suffered from bulimia. To me, lentils seem more delicately flavored than beans in general, and as far as the threat of "bombarditis" is concerned they are less dangerous than common beans, and about equal to the black-eyed variety.

This soup can be made in the same way as the bean soup. The broth of lentils and black-eyed beans, however, also makes a nice soup with rice, which is prepared and seasoned in the same way. You must, however, make sure to keep the broth more watery, because the rice absorbs so much of it. It is easier to achieve the desired consistency if you wait until the rice is cooked before adding the necessary amount of strained lentils to the broth.

62. ZUPPA DI MAGRO COLLE TELLINE
(CLAM SOUP)

Proceed as for risotto with clams (recipe 72).

If you are serving seven to eight people, two cloves of garlic and a quarter of an onion will do. This will yield an excellent dish, with no need for butter or Parmesan, provided that you know how to make a good soffritto. Slice some bread, which you will roast and then dice.

Here too, a few pieces of dried mushroom add a nice touch.

63. SPAGHETTI COLLE TELLINE
(SPAGHETTI WITH CLAMS)

As one often hears mention of spaghetti with clam sauce as a meatless first course, I will describe how to make it, though to my taste rice is preferable for this dish. If you want to try this spaghetti, follow recipe 72, chopping the spaghetti small enough to eat with a spoon, and cooking it in the water in which the clams have opened. Drain the excess water, and dress the spaghetti with the sauce, adding a little butter and Parmesan cheese.

64. ZUPPA DI RANOCCHI (FROG SOUP)

Certain customs of the Florence market are not to my taste. When they clean the frogs, if you are not careful, they will throw away the eggs, which are the best part. Eels should be skinned. The legs and loin of mutton should be sold whole. Among pig entrails, the liver and caul fat should be preserved, as should the liver and sweetbreads of milk-fed veal. The rest, including the lung, which being tender could be served, as in other countries, as part of a mixed fry, are usually given to the tripe seller, who generally sells them to the broth maker. Perhaps the so-called tripe of milk-fed veal also falls into their hands, and in any case I have never seen it at the market. In Romagna, however, it is added as an extra, and, in pea season, when roasted in a pan with a piece of loin, it is so good that it is even better than the loin itself.

Before describing frog soup to you, I wish to say a few things about this amphibian of the batrachian order (*rana esculenta*)—the metamorphosis it undergoes is truly worthy of note. In the first part of its existence, the frog can be seen darting around in the water like a fish, all head and tail. This is what the zoologists call a tadpole. Like fish, they breath through gills which are first external in the shape of plumes and then become internal. During this stage of their development, tadpoles feed on vegetables and have an intestine which, like that of all herbivores, is much longer than that of carnivores. At a certain point in its development, around two months after birth, the tadpole reabsorbs its own tail, grows lungs in place of gills and puts forth limbs—that is, the four legs which previously were invisible. It transforms itself completely, and becomes a frog. Feeding on other creatures, especially insects, its intestine shortens to adapt itself to this kind of food. The common opinion that frogs are fatter in the month of May because they eat grain is therefore incorrect.

All amphibians, toads included, are wrongly persecuted. In fact, they are very useful in agriculture, and in gardens of all kinds, where they destroy the worms, snails and many insects on which they feed. The skin of toads and salamanders exudes, it is true, a poisonous, acrid fluid, but in such small amounts in proportion to the mucus in which it is mixed that it is quite harmless. It is, in fact, this copious secretion of mucus on the part of the salamander that allows it to withstand the heat of fire for some time, thereby giving rise to the myth that this amphibian is gifted with the virtue of being able to go through fire unharmed.

The broth of frogs is refreshing and soothing, and as such is recommended for chest ailments and inflammations of the intestine. It is also suitable to be consumed at the end of any inflammatory illnesses, and in nearly all those cases where the invalid requires a mild diet.

The white meat of frogs, lamb, goat, pullet, pheasant, etc., is low in fibrin and rich in albumen, and therefore especially suited to sensitive people and people of delicate digestion, and to those whose work does not involve strenuous muscular activity.

And now for the frog soup: two dozen frogs, if large, could perhaps suffice for four or five people, but it is better to have too many than too few.

Remove the legs and set them aside. Finely chop two cloves of garlic with a generous amount of parsley, carrot, and celery, adding some basil if it is to your taste. If you have a horror of garlic, onion will do. Place the mixture on the fire with salt and pepper, and a good amount of oil; when the garlic begins to brown, toss in the frogs. Stir occasionally to prevent the frogs from sticking to the pan. When most of the moisture has come out of them, toss in some chopped tomatoes, if you have them, or, alternatively, some tomato paste thinned with water. Continue boiling and, to finish the dish, add as much water as needed for the soup. Keep this on the fire until the frogs are cooked and the flesh begins to come apart. Pass everything through a sieve, pressing well to make sure that only the little bones remain behind. Boil the legs, which you have kept separate, in a bit of this strained broth and, when they are cooked, bone them. Then mix them into the soup along with pieces of pre-soaked dried mushroom. Serve with sliced bread, toasted and cut into rather large cubes.

65. ZUPPA COL BRODO DI MUGGINE
(SOUP WITH MULLET BROTH)

One of the fish that best lends itself to a good broth is mullet, which in the Adriatic begins to grow handsome and fat in August, and often reaches a weight of over 2 kilograms (about 4 pounds). If you cannot get mullet, you can use umber or grayling, bass, or the angler fish. The flesh of these fish is more delicate and more easily digested than mullet, compensating for the fact that the broth they make is less flavorful.

If you are making a soup for seven or eight people, take a mullet (or "baldigara," as it is called in certain seaside areas), weighing at least 2 kilograms (about 2 pounds). Scrape off the scales, gut and clean it, and then poach it in a suitable amount of water.

Finely chop a generous quantity of onion, garlic, parsley, carrot and celery, and place on the fire with oil, salt and pepper. When this mixture begins to brown, add tomato sauce (recipe 6) and fish broth. Boil a while and then strain the broth. Use some of this broth to cook a small quantity of chopped celery, carrot and dried mushroom, which will add flavor.

The bread for the soup should be toasted and cubed, then placed in a soup tureen. Pour in the hot broth along with the additional seasonings, and send to the table with Parmesan cheese on the side.

The mullet family has a stomach with strong muscular walls similar to the gizzard of birds. The angler fish, *Lophius piscatorius*, of the family *Lophidae*, attracts smaller fish with a movable silver fin on its head, and then devours them. It too is prized for its broth.

66. ZUPPA ALLA CERTOSINA
(SOUP CARTHUSIAN STYLE)

With 500 grams (about 1 pound) of fillets from a variety of fish you should be able to make enough soup for four to five people.

Finely chop 1/4 of an onion, some parsley and celery. Put on the fire in a pan with oil and, when it has browned, add the fish, which you will keep moist with water, tomato sauce (recipe 6) or tomato paste. Season with salt and pepper. Allow it to cook well and then add the water for the soup—1 liter (about 1 quart) of water in total should suffice for this recipe. Pass the mixture through a sieve, pressing well against the mesh. Then put it back on the fire and bring it to a boil again. Break three eggs in a tureen and mix them with three spoonfuls of Parmesan cheese. Pour in the broth slowly, and before serving toss in small cubes of bread which you have toasted or fried in the condiment you prefer: butter, oil, or lard. If you like to see the eggs and Parmesan cheese making little lumps in the soup, you can beat them separately and pour them in the pot when the broth is boiling.

It is said that the Granduke of Tuscany first tasted this soup in a convent of friars and, having found it excellent, sent his cook there to learn how to make it. But no matter how hard he tried, the excellent cook could not make the soup as well as the friars, who did not want to tell the Granduke that the soup was made with broth of capon rather than water!

67. PASTINE O CAPELLINI SUL BRODO DI OMBRINA (PASTINA OR CAPELLINI IN BLACK UMBER BROTH)

The umber or grayling is a most excellent fish. When boiled without spices of any sort, it yields a broth that is almost like beef consommé— an eminently suitable base for a light, meatless soup.

These amounts serve three people, maybe four:

500 grams (about 1 pound) of umber
120 grams (about 4-1/4 ounces) of pastina or capellini
30 grams (about 1 ounce) of butter
1 liter (about 1 quart) of water

Immerse the umber in cold water and place on the fire. When the fish is done, pour the broth through a strainer and then use it to cook the pasta, but flavor the broth with tomato sauce (recipe 6) to cover the smell of fish. When the pasta is ready, transfer the soup to a tureen into which you have previously placed the butter. Send to the table with Parmesan cheese on the side, as is done with meat soups.

68. ZUPPA DI PURÈ DI PISELLI SECCHI (PURÉE OF DRIED PEA SOUP)

Take 1/2 liter (about 1/2 quart) of peas and place on the fire in 2 liters (about 2 quarts) of water. Meanwhile prepare a light soffritto with half an onion, one carrot, two finger-length celery stalks, and, if you have some on hand, a few sprigs of dill. Finely chop all these ingredients, and place them on the fire adding some butter. When the mixture begins to brown, add the peas half-boiled and strained. Season with salt and pepper, and allow them to fully absorb the soffritto. Now add tomato sauce (recipe 6) and the water from the peas. Simmer until completely done. Pass everything through a sieve and, if the purée turns out too thick, add hot water. Test for taste, and add a second little pat of butter which the soup will probably need. The bread for the soup should be chopped into tiny cubes and sautéed in butter.

If you make this soup with care, it will taste as if it were made with meat broth.

This recipe serves ten to twelve people.

69. TAGLIATELLE COL PROSCIUTTO
(TAGLIATELLE WITH PROSCIUTTO)

I call this dish "tagliatelle" ("little strips") because, since it is cooked in water and served dry with a sauce, the pasta dough must be rolled out to a somewhat greater thickness, and cut into somewhat broader strips than when making "taglierini" ("tiny strips"). The paste is made with the usual flour and egg dough, which should contain no water if you want a pasta that is firm and flavorful.

Cut a large thick slice of untrimmed prosciutto into little cubes. Finely chop some celery and carrot which, heaped together, should equal the amount of the diced prosciutto. Sauté all three ingredients, along with enough butter to flavor the tagliatelle. When the mixture begins to brown, add tomato sauce (recipe 6) or tomato paste, though with the latter you will also need to add a small ladleful of broth or, lacking that, of water.

Keep the tagliatelle al dente, and salt the water you are cooking them in very sparingly given that the sauce has prosciutto in it. Strain the pasta and dress it with the sauce and Parmesan cheese.

When available, you can use sausages instead of prosciutto. Mince the sausages well, and prepare as described above.

Anyone who loves the taste of butter should save half the quantity needed for the sauce and add it in only after the sauce is removed from the fire.

Spaghetti are also very tasty when served with sausages prepared in this manner.

70. TAGLIATELLE VERDI (GREEN TAGLIATELLE)

This pasta is lighter and more digestible than noodles made entirely with eggs. To give these tagliatelle their characteristic green color, boil some spinach, squeeze well, and then chop fine with a mezzaluna. On a pastry board, fold two eggs and a handful of the spinach into enough flour to obtain a very firm dough that you must knead well with your hands. Then, using a rolling pin, roll out the dough into a thin sheet, sprinkling it lightly with flour when it shows a tendency to stick (the spinach makes the dough sticky). Wrap the rolled-out dough in a cloth and, when dry, cut it into strips that are somewhat wider than the taglierini used for broth. Bear in mind that what makes this pasta beautiful is the strips' length, which demonstrates the virtuosity of its maker. As soon as the water starts boiling, remove the noodles, strain and season like the country-style spaghetti described in recipe 104, or like macaroni or tagliatelle as described in recipes 87 and 69. Or simply flavor with cheese and butter.

This recipe serves four to five people.

71. TAGLIATELLE ALL'USO DI ROMAGNA (TAGLIATELLE ROMAGNA STYLE)

"Bills should be short and tagliatelle long," the people of Bologna say, and they are right, because long bills terrify poor husbands and short tagliatelle look like leftovers, attesting to the incompetence of their maker. For this reason I do not approve of the widespread custom adopted simply to satisfy the palate of foreigners of chopping capellini, taglierini and similar types of pasta into the minutest bits and serving them in broth. Since they are unique to Italy, they ought to preserve their original characteristics.

Prepare the pasta dough and cut it as described in recipe 69. Boil for a short while, drain well, put in a saucepan and heat for a moment to help it absorb the sauce, which is the one for country-style spaghetti described in recipe 104. Also add enough butter to season the amount of pasta you are making. Toss gently, then send to the table.

To my way of thinking, this is a very tasty dish, but to digest it well, you need air like the kind that you can breathe in Romagna.

I remember traveling once with some Florentines (a toothless old codger, a middle-aged man and a young lawyer) who were on their way to claim an inheritance in Modigliana. We stopped at an inn, and you can well imagine the sort of place it was in that part of the country, this being forty or more years ago. The innkeeper gave us only tagliatelle as the pasta course and cured pork neck as an appetizer, and while this was very tough and displeasing to the taste, the effort the old fellow made to gnaw it was a sight to behold. Such was the appetite he and the other two possessed, that they found this and everything else to be very good, indeed delicious; I even heard them exclaim several times: "Oh, if only we could take this air with us to Florence!"

Speaking of that fair city, let me tell you about a certain Count from Romagna who was living in Florence when "francesconi"[18] were still in circulation. This gentleman, a fine match for Goldoni's *Marquis of Forlimpopoli*,[19] had plenty of arrogance, only a few pennies to his name, and a cast-iron stomach. In those days you could live inexpensively in Florence, which was famous for its low prices in comparison to other capital cities. There were many small restaurants that offered a *prix-fixe* meal of pasta, three main courses to choose from, fruit or pastry, bread and wine for a single Tuscan lira. The servings, though small, satisfied everyone who was not as hungry as a wolf. Even the nobility frequented these restaurants, although the count in question did not deign to do so. What trick do you suppose he had found to maintain such a façade while spending little? On alternate days he would go to the buffet table at one of the best hotels, where for half a francescone (2.80 lire), the fare offered was most sumptuous. Gobbling up everything in sight, he would stuff his stomach enough to last him two days. Then he would go home to diet, on the off day, on bread, cheese and cold cuts. Now you have his example and the recipe.

72. RISOTTO COLLE TELLINE (RICE WITH CLAMS)

In my kitchen this risotto is usually made with the following amounts:

1 1/3 kilograms (about 3 pounds) of clams, still in their shells
500 grams (about 1 pound) of rice

To remove the sand inside the clams, wash them first. Then arrange the clams on top of a serving dish, which you have turned upside

18 These are old Tuscan silver coins.
19 Carlo Goldoni (1707–1793) is considered one of the most eminent Italian playwrights.

down, and soak them in a basin filled with salted water, or prefer-ably in sea water. After at least two hours, remove the clams from the water, and put them on the fire with enough water to cook the rice. When the clams pop open, remove the shells and save the wa-ter. Before you use the water again, make sure to discard the sandy deposit that forms in the bottom of the pan.

Prepare a soffritto with olive oil, garlic, one small onion, pars-ley, one carrot and celery. Mince everything as fine as possible with a mezzaluna. When the ingredients are sufficiently browned, throw in the shelled clams, a few pieces of dried mushroom previously soaked in water, a pinch of pepper, and some of the water you have reserved. After a few minutes, throw in the rice and cook thoroughly, adding the rest of the water.

Taste to see if the natural salt of the clams and the spices you have added have given it enough flavor. If not, add tomato sauce (recipe 6) or tomato paste, and also some butter and a pinch of Parmesan cheese.

Instead of clams, you can use other varieties of shellfish such as "peocci" (mussels), as is done in Venice, where, if restaurants fol-lowed this recipe to cook rice with peocci (a specialty of that town), the results would be much improved. To preserve shellfish for a little while, store in a cool place, tightly wrapped in a kitchen towel or canvas bag. In winter, I have kept fresh clams for up to six days in this way. But avoid it if you can, as mollusks become very indigest-ible if not fresh.

73. RISOTTO COLLE TINCHE (RICE WITH TENCH)

Do not be frightened by the notion that tench can produce a good risotto, which will naturally taste of fish and which can be a bit hard on delicate stomachs. However, it will please the palate and perhaps even win praise, if you are clever enough not to name the type of fish you used.

Here are the ingredients for a first course that serves six or seven people:

500 grams (about 1 pound) of rice
400 grams (about 14 oz) of tench, more or less

Finely chop two garlic cloves, a pinch of parsley, some basil leaves (if you like its flavor), one large carrot, and two stalks of white celery the length of your palm. Place on the fire in a saucepan with olive oil, salt and pepper. Add the tench, gutted and cut into chunks, and include the fish heads. Keep turning the fish, so that it will not stick to the bottom of the pan. When the tench have browned, begin adding some liquid: first tomato sauce (recipe 6) or tomato paste, and then enough water to cook the rice. To make sure you do not use too much water pour it in slowly, especially at the beginning and the end. Also keep in mind that it is better to use too little water than too much. Boil until the flesh of the fish is quite soft and begins to come apart. Then pass everything through a sieve so that only the little bones and cartilage are left behind. In this sauce you will cook the rice until all the liquid is gone and the rice is done. To make this dish more appetizing, you can add a few pieces of dried mushroom and a small amount of butter. Send to the table with grated Parmesan cheese on the side for those who may want it.

When peas are in season, they are better for this dish than mushrooms. 200 grams (about 7 ounces) of shelled peas should be enough. Cook them separately in a little olive oil, some butter and a whole new onion. Stir in the peas when the onion starts to brown. Sauté, seasoning with salt and pepper, and then finish cooking in a little water. Discard the onion and mix the peas in the rice when it is just about done.

74. RISOTTO NERO COLLE SEPPIE ALLA FIORENTINA (BLACK RISOTTO WITH CUTTLEFISH FLORENTINE STYLE)

This invertebrate (*Sepia Officinalis*), of the order of mollusks and the family of cephalopods, is called "calamaio" ("inkwell") in Florence. The reason for such a name lies perhpas in a simile (indeed, this is the way the lovely Tuscan language often coins its words): this mollusk possesses a pouch enclosing a little bladder which nature has given it for self-defense. This bladder contains a black liquid that can be used for ink.

Tuscans, Florentines in particular, are so fond of vegetables that they would like to stick them in everything. Thus in this dish they put Swiss chard, which, in my opinion, goes with it like the bread soup with the *Credo*.[20] I fear that this excessive use of vegetables may be one of the causes, and perhaps not the least one, of the weak constitution of certain groups of people who, when struck with some illness, are unable to fight it off, and so drop to the ground in droves like leaves in late autumn.

> Skin and gut the cuttlefish to remove the useless parts such as the cuttlebone, the mouth, the eyes and the digestive tube. Set aside the small ink sacs. After having washed them thoroughly, cut the cuttlefish into tiny squares and chop the tentacles into little pieces.
>
> Mince two medium-sized onions until very fine, or better yet just one onion and two garlic cloves, and heat in a saucepan with a generous amount of the finest olive oil. When the mixture begins to brown, toss in the cuttlefish and wait until they start turning yellow. Then add about 600 grams (about 1-1/3 pounds) of Swiss chard, which you have chopped in advance while discarding the larger ribs. Stir thoroughly and let simmer for about half an hour. Then pour in 600 grams (about 1-1/3 pounds) of rice (equal to the weight of the raw cuttlefish) and the ink sacs. When the rice has soaked up this sauce, add hot water to finish cooking. Rice, as a general rule, should not be cooked too long, and when it is said to be "dry," it should make a nice mound in the bowl in which you serve it. Always accompany with grated Parmesan cheese. But if you have a delicate stomach, refrain from adding more Parmesan cheese when the rice has been prepared with ingredients that are not easily digested (as in this dish).
>
> Here is another way to prepare this dish; you can choose the one you like better. No chard, no ink, and when the cuttlefish, as I have described above, start to turn yellow, add the rice and cook thoroughly in hot water and tomato sauce (recipe 6) or tomato paste, adding some butter for more flavor and a better appearance. When almost done, combine with the Parmesan cheese.

20 A play on the Tuscan expression, "It goes with it like Pilate in the Credo," which means that the two items in question are not especially suited to each other. See Pauli, *Tuscan Proverbs Researched as to Their Origins*, p. 76.

If you wish to improve the dish still more, when it is two-thirds done, add peas as described in recipe 73 for risotto with tench.

75. RISOTTO COI PISELLI (RICE WITH PEAS)

Rice! Behold the fattening food that the Turks feed to their women, so that they will develop, as a celebrated and well-known professor would say, sumptuous adipose cushions.

500 grams (about 1 pound) of rice
100 grams (about 3-1/2 ounces) of butter
Parmesan cheese, as needed
1 medium-sized onion

Rice, as I have indicated earlier, should not be washed; it is enough to clean it and rub it in a kitchen towel.

Mince the onion very finely with a mezzaluna and put it on the fire with half the butter. When it has turned golden brown, add the rice, stirring constantly with a large spoon until it has absorbed all the butter. Then start adding hot water ladleful at a time. Make sure the rice does not boil too fast, otherwise it will remain hard in the center while becoming too soft on the outside. Salt and cook until dry, then add the rest of the butter. Before removing from the fire, stir in a suitable amount of peas prepared as in recipe 427, and flavor with a good handful of Parmesan cheese.

This recipe serves five people.

76. RISOTTO COI FUNGHI (RICE WITH MUSHROOMS)

For this risotto I avail myself of porcini (*Boletus edulis*) mushrooms, which in some places are called "morecci."

The fresh mushrooms, before they are cleaned and trimmed, should be equal to half the weight of the rice.

Finely chop a little onion, parsley, celery, and carrot, and put on the fire with three tablespoons of olive oil. This is the amount of oil needed for 300 grams (about 10-1/2 ounces) of rice, which serves three people. When the mixture begins to brown, cover it with tomato sauce (recipe 6) and water, season with salt and pepper, and bring to a boil, adding one clove of garlic. Allow to simmer for a while, then discard the garlic clove and pass the mixture through a sieve. Chop the mushrooms into pieces a little smaller than corn kernels, add them to the sauce and put everything back on the fire to cook. Once done, set the sauce with the mushroom to one side. Lightly sauté the raw rice in a little of butter, then cook adding hot water one ladleful at a time. When the rice is half done, stir in the mushroom sauce, and before serving add Parmesan cheese to taste.

This risotto is quite delightful even if you substitute the fresh mushrooms with a handful of dry ones.

77. RISOTTO COI POMODORI
(RICE WITH TOMATOES)

500 grams (about 1 pounds) of rice
100 grams (about 3-1/2 ounces) of butter
Parmesan cheese, as needed

Pour the rice into melted butter. When the butter has been fully absorbed, start adding hot water, a little at a time. When the rice is half done, flavor it with the tomato sauce described in recipe 125. Before removing from the fire, toss in a good handful of grated Parmesan cheese. You may, if you like, substitute bacon for olive oil in the tomato sauce to flavor the risotto. Alternatively, you may use the tomato sauce described in recipe 6.

78. RISOTTO ALLA MILANESE I
(RICE MILANESE STYLE I)

500 grams (about 1 pounds) of rice
80 grams (about 2-3/4 ounces) of butter
saffron, as much as will turn the risotto a bright yellow
1/2 of a medium-sized onion

For cooking instructions, follow recipe 75, keeping in mind that this risotto will be more substantial and flavorful if cooked in broth.

If you happen to have a bronze mortar and pestle, you can buy unrefined saffron, grind it finely yourself and then dissolve the powder in a drop of hot broth before adding it to the rice, which you will send to the table with Parmesan cheese on the side. Saffron is a stimulant; it whets the appetite and promotes digestion.

These amounts serve five people.

79. RISOTTO ALLA MILANESE II
(RICE MILANESE STYLE II)

This risotto is more complicated and heavier to digest than the preceding one, but it is more flavorful.

These amounts serve five people:

500 grams (about 1 pound) of rice
80 grams (about 2-2/3 ounces) of butter
40 grams (about 1-1/3 ounces) of beef marrow
1/2 of an onion
2 deciliters (about 4/5 of a cup) of good white wine
saffron as needed
Parmesan cheese as needed

Mince the onion and put it on the fire with the marrow and half the butter. When sufficiently browned, pour in the rice and, after a few minutes, add the wine, then cook with the broth. Before removing from the fire, season with the rest of the butter and the Parmesan cheese. Send to the table with more Parmesan cheese on the side.

80. RISOTTO ALLA MILANESE III
(RICE MILANESE STYLE III)

Now you can choose! Here is yet another way to prepare Milanese-style risotto, but without the pretense of taking over from the chefs of Milan, who are very learned and creative when it comes to this dish.

300 grams (about 10-1/2 ounces) of rice
50 gram (about 1-2/3 ounces) of butter

1/4 of a medium-sized onion
2 deciliters (about 4/5 of a cup) of Marsala wine
saffron as needed

Brown the onion, finely chopped, with half the butter. Add the rice, and after a few minutes the Marsala. Add broth and simmer until cooked. Then add the rest of the butter and the saffron dissolved in a bit of the broth. Lastly, toss in a handful of Parmesan.

Serves three people.

81. RISOTTO COI RANOCCHI
(RICE WITH FROGS)

A famous chef once said that to make the flesh of frogs tender you must soak them in hot water as soon as you have skinned them (but mind you, only for half a minute, otherwise they will cook), and then run them in cold water. If they are large, twelve frogs will be enough, I should think, to accompany 300 grams (about 10-1/2 ounces) of rice. Set aside the legs. I also think it is better not to use the eggs in this recipe. Prepare a battuto with a quarter of a large onion, one garlic clove, some carrot, celery and parsley. Sauté in olive oil, adding salt and pepper. When sufficiently browned, add the frogs. Stir now and then, and after they have turned a nice golden color, toss in some coarsely chopped tomatoes, which will gradually dissolve. Now add as much hot water as needed. Let simmer slowly until the frogs are well done. Then pass everything through a sieve, squeezing well. Cook the legs you have set aside in a small portion of this sauce. When the legs are done, bone them and add the flesh to the rest of the sauce.

Put the rice on the fire with some butter, stir, and when the butter has been completely absorbed, add the warm frog sauce a ladleful at a time until the rice is cooked to perfection. Before removing the rice from the fire, add a handful of Parmesan cheese, then send to the table.

82. RISOTTO COI GAMBERI
(RICE WITH PRAWNS)

It is said that a lady prawn once chided her daughter, saying, "Good Lord, how crookedly you move! Can't you walk straight?" "And you, mama, how do you walk?" replied the daughter, "How can I walk straight when everyone I see walks sideways?" And the daughter was right.[21]

300 grams (about 10-1/2 ounces) of crayfish will be enough for 700 grams (about 1-1/2 pounds) of rice and will serve eight people.

Finely chop half an onion, three garlic cloves, a carrot, a generous amount of celery and parsley, and sauté in olive oil. I find the garlic necessary in this recipe to balance the sweetness of the prawns. When the soffritto has browned, add the prawns and season with salt and pepper. Turn them often and when they are all red, baste them with tomato sauce (recipe 6) or tomato paste. Then add enough hot water to cook the rice. Allow to boil for a short while, as prawns cook quickly, then remove from the fire, and take the prawns out of the pot. Selecting the largest ones, shell 1/4 of the prawns and set them aside. Pound the rest in a mortar and pass through a sieve. Mix the paste thus obtained with the broth in which they have been cooked.

Heat some butter in a saucepan and add the cleaned unwashed rice, stirring constantly. When the rice has taken on the luster of butter, pour in the broth a little at a time. When the rice is more than half done, add the large whole prawns, already shelled. Flavor with a handful of Parmesan cheese before serving.

If you have kept some meat broth in reserve, you should use it when preparing these meatless risottos. This will make the dish more substantial and flavorful.

---

21 In Italian the expression "to walk like prawn" ("camminare come i gamberi") commonly means "to walk backwards" (or "sideways"), somewhat like the English "to move like a crab."

83. RISOTTO COL BRODO DI PESCE
(RICE IN FISH BROTH)

When you boil a fine fish, or even a large gray mullet in the way described in recipe 459, you can strain the broth and use it to make a risotto or a soup. Make a battuto with a quarter of an onion, one or two garlic cloves, parsley, some carrot and parsley. Put on the fire in olive oil, adding salt and pepper. When browned, cover in tomato sauce (recipe 6) or tomato paste diluted with a ladleful of broth. Allow to boil for a little while, and then add the rice to the sauce. Cook the rice, adding more of the broth a little at a time. When the rice is half done, add some butter, and, when the rice is completely done, toss in a small handful of Parmesan cheese. If you are making soup you may add a pinch of dried mushrooms, and then the Parmesan cheese is served on the side.

84. MACCHERONI ALLA FRANCESE
(MACARONI FRENCH STYLE)

I say French style because I found this recipe in a cookbook of that nation, but as often happens with printed recipes, which rarely coincide with what must be done in practice, I had to change the proportions of the ingredients as follows:

300 grams (about 10-1/2 ounces) of Neapolitan-style long macaroni
70 grams (about 2-1/3 ounces) of butter
70 grams (about 2-1/3 ounces) of Gruyère cheese
40 grams (about 1-1/3 ounces) of Parmesan cheese
a small pot of broth

Cook the macaroni until two-thirds done in moderately salted water. Put the broth on the fire, bring it to a boil and then add the grated Gruyère cheese and the butter, stirring well with a wooden spoon to help them dissolve. When this is done, *immediately* pour the broth over the drained, partly cooked macaroni. I say immediately, because otherwise the Gruyère sinks to the bottom and sticks together. Keep the macaroni on the fire until completely cooked, making sure that they do not absorb all the sauce. When you remove them from the stove, season the macaroni with the Parmesan cheese. Serve with more Parmesan on the side for those who like strong tastes and prefer their pasta sharp.

This, like macaroni Bolognese style, is a first course that comes in handy in family cooking: you need only a small pot of broth from the day before, so you save the time and expense of making a fresh meat broth. If you prefer the dish meatless, substitute milk for the broth.

Gruyère, also known commercially as Emmenthal, is a cheese that comes in very large round wheels. It has a soft flesh, yellow in color and full of holes. Some people do not like its distinctive smell, which can be rather sharp and unpleasant. However, you should note that during the cold season this smell is quite weak, and in pasta dishes it will be hardly noticed.

85. MACCHERONI ALLA NAPOLETANA I
(MACARONI NEAPOLITAN STYLE I)

I guarantee that this dish is genuine and well tested, as it is based on a recipe I obtained from a family in Santa Maria Capua Vetere. I must also tell you that for a long time I hesitated about trying out this recipe, not being entirely won over by the hodgepodge of spices and flavors. To tell the truth, the dish did not turn out at all badly; indeed, it may appeal to those whose taste buds are not categorically in favor of simplicity.

Take a piece of beef flank and lard it with strips of untrimmed prosciutto, zibibbo raisins, pine nuts, and a little battuto of lardoon, garlic, parsley, salt and pepper. After you have prepared the meat in this manner and bound it with twine to keep it together, put it on the fire with a battuto of salt pork, and finely chopped onion. Turn the meat often and poke it occasionally with a larding needle. Once the meat is browned and the soffritto all absorbed, add three or four pieces of peeled tomatoes. When these have dissolved, add some puréed tomato sauce a little at a time. Wait until the sauce is rather concentrated, then add enough water to cover the meat. Salt and pepper to taste, and allow it to simmer over a low flame. If you do not have any fresh tomatoes, use tomato paste. This is the sauce for the macaroni, which should also be seasoned with sharp cheese, as is done in Naples. The meat is served on the side.

As for the macaroni themselves, the Neapolitans recommend that they should be boiled in a large pot, with lots of water, and not cooked too long.

86. MACCHERONI ALLA NAPOLETANA II
(MACARONI NEAPOLITAN STYLE II)

This is a much simpler way to prepare macaroni, and the result is so tasty I advise you to try it.

300 grams (about 10-1/2 ounces) of long macaroni are sufficient for three people. Start by frying two large onion slices in 30 grams (about 1 ounce) of butter and two tablespoons of olive oil. When the onion turns a nice golden brown and begins to dissolve, press it well with a wooden spoon against the sides of the saucepan squeezing all the fat out, then discard it. Add 500 grams (about 1 pound) of tomatoes and a good pinch of coarsely chopped basil to the bubbling fat. Salt and pepper to taste. Remember to prepare the tomatoes in advance: they should be peeled and cut into chunks, removing the seeds as best you can (if some remain they will not spoil the dish).

Thicken the sauce with 50 grams (about 1-2/3 ounces) of butter and some Parmesan cheese, pour it over the macaroni and then send to the table. People who like their pasta swimming in sauce will find this dish especially appealing.

Instead of long macaroni, you can also use penne, which in fact absorb this sauce even better.

87. MACCHERONI ALLA BOLOGNESE
(MACARONI BOLOGNESE STYLE)

For this dish, the Bolognese use medium-size "denti di cavallo" ("horse teeth") whose shape, I would agree, is best suited to make this recipe. Make sure, however, to roll out the dough quite thick when you make this pasta, so that it will not get damaged while boiling. The Tuscans seem not to take sufficient precautions in this regard. Due to their preference for light food, they have developed varieties of pasta they call *genteel*, with large holes and thin walls, which hardly remain firm during cooking and collapse when boiled—something that is as unpleasant to see as it is to eat.

As everybody knows, the best pastas to use are those made of durum wheat. These can be easily identified because of their natural waxy color. Avoid yellow pastas, which are made with ordinary wheat and then colored to mask the lower quality. In the past, mostly harmless substances like saffron and crocus were used, while today an artificial dye is employed.

The following amounts should be more or less enough to make a sauce for 500 grams (about 1 pound) of pasta and maybe a little more.

150 grams (about 5-1/4 ounces) of lean veal (fillet is best)
50 grams (about 1-2/3 ounces) of bacon
40 grams (about 1-1/3 ounces) of butter
1/4 of an ordinary onion
1/2 of a carrot
2 palm-length stalks of white celery, or a little of the tender part of
    green celery
a small pinch of flour
a small pot of broth
very little salt or none at all, because of the bacon and the broth are
    both very flavorful
pepper and, for those who like it, a dash of nutmeg

Cut the meat into little cubes and mince the bacon and the herbs finely with a mezzaluna. Put all the main ingredients on the fire with the butter. When the meat has browned, add the pinch of flour and then cook in broth until done.

Drain the macaroni well; flavor them with this sauce and Parmesan cheese. The sauce can be made even tastier adding small pieces of dried mushroom, a few truffle slices, or a chicken liver cooked with the meat and cut into tiny chunks. When everything has been combined together, and the sauce is completely done, you can add as a final touch half a glass of cream—this will make an even more delicate dish. Remember, in any case, that the macaroni should not be served too dry, but rather well coated in sauce.

As we are speaking of pasta,[22] a few remarks come to mind. Pasta must not be overcooked; but let us meditate a little on this. If the pasta is al dente, it will be more pleasant to the taste and more easily digested. This may seem paradoxical, but so it is, for when pasta is overcooked, and not sufficiently chewed, it goes down in a lump, weighs heavily on the stomach and becomes an indigestible mass. Whereas, when it can only be chewed, the mastication produces saliva, which contains an enzyme called ptyalin, and this enzyme helps to break down the starch, turning it into sugar and dextrin.

Saliva has a very important physiological function not only because it helps to soften and break down food, but also because it facilitates swallowing. Furthermore, its alkaline nature promotes the secretion of gastric juices in the stomach while the food is being swallowed. For this reason nursemaids are right to engage in that disgusting practice of pre-chewing mouthfuls of food for little babies.

It is said that the Neapolitans, great consumers of pasta, always drink a glass of water with it to aid digestion. I do not know if in this case the water acts as a solvent, or if it is helpful because it is easier on the stomach than the glass of wine or similar substance which it replaces.

When it is larger and longer than the one used in this recipe, horse teeth pasta is called "cannelloni" in Tuscany and "buconotti" or "strozzapreti"[23] elsewhere in Italy.

88. MACCHERONI CON LE SARDE ALLA SICILIANA (MACARONI WITH SARDINES SICILIAN STYLE)

For this pasta I am indebted to a very clever widow whose husband, a Sicilian, used to amuse himself by experimenting with certain dishes

22 "Pasta asciutta" (literally, "dry pasta") is the common term for pasta served by itself with a sauce, and not in a broth (hence, "dry").

23 One of the many fanciful names given to the various kinds of pasta—for example, butterflies (farfalle), angel hair (capelli d'angelo), little ears (orecchiette), priest-chokers (strozzapreti), and so on.

of his homeland, among them hake Palermo style and poached sliced fish.

500 grams (about 1 pound) of long Neapolitan-style macaroni
500 grams (about 1 pound) of fresh sardines
6 salted anchovies
300 grams (about 10-1/2 ounces) of wild fennel stalks, also called
*   new fennel*
olive oil, as needed

Clean the sardines, remove the head, tail and spine; then split them in half, dredge in flour, fry, salt, and put aside.

Boil the fennel, squeeze dry, mince finely, and put to one side.

After you have cooked the pasta, whole, in salted water, drain and also place to one side.

Heat in a skillet a generous quantity of olive oil and the six anchovies until they dissolve (remember to clean and remove the spines from the anchovies before you cook them). Add the fennel to this sauce, season with salt and pepper to taste, and let boil for ten minutes in tomato sauce (recipe 6) or tomato paste diluted with water. Now that everything is ready, take a fireproof platter or baking pan, and arrange the macaroni in layers with in between the sardines, fennel and anchovy sauce. The last layer should reach the rim of the pan. Bake with embers all around, and send to the table hot.

These amounts serve six to seven people.

89. GNOCCHI DI PATATE (POTATO DUMPLINGS)

The gnocchi family is very large. I have already described gnocchi in broth in recipe 14. Here I shall present potato gnocchi, yellow flour gnocchi for stew, and, later on, semolina gnocchi, gnocchi Roman style as an *entremets* or a side dish, and finally a milk gnocchi dessert.

400 grams (about 14 ounces) of large yellow potatoes
150 grams (about 5 1/4 ounces) of wheat flour

I indicate the amount of flour required for kneading the gnocchi, so that you will not experience what happened to a woman whose cooking I was observing: the moment she put her wooden spoon into the hot water to stir them, the gnocchi disappeared. "But where did they go?" asked, with anxious curiosity, another woman to whom I had told the story for laughs. Perhaps she thought some little sprite had carried them off.

"Do not be so surprised, my dear lady," I answered. "This strange phenomenon is perfectly natural: the gnocchi had been mixed with too little flour, and as soon as they hit the water, they liquefied."

Boil the potatoes in water, or better still, steam them, and while they are steaming hot, peel them and pass them through a sieve. Then mix them with the flour, and knead the dough for a while with your hands, finally rolling it out into a slender cylinder that you can cut into little pieces about 3 centimeters (about 1-1/5 inches) long. Sprinkle each piece lightly with flour. Picking them up one at a time, roll them against the back of a cheese grater, pressing gently with your thumb (your thumb will leave a small depression on one side of each dumpling). Boil in salted water for 10 minutes. Drain and season with cheese, butter and tomato sauce (recipe 6) to taste.

If you wish them to turn out more refined, boil in milk and serve undrained. If the milk is of high quality, you will not need any other seasoning except salt, or at most a pinch of Parmesan cheese.

90. GNOCCHI DI FARINA GIALLA
(YELLOW CORNMEAL DUMPLINGS)

When you have overeaten and experience a feeling of fullness, you may find a remedy in a dish of cornmeal gnocchi, which are very light and of little substance. The benefits are even greater if after the gnocchi you eat an easily digested fish course.

The best corn flour for this purpose is the coarsely ground variety. Otherwise, it is best to use corn semolina, which you can now find at the grocer. Salt the water and when it boils, pour in the flour a little at a time with the your left hand, mixing constantly with the wooden spoon in your right hand. The corn flour must cook for a good while, until it has been reduced to the point that the mixing spoon stands up straight in it. Then with a table knife shape small pieces of dough and arrange them in layers in a deep serving dish. Flavor each layer with cheese, butter, and tomato sauce (recipe 6) or tomato paste diluted with water. Make a nice mound in the serving dish, and send to the table hot.

If you'd like to add more flavor to this dish, you can prepare the gnocchi like polenta with sausage described in recipe 232, or like the macaroni Bolognese style in recipe 7.

9 1 . PAPPARDELLE ALL'ARETINA
(PAPPARDELLE NOODLES AREZZO STYLE)

I present this not as a refined dish, but as one suitable for family cooking.

Take a domestic duck, put it into a saucepan with some butter, season with salt and pepper, and when it begins to brown, add a battuto made with prosciutto, onion, celery and carrot, which you will place under the bird to cook. Remember to turn the duck regularly. Then remove most of the fat, as it will make the dish excessively heavy, and continue cooking with broth and water, which you will added a little at a time and in such quantity as will yield enough sauce to season the pappardelle.

Take a small piece of spleen, preferably veal spleen, cut it open and scrape the inside clean with a knife. Then place the spleen under the duck to boil. It will add flavor to the sauce, which it is a good idea to season with a little tomato and a dash of nutmeg.

Make a dough with only flour and eggs, and roll it out in a rather thick sheet as for tagliatelle. Use a pastry wheel with a scalloped edge to cut the dough into strips somewhat wider than a finger. Boil these for a short time and toss with the sauce, the duck's liver cut into tiny pieces, Parmesan cheese and some butter, if necessary. The pappardelle will be the pasta course, and the duck the main dish.

9 2 . PASTA ALLA CACCIATORA
(PASTA HUNTER'S STYLE)

This is the Tuscan name for a dish of pasta—"nocette" (little nuts), "paternostri" (rosary beads), "penne" and so forth—served with a sauce of teal meat. Teals are marsh birds, with webbed feet, spoon-bills, and very similar to ducks but much smaller. In the wild they weigh from 250 to 300 grams (about 1/2 a pound). Two teals should suffice to make a sauce for 400 grams (about 14 ounces) of pasta, or enough to feed four people.

Remove and discard the teal's head, feet, rump-gland and intestines. Boil the birds with a *bouquet garni* of celery, carrot and parsley sprigs in as much salted water as you will need to cook the pasta. Once done, bone the birds and mince the flesh with a mezzaluna together with the livers and cleaned gizzards, which you have cooked along with the teals. Boil the pasta in the broth, then drain and season with the minced teal meat, butter and a good measure of Parmesan cheese, making a few layers.

The result is a pasta dish that is not only delicious, but more importantly easy to digest.

93. PASTE CON LE ARZAVOLE
(PASTA WITH TEAL)

The preceding recipe made me think of the following dish, which is every bit as appetizing.

Take one teal, clean it as described in the preceding recipe, and sauté it in a battuto made with a quarter of an onion (half if the onion is small), a good-sized stalk of celery, half a carrot, 40 grams (about 1-1/3 ounces) of untrimmed prosciutto, and some butter, seasoning with salt and pepper. Once the bird has browned, cook it in a good broth, adding a little tomato sauce (recipe 6) or tomato paste. Then bone the duck and chop it finely, adding, if you have them, a few pieces of dried mushrooms, which you should cook in the broth with the teal.

Put everything back on the fire and flavor with a dash of herbs or nutmeg. To bind the sauce add some butter mixed with flour. Then toss 350 grams (about 12-1/4 ounces) of pasta—use maca-roni, "strisce" (strips), horse-teeth or any other variety of this general size and shape—with the sauce and Parmesan cheese.

This recipe serves five people, unless the company includes hearty eaters.

By adding 50 grams (about 1-2/3 ounces) of ground beef fillet to the teal, you will get an even more substantial sauce.

94. PAPPARDELLE COL SUGO DI CONIGLIO
(PASTA IN RABBIT SAUCE)

After you have washed the rabbit, cut it into larger pieces than you would if frying it, and place these in a saucepan to draw out the water they contain. Drain the water off and when the pieces are nice and dry add some butter, a little olive oil, and a finely chopped battuto made with the rabbit liver, a little piece of bacon, and the usual seasoning—that is, onion, celery, carrot and parsley. Season with salt and pepper. Stir often and when browned, cook it with water and tomato sauce (recipe 6) or tomato paste. When done, add another small piece of butter. Use the sauce to season pappardelle or strisce, and serve the rabbit in a separate bowl as the main dish, using a bit of the sauce as gravy.

If you are not going to use the sauce to season the pasta, do not put any bacon in the battuto.

95. PAPPARDELLE COLLA LEPRE I
(PAPPARDELLE NOODLES WITH HARE I)

As it is dry and not very tasty, the meat of the hare needs in this recipe the help of a very substantial meat sauce to yield an elegant pasta dish. Here are the ingredients to serve five people. A dough made with three eggs should do, in my opinion. The rolled-out dough should be cut in the shape of pappardelle about one finger in width using a pastry wheel with a scalloped edge. Or you may use between 500 and 600 grams (between about 1 and 1-1/3 pounds) of strisce, which you can buy at the store.

*2 fillets of hare that together should weigh between 180 and 200
grams (between about 6-1/3 and 7 ounces), including the kidneys*

50 grams (about 1-2/3 ounces) of butter
40 grams (about 1-1/3 ounces) of bacon
1/2 of a medium-sized onion
1/2 of a carrot
1 palm-length celery stalk
a dash of nutmeg
Parmesan cheese, as needed
1 tablespoon of flour
6 deciliters (about 2-1/2 cups) of brown stock

The fillets should be skinned of any covering membrane and cut into small cubes. Then, using a mezzaluna, finely chop the bacon along with the onion, celery and carrot. Put the battuto on the fire with a third of the butter and the hare meat, seasoning with salt and pepper. When the meat turns brown, sprinkle the flour on top. Wait a few seconds before adding the brown stock, then simmer until done. Add the rest of the butter and the nutmeg before serving.

Prepare the pappardelle or the strisce in salted water. Drain, and then toss with the stew and Parmesan cheese.

If you have no fillets, use hare legs instead.

96. PAPPARDELLE COLLA LEPRE II
(PAPPARDELLE NOODLES WITH HARE II)

Here is another, simpler recipe that uses the same amounts of pasta and hare meat.

Make a battuto with 50 grams (about 1-2/3 ounces) of fatty prosciutto, a quarter of an onion, celery, carrot, and very little parsley. Put on the fire with 40 grams (about 1-1/2 ounces) of butter, and when it begins to brown, toss in the hare meat cut in chunks, seasoning with salt and pepper. Allow to brown, and then finish cooking in broth and tomato sauce (recipe 6) or tomato paste, which you will adding little by little, making sure that at the end there is a lot of liquid left in the pot. When the meat is done, remove it from the sauce, and mince into small but not tiny bits with a mezzaluna.

Prepare, as the French say, a roux, or as I would say, a paste with 30 grams (about 1 ounce) of butter and a tablespoon of flour.

Put on the fire and when the paste begins to turn a golden brown add it to the minced meat and the sauce, adding another 30 grams (about 1 ounce) of butter and the dash of nutmeg. Use this sauce to season the pasta; add Parmesan cheese. And do not reproach me for recommending the use of nutmeg in many of these dishes. In my opinion it goes well with them; if, however, you do not like it, you know what to do.

97. RAVIOLI

300 grams (about 10-1/2 ounces) of ricotta cheese
50 grams (about 1-2/3 ounces) of grated Parmesan cheese
2 eggs
boiled Swiss chard, as much as you can hold in your hand
a dash of nutmeg and the usual spices
salt, to taste

Pass the ricotta through a sieve; if it is too liquid, first squeeze it dry in a cheesecloth.

Cut the stalks away from the chard, steam, dry well and chop finely with a mezzaluna.

Make a firm dough with all these ingredients. Take spoonfuls of this dough and drop them on a layer of flour which you will have spread out on a pastry board. Roll each dollop well in the flour, giving it the round, oblong shape of croquettes. With these amounts you can make about two dozen ravioli. To cook them, toss them in a pot of unsalted water that is at a full boil. Remove them from the water with a slotted wooden spoon, to keep them dry. Season either with sauce or cheese and butter. Serve as a first course or as a side dish with a beef stew.

These ravioli cook fast and are done as soon as they become firm Cook them only a few at a time and they will not fall apart.[24]

---

24 Artusi clearly intends, by the term "ravioli," a different sort of dumpling from what we commonly understand by that term. This becomes even more apparent in recipe 99.

98. RAVIOLI ALL'USO DI ROMAGNA
(RAVIOLI ROMAGNA STYLE)

Because of their climate, which requires very substantial fare, and perhaps also because they have been so long accustomed to heavy foods, the Romagnoli tend to cook their vegetables in a way that makes them as pleasant as smoke in the eyes. Indeed, I have often heard people cry out in restaurants: "Waiter, some boiled meat please, but mind you, no spinach." Or, pointing to the spinach, "with that you can make a good poultice for your bottom."

Thus, leaving out chard and spinach, here is the recipe for ravioli Romagna style:

150 grams (about 5-1/4 ounces) of ricotta cheese
50 grams (about 1-2/3 ounces) of flour
40 grams (about 1-1/3 ounces) of grated Parmesan cheese
1 egg
1 egg yolk
salt, to taste

Prepare a firm dough with all the ingredients and pour it on a pastry board sprinkled with flour. Roll it into a cylindrical shape, which you will then cut into 14 or 15 pieces of equal size, molding them in the usual way as you go along. Boil for two or three minutes in unsalted water and season with cheese and brown stock, or serve as a side dish with a stew or a *fricandeau*.

99. RAVIOLI ALLA GENOVESE
(RAVIOLI GENOESE STYLE)

Actually, these should not be called ravioli, as true ravioli are not made with meat and are not wrapped in pastry shells.

1/2 breast of capon or pullet
1 lamb's brain
a few lamb sweetbreads
1 chicken liver

Put all these ingredients on the fire with some butter, and when they change color, finish cooking in brown stock. Remove them from the sauce and, using a mezzaluna, mince the meat very finely together with a thin slice of untrimmed prosciutto. Then add a little spinach, boiled and passed through a sieve, some grated Parmesan, a dash of nutmeg and two egg yolks. Mix well and then make dumplings, which you will wrap in pasta dough like the cappelletti Romagna style described in recipe 7, or even in a simpler fashion. With these quantities, you can make about 70 ravioli.

Serve as a pasta dish with cheese and butter, or with a sauce, or in broth as a soup.

100. SPAGHETTI COLLE ACCIUGHE (SPAGHETTI WITH ANCHOVIES)

This is an appetizing meatless pasta dish. Use medium-size spaghetti, which are preferable to those double-bass strings, which are excellent if you have the stomach of a lumberjack. 350 grams (about 12-1/4 ounces) are more than enough to feed four people with a normal appetite, and for this amount of pasta five anchovies should suffice. Wash, remove all spines and scales, and mince the anchovies with a mezzaluna, then put them on the fire with a generous amount of fine olive oil, adding a pinch of pepper. Do not let them sizzle, and when the anchovies start to get hot, add 50 grams (about 1-2/3 ounces) of butter, a little tomato sauce (recipe 6) or tomato paste, as you take them off the fire. Use this sauce to dress the spaghetti cooked in lightly salted water, making sure they turn out al dente.

101. SPAGHETTI COI NASELLLI (SPAGHETTI WITH HAKE)

500 grams (about 1 pound) of spaghetti
300 grams (about 10-1/2 ounces) of hake (or codfish)
60 grams (about 2 ounces) of butter
4 tablespoons of olive oil
4 tablespoons of Marsala wine
a dash of nutmeg

Chop a medium-sized onion and squeeze it in your hands to remove its sharpness. Put it on the fire with the olive oil and when it begins to brown, throw in the hake cut into chunks. Season with salt and pepper. As soon as the fish begins to brown, pour in some tomato sauce (recipe 6) or tomato paste diluted with water, and allow to cook. Then pass through a sieve, moistening the pieces of fish, if necessary, with a little hot water to extract all the pulp. Put the puréed fish back on the fire together with the butter, the Marsala wine and the dash of nutmeg. Unless the sauce is too watery and needs to cook down, as soon as it begins to boil pour it on top of the spaghetti, which you have boiled in salted water. Season with Parmesan cheese.

This recipe serves five people, and will please them all, for it is anything but a haphazard concoction, as it may at first seem from the description.

102. SPAGHETTI COL SUGO DI SEPPIE (SPAGHETTI IN CUTTLEFISH SAUCE)

Here are the approximate amounts to make enough of this pasta to feed five people.

Take three medium-sized cuttlefish, which may weigh in all between 650 and 700 grams (about 1-1/2 pounds). Remove the membrane that covers them, the cuttlebone, the mouth, the eyes, the digestive tube and the ink sac. Some cooks leave the latter, but I remove it, because it gives the dish an unpleasant appearance.

Prepare a battuto with 100 grams (about 3-1/2 ounces) of crustless bread, a good pinch of parsley, and a garlic clove. Finely chop the tentacles (there are two for each cuttlefish), season them with olive oil, as well as a good measure of salt and pepper. Then use this mixture to stuff the cuttlefish, sewing up their mouths. Chop up a medium-sized onion, squeeze it to remove its sharpness, and put on the fire with a little olive oil. When the onion begins to brown, toss in the cuttlefish and season with salt and pepper. Wait until the cuttlefish begin to turn a golden brown and then finish cooking over a low flame in lots of tomato sauce (recipe 6) or tomato paste, adding water a little at a time. Allow to simmer for 3 hours, but make sure that enough sauce remains to season 500 grams (about 1 pound) of spaghetti. Before serving, add some Parmesan cheese, and you will find that this is a delicious sauce. The cuttlefish, which when cooked in this manner become tender and easy to digest, should be removed from the sauce and served as a seafood stew for the next course.

103. SPAGHETTI DA QUARESIMA
(LENTEN SPAGHETTI)

Many who read this recipe will cry out, "Oh, what a ridiculous pasta!" I, however, like it. It is common in Romagna, and if you serve it to youngsters, you can be almost certain they will love it.

Pound some walnuts together with bread crumbs, adding confectioners' sugar and a spoonful of the usual spices. After removing the spaghetti from the water, season first with olive oil and pepper, then with a good measure of this mixture.

For 400 grams (about 14 ounces) of spaghetti, which feeds five people, you will need:

60 grams (about 2 ounces) of shelled walnuts
60 grams (about 2 ounces) of bread crumbs
30 grams (about 1 ounce) of confectioners' sugar
1 heaping tablespoon of allspice

104. SPAGHETTI ALLA RUSTICA
(COUNTRY-STYLE SPAGHETTI)

The ancient Romans left the consumption of garlic to the lower classes, while Alfonso King of Castile hated it so much he would punish anyone who appeared in his court with even a hint of it on his breath. The ancient Egyptians were much wiser—they worshipped garlic as a divinity, perhaps because they had experienced its medicinal properties. Indeed, it is claimed that garlic provides some benefit to those suffering from hysteria, promotes the secretion of urine, strengthens the stomach, aids digestion and, being also a vermifuge, protects the organism against epidemic and pestilential diseases. When sautéing it, however, you must be careful not to cook it too much, as then it acquires an unpleasant taste. There are many people who, ignorant of the ways of food preparation, have a horror of garlic merely because they can smell it on the breath of those who have eaten it raw or poorly cooked. As a result, they absolutely ban this plebeian condiment from their kitchens. This fixation, however, deprives them of healthy and tasty dishes, such as the one I present below, which has often comforted my stomach when upset.

Finely chop two garlic cloves and a few sprigs of parsley, as well as some basil leaves, if you like the taste. Sauté in a good measure of olive oil. As soon as the garlic starts to turn golden brown, toss in 6 or 7 chopped tomatoes, seasoning with salt and pepper. When everything is well cooked, purée the sauce, which will serve four to five people. Pour the sauce over spaghetti or vermicelli, adding grated Parmesan cheese. Remember to cook the pasta only for a short time in plenty of water. Send to the table immediately, so that the pasta does not have time to absorb all the moisture, and thus remains of the right consistency.

Tagliatelle are also delicious when served in this sauce.

105. SPAGHETTI COI PISELLI
(SPAGHETTI WITH PEAS)

This is a family dish, but good and tasty if prepared carefully. Besides, pasta dishes of this sort are useful alternatives to that eternal and often stringy and tasteless stew.

500 grams (about 1 pound) of spaghetti
500 grams (about 1 pound) of shelled peas
70 grams (about 2-1/2 ounces) of bacon

Make a battuto with the bacon, one new onion, one fresh garlic clove, some celery and parsley. Sauté in olive oil and when it starts to brown add the peas together with a few stems of chopped dill, if you can find some. Season with salt and pepper, and cook.

With your hands break the spaghetti into pieces shorter than half a finger, then cook them in salted water, drain well, mix with the peas and send to the table with Parmesan cheese on the side.

This recipe serves six or seven people.

106. SPAGHETTI CON LA BALSAMELLA
(SPAGHETTI IN BÉCHAMEL SAUCE)

Drain 300 grams (about 10-1/2 ounces) of spaghetti and season in a bowl with the amount of butter and Parmesan cheese you normally use. Then pour over the pasta a béchamel sauce made with:

3 deciliters (about 1 1/4 cups) of high quality milk
30 grams (about 1 ounce) of butter
1/2 a tablespoon of flour

This recipe serves four people.

107. MINESTRA DI ERBE PASSATE
(PURÉED VEGETABLE SOUP)

Take a bunch of Swiss chard, a bundle of spinach, a head of lettuce and a section of cabbage. Remove the larger ribs from the chard, then coarsely chop all these vegetables and soak them in cold water for a few hours.

Prepare a battuto with a 1/4 of an onion and all the usual seasonings, that is, parsley, celery, carrot and a few basil leaves (or a few springs of dill). Sauté in butter. When the battuto has taken on a nice golden color, add the vegetables which you will remove from the water without squeezing them dry, some chopped tomatoes and a sliced potato. Season with salt and pepper and allow to boil, stirring frequently. When the vegetables have cooked down, pour cold water over them and then cook them until they break up. Then pass the mixture through a sieve, which will remove the vegetable's rinds and filaments, which you will discard. Use some of the puréed sauce to cook rice or to provide the base for a soup. But first test for flavor, to see if it needs some additional seasoning and particularly butter, which is almost always the case.

Serve this first course with Parmesan cheese on the side. But I warn you not to make it too thick, so that it doesn't seem like plaster.

APPETIZERS

Appetizers or antipasti are, properly speaking, those delicious trifles that are made to be eaten either after the pasta course, as is practiced in Tuscany, which seems preferable to me, or before, as is done elsewhere in Italy. Oysters, cured meats such as prosciutto, salami, mortadella, and tongue, or seafood such as anchovies, sardines, caviar, "mosciame" (which is the salted back of the tuna fish), etc., may be served as appetizers, either alone or with butter. In addition, the fried breads I describe below make excellent appetizers.

108. CROSTINI DI CAPPERI
(CANAPÉS WITH CAPERS)

50 grams (about 1-2/3 ounces) of pickled capers
50 grams (about 1-2/3 ounces) of powdered sugar
30 grams (about 1 ounce) of raisins
20 grams (about 2/3 of an ounce) of pine nuts
20 grams (about 2/3 of an ounce) of untrimmed prosciutto
20 grams (about 2/3 of an ounce) of candied fruit

Coarsely chop the capers. Remove all the stems from the raisins and wash them well. Slice the pine nuts crosswise into three sections, finely dice the prosciutto, and chop the candied fruit into little chunks.

In a small saucepan heat a heaping teaspoon of flour and the two tablespoons of sugar. When the mixture begins to brown, pour in a half glass of water with a few drops of vinegar in it. Let it boil until smooth, then toss all the other ingredients into the saucepan and let simmer for 10 minutes. Test for flavor from time to time to make sure the sweet, strong taste is just right (I have not specified how much vinegar is needed, because not all vinegars are of equal strength). While the mixture is still hot, spread it over small slices of bread fried in good olive oil or lightly toasted.

You can serve these canapés cold even midway through dinner, to whet the appetites of your table companions. The best bread to use is the kind baked in a mold, as in England.

109. CROSTINI DI TARTUFI
(TRUFFLE CANAPÉS)

Preferably use baguettes cut into diagonal slices. If you cannot get baguettes, prepare small elegant slices of lightly toasted bread, which you will butter when still hot. Spread truffles prepared as described in recipe 269 over the bread, and coat with any drippings that are left over.

110. CROSTINI DI FEGATINI DI POLLO
(CANAPÉS WITH CHICKEN LIVERS)

As you know the gall bladder must be removed unbroken from a chicken liver, a procedure you can best perform in a small basin of water.

Put the chicken livers on the fire together with a battuto made with a shallot or, if you do not have any, a section of a small white onion, a small piece of fat trimmed from prosciutto, a few sprigs of parsley, celery and carrot, seasoned with a little olive oil and butter, as well as salt and pepper. Be sparing with the amounts, so that the resulting mixture will not turn out too spicy or heavy. When half done, remove the chicken livers from the saucepan and chop finely with a mezzaluna along with two or three chunks of dried mushrooms soaked in water. Put them back in the saucepan, and finish cooking, adding some broth. Before serving, however, sprinkle the mixture with a pinch of bread crumbs to bind it and add a little lemon juice.

I remind you that these canapés should turn out tender. There-fore, make sure the mixture is somewhat runny. Alternatively, soak the small bread slices lightly in broth.

111. CROSTINI DI FEGATINI DI POLLO CON LA SALVIA (CANAPÉS WITH CHICKEN LIVERS AND SAGE)

Finely chop very little onion and some untrimmed prosciutto. and sauté with butter. When well browned, add the chicken livers, finely minced, together with a few sage leaves (four or five will be enough for three livers). Season with salt and pepper. After the moisture has evaporated, add some more butter and bind with a tablespoon of flour, then finish cooking with broth. Before removing from the fire, add three or four teaspoons of grated Parmesan cheese and taste to see if properly flavored.

Make the crostini with a loaf of crustless stale bread. Each piece should be a little less than 1 centimeter thick (about 1/2 an inch). Spread the mixture generously on top of the slices when they are not too hot. After a few hours, when you are ready to serve the dish either alone or as a side dish for roast, beat an egg with a drop of water. Pick up the crostini one by one, dust the top with flour to cover the spread, then douse them in the beaten egg and fry them in the skillet, with the covered side down.

112. CROSTINI DI BECCACCIA (WOODCOCK CANAPÉS)

Gut the woodcocks and remove the entrails, discarding only the part of the intestines close to the rectum. Combine the entrails with the gizzards (without emptying them), some parsley leaves and the pulp of three anchovies for every three sets of entrails. No salt is needed. Mince everything finely with a mezzaluna. Put on the fire with but-ter and a pinch of pepper, then add brown stock.

Spread this mixture on thin bread slices. Toast lightly and serve with the woodcocks, which you will have roasted with a few bunches of sage and larded with a thin slice of salt pork.

113. CROSTINI DIVERSI
(VARIOUS CANAPÉS)

The bread that best lends itself to making crostini is fine white bread baked in a mold, in the English fashion. If this type of bread is not available, use day-old bread with lots of pulp inside and cut it in square, one-centimeter thick slices (about 1/2 of an inch), on which you will spread the following mixtures which should have the consistency of an ointment:

CROSTINI DI CAVIALE (CAVIAR CANAPÉS)

Combine equal parts of caviar and butter. If the caviar is firm, heat to soften it a little, stirring with a wooden spoon over a moderate flame. If instead of butter you would prefer to use olive oil, add a few drops of lemon juice, then fully blend all three ingredients.

CROSTINI DI ACCIUGHE
(ANCHOVY CANAPÉS)

Wash the anchovies, and remove the backbone and spines. Then mince with a mezzaluna, adding the right amount of butter. Crush the resulting mixture with a knife blade until you have a smooth paste.

CROSTINI DI CAVIALE, ACCIUGHE E BURRO
(CANAPÉS WITH CAVIAR, ANCHOVIES AND BUTTER)

I would use the following amounts, but feel free to modify them according to your taste:

60 grams (about 2 ounces) of butter
40 grams (about 1 1/3 ounces) of caviar
20 grams (about 2/3 of an ounce) of anchovies

Prepare a blend of all three and reduce to a fine, smooth paste.

114. SANDWICHES

Sandwiches can be served as appetizers or to accompany a cup of tea.

Take very fine day-old bread or rye bread, remove the crust, and cut into small round slices each about 1/2 a centimeter thick (about 1/4 of an inch), 6 centimeters long (about 2-1/2 inches), and 4 centimeters wide (about 1-1/2 inches). Spread fresh butter on one side only, place a thin slice of lean ham or salted tongue on top and cover with another slice of bread.

115. CROSTINI DI FEGATINI E ACCIUGHE
(CANAPÉS WITH CHICKEN LIVERS AND ANCHOVIES)

2 chicken livers
1 anchovy

Cook the livers in butter, and when they have absorbed it cover with broth. Add a pinch of pepper but no salt. When done, mince finely together with one anchovy, washed and boned. Then put back in the skillet where you cooked the chicken livers, add a little more butter, and heat the mixture without bringing it to a boil. To serve spread on slices of fresh bread from which you have removed the crust.

116. CROSTINI DI MILZA
(CANAPÉS WITH SPLEEN)

120 grams (about 4-1/2 ounces) of mutton spleen
2 anchovies

Remove the membrane from the spleen and cook in butter and brown stock. If you have no brown stock, sauté a little onion in olive oil and butter, adding salt, pepper and the usual spices, and then use the mixture to cook the spleen. When the spleen is done, add the anchovies, finely mincing together all the ingredients. Put the sauce back on the fire, adding a teaspoon of bread crumbs to bind the mixture. Do not allow it to come to a boil, and spread on small slices of bread that have first been dried but not toasted over the fire, and then buttered.

117. CROSTINI FIORITI
(FANCY CANAPÉS)

This type of crostini is easy to make, lovely to look at and rather delicious.

Remove the crust from some very fine bread and cut into lozenge-shaped or square slices about 1 centimeter thick (about 1/2 an inch). Spread fresh butter over them and lay two or three sprigs of parsley on top. Place anchovy fillets around the parsley like little snakes.

118. BACCALÀ MONTEBIANCO
(SALTED CODFISH MONT BLANC STYLE)

How strange is the nomenclature associated with cuisine! Why white mountain and not yellow mountain, as one would think from the color this dish takes when made? And how could the French, demonstrating their usual boldness when it comes to metaphors, have stretched their name for this dish into *Brandade de morue*?[25] *Brandade*, they say derives from *brandir*, to move, strike, wave a sword, halberd, lance and similar weapons. In fact, what is being brandished except a paltry wooden mixing spoon? No, it cannot be denied that the French are clever in everything!

Whatever the case, this is a dish that deserves your full attention, because salted codfish, when prepared in this fashion, loses its vulgar nature, becoming very delicate and worthy of gracing an elegant table, either as an appetizer or *entremets*.

500 grams (about 1 pound) of plump salted codfish, softened
200 grams (about 7 ounces) of extra fine olive oil
1 deciliters (about 1/3 of a cup) of cream or high-quality milk

Remove the bones, spine, scales, skin and sinews, which look like threads, from the cod and you will be left with about 340 grams (about 12 ounces) of flesh.

---

25 *Brandade* of cod, a traditional Provençal dish.

Grind the fish thoroughly in a mortar, then place it in a sauce-pan along with the cream, and heat over a moderate flame, stirring constantly. When the cod has absorbed the cream or milk, begin adding the oil in small droplets as you would do when preparing mayonnaise, stir constantly brandishing your kitchen weapon, the wooden spoon, so that the mix does not curdle and remains smooth. Remove from the heat when it seems perfectly cooked. Serve cold with a side dish of raw truffles cut into the thinnest slices, or else with fried bread crostini or caviar crostini, as described in this chapter. If you have prepared this dish correctly, it will not release any oil when served.

These amounts serve eight people.

SAUCES

The best sauce you can offer your guests is a happy expression on your face and heartfelt hospitality. Brillat-Savarin[26] used to say, "Inviting someone is the same as taking responsibility for their happiness and well-being for as long as they stay under your roof."

The pleasure you would like to give to the friends you have invited during these few hours is nowadays imperiled even before it starts by certain unfortunate customs that are being introduced and threaten to become widespread. I am referring to the so-called "digestion visit," to be made within eight days of the meal, and to the tips distributed to the domestics for the meal served. When you have to pay for dinner, it seems best to pay a restaurateur since that way you incur no obligation to anyone. And that bothersome second visit, which is made within a set period of time, like an obligatory rhyme, and does not issue unbidden from a sincere heart, is downright silly.

119. SALSA VERDE (GREEN SAUCE)

To prepare green sauce, squeeze the brine out of some capers and then, using a mezzaluna, finely chop them together with an anchovy, a little onion, and very little garlic. Mash the mixture with a knife blade to make it into a fine paste which you will place in a gravy dish. Add a fair amount of parsley chopped with a few basil leaves.

26 Jean-Anthelme Brillat-Savarin (1755–1826), a celebrated French gastronomist and magistrate, perhaps best known today for his book, *La physiologie du goût* (1825).

Blend everything in fine olive oil and lemon juice. This sauce goes well with boiled chicken, cold fish, hard-boiled or poached eggs. If you have no capers, brine-cured peppers may be used instead.

120. SALSA VERDE CHE I FRANCESI CHIAMANO *SAUCE RAVIGOTE* (GREEN SAUCE WHICH THE FRENCH CALL *SAUCE RAVIGOTE*)

This sauce deserves to become part of Italian cuisine because it goes well with poached fish, poached eggs, and so forth.

The sauce is made mainly with parsley, basil, chervil, pimpernel (also known as salad burnet), some celery leaves, two or three shallots, or, if you do not have any, a scallion or green onion. You also need one anchovy, two if they are small, and sweetened capers. Mince everything very finely or else crush in a mortar and then pass through a sieve. Place the purée in a gravy dish with a raw egg yolk, seasoning with olive oil, vinegar, salt and pepper. Mix well and send to the table. I use 20 grams (about 2/3 of an ounce) of capers, one egg yolk and the other ingredients in the quantities that seem suitable.

121. SALSA DI CAPPERI E ACCIUGHE (CAPER AND ANCHOVY SAUCE)

This sauce is rather hard on delicate stomachs. It is ordinarily used with steak. Take a pinch of sweetened capers, squeeze out the brine and finely chop with a mezzaluna along with an anchovy from which you have removed the scales and spine. Heat this in olive oil, and pour it over a beef steak that you have grilled and then seasoned with salt and pepper and some butter. Use the butter sparingly, however, otherwise it will clash, in the stomach, with the vinegar from the capers.

122. SALSA DI MAGRO PER CONDIRE
LE PASTE ASCIUTTE
(MEATLESS SAUCE FOR PASTA)

If I may be allowed to make a comparison between the senses of sight and taste, this sauce is like a young woman whose face is not particularly striking or attractive at first glance, but whose delicate and discreet features you might indeed find attractive upon closer observation.

500 grams (about 1 pound) of spaghetti
100 grams (about 3-1/3 ounces) of fresh mushrooms
70 grams (about 2-1/2 ounces) of butter
60 grams (about 2 ounces) of pine nuts
6 salted anchovies
7 or 8 tomatoes
1/4 of a large onion
1 teaspoon of flour

Place half the butter in a saucepan on the fire and brown the pine nuts in it. Then remove them from the pan, and grind them in a mortar, adding the flour. Finely mince the onion, place it in the butter in which you sautéed the pine nuts, and, when it begins to brown, add the tomatoes, chopped up. Season with salt and pepper. When the tomatoes are done, purée them. Put the sauce back on the fire adding the fresh mushrooms, cut into thin slices no larger than pumpkin seeds, the pine nut paste diluted in a little water, and the rest of the butter. Allow to simmer for half an hour, adding water to make the sauce rather liquid. Lastly, dissolve the anchovies by heating them with a little of this sauce, but do not let them come to a boil, and then combine with everything else.

Drain the spaghetti and toss with the sauce. If you wish to improve this dish further, add some grated Parmesan cheese.

These amounts serve five people.

123. SALSA ALLA MAÎTRE D'HÔTEL
(SAUCE MAÎTRE D'HÔTEL STYLE)

What a pompous title for a trifling little thing! Yet here, as in other matters, the French have claimed the right to lay down the law. Their dictates have prevailed and we must conform. This too is a sauce that goes well with steak. Chop some parsley and to remove the acidity wrap it (as someone has suggested) in the corner of a napkin and wring gently in cold water. Then make a paste with it, adding butter, salt, pepper and lemon juice. Heat on the fire in a baking pan or platter, taking care not to bring to a boil. Dip steak, hot off the grill, or fried cutlets in this sauce, and send to the table.

124. SALSA BIANCA (WHITE SAUCE)

This sauce should be served with boiled asparagus or cauliflower.

100 grams (about 3-1/3 ounces) of butter
1 tablespoon of flour
1 tablespoon of vinegar
1 egg yolk
salt and pepper
broth or water, as needed

First put the flour on the fire with half the butter, and when it has turned nut brown, add the broth or water slowly, stirring constantly. Without letting it boil too hard, add the rest of the butter and the vinegar. Remove from the burner, fold in the egg yolk and send to the table. It should have the consistency of cream sauce made without flour. For an ordinary bunch of asparagus, 70 grams (about 2-1/3 ounces) of butter should do, and then add a proportionate amount of flour and vinegar.

125. SALSA DI POMODORO (TOMATO SAUCE)

There once was a priest from Romagna who stuck his nose into everything, and busy-bodied his way into families, trying to interfere in every domestic matter. Still, he was an honest fellow, and since more good than ill came of his zeal, people let him carry on in his usual style. But popular wit dubbed him Don Pomodoro (Father Tomato), since tomatoes are also ubiquitous. And therefore it is very helpful to know how to make a good tomato sauce.

Prepare a battuto with a quarter of an onion, a clove of garlic, a finger-length stalk of celery, a few basil leaves and a sufficient amount of parsley. Season with a little olive oil, salt and pepper. Mash 7 or 8 tomatoes and put everything on the fire, stirring occasionally. Once you see the sauce thickening to the consistency of a runny cream, pass it through a sieve and it is ready to use.

This sauce lends itself to innumerable uses, as I shall indicate in due course. It is good with boiled meat, and excellent when served with cheese and butter on pasta, as well as when used to make the risotto described in recipe 77.

126. SALSA MAIONESE (MAYONNAISE)

This is one of the best sauces, particularly to flavor poached fish. In a china bowl break the raw yolks of two fresh eggs. After you have whisked them a little, add 6 or 7 tablespoons of olive oil, pouring it very slowly, drop by drop as it were, particularly at first. Then add the juice of one lemon and, if the eggs can absorb it, add a little more oil. A mayonnaise that has turned out well should look like a thick cream, but to obtain this consistency you will have to work it for more than twenty minutes. Lastly, season with a good pinch of salt and white pepper.

Adding a hard-boiled egg yolk to the two raw yolks makes it easier to prepare this sauce successfully.

127. SALSA PICCANTE I (TANGY SAUCE I)

Take two tablespoons of pickled capers, two anchovies and a pinch of parsley. Mince everything together until very fine, and place in a gravy dish with a generous pinch of pepper and plenty of olive oil. If the sauce is not sufficiently acidic, add vinegar or lemon juice. Serve over poached fish.

128. SALSA PICCANTE II (TANGY SAUCE II)

Finely chop one small onion, parsley, a few basil leaves, prosciutto trimmed of fat, and capers drained of brine. Sauté in good olive oil. Allow to simmer slowly and when the onion begins to brown, cool with a little broth. Bring to a boil and simmer again for a short while. Then remove from the heat, adding one or two minced anchovies and lemon juice.

This sauce can be served on poached eggs, on steak (which in this case need not be salted), and also on cutlets.

129. SALSA GIALLA PER PESCE LESSO (YELLOW SAUCE FOR POACHED FISH)

The following amounts will make a sauce for a fish fillet or a whole fish weighing between 300 and 400 grams (between 10-1/2 and 14 ounces).

Put a small saucepan on the fire with 20 grams (about 2/3 of an ounce) of butter and a heaping tablespoon of flour. When the flour begins to brown, pour in (a little at a time) two ladles of broth made with the fish you are preparing. When you see that the flour no longer rises as the sauce simmers, remove from the fire and add two tablespoons of olive oil and an egg yolk, stirring well. Lastly add the juice of half a lemon. Salt and pepper to taste. Allow to cool and pour over the fish, which should be served garnished all around by whole parsley sprigs.

This sauce should have the consistency of a cream that is not too liquid, so that it will coat the fish. You will see how fine and delicate it is. You can serve it hot for those not fond of cold fish.

130. SALSA OLANDESE (HOLLANDAISE SAUCE)

70 grams (about 2-1/3 ounces) of butter
2 egg yolks
1 tablespoon of lemon juice
1/2 an eggshell of water
salt and pepper

Melt the butter separately, without overheating it.

Put the egg yolks and the water in a bowl which you will put over a light flame or at the edge of the stove. Start beating the mixture with a whisk. Then add the butter carefully a little at a time. When the mixture has thickened, add the lemon and lastly the salt and pepper.

This sauce should be prepared just before serving. It is a very delicate sauce for poached fish or any similar dish. These amounts are sufficient for about 500 grams (about 1 pound) of fish.

131. SALSA PER PESCE IN GRATELLA (SAUCE FOR GRILLED FISH)

This sauce, simple but tasty and healthy, is made with egg yolks, salted anchovies, fine olive oil and lemon juice. Boil the eggs for 10 minutes, and for every egg yolk hard boiled in this way use either one large or two small anchovies. Clean the anchovies, remove the spines and pass through a sieve together with the egg yolks. Then dilute the mixture with olive oil and lemon juice until it becomes creamy. Cover the grilled fish with this sauce before sending it to the table, or serve on the side in a gravy dish.

132. SALSA CON CAPPERI PER PESCE LESSO (CAPER SAUCE FOR POACHED FISH)

50 grams (about 1-2/3 ounces) of butter
50 grams (about 1-2/3 ounces) of capers, drained of brine
1 heaping tablespoon of flour
salt, pepper and vinegar

These amounts are enough for a fish weighing about 500 grams (about 1 pound).

Not everyone can easily digest butter, which, being a fatty substance, is by its very nature hard on the stomach, especially when fried. When it is combined with acids, as in this and in similar instances, this is even more the case, and then butter often proves difficult to digest even by the strongest stomachs.

Cook the fish and, leaving it to stay warm in its broth, prepare the sauce. Put the flour on the fire with half the butter. Stir, and, when it starts to brown, add the remaining butter.

Allow to simmer for a while, then add a ladleful of fish broth. Season generously with salt and pepper, and remove the saucepan from the stove. Add the capers, half whole and half chopped, and then a droplet of vinegar. Taste for flavor and texture—the sauce should have the consistency of a light cream.

Place the fish well drained and hot on a large platter. Pour the sauce, equally hot, over it. Garnish with whole parsley sprigs, and send to the table.

133. SALSA TONNATA
(TUNA SAUCE)

Here is a sauce that can be served equally well with boiled meat and poached fish.

50 grams (about 1-2/3 ounces) of tuna preserved in olive oil
50 grams (about 1-2/3 ounces) of capers, drained of brine
2 anchovies
2 hard-boiled egg yolks
a good pinch of parsley
the juice of half a lemon
a pinch of pepper
olive oil, as needed

Clean the anchovies and then mince them finely with a mezzaluna, along with the tuna, the capers and the parsley. Then crush the mixture in a mortar with the egg yolks. Add a little olive oil to soften the mixture and then pass it through a sieve. After this is completed, add the lemon juice and enough olive oil to obtain the consistency of a light cream.

134. SALSA GENOVESE PER PESCE LESSO
(GENOESE SAUCE FOR POACHED FISH)

40 grams (about 1-1/3 ounces) of pine nuts
15 grams (about 1/2 an ounce) of capers, drained of brine
1 salted anchovy
1 hard-boiled egg yolk
3 pickled olives, pitted
1/2 a garlic clove
a few sprigs of parsley, including the stems
soft crustless bread soaked in vinegar, about the size of an egg
a pinch of salt
a pinch of pepper

With a mezzaluna mince the parsley and the garlic very finely. Then put them in a mortar with all the other ingredients. Pound the mixture into a very smooth mash and then pass through a sieve. Once this is done, dilute the resulting mixture with 60 grams (about 2 ounces) of olive oil and a droplet of vinegar, but taste first to ensure you put in the right amount.

This is an excellent sauce and these amounts should be enough for 600 grams (about 1-1/3 pounds) of fish.

135. SALSA DEL PAPA (POPE SAUCE)

Do not get the idea that this sauce takes its name from the Pope in the Vatican, and is therefore some sort of extravagant delight. All the same it is rather good on fried cutlets.

Take a small handful of capers, squeezing out the brine, and an equal amount of sweetened olives, from which you have removed the pits. Mince both with a mezzaluna. Finely chop a bit of onion and put it on the fire with some butter. When the onion begins to brown, moisten it a little at a time with water until it dissolves. Then add the mixture of capers and olives and allow to simmer for a while, eventually adding a droplet of vinegar, a pinch of flour and a little more butter. Finally, add a minced anchovy, and send to the table without letting the sauce simmer any further.

136. SALSA TARTUFATA
(TRUFFLE SAUCE)

Prepare a well-minced battuto with a small, nut-size chunk of onion, a half clove of garlic and a little parsley. Put on the fire with 20 grams (about 2/3 of an ounce) of butter and, when the onion begins to brown, add two fingers of Marsala or white wine in which you have first dissolved a heaping teaspoon of flour. Season the sauce with a pinch of salt, pepper and the usual spices, stirring constantly with a wooden spoon.

When the flour has thickened the sauce, add a little broth and then add some truffle shavings. Allow to stand for a moment longer on the fire, and serve as a garnish for fried cutlets of milk-fed veal, steaks or roasted meats.

I warn you that wine as a condiment is hard on some stomachs.

137. BALSAMELLA (BÉCHAMEL SAUCE)

This is the same sauce as the French *béchamel*, except that theirs is more complicated.

Heat in a saucepan a tablespoon of flour and a pat of butter as large as an egg. Use a wooden spoon to dissolve the butter and flour together. When the flour begins to color, add 1 liter (about 4 cups) of good-quality milk a little at a time, stirring constantly until the liquid has thickened to the consistency of milky cream. This is the béchamel. If it appears too thick, add milk; if too watery, reheat with another piece of butter combined with flour. These proportions produce a good amount of sauce, but you can vary them according to your needs.

A good béchamel and a brown stock prepared correctly are the foundations, as well as the principal secret of fine cooking.

138. SALSA DI PEPERONI
(BELL PEPPER SAUCE)

Take some large green peppers, cut them open and remove the seeds. Slice them lengthwise into four or five strips. Scorch them a little in a skillet with some olive oil—this makes it easier to peel off the skin. Once the skins have been removed, put a clove of finely chopped garlic on the fire in olive oil and butter. When the garlic begins to brown, add the peppers. Salt and let the peppers absorb the flavor, then add tomato sauce (see recipe 6).

Do not cook too long, otherwise the peppers will lose the tangy flavor that makes them so delicious. Serve with boiled meats.

EGGS

Eggs come immediately after meat at the top of the scale of nutritional value. During his tenure at the University of Florence, the celebrated physiologist Moritz Schiff[27] used to argue that the egg white is more nourishing than the yolk, which is composed of fatty substances, and that raw or lightly cooked eggs are less readily digested than well cooked eggs, because the stomach has to perform two operations instead of one: first coagulating the egg, then breaking it down to prepare it for assimilation by the body. Therefore it is better to abide by the middle path: eggs should be cooked neither too little nor too much.

Spring is the season in which eggs taste best. Fresh eggs are given to birthing mothers to drink, and are also considered a good food for newlyweds.

I once knew an innkeeper's son, a big, strapping young dolt who had ruined his health through bad living. He went to see a doctor who prescribed drinking two raw eggs each morning. Given the fact, at once happy and unhappy, that there was a large chicken coop at the inn, he would go there and drink the eggs as soon as the hens laid them. But as it happened, after a few days of this régime, the dunce began to think, "if two eggs are beneficial, four would be better," and

27 Moritz Schiff (Frankfurt am Main 1822–Geneva 1896), physiologist and naturalist. Director at Frankfurt of the Department of Ornithology at the Museum of Zoology, from 1854 to 1863 he taught comparative anatomy at the University of Bern; from 1853 to 1878 he was professor of physiology at the Institute of Advanced Studies in Florence. From 1876 until his death he was professor of physiology at the University of Geneva.

so down went four eggs. Then: "if four are good, six would be better," and so he drank six every morning. Finally he increased his consumption to twelve or fourteen a day; then he started to choke, and fierce gastralgia kept him in bed I do not how long until he hatched all the eggs he had drunk.

139. UOVA A BERE E SODE
(SOFT-BOILED AND HARD-BOILED EGGS)

Soft-boiled eggs should be boiled for two minutes; hard-boiled eggs for ten. Start counting from the moment you immerse them in boiling water. If you prefer them lightly boiled, six or seven minutes should be long enough. In either case, as soon as you remove the eggs from the boiling water, put them in cold water.

140. UOVA AFFOGATE
(POACHED EGGS)

Crack the eggs when the water boils, and drop them in from a very short distance. When the white coagulates and the yolk stops quivering, remove them with a slotted spoon and flavor with salt, pepper, cheese and butter. If you prefer a sauce, you can use tomato sauce, the green sauce described in recipe 119, the sauce in recipe 127, or you can make a sauce by dissolving an anchovy in hot butter and adding coarsely chopped capers drained of brine—but this is not for every stomach.

I have seen eggs served on a bed of mashed potatoes, one finger high, and also over spinach reheated in butter.

141. UOVA STRACCIATE
(SCRAMBLED EGGS)

This is a dish to be had when nothing else is available, or to be served as an appetizer for lunch. These quantities serve three people:

4 eggs
40 grams (about 1-1/3 ounces) of butter
1 deciliters (about 1/2 a cup) of cream

Heat the butter, and when it starts to sizzle, add the whisked eggs. Season with salt and pepper, and, stirring constantly, add the cream a little at a time. When the mixture firms up, cover with it three slices of toast, each about one finger thick and with the crust removed, which you have buttered while still hot and placed on a platter.

Sprinkle with Parmesan cheese and send to the table.

142. ROSSI D'UOVO AL CANAPÈ[28]
(EGG-YOLK CANAPÉS)

How repugnant it is for me to call dishes such stupid and often ridiculous names! But in order to make myself understood, I have to follow common practice.

This is a dish that can be served as an appetizer for lunch. If you follow this recipe to the letter, it should be enough for five people. Cut five square slices of crustless bread, each one about as wide as the palm of your hand and one finger thick. Carve a hole in the middle of each, but not all the way through. Fry in butter and arrange on a fireproof platter. In each depression put the whole yolk of a raw egg. Then prepare a béchamel with just under 3 deciliters (about 1-1/4 cups) of milk, 40 grams (about 1-1/3 ounces) of flour and 40 grams (about 1-1/3 ounces) of butter. After removing the béchamel from the fire, add to it three spoonfuls of grated Parmesan, a dash of cinnamon or of nutmeg, and salt. Allow to cool, then pour onto the platter, covering both the egg yolks and the toast slices. Brown for a while under the hood of the Dutch oven, making sure the eggs do not get too hard. Send hot to the table. Where English, mold-baked bread can be found, this is the best kind for these canapés.

---

28 The expression "al canapè" was formerly used to mean a layer of bread or biscuit on which a dressing of meat, fish, etc., was served.

143. UOVA RIPIENE I (STUFFED EGGS I)

After you have hard-boiled the eggs as described in recipe 139, cut them in half lengthwise and remove the yolks. Take one anchovy for every two eggs, wash, remove the spine, and mince with a little parsley and very little onion. Combine with the yolks, adding as much butter as you need to make a smooth paste, blending everything together with the blade of a knife. Fill the empty space left by the egg yolks with this paste; arrange the half-eggs in neat rows on a platter and cover with the mayonnaise described in recipe 126.

These eggs may also eaten seasoned simply with salt, pepper, olive oil and vinegar, a solution not to be scoffed at, and which will not aggrieve your stomach.

144. UOVA RIPIENE II (STUFFED EGGS II)

As a first course for lunch, these will feed five people:

6 eggs
30 grams (about 1 ounce) of butter
20 grams (about 2/3 of an ounce) of crustless bread
2 heaping spoonfuls of grated Parmesan cheese
a pinch of dried mushrooms
some parsley leaves
salt, to taste

Hard boil the eggs, slice lengthwise, remove the yolks and set them aside.

Soak the bread well in milk and then wring dry.

Reconstitute the mushroom in lukewarm water.

Grind everything as fine as possible and then fill the empty egg whites to overflowing. Then arrange the 12 half-eggs on the convex side of a platter, on a bed of mashed potatoes as described in recipe 443, but for this recipe use 350 grams (about 12-1/3 ounces) of potatoes (weighed before cooking). Instead of potatoes, you may also place the eggs on a bed of spinach, peas or other vegetables. Before sending to the table, reheat the dish by placing it under the lid of a Dutch oven with fire above.

145. FRITTATE DIVERSE (OMELETTES)[29]

Is there anyone who does not know how to make an omelette? Is there anyone in this world who has not in his life made some sort of omelette? All the same, it will not be a complete waste of time to say a few words on the subject.

It is not a good idea to beat the eggs excessively when making an omelette. Whirl them around in a soup bowl with a fork, and when you see the whites breaking up and blending with the yolks, stop. There are two kinds of omelettes: simple, egg-only omelettes and those made with some additional ingredient. A simple omelette is one made "paper-thin," Florentine style, the sort one man is said to have rolled onto his fork all at once and swallowed in a single mouthful, after which he asked for a whole ream. Nonetheless the Florentine omelette turns out very tasty when prepared in excellent Tuscan olive oil also because it is cooked on one side only, which custom is preferable for almost all omelettes. When the underside has firmed up, flip the skillet over a platter which you are holding in your hand, and send to the table.

All manner of vegetables, simply boiled or cooked in butter, may be used in omelettes, and one may add as well a pinch of grated Parmesan cheese, by itself or with parsley. Onions also go well in omelettes, but they make them harder to digest. Two of the most refined ingredients for omelettes, in my opinion, are asparagus and zucchini. If you are going to use asparagus, boil and then sauté the green portion in butter, mixing a pinch of Parmesan into the eggs. If you are using zucchini, buy the small long ones and cut them into round slices. Salt them, and after they have lost their water, sprinkle flour on top and sauté in lard or olive oil. Wait until they have browned before adding the eggs. Peas as well, prepared as described in recipe 427, when combined with the eggs, make a first-class omelette.

Sweet omelettes can also be prepared. Spread fruit preserves of any type on top of the eggs when the omelette is done. Sweet omelettes

29 The Italian term is "frittata," which nowadays is distinguished from the omelette by the fact that it is not folded in two when nearly cooked. Artusi's omelettes for Recipes 146 and 152 are, however, folded, and for this and stylistic considerations, we have translated frittata as *omelette*.

might be all right, but I do not like the idea of them, and I must say that when I see them as the only dessert offered at a restaurant, I begin to get a bad idea about the place.

146. FRITTATA IN ZOCCOLI
(OMELETTE WITH PROSCIUTTO)

This omelette deserves special mention because it requires a rather unique method of preparation.

Take some thin untrimmed slices of prosciutto, cut into pieces as wide as a 10-centesimo coin,[30] and place in a skillet with butter. When they have sautéed a short while, add the eggs, with a very small pinch of salt. When the omelette starts to firm up, fold in half. The appearance it thus assumes explains why this type of omelette is more properly called the "egg fish." Then add more butter and cook until done.

147. FRITTATA DI CIPOLLE (ONION OMELETTE)

Use preferably large white onions, sliced into half rings half a finger in width. Soak in cold water for at least an hour. Then dry well in a clean kitchen towel, and place in a skillet with lard or olive oil. When the onions begin to brown, salt them, and also salt the eggs before pouring them over the onion. Make sure that the onions do not turn too dark from overcooking.

148. FRITTATA DI SPINACI (SPINACH OMELETTE)

Remove the spinach from the water and cook it dripping wet. As soon as you take it off the fire, put it back in cold water. Then squeeze dry, mince coarsely, put into a skillet with a pat of butter, seasoning with salt and pepper. Turn frequently, and when the spinach has absorbed the butter, add the whisked eggs and some salt. When one side has browned, flip over, using a plate and put back in the skillet

30 The coin referred to here is medium size, by current North American standards.

with some more butter. You may add a pinch of grated Parmesan cheese to the eggs, if desired.

The ideal quantities for this recipe seem to me these:

200 grams (about 7 ounces) of raw spinach
40 grams (about 1-1/3 ounces) of butter in all
4 eggs

149. FRITTATA DI FAGIOLINI IN ERBA
(BABY GREEN-BEAN OMELETTE)

Boil the green beans in salted water and cut each into two or three pieces. Then sauté in a skillet with butter and olive oil and season with salt and pepper. Beat the eggs with a pinch of Parmesan and salt, and pour over the beans when you see they have shriveled.

150. FRITTATA DI CAVOLFIORE
(CAULIFLOWER OMELETTE)

To ensure that this omelette prepared with cauliflower, one of the most insipid vegetables, will turn out tasty, I will give you the precise amounts:

300 grams (about 10-1/2 ounces) of boiled cauliflower, stripped
*   of leaves and stem*
60 grams (about 2 ounces) of butter
2 heaping spoonfuls of grated Parmesan cheese
1 tablespoon of olive oil
6 eggs

Finely mince the cauliflower and place in a skillet along with the butter and the olive oil. Season with salt and pepper. When the cauliflower has absorbed the condiments, pour in the eggs which you have beaten with the Parmesan cheese and salted. Keep the omelette thin, so that you do not have to flip it. If your skillet is small, make two omelettes.

151. FRITTATA DI RICCIOLI PER CONTORNO
(OMELETTE IN CURLS AS A SIDE DISH)

Boil a bunch of spinach and pass through a sieve. Whisk two eggs, season with salt and pepper, and mix in just enough of the spinach to turn the mixture green. Put the skillet on the fire with a droplet of olive oil, just enough to grease it. When it is nice and hot, pour in a small portion of the eggs, tip the skillet in all directions so that the egg uniformly coats the bottom and the omelette turns out paper thin. Remove from the fire when it is firm and dry, flipping it if necessary. Repeat the operation with the rest of the eggs, two or three times as needed. Roll the two or three omelettes together, and then slice the roll thin to obtain thin strips that resemble taglierini needles. Sauté lightly in butter and flavor with Parmesan cheese. Then serve as a side dish for a *fricandeau* or other similar dish. In addition to looking very attractive, this side dish, which also turns out well without the spinach, is sure to make at least one of your table companions rack his brains to find out what it is made of.

152. FRITTATA COLLA PIETRA DI VITELLA DI LATTE
(OMELETTE WITH KIDNEY OF MILK-FED CALF)

Take a kidney of a milk-fed calf, and cut it open lengthwise without removing any of the fat. Season with olive oil, salt and pepper, grill it and then cut into thin diagonal slices. Whisk eggs in proportion to the kidney, season again with salt and pepper, adding a sprig of minced parsley and a little Parmesan cheese. Add the kidney to the eggs, mix well, and with these ingredients prepare an omelette cooked in butter. When the bottom has browned, fold the omelette in half so that it remains tender.

DOUGHS AND BATTERS

153. PASTA MATTA (CRAZY DOUGH)

It is called crazy not because it is likely to do something mad, but for the simplicity and ease with which it can serve as the necessary dress for a variety of dishes, as you will see.

Sprinkle water and salt in due proportion over the flour and form a dough loaf that can rolled out wafer thin.

154. PASTA SFOGLIA (PUFF PASTRY DOUGH)

This dough can be said to have turned out beautifully when it puffs up in paper-thin and feather-light layers. Thus, for those who have not had much practice making it, it is difficult to prepare. You would need to watch a master chef make it. Nonetheless, I shall do my best to teach you.

200 grams (about 7 ounces) of fine flour, or Hungarian flour
150 grams (about 5-1/4 ounces) of butter

Or:

300 grams (about 10-1/2 ounces) of flour
200 grams (about 7 ounces) of butter

In the winter, mix hot but not boiling water with the flour; salt as needed, then add a tablespoon of brandy and a nut-sized pat of butter, taking it from the above-mentioned quantities. After you have formed a loaf that is neither too hard nor too soft, knead it for half an hour at least, first with your hands, then banging it repeatedly against the pastry board. Now make a rectangular loaf, wrap it in a kitchen towel, and allow it to rest a while. Meanwhile, with one wet hand, knead the butter, if it is hard, against the pastry board until it is quite soft and tender; then shape it into a loaf like the one you have made out of the flour and put it in a small basin of cold water. When the dough has finished resting, remove the butter from the water, dry it in a kitchen towel, and sprinkle it well with flour.

Spread out the dough with a rolling pin only as far as is necessary to place the butter loaf inside it. Place the butter loaf inside the dough and draw the edges of the dough all around it, sealing them tightly with your fingers. Make sure the dough adheres firmly to the butter on all sides and that there is no air trapped inside. Now start rolling out the dough, first with your hands and then with a rolling pin, making it as thin as possible the first time, while taking care the butter does not spurt out through the dough. If that should happen, immediately cover the spot where the butter shows through with a little flour. Keep the pastry board and the rolling pin well sprinkled with flour, so that the dough rolls out smoothly and spreads evenly over the board. After you have rolled out the dough the first time, fold it into three layers, so that they form three sheets one on top of another, and roll out again to a nice thickness. Repeat the process six times, allowing the dough to rest for 10 minutes between each treatment. For the last roll-out, which makes seven such roll-outs in all, fold it into two layers and reduce to the required thickness, that is, to slightly less than 1 centimeter (about 1/2 an inch) thick.

Except for this final folding of the dough, be sure every time you roll it out to give the dough a rectangular shape three times as long as it is wide. If some bubbles start appearing due to air trapped inside, lance them with a pin.

Instead of an ordinary pastry board, you should use a marble-top table, as it is cooler and smoother. In summer, you will need to use ice to harden the butter before kneading it, as well as for better rolling out the dough. This is done by rubbing ice, when necessary, over the dough which has been wrapped inside in a thick cloth, or better still, by placing the dough between two ice-covered dishes.

Puff-pastry dough is used, as you know, to make *vols-au-vent*, tartlets filled with jam and fruit preserves, and little cakes stuffed with marzipan. If you would like to serve puff pastries as an *entremets*, stuff them with a delicate mix of meat, chicken livers, and sweetbreads. But for every purpose, this dough should be brushed with egg yolk on the surface but not on the edges, as that would hinder its puffing out while baking. If served as a dessert sprinkle with powdered sugar while still hot.

155. PASTA SFOGLIA A METÀ
(PUFF PASTRY BY HALF)

Use half a measure in weight of butter for one measure of flour, with an additional small piece of butter inside the dough.

In every other respect, follow the previous recipe.

156. PASTELLA PER LE FRITTURE
(BATTER FOR FRYING)

100 grams (about 3-1/5 ounces) of flour
1 tablespoon of fine olive oil
1 tablespoon of brandy
1 egg
salt, to taste
cold water, as needed

Fold the egg yolk and the other ingredients into the flour, adding the water a little at a time so that the batter does not turn out too runny. Stir well with a wooden spoon and let rest for several hours. When you are ready to use it, add the beaten egg white. This batter can be used for many fried dishes, particularly those made with fruit and vegetables.

157. PASTELLA PER FRITTI DI CARNE
(BATTER FOR FRIED MEATS)

Dissolve two heaping teaspoons of flour in two teaspoons of olive oil. Add two eggs, a pinch of salt and mix well.

This mixture should have the consistency of smooth cream, and can be used to fry brains, bone marrow, sweetbreads, testicles, lamb's head, head meat from a milk-fed calf and the like. Scald all these items, some more than others, according to their nature, including brains and spinal marrow, so that they firm up while boiling. Salt the water, season with a pinch of salt and one of pepper when you remove them from the water. Slice the testicles lengthwise into tiny fillets. Cut the spinal cord marrow into finger-length chunks. If the sweetbreads come from mutton, leave them whole. Dice the brains into nut-sized morsels and the head meat in somewhat larger chunks. Put the pieces into the batter after having sprinkled them with flour, and sauté in virgin lard or olive oil.

Often these fried meats are combined with liver or cutlets of milk-fed veal. Cut the liver into very thin slices and pound the cutlets with he blunt edge of a knife, or else mince the meat with a mezzaluna and then mold it into a more elegant shape. Season both the liver and the veal with salt and pepper, then marinate in whisked egg for a few hours. Before frying, dredge the slices in fine bread crumbs, repeating the procedure twice if necessary. This fry should always be served with lemon wedges.

158. PASTA PER PASTICCI DIACCI DI CARNE
(DOUGH FOR COLD MEAT PIES)

250 grams (about 8-4/5 ounce) of flour
70 grams (about 2-1/3 ounces) of butter
a generous pinch of salt
milk, as much as needed to blend and reduce the dough to the right consistency

It is not necessary to knead this dough too much. Shape into a loaf, sprinkle with flour, and allow to rest for about half an hour wrapped in a damp cloth.

With these amounts you will have enough dough for an even larger pie than the game pie described in recipe 370.

159. PASTA PER PASTICCI DI CACCIAGIONE
(DOUGH FOR GAME PIES)

For this dough see the recipe for hare pie, described in recipe 372.

STUFFINGS

160. RIPIENO PEI POLLI
(STUFFING FOR CHICKEN)

about 100 grams (about 3-1/2 ounces) lean milk-fed veal
a small piece of veal udder
the giblets from the chicken

Instead of the lean veal and veal udder, you may substitute lean pork, turkey breast, or just regular veal.

Cook the meat in a small battuto of shallot or onion, parsley, celery, carrot and butter. Season with salt and pepper and the usual spices, keeping the meat moist with broth. Remove the meat from the pan, cut the gristle away from the gizzard, add some small pieces of reconstituted dried mushroom, a little slice of untrimmed prosciutto, and mince everything very finely with a mezzaluna. In the meat juice left in the pan, toss enough crustless bread to make one tablespoon of firm pap. Combine this with the mixed meats, adding a good pinch of grated Parmesan cheese and two eggs. Stuff the chicken with this mixture, then sew it up. The chicken may be boiled or stewed. If you boil the chicken, you will notice it makes an excellent broth. But be careful when carving the bird—the stuffing should be removed in one piece and then cut into slices.

For a different chicken stuffing, see the one for roast chicken described in recipe 539.

161. RIPIENO DI CARNE PER PASTICCINI DI PASTA SFOGLIA (MEAT STUFFING FOR PUFF PASTRIES)

You can prepare this stuffing with well-stewed milk-fed veal, chicken livers, or sweetbreads. In my opinion sweetbreads are best, being the most delicate; but whatever you choose I would always add to this stuffing a dash of truffles when they are in season. If you are using sweetbreads put them on the fire with a little butter, seasoning them with salt and pepper, and when they begin to brown finish cooking with the brown stock described in recipe 4. Then cut them into chickpea-sized chunks or even smaller. Add a tablespoon or two of the béchamel sauce described in recipe 137, as well as a little salted tongue or a little untrimmed prosciutto diced into small cubes, a pinch of Parmesan cheese and a dash of nutmeg, making sure the ingredients are in the amount necessary to give the mixture a savory and delicate flavor. Allow to cool so that the mixture firms up and becomes easier to handle.

There are two ways to enclose this mixture in the puff-pastry dough described in recipe 154. For either, you may use the mold for jam cookies described in recipe 614, or a regular oval mold. The first way is to cook the dough with the stuffing inside; the second way is to cook the dough first and then add the stuffing. In the first case, place the stuffing right in the middle of the disk of dough, moisten the edges with a wet finger, cover with another similar disk and cook. In the second case, which will actually be more convenient for those who, having a whole meal to prepare, can cook the dough a day in advance, the two disks are joined together without the stuffing; but before joining them, you will use a small tin ring to make a round incision (having the diameter of a medium-sized coin)[31] in the center of the upper disk. As the tartlet is baking, it will naturally puff up with air, remaining rather hollow inside. The round of dough you have cut out on top will now look like a little lid which you can remove with the tip of a knife. Before stuffing the tartlet, you may also, if you like, widen the hollow space which you have uncovered by removing the lid. Fill the tartlets and then put the little lids back on. In this way, you need only heat them before sending

31 See the note to recipe 146.

them to the table. Remember that puff-pastry should always be brushed with egg yolk before baking, but only on top.

If you should be making *vols-au-vent*, you should make a sauce with chicken giblets and sweetbreads, chopped into large chunks.

FRIED FOODS

162. FRITTO DI PASTA RIPIENA
(STUFFED FRITTERS)

Use the dough described in recipe 212 or the puff-pastry dough described in recipe 154, roll out to the thickness of a scudo,[32] and cut it into disks with scalloped edges of the size shown below.

Place the stuffing described in the previous recipe inside one disk of dough, cover with another disk, moistening around the edges so that they will stick together, then fry and serve hot.

32 This is an old coin, much larger than the coin mentioned previously (see notes to recipes 146 and 161).

163. FRITTO DI RICOTTA (RICOTTA FRITTERS)

200 grams (about 7 ounces) of ricotta cheese
40 grams (about 1-1/3 ounces) of flour
2 eggs
2 scant teaspoons of sugar
a dash of lemon zest
1 pinch of salt
2 tablespoons of brandy

Any type of ricotta is good for this recipe as long as it hasn't become strong smelling. But if you use the ricottas that come from Rome and the Maremma,[33] which are first-rate, you may be sure the results will win you honor and praise.

Allow the mixture to rest for several hours before frying. Using the above-mentioned amounts, the mixture will turn out a little firm. This is good and enables the fritters to swell into round shapes about the size of a walnut. Sprinkle confectioners' sugar on top and serve hot as a side dish for a meat fry. As you can see, very little sugar goes into the mix, since sugar burns and with too much of it the fritters would not have that nice golden yellow hue.

To give these and similar pastries a more or less round shape, the mixture should be picked up in a spoon greased with the hot oil of the skillet and shaped with the tip of a table knife which has also been dipped in the same hot oil.

164. FRITTO RIPIENO DI MOSTARDA
(FRITTERS STUFFED WITH CHUTNEY)

This fritter may be made in Romagna, where in wintertime you can buy Savignano mostarda or a chutney made in the style of that town, which was at one time greatly appreciated, though I could not say if this is still the case.

If you do not have this type of chutney, you can use the home-made chutney described in recipe 788.

---

33 A marshy, coastal region of Tuscany on the Tyrrhenian Sea.

Prepare a rather soft dough using the following ingredients, which you will knead with your hands on a pastry board.

220 grams (about 7-3/4 ounces) of flour
30 grams (about 1 ounce) of butter
a pinch of salt
milk, as much as required for the kneading

Allow to rest for half an hour, then roll out with a rolling pin to the approximate thickness of a scudo.[34] Cut into small disks using the sample given in recipe 162. Once you have produced 80, spread chutney over 40 of them, then cover these with the other 40, first moistening the edges with a finger dipped in water, so that they stick together.

Fry and sprinkle sugar on top before sending to the table.

165. FRITTO DI MELE
(APPLE FRITTERS)

Take large good-quality apples that are not too ripe. Remove the cores with a tin corer which leaves a hole in the middle. Peel the apples and cut them into slices just under 1 centimeter (about 1/2 an inch) thick. When you are ready to fry, dip the slices in the batter described in recipe 156, adding, if you like, a pinch of anise, which goes well with this dish.

Sprinkle with confectioners' sugar and serve hot.

166. FRITTO DI CARDONI
(CARDOON FRITTERS)

Remove the filaments from the cardoons and boil them in salted water. Then cut into small chunks, and sauté in butter, adding a little more salt. Sprinkle flour on top, dip in the batter described in recipe 156, and fry. They can come in handy as a side dish for a meat fry or a stew.

34 See the note to recipe 162.

167. FRITTO DI FINOCCHI
(FENNEL FRITTERS)

Cut the fennel into wedges, remove the tougher leaves and boil in salted water. Before dipping in the batter described in recipe 156, dry them and sprinkle with flour.

168. CAROTE FRITTE
(FRIED CARROTS)

These carrots can be used as a side dish for fried meat or fish, when zucchini are no longer available.

Cut the carrots into thin finger-length slices without peeling them; salt them and, after a few hours, when they are very moist, roll in flour. Shake off the excess flour, dip both sides in egg and then throw the slices one by one into the skillet with your fingers.

169. FRITTO DI PESCHE
(FRIED PEACHES)

Take nice, fat peaches that are not too ripe, cut into medium-size sections and, like the apples and the fennel, coat them in the batter described in recipe 156. Sprinkle sugar on top after they are done. There is no need to peel them.

170. FRITTO DI SEMOLINO (SEMOLINA FRITTERS)

70 to 80 grams (about 2-1/3 to 2-2/3 ounces) of fine-grain semolina
3 deciliters (about 1-1/4 cups) of milk
1 egg
3 teaspoons of sugar
1 walnut size pat of butter
a pinch of salt
a dash of lemon zest

Put the milk on the fire with the butter and the sugar, and, when it starts bubbling, add the semolina a little at a time, stirring constantly. Salt and fold in the egg; stir, and when the egg has been thoroughly incorporated into the mixture, remove the semolina from the fire, and spread it to the thickness of about one finger on a platter greased with butter or on a pastry board sprinkled with flour. Cut into lozenge-shaped pieces, dip in a beaten egg and then in fine bread crumbs, then fry. If you wish to make this dish sweeter, sprinkle with confectioners' sugar, Serve alone, or better still as a side dish for a meat fry.

171. PALLOTTOLE DI SEMOLINO
(SEMOLINA NUGGETS)

To me it seems this fry always turns out very well, and rewards the labor it takes to grind it with a mortar and pestle.

120 grams (about 4-1/4 ounces) of semolina
15 grams (about 1/2 an ounce) of butter
1 heaping tablespoon—the equivalent to 25 grams (about 4/5 of
    an ounce)—of potato flour
1 whole egg
2 egg yolks
1 heaping teaspoon of sugar
a dash of lemon zest
4 deciliters (about 1-2/3 cups) of milk

Cook the semolina in the milk with the sugar. When you remove it from the fire add the butter, lemon peel and a pinch of salt. When it has completely cooled, grind the mixture in a mortar together with the eggs: first the yolks, one at a time, and then the whole egg. At the end, add the potato flour, still grinding well with the pestle. Pour on a platter and then fry in a skillet one teaspoon at a time, making nuggets which should be slightly larger than walnuts. Serve with confectioners' sugar sprinkled on top, once the nuggets have cooled off a little.

These fritters are light, delicate, and pleasing to the eye.

172. FRITTELLE DI POLENTA ALLA LODIGIANA (POLENTA FRITTERS LODI STYLE)

1/2 liter (about 1/2 a quart) of milk
100 grams (about 3-1/2 ounces) of cornmeal

Prepare a polenta, and before removing it from the fire, salt to taste. Pour out on a pastry board while still hot, and with a table knife dipped in water spread it out to the thickness of barely half a finger. When it has cooled off, use the sample disk described in recipe 182, or a similar one, to cut the dough into as many disks as you can, which should come to 30 or 32 if you add the leftover trimmings, rolling them up and spreading them out again by hand. Pair the disks, putting a thick slice of Gruyère cheese between each pair. In this way you will get 15 to 16 fritters. Now whisk two eggs, as they are needed to gild the fritters. Dip the pancake in the eggs and then in bread crumbs, then fry in lard or olive oil. Serve hot as a side dish for a roast.

173. FEGATO DI MAIALE FRITTO (FRIED PORK LIVER)

The higher animals are equipped with a whitish gland (the pancreas) situated between the liver and the spleen, which empties out into the duodenum through its own excretory conduit. The pancreatic humor, naturally alkaline and viscous as albumen, assists the bile in breaking down the foods we eat. However, its action is more particularly responsible for converting fats into an emulsion that renders them more digestible. These secretions, the gastric juices and the saliva contribute jointly to ensure perfect digestion. Because of its similarity to the salivary glands (the usual sweetbreads) and its delicate flavor, the pancreas is called by many people the sweetbread of the liver. Tuscans, however, call the pig's pancreas the "little stomach."

In my opinion, to taste the true flavor of pork liver, you must slice it thin and fry it on its own and without spices in virgin lard, mixing in some "little stomach" (i.e., the pancreas) diced into small pieces. When preparing it in this way, remove it from the skillet with a little of its own grease, season with salt and pepper, and squeeze a lemon on top of it, while still steaming hot—the acidity of the lemon will counteract the greasiness of the dish a little. The thin liver slices may also be dredged in flour before frying.

174. GRANELLI FRITTI (FRIED TESTICLES)

I've heard it said that in the Maremma[35] on the day when the colts are gelded, it is customary to invite one's friends to a dinner where the dish that takes top honors is a magnificent fry of colt testicles. How such testicles might taste I have no idea, as I have not tried the dish myself, although you and I have surely eaten horse and even donkey testicles countless times, without realizing it.

But let us speak instead about mutton testicles, which are just as flavorful, because they taste much like sweetbreads, but are even more delicate.

Boil the testicles in salted water, and then make a lengthwise incision in order to remove their outer membrane, which is composed, as the physiologists say, of the tunica and the epididymis. Cut them into thin slices, salt a little more, dredge in flour, dip in a beaten egg, and fry.

175. FRITTO COMPOSTO ALLA BOLOGNESE (MIXED FRY BOLOGNESE STYLE)

This fry, properly speaking, should be called "fine croquettes." Take a piece of stewed lean milk-fed veal, a small brain either boiled or cooked in sauce, and a small slice of untrimmed prosciutto. Mince everything finely with a mezzaluna and then grind well in a mortar. Then add an egg yolk or a whole egg, according to the amount you need, and a little béchamel sauce from recipe 137. Put the mixture on the fire, and stir constantly until the egg is done. At the end, add grated Parmesan cheese, a dash of nutmeg and some truffles, very finely minced. Pour on a platter and when completely cooled, make many round nuggets each about the size of a small walnut and roll in flour. Then dip in egg and in very fine bread crumbs. Repeat the procedure twice, then fry.

35 A marshy region in Tuscany, famous for its horses. See note to recipe 163.

176. FRITTO ALLA ROMANA I
(ROMAN-STYLE FRY I)

Put on the fire some finely chopped onion in a little butter. When the onion begins to brown, drop in a piece of lean milk-fed veal and cook, seasoning with salt and pepper. When the meat has adequately browned, moisten with Marsala and simmer till done.

Grind the meat in a mortar and to soften it use the juices from the pan. If this is not enough, add a droplet of broth, and at the end, an egg yolk. Bear in mind that the mixture should come out rather firm.

Now take some wafers, like host wafers, that are not too thin and cut them into little squares like those the pharmacists use when they prepare their doses.

Whisk an egg and the white left from the egg yoke. Then with your fingers pick up one of the wafers, dip in the egg, and place on a bed of bread crumbs. On the wafer place a nut-sized dab of the mixture, dip a second wafer in the egg, bread the side that will show on top, and place it over the first wafer. Coat with bread crumbs one more time if necessary, then set the completed piece to one side. Repeat the process until you run out of ingredients.

Fry in olive oil or lard and serve as an *entremets*. If you use 200 grams (about 7 ounces) of boneless meat, you will get about 20 of these morsels.

177. FRITTO ALLA ROMANA II
(ROMAN-STYLE FRY II)

This fry can be prepared when you happen to have handy the breast of a roasted chicken. For about the same amount as in the preceding recipe, here is what you will need:

50 grams (about 1-2/3 ounces) of chicken breast
40 grams (about 1-1/3 ounces) of salted tongue
30 grams (about 1 ounce) of untrimmed prosciutto
1 tablespoon of grated Parmesan
1 small truffle, or lacking that, a dash of nutmeg

Skin the chicken breast and dice it very finely. Do the same with the salted tongue and the prosciutto. Slice the truffle.

Make a béchamel with 2 deciliters (about 4/5 of a cup) of milk; 30 grams (about 1 ounce) of butter; and 30 grams (about 1 ounce) of flour.

When the sauce is done, add the other ingredients to it, and allow to cool thoroughly before using it with the wafers as described in the preceding recipe.

178. FRITTELLE DI RISO I
(RICE FRITTERS I)

1/2 a liter (about 1/2 a quart) of milk
100 grams (about 3-1/2 ounces) of rice
100 grams (about 3-1/2 ounces) of flour
50 grams (about 1-2/3 ounces) of sultanas
15 grams (about 1/2 an ounce) of pine nuts ground to the size
  of rice
3 egg yolks
1 egg white
a nut-sized pat of butter
2 small teaspoons of sugar
1 tablespoon of rum
a dash of lemon zest
30 grams (about 1 ounce) of brewer's yeast
a pinch of salt

Prepare the brewer's yeast, as described in recipe 182 for *Krapfen*, kneading it with 40 grams (about 4-1/3 ounces) of the flour.

Cook the rice in milk until firm, but put some milk aside, which you will add if needed. To prevent the rice from sticking to the pot, stir often, and then cook keeping the pot on the edge of the hearth.

Remove the rice from the fire and when it is lukewarm add the brewer's yeast, already risen, as well the eggs, the rest of the flour—the remaining 60 grams (about 2 ounces)—then the pine nuts, the rum, and a little more milk if needed. Knead well, add the raisins and put the pot back near the fire so that the mixture can rise in very moderate heat. When it has risen, fry in a skillet one tablespoon at a time. These will make big, light fritters. Sprinkle confectioners' sugar on top when they have cooled off a little, and serve warm.

179. FRITTELLE DI RISO II
(RICE FRITTERS II)

Though simpler than those described in the preceding recipe, these fritters also turn out light and tasty.

Cook 100 grams (about 3-1/2 ounces) of rice for a long time, or better yet, for a very long time in about 1/2 a liter (about 1/2 a quart) of milk. Season for flavor with a nut-sized pat of butter, a little salt, a small teaspoon of sugar and a dash of lemon peel. Once the rice has completely cooled off, add a tablespoon of rum, three egg yolks and 50 grams (about 1-2/3 ounces) of flour. Mix well and let the mixture rest for a few hours. When you are ready to fry, whisk the egg whites as stiff as you can and then fold them slowly into the mixture. Fry in a skillet one tablespoon at a time. As usual, sprinkle confectioners' sugar on top, and serve hot.

180. FRITTELLE DI SEMOLINO
(SEMOLINA FRITTERS)

1/2 a liter (about 1/2 a quart) of milk
130 grams (about 4-1/2 ounces) of semolina
1 tablespoon of rum
a dash of lemon zest
salt as needed
3 eggs

Cook the semolina in milk, and salt when done. Once cooled, add the eggs and the rum. Fry in olive oil or lard. Send to the table sprinkled with confectioners' sugar.

These amounts serve four to five people.

181. FRITTELLE DI TONDONE
(TONDONE FRITTERS)

If you do not know what a tondone is, ask Stenterello,[36] as he eats it often and likes it very much.

250 grams (about 8-4/5 ounces) of flour
6 eggs
3 deciliters (about 1-1/4 cups) of water
a pinch of salt
a dash of lemon zest

Mix the flour with the water poured in a little at a time, and then salt. Put this mix into a skillet and fry it only with some butter, olive oil or lard. When it has firmed up on the bottom, use a dish to flip it over on the other side. Now you have a tondone.[37]

Now pound it in a mortar with the lemon peel, softening with the eggs: two at once, the other four one at a time, first the yoke and then the white which you have beaten until stiff. Keep pounding and kneading the mixture throughout this operation.

To make the fritters, fry the mixture in a skillet one tablespoon at a time. The fritters will puff up hugely until they look like pastry puffs. Then sprinkle with confectioners' sugar.

If you like, you can add 100 grams (about 3-1/2 ounces) of Malaga raisins to this mixture. But then you should first soak the raisins in water for 24 hours and remove the seeds before using them. These amounts should serve six people, or, if you cut the quantities in half, four.

182. KRAPFEN I[38]

Let us try to describe this dish with so German a name, as we go about in search of the good and beautiful no matter where they are found. For our own sake, however, and for Italy's good name, let's not

36 Stenterello is a character in the "commedia dell'arte," known particularly for his cowardice and constant hunger.
37 "Tondone" literally means "large disk."
38 This is a German word denoting a doughnut-shaped fritter, related to the bagel.

imitate other countries blindly, simply in the spirit of foreigner mania.

150 grams (about 5-1/4 ounces) of Hungarian flour
40 grams (about 1-1/3 ounces) of butter
a pat of brewer's yeast the size of a large walnut
1 whole egg
1 egg yolk
1 teaspoon of sugar
a generous pinch of salt

Drop a handful of the flour on a pastry board, make a depression in the middle, and in it dissolve the brewer's yeast with lukewarm milk. Then mix it with the flour to produce a loaf of the right firmness. On this loaf, make a cross-shaped incision, which will later help you recognize if the loaf has risen.

Place this loaf in a small pan or saucepan, the bottom of which you have coated with a little milk. Cover and place near the fire so that the dough can rise in very moderate heat. You will find this will take about 20 minutes. Once the dough has risen, add it to the rest of the flour and mix in the eggs, the melted butter, the sugar and the salt. If this large dough turns out too soft, add flour as needed until you can roll it out satisfactorily with a rolling pin to the thickness of half a finger. You will thus obtain a sheet of dough, from which, using a tin ring, you can cut out many disks of the size indicated here.

OUTER CIRCUMFERENCE

Once you have made 24 such disks, take an egg or other similarly shaped object, and with the tip of it make a depression in the center of each disk. In 12 of these disks, put a teaspoon of a stuffing made with finely diced chicken livers, sweetbreads, prosciutto, salted tongue, and a dash of truffles or of mushrooms, all cooked in brown stock and béchamel.

Moisten the disks around the edges with a finger dipped in water, and then place on top of each disk one of the remaining 12 empty disks. When all disks are thus covered, make an incision on the top of each pair with another tin ring of the size shown here.

INNER
INCISION

Now that you have stuffed the 12 pastries, you must let them rise, but only in moderate heat. You can do so by placing them near the fire or inside a warming oven. When they have puffed up nicely, deep fry them in lard or olive oil. Serve hot as a fried dish or an *entremets*. They are so handsome and delicious that your guests will consider them a product of haute cuisine.

If you want to serve the *Krapfen* as a dessert, you need only stuff them with a rather firm cream or fruit preserve, and sprinkle confectioners' sugar on them when they are done.

For another *Krapfen* recipe, see recipe 562.

183. BOMBE E PASTA SIRINGA
(TUBE PASTRIES AND PASTRY PUFFS)

This recipe, which can be used both for pastry puffs and tube pastries, takes some effort, though the operations it requires are not in themselves difficult.

> *150 grams (about 5-1/4 ounces) of water*
> *100 grams (about 3-1/2 ounces) of Hungarian flour, or very fine*
> *flour*

one walnut-sized pat of butter
a pinch of salt
a dash of lemon zest
2 eggs
1 egg yolk

Put the water on the fire with the butter and salt. When it boils, add the flour all at once and stir vigorously. Keep the dough on the fire until the flour is thoroughly cooked (10 minutes), stirring constantly. Then remove from the pan and spread it out to the thickness of a finger so that it cools thoroughly. Start kneading the dough, first adding an egg yolk, and then, when that has been absorbed, an egg white, beaten stiff. Keep stirring and add another yolk and then, again, another stiffened white. If you are doubling or tripling the amounts given here, repeat this operation as many times as needed.

Due to all the kneading, the mixture should eventually have the consistency of a fine smooth paste, somewhat like an ointment. If you are making pastry puffs, drop the mixture a teaspoon at a time into a skillet. This will give them a ball shape. If you want to make tube pastries, press the dough through a pastry tube with a star-shaped opening at the end, as shown in the picture on this page. Slice into segments of between 9 and 10 centimeters (about 3-1/2 and 4 inches) long. When the puffs have cooled off a little, sprinkle them with confectioners' sugar. Doubling the quantities indicated you should have enough pastries for eight to ten people.

Pastries of this sort can also be served as stuffed fritters. In this case, make a small slit in the puffs once they are done and use it to fill them with a little delicate meat stuffing. But in that case, do not sprinkle sugar on top.

184. BOMBE COMPOSTE
(PASTRY PUFFS WITH CHEESE AND MORTADELLA)

These puffs must have first exploded in Bologna.[39] Their charge of cheese and mortadella inclines me to such belief. In any case, enjoy them, for they do honor to their inventor.

180 grams (about 6-1/3 ounces) of water
120 grams (about 4-1/4 ounces) of flour
30 grams (about 1 ounce) of Gruyère cheese
a walnut-sized pat of butter
30 grams (about 1 ounce) of Bolognese mortadella
3 eggs
a pinch of salt

Put the water on the fire with the butter and salt. When it begins to boil, add the cheese cut into small pieces and the flour all at once, stirring vigorously. Keep the flour on the fire for about 10 minutes, stirring constantly, then allow to cool. Work the dough with a wooden spoon as much as possible over and over again, adding one egg at a time, first the yolk and then the white, beaten stiff. When you are about to fry, toss in the mortadella, diced into rather large cubes about 1 centimeter (about 1/3 of an inch) thick. Should the mixture turn out too firm because of the quality of the flour used or because the eggs are too small, add another egg, and you will have enough pastries to feed six people. When they turn out well, these pastries will puff up and stay hollow inside. But it all depends on the strength and determination of whoever does the mixing.

Serve as a side dish for fried meat or liver, or mixed in with any other fried food.

---

39 Artusi here is punning on the word for pastry puff, "bomba," which also means bomb.

185. BOMBE DI SEMOLINO
(SEMOLINA PUFFS)

*3 deciliters (about 1-1/4 cups)—the equivalent of 300 grams (about
    10-1/2 ounces)—of milk*
130 grams (about 4-1/2 ounces) of fine-grain semolina
a walnut-sized pat of butter
1 teaspoon of sugar
salt, as much as needed
a dash of lemon zest
3 eggs

Put the milk on the fire with the butter and the sugar. When it starts
to boil, add the semolina a little at a time, so that it does not make
lumps. Keep on the fire until the semolina is quite firm, stirring constantly so that it does not stick to the bottom of the pan. Then remove from the fire, salt, and immediately add the first egg. Then, as
you are about to fry, add the other two eggs, one at a time, the
whites beaten stiff, stirring the mixture constantly with a wooden
spoon. When you drop it into the skillet, shape the mixture into
little nuggets that will balloon into the lightest puffs. After they have
cooled a little, sprinkle the puffs with confectioners' sugar. Remember to use a very low flame and to keep shaking the frying pan.

186. CARCIOFI FRITTI (FRIED ARTICHOKES)

This is a very basic fry, but strange as it may seem, not everyone knows
how to make it. In some places, they boil the artichokes before frying
them, which is not a good idea. In others, they first cover them in
batter. Not only is that not necessary, but it takes away their natural
flavor. Here is the method used in Tuscany, which is the best. Tuscany
is the region, where by dint of using and abusing fruits and vegetables
as much as they do, they end up cooking them best.

As an example, take two artichokes, remove the tough outer leaves,
trim off the sharp ends, cut off the stems, and slice in half. Then cut
the artichoke halves into wedges, or to be more precise in slices,

about 8 to 10 of them for each artichoke, even if they are not particularly large. As you cut them up, toss them into cold water. When
they are quite cold, take them out of the water and blot them or just
squeeze dry, then dredge them immediately in flour which will stick
well to them.

Beat the white of one egg until half-stiff, one egg being enough
for two artichokes; then combine the yolk and the white, and salt.
Put the artichokes in a colander to shake off the excess flour. Then
drop them in the egg, stir and allow to sit a while until they absorb
the egg. Place the pieces one at a time in a skillet sizzling with oil.
When they have turned a nice golden color, take them out and send
to the table with lemon wedges because, as everybody knows, lemon
juice, when squeezed on all fried food except sweet things, always
enhances their flavor and goes well with good wine. If you want the
artichokes to remain white, it is best to sauté them in olive oil and
squeeze a half lemon in the water in which you soak them.

187. COTOLETTE DI CARCIOFI
(ARTICHOKE CUTLETS)

Certain ladies complained they could not find this recipe in my book.
Now they are satisfied.

Take two large artichokes, remove the tough leaves and scrape the
stems. Then boil, but not for very long, and while they are steaming
hot, cut each of them into five slices, keeping some of the stem.
Season with salt and pepper.
  Prepare a béchamel as follows:

30 grams (about 1 ounce) of flour
30 grams (about 1 ounce) of butter
20 grams (about 2/3 of an ounce) of grated Parmesan cheese
2 deciliters (about 4/5 of a cup) of milk

When you remove the sauce from the fire, fold in one egg yolk, the
Parmesan cheese and a pinch of salt. Taking them one by one by the
stem, dip the artichokes slices in the béchamel, and then arrange
them on a platter. Use a spoon to cover the slices with the remaining

béchamel. After a few hours, when the artichokes are good and cold, brush them with a beaten egg, coat them in bread crumbs, and fry in olive oil or lard.

188. ZUCCHINI FRITTI I (FRIED ZUCCHINI I)

Just about everyone likes fried zucchini, and they lend themselves wonderfully to embellishing or accompanying other fried foods of every sort.

Take long, slender finger-length zucchini. Wash and cut lengthwise into slices about 1 centimeter (about 1/3 of an inch) thick. Remove part of the core and salt lightly. After an hour or two, drain off the water they have lost, and, without drying them further, roll them in flour. Then put them into a small colander to shake off any excess flour. Drop them right away in a skillet where a generous amount of olive oil or lard is sizzling. At first do not touch them or they may break. Only when they begin to firm up should you stir them with a slotted spoon and remove them from the pan when they start to brown.

They may also be prepared like artichokes in a baking pan, as described in recipe 246. In that case you have to cut them in thick round slices and otherwise you prepare them as if for frying.

189. ZUCCHINI FRITTI II (FRIED ZUCCHINI II)

These zucchini will turn out better and more impressive than the ones in the preceding recipe. Take large, thick zucchini that you cannot grasp in one hand. Peel them to make the dish more handsome. Split lengthwise into two halves and remove that part of the core containing the seeds. Then slice into long thin strips, as wide as a good-sized finger. Sprinkle them with salt so they will throw off their water and leave them for a few hours. When you are ready to fry them, pick them up in both hands and squeeze vigorously to get rid of any remaining water. Then toss in flour, separating the strips with your fingers. Place in a colander to shake off any excess flour, and toss immediately into a skillet with plenty of oil.

190. CIAMBELLINE (LITTLE RINGS)

This dish, too, is difficult to make well if you have not seen it prepared. I will try to describe it, but I cannot guarantee you will understand me. These little cakes were taught to me under the name of *beignets* (French for fritters), but their shape suggests they should be more properly called little rings, and as such I offer them to you.

In a saucepan heat 180 grams (about 6-1/3 ounces) of water, a nut-size butter pat, two teaspoons of sugar and a pinch of salt. When the liquid begins to boil, stir in 120 grams (about 4-1/4 ounces) of flour, adding it all at once so that no clumps form, and stirring immediately with a wooden spoon. Remove from the fire shortly thereafter, and while the mixture is still steaming hot, add an egg, stirring vigorously until totally blended. Then, once the mixture has cooled, add two more eggs at separate intervals, continuing to stir vigorously with a mixing spoon until the dough has a smooth consistency. You will know when you have reached this point by the action of the mixing spoon itself, which leaves behind a thin veil of dough over the bubbles it creates as you stir. Add a dash of vanilla and sprinkle some flour on the pastry board over which you will pour the dough. Knead the dough with your hands (also coated with flour), ensuring that the dough incorporates enough flour to become manageable while remaining quite soft.

Divide the dough into 16 to 18 sections, forming nuggets not much larger than walnuts. Make a hole through the middle of each nugget, by pushing your finger through the dough until it touches the pastry board, and then rotating the nugget upon itself. Then flip the nuggets over and repeat the operation on the other side so that the hole becomes large enough and nicely shaped. In this way your nuggets turn into little rings. Put a wide pot of water on the fire, and when it is quite hot but not boiling, drop in the rings three or four at a time. If they stick to the bottom of the kettle, free them gently with a slotted spoon. Turn them over, and when they start floating to the surface, drain them and place on a kitchen towel. Then, with the point of a knife, make an incision or two in each of them, all the way around, both on the inside and outside, so that they will puff up better.

At this point you can let them sit for a few hours, if you want to.

Fry them over a low flame in plenty of lard or olive oil, constantly shaking the skillet. They turn out well when you see them swell up to an extraordinary size, while remaining dry. While still hot but no longer steaming, sprinkle them with confectioners' sugar and serve. And the undersigned hopes that delicious and shapely as they are, they will be enjoyed by discerning palates and lovely young ladies. So be it.

191. DONZELLINE
(LITTLE DAMSELS)

100 grams (about 3-1/2 ounces) of flour
a nut-size pat of butter
milk, as much as needed

Form a dough that is neither too firm nor too soft, kneading it well with your hands on a pastry board, and spread out into a sheet as thick as a large coin. Cut into small lozenge shapes, fry in lard or olive oil and you will see them puff up. These pastries turn out tender and delicate tasting.

You will then have a batch of little damsels, which should be sprinkled with confectioners' sugar after they have begun to cool.

192. FRITTO DI *CHIFELS* (FRIED *KIPFELS*)[40]

These are trifling fritters, but they may be used instead of bread as a side dish for grilled meat.

2 kipfels
2 deciliters (about 4/5 of a cup) of milk
20 grams (about 2/3 of an ounce) of sugar

Remove the tips from the *kipfels* and cut into little rounds 1 centimeter (about 1/2 an inch) thick. Put the milk on the fire with the sugar, and when the milk starts to boil, pour it over the *kipfels*, drenching them but not excessively. When they have cooled off, dip

40 This is a German word for a small leavened bun, shaped like a crescent moon.

them in two beaten eggs, coat in bread crumbs and fry. For ladies who are easily pleased, *kipfels* may be served as a dessert, provided you add some vanilla and sprinkle them with confectioners' sugar once they are done.

193. AMARETTI FRITTI (FRIED MACAROONS)

Take 20 small macaroons, soak them briefly in rum or cognac, but do not let them become too soft. Dip them in the batter described in recipe 156—the amounts given there should do for our purposes here. Then fry in lard, butter or olive oil. Sprinkle lightly with confectioners' sugar and serve hot.

This is not the kind of desert to send you into raptures and make you ask for more, but it will do in a pinch.

194. CRESCENTE (HALF MOONS)

What a strange language they speak in learned Bologna!

They call carpets rags; wine flasks gourds; sweetbreads milks. They say "sigàre" for "piangere" (to weep), and they call an unsavory, ugly, annoying woman, who would normally be termed a "calia" or a "scamonea" a "sagoma" (Italian for silhouette and, figuratively speaking, a funny person). In their restaurants you find "trefoils" (instead of truffles), Florentine style "chops" (instead of "steaks"), and other similar expressions that would drive anybody mad. It was there that, I think, the term "batteries" was devised to describe harness races, and where "zone" is used to mean a tram route. When I first heard the Bolognese mention a crescent, I thought they were talking about the moon. Instead they were discussing the schiacciata or focaccia, the ordinary fried dough cake that everybody recognizes and all know how to make. The only difference is that the Bolognese, to make theirs more tender and digestible, add a little lard when mixing the flour with cool water and salt.

It seems the schiacciata will puff up better if you drop it in a skillet where the fat is sizzling, but which you have removed from the fire.

The Bolognese are, in any case, an active, industrious, friendly and hospitable people, and one speaks freely with the men, as well as the women, because their candid manner of conversation is quite engaging. If I had to judge in these matters, I would hold that this is the hallmark of a people's general civility and good manners, and not at all like what one encounters in certain other cities whose inhabitants are of an altogether different character.

In one of his tales, Boccaccio, speaking of the Bolognese, exclaims: "Ah, how singularly sweet is the blood of Bologna! How admirably you rise to the occasion in such moments as these (moments of love)! Sighs and tears were never to your liking: entreaties have always moved you, and you were ever susceptible to a lover's yearnings. If only I could find words with which to commend you as you deserve, I should never grow tired of singing your praises!"[41]

195. CRESCIONI (SPINACH FRITTERS)

Why they are called "crescioni" and not spinach fritters, I have no idea. I know that the spinach is cooked as it normally is, that is, without water, then squeezed well and coarsely chopped into a soffritto of olive oil, garlic, parsley, salt and pepper. Then it is seasoned with a little concentrated must[42] and raisins, from which the seeds have been removed. If you do not have any must or raisins, you may substitute sugar and dried grapes. Then the spinach, seasoned in this fashion, is wrapped in the crazy dough described in recipe 153, which has been moistened with a few drops of olive oil, rolled out into a thin sheet and cut into rounds about the size of the one shown on the following page.

---

41 *Decameron* VII, 7, translated by G.H. McWilliam (Penguin, 1972). The parenthesis is Artusi's.
42 "Must" is the juice of grapes before it has fermented to produce wine. Artusi is referring here to concentrated must, i.e., must that is boiled down to between 2/3 and 1/2 of its original volume.

CRESCIONI

These rounds are folded in two, giving them the shape of a half moon. Close the fold tightly and fry in olive oil. Serve as an *entremets*.

196. CROCCHETTE (CROQUETTES)

These can be made with every variety of leftover meat, and are prepared like the meatballs described in recipe 314, but without the raisins and pine nuts. If you like, however, you may add a little garlic combined with a few parsley leaves. These croquettes are better when given the shape of spools, and are only eaten fried, as a rule.

197. CROCCHETTE D'ANIMELLE
(SWEETBREAD CROQUETTES)

Take 150 grams (about 5-1/4 ounces) of sweetbreads, cook in brown
stock or in a soffritto of onion and butter. Season with salt, pepper,
and a dash of nutmeg. Then dice the sweetbreads and mix in two
tablespoons of rather firm béchamel, adding an egg yolk and a good
pinch of grated Parmesan cheese. Scoop up the mixture one small
spoonful at a time, roll each scoop in bread crumbs, giving it the
oblong shape of a spool. Then dip in a whisked egg, roll a second
time in bread crumbs and fry. You can make them even more delicious if you add untrimmed prosciutto and diced salted tongue to
the mixture, and if you use a few shavings of truffle instead of nutmeg.

With this amount of sweetbreads you will make 10 or 12 croquettes, which you can combine with some other fritters for a dish
of mixed fry.

198. CROCCHETTE DI RISO SEMPLICI
(BASIC RICE CROQUETTES)

1/2 a liter (about 1/2 a quart) of milk
100 grams (about 3-1/2 ounces) of rice
20 grams (about 2/3 of an ounce) of butter
20 grams (about 2/3 of an ounce) of grated Parmesan cheese
2 eggs

Cook the rice in milk until quite firm. When half cooked, add butter
and salt. Remove from the heat, add the Parmesan cheese, and while
the rice is still steaming hot break in an egg, stirring at once to incorporate it in the mixture. When it has cooled off completely, take the
rice out in tablespoons and roll each piece in bread crumbs, giving
them a cylindrical shape. With these amounts you will make 12 croquettes. Whisk the remaining egg, dip each croquette in it, roll them
once more in the bread crumbs, and fry.

They may be served alone, but are best when accompanied by
some other fried food.

199. CROCCHETTE DI RISO COMPOSTE
(RICE CROQUETTES WITH GIBLETS)

Follow the preceding recipe and combine the rice, which you have cooked in the right amount, with chicken giblets prepared in butter and brown stock, or failing that, in a soffritto of onion.

The giblets, once cooked, should be cut into chickpea-size pieces.

200. CROCCHETTE DI PATATE
(POTATO CROQUETTES)

300 grams (about 10-1/2 ounces) of potatoes
30 grams (about 1 ounce) of butter
20 grams (about 2/3 of an ounce) of grated Parmesan cheese
2 egg yolks
2 tablespoons of sugar
a dash of nutmeg

Peel the potatoes, and if they are large, slice them into quarters. Boil in salted water. Then, when the potatoes are cooked and still very hot, drain and purée, passing them through a sieve. Add butter, melted if it is winter, and then the rest of the ingredients, stirring all the while.

Allow the mixture to cool and then make the croquettes by dividing it into 10 or 12 portions which you will place over a thin layer of flour and mold in the shape of a spool. Beat an egg and dip each croquette individually in it. Roll in bread crumbs and sauté in olive oil or lard. Serve as a side dish for fried meats or a roast.

201. PALLOTTOLE DI PATATE RIPIENE
(STUFFED POTATO NUGGETS)

300 grams (about 10-1/2 ounces) of potatoes
2 heaping tablespoons of grated Parmesan cheese
2 eggs
a dash of nutmeg
flour, as much as needed

Boil the potatoes, peel and while they're still hot, pass them through a sieve onto a thin layer of flour. Make a hole in the mound of puréed potatoes, salt, and add the nutmeg, the eggs and the Parmesan cheese. Then, using as little flour as possible, make a long soft loaf, which you will divide into 18 sections. With your fingers coated in flour make a small hole in each croquette which you will then fill with meat stuffing. Pull up the sides of the croquette and join them tightly. Then, with your hands still covered in flour, remold each piece into a round ball that you will fry in lard or olive oil. Send to the table as a side dish for fried meat.

This is an impressive dish, tasty and inexpensive, since the stuffing can be made with the giblets from a single hen, if you happen to have one, as long as you use the crest, the gizzard boiled beforehand, and the unlaid eggs, which you should sauté in butter with a little finely chopped onion, later adding a slice of untrimmed prosciutto cut into tiny cubes. All the other ingredients should be finely minced.

If you do not have a hen, prepare the stuffing in some other way.

202. PERINE DI RISO (LITTLE RICE "PEARS")

100 grams (about 3-1/2 ounces) of rice
1/2 a liter (about 1/2 a quart) of milk
a little more than a walnut-size pat of butter
a generous pinch of grated Parmesan cheese
1 egg

Cook the rice in milk with the butter, keeping it firm. When done, salt and wait until cooled, then add the egg and the Parmesan cheese. Cook two chicken livers and the sweetbreads of two lambs, thus making a tasty little stew, adding a dash of nutmeg. Cut into chunks smaller than a hazelnut, and combine them with small pieces of prosciutto, truffles or mushrooms, which add a delightful flavor.

To give this rice stuffing the appearance of little pears, have a small tin funnel made, the shape and size of which I would draw if I could. But as I cannot, you shall have to content yourselves with the circle pictured here, which represents the funnel's mouth.

MOUTH OF THE
SMALL FUNNEL

This is the top section of the funnel, while the spout is a small hollow tube about 2 centimeters (about 3/4 of an inch) long. Grease the funnel with melted butter and coat it with fine bread crumbs. Then fill it half full with the rice, add two or three pieces of the stew, and finish filling the funnel with more rice. To release the little pear you have made, blow on the hollow tube at the other end of the funnel. Repeat this operation until you run out of rice. Of course, before frying these little pears, you need to dip them in egg and roll them in bread crumbs.

203. FRITTO DI STECCHINI
(FRY WITH TOOTHPICKS)

2 large chicken livers
40 grams (about 1-1/3 ounces) of salted tongue
40 grams (about 1-1/3 ounces) of Gruyère cheese

Cook the chicken livers in butter, seasoning with salt and pepper. When done, cut into 12 small pieces and do the same with the Gruyère and the tongue. Take 12 toothpicks and skewer all the aforementioned 36 pieces, three per toothpick, in this order: first a piece of tongue, then the Gruyère, and finally the chicken liver, leaving a little space between each piece and the next. Then, using the béchamel described in recipe 220, coat the three pieces on each toothpick so that they are well covered. Dip in beaten egg, roll in bread crumbs and fry.

If you like, you may add to these ingredients little pieces of sweetbread cooked in the same way as the chicken livers, and tiny chunks of raw truffle.

204. AGNELLO IN FRITTATA (LAMB OMELETTE)

Chop up a loin of lamb, which is the best cut to use for this dish, and sauté in virgin lard. A little lard will do, because this cut of meat is rather fatty. When half cooked, season with salt and pepper, and then, when completely done, add four or five beaten eggs also lightly seasoned with salt and pepper. Mix well, making sure the eggs do not become too firm.

205. POLLO DORATO I
(GOLDEN CHICKEN I)

Take a young cockerel, gut it, remove the head and the feet, wash well, and place in boiling water for one minute. Then cut it into pieces along the joints, coat the pieces in flour, season with salt and pepper and pour two beaten eggs over them. After letting them soak for at least half an hour, roll the pieces in bread crumbs. Repeat this procedure two more times if necessary. Prepare over hot coals as follows: take a tin-lined copper skillet and pour in it some olive oil or better still, put in some virgin lard; when the fat starts to sizzle, add the chicken pieces, making sure they brown well on both sides over moderate heat, so that they are cooked through and through. Serve very hot with lemon slices. Turkey wings, the most delicate part of this bird when boiled, may also be used instead of chicken for this dish. They should be cut into little pieces and prepared in the same manner.

The tip of the breast and the feet of chickens, and this holds true also for turkeys, give you some indication of the tenderness of the bird's meat since as these birds age, the breast tip hardens and will not yield as you press it with your fingers, while the feet turn from black to yellowish.

206. POLLO DORATO II
(GOLDEN CHICKEN II)

After you have cleaned the bird as described in the preceding recipe, cut it up into smaller pieces, coat with flour and soak in two beaten eggs, salting liberally. Fry in a skillet, season it again with a little salt and pepper, and serve with lemon wedges.

207. PETTI DI POLLO ALLA SCARLATTA
(CHICKEN BREASTS WITH SALTED TONGUE)

From the breast of a capon or large pullet, you should be able to carve 6 thin slices which will feed four to five people. Cook in butter and season with salt and pepper.

Prepare a béchamel with 20 grams (about 2/3 of an ounce) of butter; 40 grams (about 1-1/3 ounces) of flour; and 2 deciliters (about 4/5 of a cup) of milk.

When this sauce is done, add 50 grams (about 1-2/3 ounces) of salted tongue which you have finely minced with a mezzaluna. When cooled, spread this sauce thickly all over the chicken slices, completely covering each piece. Then dip in one whisked egg, roll in bread crumbs and sauté in butter or lard. Serve with lemon wedges.

208. POLLO ALLA CACCIATORA
(CHICKEN HUNTER'S STYLE)

Slice a large onion and soak it in cold water for more than half an hour. Then dry it and place in skillet with olive oil or lard. When the onion has turned soft and translucent, remove it from the pan and put to one side. Cut up a pullet or cockerel, sauté the pieces in the grease left in the pan, and when browned, add the onion, seasoning with salt and pepper, and sprinkling half a glass of Sangiovese or other fine red wine over it. Also add some tomato sauce (recipe 6). After cooking it for five more minutes, serve.

I warn you—this is no dish for weak stomachs.

209. POLLO FRITTO COI POMODORI
(FRIED CHICKEN WITH TOMATOES)

For frying, people normally use the best quality fat their native land produces. In Tuscany, olive oil is preferred; in Lombardy, butter; in Emilia, they make the best lard—that is, it is very white, firm and possesses a delicate, comforting aroma of bay leaves. This explains why in this region an incredible number of young poultry is slaughtered to be fried in lard with tomatoes.

For meat fry in general, I prefer lard because I find it more delicate and flavorful than olive oil.

The chicken is cut into small pieces, which are then placed in a skillet in a generous amount of lard and seasoned with salt and pepper but without adding any other spice. When done, drain off the excess fat and add the tomatoes which you have chopped in small chunks after removing the seeds. Stir constantly until the tomatoes are almost completely dissolved, then send to the table.

210. FEGATO COL VINO BIANCO
(LIVER IN WHITE WINE)

As a flavoring, wine is not among my favorites, unless we are talking about bottled wine or about dishes in which it is needed to give them their special character. But, as tastes vary, what displeases one persons is sure to delight another, so here is a dish made with wine.

Cut the liver into thin slices and sauté it in a skillet with olive oil and butter, without any additional spices. In a small pot whisk a teaspoon of flour along with fine dry white wine to form a very runny sauce. When the liver is two-thirds done, add the sauce. Finish cooking and season with salt and pepper.

2 1 1 . FEGATO ALLA CACCIATORA
(LIVER HUNTER'S STYLE)

If the liver weighs about 300 grams (about 10-1/2 ounces), slice three large onions, soaking them in cold water for one or two hours. Then, drain the water and toss the onions in a skillet to dry them out. Once dry, add lard and sauté. When the onion begins to brown, add the liver, which should be cut into thin slices. Let it cook for a while, along with the onion. Pour in just under half a glass of good red wine. Keep stirring and after five minutes have elapsed, season with salt and pepper and serve. This is not a dish for delicate stomachs.

2 1 2 . CASTAGNOLE I (LITTLE CHESTNUTS I)

This dish, peculiar to Romagna and a feature of the carnival season, is not, in all honesty, terribly refined, but can be a pleasant treat all the same.

On a pastry board prepare a firm dough with flour, two eggs, a teaspoon of "fumetto,"[43] a dash of lemon peel and salt as needed. Knead long and vigorously with your hands as if you were making ordinary bread, adding a tablespoon of fine olive oil a little at a time until it is completely absorbed. Finally roll out the dough into little cylinders, which you will then cut into nut size pieces. Toss them immediately in a skillet, which you will keep shaking over a low flame. Once they are done, sprinkle the "little chestnuts" (which they resemble) with confectioners' sugar and serve cold, since they taste better that way.

I warn you that, if you use cognac or brandy instead of fumetto, you will not get the same result, and the pastries will not puff up sufficiently.

---

43 A traditional drink of the Romagna region, composed of half anisette and half rosolio, "fumetto" (little cloud) is so called because when poured in water it makes a little cloud.

213. CASTAGNOLE II (LITTLE CHESTNUTS II)

Here is a second recipe for castagnole. Try both and use the one you prefer.

2 eggs
2 tablespoons of water
2 tablespoons of fumetto[44]
20 grams (about 2/3 of an ounce) of butter
20 grams (about 2/3 of an ounce) of sugar
a pinch of salt

Break the eggs and drop the yolks in a bowl, adding the sugar, the fumetto, the water and the salt. Mix well. Beat the whites until stiff. On a pastry board, fold all these ingredients and the butter into enough flour to make a dough that you can knead with your hands. Work the dough hard until it becomes nice and smooth. Then make nuggets the size of a small walnut and fry them, as in the previous recipe, over a low flame and in plenty of fat.

214. CREMA FRITTA I (FRIED CUSTARD I)

100 grams (about 3-1/2 ounces) of starch
30 grams (about 1 ounce) of sugar
20 grams (about 2/3 of an ounce) of butter
4 deciliters (about 1-1/3 cups) of milk
2 whole eggs
a dash of lemon zest
a pinch of salt

Beat the eggs with the sugar, then add the starch (reduced to a powder), the grated lemon peel, the butter, and the milk, which you will pour in a little at a time. Put the mixture on the fire, stirring constantly as you would when preparing an ordinary cream. When the mixture has thickened and will not grow any more, add a pinch of salt and pour on a platter or a board, spreading it to the thickness of a finger.

After it has cooled completely, cut into lozenge shapes, brush with egg and coat in bread crumbs. Fry in lard or olive oil and serve hot as a side dish for another fried course.

44 See note to preceding recipe.

215. CREMA FRITTA II (FRIED CUSTARD II)

100 grams (about 3-1/2 ounces) of flour
20 grams (about 20 grams) of sugar
2 whole eggs
5 deciliters (about 2 cups) of milk
a dash of vanilla or lemon zest

Cook by keeping on the fire until the flour no longer tastes raw. As for the rest, follow the preceding recipe. With half the quantities and mixed with another fry, this will serve four to five people.

216. TESTICCIUOLA D'AGNELLO FRITTA (FRIED LAMB'S HEAD)

If one does not wish to eat lamb's head boiled, I only know two other ways of preparing it: fried or stewed (see recipe 321). For frying, either alone or with brains, see the batter for fried meats in recipe 157.

217. CORATELLA D'AGNELLO ALLA BOLOGNESE (LAMB'S LIVER AND OFFAL[45] BOLOGNESE STYLE)

Cut the liver into little slices and the offal into small pieces, and put in a skillet with lard without spicing them. When the offal is almost done, drain off all the fat and add a small pat of butter. Continue frying, and after a short while pour in tomato sauce (recipe 6) or tomato paste dissolved in water or broth. Season with salt and pepper, then serve in its sauce, and you can be sure it will win praise.

218. FRITTO D'AGNELLO ALLA BOLOGNESE (FRIED LAMB BOLOGNESE STYLE)

The best part of the lamb for frying is the loin. But you may also use

---

45 *Coratella* is specifically the heart, lungs, and spleen of a small animal.

the shoulder and the neck. Cut into pieces and fry, following the previous recipe.

219. CONIGLIO FRITTO
(FRIED RABBIT)

The distaste many Italians have for rabbit (*Lepus cuniculus*) does not seem to me justified. Its flesh is light and not very flavorful, which can be remedied by adding spices. And it is quite satisfactory in every other respect, and its odor is not at all unpleasant. In fact it is wholesome and easy to digest, unlike lamb. It also comes in handy for those who cannot afford beef and are forced to make do with vegetables and legumes. The best way to cook rabbit is by frying it, following recipe 217.

Stewed rabbit also makes a first-rate broth, they say.

The domestication of the rabbit goes back a long way. Confucius, 500 years before the Christian era, already spoke of these animals as worthy of being sacrificed to the gods and discussed their reproductive powers.

220. *COTOLETTE*[46] IMBOTTITE
(STUFFED CUTLETS)

Take some milk-fed veal cutlets or chicken or turkey breasts, cut into thin slices, or, if you wish to give them an elegant appearance, grind the meat and then mold it as you wish by pressing it together with your hands. If you are using veal, 170 grams (about 6 ounces) of lean boneless meat will be enough to make 6 or 7 cutlets. Sauté, plain as they are, in butter, then salt and set aside.

Prepare a béchamel with 70 grams (about 2-1/3 ounces) of flour, 20 grams (about 2/3 of an ounce) of butter and 2 deciliters (about 4/5 of a cup) of milk. As soon you remove the béchamel from the fire, salt it, add a tablespoon of Parmesan cheese and one egg yolk, stirring well. When the sauce has cooled, spread it thickly over the

---

46 Artusi's wry (though inconsistent) italicization of the word cutlet, here and elsewhere in the text, is intended to underscore the word's French derivation (*côtelette*).

cutlets on both sides, smoothing it evenly with a table knife dipped in olive oil. Then dip the cutlets in beaten egg, roll in bread crumbs and sauté in olive oil or lard until golden brown.

Serve with lemon wedges.

221. BRACIOLINE DI VITELLA DI LATTE ALL'UCCELLETTO (MILK-FED VEAL CUTLETS "LITTLE BIRD" STYLE)[47]

Take a lean cut of milk-fed calf meat, slice into small thin chops, and pound with the blunt edge of a knife. Put a saucepan or a copper skillet on the fire with an equal amount of olive oil and butter and a few whole sage leaves. As soon as the sage has fried for a little, add the chops. Season with salt and pepper. Cook them over a lively flame for five or six minutes, then squeeze lemon juice over them and send to the table.

This dish should be served as a lunch course.

222. SALTIMBOCCA ALLA ROMANA (VEAL CUTLETS ROMAN STYLE)

I have eaten saltimbocca in Rome at the trattoria "Le Venete," and therefore I can describe it with precision.

Saltimbocca consists of small cutlets of milk-fed veal, lightly seasoned with salt and pepper. Over each piece you lay half a leaf of sage (a whole leaf would be too much), and over the sage, a thin slice of untrimmed prosciutto. To hold the three ingredients together, you skewer them with a toothpick. Then you cook the saltimbocca in butter in a skillet. Do not let the side with the prosciutto fry for too long, lest the prosciutto become tough. As you see, this is a simple and healthy dish.

From 300 grams (about 10-1/5 ounces) of lean veal you will get 11 to 12 pieces, which will feed three to four people.

---

47 So called (all'uccelletto) because of the sage, often used to season dishes of small wild birds.

These cutlets should be half a finger thick. Before cooking, rinse
them in water and flatten them out.

You may serve them with any kind of side dish.

223. BOCCONI DI PANE RIPIENI
(STUFFED BREAD MORSELS)

If I were writing in French and adhering to that tongue's pompous
style, I would call this dish *bouchées de dames*, which would no doubt
win it more praise than this modest name.

Take one or two chicken livers, some sweetbreads, and, if available,
a chicken or turkey gizzard, which always helps. The latter, however, are tough and should therefore be blanched first, and the gristle
removed. Mince everything with a mezzaluna, put on the fire in
butter with some minced onion and prosciutto, seasoning with salt
and pepper, a dash of nutmeg or of spices. When the mixture starts
to sizzle, add a scant teaspoon of flour and stir until it is fully absorbed, then cover with brown stock or broth. Bring to a boil, then
add a beaten egg, a little at a time, and, stirring constantly, allow the
mixture to thicken. Remove from the fire, add a pinch of grated
Parmesan cheese and pour on a plate.

Now take a loaf of stale bread, cut into slices 1 centimeter (about
1/2 an inch) thick, remove the crust, and chop into small cubes as
wide as a medium-sized coin. Spread the mixture thickly over these
cubes on one side only; a half hour before frying, coat this same side
with flour and arrange the little cubes over a platter. Pour a beaten
egg over them generously, so that the bread is soaked and the stuffing is well coated and nicely golden. Put into a skillet, with the stuffing side down.

I ought to tell you that this dish will make a very nice impression. With the giblets of one chicken, and the sweetbreads of two or
three lambs, you will make about 20 morsels, which will handsomely
accompany a fry of brains or something similar. You may also leave
out the sweetbreads; a hint of truffles, if available, can only improve
this dish.

224. FRITTO ALLA GARISENDA[48]
(GARISENDA FRY)

You ladies who take pleasure in fine cuisine, do not consign this dish to oblivion, for it will delight your husbands, and due to the ingredients it contains, may well move them to reward you.[49]

Take some stale bread, not too spongy, remove the crust and cut into diamond shapes or squares about 4 centimeters (about 1-1/2 inches) on each side. On each piece place a slice of untrimmed prosciutto, then little shavings of truffle, and over them a slice of Gruyère cheese. Cover the filling with a second slice of bread and press tightly together so that they remain joined. Remember to slice everything very fine so that the pieces do not turn out inelegantly large.

Now that you have prepared the morsels, lightly soak them in cold milk, and when that has been absorbed, dip each piece in beaten egg and then roll in bread crumbs. Repeat the procedure twice so that even the edges remain covered and tightly closed.

Fry in lard or olive and serve alone or with another fried food.

225. FRITTO DI CERVELLO, ANIMELLE, SCHIENALI, TESTICCIUOLA, ECC. (FRIED BRAIN, SWEETBREADS, BONE MARROW, HEAD, ETC.)

For these fried meats, see the batter in recipe 157.

48 Name of a famous tower in Bologna.
49 An allusion to the supposed aphrodisiacal powers of truffles.

BOILED MEATS

226. POLLO LESSO
(BOILED CHICKEN)

Boiled poultry, particularly capons and fattened pullets, will turn out whiter and more elegant, without detriment to the broth, if you boil them wrapped in cheesecloth.

For different ways to serve boiled meats, see recipes 355, 356, and 357.

ENTREMETS

Entremets are what the French call in-between courses. They are minor dishes served between main courses.

227. CRESENTINE (GARLIC BREAD)

If garlic is a vermifuge, as it is generally considered to be, this is a simple and appetizing food for babies. Toast slices of bread on both sides and while they are still hot rub them thoroughly with a garlic clove. Then season with salt, olive oil, vinegar and sugar.

228. DONZELLINE RIPIENE DI ACCIUGHE SALATE (LITTLE DAMSELS STUFFED WITH SALTED ANCHOVIES)[50]

220 grams (about 7-3/4 ounces) of flour
30 grams (about 1 ounce) of butter
milk, as needed
a pinch of salt
4 salted anchovies

Mix the flour with the butter, milk and salt until you have a doughy loaf of just the right consistency. Knead vigorously and thoroughly, so that the dough will puff up in the skillet.

Allow to rest for a short while, then slice in half and spread each half out somewhat.

50 See recipe 191.

Clean the anchovies, divide in half lengthwise, remove the spines and cut into small square pieces. Arrange these pieces on one of the dough halves, then cover with the other half. Close them tightly together. Thus joined, roll out the dough with a rolling pin into a thin sheet. Then cut into lozenge shapes and fry in olive oil. These quantities will feed six people. This dish may be served as an appetizer at lunch or as a side dish for fried fish.

229. DONZELLINE AROMATICHE
(LITTLE DAMSELS WITH HERBS)

180 grams (about 6-1/3 ounces) of flour, more or less
2 tablespoons of olive oil
2 tablespoons of white wine or Marsala
5 or 6 sage leaves
1 egg
salt, to taste

Finely chop the sage with a mezzaluna. Then mix the flour with the other ingredients, kneading well and making sure the resulting dough remains rather soft. Spread out with a rolling pin to the thickness of a large coin, sprinkling flour on top if necessary. Cut into lozenge shapes and fry in olive oil or lard. I have heard that some people eat these with figs and prosciutto.

These amounts should be enough to serve four people.

230. GNOCCHI DI SEMOLINO
(SEMOLINA DUMPLINGS)

4 deciliters (about 1-2/3 cups) of milk
120 grams (about 4-1/4 ounces) of semolina flour
50 grams (about 1-2/3 ounces) of butter
40 grams (1-1/3 ounces) of grated Parmesan cheese
2 eggs
salt, to taste

Cook the semolina in the milk and when you are about to take it off the fire, salt it and add half the butter and half the Parmesan cheese.

Then, while it is still hot, add the eggs and stir. Then pour out onto a pastry board or on a platter and spread to the thickness of one and a half fingers. Allow to cool and then cut into lozenge shapes.

Now you have the gnocchi, which you will place one on top of another in layers to make a lovely mound inside an appropriately sized serving tray. Intermingle the layers with the rest of the butter, cut into tiny pats, and sprinkle with grated Parmesan cheese, except for the last layer on top. Finally, brown in a Dutch oven and serve hot either alone or as a side dish for stews or other meat dishes.

231. GNOCCHI ALLA ROMANA (ROMAN-STYLE DUMPLINGS)

These gnocchi, for which I have modified the amounts as follows, I hope will please you as much as they have delighted those for whom I have prepared them. Should that happen, toast to my health if I am still alive or say a *requiescat* in my name, if I have gone on to feed the cabbages.

150 grams (about 5-1/4 ounces) of flour
50 grams (about 1-2/3 ounces) of butter
40 grams (about 1-1/3 ounces) of Gruyère cheese
20 grams (about 2/3 of an ounce) of grated Parmesan cheese
1/2 a liter (about 1/2 a quart) of milk
2 eggs

It is commonly said that one should not sit down to table in lesser number than the Graces or in greater number than the Muses. If you are approaching the number of the Muses, double the amounts.

In a saucepan, mix the flour and the eggs, then pour the milk in a little at a time. Add the Gruyère cheese chopped into little pieces, and put the mixture on the fire, stirring constantly. When the flour makes it thicken, salt and add half the butter. Allow to cool, and then, in the same way as you would prepare cornmeal gnocchi, place the mixture in little tidbits onto an ovenproof platter. Season them with the rest of the butter, cut into little pats, and with the Parmesan cheese, but do not cover the top layer, because Parmesan on top turns bitter when heated. Brown under an iron lid or in a Dutch oven, and serve hot.

232. POLENTA DI FARINA GIALLA COLLE SALSICCE (YELLOW CORNMEAL POLENTA WITH SAUSAGES)

Prepare a rather soft polenta using cornmeal. On a pastry board, spread it out to a thickness of one finger, and cut into lozenge shapes.

In a pan, place several whole sausages with a little water. When done, peel, crumble up and add tomato sauce (recipe 6) or tomato paste.

Arrange the polenta in layers on a baking pan or ovenproof platter, season each layer with grated Parmesan cheese, the sausages and a few small pats of butter here and there, then put in the oven with embers all around. Serve very hot, most suitably as the first course of a hot lunch. You can also make this dish with a very firm polenta, which you would then cut into slices.

233. PASTICCIO DI POLENTA[51] (POLENTA CASSEROLE)

Prepare a firm polenta of cornmeal cooked in milk. Salt as you are about to remove it from the fire and pour out on a pastry board, leveling it to the thickness of about two fingers. Once cooled, cut into lozenge shapes 1/2 a centimeter wide (about 1/5 of an inch), which you will arrange as follows in a preheated metal or porcelain baking dish. Prepare a sauce like that for macaroni Bolognese style in recipe 87, and prepare a little béchamel as in recipe 137. Sprinkle grated Parmesan cheese on the bottom of the platter and spread a layer of polenta on top of the cheese. Add more Parmesan, some sauce and béchamel; place a second layer of polenta on top of the first and season as before; repeat the operation until you run out of ingredients. It is not a bad idea to add small pats of butter here and

---

51 A "pasticcio" is a sort of baked savory pie usually containing vegetables and/or meat, bound with béchamel or eggs.

there. However, do not put too much if you do not want the dish to turn out too heavy from too many condiments.

Once you have prepared the platter as I have described, put it in a Dutch oven until the polenta browns and serve hot as an *entremets* for a full-course autumn or winter meal. Provided it turns out well, this dish will be praised for its delicate flavor.

During the hunting season, a skillful chef may cook it in a mold, stuffing it with stewed birds.

234. MACCHERONI COLLA BALSAMELLA
(MACARONI IN BÉCHAMEL SAUCE)

Take long Neapolitan-style macaroni and cook in salted water until two-thirds done. Drain, and put back on the fire with a small pat of butter. When that has been absorbed, add enough milk to allow the macaroni to finish cooking over moderate heat. Meanwhile prepare a béchamel as in recipe 137, and when it is has began to cool, bind it with an egg yolk and pour it over the macaroni together with a proportionate amount of grated Parmesan cheese. Macaroni prepared in this way is an excellent side dish for a meat stew or a *fricandeau* of milk-fed veal. In this case, take an ovenproof platter, place a tin mold in the center and arrange the macaroni all around it. Put the platter in a Dutch oven or under an iron hood heated from above. When the macaroni is lightly browned, take it off the fire and remove the tin mold, in whose place you will put the meat before serving. You may also send them to the table on a separate dish, but also lightly browned on top to add to their handsome appearance. Make sure that the macaroni remains moist.

235. MACCHERONI COL PANGRATTATO
(MACARONI WITH BREAD CRUMBS)

If it is true, as Alexandre Dumas *père* remarks, that the English live on roast beef and pudding; the Dutch on oven-cooked meat, potatoes and cheese; the Germans on sauerkraut and bacon; the Spanish on chickpeas, chocolate and rancid bacon; and the Italians on macaroni, do not be too surprised if I keep coming back to this topic, since I have, after all, always loved this pasta. Indeed, I once very nearly acquired the distinguished name of Macaroni-Eater, and I will tell you why.

One day in 1850, I found myself in the "Tre Re" (Three Kings) restaurant in Bologna in the company of several students and Felice Orsini,[52] who was a friend of one of them. It was the season for politics and conspiracy in Romagna, and Orsini, who seemed practically born for that purpose, spoke enthusiastically about these subjects. In his passion he tirelessly strove to show us that an uprising was imminent, that he and another leader he mentioned would lead it, overrunning Bologna with an armed band of followers. Listening to him so imprudently discuss in a public place such dangerous subjects and an enterprise that seemed to me utter madness, I remained indifferent to his harangues and calmly continued to eat the plate of macaroni set before me. My demeanor stung Orsini's *amour propre*, and thereafter, having felt humiliated at the time, whenever he remembered me he would ask his friends, "How's the Macaroni-Eater doing?"

In my mind's eye I still see that congenial young man, of middling height, lean build, pale round face, refined features, the blackest eyes, crinkly locks, who lisped slightly when he spoke. Another time, many years later, I ran into him in a coffeehouse at Medola just as he was bristling with anger against someone who had abused his trust and offended his honor. He was asking a young fellow to follow him to Florence, to help him, he said, execute an exemplary vendetta. A series of circumstances and events, each stranger than the last, later led him to his tragic end, which we all know and deplore, but which also perhaps prodded Napoleon III to intervene in Italy.[53] Now let's get back to our subject.

300 grams (about 10-1/2 ounces) of long macaroni that hold up
  well when cooked
15 grams (about 1/2 an ounce) of flour

---

52 Artusi was a student of letters; Orsini of jurisprudence. The latter was a famous Romagnol patriot and freedom advocate. Orsini was one of the Italian patriots responsible for the attempt on Napoleon III's life on January 14, 1858. Captured, he was the protagonist of a famous trial, at the end of which he received the death sentence and was executed.

53 Artusi is referring to Napoleon III's involvement in Italy's Second War of Independence (1859), successfully fought by Piedmont with the support of the French against the Austro-Hungarian Empire.

60 grams (about 2 ounces) of butter
60 grams (about 2 ounces) of Gruyère cheese
40 grams (about 1-1/3 ounces) of Parmesan cheese
6 deciliters (about 2-1/2 cups) of milk
bread crumbs, as needed

If you want to add more flavor, increase the amounts of the condiments.

Cook the macaroni halfway, salt, and drain in a colander. Put the flour on the fire in a saucepan with half the butter, stirring constantly. When the flour begins to change color, pour in the milk a little at a time and allow to boil for about 10 minutes. To this béchamel, add the macaroni and the Gruyère cheese, either grated or in little chunks. Move the saucepan to the edge of the hearth, so that the macaroni will absorb all the milk while bubbling slowly. Now add the rest of the butter and the grated Parmesan cheese. Then transfer to an ovenproof platter, fill the platter to the rim and cover with bread crumbs.

Put the macaroni prepared in this fashion into a Dutch oven or under an iron hood heated from above. When browned, serve hot as an *entremets*, or preferably, as a side dish for meat.

236. COSTOLETTE D'AGNELLO VESTITE (DRESSED LAMB CHOPS)

Take high-quality lamb cutlets, strip the bone to expose it, pound, smooth out, and sauté in a skillet with a little butter but without any other spices. Season while hot with salt and pepper, and put to one side.

Prepare a rather firm béchamel, add to it prosciutto and salted tongue cut into very tiny cubes, a pinch of grated Parmesan cheese, a dash of nutmeg, one sliced truffle or minced dried mushrooms reconstituted in water. Put this mixture also to one side until well cooled.

Make enough puff pastry dough (see recipe 154) to wrap the cutlets one by one, allowing the bone to show, but first generously coat both sides of the cutlets with the mixture. Once the cutlets are wrapped, brush the dough with egg yolk, and place each piece upright around the edge of a baking pan. Cook in a Dutch oven and serve hot. They will be praised by all and held to be a dish of fine cuisine.

You may cut the puff pastry using a paper pattern, so that the envelopes will turn out more even. For a tidier and more elegant look, decorate the tips of the bone in each cutlet with purled white paper before sending the dish to the table.

237. COTOLETTE NELLA CARTA
(VEAL CHOPS IN PAPER)

These cutlets, which the French call *côtelettes en papillote*, may be prepared in the following manner, as it is the simplest and therefore not to be scoffed at. Take cutlets of milk-fed veal, strip the bone of meat to better expose it, sauté in butter, and season with salt and pepper. Prepare a sufficient quantity of finely minced untrimmed prosciutto and parsley, adding butter and soft bread crumbs to bind the mixture. Generously coat the cutlets on both sides with this mixture and embellish them with shavings of raw truffle.

Take some rather thick paper and cut out a pattern to follow the curve of the cutlets, grease the paper with butter or olive oil on both sides and wrap the cutlets tightly in it, allowing the bone to show. Now place on a grill over a light flame, making sure the paper does not catch fire, then serve. For greater tidiness and elegance, wrap the tip of each cutlet in purled white paper. You can also make this dish with lamb chops, provided they are large enough.

238. SALAMI DAL SUGO DI FERRARA
(FRESH FERRARA SAUSAGES)

Ferrara sausages are a specialty of that region. They are shaped like "bondiola"[54] sausages and weigh about 500 grams (about 1 pound). They are very spicy and flavorful. Unlike other cured meats of this genre, they improve with age, and ordinarily they are eaten when they have matured. When you are ready to use them, wash them a

---

54 "Bondiole" are a linked variety of boiling sausage nearly spherical in shape. Ground pork is stuffed into turkey bladders, which are then tied together.

number of times in lukewarm water to get rid of the greasy film that covers them. Put on the fire in a generous amount of cool water and allow to simmer slowly for no more than one and a half hours, wrapped tightly in a cheesecloth so that the skin does not break. Serve hot with a side dish, as you would with cotechino. Sometimes, however, there is no sign of the sauce they are famous for, or if there is some, it is very little.

239. PAGNOTTELLE RIPIENE (STUFFED ROLLS)

In large cities, a good cook is, to use a poor simile, like an army general with many well-armed legions at his disposal in a vast well-fortified battlefield, where he can demonstrate the full extent of his military prowess. Furthermore, large cities are graced not only by all of God's bounty but also by people who make it their business to provide all sorts of little trifles, which even though unimportant in themselves, nonetheless contribute significantly to the variety, elegance and precision of your culinary efforts. This is why, just as you can find thin loaves of bread that, when sliced, slide nicely onto spits together with birds for roasting, you can also find rolls the size of ordinary apples, made just to be stuffed.

With a grater, lightly scrape off the crust from the rolls and in the middle of each remove a disk the size of an average coin making a small round hole. Carve out the inside of the roll, leaving, however, a rather thick wall all around. Bathe them inside and out in boiling milk, and when they are pretty well soaked, cap the hole with the disk you had removed, and which you have also soaked in milk. Then dip in egg, and fry in lard or olive oil, placing them in a skillet with the hole side down, so that they stay shut. Afterwards, with the point of a penknife, reopen the hole, and fill the rolls with a delicate meat stuffing which you have kept quite warm. Reseal the rolls and send them to the table. If you make them right, they will cut an excellent figure on any dinner table.

The meat stuffing, consisting of chickpea-size chunks, is best made with chicken livers, white chicken meat, sweetbreads and the like, and then cooked in brown stock and bound with a pinch of flour. But what you absolutely must have, to make the mixture tastier, are truffles.

240. MIGLIACCIO DI FARINA DOLCE VOLGARMENTE CASTAGNACCIO (CHESTNUT FLOUR CAKE, POPULARLY CALLED CASTAGNACCIO)

Here too, I can hardly refrain from railing against the disinclination we Italians have for commerce and industry. In some Italian provinces, chestnut flour is completely unknown and I think no one has ever even tried to introduce it. And yet for common folk, and for those unafraid of wind, it is a cheap, healthy and nutritious food.

I questioned a street vendor in Romagna on the subject. I described this chestnut cake to her, and asked why she did not try to earn a few pennies selling it. "What can I tell you?" she replied, "It's too sweet; nobody would eat it." "But those "cottarone" you are selling, aren't they sweet? Still, they are selling." I said. "Why don't you at least try the chestnut cake," I added. "At first, distribute them free to the children, give them a piece as a gift to see if they start liking the taste. And then the grown-ups are very likely to come after the children." It was no use; I might as well have been talking to a stone wall.

"Cottarone," for those who do not know them, are apples and pears, mostly overripe, that are stewed in the oven in a small pan with a little water in it, while the top of the pan is covered with a moist kitchen towel. But let us turn to the very simple way to make this chestnut cake.

> Take 500 grams (about 1 pound) of chestnut flour, and because it easily clumps up, sift before using it to make it soft and fluffy. Then put it into a bowl and season with a small pinch of salt. This done, add 8 deciliters (about 3-1/3 cups) of cool water, pouring it in a little at a time, until the mixture has the consistency of a runny porridge into which you will throw a handful of pine nuts. Some people supplement the pine nuts with chopped walnuts; others add raisins and a few rosemary leaves.
>
> Now take a baking pan where the chestnut cake can rise to a thickness of one and half fingers. Cover the bottom with a thin layer of olive oil, pour in the chestnut porridge, and sprinkle another two

tablespoons of olive oil on top. Take it to the baker to cook in the oven or bake it at home in a Dutch oven with fire above and below. Remove and serve hot.

You can also make fritters with this batter.

241. MIGLIACCIO DI FARINA GIALLA I
(CORNMEAL CAKE I)

This is a very ordinary dish, but it will not displease those who like corn flour, and it will not produce stomach acid. And little children will jump for joy every time mamma serves it hot for breakfast in the winter time.

Corn meal is always best when ground rather coarse.

Place in a container the amount of flour you are planning to use. Salt well and mix with boiling water until it forms a firm dough. When there is no dry flour left at the bottom of the bowl, add raisins or dried Muscat grapes in due proportion. Local raisins are preferable, in certain cases, to the sweet Muscat variety because they maintain a pleasant slight acidity. Take a copper baking pan and put it on the fire with a generous amount of virgin lard, and when the lard starts to sizzle, pour in the dough, which, if kneaded to the right consistency, needs to be spread and smoothed out with a mixing spoon. Coat the top of the cake with a little more lard and adorn with small sprigs of fresh rosemary. Bake in the oven at the baker's or in Dutch oven with fire above and below. Allow to brown and then remove from the pan. With this mixture you can also make fritters, but leave out the rosemary.

The best cornmeal I know comes from Arezzo, where the corn is carefully tended and dried in ovens.

242. MIGLIACCIO DI FARINA GIALLA II
(CORNMEAL CAKE II)

This is a fancier dish than the preceding one.

300 grams (about 10-1/2 ounces) of corn meal
100 grams (about 3-1/2 ounces) of dried zibibbo grapes or raisins

40 grams (about 1-1/3 ounces) of lard
30 grams (about 1 ounce) of pine nuts
3 teaspoons of sugar

Remove the seeds from the grapes, cut the pine nuts in half lengthwise. Grease the pan with lard and coat with flour. In every other respect follow the preceding recipe.

243. SALSICCIA COLLE UOVA
(SAUSAGE WITH EGGS)

Eggs and sausages together do not make for bad company, nor for that matter does diced bacon. Since the eggs are somewhat bland, and the sausages or bacon are very savory, their marriage produces a taste that delights many, even though we are talking about ordinary dishes.

If the sausage is fresh, cut it in two lengthwise and place in an ungreased pan without condiments, because it contains enough by itself. If dried, cut the sausage into slices and remove the skin. Once the sausage is done, crack the eggs over it and serve when they have firmed up. For every normal-sized sausage, one or at most two eggs will do.

If the sausages are too lean, prepare with a little butter or lard. If you are using bacon instead of sausage, add a small pat of butter, and then the eggs, after you have whisked them separately.

244. SALSICCIA COLL'UVA
(SAUSAGE WITH GRAPES)

This is a trivial and ordinary dish, but I mention it because sausages, combined with the bittersweet taste of grapes, might tickle someone's taste buds.

Poke the sausages with the tines of a fork and then place them whole in a kettle with a little lard or butter. When done, add a reasonable amount of whole grapes, and simmer until these have lost half their volume.

If they are to be eaten alone, sausages can be grilled or also boiled whole in a pot with a little water.

245. RISO PER CONTORNO
(RICE AS A SIDE DISH)

When you are having boiled pullet or capon, send them to the table with a side dish of rice, as they go well together. To avoid using too much broth, first blanch the rice in water, and then finish cooking it in the broth made by the chicken. Make the rice firm and when nearly done, flavor it with butter and a little Parmesan cheese. If you are using 200 grams (about 7 ounces) of rice, bind it with one egg, or better still, with two yolks as you remove it from the fire.

If you are serving the rice with a stew of milk-fed veal or veal chops, rather than with boiled chicken, in addition to the ingredients mentioned above add two or three tablespoons of spinach which you have boiled and passed through a sieve. In this way your rice will be green and have a more refined flavor.

If you want to give a more handsome appearance to these side dishes, put the rice in a mold and place in *bain-marie*, making sure it does not harden too much. That would be a serious flaw.

246. CARCIOFI IN TEGLIA
(ARTICHOKES IN A BAKING PAN)

This is another family-style dish, this time from Tuscany, inexpensive and relatively tasty. It will do for lunch, as an appetizer or an *entremets* for a family dinner. I do not know why it is not popular elsewhere in Italy.

Prepare the artichokes in the manner described in recipe 186. After shaking off the excess flour, spread them out in a baking dish where a fair amount of good olive oil is already sizzling. When the artichoke slices have browned on both sides, pour beaten eggs over them, but be sure not to overcook. Add salt and pepper to taste, some on the artichokes and some in the eggs before you pour them in.

Instead of a baking dish, you may also use a skillet. But in that case you will get an omelette that will have a rather different and inferior flavor.

247. CACIMPERIO (CHEESE FONDUE)

Those who frequently dine in restaurants can get a pretty good idea how varied people's tastes are. Leaving aside the gluttons who, like wolves, cannot distinguish, say a marzipan cake from a bowl of thistles, at times you will hear a dish praised to the skies by some, but which others judge mediocre, and still others consider dreadful and downright inedible. At such moments you might recall the great truth of that proverb that says: *De gustibus non est disputandum* (there is no arguing about tastes).

Writing about this topic in his *Del vitto e delle cene degli antichi* (*The Foods and Meals of the Ancients*), Giuseppe Averani says: "Taste is more varied and fickle than all the other senses. This is due to the fact that taste buds, through which we experience flavor, differ among people and across climates. They also often change through age or sickness or some other even more compelling reason. This is why many of the foods that delight children do not please adults. And those dishes and beverages that healthy people's palates find tasty and refined, often disgust the sick, who find those dishes displeasing to the taste. It also happens quite often that a certain fantastic perception makes dishes taste more or less delectable and luscious, depending on how our twisted imagination presents them to us. Rare and exotic foods and viands please our taste better than ordinary and local dishes do. Famine and plenty, costliness and cheapness add to and subtract from the flavor of our food: and the universal approbation of gluttons makes all food flavorful and delightful. Thus, at all times and among all nations, it generally happens that the same dishes are not universally held in the same esteem, and they are simultaneously judged both good and bad."

For example, I do not share Brillat-Savarin's opinion about *fondue* (cacimperio) which receives high praise in his *Physiologie du goût*, where he gives the following recipe for it:

"Weigh the eggs, and use a third of their weight in Gruyère cheese, and a sixth of their weight in butter, plus a little salt and a good measure of pepper."

Unlike Savarin, I do not consider fondue an important dish, as it seems to me it may only be served as an appetizer for lunch or as a last resort, when nothing better can be prepared.

In Italy, fondue is a specialty of the people of Turin. The general opinion being that they prepare it to perfection, I went to the trouble of getting the following recipe from Turin. Having personally tried it out with good results, I pass it on to you. These amounts serve six people.

400 grams (about 14 ounces) of rindless Fontina cheese
80 grams (about 2-2/3 ounces) of butter
4 egg yolks
milk, as much as needed

Fontina is a cheese not unlike Gruyère, but somewhat fattier.

Cut the Fontina into little cubes and soak in milk for two hours. Put the butter in a saucepan on the fire, and when it has began to color, add the Fontina, but only two tablespoons of the milk in which it has been soaking. Stirring constantly with a mixing spoon, do not allow it to come to a boil. When the cheese has completely melted, remove from the burner and add the egg yolks. Put back on the burner for a short while, still stirring. In winter, pour the cacimperio into a hot bowl.

If it has turned out well, it should be neither grainy or stringy. Instead it should look like heavy cream.

In Turin, I have seen fondue served with a top layer of paper-thin slices of raw white truffles.

248. TORTINO DI POMODORI (TOMATO PIE)

Simmer some chopped tomatoes in a soffritto of garlic, parsley and olive oil. Salt and pepper to taste. When they have cooked to the point of forming a dense sauce, purée them, and then put back on the fire, adding a sufficient amount of beaten egg. Season with a pinch of Parmesan cheese, stir, and when the egg has firmed up, pour onto a platter and surround the dish with diamond-shape croutons fried in butter or lard.

A few calamint leaves or a pinch of wild marjoram, added after you purée the sauce, will give the pie a pleasant aroma.

249. TORTINI DI RICOTTA
(RICOTTA CROQUETTES)

200 grams (about 7 ounces) of ricotta cheese
50 grams (about 1-2/3 ounces) of grated Parmesan cheese
30 grams (about 1 ounce) of flour
2 eggs
a pinch of chopped parsley
a dash of spices
salt, to taste

Make a dough with the above ingredients, and place on a pastry board sprinkled with flour. Keeping all the while your hands well coated with flour, knead enough flour into the dough to make 12 soft croquettes, which you should flatten a little. Put on the fire with butter in a skillet or baking pan. When the croquettes have browned on both sides, add tomato sauce (recipe 6) or tomato paste diluted with water.

They may be served as an *entremets* or as an accompaniment to a steak or hot roast beef.

250. CROSTINI DI TRE COLORI
(TRICOLOR CANAPÉS)

Take two *kipfels*,[55] cut them into little rounds 1 centimeter (about 1/2 an inch) thick and fry in butter or olive oil. Take some spinach cooked in brown stock or in butter and Parmesan cheese, mince finely, and cover the *kipfel* slices with a layer of this. Take two hard-boiled eggs, peel them, cut in half lengthwise and separate out the yolks. From the whites make several concentric rings which you will place over the layer of spinach. Cut the yolks into many little pieces or

55 See recipe 192.

cubes and position them inside the rings of egg white. In this way you will have crostini that can accompany a roast, and which, consisting of a base of fried bread a green layer of spinach covered and with the white and yellowish-red of the eggs will give you the three colors of the Italian flag. But they look better than they taste.

251. INSALATA DI MAIONESE
(MAYONNAISE SALAD)

Certain cooks with poor taste will prepare this salad with so many strange concoctions that the following day you will have to resort to castor oil or Hungary water.[56]

Some make it with boiled chicken, others with leftover roast meat of any kind. But fish is always to be preferred, particularly if it is of high quality, such as the sea bream, umber, weaver, sturgeon, or shelled prawns, Mediterranean lobster, and lastly dogfish. I will give you here the simplest recipe for this salad, which is also the best.

Take romaine or plain lettuce, cut into finger-wide strips, toss with slices of chard and boiled potatoes. Wash well some anchovies, bone them, cut them into four or five pieces, and add them to the vegetables. Lastly, add the poached fish chopped in small pieces. You may also add some capers and the flesh of two or three sweet pickled olives. Season with salt, olive oil and a little vinegar. Toss well so that the condiments are evenly distributed and then mound it in a bowl.

Prepare a mayonnaise according to recipe 126, which, using the quantities indicated there, will make enough to serve seven or eight people. However, to give it some tang use a teaspoon of mustard rather than pepper, and add a droplet of vinegar to the lemon, which you may use to dissolve the mustard. Coat the top of the salad with this sauce and then embellish it with more slices of chard and potatoes, interleaved, which will give the dish a handsome appearance. If you have an appropriate mold handy, make a little flower out of butter and place it on top of the salad, not for eating, but just for show.

56 A distilled water, named for the Queen of Hungary, for whose use it was first prepared; made with rosemary flowers infused in wine spirits, and used as a restorative.

On the subject of salads, it seems to me that cooked radicchio, with its bitter juice, goes very well with beets, which are sweet.

252. PIZZA A LIBRETTI
(ACCORDION CAKE)

A woman wrote to me: "I want to teach you, as I had promised myself to do, how to make a tasty and elegant fried pastry. But heaven help you if you call it flat, because it should turn out quite otherwise. Call it "accordion cake," which would be a fair description."

Obediently carrying out the lady's orders, I tried out this accordion cake twice, and both times it turned out well. Now I will describe it to you.

Roll out a sheet of dough that is not too firm and as thin as possible by mixing together some flour, two eggs, a pinch of salt, three tablespoons of cognac or spirits, or better yet fumetto (see note to recipe 212). Grease the dough with 20 grams (about 2/3 ounces) of melted butter and roll it up, that is fold it upon itself so that it is 10 to 11 centimeters (about 4 to 4-1/4 inches) wide. Make sure that the inner side is the greased side. Now cut the roll in half lengthwise and then slice crosswise at regular intervals to obtain a number of rectangles. Now press firmly with your fingers on the outer edge of each rectangle, that is, the uncut spine of the rolls. Fry in a skillet with a lot of oil, and before serving, sprinkle confectioners' sugar on top. If they have turned out well, you will see the accordions pop open and stay open.

These amounts serve four people.

STEWS

Generally speaking, stews are very appetizing dishes; it is a good idea, therefore, to take special care when preparing them, so that they turn out delicate, tasty and easily digestible. They are sometimes rumored to be harmful to one's health, but I do not share that opinion. This ill-conceived notion arises more than anything else from not knowing how to prepare them well. People do not think, for example, to skim off the fat, or else they are too liberal with herbs and soffritti, or what is worse, they use them inappropriately.

In great kitchens, where brown stock is never lacking, many stews may be cooked with brown stock and butter. This way they turn out simple and light. But if no brown stock is available, you must resort to soffritti; but use them sparingly, prepare just the right amount, and cook them just right.

253. STRACOTTO DI VITELLA (VEAL STEW)

Veal stew is generally used by middle-class Florentine families to season macaroni or to make risotto with brown stock. This is not a bad idea, especially if you consider that the stew then serves a double purpose; it provides an ingredient for the first course and is also eaten separately. Take care, however, not to drain off too much of the juice from the meat, simply because you want to make a lot of brown stock. And do not use only olive oil, but rather replace it wholly or in part with bacon as the Tuscans do, which gives it a stronger and more agreeable flavor. Here are the amounts for seasoning between 250 and 300 grams (about 8-4/5 and 12-1/3 ounces) of macaroni.

500 grams (about 1 pound) of lean veal, including the bone or the joint
50 grams (about 1-2/3 ounces) of bacon
50 grams (about 1-2/3 ounces) of butter
1/4 of a large onion
1 carrot
2 pieces of celery

Chop the last three items coarsely, and dice the bacon into little cubes.

Put everything together on the fire and season with salt and pepper. Turn the meat often, and when browned, sprinkle a pinch of flour over it. Then moisten with tomato sauce (recipe 6) or tomato paste. Cook until done, adding water a little at a time. The flour serves to bind the sauce and to give it a little color. Take care, however, that it does not burn, as that would give the sauce an unpleasant taste and a nearly black color, something sauce should never have. Pass through a sieve, and then it would certainly do no harm to season the mixture with some pieces of dried mushroom reconstituted in warm water and stewed a little in the sauce.

Cook the macaroni in salted water, drain well and, before serving, steep them in the sauce, keeping them near the fire. Season with butter and Parmesan cheese, not much of the latter since people can add more cheese at the table.

If you are making rice, cook it in water, which you will add a little at a time. When half done, add the sauce and a little butter. Before removing from the fire, mix in a little Parmesan cheese.

It is a good idea to serve the stewed veal with a side dish of vegetables or legumes. Round of veal is the best cut to use. If you prepare it in olive oil, about 20 grams (about 2/3 of an ounce) of bacon should suffice.

254. STRACOTTO ALLA BIZZARRA
(WHIMSICAL STEW)

If you should have, by chance, a piece of lean veal weighing between 700 and 800 grams (about 1-1/2 and 1-2/3 pounds) without the bone, lard it with 100 grams (about 3-1/2 ounces) of lardoons, first seasoning the lardoons—each one finger thick—as well as the meat, with salt and pepper. Tie up the veal to hold it together, and put on the fire half-covered in water with two sage leaves, a sprig of rosemary and half a clove of garlic. If the meat is very ripe, use less water. Once the water has boiled off, sprinkle a teaspoon of flour on the meat and let it brown; add a small pat of butter, then moisten with a ladleful of broth and one finger's worth of Marsala wine. Strain the sauce but without forcing it through, then pour it over the meat before sending the dish to the table.

255. FRICANDÒ (FRICANDEAU)

Take a solid piece of milk-fed veal, taken from the haunch, and lard it with untrimmed prosciutto. Tie the piece and salt very little, or better yet not at all, because over-salting is the worst defect in food. Spike an onion with two cloves and prepare a *bouquet garni* with carrot strips, celery and parsley. Put everything in a saucepan with a small pat of butter, brown the meat and then simmer in broth until cooked.

When done, throw away the onion and the *bouquet garni*, strain the sauce, skim off the fat, then cook down to the consistency of gelatin. Then it is ready to be added to the *fricandeau* when you send it to the table.

It should be pointed out here that broth (which plays such in large role in preparing dishes) may not always be available. For that reason some people stock up on Liebig meat concentrate, which in a pinch, dissolved in water, may replace broth.

Every variety of meat should be larded following the grain of the flesh, so that it can be carved diagonally.

256. FRICASSEA (*FRICASSÉE*)

Fricassée may be made with breast or another lean cut of milk-fed veal, lamb or chicken. Let's use the first item, veal breast, as our example—approximately the same quantities may be used for the other cuts as well.

500 grams (about 1 pound) of breast of milk-fed veal
50 grams (1-2/3 ounces) of butter
5 grams (about 1/6 of an ounce) or 1 scant tablespoon of flour
2 deciliters (about 4/5 of a cup) of hot but not boiling water
2 egg yolks
1/2 a lemon
1 bouquet garni

Break up the breast of veal, leaving the bones. Put in a saucepan with half the butter, and when it starts to melt, add the flour and stir until it turns nut brown. Now start adding the water a little at a time and throw in the *bouquet garni*, which you can make with strips of onion and of carrot, as well as stalks of parsley, celery and basil, all tied together. Leave out the leaves, because they may dissolve and spoil the appearance of the *fricassée*, which should be of a lovely uniform straw color. When the water boils, add the meat and the rest of the butter, then season with salt and white pepper, which is the flower of ordinary pepper. Cover the saucepan with a sheet of paper held firmly in place by the lid, and allow to simmer slowly. When it is two-thirds done, remove the *bouquet garni*, and if it is fresh mushroom season, you can make the *fricassée* more delicious by adding between 100 and 150 grams (about 3-1/2 and 5-1/4 ounces) of thinly sliced mushrooms. Otherwise, use a pinch of the dried variety.

When you are about to send the *fricassée* to the table, remove the saucepan from the burner and stir in the egg yolks, whisked in lemon juice, a little at a time.

If you are making chicken *fricassée*, cut the chicken into pieces along the joints, leaving out the head, neck and feet. In all other respects, prepare as described above.

Fricassée made in this way is a healthy and refined dish that particularly delights those whose palates have not been spoiled by strong and spicy flavors.

257. CIBREO
(CHICKEN GIBLET *FRICASSÉE*)

Cibreo is a simple but delicate dish, appropriate for ladies with listless appetites and for convalescents.

Take some chicken livers (first remove the gall bladder as indicated in recipe 110), coxcombs and testicles. Use boiling water to skin the coxcombs, then cut them into two or three pieces, and slice the livers in half. Put on the fire in an appropriate amount of butter, first the coxcombs, then the livers, and lastly the testicles. Season with salt and pepper, then cook until done, adding broth if necessary.

Depending on the amounts you are using, place one or two egg yolks in a small pan together with one or half a teaspoon of flour, some lemon juice and hot broth, whisking constantly so that the egg does not clump up. Once the giblets are cooked, pour this sauce over them, and allow to simmer for a while, adding more broth if needed to give the sauce a light consistency, then serve.

To serve one person, use three or four coxcombs, the same number of chicken livers and six or seven testicles, plus one egg yolk, half a teaspoon of flour, and half a lemon.

The ram testicles described in recipe 174, boiled and cut in thin slices, are also quite good prepared in this manner.

258. POLLO DISOSSATO RIPIENO
(BONELESS STUFFED CHICKEN)

To bone a chicken, the simplest way is the following: cut off the neck half way down, the tips of the wings, and the feet along the shin joint. Then, without gutting the bird, open its back lengthwise along the surface, from the wings to the rump. With a very sharp paring knife, start taking out the bones from inside the wings, stripping out the flesh as you go along. Then do the same with the thigh and leg bones and the outer bones of the carcass, scraping away continually with the knife, until you can remove the carcass whole, including the entrails. Leave the little bones in the gizzard intact, or else remove the whole gizzard, then lift the wishbone from the breast.

Having done this, turn the now boneless legs and the wings, pulling them inward, and remove any tendons you find in the meat.

Once the chicken has been boned, and assuming it is rather large, prepare the stuffing with about 300 grams (about 10-1/2 ounces) of lean milk-fed veal. If the bird is small, reduce the quantity. Mince the veal finely, then grind it in a mortar until very soft. Then add to the meat a good portion of crustless bread soaked in broth, a handful of grated Parmesan cheese, three egg yolks, salt and pepper, and a dash of nutmeg if you like. Lastly, add 20 grams (about 2/3 of an ounce) of untrimmed prosciutto and 20 grams (about 2/3 of an ounce) of salted tongue, both diced into small cubes. Once you have stuffed the bird, sew it up, wrap tightly in a cheesecloth, and tie up. Simmer in water for a couple of hours over a slow flame. Then remove the wrapping and brown it, first in butter and then in a sauce prepared as follows.

Break all the bones you have removed from the chicken, as well as the neck and head. Then put all of this in a saucepan on the fire with minced bacon, some butter, onion, celery and carrot. Season with salt and pepper, and draw out their juices by adding the water in which you have boiled the chicken, which by now has turned into good broth.

Before sending it to the table, either alone or with a side dish, remove the thread you have used to sew the stuffing inside.

259. SOUFFLET DI POLLO
(CHICKEN SOUFFLÉ)

This nourishing, light and not very exciting dish may come in handy, if, after a meal, you have some leftover roast chicken (breast and thighs), particularly if you are serving some older people in the family, or other members with sensitive and weak stomachs.

> *80 grams (about 2-2/3 ounces) of skinless chicken meat*
> *50 grams (about 1-2/3 ounces) of flour*
> *30 grams (about 1 ounce) of butter*
> *20 grams (about 2/3 of an ounce) of grated Parmesan cheese*
> *2-1/2 deciliters (about 1 cup) of milk*

4 eggs
a pinch of salt

Prepare a béchamel with the butter, the flour and the milk. When done but no longer boiling hot, add the Parmesan cheese, the salt, the egg yolks and the chicken, finely minced with a mezzaluna. Then beat the whites until they are stiff and add carefully to the mixture. Pour everything into an ovenproof platter, brown lightly in a Dutch oven, and serve hot, though it is also delicious cold.

260. POLLASTRA IN UMIDO COL CONTORNO DI RISO (STEWED PULLET SERVED WITH RICE)

1 gutted pullet, weighing about 700 grams (about 1-1/2 pound)
300 grams (about 10-1/2 ounces) of rice
100 grams (about 3-1/2 ounces) of butter
40 grams (about 1-1/3 ounces) of untrimmed prosciutto
1 onion of more than average size
1 piece of carrot
a small handful of dried mushrooms

Tie up the pullet to hold it all well together, then place in a saucepan the prosciutto, cut into small strips, and 30 grams (about 1 ounce) of the butter. Slice the onion and carrot on top, then put the bird in breast downward, seasoning with salt and pepper. Keep it covered and, when it has browned on both sides, finish cooking by adding hot water a little at a time. Take care to have enough sauce left to flavor the rice, and remember to strain it.

Put the rice on the fire with half of the remaining butter, and without other condiments or spices. Cook in hot water, adding the sauce from the pullet at the end. When completely done, add the remaining butter, and, to give it better flavor, a good handful of grated Parmesan cheese.

Cook the liver and giblets together with the bird, then chop them up and mix into the rice. Prepared in this way, the rice may also be served as a first course and should do for three people. But in that case, serve the chicken separately in its own sauce, with the mushrooms as a side dish.

261. BRACIUOLA DI MANZO RIPIENA IN UMIDO
(BEEF CUTLETS STUFFED AND STEWED)

The roasted and stuffed beef cutlets described in recipe 537 can also be stewed. Brown in butter and finish cooking with water and tomato sauce (recipe 6). They can be served with any side dish.

262. BRACIUOLA DI MANZO ALLA *SAUTÉ* O IN TEGLIA
(SAUTÉED OR PAN-BROILED BEEF CUTLETS)

When for a luncheon instead of steak you would like to serve beef cutlets, which can turn out too dry when grilled, cook them in the following way, and they will turn out very well. Pound the cutlets thoroughly with the blunt edge of a knife, and put on the fire with an appropriate amount of butter. Season with salt and pepper, turning often so that they brown on both sides. When the meat has absorbed nearly all of the butter, moisten twice with a splash of water, and when it is cooked, sprinkle a pinch of chopped parsley over it, keeping it just another moment on the flame. Serve in its own sauce.

If you like, you can accompany these cutlets with fried potatoes.

263. POLLO ALLA CONTADINA
(PEASANT-STYLE CHICKEN)

Take a young chicken and stud it with several sprigs of rosemary and with a clove of garlic cut into four or five pieces. Put on the fire with a little finely minced lardoon and season inside and out with salt and pepper. When it has browned all over, add chopped, seeded tomatoes, and when the tomatoes have dissolved moisten with broth or water. In a different pan, brown some raw potato wedges in oil, lard, or butter. Then flavor them with the juice from the chicken, and serve as a side dish. For a more delicate taste, use butter instead of lardoon.

264. POLLO COLLA MARSALA
(CHICKEN MARSALA)

Cut the chicken into large pieces and put it in a saucepan with some finely chopped onion and a bit of butter. Season with salt and pepper and when it has nicely browned, add some broth and cook until done. Strain the sauce, skim off the fat if necessary, and put the chicken back on the fire in a little Marsala wine. Remove as soon as it starts to boil again.

265. POLLO COLLE SALSICCE
(CHICKEN WITH SAUSAGES)

Chop half an onion very fine and put it in a saucepan with a bit of butter and four or five thin slices of prosciutto about a finger in width. On top of these ingredients, put a whole chicken. Season with pepper and a little salt, and put on the fire. When it has browned all over and the onion has completely dissolved, moisten with broth or water and add three or four freshly made whole sausages. Cook over a slow fire, making sure some liquid remains at the end.

266. POLLO IN SALSA D'UOVO
(CHICKEN IN EGG SAUCE)

Cut up a young chicken and place it in a saucepan with 50 grams (about 1-2/3 ounces) of butter. Season with salt and pepper. After it has cooked a while, sprinkle the pieces with a pinch of flour to brown them; then add broth and cook until done. Remove the chicken pieces and place on a platter; keep warm. Make the sauce by beating an egg yolk with the juice of half a lemon and adding it to the liquid that remains in the saucepan. Stir over the fire for a few minutes, pour over the chicken, and serve.

267. POLLO CON LA PANNA
(CHICKEN WITH CREAM)

Put the breast of a young chicken on a spit and roast until two-thirds done. Baste with olive oil, season with salt, and brown. Then cut it into pieces at the joints, and divide the breast in two down the middle. Finish cooking in the following manner.

Chop a 1/4 of a medium-sized onion and put on the fire with 50 grams (about 1-2/3 ounces) of butter. When it has thoroughly browned, sprinkle with 10 grams (about 1/3 of an ounce) of flour. Then add 3 deciliters (about 1-1/4 cups) of heavy cream, a little at a time. If you do not have heavy cream, you can use high-grade milk. When you think the flour is cooked, add the pieces of chicken and simmer until done.

268. POLLO ALLA MARENGO
(CHICKEN MARENGO)

The evening of the Battle of Marengo, after the turmoil of the day, the cook to the First Consul and to the Generals was unable to find the kitchen wagons; and so he had some chickens stolen and improvised a dish that, prepared more or less as I will describe it to you, was called "Chicken Marengo." They say it was always a favorite of Napoleon, not so much for its intrinsic merit, but because it reminded him of that glorious victory.

Take a young chicken, remove the neck and legs and cut into large pieces at the joints. Sauté in 30 grams (about 1 ounce) of butter and one tablespoon of olive oil, seasoning with salt, pepper, and a dash of nutmeg. When the pieces have browned on both sides, skim the fat and add a level tablespoon of flour and a deciliter (about 7 fluid ounces) of wine. Add broth and cover, cooking over low heat until done. Before removing from the fire, garnish with a pinch of chopped parsley; arrange on a serving dish and squeeze half a lemon over it. The result is an appetizing dish.

269. PETTI DI POLLO ALLA SAUTÉ
(SAUTÉED CHICKEN BREASTS)

I think that the following is the best way to cook chicken breasts, because they come out delicate to the taste and make such a fine show that a capon breast can serve as many as four or five people.

Cut the breasts into paper-thin slices, giving them the best shape possible; use the scraps from the breastbone to make a single piece, squeezing them together and flattening them out. Then season with salt and pepper and soak for a few hours in a mixture of beaten eggs. Then dip the pieces in fine bread crumbs and sauté them in butter. If you like them plain, you can season with lemon juice; if you prefer them with truffles, prepare them like the cutlets in recipe 312, or as follows.

Take a small metal frying pan, pour in just enough olive oil to barely cover the bottom, then line the bottom with a layer of sliced truffles, sprinkling with just a little grated Parmesan cheese and a pinch of bread crumbs. Repeat the same operation three or four times, depending on the amount of truffles, and then season with oil, salt, pepper, and a few small pats of butter; season sparingly, so that the dish does not turn out too heavy. Put the pan on the fire and when it begins to sizzle, moisten the truffles with a ladleful of brown stock or broth and a little lemon juice. Promptly remove the sauce from the fire and pour it over the chicken breasts, which you have already browned as described above.

If you do not have truffles, use dried mushrooms soaked in water and coarsely chopped, and if you do not have lemon juice you can use tomato sauce (recipe 6) or tomato paste.

270. GERMANO OSSIA ANATRA SELVATICA IN UMIDO I
(MALLARD OR WILD DUCK STEW I)

When you buy a mallard (*Anas boscas*) at the market, open its beak and examine the tongue. If the tongue is very dry, you know that the animal has been dead for some time, so smell it to make sure that it doesn't stink.

Some people suggest that ducks should be washed with vinegar before cooking, or scalded in boiling water, to take away their gamey smell. But since this odor, which is disgusting when it is too strong, resides primarily in the uropygial gland, I think that one need only remove that gland. The gland, called "stizza" in the Florentine dialect, is found at the base of the tail, and contains a yellowish, viscous fluid which water fowl produce in abundance and smear on their feathers to make them water resistant.

Clean the duck, but save the liver, heart, and gizzard. Remove the head and, after you have cut it open to remove the vertebrae, fold down the skin from the neck over the bird's breast. A dish of red cabbage or whole lentils goes well with stewed duck; whether you serve the one or the other, prepare a soffritto in the following manner.

For a duck weighing roughly 1 kilogram (about 2 pounds), finely chop 30 grams (about 1 ounce) of untrimmed prosciutto with the usual flavorings, namely some celery, parsley, carrot, and 1/4 of a large onion. Put all of this in a saucepan with some olive oil and place the duck on top. Season with salt and pepper, brown all over, add water, and simmer until done.

Cook the red cabbage or lentils in water, and then again in the bird's sauce. Taste the sauce to see if it needs a little butter to enhance its flavor, and then send it to the table with the duck. The cabbage should be coarsely chopped and seasoned with salt and pepper.

271. GERMANO OSSIA ANATRA SELVATICA IN UMIDO II (MALLARD OR WILD DUCK STEW II)

Put the duck in a saucepan with 30 grams (about 1 ounce) of butter and let it brown. Remove the duck and add a tablespoon of flour to the fat in the pan, stirring with a wooden spoon until it turns brown. Remove the pan from the fire, and when the mixture has stopped sizzling, pour in 1/2 a liter (about 1/2 a quart) of water and put the duck back in the pan. Season with salt and pepper, cover, and cook until completely done with the peel of a quarter of an orange, a stalk of celery about one palm long, and a piece of carrot—the celery and carrot should be coarsely chopped, while the orange peel should be kept in a single piece. When done, strain the sauce, cut the duck into pieces at the joints, put the pieces back in the sauce and squeeze the juice from the orange rind over them. Bring to a boil again for just a few minutes, and serve.

Domestic duck can be prepared in the same way, but, since it is very fatty, one should skim off the excess fat from the sauce before serving. One way to remove the fat is to pour the sauce into a bowl and to lay a piece of blotting paper on top of it, which will absorb the fat.

272. ANATRA DOMESTICA
(DOMESTIC DUCK STEW)

Prepare this bird in the same manner as the wild duck in recipe 270, putting it on the fire in a saucepan with a similar soffritto. When the duck has browned, add tomato sauce (recipe 6) or tomato paste and finish cooking with water or broth. Strain the sauce, skim off the fat, and put it back on the fire together with the duck and a bit of butter. You can use this sauce together with Parmesan cheese as a dressing for homemade noodles or lasagne, while serving the duck with a side dish of greens reheated in a little of the same sauce.

273. ANATRA DOMESTICA COL CONTORNO DI RISO
(DOMESTIC DUCK WITH RICE)

I think that this is a good stew that deserves special mention.

Chop a quarter of a large onion, all the usual flavorings, namely some parsley, carrot, and celery, and 50 grams (about 1-2/3 ounces) of untrimmed prosciutto. Put this on the fire with two tablespoons of olive oil and place the duck on top, seasoning with salt and pepper. When it has browned, add tomato sauce (recipe 6) or tomato paste, and enough water to cook it until done. At the same time, toss in a handful of dried mushrooms. Cook the mushrooms in the sauce, then strain and put aside—they are ready to be added to the rice. Then pass the sauce through a sieve and skim off the fat. Put 200 grams (about 7 ounces) of raw rice into a pan with 40 grams (about 1-1/3 ounces) of butter without any other flavoring; as soon as it

per Ghennaria
regina del bosco
e della tavola

G. Nebbia   *2001*

begins to brown, pour in hot water a little at a time. When you are about to remove it from the fire, season the rice with the duck sauce and Parmesan cheese.

274. FEGATO D'OCA (GOOSE LIVER)

Read recipe 548 for domestic goose, and at the end you will find instructions on how to cook goose liver. However, having come across another one, I cooked it differently and it turned out better than the other, so I will give you the new recipe here. After you have cooked the goose liver as indicated in recipe 548, drain it and bind it with a mixture consisting of 20 grams (about 2/3 of an ounce) of melted butter and a heaping tablespoon of flour. When the mixture turns nut brown, dilute it with a ladleful of broth and three tablespoons of Marsala wine. Put the liver back in, simmer for a little while, and serve.

275. FOLAGHE IN UMIDO (STEWED COOT)

The coot (*Fulica atra*) could be called a fish-bird, since the Church permits it to be eaten on fasting days without infringing on Catholic precepts. The coot comes from the warm, temperate countries of Europe and North Africa. As a migratory bird, it travels by night. An inhabitant of swamps and lakes, the coot is a good swimmer, feeding on aquatic plants, insects, and small mollusks. Only two species of coot are found in Europe.

Except during the time when they lay their eggs, coots live in huge flocks, which makes for very entertaining hunting, with huge kills. Quite famous is the coot hunt called "la tela," which takes place several times in late autumn and winter and is conducted in small boats on Lake Massaciuccoli near Pisa, on the estate of the Marquis Ginori-Lisci. During the hunt of November 1903, in which hunters in a hundred boats from every part of Italy took part, about six thousand coots were brought down, or so the newspapers reported.

Coot meat is dark and not very flavorful, and being game it should be prepared in the following manner.

Taking, for example, four coots (as I did), skin them and singe them on the fire to remove all their down, then clean and wash them well. Thread them lengthwise on a red-hot skewer, then cut the birds into four parts, discarding the head, feet, and wing tips. Marinate for an hour in vinegar and then wash repeatedly with cool water. I did not use the livers; but I did use the gizzards, which are large and chewy like those of a chicken. Cleaned, washed and cut into four pieces, they went into the marinade.

Now, finely chop a large onion, and the appropriate amount of the usual flavorings, that is, celery, carrot, and parsley. Put this battuto on the fire with 80 grams (about 2-2/3 ounces) of butter, the coots, and the gizzards. Season with salt, pepper, and a dash of spices. When the meat starts to dry out, pour in tomato sauce (recipe 6) or tomato paste diluted in a generous amount of water to finish cooking and so that there will be plenty of sauce left at the end. When the birds are done, strain the sauce and add to it half a coot breast, finely minced, and another 40 grams (about 1-1/3 ounces) of butter, along with some Parmesan cheese. You can use this sauce to flavor three eggs' worth of pappardelle or 500 grams (about 1 pound) of large flat noodles, which will be highly praised for their unique flavor. Serve the coots, with some of the sauce, as the main course, and they will not be sneered at. All of this should serve five or six people.

I have also heard that you can get quite a nice stock by boiling coots with two sausages inside.

276. PICCIONI IN UMIDO (STEWED SQUABS)

Here is a story about squabs that, as unbelievable as it may seem, is indeed true. Let it stand as proof of what I was telling you about the caprices of the stomach.

One day a lady asked a man who happened to be around to kill a couple of squabs for her. Well, he drowned them in a basin of water, right there in front of her. The lady was so shocked by the sight that from that day on she could never eat the flesh of that bird again.

Garnish the birds with whole sage leaves, and put them in a pot or saucepan on top of some slices of untrimmed prosciutto. Season with olive oil, salt, and pepper. When they have browned, add a bit of butter and some broth, and then simmer until done. Before removing from the fire, squeeze a lemon on them and serve in their sauce over toasted bread. Salt them very little, on account of the prosciutto and the broth. During the season when verjuice[57] is made, you can use that instead of lemon juice. As the old saying goes:

> *Quando sol est in leone,*
> *Bonum vinum cum popone,*
> *et agrestum cum pipione.*
> (When the sun is in Leo,
> Wine goes well with melon,
> And verjuice with pigeon.)

277. PICCIONI ALL'INGLESE
(SQUABS ENGLISH STYLE, OR SQUAB PIE)

I would like to make it clear once and for all that names do not mean much in my kitchen, and that I give no importance to high-sounding titles. If an Englishman should tell me that I have not made this dish, which also goes by the odd name of "piccion paio,"[58] according to the customs of his country, I do not care a fig. All I care is that it be judged tasty, and that is the end of the matter. Take:

a young but large squab
100 grams (about 3-1/2 ounces) of lean milk-fed veal, or a chicken
  breast
40 grams (about 1-1/3 ounces) of thinly sliced untrimmed
  prosciutto
30 grams (about 1 ounce) of thinly sliced salted tongue
40 grams (about 1-1/3 ounces) of butter
1/2 a glass of good skimmed broth
1 hard-boiled egg

57 The acid juice (literally "green juice") from unripened grapes, used as a condiment and for deglazing.
58 Artusi is making fun of an Italian transcription of the English "pigeon pie."

Cut the bird into small pieces at the joints, discarding the head and legs. Cut the veal or chicken breast into small cutlets and pound them with the blunt edge of a knife. Cut the prosciutto and the tongue into strips about one finger wide. Cut the egg into 8 sections.

Take an ovenproof oval platter made of metal or porcelain and arrange on it, in layers, first half of the squab and veal, then half of the prosciutto and tongue, half of the butter scattered here and there in tiny bits, and half (or four sections) of the egg. Season with very little salt, pepper, and some aromatic spices, and repeat the procedure with the rest of the ingredients until you have formed a mound. Then pour in the broth, making sure that it is cold; it should reach the inner rim of the platter. Very little of the broth will be absorbed during cooking.

Now make the dough to cover the dish, using the following amounts:

150 grams (about 5-1/4 ounces) of flour
50 grams (about 1-2/3 ounces) of butter
1 teaspoon of wine spirits
1 teaspoon of sugar
the juice of one lemon wedge
1 egg yolk
salt to taste

Mix the flour with the other ingredients; add warm water if necessary to make a rather soft dough. Knead thoroughly, throwing it down hard on the pastry board. Let it rest a little, and then roll it out, folding it over four or five times and finally using a ridged rolling pin to make a sheet about the thickness of a large coin. Cover the dish with this dough; if you have some left over, garnish the top with decorations cut out of the extra dough. Brush it with egg yolk, and then bake this pasticcio (for that's really what it is) in a Dutch oven. Serve hot.

I think that this dish turns out even better if it is prepared in the following way, which gives it a more Italian character and taste. First cook the squab and other meats halfway with the same amount of butter, seasoning with salt, pepper, and spices. Then arrange the meats on the platter as indicated, also adding the sauce from the meats as well as the skimmed broth. You can also add chicken giblets, sweetbreads, and truffles, adjusting the seasoning as necessary.

278. MANICARETTO DI PICCIONI
(SQUAB DELIGHT)

Cut the squabs into quarters or large pieces at the joints and put them on the fire with a slice of prosciutto, a little butter, and a *bouquet garni*. Season with salt and pepper. When the squabs start to dry out, add some broth, and when they are halfway done, add their giblets, some chopped sweetbreads, and sliced fresh mushrooms or dried mushrooms (soaked first in warm water), or truffles. If you use truffles, however, they should be added almost at the end of the cooking process. Blanch the sweetbreads before adding them, and skin them if they come from a large animal. After moistening the birds with stock, pour in half a glass of white wine for each two squabs. But first reduce the wine by about half in a separate pan. Continue to simmer the squabs, then add another bit of butter rolled in flour, or else just flour, to thicken the sauce. Lastly, just before serving remove the prosciutto and the *bouquet garni*, and squeeze a lemon over the squabs.

You can also cook young chickens this way, garnishing them with giblets instead of sweetbreads.

279. TIMBALLO DI PICCIONI (SQUAB TIMBALE)

The name of this dish comes perhaps from its shape, which is similar to the musical instrument of the same name.[59] Chop some prosciutto, onion, celery, and carrot, add a bit of butter and put on the fire with one or two squabs, depending on the number of people you are serving. Add the giblets from the squabs and some chicken giblets, if you have them. Season with salt and pepper, and when the pigeons have browned, add broth and simmer until done. Make sure, however, that there is some sauce left over. Strain the sauce and toss in some macaroni which you have cooked beforehand, but not completely, in salted water, and keep near the fire, stirring from time to time. Make a little béchamel sauce, then break the squabs apart at the joints and discard the neck, head, legs, and backbones if you do not want to bone them completely, which would be better. Cut the giblets into rather large pieces and remove the gristle from the gizzards.

59 In Italian "timballo" also means timbal or kettledrum.

When the macaroni has absorbed the sauce, season with Parmesan cheese, bits of butter, small cubes or, better yet, thin slices of untrimmed prosciutto, nutmeg, and truffle shavings—if you do not have truffles, use a handful of dried mushrooms softened in water. Lastly, stir in the béchamel sauce.

Take a casserole of the appropriate size, grease it with cold butter and line it with shortcrust pastry dough. Pour in the squab mixture, cover with the same dough, and bake. Remove from the oven while still hot, and serve immediately.

With 300 grams (about 10-1/2 ounces) of macaroni and two squabs you can make a timbale for ten to twelve people, if they are not big eaters. If you want, you can also make this dish as a pasticcio, as in recipe 349.

280. TORDI COLLE OLIVE
(THRUSHES WITH OLIVES)

Thrushes and other small birds can be stewed like the squabs in recipe 276; in fact, I recommend that you cook them that way, for they are excellent. Pickled olives—that is, olives soaked in brine—are usually added whole, with the pits, when the thrushes are half cooked. Still, it is better to remove the pits by cutting the flesh of the olive with a penknife into a spiral that looks like a whole olive when wrapped on itself.

There was once a gentleman who received six thrushes as a gift. Since his family was in the country at the time, he decided to take the birds to a restaurant and have them roasted for himself. The thrushes were beautiful, fresh and plump like garden warblers. The man was afraid lest they be switched on him, so he marked each thrush by cutting out its tongue. The waiters at the restaurant, who had their suspicions, began to examine the birds to see if they had any distinctive mark, and lo and behold, aided by their own shrewdness they found it. Unwilling to let themselves be outdone in cleverness, or perhaps because the gentlemen's only generous side was his waistline, they all cried out at once "We will show *him*!" So they cut the tongues out of six of the scrawniest thrushes they had in the kitchen and prepared those for him, keeping his thrushes for more honored customers. When our friend arrived looking forward to a scrumptious meal and saw the dry, puny birds, his eyes started out of his head. Turning the birds over and over, he kept saying to himself: "I am confounded! Can these really be my thrushes?" Then, seeing that their tongues had been cut out, sadly he resigned himself to believing that the spit and the fire had worked this metamorphosis.

The first thing the waiters offered to the customers who came in afterward was: "Would you like some nice thrushes today?" And then they proceeded to tell the story of their prank, as it was later recounted to me by one of those who ended up eating the gentleman's birds.

281. TORDI FINTI (MOCK THRUSHES)

This dish is called mock thrushes because of the flavor that juniper berries and the combination of ingredients lend to it. It is a dish that many people like, and you would do well to try it.

To make six "thrushes" you need:

300 grams (about 10-1/2 ounces) of lean, boneless milk-fed veal
6 juniper berries
3 chicken livers
3 salted anchovies
3 tablespoons of olive oil
lardoon, as needed

These mock thrushes should look like small, stuffed cutlets; therefore cut the veal into six thin slices, flatten them out, give them a nice shape, and put the scraps aside. The scraps, along with the chicken livers, a bit of lardoon, the juniper berries, the anchovies (cleaned and boned), and a sage leaf, make up the mixture you will use to stuff the veal. So mince everything very fine and season with a little salt and pepper. After filling the veal slices with this mixture and rolling them up, wrap them in a thin slice of lardoon with half a sage leaf between the veal and the salt pork, and then tie them crosswise. I think that 60 grams (about 2 ounces) of lardoon in all should be enough.

Now that you have prepared the cutlets, put them over a high flame in a skillet or an uncovered saucepan with the three tablespoons of olive oil and season again lightly with salt and pepper.

When they have browned all over, pour out the fat, but leave the burnt bits on the bottom of the pan; finish cooking, adding broth a little at a time, because when they are done the cutlets should be almost dry.

Untie and serve over six slices of lightly toasted bread, pouring over them the concentrated sauce that remains in the pan.

These mock thrushes are even good when served cold.

282. STORNI IN ISTUFA (STEWED STARLINGS)

The meat of starlings is tough and of low quality. Therefore these birds need to be prepared in the following way to be edible.

For six starlings, finely chop 1/4 of a large onion with 30 grams (about 1 ounce) of fat trimmed from prosciutto, then put on the fire with 20 grams (about 2/3 of an ounce) of butter, three or four small strips of untrimmed prosciutto, and two juniper berries. Place the starlings (whole and ungutted) on top of this mixture; garnish with sage leaves and season with salt and pepper. Turn the birds often, and when they have absorbed the flavor of the battuto, and the onion is nice and golden brown, moisten with a little dry white wine. When that has been absorbed, pour in more wine to make a total of 3 deciliters (about 1-1/4 cups). If you do not have white wine, you can substitute 2 deciliters (about 4/5 of a cup) of water and 1 deciliter (about 3-1/2 fluid ounces) of Marsala wine. Cover the saucepan with a sheet of paper folded four times and held in place by a heavy lid. Simmer over a low fire until completely cooked. Serve with the sauce from the pan.

283. UCCELLI IN SALMÌ (BIRDS IN WINE SAUCE)

Cook the birds, but not completely, by roasting them on a spit, seasoning them with salt and olive oil. Remove them from the spit and leave them whole, if they are small birds or thrushes; if they are large, cut the birds into four parts and remove the heads, which you will crush in a mortar along with some other small roasted bird or with some scraps from larger birds. Put a small saucepan on the fire with some butter, some bits of prosciutto, brown stock or broth, Madeira or Marsala wine in roughly the same amount as the broth, a finely chopped shallot, one or two juniper berries (if you are cooking thrushes), or a bay leaf (if they are some other kind of bird). Season with salt and pepper, and when the mixture has boiled for half an hour strain it, then placing the partially roasted birds in it. Cook until completely done, and serve over small slices of toasted bread.

284. STUFATO DI LEPRE (HARE STEW)

I will describe to you later how to make hare pie, and I will also tell you about roasting hare. For now I will add that, if you want to cook it sweet-and-sour, you can use the recipe for boar, 285. This is the way to stew hare.

Let's take, for example, half a hare. First cut it into pieces, then finely chop a medium-sized onion, two cloves of garlic, a piece of celery as long as the palm of your hand, and a few sprigs of rosemary. Put on the fire with a bit of butter, two tablespoons of oil, and four of five strips of prosciutto as wide as a finger. Let this fry for five minutes, then toss in the hare and season with salt, pepper, and spices. When the hare has browned, add half a glass of white wine or Marsala and then throw in a handful of fresh mushrooms or reconstituted dry mushrooms. Cook until done with broth and tomato sauce (recipe 6) or tomato paste diluted with water. Before serving, taste to check whether you need to add a little more butter.

285. CINGHIALE DOLCE-FORTE (SWEET-AND-SOUR WILD BOAR)

I think that when you prepare sweet-and-sour wild boar you should leave a layer of fat about the thickness of a finger inside the skin, because when cooked the fat of this wild pig remains firm, is not sickeningly greasy, and has a very pleasant, crispy texture.

Supposing that you have a piece of boar meat weighing roughly 1 kilogram (about 2 pounds), these are the proportions for the flavorings.

Take half an onion, half a large carrot, two stalks of white celery the length of the palm of your hand, a pinch of parsley and 30 grams (about 1 ounce) of untrimmed prosciutto. Chop finely with a mezzaluna and put the mixture at the bottom of a saucepan with olive oil, salt, and pepper, placing the wild boar on top to cook. When the meat has browned all over, pour out most of the fat, sprinkle a pinch of flour over it, and add hot water from time to time to finish cooking. In the meantime, prepare the sweet-and-sour sauce in a glass with the following ingredients—you will add it to the meat but only after straining the liquid already in the pan.

40 grams (about 1-1/3 ounces) of raisins
30 grams (about 1 ounce) of chocolate
30 grams (about 1 ounce) of pine nuts
20 grams (about 2/3 of an ounce) of diced candied fruit
50 grams (about 1-2/3 ounces) of sugar

Add vinegar to taste, but not too much, because you can always add more later. Before sending it to the table, simmer for a while so that all the seasonings blend well. In fact, I should tell you that sweet-and-sour sauce turns out better if you make it a day ahead. If you like it simpler, you can make the sweet-and-sour sauce with just sugar and vinegar.

You can cook hare the same way.

286. CINGHIALE FRA DUE FUOCHI
(OVEN-ROASTED WILD BOAR)

Keep the boar in a marinade (like the one for hare described in recipe 531) for 12 to 14 hours. Remove from the marinade, dry with a cloth, and then prepare as follows.

Place three or four paper-thin slices of lardoon in the bottom of a saucepan, place the piece of boar meat on top and season with salt and pepper, adding a whole onion, a *bouquet garni*, a bit of butter and, for a piece of meat weighing about 1 kilogram (about 2 pounds), half a glass of white wine. Lay another three or four slices of lardoon on top of the meat, and cover snugly with a sheet of paper greased with butter. Roast in the oven with embers all around, and if it looks like it is starting to dry out, moisten with broth. When the meat is cooked, strain the sauce, skimming the fat, and add it to the boar meat when you send the dish to the table.

287. COSTOLETTE DI DAINO ALLA CACCIATORA (VENISON CUTLETS HUNTER'S STYLE)

The meat of fallow and roe deer and similar game is dry and tough, so it is necessary to let it ripen for some time before it can be properly enjoyed.

For this dish, use the loin, from which you will cut the cutlets, making sure to keep them thin. Place on the fire the amount of butter and oil you need to cook the meat, a whole clove of garlic, and several sage leaves. When the garlic has browned, put the cutlets in the pan, season with salt and pepper, and cook quickly over high heat, moistening them with Marsala wine.

288. CONIGLIO IN UMIDO (RABBIT STEW)

To prepare this dish, see recipe 94 for pappardelle with rabbit sauce.

289. LINGUA DOLCE-FORTE (SWEET-AND-SOUR TONGUE)

Take a whole tongue of a milk-fed calf, including the root, which is the most delicate part. Skin the tongue and boil it until half done. For the rest of the dish, follow the directions for wild boar in recipe 285, using the water in which you have boiled the tongue to finish cooking it. To skin the tongue, take a red-hot spatula and place it on the tongue, repeating the operation several times if necessary.

290. LINGUA DI BUE AL SUGO DI CARNE
(BEEF TONGUE WITH BROWN STOCK)

Here's another way to cook a beef tongue that weighs, without the root, more than 1 kilogram (about 2 pounds).

Skin the tongue as indicated in recipe 289 and stud it with 60 grams (about 2 ounces) of lardoons seasoned with salt and pepper. Truss the tongue so that it will stay flat and put it on the fire with 30 grams (about 1 ounce) of butter. Season with salt and pepper and brown for quite a while. Then finish cooking with brown stock, which you will add a little at a time. When it is done, strain the sauce and reduce it over the fire with a bit of butter and less than half a tablespoon of flour. Serve over the tongue, which you will send to the table cut into slices with a side dish of boiled greens re-heated with butter and with some of the sauce.

291. ARNIONI SALTATI
(SAUTÉED KIDNEYS)

Take a "pietra" (stone), as it is called in Florence—that is, the kidney of a large animal or several kidneys of small animals—open it and remove all the fat, which has an unpleasant odor. Cut it crosswise into thin slices, place it in a bowl, salt it and pour in enough hot water to cover it. When the water has cooled, drain it and put it in a pan to make it sweat out whatever water is left, which you will then pour out. Sprinkle a pinch of flour over it, toss in a bit of butter and let it sizzle for just five minutes, stirring often. Season with salt, pepper, and less than half a glass of white wine. Leave it on the fire for a little while longer, and when you are about to remove it add another bit of butter, a pinch of chopped parsley, and a little broth, if necessary.

Keep in mind that kidneys become tough if left on the fire too long. It is a good idea to boil the wine and reduce it by 1/3 before using it. If you use Marsala or champagne instead of white wine, so much the better.

292. ARNIONI PER COLAZIONE
(KIDNEYS FOR LUNCH)

The kidneys of milk-fed calves, mutton, pigs, and similar animals are good for a midday meal when prepared in the following way. Before you start to cook the kidneys, have ready some parsley finely chopped with half a clove of garlic, the juice of half a lemon, and five to six slices of crustless bread which you have dried out over the fire.

Open the kidneys, remove the fat, and cut them crosswise into thin slices. If you have a total of between 400 and 500 grams (between about 14 ounces and 1 pound) of kidneys, toss them in a pan with between 50 and 60 grams (about 1-2/3 and 2 ounces) of butter over a high flame. Stir often, and as soon as the kidneys start to sizzle, toss in the parsley and garlic mixture. Season with salt and pepper. As you keep stirring with a wooden spoon, pour in the lemon juice, and at the very end add a ladleful of broth.

This should all take about five minutes. Send the kidneys to the table over the slices of bread.

This recipe serves four people.

293. ARNIONI ALLA FLORENTINA
(KIDNEYS FLORENTINE STYLE)

Open the kidneys and remove the fat as in recipe 291. Cook them just as they are—that is, cut in half lengthwise—in the following manner. Put a frying pan on the fire with an appropriate amount of butter; as soon as the butter starts to bubble, put the kidneys in the pan for just a little while; then remove them from the fire and season with salt, pepper, and a pinch of chopped parsley. Coat well with the seasonings and after several hours dip in bread crumbs and cook in the same pan, or on the grill.

294. COSCIOTTO O SPALLA DI CASTRATO IN CAZZARUOLA I (POT-ROASTED LEG OR SHOULDER OF MUTTON I)

By association of ideas, the word "castrato" brings to my mind those manservants who shave their mustaches and sideburns so that they look like so many eunuchs, with faces like Franciscan friars. This ridiculous practice is the result of the perverse vanity of their masters.

For the same reason, that is, their mistresses' vanity, maidservants scowl and complain that they do not want to wear those white caps otherwise known as bonnets. In fact, when they are no longer young or beautiful, they look like Barbary apes with that contraption on their heads. Wet nurses, on the other hand, who come from the country and have little concern for their own dignity, sport their bonnets decorated with colorful bows and ribbons—"indegne pompe, di servitù misere insegne" (unworthy pomp, of servitude the miserable banner)—strutting around unaware that they look like cows being led to market.

> To come to the subject at hand, I believe that these two cuts of meat are best when prepared in the following way. Let's take, for example, a shoulder of mutton, and you can calculate the amounts you will need for a leg accordingly. I do not need to tell you that the animal should be of excellent quality, nice and fat. Let's suppose that the shoulder weighs between 1 and 1-1/2 kilograms (about 2 to 3 pounds). Bone it, stud it with lardoons, and season inside and out with salt and pepper; then roll it and tie it into a nice shape. Place the meat in a casserole with 40 grams (about 1-1/3 ounces) of butter and brown it. Then add the following ingredients:

> *several lardoon or prosciutto rinds*
> *1 bouquet garni made of parsley, celery, and carrot*
> *1 whole medium-sized onion*
> *the bones you have removed from the shoulder or leg, cracked*
> *some scraps of raw meat, if you have any*
> *1 glass of broth (1/2 glass will do)*
> *2 or 3 tablespoons of brandy*

Put the mutton in enough cold water to almost cover it. Cover the pan tightly and simmer until the meat is cooked, which should take four or more hours if the meat is tough. Then strain the sauce, discarding what does not go through, skim off the fat, and serve only the mutton meat.

This dish is usually garnished with carrots, turnips, or shelled beans. If you use carrots, put two large whole carrots in with the meat. When they are done remove them and cut into small wheels, which you will add later. If you use turnips, make sure they are not too strong tasting if the weather has not been cold yet. Cut the turnips into four sections, blanch them, dice, brown lightly in butter and add to the sauce, which should be quite abundant. If you use beans, cook them first and then re-heat in the mutton sauce.

295. COSCIOTTO O SPALLA DI CASTRATO IN CAZZARUOLA II (POT-ROASTED LEG OR SHOULDER OF MUTTON II)

This is a simpler recipe, and preferable to the preceding one when you do not intend to accompany it with greens or legumes.

Take a shoulder of mutton, bone it, and stud it with lardoons rolled in salt and pepper. Salt the meat a bit, then roll it and tie tightly, before placing it to brown on the fire with 40 grams (about 1-1/3 ounces) of butter and half an onion studded with a clove. Remove the saucepan from the fire, and pour in a glass of water or, better yet, broth, a tablespoon of brandy, a *bouquet garni*, and a few chopped fresh tomatoes if they are in season. Cover the pan with a double sheet of paper and simmer for around three hours, turning the piece of meat often. When it is cooked, discard the onion, strain the sauce, skim off the fat, and pour the sauce over the meat before you send the dish to the table.

Be careful not to overcook the meat, otherwise you will not be able to slice it.

You can prepare a leg of mutton in the same way, using the appropriate amounts of seasonings. If you find the distinctive smell of mutton sickening, trim the fat while the meat is still raw.

296. LOMBATA DI CASTRATO RIPIENA
(STUFFED LOIN OF MUTTON)

Take a piece of loin of mutton with its fatty underskin weighing 1 kilogram (about 2 pounds). Remove most of the fat, but not all, bone it, and season with salt and pepper. Make the stuffing with the following:

150 grams (about 5-1/4 ounces) of lean milk-fed veal
50 grams (about 1-2/3 ounces) of untrimmed prosciutto
40 grams (about 1-1/3 ounces) of grated Parmesan cheese
1 egg
salt and pepper

Finely chop the veal and prosciutto; add the other ingredients, and spread over the whole inside of the loin. Roll up the meat and sew it up so that the stuffing will not burst out. Now put it on the fire with 50 grams (about 1-2/3 ounces) of butter; when it has browned, moisten with a finger's worth of Marsala wine. Then toss into the saucepan to simmer with the meat half of a rather small onion cut into two pieces, two or three pieces of celery, two or three pieces of carrot, and some sprigs of parsley. As the last step, strain the sauce, skim the fat, and serve. This dish will serve eight people, and deserves to be recommended.

You already know that to skim the fat from a sauce all you have to do is place a few pieces of absorbent paper on top of it.

297. BUE ALLA MODA
(BEEF À LA MODE)

The preparation of this dish is not much different from that of recipe 294.

Take a piece of lean leg or rump of beef weighing no less than 1 kilogram (about 2 pounds) and stud it with nice lardoons—as thick as a finger—that you have rolled in salt and pepper. Tie the piece of meat into a nice shape, season generously with salt, and put it in a saucepan to brown with 50 grams (about 1-2/3 ounces) of butter.

Then add the following ingredients: half a foot of a milk-fed calf, or one piece of a large calf's foot; one whole large onion; two or three whole carrots; one *bouquet garni* of aromatic herbs such as parsley, celery, basil, and the like; several pork rinds; a glassful of water or, better yet, of skimmed broth; and lastly half a glass of white wine or two tablespoons of brandy. Put the pan, tightly covered, on the fire and simmer until the meat is cooked. Since the carrots will be done first, remove them so that they will stay whole. Remove and discard the *bouquet garni* and then strain the sauce, skimming off the fat if necessary. Take care not to overcook the meat and serve it with the calf's foot, garnishing the dish with the carrots sliced into rounds. If it turns out right, you will taste a delicate, light stew.

Some people stud the onion with cloves, but this spice is not recommended for those with delicate stomachs. In my opinion, shelled beans cooked and then re-heated in the sauce from the meat make a better accompaniment than carrots.

298. BUE ALLA BRACE
(BRAISED BEEF)

This is what the French call *boeuf braisé*. Find a nice piece of lean, tender beef. Take a piece that weighs 500 grams (about 1 pound) without the bone, and stud it with 50 grams (about 1-2/3 ounces) of rather thick, finger-length lardoons, seasoned with salt and pepper.

Chop with a mezzaluna a quarter of a medium-sized onion, half a carrot, and a stalk of celery as long as your palm. Place on the fire with 30 grams (about 1 ounce) of butter and then add your piece of meat, tied and seasoned with salt and pepper.

When the seasonings are almost entirely dissolved, moisten twice with a droplet of cold water. When this too has been totally absorbed and the meat has browned, pour in two ladles of hot water, cover the pan with a double sheet of paper, and simmer until the meat is cooked. Then strain the sauce, skim off the fat, and put it back on the fire with another bit of butter to enhance the flavor of the meat and the sauce. You can use this meat sauce to flavor a side dish of vegetables such as spinach, Brussels sprouts, carrots, or fennel, whichever you prefer.

299. GIRELLO ALLA BRACE
(BRAISED TOP ROUND OF BEEF)

Would you like a meat dish from Bologna, one of the simplest dishes imaginable? Then make "garetto."

> Garetto is the Bolognese name for top round, which is the boneless cut of beef situated almost at the top of the thigh, between the round and the rump. It can weigh up to around 700 grams (about 1-1/2 pounds), and is the only cut of beef that lends itself to this type of dish. Put the meat on the fire in a saucepan, with no other seasoning than salt and pepper—no water, and no other ingredients. Cover the saucepan with a sheet of paper folded in half several times and kept in place by the lid. Simmer very slowly. You will see that it gives off a copious amount of juice, which it later reabsorbs little by little. When the meat has reabsorbed all the juice, remove it from the saucepan and serve. It is almost better cold than hot. No one can doubt that this is a healthy, nutritious dish; but I am not sure that everyone will like it because it is so simple.

300. BUE ALLA CALIFORNIA
(BEEF CALIFORNIA STYLE)

Whoever concocted this dish probably did not know what to call it, so he gave it this strange name. But for that matter, almost all culinary terms are either strange or ridiculous.

After testing the recipe several times, I recommend the following amounts:

> 700 grams (about 1-1/2 pounds) of lean, boneless beef or veal
>   from the rump, loin, or fillet
> 50 grams (about 1-2/3 ounces) of butter
> 2 deciliters (about 4/5 of a cup) of heavy cream
> 2 deciliters (about 4/5 of a cup) of water
> 1 tablespoon of strong vinegar, or more if the vinegar is weak

Put the meat on the fire with the butter, half an onion cut into four sections, and a carrot cut into small pieces; season with salt and pepper. When the meat is nicely browned, pour in the vinegar; after a while add the water, and then the cream. Simmer for about three hours, but if the sauce begins to dry up add a little more water.

Slice the meat and serve with its sauce, which you will strain first. As part of a meal of several courses, this should serve five to six people.

301. SCANNELLO ANNEGATO
("DROWNED" RUMP ROAST)

I did not know what to call this simple, healthy pot roast, so I gave it the name drowned rump roast.

800 grams (about 1-3/4 pounds) of lean, boneless rump of beef or veal
80 grams (about 2-2/3 ounces) of fat trimmed from prosciutto
1 large or 2 medium-sized carrots
3 or 4 ribs of celery as long as the palm of your hand
1/2 a glass of dry white wine, or, lacking that, 2 fingers of Marsala wine

Cut the fat from the prosciutto into small pieces, roll in salt and pepper, and lard the meat with it; salt the meat and tie it so that it will stay together.

Cut the carrot and celery into small pieces and place them on the bottom of a rather small saucepan; place the piece of meat on top of this, and cover with water. Simmer in the covered saucepan, and when the meat has absorbed the water, strain the sauce and the vegetables. Then put the sauce back on the fire with the meat and the wine. When the meat is cooked, slice and serve with the sauce poured over it. These amounts should serve six people.

As you have probably noticed in this recipe and in many others in this collection, my cooking tends to be simple and light. I try as much as possible to avoid dishes that are too elaborate and contain a heterogeneous mixture of ingredients, and that, as a result, upset the stomach. Nevertheless, a good friend of mine unjustly slandered my cooking, mistaking it for someone else's. He had been struck by progressive paralysis, which kept him an invalid for more than three years. The only consolation he could find in his misfortune was eating well, and when he would ask his daughter to prepare him a meal, he never failed to say: "And make sure not to give me any of Artusi's swill!"

This young lady, who ran her father's household, had received her education in a girls' school in the French part of Switzerland; and while she was in there, she had acquired Madame Roubinet's treatise on cooking. She wholeheartedly admired this cookbook, and thus paid little or no heed to mine. Thus the "swill" so bemoaned by her father came from this Madame "Faucet,"[60] who evidently let her spigot flow with dirty kitchen water, something *I* would never do.

302. SCALOPPINE ALLA LIVORNESE
(VEAL CUTLETS LIVORNO STYLE)

Why they are called "scaloppine" I have no idea, nor do I know what they have to do with the city of Livorno. At any rate, take some boneless cutlets from a large piece of meat, pound them well to make them tender, and throw them in a pan with a bit of butter. When the meat has absorbed the butter, finish cooking with a few tablespoons of broth. Season with salt and pepper, bind with a pinch of flour, and add a dash of Marsala wine. Before removing the cutlets from the pan add a pinch of minced parsley as a final flavoring touch.

303. SCALOPPINE DI CARNE BATTUTA
(GROUND MEAT CUTLETS)

Take a lean cut of meat from a large animal, remove the tendons and any membranes, and, if you do not have a meat grinder, chop very fine first with a knife and then with a mezzaluna. Season with salt, pepper, and grated Parmesan cheese. Add aromatic herbs if you like, but then you might run the risk of it tasting like a dish made with leftovers. Mix well and form the meat into a ball. Sprinkling the top and bottom with bread crumbs so that it will not stick, flatten the meat out with a rolling pin on a pastry board, moving it often, to form a patty a little thicker than a good-sized coin. Cut the patty

60 Artusi is making a pun on the word "robinet," meaning "faucet."

into squares the width of the palm of your hand and cook with butter in a frying pan. When the cutlets have browned, moisten them with tomato sauce (recipe 6) or tomato paste diluted with broth or water, then serve. Without using a rolling pin, you can also flatten out the chopped meat with your hands, and form it into heart-shapes for a fancier look.

If you have some leftover stewed meat, you can add it to the raw meat to make these cutlets.

304. SCALOPPINE ALLA GENOVESE
(CUTLETS GENOESE STYLE)

Slice lean veal into cutlets. To prepare 500 grams (about 1 pound) of boneless meat, chop a quarter of a medium-sized onion and put it on the bottom of a saucepan with some olive oil and a bit of butter. Arrange the cutlets in layers on top of the chopped onion, season with salt and pepper, and put on the fire without touching them; in this way they stick to each other and do not shrivel. When the cutlets have browned on the bottom, pour in a teaspoon of flour and after a little while add a pinch of parsley and half a clove of garlic (both chopped), as well as a little less than two fingers of good white wine or, if you do not have that, Marsala wine. Now separate the cutlets from one another, stir, and let them absorb the liquid. Then pour in hot water and a little tomato sauce (recipe 6) or tomato paste. Simmer slowly, but not for too long, until cooked. Serve over slices of toasted bread, with a generous amount of the sauce from the pan. Or if you prefer, serve with a side dish of rice cooked in water until quite firm and seasoned lightly with butter, Parmesan cheese, and the sauce from the cutlets. In fact, rice goes very well with this dish, and everyone will like it this way.

305. SCALOPPINE CON LA PANNA ACIDA
(CUTLETS IN SOUR CREAM)

Sour cream is ordinary cream—that is, the cream that rises to the top of milk—when it has naturally soured, a "defect" that does not harm but rather improves this dish, which is very delicate.

Take lean veal or milk-fed veal, cut it into small cutlets, pound, dredge in flour, and put on the fire with an appropriate amount of butter. Season with salt and pepper and cook over a low flame until the cutlets have browned on both sides. Then add the sour cream. If you are using milk-fed veal, add a little water or broth at the end so that the sauce does not turn out too thick and the cutlets cook better.

Serve with lemon wedges on the side.

For four people, use 500 grams (about 1 pound) of boneless, lean veal, 70 grams (about 2-1/3 ounces) of butter, and 2 deciliters (about 4/5 of a cup) of sour cream.

306. SCALOPPINE DI VITELLA DI LATTE IN TORTINO

(LAYERED MILK-FED VEAL CUTLETS)

Take 70 grams (about 2-1/3 ounces) of thinly sliced lardoons and 300 grams (about 10-1/2 ounces) of lean, boneless, milk-fed veal, remove the membranes covering it (if any) and cut into very thin slices.

Melt a little butter in an appropriately sized saucepan and line it with the lardoons, on top of which you will arrange a first layer of cutlets seasoned with salt, pepper, a hint of spices, grated Parmesan cheese, and chopped parsley. Then add another layer of cutlets seasoned in the same way, and so forth until you have used all up all the veal. Scatter several pieces of butter over the last layer of veal, and cook with embers all around, but with the fire below stronger than the fire above, until the veal is almost dry and the lardoons have browned. Pour the contents of the saucepan over a bed of spinach cooked in butter and send to the table. These amounts serve four people.

307. BRACIOLINE RIPIENE

(STUFFED VEAL CUTLETS)

300 grams (about 10-1/2 ounces) of thin veal cutlets
70 grams (about 2-1/3 ounces) of lean veal or milk-fed veal
40 grams (about 1-1/3 ounces) of rather lean prosciutto
30 grams (about 1 ounce) of veal marrow
30 grams (about 1 ounce) of grated Parmesan cheese
1 egg

You should get 6 or 7 cutlets if you cut them the width of the palm of your hand. Pound very well with a meat mallet or the handle of a knife dipped frequently in water to flatten them out. Then finely chop the prosciutto with the other 70 grams (about 2-1/3 ounces) of meat; add the Parmesan cheese and the bone marrow, which you have first turned into a paste with the blade of a knife. Lastly, add the egg to bind the mixture, and a dash of pepper (it is not necessary to add salt because of the prosciutto and the Parmesan cheese). Spread out the chops and cover half of each with this mixture; then roll them up and tie with twine.

Now that the cutlets have the proper shape, chop a bit of onion, a small piece of white celery, a small piece of carrot, and 20 grams (about 2/3 of an ounce) of bacon; put on the fire in a saucepan with the cutlets and 20 grams (about 2/3 of an ounce) of butter. Season with salt and pepper, and, when the chops have browned, pour in some tomato sauce (recipe 6) or tomato paste and finish cooking with water. You can also add a little of white wine if you like. Before serving, remove the twine you used to tie them.

308. BRACIOLINE ALLA BARTOLA
(CUTLETS BARTOLA)

The best cut of beef or veal for this dish is the fillet or top of the round, but you can also use the rump or the thigh.

500 grams (about 1 pound) net weight of boneless beef or veal
50 grams (about 1-2/3 ounces) of untrimmed prosciutto
1 small clove of garlic
1 small section of onion
1 stalk of celery as long as the palm of your hand
1 good-sized piece of carrot
a pinch of parsley

Cut the meat into slices almost as thick as your finger to obtain no more than 7 or 8 cutlets, which you should try to shape nicely. Pound with the back of a knife blade. Chop the prosciutto and the other ingredients described above very finely. Pour six tablespoons of oil into a skillet or a copper pan. Put the cutlets in the oil, still cold, and spread a little of the chopped mixture on top of each cutlet. Season with a little salt, pepper, and the flower from four or five cloves. Brown the bottom of the cutlets over a high flame. Then turn one by one and brown the other side with the bit of soffritto, and when this has browned sufficiently turn the cutlets again so that the soffritto is on top again; scrape off whatever has stuck to the bottom of the pan. Now moisten the cutlets with tomato sauce (recipe 6) or tomato paste diluted with water, cover, and simmer for almost two hours. A half hour before you intend to serve them, cook in this sauce a large peeled potato, cut into ten or twelve pieces, arranging the pieces of potato in the spaces between the cutlets.

It is best to serve this dish directly from the pan in which it is cooked; but if this seems improper, layer the cutlets on a platter with the potatoes all around. These amounts should serve four or five people. This is not a dish to be sneered at, because it is not hard on the stomach.

309. BRACIOLINE ALLA CONTADINA
(COUNTRY-STYLE CUTLETS)

These are not to my taste, so I would just as soon let the peasants eat them. But since some people may like them, I will describe them to you.

Form the cutlets from lean, well-pounded veal. Rub with olive oil and season with a little salt and pepper. Finely chop some pickled olives, capers drained of brine, and an anchovy. You may leave the mixture simple, as I have described it, or you can also add one egg yolk and a pinch of grated Parmesan cheese. Stuff the cutlets with this mixture, tie them, and cook with butter and tomato sauce (recipe 6), or else in a little fried onion.

310. BRACIUOLE DI MAIALE NELLA SCAMERITA
(SCAMERITA CUTLETS)

Here is a typically Florentine dish for you. The "scamerita" is the part of a butchered pig where the loin ends and the leg begins. This cut is marbled with fat, enough to please without turning the stomach.

Place the cutlets in a pan with very little oil and two or three slightly crushed, unpeeled cloves of garlic, and season with salt and pepper. When they have browned on both sides, pour in two or three fingers of red wine, and simmer until the liquid is reduced by half. Remove the cutlets from the liquid and set aside, keeping them warm. Use the sauce to reheat some boiled red cabbage which you have squeezed dry, chopped not too fine, and also seasoned with salt and pepper. Serve the cutlets on top of the cabbage.

311. COTOLETTE DI VITELLA DI LATTE IN SALSA D'UOVO (MILK-FED VEAL CUTLETS IN EGG SAUCE)

After you have brushed the cutlets with egg yolk and sautéed them as in recipes 312 and 313, spread over them a sauce made of egg yolk, butter, and lemon juice. Keep on the fire a little longer, then serve. For seven or eight cutlets, you need three egg yolks, 30 grams (about 1 ounce) of butter, and the juice of half a lemon. Beat these ingredients together in a little saucepan before adding them to the meat.

312. COTOLETTE DI VITELLA DI LATTE O DI AGNELLO COI TARTUFI ALLA BOLOGNESE (MILK-FED VEAL OR LAMB CUTLETS WITH TRUFFLES BOLOGNESE STYLE)

The best cut of veal for this dish is the *sous-noix* or lower part of the thigh, but you can also use the lean part of the rest of the thigh or rump. Cut the meat into thin slices the size of the palm of your hand. Pound the cutlets and give them a rounded, elegant shape such as, for example, a heart shape—that is, wide on top and narrow at the bottom. This is easier to do if you mince the meat first with a mezzaluna. Then arrange the cutlets on a plate and season them with lemon juice, pepper, salt, and very little grated Parmesan cheese. After they have been sitting in this infusion for an hour or two, soak the cutlets in beaten egg for the same amount of time. Then roll in fine bread crumbs, and sauté them in butter in a copper skillet. When they begin to brown on one side, turn them over and lay on top first the sliced truffles and then slices of Parmesan or Gruyère cheese. Whichever cheese you use, slice it as thin as possible. Once this is done, finish cooking with heat above and below, adding broth or brown stock. Then remove them one by one and arrange on a platter, accompanying them with their sauce and squeezing on top the juice of one lemon, or half a lemon if you have just a few cutlets.

Lamb chops can be cooked in the same way, after having stripped the rib bones.

313. COTOLETTE COL PROSCIUTTO (CUTLETS WITH PROSCIUTTO)

Prepare these cutlets like the ones in the preceding recipe and dip in beaten egg with a very thin slice of untrimmed prosciutto about the same size as the cutlet itself. Roll in bread crumbs with the prosciutto, salt lightly, and brown in butter on the side without the prosciutto. On top of the prosciutto lay very thin slices of Parmesan or Gruyère cheese rather than truffles. Finish cooking in the oven with embers all around, and serve with brown stock and lemon juice, or with tomato sauce.

314. POLPETTE (MEATBALLS)

Do not think for a moment that I would be so pretentious as to tell you how to make meatballs. This is a dish that everyone knows how to make, beginning with the jackass, which was perhaps the first to provide the model for the meatball for the human race. My sole intention is to tell you how to prepare them when you have leftover boiled meat. Should you wish to make them more simply, or with raw meat, you will not need as much seasoning.

Chop the boiled meat with a mezzaluna; separately, mince a slice of untrimmed prosciutto and add to the chopped meat. Season with grated Parmesan cheese, salt, pepper, a dash of spices, raisins, pine nuts, and a few tablespoons of a mash made with crustless bread cooked in broth or milk. Bind this mixture with an egg or two, depending on the amount. Shape the meat into balls the size of an egg, "flattened at the ends like the terrestrial globe," roll in bread crumbs, and fry in oil or lard. Then, transfer them to a baking dish with some chopped garlic and parsley, which you have fried in the grease left in the pan, garnishing with a sauce made with an egg and lemon juice.

If your stomach cannot tolerate soffritti, put the meatballs in the baking pan with a bit of butter, but I assure you that a soffritto, when done right, does not irritate but rather stimulates the stomach to digest better. I remember the time I was at lunch with some ladies in a fashionable restaurant which had pretensions of cooking food in the French style—too French indeed!—where we were served a dish of sweetbreads and peas. Both were fresh and of the highest quality, but they had been cooked with butter alone, with no soffritto, not even a nice broth, and no herbs of any kind. They could have made for a excellent, tasty dish, but instead we could feel that it was not agreeing with our stomachs, and everybody had trouble digesting it.

315. POLPETTONE (MEAT LOAF)

Dear Mr. Meat Loaf, please come forward, do not be shy. I want to introduce you to my readers.

I know that you are modest and humble, because, given your background, you feel inferior to many others. But take heart and do not doubt that with a few words in your favor you shall find someone who wants to taste you and who might even reward you with a smile.

This meat loaf is made with leftover boiled meat, and, though simple, it is an agreeable dish. Remove the fat from the meat and chop the rest with a mezzaluna. Season with an appropriate amount of salt, pepper, grated Parmesan cheese, one or two eggs, and two or three tablespoons of a mash made with crustless bread cooked in milk, broth, or simply in water, and flavored with a little butter. Mix everything together, shape into an oblong loaf, and sprinkle with flour. Then fry it in lard or oil, and you will see that soft as it was before, it will become firm and will acquire a delicate crust on the surface. Remove from the pan, and sauté on both sides in a skillet with butter. When you are about to serve it, coat it with two beaten eggs, a pinch of salt, and the juice of half a lemon. Make this sauce separately in a small saucepan, treating it as you would a cream sauce, and pour it over the meat loaf, which you have placed on a platter.

If the meat loaf is large, turn it over in the pan using a plate or a copper lid, as you would for a frittata; this ensures that you will not spoil it.

316. POLPETTONE DI CARNE CRUDA ALLA FIORENTINA (FLORENTINE-STYLE MEAT LOAF WITH FRESH MEAT)

Take 1/2 a kilogram (about 1 pound) of boneless lean veal. Remove the membranes and the gristle, and then chop finely, together with a slice of untrimmed prosciutto, first with a knife and then with a mezzaluna. Season with a little salt, pepper, and spices; add an egg, mix well. Wet your hands before shaping the meat into a ball, which you will then roll in flour.

Chop a little bit of onion (about the size of a walnut), some parsley, celery, and carrot, and put on the fire with a bit of butter. When this begins to brown, toss in the meat loaf. Brown all over and then pour in a generous half glass of water in which you have dissolved one tablespoon of flour. Cover and simmer very slowly, making sure that it does not stick. Serve it with its dense sauce all around it, squeezing half a lemon over it.

If you want to prepare meat loaf in the Piedmontese style, all you have to do is to place a peeled, hard-cooked egg in the center of the ball of meat when you shape it; this gives the meat loaf a more attractive appearance when it is sliced. This is not a dish to be sneered at.

317. QUENELLES (FRENCH STYLE DUMPLINGS)

Quenelles are a dish of French origin as well as type, as you can tell by the name, for which there is no equivalent in Italian. Perhaps they were invented by a cook whose master had no teeth.

120 grams (about 4-1/4 ounces) of milk-fed veal
80 grams (about 2-2/3 ounces) of fat from the kidney of a milk-
*   fed calf*
50 grams (about 1-2/3 ounces) of flour
30 grams (about 1 ounce) of butter
1 whole egg
1 egg yolk
2 deciliters (about 4/5 of a cup) of milk

Remove and discard the membranes covering the meat, as well as the thin casing around the kidney fat. Now weigh the meat and the kidney, chop them as finely as you can first with a knife and then with a mezzaluna, and then grind in a mortar until they have been reduced to a very fine paste.

Make a béchamel sauce with the flour, butter, and milk mentioned above, and when it has cooled add the ground meat and the eggs. Season with salt only, and blend well. Spread a thin sheet of flour over a pastry board, pour the meat mixture onto the board, lightly flour it, and then roll into 18 or 20 finger-long spool shapes, similar to sausages.

Put the water on the fire in a large pan, and when it begins to boil throw in the quenelles. Boil for 8 or 10 minutes, and you will see them swell up. Then remove them from the water with a slotted spoon, and serve them smothered in the tomato sauce of recipe 125, to which you can add some fresh or dried mushrooms (cooked beforehand in the same sauce) and some pitted brine-cured olives. You can use brown stock instead of tomato sauce, or you can flavor the quenelles with a sauce of giblets and sweetbreads. They can also be made with the white meat of chicken or with fish. These amounts should serve five people.

If you use tomato sauce, which is the best suited to this very delicate-tasting dish, thicken it with a mixture of 30 grams (about 1 ounce) of butter and one tablespoon of flour. Pour the tomato sauce into this roux when it has turned nut-brown over the fire.

318. AGNELLO TRIPPATO
(*FRICASSÉE* OF LAMB)

Break 500 grams (about 1 pound) of lamb loin into pieces and fry them in virgin lard. Then pour the leftover fat into a different pan where you will sauté some chopped garlic and parsley. When the garlic has browned, toss in the lamb, season with salt and pepper, stir thoroughly, and leave it on the fire for a while so that it absorbs the seasoning. Then bind it with the following sauce: beat two eggs with a generous pinch of grated Parmesan cheese and the juice of half a lemon. Pour over the lamb, stir, and when the egg has thickened somewhat, serve.

319. AGNELLO COI PISELLI ALL'USO DI ROMAGNA
(LAMB WITH PEAS ROMAGNA STYLE)

Take a lamb hindquarter and stud it with two cloves of garlic (cut into tiny strips) and a few sprigs of rosemary. I said sprigs rather than leaves, because sprigs may be more easily removed once the lamb is cooked. Take a piece of lardoon or a slice of bacon and chop fine with a knife. Put the lamb on the fire in a pan with the chopped lardoon and a little oil. Season with salt and pepper, and brown. When the lamb has browned, add a bit of butter, tomato sauce (recipe 6) or tomato paste diluted with broth or water, and cook until perfectly done. Then remove the lamb from the pan for a moment, pour the peas into the sauce, and when they have boiled a little put the lamb back on top of them, cook until the peas are done, and serve them as a side dish.

You can cook a piece of milk-fed veal loin or rump in the same manner.

These dishes are prepared in almost the same way in Tuscany as in Romagna, but in Tuscany olive oil is all they use as a condiment.

320. SPALLA D'AGNELLO ALL'UNGHERESE
(SHOULDER OF LAMB HUNGARIAN STYLE)

If it is not Hungarian, it might be Spanish or Flemish—the name does not matter, as long as it is to the taste of whoever eats it, which I believe it will be.

Cut the shoulder into thin square pieces about three fingers wide. Finely chop two spring onions, or three or four small white onions and sauté them with a bit of butter. When the onions have turned dark brown, toss in the lamb and season with salt and pepper. Wait until the meat itself begins to brown, then add another bit of butter rolled in flour. Stir until it turns a nice color, then finish cooking with broth which you will add a little at a time. Take care not to serve dry, but rather send to the table with a good amount of its own sauce.

321. TESTICCIUOLA D'AGNELLO
(LAMB'S HEAD)

To stew a lamb's head, do not cut it in half crosswise like the maid-servant whose master told her to divide it in two. It was this same gifted girl who on another occasion skewered some thrushes on a spit from back to front.

Cut the head lengthwise along its natural division and put both pieces in a large pan. But first sauté some chopped garlic and parsley in olive oil, and when this has browned, stop it from cooking with a ladleful of broth. Toss in the lamb's head and season with salt and pepper. When it is halfway done, add a bit of butter and a little tomato sauce (recipe 6) or tomato paste, and finish cooking with more broth, if necessary.

This is not a dish to serve to guests, but for the family it is inexpensive and tasty. The part around the eye is the most delicate.

322. COTEGHINO FASCIATO[61]
(SPICED PORK SAUSAGE OR
COTECHINO BOILED IN A WRAP)

I will not pretend that this is an elegant dish, but rather one for the family, and as such it does the job perfectly well, and indeed you could even serve it to close friends. Speaking of close friends, Giusti says that people who are in a position to do so, should occasionally invite their close friends to get their mustaches greasy at their table. I am of the same opinion, even if the guests will probably proceed to speak ill of you, and of how they were treated.

Skin an uncooked cotechino weighing about 300 grams (about 10-1/2 ounces). Take a large, thin cutlet of lean veal or beef weighing between 200 and 300 grams (about 7 and 10-1/2 ounces), and pound well. Wrap the cutlet around the cotechino, tie it all up with twine and put on the fire in a saucepan with a bit of butter, some celery, carrot, and a quarter of an onion, all coarsely chopped. Salt and pepper are not necessary, because the cotechino contains plenty of these ingredients. If you plan to use the sauce on a first course of macaroni, add some slices of untrimmed prosciutto or some bacon. When the piece of meat has browned all over, pour in enough water to cover it halfway, and throw in some little pieces of dried mushrooms; simmer slowly until completely cooked. Strain the sauce, but add back the mushrooms, then use the sauce, along with cheese and butter, to season macaroni. Serve the cotechino as the main course, keeping it wrapped in the cutlet, but removing the twine, and garnishing it with a good amount of its own sauce.

It is a good idea to thicken the sauce for the pasta a bit with a pinch of flour. Put the flour in a saucepan with a bit of butter, and when it starts to brown pour in the sauce and boil for a while.

A side dish of carrots goes very well with this dish. First boil the carrots until two-thirds done and then finish cooking in the meat sauce.

---

61 "Coteghino," or today more commonly "cotechino," is a rather large sausage made with pork rind mixed with lean pork and back fat, usually flavored with salt, pepper, cloves, and cinnamon. This sausage is meant to be cooked before it is eaten. It is a fat-rich, hearty food.

3 2 3 . STUFATINO DI MUSCOLO
(LEAN VEAL STEW)

Everyone knows that the muscles of animals, including the human *animal*, are the bundles of fibers making up the flesh. But in the Florentine dialect, "muscolo" is also the name for the cut of veal where the leg ends and the shoulder begins. This cut of meat contains tender, gelatinous tendons that lend themselves to this cooking method.

Cut 500 grams (about 1 pound) of "muscolo" of veal or of milk-fed veal into small pieces. Put some oil on the fire with two unpeeled, slightly crushed cloves of garlic. Sauté the garlic and then toss in the meat, seasoning with salt and pepper. When the meat has browned, sprinkle half a tablespoon of flour over it, adding tomato sauce (recipe 6) or tomato paste and a bit of butter; then add water or broth a little at a time to finish cooking. Make sure to have some sauce left in the pan at the end. Arrange slices of toasted bread on a platter, pour the stew over them, and send to the table. You can also serve this stew without toasted bread, adding sliced fresh mushrooms or potatoes when the meat is almost done.

3 2 4 . STUFATINO DI PETTO DI VITELLA DI LATTE
COI FINOCCHI (STEWED BREAST OF
MILK-FED VEAL WITH FENNEL)

Cut into pieces a breast of milk-fed veal, without removing the bones. Finely chop some garlic, parsley, celery, carrot, and an appropriately sized slice of bacon; add oil, pepper, and salt and put on the fire with the veal. Turn often, and when the meat has browned, sprinkle with a pinch of flour, add a little tomato sauce (recipe 6) or tomato paste, and finish cooking with broth or water. At the end, add a bit of butter and some fennel, cut into large sections that have been parboiled and sautéed in butter. As with all other stews, keep the saucepan covered.

When I say "saucepans," I mean copper pans, well coated inside with a layer of tin. People can say what they like, but copper, when kept clean, is always preferable to iron or earthenware, which get too hot and tend to burn the food cooking in them. Earthenware cracks and absorbs grease, and after too much use starts to give off a bad smell.

325. VITELLA DI LATTE IN GUAZZETTO
(MILK-FED VEAL STEW)

This stew is not particularly flavorful, but it is simple and healthy, so I will describe it. Take a *sous-noix* or rump of veal, pound it, tie it to hold it together, and put in a saucepan as follows.

If the piece of meat weighs 500 grams (about 1 pound) without the bones, cover the bottom of the saucepan with 30 grams (about 1 ounce) of very thinly sliced bacon and 30 grams (about 1 ounce) of butter. On top of this layer arrange less than half a lemon cut into four thin rindless and seedless slices. Place the veal on top of all this, and brown it well all over; but take care not to let it burn, since there is very little liquid. When the meat has browned, pour off the extra fat, season with salt and pepper, and, after a little while, add a glass of hot milk that you have boiled separately; do not get upset if the milk curdles, which it probably will do.

Cover the saucepan with a sheet of paper folded in two, and finish cooking the piece of meat over a slow fire. Strain the sauce just before serving.

This recipe serves four people.

326. PETTO DI VITELLA DI LATTE RIPIENO
(STUFFED BREAST OF MILK-FED VEAL)

In culinary terms this would be called "petto farsito" (stuffed breast).

500 grams (about 1 pound) of milk-fed veal breast in a single piece
170 grams (about 6 ounces) of lean boneless milk-fed veal
40 grams (about 1-1/3 ounces) of untrimmed prosciutto
40 grams (about 1-1/3 ounces) of mortadella from Bologna
15 grams (about 1/2 an ounce) of Parmesan cheese
1 egg
less than 1/4 of a clove of garlic
4 or 5 parsley leaves

Make a mixture with the lean veal in the following way: remove the tendons and gristle, if any, and mince very fine with a bit of fat taken from the 40 grams (about 1-1/3 ounces) of prosciutto. To this minced meat add the garlic and parsley, both chopped very fine, the Parmesan, the egg, a pinch of pepper and very little salt, then blend thoroughly. If you happen to have a little truffle, chop it up and add it as well to the mixture—you will find it a marvelous addition.

Remove the hard bones from the breast of veal, and leave the soft ones. Cut open the breast as follows: run a knife under the ribs, slicing the connecting tissues in half; now double the surface area by "opening" the meat, as if it were a book. Spread part of the chopped veal mixture over the half of the breast where the softer bones remain, and on top of this arrange in turn some of the prosciutto and mortadella, cut into strips as wide as your finger, leaving a little space between each strip. On top of this first layer place a second and then a third, if you have enough ingredients to do so, always alternating between the veal mixture and the layer of cured meat strips. When you are done, fold over the other half of the breast of veal, closing the "book," so to speak, and sew the edges with a large needle and thread, so that the filling does not leak out. In addition, tie the breast firmly crosswise with twine. Once you have dressed the meat in this manner, put it on the fire in a saucepan with a bit of butter, salt, and pepper, and when it has browned on both sides finish cooking with water added a little at a time.

Serve warm with its own concentrated juice; but first remove the twine and thread. If it has turned out right, you should be able to slice the veal, which will look quite handsome with the layers of prosciutto and mortadella. You can serve it with fresh peas cooked in the meat sauce, or with sections of fennel that you have boiled in advance.

327. ARROSTINI DI VITELLA DI LATTE ALLA SALVIA (ROASTED MILK-FED VEAL CHOPS WITH SAGE)

Prepare this dish with loin of milk-fed veal (remove the gristle but do not bone), cut into thin chops. Using a saucepan or a copper skillet, sauté some whole sage leaves in an appropriate amount of butter. Once the sage has fried a little, toss in the chops, and while they are browning over a high flame, salt on both sides and then sprinkle with a little flour; then finish cooking with Marsala wine. The chops should remain a little moist.

With 500 grams (about 1 pound) of veal loin, weighed after the gristle has been cut away, you will make about six chops. For this amount of meat, less than a finger of Marsala wine will suffice, and if necessary a little tomato sauce. As to flour, a teaspoon will do.

3 2 8 . LOMBO DI MAIALE RIPIENO
(STUFFED PORK LOIN)

Use a piece of pork loin from the part without ribs.

1 kilogram (about 2 pounds) of pork loin
100 grams (about 3-1/2 ounces) of pork caul[62]
100 grams (about 3-1/2 ounces) of lean milk-fed veal
50 grams (about 1-2/3 ounces) of untrimmed prosciutto
50 grams (about 1-2/3 ounces) of mortadella
30 grams (about 1 ounce) of bone marrow
30 grams (about 1 ounce) of grated Parmesan cheese
1 egg yolk
a dash of nutmeg, if you like it

Brown the pork in butter and then chop it with a knife, along with the prosciutto and mortadella; then grind them in a mortar until very fine. Pour this mixture onto a cutting board, add the marrow, Parmesan cheese, and egg yolk, and season lightly with salt, pepper, and nutmeg. Using the blade of a knife, reduce the mixture to a smooth paste. Now remove the surface fat from the pork loin, bone it, and then cut it into seven or eight cutlets; but make sure that they all remain joined at the base, so that they can be opened like the pages of a book. Spread a tablespoon of the veal mixture on each cutlet, and then put them together to form a roll, which you will sprinkle with salt and pepper and tie tightly with twine. This done, cover the loin with the caul, tying it in place with a piece of thread so that it adheres to the meat, and cook over a slow fire in a saucepan, all by itself. It should be done in three hours, and serves eight people.

62 The fatty membrane that lines the stomach of a pig.

This dish is good hot or cold, and does not lie heavy on the stomach. If you serve it hot, you can accompany it with some greens warmed in the drippings from the pan. To slice, cut in the opposite direction from the way you sliced the cutlets, which makes for a nice appearance.

329. BUE GAROFANATO
(BEEF WITH CLOVES)

By "beef" here I mean meat from a large animal, either cow or calf.

Take a nice cut of lean meat from the leg or the rump, pound it, and put it in a marinade of wine the evening before you intend to cook it. If the meat weighs about 1 kilogram (about 2 pounds), stud it with lardoons and four cloves, tie it, and place on the fire with half an onion cut into thin slices, butter and oil in equal amounts, and salt. Brown all over. When the onion has dissolved, pour in a glass of water, cover the saucepan with a sheet of paper folded in half two or three times and held in place by the lid, and simmer until done. Remove the thread and serve in its own sauce, which you have strained and skimmed. As I have told you before, it is good to make the lardoons about one finger thick, and to season them with salt and pepper.

This is not, in my opinion, a dish for people with delicate stomachs.

330. ANIMELLE ALLA BOTTIGLIA
(SWEETBREADS WITH WINE SAUCE)

While lamb sweetbreads do not need any prior preparation, sweetbreads from larger animals must first be cooked halfway in water, and skinned if necessary. Leave the former whole but cut the latter into pieces. Dredge well in flour, brown in butter, and season with salt and pepper. Then moisten with Marsala or Madeira wine, and bring to a boil. You can also make a sauce separately with a pinch of flour, a bit of butter, and the wine.

If you enhance them with brown stock, instead of being just good, they will become delicious.

331. TRIPPA COL SUGO (TRIPE IN SAUCE)

No matter how it is cooked or seasoned, tripe remains just an ordinary dish. To my mind, it is not a dish for weak, delicate stomachs, except perhaps when cooked by the Milanese, who have found a way to make it tender and light, or in the Corsican manner, which I will describe below. In some cities tripe is sold boiled, which is convenient. If you cannot find it already boiled, boil it at home, and try to use the large, ridged variety. After boiling it, cut it into strips half a finger wide and dry between the folds of a kitchen towel. Then put it in a saucepan and sauté it in butter, and when it has absorbed the butter add brown stock, or tomato sauce (recipe 6) if you do not have any stock. Season with salt and pepper, let it cook at long as possible, and when you are about to remove it from the pan, toss in a pinch of grated Parmesan cheese.

332. TRIPPA LEGATA COLLE UOVA
(*FRICASSÉE* OF TRIPE)

Boil and cut the tripe as in the preceding recipe. Then put it on the fire with butter and chopped garlic and parsley; season with salt and pepper, and when you think it is cooked, bind it with beaten eggs, lemon juice, and grated Parmesan cheese.

333. TRIPPA ALLA CÔRSA
(TRIPE CORSICAN STYLE)

This a unique tripe dish in its way, pleasant to the taste and easy to digest, superior to all other tripe dishes I know. But the secret lies in preparing it with brown stock, well made and in great abundance, because the tripe absorbs a great deal of stock. Moreover, it is a dish that can only be made in countries where they normally sell the feet of bovine animals with the hide left on, though shaved. The reason for this is that the gluey hide is needed to bind the sauce.

700 grams (about 1-1/2 pounds) of raw tripe
100 grams (about 3-1/2 ounces) of boned calf foot

80 grams (about 2-2/3 ounces) of butter
70 grams (about 2-1/3 ounces) of lardoon
1/2 a large onion
2 small cloves of garlic
a dash of nutmeg and spices
brown stock, as needed
a handful of grated Parmesan cheese

I specify *raw* tripe, because in many places it is sold boiled.

After washing the tripe thoroughly, cut it into strips no wider than half a finger; do the same to the calf's foot. Once this is done, finely chop the onion and put it on the fire; when the onion starts to brown, add the lardoon and garlic, chopped together finely with a mezzaluna. When the lardoon and garlic have began to turn nut brown, toss in the tripe and the calf's foot, seasoning with salt, pepper, and the spices indicated, but use the latter sparingly. Boil until dry, then moisten with the brown stock and finish cooking over a slow fire until the tripe is tender, which should take between 7 and 8 hours in all. If you do not have enough brown stock, you can substitute broth. When you are ready to serve the tripe, give it more flavor with the grated Parmesan cheese, and pour it over sliced, toasted bread, which should be well drenched with the sauce. Serves five people.

334. POLPETTE DI TRIPPA
(TRIPE MEATBALLS)

This dish, taken from a treatise on cooking dating from 1694, might seem strange to you, and the mere mention of tripe will probably make you reluctant to try it. But in spite of its homely character, when prepared with the proper seasonings it turns out quite pleasant and does not lie heavy on the stomach.

350 grams (about 12-1/3 ounces) of boiled tripe
100 grams (about 3-1/2 ounces) of partly trimmed prosciutto
30 grams (about 1 ounce) of grated Parmesan cheese
20 grams (about 2/3 of an ounce) of beef marrow
2 eggs

a generous pinch of parsley
a dash of spices or of nutmeg
2 tablespoons of a mash (not too runny) made with bread soaked
  in broth or milk

Chop the tripe as fine as you can with a mezzaluna. Do the same with the prosciutto, marrow, and parsley; then add the eggs and other ingredients, a little salt, and blend. With this mixture, make 12 or 13 balls, which should serve four people; roll well in flour and fry in oil or lard.

Now finely chop a 1/4 or less of a medium-sized onion and put it in an appropriately sized pan with 60 grams (about 2 ounces) of butter; when the onion has browned, put in the meatballs. After a little while moisten the meatballs with tomato sauce (recipe 6) or tomato paste diluted with water; cover, and simmer for about ten minutes. Remember to turn the meatballs. Send to the table with a little of their sauce, and sprinkled with Parmesan cheese. The seventeenth-century author adds raisins and pine nuts to the tripe mixture, but one can do without them.

335. ZAMPA BURRATA (CALF'S FOOT IN BUTTER)

Because of its similar cooking method and appearance, tripe brings to mind buttered calf's foot, which is a typically Florentine dish both in character and preparation. This dish is worthy of praise because it is nutritious and easy to digest. Since in Florence it is customary to butcher young cattle, the Florentines take advantage of this to use as food what in other places is left attached to the hide to make leather— I am referring to calves' feet, which are shaved of their hair from the knee down, and sold, all nice and white, in pieces or whole.

So take a nice piece of calf's foot and boil it, remove the bones, cut into small pieces and put on the fire with butter, salt and pepper, and a little brown stock, adding Parmesan cheese when you remove it from the fire. If you do not have brown stock, you can make do with tomato sauce (recipe 6) or tomato paste.

Once in my home an elderly lady suffered a serious case of indigestion from this dish, perhaps because she ate too much of it, and it had not been cooked long enough to make it sufficiently soft.

336. LINGUA IN UMIDO (STEWED TONGUE)

Take a beef tongue weighing about a kilogram without the root. Boil it just enough so that you can skin it, and then prepare it in the following manner.

Make a generous battuto with 50 grams (about 1-2/3 ounces) of untrimmed prosciutto, half a medium-sized onion, celery, carrot, and parsley. Put on the fire with 50 grams (about 1-2/3 ounces) of butter and the peeled tongue, seasoned with salt and pepper. When the tongue has browned, finish cooking with broth, added a little at a time, and tomato sauce (recipe 6) or tomato paste; then strain the sauce. In a separate pan, make a roux with 20 grams (about 2/3 of an ounce) of butter and a level tablespoon of flour. When the roux has turned golden brown, pour the sauce from the tongue into it and then add the tongue. Keep the tongue on the fire a while longer, and then serve cut into slices one centimeter thick, with a side dish of celery or some other vegetable reheated in the tongue's sauce.

This dish serves seven to eight people.

337. FEGATO DI VITELLA DI LATTE ALLA MILITARE (MILK-FED CALF'S LIVER MILITARY STYLE)

Finely chop a shallot or a spring onion, sauté in oil and butter, and when it has turned dark brown, toss in the calf's liver, cut into thin slices. When the liver is halfway done, season with salt, pepper, and a pinch of chopped parsley. Simmer slowly so that it stays juicy. Serve in its own sauce, adding lemon juice just before sending it to the table.

338. BRACIUOLE DI CASTRATO E FILETTO DI VITELLA ALLA FINANZIERA (MUTTON CHOPS AND VEAL FILLET WITH FINANCIÈRE SAUCE)

Put a slice of prosciutto in the bottom of a saucepan with some butter and a *bouquet garni* made of carrot, celery, and sprigs of parsley; on top of this place the mutton chops, carved from the loin and left whole; season with salt and pepper. Brown the meat on both sides, add another bit of butter if necessary, and then add chicken gizzards, livers, sweetbreads, and fresh mushrooms or reconstituted dried mushrooms, all chopped. When everything has browned, moisten with broth and cook over a slow fire. Bind the sauce with a little flour, and lastly add half a glass, or even less, of good white wine that you have boiled in a separate pan until reduced by half. Boil a little longer until the wine is absorbed in the sauce. Just before serving, remove the prosciutto and the *bouquet garni*, strain the sauce, and skim off the fat.

Instead of mutton, you can prepare a fillet of veal in the same way, adding peas to the other ingredients. If you make these two dishes carefully, they will come out delicious.

339. BRACIOLINE RIPIENE DI CARCIOFI
(CUTLETS STUFFED WITH ARTICHOKES)

Remove all the tough leaves from the artichokes and cut them into four or five wedges. Take a slice of untrimmed prosciutto, chop it very fine, mix it with a little butter, and spread this mixture on the artichoke wedges. Pound and flatten the chops, which can be of veal or beef, season with salt and pepper, and place two or three artichoke sections in the center of each cutlet. Then roll them up and tie them crosswise with twine.

Finely chop a little onion and place it in a saucepan with butter and oil; when the onion is nice and brown, arrange the cutlets in the saucepan and season again with salt and pepper. When the cutlets have browned, finish cooking with tomato sauce (recipe 6) or tomato paste diluted with water. Remove the twine before sending to the table.

340. FILETTO COLLA MARSALA
(FILLET WITH MARSALA WINE)

The meat of the fillet is the most tender, but if some knave of a butcher should give you the part with all the tendons, you can rest assured that your cat will end up getting half of it.

Take a fillet weighing about 1 kilogram (about 2 pounds), roll it up, tie it, and put on the fire with a medium-sized onion cut into thin slices, along with several small slices of prosciutto and a bit of butter. Season sparingly with salt and pepper. When the meat is browned all over and the onion has dissolved, sprinkle with a pinch of flour. Let the flour brown, and then moisten with broth or water. Simmer slowly, then strain the sauce, and skim off the fat. This done, put the meat back on the fire in the sauce, along with three fingers of Marsala wine. Simmer again slowly. Send to the table with the reduced sauce (be careful not to make it too thick by using too much flour).

You can also stud the fillet with lardoons and cook just with butter and Marsala wine.

341. FILETTO ALLA PARIGINA
(FILLET PARISIAN STYLE)

Since one often hears people in restaurants asking for fillet Parisian style—perhaps because it is a simple, healthy, nutritious dish—I suppose I should say a few things about it, and describe how it is cooked. Have the butcher cut you some round cutlets about as thick as your finger from the best part of the beef fillet. Sauté in butter that has already browned a little over a high flame. Season with salt and pepper, and when the cutlets have formed a crust all over so that they stay juicy and rare on the inside, sprinkle a pinch of chopped parsley over them and remove immediately from the fire. But before taking it to the table, cover the fillet with brown stock or some similar sauce, or—more simply yet—serve the cutlets with the juice left over in the pan, adding a pinch of flour and some broth to make a sauce.

342. CARNE ALLA GENOVESE (VEAL GENOESE STYLE)

Take a lean veal cutlet weighing between 300 and 400 grams (about 10-1/2 and 14 ounces); pound and flatten well. Beat three or four eggs, seasoning them with salt and pepper, a pinch of grated Parmesan cheese, and some chopped parsley. Fry the eggs in butter as if you were making an omelette about as wide as the cutlet. Lay the omelette on top of the cutlet, cutting off the excess and using these pieces to fill in any empty spots. Once you have done this, roll up the veal chop tightly with the egg inside, and tie it; then roll in flour and put in a saucepan with butter, seasoning with salt and pepper. When the veal is nice and brown all over, finish cooking in broth. Serve in its own sauce, which will turn out quite thick on account of the flour.

343. SFORMATO DI SEMOLINO RIPIENO DI CARNE[63]
(SEMOLINA MOLD FILLED WITH MEAT)

Sformati filled with cutlets or giblets are usually made with vegetables, rice, or semolina. If you choose semolina, use recipe 230, blend all the butter and Parmesan cheese into the mixture, pour into a plain mold, or a mold with a hole in the center, which you have greased with butter while lining its bottom with a sheet of buttered paper. The meat stuffing, which you will put in the middle of the semolina or as a sauce in the hole in the mold, should be cooked with a dash of truffles or of dried mushrooms, which will give it a delicate flavor. Cook in *bain-marie* and serve hot with the sauce poured over it to give it a nicer appearance.

344. SFORMATO DI PASTA LIEVITA
(LEAVENED DOUGH PUDDING)

This dough takes the place of bread to eat with the filling, which can be any kind of stewed meat or mushrooms.

300 grams (about 10-1/2 ounces) of Hungarian flour
70 grams (about 2-1/3 ounces) of butter
an additional 30 grams (about 1 ounce) of butter
30 grams (about 1 ounce) of brewer's yeast
3 egg yolks
2 deciliters (about 4/5 of a cup) of heavy cream or high-grade milk
salt to taste

I should warn you that you will have a little more cream than you need.

---

63 A "sformato" is a kind of savory pudding, usually made in a mold with a coarse purée of vegetables, chicken, or fish, usually bound with eggs and béchamel sauce.

With a quarter of the flour, the yeast, and a little of the cream, which should be lukewarm, make a small loaf like a *Krapfen* and set it aside to rise. Knead the rest of the flour together with 70 grams (about 2-1/3 ounces) of butter (softened beforehand in wintertime), the egg yolks, the salt, the little loaf after it has risen to twice its original size, and enough lukewarm cream to make a dough of the right consistency, which you should be able knead in a bowl with a wooden spoon. You will know that you have worked the dough enough when it begins to come away from the sides of the bowl as you knead; then set it aside to rise in a warm place. When the dough has risen, pour it on a floured pastry board, and after dusting your hands with flour, roll it out to a thickness of 1/2 a centimeter (about 1/5 of an inch).

Take a smooth mold with a hole in the middle; the mold should have a capacity of about 1 1/2 liters (about 1-1/2 quarts), so that the dough will fill it only halfway. Grease the mold and dust it with flour, cut the dough into strips, and arrange them in layers until you run out of dough. Melt the 30 grams (about 1 ounce) of additional butter, and us it to brush each layer of dough before adding the next. Cover the mold and set aside so that the dough can rise again; when it reaches the rim of the mold, bake in an oven or a Dutch oven.

Add the filling after you have removed the pudding from the mold. Serves five to six people.

345. SFORMATO DI RISO COL SUGO GUARNITO DI RIGAGLIE
(RICE PUDDING WITH GIBLET SAUCE)

Prepare a good brown stock to use both for the rice and for the giblets. First sauté in butter the giblets (to which you can add a few thin slices of prosciutto if you like), seasoning with salt and pepper. Then finish cooking with brown stock. Adding a dash of mushrooms or truffles can only make the giblets taste better.

Sauté the rice in butter and nothing else, then cook until done with boiling water. Season with brown stock, and when done, with Parmesan cheese. When the rice has cooled a little, add beaten egg in the proportion of two eggs per 300 grams (about 10-1/2 ounces) of rice.

Take a smooth round or oval-shaped mold, grease with butter and line the bottom with buttered paper. Pour in the rice and bake until solid. After removing the rice from the mold, pour over it the giblet sauce, which you have first thickened a little with a pinch of flour. Serve the sformato surrounded with the giblets, swimming in more of the sauce.

346. SFORMATO DELLA SIGNORA ADELE
(SIGNORA ADELE'S GRUYÈRE MOLD)

The lovely and most gracious Signora Adele wishes me to tell you how to make this mold of hers, which has a very delicate flavor.

100 grams (about 3-1/2 ounces) of butter
80 grams (about 2-2/3 ounces) of flour
70 grams (about 2-1/3 ounces) of Gruyère cheese
1/2 a liter (about 1/2 a quart) of milk
4 eggs

Make a béchamel sauce with the flour, milk, and butter, and before removing it from the fire add the Gruyère, grated or cut into small pieces, and salt. Once the sauce has cooled a little, add the eggs, first the yolks one at a time, and then the whites, beaten until stiff.

Pour this mixture into a smooth mold with a hole in the middle after greasing the mold with butter and dusting it with bread crumbs. Bake in a Dutch oven and serve filled with stewed giblets or sweetbreads.

Serves six people.

347. BUDINO ALLA GENOVESE
(PUDDING GENOESE STYLE)

150 grams (about 5-1/4 ounces) of milk-fed veal
1 chicken breast weighing about 130 grams (about 4-1/2 ounces)
50 grams (about 1-2/3 ounces) of untrimmed prosciutto
30 grams (about 1 ounce) of butter
20 grams (about 2/3 of an ounce) of grated Parmesan cheese

3 eggs
a dash of nutmeg
a pinch of salt

Using a mezzaluna, chop the veal, chicken breast, and prosciutto and then put them in a mortar along with the butter, Parmesan cheese, and a bit of crustless bread soaked in milk. Crush it all very well until the mixture is fine enough to pass through a sieve. Put the puréed mixture in a bowl and add three tablespoons of béchamel sauce (recipe 137). For this dish, the béchamel should have the consistency of a soft paste. Add the eggs and nutmeg and blend well.

Take a smooth tin mold, grease it with butter and line the bottom with a sheet of buttered paper cut to size; pour in the mixture and bake in *bain-marie*.

After removing the pudding from the mold, remove the paper from the top and in its place sprinkle a mixture made up of chopped chicken livers cooked in brown stock. Serve hot. If it turns out well, everyone will praise it for its delicacy.

But now is a good time to say that all dishes made with fillings of ground meat are heavier on the stomach than foods that need to be chewed because, as I have said before, saliva is one of the elements that contribute to digestion.

348. BUDINO DI CERVELLI DI MAIALE
(PORK BRAIN PUDDING)

Because of its ingredients, this is a nutritious pudding that I believe can satisfy the delicate taste of the ladies.

Using three pork brains, which can weigh up to about 400 grams (about 14 ounces), you will need:

2 whole eggs
1 egg yolk
240 grams (about 8-1/2 ounces) of cream
50 grams (about 1-2/3 ounces) of grated Parmesan cheese
30 grams (about 1 ounce) of butter
a dash of nutmeg
salt to taste

By cream I mean the heavy cream that dairies prepare for whipping.

Put the brains on the fire with the butter; salt them and cook, stirring often so that they do not stick to the pan. Take care not to let them brown. Then pass them through a sieve. Add the Parmesan, nutmeg, beaten eggs, and cream, and blend well. Pour this mixture into a smooth mold greased with cold butter and cook in *bain-marie*.

This dish is almost better cold than hot. These quantities serve six people.

349. PASTICCIO DI MACCHERONI
(MEAT AND MACARONI PIE)

The cooks of Romagna are generally very capable when it comes to making this dish, which is very complicated and costly but excellent when properly prepared—not an easy task. In that region, this dish is featured during Carnival, during which period one might say that no meal begins without it. It is mostly served as a first course.

I once met a man from Romagna famed for his eating abilities. One evening he unexpectedly turned up among a group of friends who were about to dig eagerly into a pasticcio that had been prepared for twelve people. Seeing the pasticcio, which was sitting in all its glory on the table, the man exclaimed: "What! For so many people, a pasticcio that would barely be enough for me?" "Very well," they replied, "if you eat the whole thing, we will pay for your supper." The good man took up the challenge, and immediately set to work, devouring the entire thing. Amazed at such a spectacle, all his friends said: "Tonight he will split his gut for sure!" Fortunately, nothing serious happened, but his body swelled so much that the skin was stretched tight as a drum. He ranted and raved, tossed and turned, and his belly contracted as if he were about to give birth. But a man armed with a rolling pin came to his aid and, working on the patient like someone making chocolate, managed to deflate his belly, into which who knows how many other pasticci went on later occasions.

Big eaters and parasites are no longer as common today as they were in antiquity, I believe, for two reasons: one, the constitution of the human body has weakened, and two, certain pleasures of the spirit, which are an appurtenance of civilization, have taken the place of sensual pleasures.

In my opinion, the best macaroni for this dish is the long Neapolitan kind, made from extra-fine dough, with thick walls and a narrow hole in the middle. This type of pasta holds up well when cooked and absorbs more of the seasoning.

Here are the portions for a Romagna-style pasticcio for twelve people. You can modify the recipe as you please, because a pasticcio always comes out good no matter how it is prepared.

> 350 grams (about 12-1/3 ounces) of macaroni
> 170 grams (about 6 ounces) of Parmesan cheese
> 150 grams (about 5-1/4 ounces) of sweetbreads
> 60 grams (about 2 ounces) of butter
> 70 grams (about 2-1/3 ounces) of truffles
> 30 grams (about 1 ounce) of untrimmed prosciutto
> a handful of dried mushrooms
> the giblets from 3 or 4 chickens, and their gizzards, provided you
>   remove the gristle
> cockscombs, testicles, and unlaid eggs, if you have any
> a dash of nutmeg

Do not be alarmed by all this quantity of dressing; it will disappear beneath the shortcrust dough.

Blanch the macaroni—that is, cook until halfway done in salted water. Remove from the water and then cook over a very low flame in brown stock (recipe 4) until the macaroni has absorbed the stock and is cooked through.

In the meantime, make a half portion of the béchamel sauce in recipe 137, and cook the giblets in butter, salt, and a pinch of pepper, moistening them with brown stock. Cut the giblets and sweetbreads into pieces the size of a small nut, and after they have cooked, add the prosciutto cut into strips, the truffles thinly sliced, the dried mushrooms softened in warm water, and a few dashes of nutmeg. Blend everything together well.

I am assuming that you have already prepared your shortcrust dough, since it needs to rest for a few hours. To make the dough, use the same portions as in 589, recipe A, and add some lemon rind for extra flavor. Now that everything is ready, you can begin to fill your pasticcio, which you can do in various ways. But I always stick to the way they do it in Romagna, where they use specially made copper pans, well lined with tin. So take an appropriately sized pan and grease it well with butter. Drain the macaroni of excess sauce and make a first layer on the bottom of the pan; season with grated Parmesan cheese, bits of butter scattered here and there, a few tablespoons of béchamel sauce, and some giblets. Repeat the same operation until you run out of ingredients and the pan is full.

Now roll out a sheet of shortcrust dough, first with a smooth rolling pin and then with a ridged one, until it is the thickness of a coin. Use this to cover the macaroni completely. Then roll two strips of dough two fingers wide and place them crosswise on top to strengthen the dough covering. Bind the crust all around the pan with a wide strip of dough, and if you have a flair for decoration, use the leftover dough to make as many decorations as will fit; do not forget to garnish the top with a nice bow. Brush the entire surface with egg yolk, and send the pasticcio to the baker or bake it at home in a Dutch oven. Then, serve it up hot to anyone wishing to eat his fill.

350. UMIDO INCASSATO
(STEW IN A SHELL)

Make a béchamel sauce with:

150 grams (about 5-1/4 ounces) of flour
70 grams (about 2-1/3 ounces) of butter
30 grams (about 1 ounce) of grated Parmesan cheese
6 deciliters (about 2-1/2 cups) of milk

Then take:

3 eggs
a bunch of spinach
salt, to taste

Boil the spinach, squeeze dry, and pass though a sieve.

When you remove the béchamel sauce from the fire, break in the eggs, and use the spinach purée to make half of the sauce green.

Take a ring-shaped copper mold with a hole in the middle and ridges all around. Grease it well with cold butter, and fill it first with the green béchamel sauce and then with the yellow sauce. Bake in *bain-marie* until firm. Remove from the mold while still hot, and fill the middle with a nice mixture of chicken giblets and sweetbreads, or milk-fed veal cutlets seasoned with a few mushrooms or truffles. Finish off this tasty treat with butter and brown stock, taking care that it turns out delicate to the taste. You will see what a fine impression this dish will make, and how it will be praised.

351. SFORMATO DI RISO CON RIGAGLIE
(SAVORY RICE PUDDING WITH GIBLETS)

150 grams (about 5-1/4 ounces) of rice
30 grams (about 1 ounce) of Parmesan cheese
20 grams (about 2/3 of an ounce) of butter
7 deciliters (about 3 cups) of milk
3 eggs
salt, to taste

Cook the rice in the milk, add the butter and salt, and then, when it is cold, add the other ingredients. Pour into a smooth mold with a hole in the middle and lined with buttered paper on the bottom. Bake in *bain-marie* for a short time, so that it does not get too hard. Remove from the mold while still hot, and serve with giblets in the middle. These amounts serve five people.

352. UMIDO DI RIGAGLIE DI POLLO COL SEDANO
(CHICKEN GIBLET STEW WITH CELERY)

When you add necks, heads, and feet to chicken giblets, they become the homely dish that everyone is familiar with. But when you want to make it more refined, using only the livers, combs, unlaid eggs, testicles, and gizzards scalded in broth and without the gristle, you can make it more flavorful and delicate by preparing it in the following way.

First cut some celery into pieces about half a finger long, and cook till one-third done in salted water. Then chop some untrimmed prosciutto and a little onion, put on the fire in butter, and when it is nicely browned, pour in first the gizzards, cut into three pieces, then a pinch of potato flour, and finally the livers cut into two pieces, and all the rest. Season with salt, pepper, and a dash of spices, and when it has absorbed the flavors add some broth or a little tomato sauce (recipe 6) or tomato paste. Sauté the celery separately in butter. When it is cooked, pour in the giblets and cook for a while longer, adding broth if necessary, and serve.

353. SCALOPPINE ALLA BOLOGNESE
(VEAL CUTLETS BOLOGNESE STYLE)

This is a simple, healthy dish that can be served for lunch or as a second course in a family meal.

300 grams (about 10-1/2 ounces) of lean boned milk-fed veal
300 grams (about 10-1/2 ounces) of potatoes
80 grams (about 2-2/3 ounces) of thinly sliced untrimmed prosciutto
70 grams (about 2-1/3 ounces) of butter
30 grams (about 1 ounce) of grated Parmesan cheese
a dash of nutmeg

Boil the potatoes, making sure not to overcook them, or steam them, which would be better, then slice as thin as possible. Cut the prosciutto crosswise into strips barely a finger wide.

Chop the meat very fine with a meat cleaver and season with salt, pepper, and a little nutmeg, because, as you know, it is good to use nutmeg and spices in general in foods that cause flatulence. Divide the meat into twelve portions and form into the same number of cutlets, flattening each with a knife. Then cook in half the butter, but do not let them brown.

Take a metal dish or platter, pour in the fat left in the pan from cooking the meat, and arrange four cutlets on it. Cover the cutlets with a third of the prosciutto, and over this arrange a third of the potatoes, seasoning them with the Parmesan cheese and bits of the remaining butter. Repeat this operation three times, and cook on the metal platter in moderate heat with fire above and below. Then serve. These amounts are enough for four to five people.

354. PICCIONI COI PISELLI (SQUAB WITH PEAS)

They say that the best way for a squab to end its life is in a stew with peas. So place the squabs in a pan on top of a mixture of finely chopped onion, prosciutto, oil, and butter. After they have browned all over, finish cooking with water or broth. Strain the sauce, skim off the fat, and cook the peas in it. Send the squabs to the table surrounded by the peas.

355. LESSO RIFATTO (TWICE-COOKED MEAT)

Sometimes to make boiled meat more appetizing, it is cooked again in a stew. But you should wait until you have a thick cut of meat weighing no less than 1/2 a kilogram (about 1 pound). Remove the meat from the broth before it is completely cooked, and place it in a saucepan on top of a mixture of chopped bacon, onion, celery, carrot, and a bit of butter, seasoning it with salt, pepper, and spices. When this battuto has mostly dissolved, finish cooking the meat with tomato sauce (recipe 6) or tomato paste diluted with broth. Strain the sauce, skim off the fat, and put it back on the fire with the meat and a handful of dried mushrooms softened in water.

3 5 6. LESSO RIFATTO ALL'INGLESE
(TWICE-COOKED MEAT ENGLISH STYLE)

The art of cooking could be called the art of whimsical, strange names. *Toad in the Hole* is the name of this twice-cooked meat. As you will see from the recipe, and as you will find out when you eat it, if it is a delicious dish it would be an insult to call it a toad.

In Florence, 1/2 a kilogram (about 1 pound) of meat for boiling, which can usually serve three people, weighs about 350 grams (about 12-1/3 ounces) when the bones have been removed. Starting with this amount of meat, beat an egg in a saucepan along with 20 grams (about 2/3 of an ounce) of flour, and 2 deciliters (about 4/5 of a cup) of milk. Cut the meat into thin slices. Take an ovenproof platter, melt in it 50 grams (about 1-2/3 ounces) of butter, and then arrange the sliced boiled meat over the butter. Season with salt, pepper, and spices. When the meat has browned on both sides, sprinkle a heaping tablespoon of grated Parmesan cheese over it, and then pour in the contents of the saucepan. Let the mixture firm up, and then send to the table.

3 5 7. LESSO RIFATTO ALL'ITALIANA
(TWICE-COOKED MEAT ITALIAN STYLE)

If onions don't bother you, this dish will prove better than the last one. For the same amount of boiled meat, chop 150 grams (about 5-1/4 ounces) of pearl onions, put them in a pan with 50 grams (about 1-2/3 ounces) of butter, and when they begin to brown toss in the boiled meat, thinly sliced, and a whole unpeeled but lightly crushed clove of garlic, which you will later discard. Season with salt and pepper. As the meat begins to dry up, moisten with broth. After seven or eight minutes, add a pinch of chopped parsley and the juice of half a lemon. Then serve.

3 5 8. OSSO BUCO (BRAISED VEAL SHANKS)

The preparation of this dish should be left to the Milanese, since it is a specialty of Lombardy. I will describe it in the most straightforward manner possible, lest I should be ridiculed.

The "osso buco" is a meaty piece of bone with a hole in it, taken from the end of the shank or shoulder of a milk-fed calf. It is stewed in such a way that it becomes delicate and tasty. Using as many pieces as there are people to be fed, place the veal shanks on top of a mixture of chopped onion, celery, carrot, and a bit of butter; season with salt and pepper. When the veal has absorbed the flavors of the seasonings, add another bit of butter rolled in flour to give it color and to thicken the sauce, and finish cooking with water and tomato sauce or tomato paste. Strain the sauce, skim the fat, and put the shanks back on the fire. Season with lemon peel cut into tiny pieces and a pinch of chopped parsley before you remove it from the fire.

359. CARNE ALL'IMPERATRICE (EMPRESS BEEF)

The name is pretentious, but this dish is fine for a family luncheon. The amounts given here serve five people.

500 grams (about 1 pound) of lean beef taken from the rump
50 grams (about 1-2/3 ounces) of untrimmed prosciutto
3 heaping tablespoons of grated Parmesan cheese
2 eggs

If you do not have a meat grinder, use a knife and a mortar to chop both the meat and the prosciutto very finely. Add the Parmesan cheese and the eggs, season the mixture with salt and pepper, and blend well. Then, using your wet hands, form a flat loaf two fingers high.

Put 30 grams (about 1 ounce) of butter and two tablespoons of oil in a pan or a skillet. When the fat begins to sizzle, place the loaf of meat in the pan and sprinkle over it a clove of thinly sliced garlic and a few rosemary leaves. Cook, and when the meat starts to dry out, moisten it with tomato sauce or tomato paste diluted with water. Send to the table with its sauce all around.

COLD DISHES

360. LINGUA ALLA SCARLATTA
(CORNED TONGUE)

We call this "alla scarlatta" (scarlet style) because it turns a nice red color. And it is a very fine dish, both in its appearance and its taste.

This talk of tongues brings to mind the following lines by Leopardi:[64]

Il cor di tutte
Cose alfin sente sazietà, del sonno,
Della danza, del canto e dell'amore,
Piacer più cari che il parlar di lingua,
Ma sazietà di lingua il cor non sente.

(Of all things the heart grows sated—of sleep, of love, of sweet song, and merry dance—things which give more pleasure than the tongue does in speech, and yet of the tongue the heart is never sated.)

It is true that the itch of loquacity is not satisfied as one ages; indeed, it grows in proportion as we grow older, as does the desire for good food, sole comfort of the aged who, however, ruled as they are by the inexorable dictates of nature, cannot abuse the comforts of the table, under penalty of grave discomforts. In old age, man consumes

---

64 Giacomo Leopardi (1798–1837) a celebrated Italian poet and essayist, best known for his lyrical verses.

less; his organs become less and less active, his secretions imperfect, thus generating in the human body superfluous, harmful humors that cause rheumatism, gout, apoplectic fits, and similar offspring of Lady Pandora's box.

> To return to the subject of tongue, take one from a large animal, (veal or beef) and rub it all over with between 20 and 30 grams (about 2/3 and 1 ounce) of saltpeter, depending on the size of the tongue, until it is thoroughly absorbed. After 24 hours, wash the tongue several times with cold water, and while still wet rub it with a great deal of salt; then leave it for eight days. Be sure to turn it every morning in its brine, which is produced as the salt draws the water out of the tongue. Since the best way to cook it is to boil it, put the tongue on the fire in cold water, with its natural brine, a *bouquet garni*, and half an onion studded with two cloves; boil for three to four hours. Skin the tongue while it is still steaming hot, let it cool, and then send to the table. It makes an excellent, elegant cold dish if you accompany it with the aspic in recipe 3.
>
> Tongue can also be served hot, either by itself, or accompanied by potatoes or spinach.
>
> Do not try this dish during the hot summer months, because the salt might not be sufficient to preserve it.

361. LINGUA DI VITELLA DI LATTE
IN SALSA PICCANTE
(TONGUE OF MILK-FED VEAL IN TANGY SAUCE)

Take a whole tongue of milk-fed veal and boil it in salted water, which should take about two hours. Finely chop some celery and carrot, and place on the fire with a generous amount of oil for five minutes, then set aside. Chop two salted anchovies, washed and with the spine removed, along with 50 grams (about 1-2/3 ounces) of capers drained of brine, a good pinch of parsley, a piece of crustless bread about the size of an egg, slightly moistened with vinegar, very little onion, and less than half a clove of garlic. When all of this has been thoroughly chopped, work it with the blade of a knife and a drop of oil until you have reduced it to a paste. Then blend this mixture with the battuto of chopped celery and carrots. Dilute it with more oil and the juice of half a lemon; season with pepper and salt, if necessary. This is the sauce.

Skin the tongue while it is still hot, discard the root with its little bones (this part is good eaten boiled), and cut the rest of the tongue into thin slices. Cover with the sauce, and serve cold.

This is an appetizing dish, good for hot summer days when the stomach does not feel hungry.

362. SCALOPPE DI LINGUA FARSITE IN BELLA VISTA (STUFFED TONGUE CUTLETS IN ASPIC)

This is one of the best—and best looking—cold dishes.

Have your pork butcher cut you ten slices from the thickest part of a salted tongue; the total weight should be about 130 grams (about 4-1/2 ounces). Also have him cut 100 grams (about 3-1/2 ounces) of untrimmed cooked ham, sliced very thinly. Trim the edges of the tongue slices all around to give them an elegant shape, and put the scraps aside. Then take ten slices of the ham and trim them so that they are the same size and shape as the tongue slices. Toss the scraps of ham and tongue into a mortar with 70 grams (about 2-1/3 ounces) of butter and 20 grams (about 2/3 of an ounce) of fragrant white truffles. Grind these ingredients together to reduce them to the consistency of a paste, which you will spread onto the slices of tongue on one side only. Then press the slices of ham on top.

Once you have assembled these ten pieces, you have all the time you want to prepare the aspic. This is described in recipe 3, and those amounts should be sufficient. But there are two ways to garnish the pieces of tongue with the aspic. The first consists of taking a wide platter or baking pan, pouring in a shallow layer of liquid aspic, and when the aspic starts to stiffen, arrange the pieces of tongue on the platter, then covering with another layer of liquid aspic. When the aspic has hardened, you will then remove the pieces one by one.

The second way is to arrange the pieces of tongue upright in a mold with a little space between them, after pouring a thin layer of liquid aspic on the bottom. Then you would cover them completely with aspic. When the aspic has hardened, you will remove it from the mold and serve as one piece, which makes a prettier presentation.

In a meal with several courses, I think that these amounts should be enough to serve up to ten people, but to be on the safe side it would be better not to serve it to more than eight.

363. VITELLO TONNATO (VEAL IN TUNA SAUCE)

Take 1 kilogram (about 2 pounds) of milk-fed veal from the thigh or the rump, all in single piece and boneless. Remove the membrane (if any) and fat and then stud it with two anchovies which you have cleaned, boned and cut crosswise to make 8 pieces in all. Tie up the meat—not too tightly—and put in enough water to cover it. The water must be boiling hot, well salted and already have in it 1/4 of an onion studded with two cloves, a bay leaf, celery, carrot, and parsley. Cook for 1-1/2 hour. Once the meat is cooked, untie it, dry it, and when it has cooled, cut it into thin slices which you will marinate for a day or two in a tight container. Make enough marinade to cover the meat as follows.

Crush 100 grams (about 3-1/2 ounces) of tuna packed in oil with two anchovies. Mash well with the blade of a knife, or better yet, pass through a sieve, adding a generous amount of fine olive oil, a little at a time, and the juice of one or more lemons, so that the sauce becomes liquid. Then, mix in a handful of capers with the brine squeezed out. Serve the veal with the tuna sauce and lemon wedges.

Save the broth to use for cooking rice.

364. RIFREDDO DI VITELLA DI LATTE (COLD MILK-FED VEAL)

1 boneless, lean milk-fed veal chop, weighing about 400 grams (about 14 ounces)
an additional 120 grams (about 4-1/4 ounces) of lean veal
1 thick slice of untrimmed prosciutto weighing 50 grams (about 1-2/3 ounces)
an additional slice of untrimmed prosciutto weighing 20 grams (about 2/3 of an ounce)
1 slice of mortadella, weighing 50 grams (about 1-2/3 ounces)

30 grams (about 1 ounce) of grated Parmesan cheese
20 grams (about 2/3 of an ounce) of butter
1 raw chicken breast
1 egg

Moisten the chop with water and pound it with a meat mallet until it is about 1 centimeter (about 1/2 an inch) thick.

Using a mezzaluna, chop the 120 grams (about 4-1/4 ounces) of lean veal along with the 20 grams (about 2/3 of an ounce) of prosciutto, and then pound in a mortar, adding the Parmesan cheese, butter, egg, and a little salt and pepper. You will use this the mixture to bind the filling, which is prepared as follows.

Cut the chicken breast and the slices of prosciutto and mortadella into strips a little wider than 1 centimeter (about 1/2 an inch). Spread the veal mixture on one side of the cutlet and arrange a third of the strips over it, alternating between the chicken, prosciutto, and mortadella; then spread more of the mixture on top of this. Repeat this operation twice. When done, roll up the cutlet with the filing inside and tie it in the shape of a salami. Put on the fire with 30 grams (about 1 ounce) of butter, and season sparingly with salt and pepper. When it has browned, pour off the fat, which you can use for some other dish, and cook for about three hours, adding a little broth from time to time. When it has completely cooled, remove the string, slice, and serve.

This can serve 10 or 12 people, especially if you garnish it with aspic, which goes marvelously with it.

365. POLLO IN SALSA TONNATA
(CHICKEN IN TUNA SAUCE)

Take a whole young chicken—by "whole chicken" I mean one cleaned of its innards, and with the neck and feet removed—and toss it into a pot of boiling water. Half an hour should suffice to cook it. When you take it out of the pot, remove the skin, which is not needed for this dish, remove all the bones, and cut it into pieces which you will season with salt—not too much—pepper, and two tablespoons of olive oil. After letting the chicken pieces sit in a pile on a platter for several hours, cover them with the following sauce. For about 600 grams (about 1-1/3 pound) of chicken (before cooking and boning), take:

50 grams (about 1-2/3 ounces) of tuna packed in oil
30 grams (about 1 ounce) of capers with the brine squeezed out
3 anchovies
a handful of parsley, that is, enough to make the sauce green

Remove the scales and spines from the anchovies. Using a mezzaluna, finely chop the parsley and then grind it in a mortar along with the other ingredients until the mixture comes out very soft and smooth. Remove it from the mortar, put it in a bowl, and dilute with four tablespoons of olive oil and half a tablespoon of vinegar. Toss the pieces of chicken with half of this sauce, and pour the other half over them, to give the dish a more pleasant appearance. Nonetheless, it is not a very pretty dish; so you might do well to decorate it before you send it to the table with two hard-boiled eggs cut into wedges and arranged around the chicken. This should be enough to serve six people, and it is an appetizing dish, good for starting off lunch or dinner on hot days when people don't feel very hungry.

To scour and clean the mortar of soft and runny sauces like this one, you can use a large slice of raw potato.

366. CAPPONE IN GALANTINA
(CAPON GALANTINE)

I am going to describe to you a galantine of capon I made at home and served at a luncheon for ten people. But it could have served twenty, since the capon weighed 1.5 kilograms (about 3 pounds) skinned.

Cleaned and boned (to bone a chicken, see recipe 258), the capon weighed 700 grams (about 1-1/2 pounds). It was stuffed with the ingredients described below:

200 grams (about 7 ounces) of lean milk-fed veal
200 grams (about 7 ounces) of lean pork
1/2 of a pullet breast
100 grams of salt pork
80 grams (about 2-2/3 ounces) of salted tongue

40 grams (about 1-1/3 ounces) of untrimmed prosciutto
40 grams (about 1-1/3 ounces) of black truffles
20 grams (about 2/3 of an ounce) of pistachios

If you do not have pork, you can use turkey breast.

Cut the truffles into pieces the size of hazelnuts and blanch the pistachios in hot water. Cut the rest of the ingredients into strips barely as wide as a finger, and set aside; salt the meat.

Finely chop some more pork and veal—200 grams (about 7 ounces) of meat in total—and then grind in a mortar with 60 grams (about 2 ounces) of crustless bread moistened with broth. Add an egg, the skins of the truffles, and the scraps from the tongue and the prosciutto, seasoning with salt and pepper. When everything is thoroughly mashed, pass the mixture through a sieve.

Now spread the capon wide open and salt it lightly. Dab it with a little of the mixture and over it place a layer of meat strips (alternating in each layer the different kinds of meat), and then a few bits of truffle and a few pistachios. Continue in this fashion, a layer of flavoring mixture followed by a layer of meat strips, truffles and pistachios, until you run out of ingredients. Remember that it is better to place the strips of chicken toward the tail of the capon so as not have too much of the same kind of meat at the breast. Once this is done, pull the two sides of the capon together. Don't worry if they don't come together perfectly, because it doesn't matter. Then sew it up. Tie it lengthwise with twine and wrap it tightly with a cheesecloth that you have rinsed so as to eliminate the smell of laundry. Finally, tie the two ends of the cheesecloth and put the capon to boil in water for about 2-1/2 hours. Then, untie it, wash out the cloth, wrap the capon in it again, and place it flat with something heavy on top of it. Keep the capon in this position for at least a couple of hours, so that it becomes quite flat.

The water in which you have boiled the capon can be used for broth, or for the aspic described in recipe 3.

367. CAPPONE IN VESCICA
(CAPON COOKED IN A BLADDER)

People will say that I have the virtue of a jackass—and so be it!—
when they hear that after four unsuccessful attempts, I finally succeeded on the fifth and sixth in cooking a capon in a bladder. The first
four were sacrificed to Comus, the god of the table: I had not taken all
the necessary precautions, and the bladders burst in the boiling water.
But it is a dish worth the trouble, since capon, in itself an excellent
dish, becomes delicious when cooked in this manner.

Take a large, heavy bladder without any defects; it is best to use a
pork rather than a beef bladder, since the former seems to be more
heat resistant. Wash it well with lukewarm water and then let it
soak for a day or two. Clean the capon, remove the neck and feet,
toss a generous handful of salt inside, turn the ends of the legs inward and fold the wings against the body so that the tips of the
wings will not puncture the bladder. Then sew up the openings in
the rump and neck, and wrap the whole thing in 150 grams (about
5-1/4 ounces) of trimmed prosciutto sliced very thin, tying the slices
so that they adhere to the capon. Once the capon has been dressed
in this manner, make an incision in the bladder just big enough for
the capon to be inserted in it. Then place the bird inside and sew it
up tightly.

Now take a tube at least as long as your palm. With this you
will make a device to let the steam escape as the bird is cooking.
Make a spout like a whistle on one end and a notch on the other,
which goes into the bladder. Then attach the tube to the neck of the
bladder. With this apparatus, put the capon on the fire in a pot of
lukewarm water, bring to a boil and let cook for three continuous
hours with the tube sticking out. But be careful, because this is the
most difficult part: it must boil in such a way that you see only a few
small bubbles rise to the surface. If the fat or some other liquid should
spurt out of the tube, do not be alarmed; catch it in a small pan.
When the capon is cooked, let it cool in the water in which you have
boiled it, and serve it the next day, discarding the prosciutto, which
will have lost all its flavor. You will find some gelatin inside the

capon, and you can add some aspic if you want to make a nice accompaniment. It will be a cold dish fit for a king. Should you not have a capon, a fattened pullet will do.

I should advise you that I was assured that the last bladder I used was a pig bladder, and that it could withstand the heat better than a cow bladder.

368. TORDI DISOSSATI IN GELATINA (BONED THRUSHES IN ASPIC)

For six thrushes, take:

100 grams (about 3-1/2 ounces) of lean milk-fed veal
40 grams (about 1-1/3 ounces) of salted tongue
30 grams (about 1 ounce) of untrimmed prosciutto
about 30 grams (about 1 ounce) of black truffles

Put aside half of the tongue and a third of the prosciutto (more of the fat than of the lean part). Chop the veal with the rest of the tongue and prosciutto, and then grind in a mortar along with the skin of the truffles, softening the mixture with a drop of Marsala wine. Then pass it through a sieve, adding an egg yolk.

Bone the thrushes as you would the stuffed chicken in recipe 258, leaving the neck and the head attached. Then stuff them with the veal mixture, to which you have added the truffles, as well as the tongue and prosciutto you set aside, all diced. Now tie the thrushes so that the string can be easily removed once they are cooked, wrap each one in cheesecloth, and boil for an hour in the broth for the aspic in recipe 3.

Serve cold, on top of the aspic they have flavored. If you make six little molds with the aspic, the size of birds' nests, it will look like the thrushes are sitting on their eggs.

The result is an elegant, delicate dish.

369. ÀRISTA (ROAST SADDLE OF PORK)

In Tuscany, spit- or oven-roasted saddle of pork is called "àrista." It is usually eaten cold, since it is much better cold than hot. In this case, pork "saddle" means the piece of the loin with the ribs still attached, which can weigh between 3 and 4 kilograms (between about 6 and 8 pounds).

Stud it with garlic, sprigs of rosemary, and a few cloves, but be parsimonious, because these herbs can come back to haunt you; season with salt and pepper.

Roast it on a spit—the best way—or in the oven without anything else, and use the drippings to brown potatoes or re-heat vegetables.

This is a convenient dish for families, because it keeps for a long time during the winter.

During the Council of 1430, convened in Florence to resolve some differences between the Roman and Greek Churches, this dish, which was known by another name at the time, was served up to the bishops and their entourage. When they found it to their liking, they began to cry "*arista, arista*" (good, good!), and that Greek word continues, four and a half centuries later, to denote saddle of pork cooked in this manner.

370. PASTICCIO FREDDO DI CACCIAGIONE
(COLD GAME PIE)

Let's take, for example, a gray partridge or a common partridge and make a pie that will serve six or seven people. The gray partridge (*Perdrix cinerea*) can be distinguished from the common partridge (*Perdrix rubra*) because the latter has red feet and a red beak and is somewhat larger.

These fowl are of the order of *Rasores*. They feed only on plants, particularly grains, and therefore the walls of their gizzards are particularly muscular; they dwell in the mountains of temperate regions. Their meat is excellent and delicate in flavor. But of the two species, the common partridge is preferable.

Here are the ingredients for this pie:

1 gray partridge or 1 common partridge that has hung for some time
3 chicken livers

1 egg yolk
2 bay leaves
2 fingers of Marsala wine
50 grams (about 1-2/3 ounces) of black truffles
50 grams (about 1-2/3 ounces) of salted tongue
30 grams (about 1 ounce) of untrimmed prosciutto
30 grams (about 1 ounce) of butter
crustless bread, the equivalent in volume of a fist
some chopped onion, carrot, and celery
a little broth

Clean and wash the partridge and put it on the fire with the chopped onion, carrot, and celery, as well as the butter, the prosciutto (cut into thin slices), and the whole bay leaves; season with salt and pepper. When the onion begins to brown, moisten it with the Marsala wine, poured in a little at a time; if this is not enough liquid to cook the partridge halfway, add broth. Take the partridge off the fire, remove the breast and cut it into 8 slices, and put them aside. Cut the rest of the partridge into small pieces and finish cooking them with the chicken livers and the liver from the partridge as well.

When all of this is cooked, strain it and put it in a mortar, discarding the bay leaves. Toss the bread into the liquid that remains in the pan, along with a little broth. Stir to form a mash which you will also pour into the mortar, along with the skin you grated off the truffles. Grind it all well, and then pass through a sieve. Add the egg yolk to the puréed mixture and work it well with a wooden spoon to blend it all together.

Now make the dough to cover the pie, following the instructions in recipe 372. Take one of those round or boat-shaped tinned steel molds with a hoop that can be unlocked made specially for pasticci. Grease the mold with butter, roll the dough out until it is a little thicker than a coin, and line the mold with it. Also make what will be the bottom of the pie, laying it on a copper baking pan greased with butter.

First pour part of the mixture over the bottom of the pie, and on top of this arrange some of the meat slices—the partridge breast and salted tongue—and a few pieces of raw truffle the size of a nut; then add more mixture, topping it again with a layer of slices and truffles, and so on if the pie is bigger. Press all of it down firmly so that it well packed, and cover it with the same dough, making some decorations. Leave a hole in the middle to let the steam escape.

Brush the outside with egg yolk and bake in the oven or in a Dutch oven. When you remove it from the fire, cover the hole on the top with a bow-shaped piece of dough, made to fit into the space and baked separately.

Using this same recipe, you can make a pie with two woodcocks, which do not need to have the intestines or gizzard removed. Just make sure there is no unpleasant smell coming from their nether parts.

371. PASTICCIO DI CARNE (MEAT PIE)

200 grams (about 7 ounces) of lean, milk-fed veal
100 grams (about 3-1/2 ounces) of lean pork
60 grams (about 2 ounces) of butter
60 grams (about 2 ounces) of cooked ham, thickly sliced
50 grams (about 1-2/3 ounces) of salted tongue, thickly sliced
50 grams (about 1-2/3 ounces) of crustless bread
1 chicken breast
1 chicken liver
1 lark or similar bird
1 truffle
1 deciliter (about 1/3 of a cup) of Marsala

Remove the beak and feet from the bird, and put it on the fire with the butter, veal, pork, chicken breast, and lastly, the chicken liver. Moisten with the Marsala, then with broth, and cook until done. Before straining, put the truffle in for a little while. Toss the bread into the liquid left in the pan, and make a mash. Put the mash in a mortar with the small bird, an egg yolk, about 1/4 of the veal and pork, and pound to make a mixture that you will then pass through an iron-wire sieve. If the mixture turns out too thick, dilute it with broth.

Dice all of the remaining meat, the ham, the tongue, the liver, and the truffle into cubes the size of hazelnuts and blend all this together with the puréed mixture. Now take a round pasticcio mold, and line it with the dough described in recipe 372. But after you have lined the bottom and sides of the mold with dough, line it again with paper-thin slices of salt pork. After you have filled the mold, make a cover for the pie, and in every other respect follow the instructions in recipe 370 for game pie.

If you want to make a more elegant pie, do not fill it all the way to the top. After it is cooked, fill the empty space with a little of the aspic described in recipe 3, and serve it cold with more aspic on the side.

These amounts serve eight people.

372. PASTICCIO DI LEPRE
(HARE PIE)

If you do not have strong arms, do not attempt to make this pasticcio. This animal's tough flesh and many bones require a tremendous effort to extract all the usable meat, without which you could not make anything really good.

What I am about to describe was made in my presence, with these amounts. If you use them as your guide, I think your money will have been well spent.

1/2 a hare, weighing 1 kilogram (about 2 pounds) without the
head and feet
230 grams (about 8 ounces) of lean milk-fed veal
90 grams (about 3 ounces) of butter
80 grams (about 2-2/3 ounces) of salted tongue
80 grams (about 2-2/3 ounces) of prosciutto fat
50 grams (about 1-2/3 ounces) of untrimmed prosciutto, sliced
half a finger wide
30 grams (about 1 ounce) of untrimmed prosciutto, sliced thinly
60 grams (about 2 ounces) of black truffles
30 grams (about 1 ounce) of flour for the béchamel sauce
3 deciliters (about 1-1/4 cups) of Marsala
2 eggs
1/2 a glass of milk
broth, as needed

After cleaning and drying the hare, take 80 grams (about 2-2/3 ounces) of lean meat from the fillet or other parts and set it aside.

Then strip the bones to remove the meat, break them, and set them aside as well. Chop the meat and put it, along with the 80 grams (about 2-2/3 ounces) of meat from the fillet, which you will leave whole, in a marinade consisting of about 2/3 of the Marsala with the following ingredients, coarsely chopped: one quarter of a large onion, half a carrot, one rib of celery as long as the palm of your hand, several sprigs of parsley, and two bay leaves. Season with salt and pepper, mix everything well, and let it sit for several hours. In the meantime, remove any membrane from the veal, mince it with a knife, and grind it in a mortar as fine as you can.

Strain the meat and the seasonings from the Marsala wine in which they were marinating, and place them in a saucepan along with all of the bones, the prosciutto fat cut into small pieces, and 30 grams (about 1 ounce) of butter. Cover the saucepan and brown the meat over a high flame, stirring frequently with a wooden spoon. When the meat begins to dry, moisten it with Marsala wine (you can use the Marsala left over from the marinade if you want) and then broth until it is completely cooked. Then separate the meat and the bones again, and put the 80 grams (about 2-2/3 ounces) of lean hare meat aside. Use this, along with the 50 grams (about 1-2/3 ounces) of prosciutto and salted tongue, to prepare a number of strips slightly more than half a finger wide.

Grind all of the remaining hare meat in a mortar, moistening it from time to time with the rest of the Marsala and some broth to make it softer, but not too watery; then pass it through a sieve. Then crush the bones and try to pass as much as you can from them through a sieve. Remember, you will need an iron-wire sieve to do this.

Now make a béchamel sauce with 30 grams (about 1 ounce) of butter, the flour, and the milk, and when it is cooked pour all of the puréed meat (both hare and veal) into the same saucepan; add the two eggs, mix well, and taste the mixture to see if the seasoning is right. Add salt and the rest of the butter if necessary.

Now make the pie with the dough described here below and follow the instructions in recipe 370 to fill it. Slice the truffles into pieces the diameter of hazelnuts, and arrange them in layers with the strips of prosciutto, lean hare meat, and tongue, alternating this with the puréed meat mixture. Press the mixture down firmly so that the strips are spread out evenly and will look nice when the pie is cut. Lastly, arrange the 30 grams (about 1 ounce) of thinly sliced prosciutto over the top, and cover.

You can cover it with the dough described in recipe 155, or with the following:

250 grams (about 8-4/5 ounces) of flour
80 grams (about 2-2/3 ounces) of butter
2 teaspoons of wine spirits
2 teaspoons of sugar
2 egg yolks
the juice from a lemon wedge
5 grams (about 1/5 of an ounce) of salt
cold water, if needed

With a few variations, you can use this recipe to make other pasticci with game, such as wild boar or venison. I think that it should be enough to serve up to twenty people.

373. PANE DI LEPRE
(HARE LOAF)

Here is another cold dish for you:

250 grams (about 10-4/5 ounces) of lean, boneless hare
100 grams (about 3-1/2 ounces) of butter
50 grams (about 1-2/3 ounces) of flour
30 grams (about 1 ounce) of grated Parmesan cheese
6 egg yolks
1/2 a liter (about 1/2 a quart) of milk

Cut the hare in small pieces and salt it. Finely chop about 20 grams (about 2/3 of an ounce) of prosciutto and a piece of onion and put on the fire with half the butter and the hare. When the butter is almost all gone but before the meat has browned, add some good broth and cook until done. When it is cooked, grind the hare meat in a mortar, moistening it with its own sauce, and then pass through a sieve.

Make a béchamel sauce with the flour, the rest of the butter, and the milk. When it has cooled, beat the egg yolks well and blend in, along with all the other ingredients. Place the mixture in a smooth mold with buttered paper lining the bottom and bake in *bain-marie*. Serve cold, with aspic around and on top. But since nowadays beauty and elegance—and even a few nice surprises—are much sought after in the presentation of dishes, it would be better to serve the loaf inside a single block of aspic, which is easy to do. Take a mold larger than the one you used to make the loaf, cover the bottom with aspic, and when it has hardened place the loaf in the middle and fill the empty space around it with more liquid aspic.

374. PANE DI FEGATO
(LIVER LOAF)

This is one of the best cold dishes I know. Its delicate flavor makes it worthy of any table.

500 grams (about 1 pound) of milk-fed calf's liver
70 grams (about 2-1/3 ounces) of butter
50 grams (about 1-2/3 ounces) of fresh crustless bread
20 grams (about 2/3 of an ounce) of grated Parmesan cheese
4 chicken livers
1 deciliter (about 2/5 of a cup) of Marsala
6 tablespoons brown stock or broth
1 whole egg
2 egg yolks
1 bay leaf
salt and pepper to taste

Cut the calf's liver into thin slices and cut the chicken livers in half. Toss both into a pan with the bay leaf and half the butter. When the liver has absorbed the fat, add the other half of the butter and season with salt and pepper. Then add the Marsala wine, and cook over a high flame for four or five minutes (so that the liver will stay tender). Then strain the liver from the liquid and pound it in a mortar along with the bay leaf. Crumble the bread into the sauce remaining in the pan to make a mash. Toss the mash into the mortar as well, and then pass everything through a sieve. Then add the Parmesan cheese and the eggs, diluting the mixture with the 6 tablespoons of brown stock or broth. Finally place the mixture in a smooth mold, lining the bottom with a sheet of buttered paper. Bake in *bain-marie* until done. Remove from the mold while still lukewarm, and when it has cooled completely, cover it with the aspic described in recipe 3, using a larger mold than the first one. It should serve twelve people.

375. PASTICCIO DI FEGATO
(LIVER PIE)

Use the mixture in recipe 374, just adding 30 grams (about 1 ounce) of black truffles cut into wedges. Bring the truffles to a boil in the Marsala before sprinkling them into the liver mixture. Cover with the pasticcio dough described in recipe 372, bake in the oven or a Dutch oven, and serve cold.

This, too, should serve twelve people.

VEGETABLES AND LEGUMES

When they are not misused, vegetables are a healthy part of cooking. They thin the blood, and when served with meat, they make it easier on the stomach. But the amount of vegetables used anywhere depends to a great extent on the climate of the place.

376. ZUCCHINI COL REGAMO
(ZUCCHINI WITH OREGANO)

Oregano (*Origanum vulgare*) is the fragrant seed of a small wild plant of the mint family or *Labiatae*.

Take some long zucchini—a goodly amount, since they shrink a great deal—and cut into round slices as thick as a large coin. Put a frying pan or copper skillet on the fire with a generous amount of olive oil. When the oil starts to sizzle, toss in the sliced zucchini just as they are, and cook over a high flame, stirring often. When they are half-way done, season with salt and pepper. When they look like they are beginning to brown, sprinkle a good pinch of oregano over them, and remove them immediately from the fire with a slotted spoon. They can be served by themselves or as a side dish, and they are sure to please.

Oregano is good for seasoning other foods as well, such as stewed mushrooms, fried eggs, anchovies, etc.

377. ZUCCHINI RIPIENI, DI GRASSO
(ZUCCHINI WITH MEAT FILLING)

To stuff zucchini, you can cut them in half lengthwise, crosswise, or even leave them whole. I prefer to leave them whole, because it is more elegant and the zucchini make a better presentation that way. No matter which method you choose, they must be hollowed out to make room for the stuffing. If you leave them whole, the best way to do this is to use a tin tube inserted all the way through. If the zucchini are so large that the tube does not make a large enough cavity, use a small, thin knife to enlarge it.

To make the filling, take some lean milk-fed veal, cut it up and put it on the fire in a saucepan with some chopped onion, parsley, celery, carrot, a little finely chopped bacon, a little oil, salt, and pepper. Stir frequently with a wooden spoon, and when the meat has absorbed all the liquid and begins to brown, pour in a ladleful of water. After the meat has absorbed the water, pour in another ladleful, and after a little while yet another, to finish cooking. Make sure that some sauce is left. Then strain the sauce and set it aside.

Chop the strained meat very fine with a mezzaluna, and mix it with an egg, a little grated Parmesan cheese, some crustless bread boiled in broth or milk, and a dash of spices; this will serve as the stuffing. Fill the zucchini with this mixture and then sauté in browned butter; cook until done with the sauce that you have set aside.

Zucchini can also be stuffed with the mixture in recipe 347. If you do not have any brown stock, you can cook them just in butter, or in butter and the tomato sauce from recipe 125.

378. ZUCCHINI RIPIENI, DI MAGRO
(MEATLESS STUFFED ZUCCHINI)

Prepare the zucchini as in the preceding recipe, and stuff with a mixture made with tuna preserved in oil, finely chopped with a mezzaluna and blended with egg, a pinch of grated Parmesan cheese, a little of the pulp that you have removed from the zucchini, a dash of spices, a dash of pepper, and no salt. Sauté the zucchini in browned butter, and add some extra flavor with the tomato sauce from recipe 125.

If you prepare this dish carefully, you won't believe how good it will turn out.

379. FAGIUOLINI E ZUCCHINI
ALLA *SAUTÉ*
(SAUTÉED GREEN BEANS
AND ZUCCHINI)

Cooked this way, these vegetables are served mainly as a side dish. Now, so-called "refined cooking" has reduced and simplified the use of condiments and seasonings. This might be healthier, and lighter on the stomach, but flavor suffers considerably as a result, and that little something that some people need to stimulate their digestion is lacking. This is a case in point. If you are using green beans, parboil them; if zucchini, keep them raw and cut them into wedges or rounds, then sauté in browned butter. Season with only small amounts of salt and pepper.

If you then add a little brown stock or some of the tomato sauce from recipe 125, you will have gone beyond the rules of foreign or modern cooking. But in my opinion, they will taste better, and your stomach will feel more satisfied. If you do not have brown stock or tomato sauce, at least sprinkle the vegetables with Parmesan cheese when you remove them from the fire.

380. FAGIUOLINI IN SALSA D'UOVO
(GREEN BEANS IN EGG SAUCE)

Take about 300 grams (about 10 1/2 ounces) of small, tender green beans, remove the ends and the strings, and, as cooks who like to use Frenchified language say, *blanch* them—that is, parboil them in salted water. Then strain, cut into thirds, and finish cooking in butter, seasoning with salt and pepper. In a small pot, beat an egg yolk with a teaspoon of flour and the juice from a 1/4 of a lemon; thin this mixture with a ladleful of cold skimmed broth, and put this liquid on the fire in a small saucepan, stirring continuously with a wooden spoon. When it thickens to the consistency of a smooth cream, pour it over the green beans. Keep the beans on the fire a little longer so that they will absorb the sauce nicely, and serve as a side dish for boiled meat.

In addition to salt, a teaspoon of soda thrown into the boiling water gives green beans and zucchini a nice green color.

381. FAGIUOLINI CON LA BALSAMELLA
(GREEN BEANS WITH BÉCHAMEL SAUCE)

Parboil the beans, adding a teaspoonful of soda so that they stay nice and green. Then sauté them in butter—but lightly, so they do not lose their nice color; season with salt and pepper. Pour over them a fairly runny béchamel sauce made with cream, butter, and flour, but not too much of it. Serve with an accompaniment of fried croutons. This dish can be served as an *entremets*.

382. FAGIUOLINI CON L'ODORE DI VANIGLIA,
O DI NEPITELLA
(GREEN BEANS WITH VANILLA OR CALAMINT)[65]

Soak the green beans in cold water. If they are tender, use them whole and raw, and when you put them in the pot do not shake off too much of the water.

Finely chop a shallot, parsley, carrot, and celery, and sauté in oil. You can also use a pearl onion or an ordinary onion instead of a shallot. Season with salt and pepper, and when this has browned, add broth and strain, pressing hard against the mesh. Add some tomato sauce to the strained sauce, and then cook the green beans in it. Before removing the beans from the fire, season with two teaspoons of vanilla sugar. If you do not like this spice, use calamint instead.

383. FAGIUOLINI DALL'OCCHIO
IN ERBA ALL'ARETINA
(BABY BLACK-EYED PEAS AREZZO STYLE)

Snap off the ends of the unshelled peas and cut them into thirds. Put them in a saucepan with two whole cloves of garlic, uncooked tomato sauce, and enough cold water to cover them. Season with olive oil, salt, and pepper, and then put on the fire and simmer until done,

---

65 An aromatic plant of the mint family, also called "basil thyme."

making sure that enough concentrated sauce is left to make the beans more flavorful. They can be served as an *entremets*, or as a side dish with boiled meat.

384. FAGIUOLI A GUISA D'UCCELLINI (BEANS "LITTLE BIRDS" STYLE)

In the trattorie of Florence I have heard shelled beans cooked in this way called "fagiuoli all'uccelletto."

First cook the beans in water and then strain. Put a pan on the fire with an appropriate amount of oil and several sage leaves. When the oil starts to sizzle, toss in the beans and season with salt and pepper. Sauté them until they absorb the oil, shaking the pan every so often. Then pour a little plain tomato sauce (recipe 6) over the beans, and when this has been absorbed, take them off the fire. You can also use boiled thin-skinned dried beans.

If you do not want to eat them by themselves, these beans go very well as a side dish with boiled meat.

385. FAGIUOLI SGRANATI PER CONTORNO AL LESSO (SHELLED BEANS AS A SIDE DISH FOR BOILED MEAT)

300 grams (about 10-1/2 ounces) of shelled beans
100 grams (about 1 ounce) unsliced bacon
2 deciliters (about 4/5 of a cup) of water
4 tablespoons olive oil
a sprig of sage (4 or 5 leaves)
salt and white pepper

Put the beans on the fire with all of the other ingredients. Simmer, stirring often. Remove the sage and bacon, and serve. This side dish serves four people.

386. SFORMATO DI FAGIUOLINI
(GREEN BEAN MOLD)

Take 500 grams (about 1 pound) of tender green beans and remove the tips and any strings they may have. Toss into boiling water with a pinch of salt, and as soon as the water comes to a boil again, strain the beans and plunge them into cold water.

If you have some brown stock, use it, along with some butter, to finish cooking the beans. If not, sauté a 1/4 of an onion, a few parsley leaves and a piece of celery, all finely chopped, and when the onion has browned toss in the beans, seasoning them with salt and pepper. Finish cooking, adding a little water if necessary.

Prepare a béchamel sauce with 30 grams (about 1 ounce) of butter, one scant tablespoon of flour, and 2 deciliters (about 4/5 of a cup) of milk. Use this sauce, along with a handful of grated Parmesan cheese and four beaten eggs, to bind the beans after they have cooled. Blend this mixture and pour into a smooth mold greased with butter and with a sheet of paper lining the bottom. Cook (in *bain-marie* if you like), and serve hot.

387. SFORMATO DI CAVOLFIORE
(CAULIFLOWER MOLD)

Take a head of cauliflower, and if it weighs, say, 350 grams (about 12-1/3 ounces) without the stalk and leaves, use the following ingredients to season it:

3 deciliters (about 1-1/4 cups) of milk
3 eggs
60 gram (about 2 ounces) of butter
30 gram (about 1 ounce) of grated Parmesan cheese

Parboil the head of cauliflower and then cut it into small pieces. Sauté these with half of the butter, and season with salt. When the cauliflower has absorbed the butter, finish cooking with a little of the milk. Then you can leave it as is, or purée it by passing it through a sieve. Make a béchamel sauce with the rest of the butter and milk and one scant tablespoon of flour, and add this to the cauliflower along with the eggs, beaten, and the Parmesan cheese.

Bake in a smooth mold as for the green bean sformato, and serve hot.

These amounts serve six.

388. CAVOLFIORE ALL'USO DI ROMAGNA (CAULIFLOWER ROMAGNA STYLE)

Divide a large head of cauliflower, or two heads if they are small, into small sections. Wash the sections, do not dry them, and then cook in the following manner. Chop an appropriate amount of garlic and parsley and sauté in oil; when they start to brown, add a splash of water. Then toss in the cauliflower, seasoning it with salt and pepper. When it has absorbed the seasoning, finish cooking in tomato paste diluted with hot water. Enhance the flavor with some grated Parmesan cheese just before serving. Use as a side dish for boiled meats, stews, or cotechino.

389. SFORMATO DI CARDONI (CARDOON MOLD)

Follow all the instructions in recipe 387 for cauliflower sformato. Cut the cardoons into small pieces so that they will absorb the seasoning well. Taste the mixture before pouring it into the mold.

390. SFORMATO DI SPINACI (SPINACH MOLD)

Parboil the spinach in very little water, or in just the water that remains on the spinach after you remove it from the cold water in which you have soaked it. Pass the spinach through a sieve, and add an appropriate amount of salt, pepper, powdered cinnamon, a few tablespoons of the béchamel sauce in recipe 137, butter, eggs, Parmesan cheese, and a handful of raisins or dried zibibbo[66] grapes

66 A flavorful dried grape from the Middle East.

with the seeds removed. Blend well, and pour the mixture into a smooth mold with a hole in the center. Bake in *bain-marie*. Remove from the mold while still hot, and fill the center with a delicate stew of chicken giblets or sweetbreads, or milk-fed veal—or even both together—mixed with little bits of dried mushrooms.

391. SFORMATO DI CARCIOFI
(ARTICHOKE MOLD)

You should make this sformato at a time when artichokes are not too expensive. I think it is one of the most delicate.

Remove the toughest outer leaves, and trim the artichokes. Peel the stalks, keeping them all, even if they are long.

Cut each artichoke into four sections and boil in salted water for five minutes only. If you leave them on the fire longer, besides soaking up too much water, they will lose much of their flavor. Strain them, grind in a mortar, and pass through a sieve. Blend this purée with all of the ingredients usually used in vegetable sformati, namely eggs (don't be too stingy to add an extra egg, this will bind the mixture better), two or three tablespoons of béchamel sauce (not skimping on butter), grated Parmesan cheese, salt, and a dash of nutmeg. Taste the mixture several times to make sure that the seasonings are just right.

If you have some brown stock or sauce from stewed meat, it's not a bad idea to put a little bit in. If the artichokes are quite tender, you can leave them in small sections instead of passing them through a sieve.

Bake, set in a pan of hot water, in a mold with a hole in the middle, if you have some meat stuffing to fill it with; if not, bake in a plain mold and serve as an *entremets*.

392. SFORMATO DI FINOCCHI (FENNEL MOLD)

Because of the pleasant aroma and sweet taste of fennel, this sformato is one of the most delicate tasting.

Remove the toughest leaves from the fennel bulbs, then cut the bulbs into small sections, and boil until 2/3 done in salted water. Strain well, and then sauté in a little butter, seasoning with salt. When the fennel has absorbed the butter, moisten with a little milk. When it has absorbed the milk as well, add a little béchamel sauce. Remove from the fire and leave as is, or pass through a sieve. When the fennel has cooled, add some grated Parmesan cheese and three or four beaten eggs, depending on how much fennel you have. Pour the mixture into a plain mold, or a mold with a hole in the center, and treat as you would any other sformato. Bake in *bain-marie*, and serve hot as an *entremets* or as an accompaniment to boiled capon. You can also garnish it with a tasty mixture of giblets and sweetbreads.

393. FUNGHI MANGIERECCI
(EDIBLE MUSHROOMS)

Because of their nitrogenous properties, mushrooms are the most nutritious of vegetables. Their unique aroma makes mushrooms delicious food, and it is a great shame that among its many varieties there are some poisonous ones, which only an expert, practiced eye can distinguish from the harmless varieties. Some guarantee can be provided when they are gathered in a place known by long experience to be free from danger.

In Florence, for example, they use a great many mushrooms that come from the woods in the surrounding mountains. If the season is rainy, they begin to appear in June; but the height of production is in September. In truth, it must be said that Florence has never been afflicted by misfortunes from these vegetables, perhaps because the two species that are almost exclusively consumed there are the bronze-colored "porcini," or *boletus* mushroom, and the "ovoli" or Caesar's mushrooms. So great is the faith in their harmlessness that no precautions are taken with regard to their consumption, not even the one suggested by some people of boiling them in water acidulated with vinegar—a precaution which, for that matter, would come at the cost of their flavor.

Of the two varieties mentioned above, porcini are best fried or stewed; ovoli are best prepared like tripe, or grilled.

394. FUNGHI FRITTI (FRIED MUSHROOMS)

Select medium-sized mushrooms that are also at the right stage of ripeness. The bigger ones tend to be mushy, while the very small ones would be too tough.

Scrape the stems, remove any earth from the mushrooms, and wash them whole without letting them soak, because the water causes them to lose their pleasant aroma. Then cut into rather large slices and dredge in flour before tossing them into the frying pan. Olive oil is the best thing for frying mushrooms, and seasonings should be limited to salt and pepper sprinkled over them while they are still sizzling. To give the mushrooms a golden color, you can dip them in beaten egg after you flour them, but this is superfluous.

395. FUNGHI IN UMIDO
(STEWED MUSHROOMS)

For stewing, it is preferable to use mushrooms that are slightly smaller than medium size. Remove the dirt, wash them, and cut into thinner slices than for the preceding recipe. Put a pan on the fire with oil, a few slightly crushed whole cloves of garlic, and a good pinch of calamint leaves. When the oil starts to sizzle, toss in the mushrooms without flouring them, season with salt and pepper, and when they are halfway done, moisten with some plain tomato sauce. But use the seasonings sparingly, because the mushrooms do not absorb them.

396. FUNGHI TRIPPATI
(MUSHROOMS TRIPE STYLE)

Ovoli are best for this dish, which probably gets its name because the mushrooms are prepared like tripe. Ovoli or Caesar's mushrooms, as you know, are orange-yellow in color. The youngest ones are closed, and shaped like an egg, while the riper ones are open and flat. For this recipe, select young mushrooms, and after you have cleaned and washed them cut them into thin slices. Cook in butter and season with salt, pepper, and grated Parmesan cheese. They will turn out even better if you add some brown stock.

397. FUNGHI IN GRATELLA
(GRILLED MUSHROOMS)

Open, ripe ovoli are best for this recipe. After you have cleaned and washed them, dry them with a kitchen towel and season with olive oil, salt, and pepper. They go very well as a side dish with steak or any roasted meat.

398. FUNGHI SECCHI (DRIED MUSHROOMS)

Every year in September, when they do not cost so much, I buy my supply of porcini mushrooms and dry them at home. Wait for a stretch of good weather to do this, because the heat of the sun is indispensable; without it, the mushrooms could go bad. Select young, firm, medium-sized mushrooms. You can also choose large ones, but make sure they are not mushy. Scrape the stems, remove any earth without washing the mushrooms, and cut into quite large pieces because they shrink a great deal as they dry. If you find any tiny worms in the stems, cut off just the part the worms had begun to spoil. Keep them exposed to the sun continuously for two or three days, then string them and keep them in a well-ventilated place, and even out in the sun again, until they are completely dry. Then take them down and keep them closed tightly in a paper bag or sack. But do not forget to check on them once in a while, because mushrooms have the bad habit of going soft again. If that should happen, you need to put them out in the open air again for several hours. If you do not check them in this manner, you run the risk of finding them all infested with worms.

When you are ready to use them, they should be softened in hot water; but keep them in the water as little as possible, so they do not lose their aroma.

399. PETONCIANI (EGGPLANT)

The aubergine or eggplant is not a vegetable to be scorned, for it causes neither flatulence nor indigestion. It is very good in side dishes; even eaten by itself as a vegetable main dish, it is anything but unpleasant, especially the less bitter varieties grown in certain regions.

Small and medium-sized eggplants are preferable to the larger ones, which may be overripe and bitter.

Forty years ago, one hardly saw eggplant or fennel in the markets of Florence; they were considered to be vile because they were foods eaten by Jews. As in other matters of greater moment, here again the Jews show how they have always had a better nose than the Christians.

Fried eggplant can be served as an accompaniment to fried fish dishes; stewed eggplant goes with boiled meats; grilled eggplant goes with steak, milk-fed veal chops, or any roasted meat.

400. PETONCIANI FRITTI (FRIED EGGPLANT)

Peel the eggplant and cut it into rather thick round slices. Salt the slices and let them sit for a few hours. Dry off the moisture that it has given off, roll in flour, and fry in oil.

401. PETONCIANI IN UMIDO (STEWED EGGPLANT)

Peel the eggplant, dice it, and put on the fire with a little butter. When the eggplant has absorbed the butter, finish cooking it in the tomato sauce from recipe 125.

402. PETONCIANI IN GRATELLA
(GRILLED EGGPLANT)

Cut the unpeeled eggplant in half lengthwise. Make some crisscrossed cuts on the white part, season with salt, pepper, and olive oil, and put on the grill with the skin side down. Then cover with a lid or an iron pan and cook with embers all around; that way you do not have to turn it. When the eggplant is halfway done, brush it with a little more olive oil. When the pulp has become soft, it is done.

403. TORTINO DI PETONCIANI
(EGGPLANT CASSEROLE)

Peel 7 or 8 eggplants, cut into thin round slices, and salt them to draw out some of their water. After letting them sit for a few hours, dredge them in flour and fry in oil.

Take an ovenproof platter and layer the slices of eggplant with grated Parmesan cheese and the tomato sauce from recipe 125, arranging them so that they form a nice mound. Beat an egg with a pinch of salt, one tablespoon of the same tomato sauce, one teaspoon of grated Parmesan, and two teaspoons of bread crumbs, and cover the surface of the mound with this mixture. Place the platter under the lid of a Dutch oven, with fire above, and when the egg mixture has hardened, serve. This dish can be served by itself, as an *entremets*, or accompanied by a meat dish.

The purpose of the egg covering is to give the dish a nicer appearance.

404. CARDONI IN TEGLIA
(PAN-FRIED CARDOONS)

Cardoons, which are colloquially called "gobbi" (hunchbacks) because their plant resembles that of the artichoke, can be cooked like that vegetable (see recipe 246). Otherwise, after carefully removing the prickly fibers that cover the outside of the cardoons, parboil them in salted water and plunge them immediately into cold water so that they do not turn black.

Cut them into small pieces, roll in flour, and when the oil starts to sizzle, toss them in the pan and season with salt and pepper. Beat some eggs and pour them in the pan after the cardoons have browned on both sides.

The cardoon is a healthy vegetable, easy to digest, refreshing, but not very nutritious and rather bland. Accordingly, it is a good idea to season it generously, as indicated in recipe 407.

The cardoon's resemblance to the artichoke is so great that when the artichoke plant ceases to bear fruit and its stalk is buried in the ground, the resulting leaf stalks are called "carducci."

405. CARDONI IN UMIDO (STEWED CARDOONS)

After parboiling the cardoons as in the preceding recipe, stew them with some chopped garlic and parsley, olive oil, salt, and pepper.

If you want to make them tastier and give them a nicer appearance, cover them with a sauce made with egg and lemon after you have arranged them on a platter. Beat a few eggs with some lemon juice; put this liquid on the fire in a saucepan, stirring with a wooden spoon. When it starts to thicken, pour it over the cardoons. If you do not use the sauce, at least season the cardoons with a pinch of grated Parmesan cheese.

406. CARDONI IN GRATELLA
(GRILLED CARDOONS)

This is not a dish to be highly recommended, but if you want to try it, please do.

After parboiling the cardoons, dry them well, leave the stalks as long as the palm of your hand, season generously with olive oil, pepper, and salt, and brown them on the grill. They can be served as a side dish with steak or grilled fish.

407. CARDONI CON LA BALSAMELLA
(CARDOONS WITH BÉCHAMEL SAUCE)

Discard the toughest stalks, remove the prickly outer fibers from the others, and parboil. Let it be said here, once and for all, that vegetables should be put on the fire in boiling water, while legumes should start out in cold water. Cut the stalks of the cardoons into pieces about three fingers long, and cook with butter and a sufficient amount of salt. Finish cooking with milk—or, better yet, heavy cream—and then bind with a little of the béchamel sauce from recipe 137. Add a pinch of grated Parmesan cheese and remove immediately from the fire. This is an excellent side dish for meat stews, chops, giblet stews, and other similar dishes.

You can cook diced turnips and potato or zucchini wedges in the same way, but the zucchini should not be parboiled first.

408. TARTUFI ALLA BOLOGNESE, CRUDI, ECC.
(TRUFFLES BOLOGNESE STYLE, RAW, ETC.)

The great quarrel between the Blacks and the Whites that prolonged strife in Italy after the devastating struggles between Guelphs and Ghibellines[67] is threatening to erupt again with regard to truffles. But fear not, dear readers, for this time no blood will be shed—the present-day partisans of the black and the white are much more benevolent than the fierce adversaries of yesteryear.

I am a supporter of the whites, and in fact I openly declare and maintain that the black truffle is the worst there is. Other people do not share my opinion; they believe that the black truffle is more fragrant, while the white truffle has a subtler taste. But they are not taking into account the fact that black truffles quickly lose their aroma. The white truffles from Piedmont are universally prized, and the white truffles from Romagna, which grow in sandy soil, are very fragrant, although they taste of garlic. In any case, let us leave the great issue unresolved so that I can tell you how they cook truffles in Bologna, "Bologna la grassa per chi vi sta, ma non per chi vi passa" (Bologna whose bounty is for those who live there, but not for those just passing through).

> After washing the truffles and cleaning them with a little brush dipped in cold water, as is usually done, the Bolognese cut them into very thin slices and arrange them on a tin-lined copper platter in alternating layers with very thin slices of Parmesan cheese; the first layer should be of truffles. They season them with salt, pepper, and a generous amount of their best olive oil. As soon as the truffles start to sizzle, they squeeze a lemon over them and then remove them immediately from the fire. Some people add a few little pieces of butter; but if you do add butter, use only very little, otherwise the dish will turn out too

67 Artusi is referring here to the bloody struggles between the supporters of the Emperor (Ghibellines) and the supporters of the Pope (Guelphs) that brought strife to Italy in the late Middle Ages. The Ghibellines were defeated, but the antagonism between the two parties resurfaced as a struggle between the White and the Black factions in the Guelph party.

heavy. Truffles are also eaten raw, very thinly sliced and seasoned with salt, pepper, and lemon juice.

They also go well with eggs. Beat the eggs and season them with salt and pepper. Put an appropriate amount of butter on the fire, and when it has melted, pour in the eggs and shortly thereafter the thinly sliced truffles, stirring until cooked.

Everyone knows about the aphrodisiacal properties of this food, so I will refrain from speaking about it, though I could tell some very amusing stories. It seems that truffles were discovered for the first time in the Périgord region of France, under Charles V.

I have preserved truffles for quite a long time, but not always successfully, in this way: sliced very thin, dried over the fire, seasoned with salt and pepper, covered with olive oil and then put on the fire just until the oil is heated through. Raw truffles are sometimes stored in rice to impart their fragrance to the rice.

409. CIPOLLINE AGRO-DOLCI
(SWEET-AND-SOUR PEARL ONIONS)

This dish does not require much thinking about, but only good taste, to get the amounts right. When prepared properly, it is an excellent accompaniment for boiled meats.

By pearl onions I mean the white ones that are a little larger than a walnut. Peel them, remove any superfluous parts, and scald in salted water. For about 300 grams (about 10-1/2 ounces) of onions, put 40 grams (about 1-1/3 ounces) of sugar in a saucepan on the fire without any water. When the sugar has melted, add 15 grams (about 1/2 an ounce) of flour. Stir constantly with a wooden spoon, and when the mixture has turned reddish-brown add 2/3 of a glass of vinegar water a little at a time. Let the liquid boil until any lumps that may have formed have dissolved. Then toss in the onions and shake the pan frequently; do not stir them with the spoon, because they will break apart. Taste before serving, because if they need more sugar or vinegar you are still in time to add some.

410. CIPOLLINE IN ISTUFA
(STEWED PEARL ONIONS)

Peel the onions, cut off the tops and bottoms evenly, toss into boiling salted water and boil for ten minutes. Sauté a bit of butter, and when it has turned golden brown arrange the onions evenly in the pan and season with salt and pepper. When they have browned on one side, turn them over and then moisten with brown stock, thickening the sauce with a pinch of flour mixed with butter.

If you do not have any brown stock, cook them as follows. After you have boiled them and plunged them into cold water, place them in a pan with a *bouquet garni*, a small slice of prosciutto, a bit of butter, and a ladleful of broth. Season with pepper and a little salt, cover with very thin slices of salt pork and then cover these with a piece of paper greased with butter. Finish cooking with fire above and below, and serve as a side dish, pouring the reduced sauce that is left in the pan over them.

411. CIPOLLINE PER CONTORNO AI COTEGHINI
(PEARL ONIONS AS A SIDE DISH FOR COTECHINO)

After boiling the onions as in the preceding recipe, sauté them in butter, season with salt and pepper, moisten with the broth from the cotechino, and enhance with some vinegar and sugar. For 28 to 30 pearl onions, the following amounts should do: 50 grams (about 1 2/3 ounces) of butter, half a ladle of skimmed broth from a cotechino sausage, half a tablespoon of vinegar, and one teaspoon of sugar.

412. SEDANO PER CONTORNO
(SIDE DISH OF CELERY)

At banquets, the ancients used to wear crowns made of celery plants, believing that this would neutralize the fumes of wine.

Celery is pleasing to the taste because of its special flavor; for this reason, and because it does not cause flatulence, it merits a place among the healthy vegetables. Select celery with a thick stalk, and serve only the white stalks and stems, which are the tenderest parts.

Here are three different ways to cook celery. For the first two, you should make the pieces 10 centimeters (about 4 inches) long, and for the third, only 5 centimeters (about 2 inches). For all three methods, you should trim the rib, cut it crosswise, and leave it attached to the stalk; then boil in salted water for no more than five minutes and strain.

1st method. Sauté the celery lightly in butter, then cook with brown stock and add grated Parmesan cheese when you are about to send it to the table.

2nd method. For between 200 and 250 grams (about 7 to 8-4/5 ounces) of raw celery, put 30 grams (about 1 ounce) of butter in a saucepan with a little battuto made of 30 grams (about 1 ounce) of untrimmed prosciutto finely chopped along with a quarter of a medium-sized onion. Add two cloves and bring to a boil. When the onion has turned golden, add some stock and continue cooking. Then strain well, and put the sauce in a pan where the celery stalks have been arranged. Season with a dash of pepper—salt is not necessary—and serve with the sauce.

3rd method. Roll the celery in flour, coat with the sauce from recipe 156, and fry in lard or oil; or, better yet, after rolling the celery in flour, dip it in egg, coat with bread crumbs, and fry. This last method for cooking celery is better than the others if you serve the celery as a side dish with stewed meats; you can pour the sauce from the meat over the celery.

413. SEDANO PER CONTORNO AL LESSO (CELERY AS A SIDE DISH FOR BOILED MEAT)

Use white ribs of celery, cutting them into small pieces about 2 centimeters (about 1/2 an inch) long. Boil for five minutes in salted water, then sauté lightly in butter. Bind with the béchamel sauce in recipe 137, kept rather thick, and season with grated Parmesan cheese.

414. LENTICCHIE INTERE PER CONTORNO
(SIDE DISH OF WHOLE LENTILS)

As a side dish with "zampone,"[68] lentils should first be cooked in water, then seasoned with butter and brown stock. If you have no brown stock, boil the lentils with a *bouquet garni*. When done, strain well, and sauté in a battuto of untrimmed prosciutto, a bit of butter, and a little onion. When the onion is nice and golden, add one or two ladles of the skimmed broth from a cotechino sausage or zampone. Let boil a while, strain, and reheat the lentils in this sauce, adding another bit of butter, salt, and pepper.

If the cotechino is not nice and fresh, use broth.

415. LENTICCHIE PASSATE PER CONTORNO
(SIDE DISH OF PURÉED LENTILS)

This dish could be called *purée* of lentils, as the French do, but Rigutini[69] tells us that the real word in Italian is "passato," which can be applied to any type of vegetables or legumes, including potatoes. So, to make a "past" rather than a "present"[70] with lentils, put the lentils in water with a little bit of butter and when they are cooked, but not mushy, pass them through a sieve. Make a little battuto with onion (not too much, because its flavor should not overpower the others), parsley, celery, and carrot; put it on the fire with just enough butter, and when it is golden brown, stop the cooking with a ladleful of broth, which could be the skimmed broth from a cotechino. Strain, and serve the lentils seasoned with this sauce, not forgetting to add salt and pepper. Keep in mind that the consistency should be as thick as possible.

---

68 A sausage mixture stuffed into a boned pig's foot.

69 Giuseppe Rigutini (1829–1903), a lexicographer whose works include a *Dictionary of Spoken Italian.*

70 In the original Italian, this is a pun on the word "passato" (meaning "purée" in this context), which also means "past." The pun also plays on Artusi's running polemic against the "modern" fashion of using French words in gastronomy.

416. CARCIOFI IN SALSA
(ARTICHOKES IN SAUCE)

Remove the tough leaves from the artichokes, cut off the tips, and peel the stalk. Cut them into four parts, or six at the most if they are large, put them on the fire with butter in proportion to their size, and season with salt and pepper. Shake the pan to turn the pieces, and when they have absorbed a good part of the melted butter, cover with broth and cook until done, then strain them. Keep the liquid in the pan, and add a pinch of finely chopped parsley, one or two spoonfuls of very fine bread crumbs, lemon juice, and more salt and pepper if necessary. Let this mixture simmer a little, while stirring it. Then remove the pan from the fire, and when the sauce has stopped boiling, add one or two egg yolks, depending upon the number of artichokes, and put it back on the fire for a little while with some more broth to make it smooth. Toss the artichoke pieces into this mixture to warm them up again, and serve as a side dish especially with boiled meats.

417. CARCIOFI IN UMIDO COLLA NEPITELLA
(STEWED ARTICHOKES WITH CALAMINT)

If you like the taste of artichokes with the aroma of calamint,[71] here is how you should proceed. Remove all the inedible leaves from the artichokes and cut them into four parts each, or into six parts if they are large. Dredge in flour and put them on the fire in a copper skillet with oil in proportion to the size and number of pieces; season with salt and pepper. When you have browned them, add a little battuto made of a clove of garlic, or only half a clove if you are cooking only a few artichokes, and a good pinch of fresh calamint. When they have absorbed the oil, finish cooking with tomato sauce or tomato paste diluted in water.

They can be served as a side dish, or eaten alone.

71 See note to recipe 382.

418. CARCIOFI RITTI
(ARTICHOKES COOKED STRAIGHT UP)

In Florence this is what they call artichokes cooked simply in the following way. Remove only the small, useless leaves near the stalk, and cut off the stalk. Trim the top with a knife, and loosen the inner leaves. Place them upright in a pot, along with the whole, peeled stalks; season with salt, pepper, and oil, all in good measure. Cook them, keeping them covered, and when they are nice and brown, pour a little bit of water into the pan to finish cooking.

419. CARCIOFI RIPIENI
(STUFFED ARTICHOKES)

Cut off the stalks at the base, remove the small outer leaves, and rinse. Then trim the top as in the preceding recipe, and open up the inner leaves so that you can remove the choke with a small knife. Discard the hairy part of the choke, if any, and keep only the small, tender surrounding leaves, which you will add to the stuffing. To make enough stuffing for, say, six artichokes, use the tiny tender leaves just mentioned, 50 grams (about 1-2/3 ounces) of fatty prosciutto, 1/4 of a spring onion, very little garlic (as much as you could gather on the tip of your fingernail), a few parsley and celery leaves, a pinch of dried mushrooms soaked in water, a small handful of crustless day-old bread crumbled into small pieces, and a pinch of pepper.

First chop the prosciutto finely with a knife, then chop all the ingredients together with a mezzaluna and stuff the artichokes with the mixture, seasoning and cooking the artichokes as in the preceding recipe. Some French cookbooks suggest parboiling the artichokes before stuffing them, which I do not approve of, because it seems to me that this would make them lose the best thing about them—their special fragrance.

420. CARCIOFI RIPIENI DI CARNE
(ARTICHOKES STUFFED WITH MEAT)

For 6 artichokes, make the following stuffing:

100 grams (about 3-1/2 ounces) of lean milk-fed veal
30 grams (about 1 ounce) of fatty prosciutto
the soft inner core of 1 artichoke
1/4 of an onion
some parsley leaves
a pinch of dried mushrooms, soaked in water
a pinch of crumbled bread
a pinch of grated Parmesan cheese
salt, pepper, and a dash of spices

After browning the artichokes in oil, add a little water and cover with a damp cloth kept in place by the lid of the pan. The steam, enveloping the artichokes on all sides, will cook them better.

421. PASTICCIO DI CARCIOFI E PISELLI
(ARTICHOKE AND PEA PIE)

This is a strange pasticcio, but many people might like it, so I will describe it:

12 artichokes
150 grams (about 5-1/4 ounces) of shelled peas
50 grams (about 1-2/3 ounces) of butter
50 grams (about 1-2/3 ounces) of grated Parmesan cheese
brown stock to taste

Remove all of the inedible leaves from the artichokes, cut them into two pieces, and remove the hairy choke or core, if any. Parboil both the artichokes and the peas for a few minutes in salted water, then drop in cold water. Strain, dry well, and cut the sections of artichoke in two again. Put both the artichokes and the peas on the fire with 40 grams (about 1-1/3 ounces) of the butter, season with salt and pepper, and cook with the brown stock until done. With the remaining 10 grams (about 1/3 of an ounce) of butter, one tablespoon of flour, and the brown stock, make a sort of béchamel sauce to bind the vegetables. Place the artichokes and peas in an ovenproof pan and arrange them in layers with the béchamel sauce and the Parmesan cheese.

Now cover the pasticcio with the dough described below; gild with egg yolk, and bake in a Dutch oven; serve hot, because this dish loses a great deal if allowed to cool. This recipe serves seven to eight people.

Dough:

230 grams (about 8 ounces) of flour
85 grams (about 3 ounces) of confectioners' sugar
70 grams (about 2-1/3 ounces) of butter
30 grams (about 1 ounce) of lard
1 egg

422. CARCIOFI IN GRATELLA
(GRILLED ARTICHOKES)

Everyone knows that you can grill artichokes and serve them with any kind of steak or roasted meat. For this recipe, choose tender artichokes, trim the tops, cut off the stalk at the base, and do not remove any of the leaves. Loosen the leaves well so that they can easily absorb the seasoning, which should consist simply of olive oil, salt, and pepper. Place them upright on a grill, and if necessary insert a stick into the bases of two or three at a time to keep them in place. Midway through the cooking process, season again with oil, and leave on the fire until the outer leaves are charred.

423. CARCIOFI SECCATI PER L'INVERNO
(ARTICHOKES DRIED FOR THE WINTER)

In southern Italian cities, where artichokes are found almost every month of the year, it is useless to bother drying them, especially as there is a big difference between fresh artichokes and dried ones. But it is convenient to have dried artichokes if you live where you cannot get them out of season.

Prepare them at the height of the season, when they don't cost much; but choose artichokes of good quality, at the right stage of maturity. Remove all the tough leaves, trim the tops, cut off a good portion of the stalk, and cut them into four sections, removing the hairy part of the core, if any. As you are cutting them up, toss the artichokes into cold water with either vinegar or lemon juice to prevent them from turning black. For the same reason, place them on the fire in an earthenware pot of boiling water, to which it is good to add a *bouquet garni* consisting of herbs such as thyme, basil, celery leaves, and the like. Ten minutes' boiling time, or even five if the artichokes are tender, should suffice to cook them halfway. Drain, and put on a grate to dry in the sun; then string them together and finish drying in a shady, well-ventilated place. Try not to keep them in the sun too long, or else they will start to smell like hay. Soften them with boiling water when you are ready to fry them or serve them as a side dish with stewed meats.

424. PISELLI ALLA FRANCESE I
(PEAS FRENCH STYLE I)

This recipe is for 1 liter (about 4 cups) of fresh peas. Take two spring onions, cut them in half lengthwise, put a few sprigs of parsley in the middle, and tie them together. Having done this, place them on the fire with 30 grams (about 1 ounce) of butter, and when they are golden brown, pour a generous ladleful of broth over them. Bring to a boil, and when the onions have fallen apart, pass them through a sieve along with the liquid, squeezing them well. Put the liquid back on the fire with the peas and two hearts of lettuce, left whole. Season with salt and pepper and boil slowly. When half done, add 30 more grams (about 1 ounce) of melted butter mixed with a level tablespoonful of flour, and more stock if necessary. Before sending to the table, bind with two egg yolks dissolved in a little stock. They come out very delicate this way.

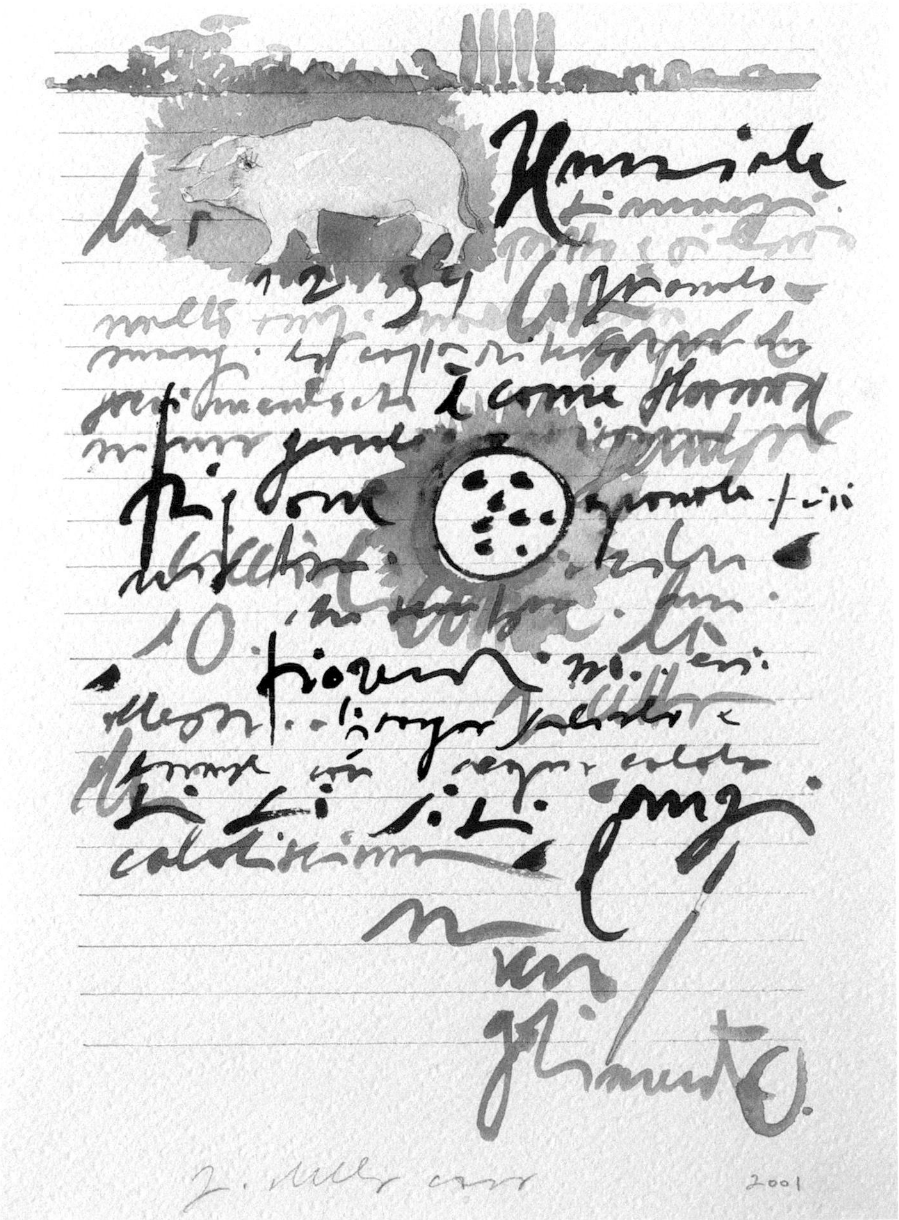
2001

425. PISELLI ALLA FRANCESE II
(PEAS FRENCH STYLE II)

This recipe is simpler and quicker to make than the preceding one, but it is not as refined. Cut some onion into very thin slices and put on the fire in a saucepan with a little butter. When the onion has browned well, add a pinch of flour, stir, and then add a ladleful or two of broth (depending on the amount of peas), then let the flour cook. Add the peas, season with salt and pepper, and when they are about half cooked add one or two hearts of lettuce, left whole. Boil slowly, making sure that the sauce does not become too thick.

Some people sweeten the peas with a teaspoon of sugar; but add only a small amount, because the sweetness should seem natural and not artificial.

Remove the lettuce before serving.

426. PISELLI COL PROSCIUTTO
(PEAS WITH HAM)

Let's leave to the English the taste for eating boiled vegetables without any seasoning, or at the most with a little butter; we southern types need our food to be a little more exciting.

I have never found peas anywhere as good as the ones they serve in the restaurants of Rome, not so much on account of the excellent quality of the vegetables from that part of the country, but because in Rome they flavor peas with smoked ham. Having experimented a bit trying to discover how they prepare them, I might not have yet fully succeeded in reproducing their delicious flavor, but I am pretty close. Here is how to do it.

Cut in half lengthwise one or two spring onions (depending on the amount of peas), and put them on the fire with oil and a generous amount of untrimmed smoked ham diced into small cubes. Fry lightly until the ham shrinks, then toss in the peas, seasoning them with little or no salt and a pinch of pepper; stir, and finish cooking with broth, adding a little butter.

Serve either alone as a vegetable course, or as a side dish; but first discard all the onion.

427. PISELLI COLLA CARNESECCA
(PEAS WITH BACON)

Peas are also good prepared in the following way, but, unlike the preceding recipes, this one cannot be said to belong to fine cuisine.

Put on the fire some finely chopped bacon, garlic, parsley, and oil; season with a little salt and pepper, and when the garlic is golden brown, toss in the peas. When they have absorbed all the oil, finish cooking them in broth, or lacking that, in water.

If the pea pods are tender and fresh, they can be cooked in water and passed through a sieve. You thus obtain a purée which, when dissolved in broth, adds a delicate flavor to a vegetable soup or a soup of rice and cabbage. It can also be mixed with the water for risotto with peas described in recipe 75.

428. SFORMATO DI PISELLI FRESCHI
(FRESH PEA MOLD)

600 grams (about 1-1/3 pounds) of shelled peas
50 grams (about 1-2/3 ounces) of untrimmed prosciutto
30 grams (about 1 ounce) of butter
20 grams (about 2/3 of an ounce) of flour
3 eggs
1 tablespoon of grated Parmesan cheese

Finely chop the prosciutto, a spring onion, and a pinch of parsley. Put on the fire with oil, and when the onion is golden brown toss in the peas, seasoning them with salt and pepper. When they are cooked, pass 1/4 of them through a sieve, and add this purée to a mixture of melted butter and flour in the amounts indicated above. Dilute the mixture over the fire with brown stock or broth. Then blend all of the ingredients together, including the Parmesan cheese, and bake in *bain-marie* in a smooth mold lined with a buttered sheet of paper.

429. FAVE FRESCHE IN STUFA
(STEWED FRESH FAVA BEANS)

Choose large, ripe pods; shell and skin the fava beans.

Finely chop a spring onion, put it on the fire with oil, and when it begins to brown toss in some untrimmed diced prosciutto into small cubes. Shortly thereafter, add the fava beans, season with pepper and a little bit of salt, and when the fava beans have absorbed the condiments, add one or two coarsely chopped hearts of lettuce, depending on the amount of beans. Finish cooking with broth, if necessary.

430. POMODORI RIPIENI
(STUFFED TOMATOES)

Choose medium-sized ripe tomatoes; cut them in half, remove the seeds, season with salt and pepper, and stuff the cavities with the following mixture, which should form a nice mound on top.

Make a little battuto of onion, parsley, and celery, put it on the fire with a bit of butter, and when it has browned add a handful of dried mushrooms moistened with water and chopped very fine. Add a tablespoon of crustless bread soaked in milk, season with salt and pepper, and boil for a while, adding milk if necessary. Remove from the fire, and when the mixture has cooled, add grated Parmesan cheese and a whole egg, or an egg yolk alone, if that is sufficient to thicken the mixture. Once the tomatoes have been prepared in this way, bake them in a pan with a little butter and oil, and serve as a side dish with any roasted meat or grilled steak. They can be made more simply with a little battuto of garlic and parsley mixed with a very small amount of bread crumbs, salt, and pepper. In this case they should be sprinkled with oil when they are in the baking pan.

As a side dish for boiled meats, they are excellent prepared as follows. Take a large skillet or baking pan, sprinkle with little bits of butter, and cover with tomatoes that have been cut in half and cored. Arrange the tomatoes with the skin side down. Season with salt, pepper, and a little oil, sprinkle more bits of butter on top, and bake uncovered.

431. CAVOLFIORE COLLA BALSAMELLA (CAULIFLOWER WITH BÉCHAMEL SAUCE)

All members of the cabbage family, be they white, red, yellow, or green, are children or stepchildren of Aeolus, god of the winds. Therefore people who cannot tolerate wind should have no difficulty remembering that these plants are called *crucifers*, since for such people these vegetables are truly a cross to bear. The real reason for the name, however, is that the flowers of these plants have four petals arranged in the shape of a cross.

Remove the leaves and the green stems from a large head of cauliflower, make a deep crosslike cut in the stalk, and cook in salted water. Then cut into small sections and season with butter, salt, and pepper. Place in an ovenproof dish, sprinkling with a little grated Parmesan cheese and covering with the béchamel sauce from recipe 137. Cook until the surface is golden brown.

Serve hot as an *entremets*, or better yet accompanied by a stewed meat or boiled chicken.

432. SAUERKRAUT I

This is not true *sauerkraut*, which we must leave to the Germans to make: it is a pale imitation of it, but it is not unpleasant as a side dish with cotechino, zampone, or simple boiled meats.

Take a head of white cabbage, remove the green leaves and large ribs, and cut into four sections, starting at the stem. Wash well in cold water and then, with a long, sharp knife, cut the sections crosswise into thin strips, much like taglierini pasta. Once all the cabbage has been cut in this way, place it in an earthenware dish with a pinch of salt and cover it with boiling water. When it has cooled completely, rinse the cabbage, squeezing it well and discarding the water; then put it back in the dish with a finger of strong vinegar mixed in a glass of cold water. If the head of cabbage is very large, double the amount. Leave it to soak in this infusion for several hours, squeeze it well again, and cook in the following way.

Finely chop a slice of fatty prosciutto or bacon, and place with a little butter in a saucepan; when this has browned a little, toss in the cabbage and cook with broth from a cotechino or zampone sausage, if they have been freshly made and are not too spicy; otherwise, use broth. Taste the cabbage before sending it to the table to make sure that it is sufficiently salted and that a perceptible vinegar flavor remains.

Speaking of cured meats, in some Italian provinces people have acquired the vice of abundant and frequent libations in honor of Bacchus. As a result their palates have become jaded, and since the pork butchers have to cater to a perverted sense of taste, they cram their cured meats with salt, pepper, and pungent spices, much to the annoyance of the connoisseurs of good food who would prefer these meats lightly seasoned and with a delicate flavor like the ones that you are likely to find especially in the province of Modena.

433. SAUERKRAUT II

This can be used as a side dish with cotechino and boiled meats, as in the preceding recipe. Take a head of white or Savoy cabbage, cut it into strips about a centimeter wide and keep it immersed in cold water. Remove it from the water without squeezing, place it in a saucepan on the fire, and press it down to draw out all the water, which you will remove with a ladle. Finely chop a 1/4 of a large onion and a little bacon and fry in a bit of butter; when the onion has browned, add the cabbage along with a whole piece of bacon, which you will later remove, and season with salt and pepper. Simmer, adding broth until it is cooked. At the end add a little vinegar and a teaspoon of sugar; you should barely be able to taste the vinegar.

434. BROCCOLI O TALLI DI RAPE
ALLA FIORENTINA[72]
(TURNIP GREENS FLORENTINE STYLE)

"Broccoli di rapa" are nothing more than the sprouts or shoots of turnips, which are usually brought to market with a few leaves attached. It is one of the most healthy greens, very popular in Tuscany;

---

72 As Edward Giobbi points out, what Artusi means by "broccoli di rapa" is not what is now known in English as "broccoli rabe" or "rapini," but rather "cime di rapa" or turnip greens.

but on account of its bland, slightly bitter taste it is not appreciated in other parts of Italy; it does not appear even on the tables of the poor.

Remove the toughest leaves from the greens and boil them. Squeeze out the water, and chop coarsely. Finely chop two or three cloves of garlic, or leave them whole, and when you have browned them in a generous amount of olive oil in a pan, add the greens, season with salt and pepper, stirring frequently, and sauté for quite some time. Turnip greens can be served either as a side dish with boiled meats, or alone.

If you do not like them cooked in this way, boil them and then season with olive oil and vinegar. The sprouts of this plant, which are tender and delicate, are sold in February and March.

In places where the olive oil is not of very high quality, you can substitute lard. In fact, to my taste, turnip greens are better sautéed in lard.

435. BROCCOLI ROMANI
(BROCCOLI ROMAN STYLE)

Broccoli, which the Romans consume in great quantities, has dark green leaves and black or purple florets.

Remove the toughest leaves and blanch the broccoli. Strain and plunge into ice-cold water. After you have squeezed it well, chop coarsely and toss in a pan with virgin lard, seasoning with salt and pepper. When the broccoli has absorbed all the fat, sprinkle with sweet white wine and continue to stir until all the wine has been absorbed and has evaporated; then serve, and it will be praised.

Here is another way to cook broccoli which turns out better without parboiling. Use only the tenderest florets and leaves; chop the leaves coarsely and cut the florets into small sections. Put a pan on the fire with sufficient oil and a clove of garlic cut into little slices crosswise. When the garlic begins to brown, toss first the raw leaves and then the florets into the pan, with salt and pepper as seasoning. As the broccoli cooks and begins to dry out, stir constantly, sprinkling it at first with warm water and then, when it is almost done, with white wine. Since I cannot give you the exact amounts for this dish, have the patience to test it out a few times (that is what I do, again and again!) to make sure you get the best taste out of it.

436. CAVOLO RIPIENO
(STUFFED CABBAGE)

Take a large head of white or Savoy cabbage, remove the toughest outer leaves, cut the stem off at the base, and parboil in salted water. Place it upside down to drain, then open the leaves one by one until you reach the center, which you will fill with the stuffing. Pull the leaves nicely over the stuffing, close the cabbage and tie it securely crosswise.

You can make the stuffing with stewed milk-fed veal alone, or with chicken livers and sweetbreads, all finely minced. To make the mixture more subtle and delicate, add a little béchamel sauce, a sprinkle of grated Parmesan cheese, an egg yolk, and a dash of nutmeg. Finish cooking the cabbage with the sauce from the stewed veal, adding a bit of butter, in a Dutch oven with a low fire under and over it.

If you do not want to stuff an entire head of cabbage, you can stuff the broadest leaves one by one, rolling them up on themselves like so many little logs.

Instead of béchamel sauce you can use crustless bread soaked in broth or brown stock.

437. CAVOLO BIANCO PER CONTORNO
(SIDE DISH OF WHITE CABBAGE)

Take a head of white or Savoy cabbage, cut it crosswise at the base to form four sections, and cut each section into small wedges. Soak in cold water, and then blanch in salted water. When you have removed the cabbage from the fire, drain well without squeezing it.

Finely chop some prosciutto and onion and put on the fire with a bit of butter. When the onion is quite brown, add a ladleful of broth to stop the frying, then simmer for a little while, and then strain. Put the cabbage in this sauce with a small piece of prosciutto, season with pepper and a little salt, and boil slowly until it is completely cooked. Remove the prosciutto and serve the cabbage as a side dish with boiled meats.

438. CAVOLO NERO PER CONTORNO
(SIDE DISH OF RED CABBAGE)

Remove the tough ribs from the cabbage, blanch, and chop finely. If you have no brown stock, finely chop some prosciutto and onion, put it on the fire with a bit of butter, and when the onion is nice and brown, moisten it with a little broth and strain the resulting sauce. Cook the cabbage in this sauce, seasoning with pepper, little or no salt, and adding another small piece of butter and more stock if necessary. Serve as a side dish with boiled meat or cotechino.

Some people toast finger-thick slices of bread, rub them with garlic, and very briefly dip them in the water in which the red cabbage has been boiled. Then they put the cabbage on top of the bread while it is still hot, and season with salt, pepper, and oil. This dish, which in Florence is called "cavolo con le fette" ("cabbage with bread slices"), is something fit for a Carthusian monk,[73] or to be inflicted on a glutton as penitence.

439. FINOCCHI COLLA BALSAMELLA
(FENNEL WITH BÉCHAMEL SAUCE)

Take nice plump fennel bulbs, remove the tough leaves, cut into small wedges, rinse, then blanch in salted water. Sauté in butter, and when the fennel has absorbed the butter, finish cooking with milk. Salt to taste, then strain and place in an ovenproof dish. Sprinkle with Parmesan cheese and cover with béchamel sauce. Broil them until golden brown and serve with boiled or stewed meats.

440. FINOCCHI PER CONTORNO
(SIDE DISH OF FENNEL)

This recipe is simpler than the preceding one, and it is just as suitable as a side dish for boiled meat.

---

73 Needless to say, this is a monastic order known for its austere way of life.

After cutting the bulbs into sections and blanching in salted water, sauté in butter and finish cooking with broth thickened with a pinch of flour. When you remove the fennel, season it with a little Parmesan cheese.

441. PATATE ALLA SAUTÉ
(SAUTÉED POTATOES)

In plain language, this means potatoes browned in butter. Peel raw potatoes and cut into thin slices, then cook in a pan with butter, seasoning with salt and pepper. These are very good served with a steak on top of them. You can also fry them in a pan with oil in the following way. If they are new potatoes, they need not be peeled; you can simply scrub them with a rough cloth. Cut them into very thin slices and leave them in cold water for about an hour; then dry them well with a towel and dredge in flour. Make sure not to over-cook them; salt them after cooking.

442. PATATE TARTUFATE (TRUFFLED POTATOES)

Cut parboiled potatoes into thin slices and place them in layers in a pan, alternating with layers of thinly sliced truffles and grated Parmesan cheese. Add a few pats of butter, salt, and pepper, and when they start to sizzle, moisten with broth or brown stock. Before removing them from the fire, sprinkle with a little lemon juice. Serve hot.

443. PASSATO DI PATATE (MASHED POTATOES)

Nowadays in Italy, if you do not talk like a foreigner, especially in matters of fashion or food, nobody understands you; so in order to be understood, I should call this side dish not mashed potatoes, but *purée* of potatoes, or, to use an even more barbarous name,[74] potatoes *mâchées*.

---

74 The term barbarous is derived from a Greek root which literally means "foreign."

500 grams (about 1 pound) of nice, big, starchy potatoes
50 grams (about 1-2/3 ounces) of butter
1/2 a glass of fresh milk or heavy cream
salt to taste

Boil the potatoes, peel, and while they are still steaming hot, pass them through a sieve. Then put them on the fire in a saucepan with the other ingredients, stirring vigorously with a wooden spoon until smooth. You can tell whether the potatoes are cooked if you can easily pass a sharp stick through them from side to side.

444. INSALATA DI PATATE
(POTATO SALAD)

Even though this is a potato dish, I can tell you that, in its own modest way, it is worthy of praise. But it is not for every stomach.

Boil or steam 500 grams (about 1 pound) of potatoes, peel while still hot, cut into thin slices, and place in a salad bowl. Then take:

30 grams (about 1 ounce) of pickled capers
2 pickled peppers
5 pickles
4 pickled pearl onions
4 salted anchovies, cleaned
1 small stalk of celery
a pinch of basil

Chop all these ingredients together very finely and place in a bowl.
    Take two hard-boiled eggs, chop finely as above, then crush with the blade of a knife and add to the above mixture. Season with a generous amount of olive oil, a little vinegar, and salt and pepper. Pour this dressing, which has become almost liquid, on the potatoes, mixing well. Add oregano it you like.
    This recipe serves six or seven people, and keeps for several days.

445. TORTINO DI ZUCCHINI (ZUCCHINI PIE)

Cut zucchini into small chunks a little larger than hazelnuts, sauté in butter, and season with salt and pepper. Then place in an ovenproof dish, sprinkle lightly with grated Parmesan cheese mixed with a pinch of nutmeg, and cover with a nice thick béchamel sauce. Cook under the lid of a Dutch oven until golden brown and serve as an *entremets* or to accompany boiled or stewed meat.

446. TORTINO DI PATATE I (POTATO PIE I)

This dish, like the one in recipe 443, can be served as an *entremets* or with cotechino or zampone.

500 grams (about 1 pound) of nice, big, starchy potatoes
50 grams (about 1-2/3 ounces) of butter
1/2 a glass of fresh milk or heavy cream
2 tablespoons grated Parmesan cheese
2 eggs
salt to taste

After you have gone through the same steps as in recipe 443, let the potatoes cool and add the Parmesan cheese and eggs.

Take a copper pie pan or a similar sized baking dish, grease it with butter, and dust with fine bread crumbs, then pour in the above mixture, well blended. Smooth out to a thickness of one or one and a half fingers, and cook in a Dutch oven until golden brown. Serve hot right side up or upside down, depending upon which side looks better. Instead of a large pie you can make several small pies, or for a more elegant shape, you can pour the mixture into several small molds.

447. TORTINO DI PATATE II (POTATO PIE II)

I think this recipe makes a better potato pie than the preceding one:

500 grams (about 1 pound) of potatoes
50 grams (about 1-2/3 ounces) of butter
30 grams (about 1 ounce) of flour

2 eggs
2 tablespoons Parmesan cheese
milk as needed
salt to taste

Make a béchamel sauce with the flour, half of the butter, and as much milk as necessary. Pour cooked potatoes that have been passed through a sieve into the sauce. Put on the fire, stirring as you add the remaining butter, salt, and as much milk as makes it not too soft. When it has cooled, add the remaining ingredients and bake until golden brown as in the preceding recipe.

448. SPINACI PER CONTORNO
(SIDE DISH OF SPINACH)

Spinach is a healthy, refreshing, soothing vegetable, with a laxative effect, and easy to digest when chopped. After boiling and chopping finely with a mezzaluna, you can cook spinach in the following ways:

1) just with butter, salt, and pepper, adding a little brown stock, if you have any, or a few tablespoons of broth or even of heavy cream;

2) with a little bit of onion chopped very fine and sautéed in butter;

3) just with butter, salt, and pepper as above, adding a little Parmesan cheese;

4) with butter, a tiny bit of olive oil, and tomato sauce (recipe 6) or tomato paste.

449. SPINACI DI MAGRO ALL'USO DI ROMAGNA
(MEATLESS SPINACH ROMAGNA STYLE)

Cook with just the water that drips off the spinach after it has been soaked and strained, then squeeze well, and sauté in olive oil with garlic, parsley, salt, and pepper. Leave the leaves whole, and sweeten with a pinch of sugar and a few seedless raisins.

450. SPARAGI (ASPARAGUS)

To make asparagus look better, before cooking scrape the white part with a knife and cut off the end of the stem; then tie the stalks in bunches—not too large—with a string. To keep them green, drop them into salted water when it is boiling hard, and fan the fire so that the water boils up again immediately. When the spears start to bend, they are cooked just right; still you should check from time to time, testing them with your fingers to see if they give a little when you exert some pressure—it is better to undercook them a little than to overcook them. After you have strained the asparagus spears, drop them in cold water, and then strain them again immediately so that you can serve them warm, the way most people like them.

This vegetable, which is prized not only for its diuretic and digestive qualities, but also for the high price it commands, can be prepared in various ways once it is blanched. The simplest and best is the most common way, which is to season with the very finest olive oil and vinegar or lemon juice. Nevertheless, for variety, here are some other ways to prepare asparagus after it has been parboiled. Place the stalks whole in a pan and sauté lightly in butter. After seasoning with salt, pepper, and a tiny pinch of Parmesan cheese, remove the stalks from the pan and pour the browned butter over them. Or, separate the green part from the white part and, taking an ovenproof dish, arrange them like this: sprinkle the bottom of the dish with grated Parmesan cheese and arrange the asparagus spears next to one another, season with salt, pepper, grated Parmesan, and dabs of butter; make another layer of asparagus and season in the same way, continuing until you have used them all. Be spare with the other ingredients, however, so that the dish does not turn out excessively rich. Crisscross the layers of asparagus like a tight lattice, place under the lid of a Dutch oven to melt the butter, and serve hot. If you have some brown stock, parboil the asparagus and finish cooking in the stock, adding a little butter and a light sprinkling of Parmesan cheese.

You can also serve asparagus spears in a mixed fry, dipping them in the batter described in recipe 156.

There are other ways to prepare asparagus given in cookbooks; but most frequently these turn out to be concoctions that are not pleasing to connoisseurs of good food. Nevertheless, I should point out that the sauce in recipe 124 can go well with asparagus, if served hot in a separate gravy dish, from where it can be poured over asparagus, as well as over artichokes cut in quarters and boiled.

The bad smell that results from eating asparagus can be turned into the pleasant fragrance of violets by pouring a few drops of turpentine into the chamber pot.

451. SFORMATO DI ZUCCHINI PASSATI
(PURÉED ZUCCHINI MOLD)

600 grams (about 1-1/3 pounds) of zucchini
40 grams (about 1-1/3 ounces) of Parmesan cheese
4 eggs

Make a battuto with 1/4 of an onion, celery, carrots, and parsley. Put on the fire with some oil, and when it starts to brown add the zucchini, cut into small pieces, and season with salt and pepper. When the zucchini has browned, finish cooking with water, pass through a sieve, and add the Parmesan cheese and eggs.

Make a béchamel sauce with 60 grams (about 2 ounces) of butter, two tablespoons of flour, and 4 deciliters (about 1-2/3 cups) of milk. Mix all the ingredients together, and bake in *bain-marie* in a smooth mold with a hole in the middle. Remove while still hot, fill the hole in the center with a delicate meat stew, and serve.

This recipe serves eight to ten people.

452. SFORMATO DI FUNGHI
(MUSHROOM MOLD)

Any kind of mushroom can be used for this recipe; I think that porcini mushrooms are the best, but not really large ones. Carefully remove all the dirt from the mushrooms, wash them, then chop into pieces about the size of a chickpea or even smaller. Put on the fire with butter, salt, and pepper, and when the mushrooms have sautéed a good while, finish cooking with brown stock. Remove from the fire, bind with béchamel, egg, and grated Parmesan cheese. Bake in a mold in *bain-marie* until firm.

600 grams (about 1-1/3 pounds) of fresh mushrooms with five eggs will make a sformato that serves ten people.

Serve warm as an *entremets*.

453. CAVOLO VERZOTTO PER CONTORNO (SIDE DISH OF SAVOY CABBAGE)

Parboil the cabbage, squeeze out the water, chop with a mezzaluna, put on the fire with butter and milk, add salt, and cook until done. When it is well cooked, add a rather thick béchamel sauce and stir over the fire until well blended; add grated Parmesan cheese. Taste for seasoning; if it's right, then serve as a side dish with boiled or stewed meat; you will see that people will like it for its delicate flavor.

454. INSALATA RUSSA (RUSSIAN SALAD)

Cooks make so-called Russian salad, which is now fashionable for dinner parties, by using the basic recipe and adding whatever concoctions they like. This recipe, invented in my kitchen, may seem complicated, but it is one of the simpler versions:

120 grams (about 4-1/4 ounces) of salad greens
100 grams (about 3-1/2 ounces) of beets
70 grams (about 2-1/3 ounces) of fresh baby green beans
50 grams (about 1-2/3 ounces) of potatoes
20 grams (about 2/3 of an ounce) of carrots
20 grams (about 2/3 of an ounce) of pickled capers
20 grams (about 2/3 of an ounce) of pickled gherkins
3 salted anchovies
2 hard-boiled eggs

You can use two or three kinds of salad greens, such as romaine, radicchio, or other lettuce, cut into thin strips. Weigh the beets, green beans, potatoes, and carrots after they have been boiled, and cut into cubes smaller than a chickpea; dice in the same way the two whites and one of the yolks of the hard-boiled eggs. Leave the capers whole, and cut the pickles into pieces about the size of the capers.

Clean and bone the anchovies, cut them into small pieces, then mix everything together thoroughly.

Now prepare a mayonnaise (see recipe 126) with two raw egg yolks, the remaining hard-boiled egg yolk and 2 deciliters of extra fine olive oil. Blend until smooth, adding the juice of one lemon and seasoning with salt and pepper. Pour the mayonnaise over the ingredients already combined, stirring to make sure that everything is well coated with dressing.

Soak three sheets of isinglass in cold water for several hours; then dissolve them in two fingers of hot water in a pot on the fire. Once melted, pour a thin layer of the liquid into the bottom of a smooth mold and blend the rest with the other ingredients, which you will later pour into the mold and chill. To remove the chilled mixture easily, dip the mold in hot water. If you want to make the salad prettier and more elegant looking, you can make a colorful decoration with the greens, egg yolks, and egg whites mentioned above, which you will place over the thin layer of gelatin lining the bottom of the mold before adding the other ingredients.

This recipe serves eight to ten people.

SEAFOOD

Types and Seasons of Fishes

Of the common types of fish, the finest are: sturgeon, dentex, sea bass, weever, sole, turbot, John Dory, gilthead sea bream, rock mullet, and fresh-water trout; these are excellent year round, but sole and turbot are especially good in the winter.

The seasons for the other best-known fish are: for hake, eel, and flying squid, year round, while eel is better in winter and flying squid in the summer.

For large gray salt-water mullet, July and August; for small mullet, October and November, and all winter. For gudgeon, whitebait, and cuttlefish, March, April, and May. For octopus, October. For sardines and anchovies, all winter, until April. For red mullet, September and October. For tuna, from March to October. For mackerel, springtime, especially May; this fish, on account of its tough and fibrous flesh, is usually used in stews—if you want to grill it, it is a good idea to put it on the fire on a large sheet of greased cooking paper and season it with oil, salt, pepper, and a few sprigs of rosemary.

Of the crustaceans, one of the most prized is lobster, which is good year round, but better in springtime, and of the shellfish, oysters, which are harvested from October to April in oyster beds.

When a fish is fresh, its eyes are bright and clear; if it is not fresh, the eyes are pale and cloudy. Another indication of freshness is the red color of the gills; but since these can be artificially colored with blood, touch them and then smell your finger; your nose will tell you whether it is fresh or not. Another characteristic of fresh fish is the firmness of the flesh, because if it is kept on ice too long it begins to decay and becomes soft to the touch.

Sailors say that crustaceans and sea urchins are meatier when gathered during a full moon.

455. CACCIUCCO I
(FISH STEW I)

Cacciucco! Let me say just a little bit about this word, which is understood perhaps only in Tuscany and on the shores of the Mediterranean, since on the shores of the Adriatic it is called "brodetto" (literally, "little broth").[75] In Florence, "brodetto" means a soup with bread and broth, bound with beaten eggs and lemon juice. In Italy the confusion between these and other names from province to province is such that it is almost a second Tower of Babel.

After the unification of Italy,[76] it seemed logical to me that we should think about unifying the spoken language, and yet few can be bothered with such an undertaking and many are outright hostile to it, perhaps because of false pride and the ingrained habit that Italians have of speaking their own regional dialect.

To return to cacciucco, let me say that, naturally enough, this is a dish prepared in seaside towns more than anywhere else, because it is there that you can find fresh fish of the kind needed to make it. Any fishmonger can tell you the varieties of fish that are best suited to a good cacciucco. Good as it may be, however, it is still quite a heavy dish, so one needs to be careful not to gorge oneself on it.

75 Lest the reader be confused, we should note a small lapse on Artusi's part. The author says "Mediterranean (Sea)" when he means the Tyrrhenian Sea (Italy's west coast) in contrast to the Adriatic Sea (Italy's east coast), both of which are part of the Mediterranean Sea.
76 In 1861.

For 700 grams (about 1-1/2 pounds) of fish, finely chop an onion and sauté it with oil, parsley, and two whole cloves of garlic. The moment the onion starts to brown, add 300 grams (about 10-1/2 ounces) of chopped fresh tomatoes or tomato paste, and season with salt and pepper. When the tomatoes are cooked, pour in one finger of strong vinegar or two fingers of weak vinegar, diluted in a large glass of water. Let boil for a few more minutes, then discard the garlic and strain the rest of the ingredients, pressing hard against the mesh. Put the strained sauce back on the fire along with whatever fish you may have on hand, including sole, red mullet, gurnard, dogfish, gudgeon, mantis shrimp, and other types of fish in season, leaving the small fish whole and cutting the big ones into large pieces. Taste for seasoning; but in any case it is not a bad idea to add a little olive oil, since the amount of soffritto was quite small. When the fish is cooked, the cacciucco is usually brought to the table on two separate platters: on one you place the fish, strained from the broth, and on the other you arrange enough finger-thick slices of bread to soak up all the broth. The bread slices should be warmed over the fire but not toasted.

456. CACCIUCCO II
(FISH STEW II)

This cacciucco, which I learned to make in Viareggio, is much less tasty than the one in the preceding recipe, but it is lighter and more digestible.

For the same amount of fish as above, crush three large cloves of garlic and some fresh or dried hot red chili peppers in a mortar. Since you are already using a hot spice, no black pepper should be added. Put this mixture on the fire in a pot or an earthenware pan with an appropriate amount of oil, and when it is sautéed, pour in a glass of liquid consisting of 1/3 dry white or red wine and 2/3 water. Place the fish in the pot, salt it, and then add tomato sauce (recipe 6) or tomato paste diluted with a little water. Then boil over a lively flame, keeping it covered; never touch the fish because you do not want it to crumble. You will find that it cooks in a few minutes.

Serve as in the preceding recipe, with slices of bread that have been warmed in the oven without toasting them.

If you are not going to cook fish you have bought right away, you can preserve it better by salting it; but then you should rinse it before cooking it.

457. PESCE AL PIATTO (FISH ON A PLATTER)

Since fish is not a highly nourishing food, I believe that it is healthier to serve it along with meat dishes rather than eating it alone as on fasting days, unless you feel the need to re-balance your system after having eaten too many rich foods. Moreover fish, especially crustaceans and shellfish in general, on account of the significant quantities of hydrogen and phosphorus they contain, have a stimulant effect and are not recommended for anyone wishing to live a continent life.

For this dish, it is best to use different kinds of small fish; but larger fish cut into thin slices can also be prepared in the same way. When I have made it with sole and red mullet, I have cut the sole into thirds. After boning, washing, and drying the fish, you will bake it on an ovenproof metal or porcelain dish seasoned with a battuto of garlic, parsley, salt and pepper, olive oil, lemon juice, and good white wine.

Place half of the battuto with a little oil in the bottom of the dish, arrange the fish on top of it, and then pour on top more oil and the rest of the battuto, ensuring that the fish is well soaked in the condiments. Bake in the oven with fire above and below; if the dish is porcelain, place it directly in hot ashes.

This is not a difficult dish to make, so I advise you to try it. I am sure you will be happy with it.

458. PESCE MARINATO (MARINATED FISH)

There are several types of fish that can be marinated, but I prefer sole and large eels. If you are using sole, sauté it first in oil, and salt it; if you use eel, cut it into pieces about half a finger long, without skinning it, and cook on a grill or a spit. When the eels have lost their fat, season with salt and pepper.

Take a saucepan and pour in vinegar, concentrated must[70] (which goes with this dish like cheese goes with macaroni), whole sage leaves, whole pine nuts, raisins, a few cloves of garlic cut in half crosswise, and some small pieces of candied fruit, all in proportion to the amount of fish. If you do not have concentrated must, use sugar as a substitute and taste to correct the flavor of the vinegar, which should not be too strong. Boil this mixture and then pour it in an earthenware pan in which you have arranged the fish in such a way that the liquid completely covers it. Bring to a boil again with the fish in the liquid; then cover the pan and put it aside.

When you serve this dish, take out the amount you need with a little of the sauce. If the fish should dry out after a while, moisten it with a little more of the marinade. You can also prepare in this way the "scorpionata" eel sold in stores.

459. PESCE LESSO (POACHED FISH)

I ought to tell you that the customary way to prepare poached fish is as follows. Place on the fire the water for poaching, but not too large an amount; salt the water. Before adding the fish let the water boil for about a quarter of an hour with the following seasonings: a quarter or half of an onion (depending on the amount of fish) with two cloves stuck into it, some pieces of celery and carrot, a bit of parsley, and two or three thin slices of lemon. Another way, which some people think is better, is to put the fish into cold water and put it on the fire with the same seasonings. After the fish is cooked, leave it in the liquid until you are about to serve it. Rub the fish all over with the lemon slices while it is still raw, so that the skin is more likely to remain intact.

The fish is properly done when the eyes pop out, the skin can be easily removed with one's fingers, and the flesh is tender. Serve hot, not too thoroughly drained. If you want to make a better impression, cover it with chopped raw parsley and surround it with a side dish of beets (cooked in water if small or baked if large) and boiled potatoes. Both should be sliced very thin so that they absorb the seasoning better; finally, add some wedges of hard-boiled egg.

If you do not make the side dish of beets and potatoes, you can

70 The juice of grapes before it has fermented to produce wine.

serve this dish with the sauces in recipes 128, 129, 130, 133, or 134.

You can also serve poached fish garnished in the following way, which makes a better presentation. Cut it into small pieces enough to fill a platter. Thoroughly cover the fish with mayonnaise (recipe 126) and decorate with salted anchovy fillets and whole capers.

460. PESCE COL PANGRATTATO
(BREADED FISH)

This dish, which can also be used as an *entremets*, is made especially when you have high-quality poached fish left over. Cut the fish into small pieces, carefully remove all the bones, then put the pieces in béchamel sauce (recipe 137) and season with salt to taste, grated Parmesan cheese, and finely chopped truffles. If you do not have truffles, use a handful of dried mushrooms that have been soaked in water. Then take an ovenproof dish, grease it with butter, and sprinkle with bread crumbs; pour the fish mixture into the dish and coat with a thin layer of bread crumbs. Finally, place a dab of butter on top, brown in a Dutch oven until golden, and serve hot.

461. PESCE A TAGLIO IN UMIDO
(STEWED FISH)

For this excellent-tasting dish you may use tuna, umber, dentex, or weever, which is incorrectly called sea bass along the Adriatic coast. Whatever fish you choose, use a piece weighing about 600 grams (about 1-1/3 pounds), which serves five people.

Remove the scales from the fish, wash and dry it, then coat well with flour and brown in a little oil. Remove from the pan, discard the small amount of oil that is left, and wipe the pan clean. Finely chop together a medium-sized onion, a stalk of white celery as long as the palm of your hand, and a generous pinch of parsley. Put on the fire with a sufficient amount of oil, and season with salt, pepper, and a whole clove. When the mix has browned, add a generous amount of tomato sauce (recipe 6) or tomato paste diluted with water. Let this boil a bit and then add the fish to finish cooking, turning it frequently. Be sure to serve the fish nicely covered with a generous amount of the thick sauce it has been cooking in.

462. PESCE SQUADRO IN UMIDO
(STEWED ANGEL SHARK)[77]

The angel shark (*Rhina squatina*) has a flat body similar to the ray. The skin, which is rough and hard, is used to polish wood and ivory, and to line sheaths for knives, swords and the like. The flesh of this fish is rather ordinary, but when prepared in the following manner it makes a family dish that is not only edible, but more than passingly good. And it is economical, because it is easy to find, at least in Italy.

Chop together very finely a generous handful of parsley, half a carrot, a piece of celery, half a clove of garlic and, if the fish weighs about 600 grams (about 1-1/3 pounds), an onion the size of a large walnut. Place the mixture on the fire with an appropriate amount of oil, and when it has browned add tomato sauce (recipe 6) or tomato paste diluted with half a glass of water. Season with salt and pepper and then put in the piece of fish (preferably a piece from the tail end, which is quite thick). Cook slowly, and when it is about two-thirds done add a dab of butter well rolled in flour to bind the sauce and give it a more delicate flavor; then cook until done.

463. NASELLO ALLA PALERMITANA
(HAKE PALERMO STYLE)

Take a hake or cod weighing between 500 and 600 grams (between about 1 and 1-1/3 pounds) and trim all the fins, except the one on the tail, but leave the head on. Cut along the belly to remove the innards and the spine, bone it, and season with a little salt and pepper. Turn the fish backside up, grease it with olive oil, season with salt and pepper, coat it with bread crumbs, and then place it flat with two tablespoons of oil in an ovenproof platter or baking pan.

Take three large salted anchovies, or four if they are small, remove the scales and bones, chop, and place on the fire with two tablespoons of oil until they dissolve; but make sure that they do not boil. Coat the inner part of the fish with this sauce and then cover it with bread crumbs; you can toss in a few sprigs of rosemary if you like. Bake with fire above and below until the bread crumbs form a

77 Also called angel fish or monk fish.

golden crust, but be careful not to let it get too dry. In fact, sprinkle some more olive oil over it, and before you remove it from the fire squeeze half a large lemon over it. I think that this should be sufficient for four to five people if you serve it with toasted bread rounds spread with caviar or a paste made with anchovies and butter.

464. ROTELLE DI PALOMBO IN SALSA
(DOGFISH ROUNDS IN SAUCE)

The smooth dogfish (*Mustelus*) is a fish from the shark family, and therefore in some places it is called shark. (This explanation is for those who do not know what dogfish is.) It can be quite large, and its flesh is perhaps the best among all the *Selachii*, the order to which it belongs.

Take some dogfish rounds half a finger in thickness; rinse, dry with a kitchen towel, remove the skin with a sharp knife, season with salt and pepper, and soak for several hours in beaten egg. Coat in bread crumbs twice, dipping them again in the beaten egg, and fry in olive oil.

Now make the sauce in the following way.

Take a wide baking dish or pan and add oil in proportion to the amount of fish, a dab of butter dredged in flour (which helps to bind the sauce), a handful of chopped parsley, tomato sauce (recipe 6) or tomato paste diluted with water, and a dash of salt and pepper. When this sauce has sautéed for a little while, place the fried dogfish rounds in it, turn on both sides, and add enough water to make the sauce liquid. Remove from the fire, sprinkle with a little grated Parmesan cheese, and serve. They will be highly praised.

465. SOGLIOLE IN GRATELLA (GRILLED SOLE)

When sole (*Solea vulgaris*) are large, it is better to grill them and season with lard instead of olive oil; they take on a more pleasing flavor this way.

Clean the fish, scrape off the scales, rinse, and dry well. Then dab them lightly with cold virgin lard (making sure that it does not taste rancid); season with salt and pepper and coat with bread crumbs.

Melt a little more lard in a frying pan and brush this on the fish; brush again with melted lard when you turn them on the grill.

When you prepare sole for frying, you can skin them on both sides or just on the dark side, then dredge in flour, keeping in beaten egg for several hours before tossing them in the pan.

A singular thing about this fish that merits mentioning is the fact that, like all well-constructed animals, it is born with one eye on its right side and the other on the left. But at a certain period in its life the eye that was on the white (or left) side migrates over to the right side and settles, like the other eye, on the dark side. Sole and turbot swim on their blind sides. Because of the quality and delicacy of its flesh, the French call sole the "partridge of the sea." It is a fish that is easy to digest, it resists decomposition better than many other fish, and it does not go out of season. It is found in abundance in the Adriatic, where it is caught at night with huge sack-like nets weighted down heavily at the mouth; when these nets scrape the bottom of the sea, they lift up the fish along with the sand and mud in which they lie.

Turbot, the flesh of which is not very different from that of sole, and is even more delicate, is called the "pheasant of the sea."

466. FILETTI DI SOGLIOLE COL VINO
(SOLE FILLETS IN WINE)

Take sole that weigh no less than 150 grams (about 5-1/4 ounces) each, cut off the heads and remove the skin. Then separate the bones from the flesh with a sharp knife to obtain four long fillets for each sole, or even eight if they should be very large. Gently pound the fillets with the blunt edge of the knife, flatten them with the flat side of the blade, and then leave them for several hours in beaten egg seasoned with salt and pepper. Then coat them with bread crumbs and fry in oil. Once done, pour a bit of the oil from the frying pan into a pan or baking dish in which the fillets will fit lying flat. Add a little butter on the bottom of the dish and arrange the fillets on top, season again with a little salt and pepper, and when they have sautéed for a while moisten them with dry white wine, and cook for five minutes with a little chopped parsley. Serve with their own sauce, sprinkling a pinch of grated Parmesan cheese over them. This dish makes a very nice presentation. Serve it with lemon wedges. Hake can also be cooked in the same way.

It is absolutely necessary that the wine you use be dry; otherwise, the dish will taste too sweet. A sole of ordinary size serves one person.

467. CONTORNO DI FILETTI DI SOGLIOLE A UN FRITTO DELLO STESSO PESCE (SIDE DISH OF FRIED SOLE FILLETS)

Take a couple of medium-sized sole or even just one. Remove the skin and bones to obtain four fillets which you will then cut crosswise into tiny strips the size of matches. If you cut them at a slant, they will turn out a little longer, which is better. Place the strips of sole in a bowl with the juice of one lemon, or more if necessary, and let them marinate for two or three hours. This will make them stiffen, otherwise they would be too soft. Shortly before you intend to serve them, dry them with a cloth, dip in milk, dredge in flour, trying not to let them curl up, and fry in oil; then salt lightly.

468. TRIGLIE COL PROSCIUTTO (RED MULLET WITH PROSCIUTTO)

The saying "mute as a fish" is not always true, because red mullet, umber, and some other fish emit odd sounds caused by the vibration of special muscles; these vibrations are increased by the movement of the air in their swimming bladder.

The largest, most flavorful red mullet are rock mullet or striped surf mullet. However, this recipe can also be used for cooking medium-sized red mullet, which are called "rossioli" or "barboni" in the regions bordering the Adriatic. After gutting and rinsing the fish, dry them well with a kitchen towel, and then place them in a bowl and season with salt, pepper, oil, and lemon juice. Leave them like this for several hours, and when you are about to cook them, cut thin slices of untrimmed prosciutto. The slices should be as wide as and equal in number to the pieces of fish. Take a metal dish or pan and scatter a few whole sage leaves on the bottom. Coat the fish well in bread crumbs, and arrange them upright side by side with the slices of prosciutto between them, scattering more sage leaves on top.

Finally, pour the remaining liquid over the fish and bake with fire above and below. If you want this dish to turn out more refined, remove the spine from the raw mullet by cutting open the belly side, and then close the fish.

469. TRIGLIE IN GRATELLA ALLA MARINARA (GRILLED RED MULLET MARINARA STYLE)

After removing the intestines with the tip of a knife passing through the gills, rinse and dry the fish, and place a little piece of garlic where the intestines used to be. Season with salt, pepper, olive oil, and sprigs of rosemary; set aside. When you are ready to cook them, dredge the fish in bread crumbs and then pour the seasonings over them when they are on the fire. Or, after cleaning, rinsing, and drying them, simply season with a little salt and pepper and cook over a high flame. Once done, arrange them on a platter, and only then season them with olive oil and a little more salt and pepper.

Serve with lemon wedges.

470. TRIGLIE DI SCOGLIO IN GRATELLA (GRILLED ROCK MULLET)

This beautiful, bright red, excellent-tasting fish, which reaches a weight of 500 to 600 grams (between about 1 and 1-1/3 pounds), is usually grilled in the following way.

Season with oil, salt, and pepper, grill over a high flame, and when you remove the fish, dab it while it is still very hot with a mixture of butter, chopped parsley, and lemon juice that you have prepared in advance. This method can also be used for other large fish cooked on the grill.

The ancient Romans prized fish with the most delicious flesh; the kinds they favored were sturgeon, weever, lamprey, rock mullet, and hake caught in the sea of Syria, not to mention moray eels, which they raised in the most lavish fashion in special ponds, even feeding them with the flesh of their slaves.

Publius Vedius Pollio is famous in history for his wealth and his cruelty. Once when he was dining with Augustus, he commanded that a servant who had carelessly broken a crystal goblet be thrown to the morays. Augustus, at whose feet the slave fell, invoking his intercession, barely managed to save his life with an ingenious stratagem.[78]

Large striped mullet, which reach a weight of not merely of 500 to 600 grams (about 1 to 1-1/3 pounds), as I said above, but even 4 to 6 pounds, were highly prized and bought at fabulously high prices. The Romans, whose sense of taste had been refined by a life of luxury and gluttony, tried to satisfy their appetite with the most delicate foods; so they invented a sauce called *garum*[79] made with the minced and cured innards of this large fish, into which they would dip the flesh of the fish.

471. TRIGLIE ALLA LIVORNESE (RED MULLET LIVORNO STYLE)

Mince a little garlic, parsley, and a piece of celery; place on the fire with a generous amount of olive oil, and when the garlic has browned add chopped fresh tomatoes seasoned with salt and pepper. Let the tomatoes cook well, stirring frequently, and then strain. Cook the mullet in the strained sauce. If small, they need not be turned, and if the pan in which they have been poached is not presentable enough, remove them one by one so as not to break them, and place on a platter.

Just before removing them from the fire, sprinkle lightly with chopped parsley.

78 An official in the government of Augustus, Pollio died in 15 B.C. The stratagem used by Augustus (ruled 27 B.C.–14 A.D.) was to break all of the remaining crystal goblets himself.

79 Highly prized by the ancient Greeks and Romans, "garum" was a sauce made by soaking fish intestines and pieces of fish in brine with aromatic herbs; it was used as a condiment in cooking, as well as added to dishes at the table.

It is easier and more productive to fish for red mullet during the day than at night, and the season for it, as I already mentioned, is September and October.

472. TRIGLIE ALLA VIAREGGINA
(RED MULLET VIAREGGIO STYLE)

If you have about 1/2 a kilogram (about 1 pound) of red mullet, take two cloves of garlic and a nice handful of parsley and chop them very finely. Place on the fire with a generous amount of oil in a skillet or baking dish in which the mullet can lie flat; when the garlic has browned, add plain tomato sauce (recipe 6). Let the sauce boil a while, and then add the mullet one at a time, turning them so that they become coated with sauce. Cover and boil slowly, and when the fish have absorbed a good part of the liquid, pour in a finger of red wine diluted in two fingers of water.

Boil a little longer and serve.

473. TONNO FRESCO COI PISELLI
(FRESH TUNA WITH PEAS)

Tuna, a fish from the mackerel family, is native to the Mediterranean basin. During certain seasons, it lives in the deepest parts of the sea, while at other times of the year it moves near the shore, where it is caught in great numbers. On account of its oiliness, its flesh is reminiscent of pork, and therefore is not easy to digest. They say that tuna are found weighing as much as 500 kilograms (about 1100 pounds). The tenderest, most delicate part of this fish is the belly, which in Tuscany is called "sorra."

Cut the tuna into half a finger thick slices. Place on the fire a generous soffritto of garlic, parsley, and oil and, when the garlic starts to brown, put in the fish. Season with salt and pepper, turn the slices on both sides, and when half cooked, add tomato sauce (recipe 6) or diluted tomato paste. When it is cooked through, remove the tuna and cook some peas in the sauce; then put the tuna back on top of the peas to warm it up, and send it to the table with this accompaniment.

474. TONNO IN GRATELLA (GRILLED TUNA)

Slice as in the preceding recipe, but try to cut slices mostly from the belly. Season with oil, salt, and pepper, coat with bread crumbs, and grill. Serve with lemon wedges.

475. TONNO SOTT'OLIO IN SALSA ALLA BOLOGNESE (OIL-PRESERVED TUNA WITH BOLOGNESE SAUCE)

Take a whole piece of tuna preserved in oil weighing 150 grams (about 5-1/4 ounces), place on the fire in boiling water, and boil slowly for half an hour, adding water every ten minutes (that is, three times). In the meantime, finely chop half a small onion as in recipe 409, with a clove of garlic, two ribs of white celery as long as the palm of your hand, a nice piece of carrot, and a generous handful of parsley. Put this mixture on the fire with three tablespoons of oil and 15 grams (about 1/2 an ounce) of butter, and when it is browned add two fingers of water and let boil a little while. Cut the tuna, which you have let cool, into the thinnest slices possible and layer the slices flat in a pan, alternating with the sauce and 15 more grams (about 1/2 an ounce) of butter, scattered in small pieces over the fish. Raise the heat so as to melt the butter, squeeze half a lemon over the tuna, and serve hot. This recipe serves four people as the first course in a meatless lunch, or it can be served as an *entremets* at a family dinner. It is not a dish to be scoffed at, because it does not lie heavy on the stomach.

476. ARIGUSTA (ROCK LOBSTER)[80]

This type of lobster, one of the finest, most delicate crustaceans, is common on the coasts of the Mediterranean. The weight of rock lobsters, true lobster, and crustaceans in general in proportion to their size is an indication of their freshness and good quality; but it is always preferable that they still be alive, or at least that they give some sign of

80 This type of lobster is smaller than the lobster familiar to North Americans, and does not have claws. Also called spiny lobster or langouste.

life, in which case one usually folds the lobster's tail under the lower portion of the body and ties it before tossing it in boiling water.

Depending on the size of the lobster, boil it for thirty to forty minutes; but first season the water in which it is to boil with a *bouquet garni* consisting of onion, carrot, parsley, and two bay leaves, adding two tablespoons of vinegar and a pinch of salt. Let the lobster cool in its broth, and when you remove it, shake the water off, holding it by the tail. After drying it, rub with a few drops of oil to make it shiny.

Send it to the table with a cut from the head to the tail so that the meat can be easily removed, and accompany it with mayonnaise or some other tasty sauce, if you do not want to eat it simply with oil and lemon juice. But you can also serve it with a lobster sauce made in the following way.

Remove the meat from the head of a lobster and chop finely with a hard-boiled egg yolk and a few parsley leaves. Place this mixture in a gravy dish, seasoning it with pepper and a little or no salt, and thinning it with fine olive oil and the juice of half a lemon, or vinegar.

477. COTOLETTE DI ARIGUSTA
(LOBSTER PATTIES)

Take a lobster weighing about 650 grams (about 1-1/2 pounds), boil as in the preceding recipe, then remove all the meat from the shell and chop coarsely with a mezzaluna. Make a béchamel sauce, using the amounts described in recipe 220, and when you remove it from the fire toss the chopped lobster into it, add salt, and, after mixing well, pour onto a plate where you will leave it to cool for several hours.

When you are ready to make the patties, divide the mixture into ten equal parts, roll each of them in bread crumbs, and mold with the palms of your hands into patties a little more than half a finger thick. Dip the patties in beaten egg, roll again in bread crumbs, and fry in oil. Break the long antennae of the lobster into ten pieces, and insert them into the patties just before serving to indicate the noble material of which they are made. This recipe serves five people and is a very delicate dish.

478. CONCHIGLIE RIPIENE
(STUFFED SCALLOP SHELLS)

This is a delicate seafood dish that can be served as the first course of a luncheon.

The scallop shells used for this recipe should each be as wide in their concave part as the palm of your hand, so that the contents of each one will be enough for one person. Scallops belong to the genus *Pecten Iacobaeus*; colloquially they are called "cappa santa" (holy cowl) because scallop shells used to be worn by pilgrims.[81] The edible flesh of this shellfish is highly prized for its delicate flavor.

In some aristocratic homes they use silver scallop shells, which can also be used to serve ice cream. But in this case, since we are dealing with seafood, natural scallop shells seem more appropriate to me.

Take the flesh of a high-quality poached fish—though you can also use hake, mullet or dogfish—and make the mixture with the following amounts, which are enough to fill six scallop shells:

130 grams (about 4-1/2 ounces) of poached fish
20 grams (about 2/3 of an ounce) of grated Parmesan cheese
20 grams (about 2/3 of an ounce) of flour
20 grams (about 2/3 of an ounce) of butter
2 egg yolks
2-1/2 deciliters (about 1 cup) of milk

Make a béchamel sauce with the milk, butter, and flour, and when you remove it from the fire add the Parmesan cheese. When it is no longer boiling hot, add the egg yolks and chopped fish, seasoning with salt and pepper. Pour into the shells, which you have greased with cold butter, bake in a Dutch oven just until golden brown, and serve.

You can also fill the scallop shells with finely chopped boiled chicken, using the same proportions.

---

81 The cockle shell or scallop is a symbol of St. James the Greater, and was traditionally worn by pilgrims traveling to the shrine of the saint in Santiago de Compostela, Spain.

fritto
in pesce gatto
come in [illegible]
[illegible]
fritte
alla fiorentina

J. Mellocaro   2001

479. STORIONE (STURGEON)

I hope my readers will allow me to give a little of the history of this very interesting fish.

The sturgeon belongs to the order of the *Ganoidei*, from the Latin *Ganus*, which means shiny, owing to the shine of its scales, and to the sub-order of the *Chondrostei*, since it has a cartilaginous skeleton. It constitutes the family of the *Acipenser*, which is defined by those two characteristic qualities, as well as by a skin made up of five longitudinal series of shiny scales. The mouth of this fish is located on the underside of the head; it has no teeth and is shaped like a protractile suction device, with nasal barbels or tentacles for searching in the mud for its food, which apparently consists of tiny creatures.

Sturgeon are highly prized for their flesh, as well as for their eggs, which are used for caviar, and for their enormous air bladder, which is used to make isinglass or fish glue. In the springtime, they swim upstream in rivers to deposit their eggs in calm waters along the banks.

Italy is home to several species of sturgeon, of which the most highly prized for its food is the *Acipenser sturio* (common sturgeon). It can be recognized by its sharp snout and thick lower lip split in the middle, as well as by its simple nasal tentacles, which are all the same size. It prefers the mouths of the Ticino and Po rivers, where not long ago one weighing 215 kilograms (about 475 pounds) was caught. But the sturgeon that grows largest is the *Acipenser huso*, which can reach up to two meters or more in length, with egg sacs one-third the size of the entire fish. It is this fish in particular that provides caviar and gelatin. Caviar is made from the raw eggs of the sturgeon, which are carefully strained through a sieve to remove the filaments that envelop them; they are then salted and tightly packed. Isinglass is made on the beaches of the Caspian Sea and along the banks of the rivers that run into it, but more than anywhere else in Astrakhan. It is hardly surprising that there is such an extraordinary amount of it on the market (since isinglass has many uses), if one considers that sometimes in the Volga from fifteen to twenty thousand sturgeon are caught daily; for it is from there—that is, the southern regions of Russia—that we get caviar. It was announced not long ago that some fishermen on the Danube caught a sturgeon weighing 800 kilograms (about 1950 pounds). The skeleton of this enormous fish, 3.3 meters (about 11 feet) long, is now on display at the Museum of Vienna.

The extinct species of sturgeon include the *Magadictis*, which reached a length of 10 to 20 meters (about 33 to 34 feet).

480. STORIONE IN FRICANDÒ
(STURGEON *FRICANDEAU*)

Sturgeon is good no matter how you prepare it: poached, stewed, or grilled. To stew it, proceed as follows. Take a large piece of sturgeon weighing at least 500 grams (about 1 pound), remove the skin, and stud it with lardoons seasoned beforehand with salt and pepper. Then tie it crosswise, dredge in flour, and place on the fire with oil and butter, seasoning again with salt and pepper. When it is browned on both sides, moisten with stock and cook until done. Before removing, squeeze lemon juice over it, and serve in its own sauce.

481. ACCIUGHE ALLA MARINARA
(ANCHOVIES MARINARA)

This small fish, with its bluish, almost silvery skin, known on the shores of the Adriatic by the name of "sardone," differs from the sardine in that the sardine is flat, whereas the anchovy is round and has a more delicate flavor. Both species belong to the same family, and when they are fresh, they are usually eaten fried. But anchovies are more appetizing when cooked with finely chopped garlic, parsley, salt, pepper, and oil; once done, add a little water mixed with vinegar.

You probably already know that blue fish are the least digestible of the bony species.[82]

82 The term "pesce azzurro" (blue fish), or, as Artusi more poetically writes, "pesci turchini," includes tuna, sardines, anchovies, mackerel, and herring.

482. ACCIUGHE FRITTE (FRIED ANCHOVIES)

If you want to give a nicer appearance to fried anchovies or sardines, after you've removed the heads and dredged them in flour, pick them up by the tail one by one, dip them in well-salted beaten egg, and then again in the flour, before tossing them in a pan of hot oil. If the anchovies are large, it is even better to make a slit along the back with a sharp knife and remove the spine, leaving the tail to keep them in one piece.

483. SARDE RIPIENE (STUFFED SARDINES)

For this dish you need the largest sardines available. Take 20 to 24 sardines, which are enough for the amount of filling described below. Wash the sardines, remove the heads, and open them out flat on the belly side with your fingers to remove the spine. Make a mixture with:

30 grams (about 1 ounce) of crustless bread
3 salted anchovies
the yolk of 1 hard-boiled egg
1/2 a clove of garlic
a pinch of oregano

Dip the bread in milk and then squeeze it dry. Remove the scales and spine from the anchovies, then finely chop them. Mix all the ingredients together; then use the blade of a knife to reduce the mixture to a fine paste. Spread this paste on the open sardines and close them up. Then dip them one by one into the egg white (lightly beaten) left over from the egg yoke, then coat the fish with bread crumbs, fry in oil, salt a bit, and serve with lemon wedges.

484. BROCCIOLI FRITTI
(FRIED FRESHWATER FISH FROM PISTOIA)

If you find yourselves some day in the mountains near Pistoia in search of cool weather, fresh air, and enchanting landscapes, ask for "broccioli," a fresh-water fish that looks like a gudgeon, and has a flavor as delicate as trout, and perhaps even more so.

So invigorating is that mountain air, that once a lady I know, after a long walk in those mountains, found meatballs made by the parish priest of Pianosinatico so delicious that she gobbled them all up.

485. TOTANI IN GRATELLA
(GRILLED FLYING SQUID)

Flying squid (*Loligo*) belong to the order of cephalopods and are known by the name of "calamaretti" on the coast of the Adriatic. Since that sea produces them small, but meaty and flavorful when fried, connoisseurs of good food judge them to be an excellent dish. By comparison, the Mediterranean produces a larger fish,[83] and I have seen "calamari" that looked like they weighed between 200 and 300 grams (between about 7 and 10-1/2 ounces); but they are not as good as the ones from the Adriatic. Even when cut into pieces, large calamari would turn out tough when fried, so it is better to stuff and then cook them on a grill, or to stew them if they are very large. This fish has inside it a little flexible blade, which is nothing more than a rudimentary shell and should be removed before stuffing.

Cut off the tentacles (which are the arms of the flying squid), leaving the sac and the head. Using a mezzaluna, chop the tentacles with some parsley and very little garlic. Mix this with a generous amount of bread crumbs, season with oil, pepper, and salt, and use this mixture to stuff the sac of the fish; to close the mouth of the sac, insert a toothpick, which you will later remove. Season with oil, pepper, and salt, and cook, as I said, on a grill.

If you find yourselves in Naples, do not forget to visit the aquarium in the gardens of the Villa Nazionale, where, among many zoological marvels, you will observe with pleasure this slender, graceful cephalopod swimming and darting about with great dexterity. You will also admire the speed and dexterity of sole as they suddenly disappear in the sand, with which they cover themselves, perhaps to hide from some pursuing enemy.

To return to squid—which are quite a difficult fish to digest, but excellent year round—after you have removed the cuttlebone and

83 If you find this confusing, see the note to recipe 455.

popped the eyes out, wash and dry them, roll in flour, and fry in oil. But be careful not to overcook them, which is easy to do if you do not pay close attention. If you do overcook them, they shrivel up and become even harder to digest. Season while hot with salt and pepper.

486. CICALE RIPIENE
(STUFFED SQUILL)

Do not think that I want to talk to you about the cicadas[84] that sing up in the trees; what I mean to talk about is the crustacean, *Squilla mantis*, so common in the Adriatic, where it is known by the name of "cannocchia."

This is a crustacean that is always tasty to eat; but it is much better during certain months of the year, from the middle of February to April. During this season, it is meatier than usual, and contains a red tube along its spine colloquially called the "cera" or "corallo," which is nothing more than the egg receptacle. It is good poached, and when cut into pieces it shows to advantage in a nice stew; it is also excellent grilled, seasoned with olive oil, pepper, and salt.

If you like it even tastier, cut it open along the back, stuff it with a mixture of bread crumbs, parsley, and garlic, and season both the filling and the fish itself with olive oil, pepper, and salt.

487. CICALE FRITTE
(FRIED SQUILL)

When they are in season, that is, when they have their egg sac as described in the preceding recipe, squill can be fried in the following way, which merits consideration.

After cleaning the squill, poach in a small amount of water, covering the pan with a cheesecloth kept in place by a weight; I think 15 minutes should be sufficient. Then remove the shell, cut the flesh into two pieces, dip in salted beaten egg, and fry in oil.

---

84 In Italian, "cicale" can mean both cicadas and squill.

488. CICALE IN UMIDO (STEWED SQUILL)

If you do not mind using your fingernails, getting your hands dirty, and maybe even cutting your lips, here is a tasty treat.

> Before cooking, soak the squill in cold water so that they do not shrivel up; in fact, this causes them to swell. Make a mixture of chopped garlic, parsley, and oil; when it has browned, add the whole squill and season with salt and pepper. When they have absorbed the seasonings, pour tomato sauce or diluted tomato paste over them and serve on top of slices of bread that have been warmed over the fire. Before serving, make an incision with scissors along the back of each one, so that they are easier to peel.

489. SPARNOCCHIE (MANTIS SHRIMP)

Talking about squill I am reminded of mantis shrimp,[85] which at first sight resemble them. But upon careful examination, this crustacean looks like a large shrimp usually weighing between 50 or 60 grams (between about 1-2/3 and 2 ounces). Its flavor is more delicate than that of the lobster and like lobster it is usually eaten boiled. But so that it doesn't lose flavor, it is better to grill it, without any seasoning, and afterwards peel it and season with olive oil, pepper, salt, and lemon juice. Like all shrimps, small sparnocchie can also be floured and fried just as they are, or it can be poached first as in the recipe for fried squill.

490. ANGUILLA (EEL)

The *Anguilla vulgaris* is a singular fish. Although the people of the Comacchio Valley claim to be able to tell the male from the female, no one has yet succeeded, in spite of much study, in distinguishing the sexes on the basis of external characteristics, perhaps because the sperm sac of the male is similar to the ovary of the female.

The common eel lives in fresh water but to reproduce it needs to

85 Actually, they are both *Squilla mantis*.

go to the sea. This descent to the sea, which is called the "calata," takes place chiefly on dark, stormy nights during the months of October, November, and December, and it is then that the catch is easier and more abundant.

Newborn eels leave the sea and enter marshes or rivers toward the end of January or February, and during this period, which is called the "montata" or ascent, they are caught at the mouths of rivers in great quantities and are called glass eels or elvers. The fishing industry takes advantage of these catches to re-populate ponds and lakes in which eels cannot reproduce because there is no connection to the salt water of the sea.

Recent studies in the Strait of Messina have shown that this fish, and its relatives the muraenids or morays, need to deposit their eggs in the depths of the sea, at a depth of no less than 500 meters (about 1640 feet), and that, like frogs, they undergo a metamorphosis. The *Leptocephalus brevirostris*, which looks like an oleander leaf as transparent as glass, was until now believed to be a species unto itself; really, it is nothing but the first stage of life, or larva, of this creature, which later is transformed into an elver, the so-called glass eel that swims upriver in search of fresh water and is never less than 1/2 a centimeter (about 1/5 of an inch) long. We do not know what becomes of the adult eels that swim down river to the sea; perhaps, remaining in the profound darkness of the depths of the sea, they die under that enormous pressure, or else they undergo a change to adapt themselves to the environment in which they find themselves.

Another peculiarity of muraenids in general is their blood, which if injected into the bloodstream of man is poisonous and deadly, whereas it is innocuous when cooked and eaten.

Because of the special conformation of its gills (which are simple slits), its cylindrical shape, and its very tiny, delicate scales, the eel can live for a long time out of water. But whenever eels have been found slithering on the ground (which happens especially at night), they have always been seen to be heading in the direction of a water course. Perhaps they do this in order to move from one place to another, or to search for food, consisting of small animals, in the fields surrounding their home.

The eels of the Valley of Comacchio in the lower Romagna region are famous. In fact, one might say that this whole area lives off this fish, which, fresh or marinated, is distributed not only throughout Italy, but also sent abroad. This area is so productive that on a single dark, stormy night in October 1905, 150,000 kilograms (about 330,000 pounds) of eels were caught; even more amazing is the final result of fishing for that year, which you will find described in recipe 688.

In some places in Italy eels are called "capitoni" when they are large and "bisatti" when they are small. They live in all the rivers of Europe except the ones that flow into the Black Sea, including the Danube and its tributaries.

The only difference between the freshwater eel and the saltwater eel, known by the name of conger, is that the former has a shorter upper jaw and does not grow as large as the latter. Indeed, there are conger eels up to 3 meters (about 9 feet) long. Perhaps this large, snake-like fish is the origin of the legend of the sea serpent, once perpetuated even by usually reliable people who exaggerated its size, probably owing to some hallucination.

491. ANGUILLA ARROSTO
(ROASTED EEL)

If you can, always select eels from the Comacchio Valley, which are the best in Italy; only those from Lake Bolsena, mentioned by Dante,[86] might surpass them.

When eels are large and you want to cook them on a spit, they

---

86 Purgatory, XXIV, 24.

should be skinned. Cut them into sections 3 centimeters (about 1-1/5 inches) long and skewer them on a spit between two rounds of toasted bread with a few sage leaves or bay leaves, if you are not afraid that the latter's sharp aroma will repeat on you. Cook without condiments over a moderate fire, and at the end over a nice hot flame to obtain a crisp crust. Season only with salt and lemon wedges when you are about to send them to the table.

In my opinion, medium-sized eels come out tastier cooked on a grill without removing the skin which, when seasoned with lemon juice at the moment of serving, is not unpleasant to the taste when you suck on it. Season only with salt and pepper. The people of the Comacchio Valley use medium-sized eels for grilling. They skin them if they are a little large, but only clean them if they are slender; then they nail the eels' head to a wooden board, split the fish open with a sharp knife, remove the spine, and spread them open on a grill, seasoning only with salt and pepper at the midway point. They are eaten piping hot.

Dry red wine should be drunk when eating eels.

492. ANGUILLA ALLA FIORENTINA
(EEL FLORENTINE STYLE)

Take medium-sized eels, and remove the skin by making a circular incision under the head, which you will hold tightly with a kitchen towel so that it will not slip from your hands in spite of the notoriously slippery skin of this fish. Then pull down the skin, which will come off whole. Cut the eel into finger-length pieces or a little shorter, and season with oil, salt, and pepper, letting them stand for an hour or two.

Take an iron pan, coat the bottom with oil, add two whole cloves of garlic, and fresh sage leaves; sauté for a little while, and roll the pieces of eel one at a time in bread crumbs, then arrange them in the pan one next to the other, pouring the rest of the seasonings on top. Cook in a Dutch oven with fire above and below, and when they start to brown, add a little water to the pan.

The flesh of this fish, which is very delicate and tasty, is rather difficult to digest on account of its high fat content.

493. ANGUILLA IN UMIDO
(STEWED EEL)

This dish is best made with eels that are rather large, which you will cut into short pieces without removing the skin.

Finely chop a rather generous amount of onion and parsley, put it on the fire with a little oil, pepper, and salt, and when the onion has browned toss in the eel. Wait until it has absorbed the flavor of the seasonings, and then finish cooking with tomato sauce or tomato paste diluted with water. Make sure to have a good amount of sauce left, if you intend to serve the eel on top of lightly toasted rounds of bread. This is a delicate tidbit, but it is not suited to all stomachs.

494. ANGUILLA COL VINO (EEL IN WINE)

Take an eel weighing about 1/2 a kilogram (about 1 pound), or several adding up to about the same weight; it is not necessary to use large eels for this dish. Rub them with sand to clean them of mucus, then rinse and cut into log-like segments. Put a thinly sliced clove of garlic, three or four coarsely chopped sage leaves, the peel of a quarter of a lemon, and a little oil in a skillet. Put on the fire, and when the garlic has browned, put in the eel and season with salt and pepper. When the liquid starts to evaporate, keep moving the eel segments with the point of a knife so that they do not stick to the pan; once they are browned on one side, pour in some tomato sauce or diluted tomato paste and turn them. When they are browned on the other side, pour in a good finger of dry red or white wine mixed with two fingers of water, cover the pot and finish cooking the eel over a low flame. Send to the table with a generous amount of their own sauce. This recipe serves four people.

495. ANGUILLA IN UMIDO ALL'USO DI
COMACCHIO (STEWED EEL COMACCHIO STYLE)

The people of Comacchio never use oil to season eel, no matter how they cook it. This can be seen in this eel stew, which could also be called eel soup or "cacciucco." In fact, this fish contains so much fat that adding oil spoils it rather than enhancing the flavor. I will transcribe here a recipe that was kindly given to me and which I have successfully tested.

"For 1 kilogram (about 2 pounds) of eels, take three onions, a stalk of celery, a good sized carrot, parsley, and the peel of half a lemon. Coarsely chop everything but the lemon, and boil in water with salt and pepper. Cut the eels into segments, but leave the segments connected by a strip of flesh. Take an appropriately sized pot and lay a layer of eel on the bottom, covering it with a layer of the parboiled chopped vegetables (but discard the lemon), then another layer of eel, another of vegetables, and so on, as much as will fit in the pot. Cover with the water in which you cooked the vegetables; boil slowly in a tightly covered pot, shaking and turning the pot, but never stirring, because you would break it all up. We usually bury the pot in ashes and coals to just above the middle point in front of a clear-burning wood fire, constantly shaking and turning the pot. When the pieces of eel that were held together by a strip of flesh start to come apart, they are almost cooked. At this point add a generous tablespoon of strong vinegar and some tomato paste. Taste the broth to adjust it for salt and pepper (be generous); boil just a little longer. You might even serve from the same pot, because this is a homey dish. Serve on top of slices of bread, on heated plates."

I should point out that here we are talking about medium-sized eels, not skinned, and that if the onions are large, two will suffice, and that two glasses of water are enough to cook the vegetables. It is a good idea to warm the sliced bread in the oven, without toasting it.

496. ANGUILLA COI PISELLI
(EEL WITH PEAS)

Stew the eel as in recipe 493, and when it is cooked remove it from the pot and cook the peas in the broth. Then return the eel to the pot to warm it, and serve. Tomato sauce is out of place here; but add water if necessary.

497. CEFALI IN GRATELLA
(GRILLED GRAY MULLET)

The eels of the Comacchio Valley bring to mind the gray mullet that live in the same valley, which are nice and fat and of excellent flavor when they are brought to market toward the end of autumn. The people of Comacchio prepare them in the following way, which is quite good. They remove the scales and the gills, but not the innards, because, as with woodcock, they say that this is the best part. They season them with salt and pepper only, and place them on the grill over a high flame. When they are cooked, they place them between two warm plates not far from the fire for five minutes. Just before serving, they turn the plates over, so that the one that was on top is on the bottom, and the fat that has dripped remains sprinkled over the fish. This dish is served with lemon that is squeezed over it.

Recipe 688 gives an indication of how they serve gray mullet in Romagna.

498. TELLINE O ARSELLE IN SALSA D'UOVO
(CLAMS IN EGG SAUCE)

The variety of clams called "arselle" do not retain sand like the ones called "telline" (tellina or sunset clams), so one need only rinse them thoroughly in cool water. Both types of clam should be cooked with a soffritto of garlic, olive oil, parsley, and a dash of pepper. Shake the pot, and keep it covered so that clams do not dry out. Remove them when the shells open, and garnish them with the following sauce: one or more egg yolks (depending on the amount of clams), lemon juice, a teaspoon of flour, broth, and a little of the liquid from the clams. Cook until creamy, and pour over the clams just before serving.

I prefer them without sauce, and serve them over slices of bread warmed (but not toasted) over the fire; you can taste the natural flavor of the shellfish that way. I do not put tomatoes in clam risotto for the same reason.

499. ARSELLE O TELLINE ALLA LIVORNESE
(CLAMS LIVORNO STYLE)

Finely chop a bit of onion and put it on the fire with oil and a dash of pepper. When the onion has browned, add a pinch of parsley chopped not too fine and shortly after toss in the clams with tomato sauce or tomato paste. Shake the pot frequently, and when the shells have opened, pour the clams over toasted bread slices that you have arranged on a platter beforehand.

Clams are good cooked this way; but to my taste they are inferior to the ones in the preceding recipe.

500. SEPPIE COI PISELLI
(CUTTLEFISH WITH PEAS)

Finely chop a rather generous mixture of onion, a clove of garlic, and parsley. Put it on the fire with oil, salt, and pepper. Strain when it has browned, squeezing well against the mesh. Cut the cuttlefish into strips, but first clean them as indicated in recipe 74; toss them into the pot with the strained soffritto, add water if necessary, and when they are almost cooked, pour in the peas dripping with the cold water in which they have been soaking.

501. TINCHE ALLA SAUTÉ (SAUTÉED TENCH)

As everyone knows, this fish (*Tinca vulgaris*) from the family of the *Cyprinidae* or carp, prefers to live in the still waters of marshes, although it is also found in deep lakes and rivers. But what many people may not know is that the tench, like the carp, is an example of a ruminant fish. When food reaches its stomach, it is sent back up the pharynx by antiperistaltic motion and further chewed and broken up by the pharyngeal teeth, which have evolved especially for this use.

Take some large tench (the ones sold live at the market in Florence are among the best, though tench is considered an inferior fish) and cut off the fins, head, and tail. Slit them open along the back, remove the spine and bones and cut in two lengthwise. Dredge in flour, then dip in beaten egg that you have seasoned with salt and pepper; coat with bread crumbs and repeat this last step twice. Sauté in butter and serve with lemon wedges and a side dish of sautéed mushrooms, if in season.

It is a good idea to mention here how to eliminate or lessen the bad smell of still-water fish. Toss the fish into boiling water, leaving it for several minutes until the skin starts to crack, and then plunge into ice-cold water before cooking. The French call this operation *limoner*, from the word *limon*, meaning silt.

502. PASTICCIO DI MAGRO (SEAFOOD PIE)

I would be failing to give credit where it is due if I didn't tell you that I owe quite a few recipes in this book to the kindness of several ladies, who also favored me with this one. Although it looks like a true pasticcio, when I tried it, it came out worthy to be served at a dinner party, if prepared properly.

a fish weighing between 300 and 350 grams (between about 10 1/2 and 12-1/4 ounces)
200 grams (about 7 ounces) of rice
150 grams (about 5-1/4 ounces) of fresh mushrooms
300 grams (about 10-1/2 ounces) of green peas
50 grams (about 1-2/3 ounces) of toasted pine nuts
butter, as needed
Parmesan cheese
6 artichokes
2 eggs

Cook the rice in 40 grams (about 1-1/3 ounces) of butter with a quarter of a chopped onion and salt it. When it has cooked in the necessary amount of water, bind it with the two eggs and 30 grams (about 1 ounce) of Parmesan cheese.

Make a soffritto of onion, butter, celery, carrot, and parsley, and cook the sliced mushrooms, peas, and parboiled quartered artichokes in it. Finish cooking these ingredients with a few tablespoons of hot water and season with salt, pepper, and 50 grams (about 1-2/3 ounces) of grated Parmesan cheese after you remove it from the fire.

Cook the fish, which can be mullet, weever, or some other large fish, in a mixture of oil, garlic, parsley, and tomato sauce or tomato paste; season with salt and pepper. Remove the fish from the fire, strain the sauce, and stir in the pine nuts, which you have toasted and crushed. Remove the head, spine, and bones from the fish, cut it into small pieces, put it back in the broth, and add all the other ingredients except the rice.

Now that all the ingredients for the filling are ready, make the dough for the pie to contain it. Here are the proportions:

400 grams (about 14 ounces) of flour
80 grams (about 2-2/3 ounces) of butter
2 eggs
2 tablespoons white wine or Marsala
a pinch of salt

Roll out the dough and use it to line a mold greased with butter. Pour in first half of the rice, then all the filling, and finally the remaining rice over the filling; cover the top with more of the same dough. Bake in the oven, remove from the mold, and serve lukewarm or cold.

Made with the amounts indicated, this recipe serves twelve people.

503. RANOCCHI IN UMIDO (STEWED FROGS)

The simplest way is to make them with a soffritto of olive oil, garlic, parsley, salt, and pepper, adding lemon juice when they are done. Instead of lemon, some people use tomato sauce, but lemon is preferable.

Never remove the eggs, which are the best part of the frog.

504. RANOCCHI ALLA FIORENTINA
(FROGS FLORENTINE STYLE)

Immediately after the frogs have been killed, plunge them briefly in hot water, and then keep them in cool water until you are ready to cook them. Dry thoroughly between the folds of a kitchen towel, and dredge in flour. Place a pan on the fire with good olive oil, and when it starts to sizzle, toss in the frogs. Season with salt and pepper, stirring frequently because they stick easily. When they have browned on both sides, pour over them beaten eggs seasoned with salt and pepper, and lemon juice if you like. Do not stir; let the eggs harden like a frittata and send them to the table in the pan.

The bile duct should always be removed from frogs.

If you want to fry them, dredge in flour, and before tossing in the pan leave them for a few hours in beaten egg seasoned with salt and pepper. Or, after flouring them, brown lightly on both sides and then dip them one by one in egg seasoned with salt, pepper, and lemon juice. Put back in the pan to finish cooking.

505. ARINGA INGENTILITA
("CIVILIZED" HERRING)

All you drinkers out there can put your forks down; this herring (*Clupea harengus*) is not for your jaded palates.

Ordinarily, people want the female herring because it is showier on account of the large amount of eggs; but the male, with its milky sperm sac, is more delicate and therefore preferable. Whether male or female, open the herring along the back, discard the head, and flatten it; then place it in scalded milk and let it sit for eight to ten hours. It would be well to change the milk once during this time. After drying it with a kitchen towel, cook on the grill like ordinary herring and season with oil and a very small amount of vinegar, or with oil and lemon juice if you prefer.

There is also another way to remove the salty flavor from herring. Place it on the fire in cold water, bring to a boil and simmer for three minutes, and then soak in cool water for a moment. Dry, discard the head, open along the back, and season as above.

Clupea harengus is the most common variety of the very important family of the *Clupeidae*, which also includes allice shad, pilchards, anchovies, sardines, and the *Alosa vulgaris*, or *Clupea comune*, which is called "cheppia" ("shad") in Tuscany. In the spring, they swim upriver to deposit their eggs; at this time they are caught even in the Arno River in Florence.

Herring live in huge numbers at the bottom of the seas at the outer reaches of Europe, and are seen on the surface only at mating time—that is, during the months of April, May, and June. After they deposit their eggs they disappear into the depths of their usual abode. Sometimes the sea appears shimmering and translucent for several miles around because of the frenzy of the spawn and the scales that come loose during it. In England the herring run from July to September; the catch, done with round nets, is at times so abundant that on the shores of Yarmouth they have filled as many as five hundred thousand barrels with herrings.

506. BACCALÀ ALLA FIORENTINA
(SALT COD FLORENTINE STYLE)

"Baccalà" belong to the family of *Gadidae*, the most typical variety being cod. The most common species in our seas are the *Gadus minutus* and the *Merlucius esculentus* or hake, quite a bland fish but one that is easy to digest on account of its light flesh. It is good for convalescents, especially when poached and seasoned with oil and lemon juice.

The genus *Gadus morrhua* is the cod from the Arctic and Antarctic regions which, depending upon how it is prepared, is called either "baccalà" (salt cod) or "stoccafisso" (stockfish). As everyone knows, an oil used for medicinal purposes is extracted from the liver of this fish. It is fished with a hook; a single man can catch up to 500 in one day. It is perhaps the most fecund of all fish—nine million eggs have been counted in a single individual.

There are two well-known types of cod on the market, Gaspé and Labrador. The former comes from the Gaspé Peninsula, that is the Banks of Newfoundland (where every year more than 100 million kilograms of cod are caught); it is dry, tough, and difficult to soften. The latter, which is caught along the coast of Labrador, is fat and tender, perhaps on account of a more copious food supply; it softens easily and is much better tasting.

Salt cod enjoys a good reputation in Florence, and deservedly so, because the Florentines know how to soften it well, cleaning it frequently with a little hard brush. Moreover, the cod consumed in Florence is usually the best Labrador cod, which is fatty by nature and relatively tender, considering the tough, fibrous flesh of this type of fish, which is not suited to weak stomachs. For this reason, I have never been able to digest it. On days of fasting, this salted fish competes on the market to great advantage with fresh fish, which is limited in quantity, high in price, and often not particularly fresh.

Cut the salt cod into pieces as wide as the palm of your hand and coat thoroughly with flour. Then put a large pan on the fire with a generous amount of oil and two or three whole garlic cloves, slightly crushed. When the garlic begins to brown, toss in the pieces of cod and brown on both sides, moving the fish around constantly to keep it from sticking. It is not necessary to add salt, or if you do, very little and only after tasting; but a pinch of pepper will not do any harm. At the end, pour in a few tablespoons of the tomato sauce from recipe 6, or tomato paste diluted in water. Boil a little longer and serve.

507. BACCALÀ ALLA BOLOGNESE
(SALT COD BOLOGNESE STYLE)

Cut into pieces as in the preceding recipe, and toss these just as they are into a large pan or skillet coated with oil. Sprinkle with chopped garlic and parsley and season with a few dashes of pepper, oil, and bits of butter. Cook over a high flame, turning slowly, because the fish breaks easily, since it has not been floured. When it is cooked, squeeze a lemon over it and send it to its fate.

508. BACCALÀ DOLCE-FORTE
(SWEET-AND-SOUR SALT COD)

Cook as in recipe 506, but without the garlic, and when it is browned on both sides, pour some sweet-and-sour sauce over it, boil a little longer, and serve hot.

Prepare the sweet-and-sour sauce beforehand in a glass. If the cod weighs around 500 grams (about 1 pound), you will need a finger of strong vinegar, two fingers of water, a sufficient amount of sugar, and pine nuts and raisins in due proportion. It is not a bad idea to boil the sauce for a little while separately before pouring it over the cod. If it comes out right, you will find that it will please those who like this kind of dish.

509. BACCALÀ IN GRATELLA
(GRILLED SALT COD)

You can cook salt cod over a slow fire on a strong sheet of oiled white paper so that it does not come out dry. Season with olive oil, pepper and, if you like, a few sprigs of rosemary.

510. BACCALÀ FRITTO
(FRIED SALT COD)

The frying pan is an implement used for many lovely things in the kitchen; but, in my opinion, salt cod comes to a most deplorable end in it. This is because, since it has to be boiled first and then coated with batter, there is no seasoning that can give it a proper flavor. And yet some people, perhaps not knowing a better recipe, make the concoction that I am about to describe. To boil it, put it on the fire in cold water, and the moment it starts to boil, take it off the hearth, for it is already cooked. Without doing anything else, it can be eaten like this, seasoned with oil and vinegar.

But let's return to the concoction I mentioned. Feel free to try it, or to send both the recipe and whoever wrote it to the devil. After you have boiled the cod, marinate it whole in red wine for several hours; then dry it with a kitchen towel and cut it into small pieces, removing the spine and bones. Coat lightly with flour and dip in a simple batter made with water, flour, and a drop of oil, with no salt. Fry in oil and sprinkle with sugar after it stopped sizzling. If eaten hot, the aroma of the wine is barely noticeable. If, however, you still find this to be an inferior dish, it is your fault for wanting to try it.

511. COTOLETTE DI BACCALÀ
(SALT COD CUTLETS)

Since we are still talking about salt cod, do not expect anything special; but prepared in this way it will be less offensive than in the preceding recipe. If nothing else, it will please the eye with its golden brown appearance, resembling cutlets of milk-fed veal.

Boil as in the preceding recipe and for about 500 grams (about 1 pound) of cod, add two anchovies and a pinch of parsley, and chop everything very fine with a mezzaluna. Then add a few dashes of pepper, a handful of grated Parmesan cheese, two eggs and finally, to make the mixture softer, three or four tablespoons of a paste made with crustless bread, water and butter. Drop this mixture by the spoonful into bread crumbs, flatten with your hands to shape into cutlets, and dip into beaten egg and again in bread crumbs. Fry in oil and serve with lemon wedges or tomato sauce (recipe 125).

Half of this amount will make nine or ten cutlets.

512. BACCALÀ IN SALSA BIANCA
(SALT COD IN WHITE SAUCE)

400 grams (about 14 ounces) of softened salt cod
70 grams (about 2-1/3 ounces) of butter
30 grams (about 1 ounce) of flour
a potato weighing about 150 grams (about 5-1/4 ounces)
3-1/2 deciliters (about 1-1/2 cups) of milk

Boil the cod and remove the skin, bones, and spine. Boil the potato as well, and cut it into rounds. Make a béchamel sauce with the milk and flour, and when it is cooked add a little chopped parsley, a dash of nutmeg, salt, and the potato. Then stir in the pieces of cod. After letting it rest a little, serve. It will be liked and praised.

This recipe serves four people, if they are not big eaters. To garnish, surround it with wedges of hard-boiled egg.

513. STOCAFISSO IN UMIDO
(STEWED STOCKFISH)

500 grams (about 1 pound) of softened stockfish, divided as fol-
lows: back, 300 grams (about 10-1/2 ounces) and belly, 200
grams (about 7 ounces)

Remove the skin and all the bones, then cut the back part into thin
slices and the belly into squares two fingers wide. Make a soffritto
with a generous amount of oil, one large or two small cloves of
garlic, and a good pinch of parsley. When the garlic has browned,
toss in the stockfish, season with salt and pepper, and stir so that it
absorbs the flavor. After a little while, pour in six or seven tablespoons of tomato sauce (recipe 125), or chopped fresh tomatoes
(peeled and seeded); boil slowly for at least three hours, adding hot
water a little at a time, and after two hours add a potato cut into
thick pieces. This amount is sufficient for three or four people. It is
an appetizing dish, but not for weak stomachs.

A friend of mine, certain that he will please his company, does
not hesitate to serve this dish for lunch to distinguished guests.

514. CIECHE ALLA PISANA
(BABY EELS PISA STYLE)

See the eel recipe 490.

Wash the eels several times, and when they have stopped foam-
ing pour them into a colander to drain.

Put on the fire oil, one or two slightly crushed whole cloves of
garlic, and a few fresh sage leaves. When the garlic has browned,
toss in the eels. If they are still alive, cover the pan with a lid so that
they do not jump out. Season with salt and pepper, stirring frequently
with a wooden spoon, and moisten with a little water if they start
to dry out. When they are cooked, bind with egg you have beaten
separately, and then mix in Parmesan cheese, bread crumbs, and
lemon juice.

If you have between 300 and 350 grams (between about 10-1/2
and 12-1/3 ounces) of baby eels, which is enough for four people,
you can bind them with:

2 eggs
2 tablespoons grated Parmesan cheese
1 tablespoon bread crumbs
the juice of 1/2 a lemon
a little water

If you serve them in the pan in which you have cooked them, place it to broil at the last minute in a Dutch oven with fire above and below until a light crust forms on top.

The illustrious Professor Renato Fucini (also known as the delightful *Neri Tanfucio*)[87] who apparently is a great lover of eels with sage, was good enough to inform me that it would be a desecration and a sacrilege to cook baby eels—even if they do look like tender little fish—for less than at least twenty minutes or so.

515. CIECHE FRITTE I
(FRIED BABY EELS I)

Cook with oil, whole garlic cloves, and sage, as in the previous recipe. Then discard the garlic and chop the eels very fine. Beat some eggs in proportion to the amount of eels, add salt and grated Parmesan cheese and a small amount of bread crumbs, and mix with the eels. Drop by the tablespoon into oil to make little fritters, which you will serve with lemon wedges. Upon eating them, few people will realize that this is a fish dish.

516. CIECHE FRITTE II
(FRIED BABY EELS II)

I have seen in Viareggio that baby eels can be fried like other fish, simply dredged in flour or cornmeal and tossed in a pan. They are simpler this way, but much less tasty than those described in the preceding recipe.

---

87 Renato Fucini (1843–1921) was the author of poetry and prose in both the Italian language and the Tuscan dialect, and very knowledgeable about the Tuscan countryside; some of his works were written under the anagrammatic pseudonym *Neri Tanfucio*.

5 1 7 . TINCHE IN ZIMINO[88]
(TENCH IN ZIMINO SAUCE)

The tench said to the pike: "My head is worth more than your body."
Then there is the proverb: "Tench in May and pike in September."

Finely chop the usual flavorings, that is, some onion, garlic,
parsley, celery, and carrot, and place on the fire with oil. When this
begins to brown toss in some tench heads cut into small pieces and
seasoned with salt and pepper. Cook well, moistening with tomato
sauce (recipe 6) or tomato paste diluted in water; then strain the
sauce and set aside. Clean the tench, cut off the fins and tail, and put
them on the fire, dropping them whole in sizzling oil. Season with
salt and pepper and finish cooking with the sauce you have already
prepared, adding it a little at a time. You can eat them just like this,
and they are excellent; but to give the "zimino" its true character,
you need a side dish of beet greens or spinach, which should first
be boiled and then reheated in the tench sauce. Peas also go well
with zimino.

Salt cod in zimino should be cooked the same way.

5 1 8 . LUCCIO IN UMIDO (STEWED PIKE)

Pike, a common freshwater fish in Italy, is noted for certain peculiarities. It is a very voracious animal, and since it feeds exclusively
on fish, its flesh is very delicate to the taste. But since it has many
bones, it is necessary always to select pike that weigh between 600
and 700 grams (between about 1-1/3 and 1-1/2 pounds). Also, pike
that live in running water are preferable; they are distinguished by
their greenish back and silvery white belly, while those from still
waters can be recognized by their dark skin. Some pike reach a weight
of up to 10, 15, or even 30 kilograms (about 22, 33 or 66 pounds),
and reach quite an advanced age. Some are believed to be more than
200 years old. The female's eggs and the male's milky sperm sacs
should not be eaten, because they have a highly purgative effect.

Let's say you have a pike of the weight I have suggested. Scrape
off the scales, gut it, cut off the head and tail and divide into four or

88 A sauce for fish, usually made with some kind of greens, parsley, garlic, and olive oil;
probably derived from the Arabic word *samîn*.

five pieces, which should serve four or five people. Stud each piece lengthwise with two lardoons seasoned with salt and pepper. Then make an appropriate amount of battuto with an onion the size of a large walnut, a small clove of garlic, a celery rib, a small piece of carrot, and a pinch of parsley, all finely chopped so that you do not need to strain the sauce. Place on the fire in oil, and when it has browned add tomato sauce (recipe 6) or tomato paste diluted with water; season with salt and pepper. Then thicken this sauce with a piece of butter dredged in flour, stir well, and put in the fish, which you will simmer slowly and turn regularly. Finally, pour in a tablespoon of Marsala wine, or lacking that, a drop of regular wine, and let boil a little longer before sending to the table in its own sauce.

519. PALOMBO FRITTO
(FRIED DOGFISH)

Cut the dogfish into rounds that are not too thick and let it sit in salted egg for several hours. A half hour before frying it, coat it with a mixture of bread crumbs, Parmesan cheese, chopped garlic and parsley, salt, and pepper. A small clove of garlic will be enough for 500 grams (about 1 pound) of fish. Surround with lemon wedges.

520. PALOMBO IN UMIDO
(STEWED DOGFISH)

Cut into rather large pieces and then finely chop some garlic, parsley, and a very small amount of onion. Place on the fire in oil, and when it has sautéed enough, put in the dogfish and season with salt and pepper. When the fish has browned, pour in a little dry red or white wine and tomato sauce (recipe 6) or tomato paste and simmer until done.

ROASTED MEATS

With the exception of birds and squabs, with which whole sage leaves go well, it is no longer customary to lard or baste spit-roasted meats, or to stud them with garlic, rosemary, or other aromatic herbs that tend to leave an aftertaste. If you have some good olive oil, baste them with that; otherwise, use lard or butter, depending on local preference.

People generally prefer roasted meats savory, so be generous with salt when you prepare milk-fed veal, lamb, kid, poultry, and pork. Be more sparing with meat from larger or older animals and with birds, because these meats are already quite flavorful in themselves. But always salt meat halfway or even two-thirds of the way through the cooking. People who salt any kind of meat before putting it on the spit are making a serious mistake, because the fire will dry it out and make it tough.

Pork and the meat of nursing animals such as veal, lamb, kid, and the like, should be cooked well in order to dry out their excessive moisture. Cook beef and mutton much less; being dry meats, you want them to remain juicy. Cook birds over a flame, but be careful not to overdo them, for they would lose a great deal of their fragrance. But take care that birds are not undercooked when you want to remove them from the fire; you can test for this by pricking them under the wing to check whether any blood still runs out. You can tell whether chickens are done by pricking them in the same way.

Poultry will come out more tender and with a better color if you roast it wrapped in paper that has been buttered on the side touching the meat; to prevent the paper from burning, baste it frequently on the outside. Halfway through the cooking, remove the paper and finish cooking the chicken, turkey, or what have you, salting and basting it. If you use this method, it is also a good idea to put a little salt inside the bird before putting it on the spit, and to stud the breast of turkeys and guinea fowl with lardoons. I should point out here that squab and fattened capon, whether roasted or boiled, are better eaten cold than hot; they also have less of an aftertaste when eaten cold.

More than any other way of preparing meats, roasting preserves their nourishing properties, and makes them easier to digest.

5 2 1 . ROAST BEEF I

This English word has come into Italian as "rosbiffe" and it means exactly what it says. A good roast beef is a very satisfying dish at a meal where the male gender predominates, since men are not satisfied with trifles the way women are. They want to sink their teeth into something solid and substantial.

The best cut for roast beef is the loin, as indicated in recipe 556 for steak Florentine style. In order to turn out tender, it should be from a young animal. It should weigh more than 1 kilogram (about 2 pounds) so that the fire will not dry it out, for the beauty and succulence of this dish depend on it being cooked just right, as is shown by a pink color on the inside and the copious juice that runs out when you slice it. Cook over a very hot fire from the start, so that the outer surface cooks quickly; baste with oil, which you will later drain from the dripping pan, and at the end pour a ladleful of broth over it; this, along with the fat that has dripped from the meat, will provide the sauce that you serve with the roast. At the halfway point, salt sparingly, because this type of meat is savory by itself, as I have already said. Always remember that salt, which is good in itself, is the worst enemy of good cooking when used to excess.

Put the meat on the spit half an hour before you serve the first course; this should be sufficient if the piece is not too large. To test for doneness, prick it at the thickest part with a thin larding needle, but do not make too many holes in it, or it will dry out. The juice that runs out should not be blood colored, nor too dark. Pan fry some raw, peeled potatoes in oil to serve as a side dish. If they are small, leave them whole; if large, cut into quarters.

Roast beef can also be made in the oven, but it doesn't come out as well as when cooked on a spit. If you make it in the oven, season with salt, oil, and a bit of butter, surround it with raw, peeled potatoes, and pour a glassful of water into the roasting pan.

If you do not like leftover roast beef cold, slice it and sauté in butter and brown stock or tomato sauce (recipe 6).

5 2 2 . ROAST BEEF II

I think that this second way to cook roast beef is preferable to the first, because the meat stays juicier and more fragrant.

After putting the meat on the spit, wrap it in a fairly thick sheet of paper well greased with cold butter. Tie the two ends so that it stays tightly closed and put it over a hot charcoal fire. Turn, and when it is almost cooked tear off the paper, salt the meat and brown it. Then remove it from the fire, place between two plates and let it rest for ten minutes before serving.

5 2 3 . SFILETTATO TARTUFATO
(TRUFFLED BEEF LOIN)

Florence butchers call beef or veal loin from which the fillet has been removed "sfilettato" ("without fillet").

Take a large piece of loin of beef without the fillet and stud it all over with truffles (better white than black) cut into slivers about 3 centimeters (about 1 inch) long. Also put with each piece of truffle a little bit of butter to fill the hole that you have made with the point of the knife to insert them. Make several slits in the rind so that the meat does not curl, tie the ends, and put on the spit. When it is two-thirds done, baste lightly with olive oil and salt sparingly, because this type of meat from large animals is quite flavorful and does not need a great deal of seasoning.

524. ARROSTO DI VITELLA DI LATTE
(ROAST OF MILK-FED VEAL)

Milk-fed veal is butchered year-round, but in the spring and summer you will find it fatter, better fed, and better tasting. The cuts that are best for roasting on the spit are the loin and the rump, and they need only oil and salt for seasoning.

The same cuts, lightly studded with garlic and rosemary, can be cooked in a pan with oil, butter, a little minced bacon, salt, and pepper, and some tomato sauce (recipe 6) in which you can cook fresh peas. This is a dish that many people like.

525. PETTO DI VITELLA DI LATTE IN FORNO
(OVEN-ROASTED BREAST OF MILK-FED VEAL)

If I knew who invented the oven, I should like to erect a monument to him at my own expense. In this age of monument mania, I think he would deserve it more than anyone else.

Since this is a family dish, leave the cut of meat as is with all the bones in it, and if it doesn't weigh more than between 600 and 700 grams (between about 1-1/3 and 1-1/2 pounds) you can cook it in the Dutch oven. Stud the meat with between 50 and 60 grams (between about 1-2/3 and 2 ounces) of lean partly trimmed prosciutto cut into small strips, tie it securely, baste generously with lard, and salt it. Place in a baking pan, and about ten minutes before you remove it from the oven add some parboiled potatoes, which will turn out very tasty cooked in the pan drippings.

Instead of lard you can use butter and olive oil, and instead of prosciutto you can salt the meat generously.

526. ARROSTO MORTO (POT ROAST)

You can make any kind of meat this way, but in my opinion the best suited to this cooking method is milk-fed veal. Take a good-sized cut from the loin, with the kidney still attached. Roll it up and tie it with a string to keep it together and place on the fire in a saucepan with fine olive oil and butter, both in small amounts. Brown on all sides, salt at the midway point, and finish cooking with broth until little or no juice is left.

What you will taste is a roast that does not have the fragrance and flavor of spit-roasted meat, but makes up for it in tenderness and delicacy. If you do not have any broth, use tomato sauce (recipe 6) or tomato paste diluted with water. If you like your meat more flavorful, add some finely chopped bacon.

527. ARROSTO MORTO COLL'ODORE DELL'AGLIO E DEL RAMERINO (POT ROAST WITH GARLIC AND ROSEMARY)

If you like these seasonings but do not like the aftertaste they can have, do not stud chicken, fillet of beef, or any other meat with pieces of garlic and rosemary. Instead, make a pot roast as in the preceding recipe, and toss a whole clove of garlic and two sprigs of rosemary into the saucepan. When you are ready to send the roast to the table, strain the concentrated juice (but do not press hard against the mesh), and if you like, accompany the meat with potatoes or vegetables reheated separately. If you want, you can also enhance the flavor of the meat with a very small amount of tomato sauce (recipe 6) or tomato paste.

Leg of lamb comes out very well this way, when cooked in a Dutch oven with fire above and below.

528. UCCELLI ARROSTO (ROAST BIRDS)

Birds must be fresh and fat, but above all fresh. In places where they are sold already plucked, you have to be very careful not to be fooled. If the birds look green, or their bellies are dark, walk away. Nevertheless, if on some occasion you find you have been cheated, you should cook them like the stewed pigeons in recipe 276. Otherwise, if you cook them on the spit they will not only burst open during cooking, they will also give off (much more than if you stew them)

that foul odor of meat gone bad, or *faisandée* as the French call it—
a stench that is intolerable to people of good taste, but unfortunately
is not disdained in some Italian provinces where over time people's
tastes have become jaded, perhaps to the detriment of their health as
well as their palates.

An exception could be made for the meat of pheasants and
woodcocks, which seem not only to become more tender, but also to
acquire a particular fragrance when they are very ripe. This is especially true of pheasant when it is allowed to ripen unplucked.

But let's try not to let them go beyond the first sign of ripeness;
otherwise what happened to me on one occasion might happen to
you. A gentleman had invited me to dine in a very famous trattoria,
and to honor me, he ordered among other things a woodcock with
toasted bread slices. Well, that woodcock gave off such a stench
from the middle of the table that it turned my stomach to the point
that I could not even bring it to my mouth. My friend was mortified,
and I was sorry that I had not been able to appreciate his kindness.

Birds, in any case, whether thrushes, larks, or smaller species,
should never be gutted. Before you put them on the spit, prepare
them as follows. Fold their wings over their back so that each wing
holds one or two sage leaves in place. Cut the feet at the ends, then
cross them by pulling each stump over the knee joint opposite and
punching a hole in the tendon. Place a little bunch of sage where the
legs cross. Then put them on the spit, placing the larger birds in the
middle and separating them with a slice of day-old bread about 1-1/
2 centimeters (about 1/2 an inch) thick placed between one bird and
the other; alternatively, if you can find them, you can keep the birds
apart with little sticks cut on the slant.

Take paper-thin slices of larding fat, salt them, and wrap them
around the bird's breast so that it can be put on the spit along with
the bread slices.

Cook over a high flame, and if you have not tucked the birds'
beaks into their sternums, hold them still on the spit for a while with
their heads hanging down so that their necks will stretch out. Baste
once only with olive oil when they start to brown, using a brush or
a feather so that you do not touch the bread slices (which are already
seasoned enough with the larding fat), and salt once only. Put them
on the fire at the last minute, because they should cook fast, and

might cook too soon and then dry out. When you send them to the table, remove them carefully from the spit and arrange in a row on a platter, which will make a nice presentation.

Some people squeeze a lemon over roast duck or mallard (which have a gamey flavor) just as they start to brown, and baste them with the lemon juice and oil from the dripping pan.

529. ARROSTO D'AGNELLO ALL'ARETINA (ROAST LAMB AREZZO STYLE)

Lamb starts to be good in December, and by Easter it has begun or is about to begin its decline.

Take a lamb leg or quarter, season it with salt, pepper, olive oil, and a drop of vinegar. Prick it here and there with the point of a knife and let it rest in the oil and vinegar mixture for several hours. Put it on a spit and using a little rosemary branch, baste it often with the same liquid until it is cooked. The oil and vinegar mixture will remove the smell of the stable, if you are afraid there is one, and will give the meat a pleasant taste. If you like a more pronounced aroma of rosemary, you can stud the meat with several sprigs of it, removing them before serving.

530. COSCIOTTO DI CASTRATO ARROSTO (ROAST LEG OF MUTTON)

The season for mutton is from October to May. They say that a short leg, with dark brownish-red meat, is the best. Roast leg of mutton is healthful and nutritious, and is specially recommended for anyone who has a tendency to corpulence.

Before cooking, let the meat ripen for several days; the exact number will depend on the temperature at the time. Before skewering it on the spit, pound well with a wooden mallet; then skin it and remove the bone from the center, trying not to tear the meat. Then tie it, so that it stays together, and cook over a high flame at first; when it is half cooked, reduce the heat. When it begins to drip, baste with the sauce from the dripping pan and some skimmed broth, nothing else. Salt when it is nearly done. Make sure that it is neither overcooked nor undercooked, and serve with its own juice in a gravy dish. For a nicer presentation, wrap the end of the leg bone in ruffled white paper.

531. ARROSTO DI LEPRE I (ROAST HARE I)

The parts of the hare (*Lepus timidus*) that are best for cooking on a spit are the hindquarters; but the legs of this animal are covered with membranes that must be carefully removed before cooking, without injuring the muscles too much.

Before roasting, marinate the hare for twelve or fourteen hours in the following liquid. Put three glasses of water on the fire in a saucepan with half a glass of vinegar, or even less depending on the amount of meat; add three or four minced shallots, one or two bay leaves, a small bunch of parsley, a little salt, and a dash of pepper. Boil for five or six minutes, let cool completely, and pour over the hare. When you remove the hare from the marinade, dry it and stud it all over with thinly sliced high-quality lardoons, using a larding needle. Cook over a slow fire, salt to taste and moisten with heavy cream and nothing else.

They say that you should not eat hare liver because it is bad for your health.

532. ARROSTO DI LEPRE II (ROAST HARE II)

If the hare has hung for quite a while, and is therefore quite tender, you can roast the hindquarters without marinating them first. Remove the thickest membranes from the outer muscles and stud the entire piece of meat with lardoons that you have salted in advance. Skewer the meat on the spit and wrap it in buttered paper sprinkled with salt. When it is done, remove the paper and baste with a little rosemary branch dipped in melted butter until it browns, then lightly salt again.

533. CONIGLIO ARROSTO (ROAST RABBIT)

For spit-roasted rabbit as well, the hindquarters are the best part. Stud it with lardoons, baste with olive oil, or better with butter, and salt when it is almost completely cooked.

534. ARROSTO MORTO LARDELLATO
(LARDED POT ROAST)

Take a short, thick, lean and ripe cut of veal or beef from the leg or rump, weighing 1 kilogram or so (about 2 pounds); stud it with 30 grams (about 1 ounce) of thinly sliced untrimmed prosciutto. Tie it with twine to keep it together and place it in a saucepan with 30 grams (about 1 ounce) of butter, a quarter of an onion cut into two pieces, three or four pieces of celery less than a finger long, and three or four strips of carrot. Season with salt and pepper, and brown the meat, turning it often; then moisten with two small ladles of water and finish cooking over a slow fire, until most of the liquid has boiled off. But take care that the meat does not dry out and turn dark. When you are ready to send it to the table, strain the small amount of juice remaining and pour it over the meat, which you can accompany with potato wedges browned in butter or oil.

You can also make a pot roast with just butter, cooking until done with the saucepan covered with a shallow bowl filled with water.

535. PICCIONE A SORPRESA (SQUAB SURPRISE)

No surprise here. Still, it is a good recipe to know because it is a dish not to be scoffed at.

If you have a squab to roast on the spit and want to serve it to more than one person, stuff it with a veal or milk-fed veal cutlet. Obviously, this cutlet should be of proportionate size to the squab. Pound the cutlet well to make it thinner and more tender, season it with salt, pepper, a pinch of spices and a few bits of butter; roll it and place it inside the squab, sewing up the opening. If you add some thinly sliced truffles to the seasonings, it will be even better. You can also cook the gizzard and the liver of the squab separately in brown stock or butter, then grind them and spread the mixture on the cutlet. In this way the different fragrances of the two types of meat blend to create a better taste. You can cook a cockerel in the same way.

536. QUAGLIETTE
(QUAIL)

Use the stuffed veal cutlets from recipe 307 (you can also use milk-fed veal) to stuff the birds. Once stuffed, wrap the quails with a very thin slice of lardoon, and tie each of them crosswise with twine. Put on the fire on a spit, placing slices of toasted bread and a few sage leaves in between each bird. Baste with olive oil, salt them, moisten with a few tablespoons of broth, and remove the twine before serving.

Beef fillet also makes an excellent spit-roast when cut into pieces, wrapped in lardoon with sage, and cooked on the spit between slices of toasted bread.

537. BRACIUOLA DI MANZO RIPIENA ARROSTO
(ROASTED STUFFED RIB STEAK)

A beef rib steak a finger thick, weighing 500 grams (about 1 pound)
200 grams (about 7 ounces) of lean milk-fed veal
30 grams (about 1 ounce) of untrimmed prosciutto
30 grams (about 1 ounce) of salted tongue
30 grams (about 1 ounce) of grated Parmesan cheese
30 grams (about 1 ounce) of butter
2 chicken livers
1 egg
a fistful of fresh crustless bread

Make a little battuto with an onion the size of a walnut, a little celery, carrot, and parsley; place on the fire with the butter, and when it begins to brown, toss in the chicken livers and veal cut into small pieces, season with a little salt and pepper, and cook with a little broth until the meat is done. Strain the meat, and chop it finely with a mezzaluna. Dissolve the crustless bread in the sauce that is left in the pan, making a firm paste, and adding a little broth if necessary. Now mix together the chopped meat and the bread paste, adding the egg, Parmesan, prosciutto, as well as the tongue, cut into small cubes. When this filling is ready, dip the steak in water for just a moment so that you can better stretch it out. Pound it with the blunt edge of a knife, and flatten it out with the blade. Then place the filling in the middle and roll the steak up, tying it tightly as you would a salami, first the long way and then all the way across. Place on the spit lengthwise and roast with olive oil and salt. This delicate roasted meat serves six to seven people.

538. COTOLETTE DI VITELLA DI LATTE ALLA MILANESE (MILK-FED VEAL CUTLETS MILANESE STYLE)

You are all familiar with simple veal cutlets "alla milanese," but if you like them more flavorful, make them this way. After removing the bone from the rib and discarding the scraps, flatten the cutlets with the blade of a large knife until they are quite thin. Then make a battuto with prosciutto (more of the fatty part), a little parsley, grated Parmesan cheese, truffle shavings (if you have any), and a little salt and pepper. Spread this mixture on one side of the flattened cutlets, dip them in beaten egg, coat with bread crumbs and sauté in butter. Serve with lemon wedges. For five cutlets, if they are not very large, 50 grams (about 1-2/3 ounces) of prosciutto and two heaping tablespoons of Parmesan will suffice.

539. POLLO ARROSTO RIPIENO (ROAST STUFFED CHICKEN)

This is a family-style stuffing, not a fancy one. For a medium size chicken, here are the approximate amounts of ingredients:

2 sausages
the liver, combs, and wattles from the same chicken
8 or 10 well-roasted chestnuts

a small handful of truffles, or if you do not have them, several
small pieces of dried mushrooms
a dash of nutmeg
1 egg

If you are cooking a turkey instead of a chicken, double the amounts.

Begin by cooking the sausages and giblets in butter, moistening with a little broth if necessary. On account of the sausages, season with only a little salt and pepper. Remove the sausages and giblets, and toss in the liquid some fresh crustless bread, enough to make, with a little broth, two tablespoons of a thick paste. Skin the sausages, finely chop the giblets and reconstituted mushrooms with a mezzaluna, and then put these ingredients in a mortar along with the roasted chestnuts, egg, and bread paste and grind well. The truffles, however, should be sliced thin and left raw. This is the mixture you will use to stuff the chicken, which will be easier to carve cold than hot; it will also taste better cold.

540. CAPPONE ARROSTO TARTUFATO
(ROAST TRUFFLED CAPON)

The Florentines say that cooking is a fanciful art, which is true since all dishes can be modified in various ways depending upon the fancy of the particular cook. But in modifying dishes one should never lose sight of the need for simplicity, delicacy, and a pleasing taste; thus everything depends on the good taste of the cook. I have attempted to adhere to these principles in making this expensive dish; I leave it to others to indicate a better way. I would stuff a gutted capon without the head, neck, and legs, killed the day before and weighing about 800 grams (about 1-4/5 pounds), in the following way:

250 grams (about 8-4/5 ounces) of truffles (it does not matter
much whether they are black or white, as long as they are
fragrant)
80 grams (about 2-2/3 ounces) of butter
5 tablespoons Marsala

Carefully peel the truffles, which should be about the size of walnuts, and put the raw peelings inside the capon; you can also insert a few slices of raw truffle under the skin. Place the butter on the fire, and when it has melted toss in the truffles with the Marsala, season with salt and pepper, and cook over a high flame for two minutes only, stirring constantly. Remove the truffles from the pan and let them cool until the butter congeals; then toss them whole into the capon, and sew it up at both ends, both at the bottom and at the top where the neck was removed.

Keep in a cool place and cook it after 24 hours; that way it will have ripened for a total of three days.

If you are preparing a pheasant or a turkey, make the necessary adjustments to the proportions. During the winter, it is good to keep turkeys and pheasants stuffed for three or four days before cooking them. In fact, for the pheasant, you should wait until the first signs of ripeness appear, for that is when the meat takes on that special fragrance that distinguishes it. When you are ready to cook it, wrap in a sheet of paper and follow the instructions for cooking guinea hen in recipe 546.

541. POLLO AL DIAVOLO (CHICKEN DEVIL STYLE)

It is called this because it is supposed to be seasoned with strong cayenne pepper and served with a very spicy sauce, so that whoever eats it feels his mouth on fire and is tempted to send both the chicken and whoever cooked it to the devil. I shall give a simpler, more civilized way to prepare it.

Take a cockerel or young chicken, remove the head, neck and feet, and, after cutting it open all the way down the front, flatten it out as much as you can. Wash and dry it well with a kitchen towel, then place it on the grill. When it begins to brown, turn it over, brush with melted butter or olive oil and season with salt and pepper. When the other side begins to brown, turn the chicken over again and repeat the procedure. Continue to baste and season as necessary until done.

Cayenne pepper is sold as a red powder, which comes from England in little glass bottles.

542. POLLO IN PORCHETTA
(CHICKEN STUFFED WITH PROSCIUTTO)

This is a family dish, not one for a distinguished company. Stuff a chicken with thin slices of untrimmed prosciutto a little more than a finger in width; add three whole cloves of garlic, two small tufts of wild fennel, and a few peppercorns. Season on the outside with salt and pepper and cook in a pot in the oven, with butter only. During the sausage season, you can substitute sausages for the prosciutto, splitting them lengthwise before inserting them into the bird.

543. ARROSTO MORTO DI POLLO ALLA BOLOGNESE
(POT ROAST OF CHICKEN BOLOGNA STYLE)

Place on the fire with olive oil, butter, a finely chopped slice of untrimmed prosciutto, a few small pieces of garlic, and a small bunch of rosemary. When the chicken has browned, add seeded chopped tomatoes, or tomato paste diluted in water. When it is done, take out the chicken and cook potatoes in the liquid remaining in the pot. Then put the chicken back into the pot to warm it up before serving.

544. POLLO ALLA RUDINÌ
(CHICKEN RUDINÌ)

Nobody knows the reason this dish is called this way, but it is a simple, healthy, delicately flavored dish, and that is why I describe it here. Take a young cockerel, clean it and remove the neck and the tips of the wings, and cut off the feet two inches below the knee joint. Then cut the bird into six pieces: two with the wings and breast, two with the legs including the thigh, and two from the back (but remove the front part). Bone the thighs and remove the wishbone from the breast; flatten the two pieces from the back.

Beat an egg with as much water as half an eggshell will hold; flour the pieces of chicken, season with pepper and a generous amount of salt, and put them in the beaten egg mixture, leaving them there until you are ready to cook them. Then take the pieces one by one, coat with bread crumbs, and cook them in a copper skillet with 100 grams (about 3-1/2 ounces) of butter. When the butter starts to sizzle, place the chicken pieces in, skin side down, for a second or so; then turn them, put a cover on the skillet, and cook with a high flame on top and a moderate flame below for about ten minutes. Serve with lemon wedges; you will find it is just as good hot as it is cold.

To speak a language that everybody understands, the Holy Scriptures say that Joshua stopped the sun and not the earth. Well, we do the same when we talk about chickens, because the hip should be called the thigh, the thigh should be called the leg, and the leg should be called the tarsus.[89] In fact, the hip has only one bone that corresponds to the femur in humans, the thigh has two, which correspond to the tibia and the fibula, and the chicken's foot represents the first bone of the human foot, that is, the tarsus. Thus the wings, because of the structure of their bones, correspond to the arms of a human, which are of a single piece from the shoulder to the elbow (humerus) and two pieces (radius and ulnus) in the forearm; the tips of the wings are like the first signs of rudimentary hands.

Apparently—and you can find out for yourselves whether or not this is true—chickens that have just been killed are more tender before *rigor mortis* has set in.

545. POLLO VESTITO
("DRESSED" CHICKEN)

This is not an extraordinary dish, but it might make a nice surprise in a family meal.

Take the body of a young cockerel, that is, gutted and without the feet, neck and head. Grease it all over with cold butter, sprinkle with salt, also sprinkling a pinch of salt inside. Then, with the wings folded, truss it with two wide, thin slices of lean, partly trimmed prosciutto and cover with the dough described in recipe 277, rolled out until it is about as thick as a coin. Brush the dough with egg yolk and bake

89 This is the case in Italian, where the thigh is called "anca" (hip), the leg "coscia" (thigh), and so on.

the chicken, thus "dressed," in a moderately hot oven. Serve it as is, so that it can be carved at the table.

I like it better cold than hot.

546. GALLINA DI FARAONE
(GUINEA HEN)

This fowl, originally from Numidia and therefore erroneously called Indian hen, was a symbol of brotherly love in ancient times. When Meleager, king of Calydon, died, his sisters mourned him so deeply that Diana transformed them into guinea hens. The *Numida meleagris*, which is the domestic guinea hen, is still half wild, unfriendly and restless; it resembles the partridge both in its habits and in the flavor of its delicate flesh. Poor creatures, they are so pretty! They are usually killed by cutting their throats, although some people prefer to drown them, keeping them under water by force—a cruel practice, like so many others invented by the gluttony of man. The meat of this bird needs to ripen for quite some time; during the winter, it will keep ungutted for at least five or six days.

> The best way to cook guinea hens is to roast them on a spit. Place a ball of butter rolled in salt inside the bird, stud the breast with lardoons, and wrap in a sheet of paper greased with cold butter and sprinkled with salt. Remove the paper when the bird is two-thirds cooked; then brown it over the flame until done, basting with oil and salting it again.
>
> A young turkey can be cooked in the same way.

547. ANATRA DOMESTICA ARROSTO
(ROAST DOMESTIC DUCK)

Salt the inside and wrap the entire breast with wide, thin strips of lardoon held in place with twine. Baste with oil and salt when it has almost finished cooking.

The mallard or wild duck, being naturally lean, gives off little juice, so it is better to baste it with butter.

548. OCA DOMESTICA (DOMESTIC GOOSE)

The goose had already been domesticated at the time of Homer, and the Romans (388 years before Christ) kept geese, which were sacred to Juno, on the Capitoline Hill.

The domestic goose, compared to the wild species, has grown larger in size, more fecund, and fatter. For this reason, it takes the place of pork in Jewish cooking. I do not cook with it much, because it is not sold in the markets in Florence, and its meat is used little or not at all in Tuscany; but I have tasted it boiled and I liked it. By itself, goose would make too sweet a broth, but mixed with beef it enhances the flavor of the broth, provided that the fat is carefully skimmed off.

They tell me that you can roast or stew goose as you would a domestic duck, and that when you grill a breast of goose it is usually studded with prosciutto (or with salted anchovies, for those who cannot eat pork), and seasoned with oil, pepper, and salt.

In Germany, goose is stuffed with apples and roasted. This dish is not suited to us Italians, because we cannot trifle with fatty foods that are heavy on the stomach. The following anecdote illustrates this point.

One year one of the farmers on my country estate, who always celebrated the feast of St. Anthony Abbot, wanted to celebrate that day more lavishly than usual by putting on a fine dinner for his friends, including the bailiff of the estate.

Everything went well, because things were done properly. But one of the guests, a well-to-do farmer, feeling expansive because he had eaten and drunk his fill, said to the assembled company: "By St. Joseph, who is the patron saint of my parish, I want to invite you all to my home on St. Joseph's day, and we shall make merry." The invitation was gladly accepted, and no one failed to appear on the appointed day.

When they got to the moment most anticipated at such festivities—the moment of sitting down to eat—the fun truly began, because the first course was broth—goose broth. This was followed by fried goose, boiled goose, stewed goose, and what do you think the roast was? It was goose! I do not know what became of the others, but toward evening the bailiff began to feel so poorly that he could not eat supper, and during the night such a hurricane burst inside him—complete with thunder, wind, rain, and hail—that to see him the next day, so downcast and defeated in spirit, you wondered whether he had not become a goose himself.

The pastries made with goose liver in Strasbourg are renowned. The liver is enlarged by means of a special treatment, long and cruel, that is inflicted on the poor creatures.

À propos of goose liver, I was once given one from the Veneto; with its abundance of fat and along with the heart, it weighed 600 grams (about 1-1/3 pounds). Following the instructions I had been given, I cooked it simply in the following way. First I put on the fire the fat, cut into thick slices; then the heart, cut into sections; and finally the liver, cut into thick slices, seasoning with salt and pepper only. I served it with lemon wedges, after draining the excess fat. I must admit it is a very delicate morsel.

See also recipe 274 for goose liver.

549. TACCHINO (TURKEY)

The turkey belongs to the order of the *Rasores*, or gallinaceous birds, to the family *Phasanidae*, and to the genus *Meleagris*. It is originally from North America, its habitat extending from the Northwest of the United States to the Panama Canal. It is called "chicken of India" because Columbus, believing that he could open a route to the East Indies by sailing West, discovered lands that were later called the West Indies. It seems certain that the Spaniards brought this bird to Europe at the beginning of the sixteenth century, and they say that the first turkeys introduced into France cost a gold sovereign.

Since this animal feeds on every kind of filth it comes across, its meat may acquire a sickening taste if it is not properly fed. But it can be excellent and very flavorful if it eats corn and warm bran mash. It can be cooked virtually any way you wish: boiled, stewed, grilled, or roasted; the meat of the hen is more delicate than that of the tom. They say that turkey broth makes you hot; that may be so, but it is very tasty and lends itself well to soup with malfattini, rice with cabbage or turnips, spelt[90] or cornmeal made more flavorful with

90 An ancient variety of hard wheat, made up of small brown grains.

two sausages crumbled up in it. The best parts for boiling are the forequarters, including the wing, which is the most delicate piece; the hindquarters are better for pot roast or roasting on the spit. It is a good idea to stud the breast lightly with garlic and rosemary and flavor it with some chopped bacon or lardoons, a little butter, salt and pepper, and tomato sauce (recipe 6) or tomato paste diluted in water. Then you can cook potatoes in the sauce to accompany the turkey. To roast on the spit, baste with olive oil and, if you like, you can serve it with fried polenta. The breast, pounded to about the thickness of a finger and seasoned several hours ahead of time with a generous amount of oil, salt and pepper, is excellent grilled. Indeed, it is a dish that is loved by drinkers, who add the liver and the gizzard seasoned in the same way but finely minced, the better to absorb the seasoning.

A young turkey weighing about 2 kilograms (about 4 pounds), cooked whole on the spit like the guinea hen, makes a fine showing at any dinner party, especially if it is early in the season.

550. PAVONE (PEACOCK)

Now that I have mentioned several birds of exotic origin, I realize that I have not yet spoken of the peacock, *Pavo cristatus*, whose meat I remember as being excellent for young people.

The most splendid of the gallinaceous birds, for its magnificent display of colors, the peacock inhabits the forests of the East Indies and can be found in its wild state in Gursarai in Hindustan, in Cambodia on the coasts of Malabar, in the kingdom of Siam, and on the island of Java. When Alexander the Great invaded Asia Minor and saw these birds for the first time, they say that he was so struck by their beauty that he forbade them to be killed, under pain of severe punishment. It was that monarch who introduced them into Greece, where they were the object of such curiosity that everyone ran to see them. But later, when they were taken to Rome during the decline of the Republic, the first to eat them was the orator Quintus Hortensius, the follower of Cicero. The Romans loved the taste of these birds, which came to be highly prized after Aufidius Lurco taught his countrymen how to fatten them. He kept his peacocks in a poultry pen that apparently earned him an income of one thousand five hundred crowns. This is probably not far from the truth, if they were sold at a rate of five crowns each.

551. MAIALE ARROSTITO NEL LATTE
(PORK COOKED IN MILK)

Take a piece of pork loin weighing about 500 grams (about 1 pound), salt it, and place in a saucepan with 2-1/2 deciliters (about 1/2 a cup) of milk. Cover and simmer, until the milk is all gone; then increase the heat to brown the pork. Once the meat has browned, skim off the fat and remove the meat from the pan. Add a droplet of fresh milk to the coagulated milk remaining in the pan, mix well, bring to a boil and then spread this mixture on lightly toasted slices of bread to use as an accompaniment to the pork, which should be served hot.

A total of 3 deciliters (about 1-1/4 cups) of milk should be enough. Cooked this way, pork has a delicate flavor, and does not cause indigestion.

552. PESCE DI MAIALE ARROSTO
(ROAST PORK LOIN)

The loin is that oblong muscle on either sides of the spinal column, which the Florentines call "lombo di maiale." In Florence, they leave the kidney attached to it, and it makes for an excellent roast. Cut into small pieces and put these on a spit, with slices of toasted bread and fresh sage leaves between the pieces of meat, as with roasted birds. Baste, like the birds, with olive oil.

553. AGNELLO ALL'ORIENTALE
(LAMB ORIENTAL STYLE)

They say that the people of the Orient still consider shoulder of lamb roasted and basted with butter and milk one of the most appetizing delicacies. So I tried it, and I have to agree that both shoulder and leg of lamb make a spit roast that is tender and delicate. If you are cooking the leg, I would prepare it in this way, which seems the best to me. Using a larding needle, stud it all over with pork lardoons seasoned with salt and pepper, baste with butter and milk or with milk alone, and salt when half done.

554. PICCIONE IN GRATELLA (GRILLED SQUAB)

Squab meat is very nutritious on account of the large amount of fibrin and albumin it contains; it is prescribed for people who are weak because of illness or any other reason. To prepare himself for a love joust, the old man Nicomaco in Machiavelli's comedy *Clizia* planned to eat a "uno pippione grosso, arrosto così verdemezzo che sanguigni un poco"[91] ("a large roast squab so rare that it bleeds a little").

Take a squab that is large, but young; cut it into two parts lengthwise and press down with your hands until it is nice and flat. Then brown in oil for four or five minutes, just until the meat becomes firm. Season with salt and pepper while it is hot and the complete the preparation as follows.

Melt 40 grams (about 1-1/3 ounces) of butter, but do not let it boil; beat an egg and mix with the butter. Place the sautéed pieces of squab in this mixture and let stand for a while; then coat thoroughly with bread crumbs. Grill over a slow fire and serve with a sauce or a side dish.

555. FEGATELLI IN CONSERVA (PRESERVED PORK LIVERS)

Everybody knows how to make pork liver seasoned with oil, pepper, and salt, wrapped in caul[92] and cooked on the grill, on the spit, or in a pan. But many people may not know that pork liver can be preserved for several months. This is how they do it in the countryside around Arezzo and perhaps elsewhere. After the livers are cooked, they are put in a metal receptacle and covered with boiling rendered pork fat. After the fat cools and solidifies, it acts as a

91 Act IV, scene 2 (published in 1524).
92 See note to recipe 328.

preservative, and the pork livers can be taken out one by one as needed and reheated. This is convenient for those who cure their own pork, because there will be fewer scraps to use up.

Some people cook pork liver between two bay leaves or add a few fennel seeds to the seasoning, as they do in Tuscany. But these are strong flavors that many stomachs cannot tolerate, and they have a tendency to repeat on you.

556. BISTECCA ALLA FIORENTINA
(STEAK FLORENTINE STYLE)

The English word "beefsteak" means rib steak. This is the origin of our word "bistecca," which is simply a steak with the bone left in,[93] about a finger or a finger and a half thick, cut from the loin of a young animal. Florentine butchers call both yearlings and any bovine animal about two years old a "calf." But if these animals could speak, they would tell you not only that they are no longer calves, but that they have already had a mate and a few offspring as well.

This is an excellent dish. It is healthy, tasty, and strengthening. Yet it has not yet spread to the rest of Italy, perhaps because in many Italian provinces they almost exclusively butcher old work animals. In such cases, they use the fillet, which is the tenderest part, and they incorrectly call "beefsteak" rounds of fillet cooked on the grill.

To return to true steak Florentine style: Charcoal grill it over a high flame, just as it comes from the beast, or at the very most after rinsing and drying it. Turn several times, season with salt and pepper when it is cooked, and serve with a pat of butter on top. It should not be too cooked, because the beauty of this dish is that when you cut into it, juice spurts out abundantly onto the plate. If you salt the steak before cooking, the fire will dry it out, and if you season it ahead of time with olive oil or something else, as many people do, it will taste sickeningly like snuffed candles.

---

93 Similar to a T-bone steak. In contemporary Italian the term "bistecca" is mostly used to identify a method of cooking rather than a particular cut of meat.

557. BISTECCA NEL TEGAME
(PAN-FRIED STEAK)

If you have a large beefsteak that you doubt will be tender because the animal was not so young, or was not recently butchered, instead of cooking it on the grill, place it in a frying pan with a pat of butter and a drop of oil. Then, as in recipe 527, season with garlic and rosemary. If necessary, add a little stock or water or tomato sauce (recipe 6), and serve with potatoes chopped into large pieces and cooked in the sauce from the pan. If there is not enough sauce, add some more stock, butter, and tomato paste.

558. ARNIONI ALLA PARIGINA
(KIDNEYS PARISIAN STYLE)

Take a veal kidney, remove the fat, open it, and cover with boiling water. When the water has cooled, dry the kidney well with a kitchen towel and insert clean sticks into it lengthwise and crosswise to keep it open (in Paris they use large silver needles). Season with 30 grams (about 1 ounce) of melted butter, salt, and pepper, and let stand for an hour or two.

If the kidney weighs between 600 and 700 grams (between about 1-1/3 and 1-1/2 pounds), take one large or two small anchovies, bone them, chop them finely and, using the blade of a knife, reduce them into a paste adding another 30 grams (about 1 ounce) of butter. Form a ball with this paste and set it aside. Cook the kidney on the grill, but do not overcook it, because you want it to stay tender; place on a platter, smear it while still steaming hot with the ball of butter and anchovy, and send to the table.

PASTRIES, CAKES, AND SWEETS

5 5 9 . STRUDEL

Do not be alarmed if this dessert seems to you to be a strange concoction, or if it looks like some ugly creature such as a giant leech or a shapeless snake after you cook it; you will like the way it tastes.

> *500 grams (about 1 pound) of reinette apples, or tender, good*
>   *quality apples*
> *250 grams (about 8-4/5 ounces) of flour*
> *100 grams (about 3-1/2 ounces) butter*
> *85 grams (about 3 ounces) of dried currants*
> *85 grams (about 3 ounces) of powdered sugar*
> *grated rind of one lemon*
> *2 or 3 pinches of ground cinnamon*

Make a fairly firm dough with the flour, warm milk, a piece of butter about the size of a walnut, an egg, and a pinch of salt. Allow the dough to rest a little before using it, then roll it out in a sheet as thin as the one for taglierini noodles. Cover the sheet of dough with a layer of apples (peeled, cored and thinly sliced), leaving the edges free. Scatter the currants, lemon peel, cinnamon, sugar, and finally the 100 grams (about 3-1/2 ounces) of melted butter over the layer of apple slices. Reserve a little of the butter to use later. This done, roll the sheet of dough up so that if forms a nice cylinder of dough and filling, which you will fit into a round copper pan greased with butter. Pour the leftover melted butter all over the outside of the roll, and place it in the oven. Remember that dried currants or sultanas are different from raisins, which are small and dark. Currants and sultanas are twice as large, light brown in color, and seedless. Scrape the lemon peel with a piece of glass.

560. PRESNITZ

Here is another German sweet, and how good it is! I saw one that had been made by the leading confectioner in Trieste, tasted it, and liked it very much. I asked for the recipe and tested it, and it came out perfectly. So, as I describe it to you, I also take the opportunity to express my gratitude to the person who favored me with this recipe.

160 grams (about 5-2/3 ounces) of sultanas
130 grams (about 4-1/2 ounces) of sugar
130 grams (about 4-1/2 ounces) of shelled walnuts
110 grams (about 3-4/5 ounces) of stale cake
60 grams (about 2 ounces) of shelled sweet almonds
60 grams (about 2 ounces) of pine nuts
35 grams (about 1 1/4 ounces) of candied citron
35 grams (about 1-1/4 ounces) of candied orange
5 grams (about 1/5 of an ounce) of spices, including cinnamon,
    cloves, and mace
2 grams (about 1/14 of an ounce) of salt
1 deciliter (about 2/5 of a cup) of Cyprus wine[89]
1 deciliter (about 2/5 of a cup) of rum

After cleaning the sultanas, soak them in the Cyprus wine and rum mixed together. Let stand for several hours and remove from the liquid when they begin to swell. Cut the pine nuts into three pieces each, dice the candied fruit into tiny cubes, and with a mezzaluna chop the walnuts and the almonds into pieces about the size of a grain of rice. Grate or crumble the stale cake, which can be something like a brioche or a Milanese "panettone." Leave the sultanas whole. Blend all of these ingredients, including the rum and the wine.

That is the filling; now it must be enclosed in a puff pastry, for which you can use recipe 155, with 160 grams (about 5-2/3 ounces) of flour and 80 grams (about 2-2/3 ounces) of butter. Roll out into a long, narrow sheet a little thicker than a coin.

Spread the filling over the pastry dough and roll it up into the

89 A deep brown dessert wine.

shape of a log or a large sausage, pulling the pastry over the edges to keep it together. Make the roll about 10 centimeters (about 4 inches) in diameter; then flatten it a little or leave it round, and place it in a copper baking pan greased with butter, coiled around itself like a snake, but not too tightly. Finally, brush it with a mixture of melted butter and egg yolk.

Instead of one *Presnitz* you can make two if you like, using the same amounts of ingredients. Half of this recipe should serve, I believe, seven to eight people.

561. KUGELHUPF

200 grams (about 7 ounces) of Hungarian flour or other very fine flour
100 grams (about 3-1/2 ounces) of butter
50 grams (about 1-2/3 ounces) of sugar
50 grams (about 1-2/3 ounces) of sultanas
30 grams (about 1 ounce) of brewer's yeast
1 whole egg
2 egg yolks
a pinch of salt
a dash of lemon zest
milk as needed

Mix the yeast with lukewarm milk and a handful of the flour to form a small, rather firm loaf; make a cross-shaped cut on the loaf and place it in a small saucepan, the bottom of which you have coated with a little milk. Cover the saucepan and place it close to the fire, but take care that it does not get too hot.

In the winter, melt the butter in *bain-marie* and then blend it for a while with the whole egg. Then pour in the sugar and then the flour, the egg yolks, the salt, and the lemon zest, blending thoroughly. Now add the leaven dough, which will have risen in the meantime, and then lukewarm milk a spoonful at a time, stirring the mixture in the bowl with a wooden spatula until it has an almost liquid consistency, but not quite. This operation might take more than half an hour. Finally, add the sultanas and place the dough in a smooth mold greased with butter and dusted with confectioners' sugar mixed with flour. The mixture should not fill more than half the mold, which you will place, well covered, in a warming oven or other warm place until it rises; this should take two or three hours.

When it has risen to the top of the mold, place it in a moderately warm oven. Remove the cake from the mold after it has cooled, and sprinkle it with confectioners' sugar, or if you like, moisten it with rum (this is optional).

562. KRAPFEN II

The *Krapfen* made with this recipe are more delicate than the ones in recipe 182, especially if they are to be used as a dessert. They should look like smooth balls.

200 grams (about 7 ounces) of fine Hungarian flour
50 grams (about 1-2/3 ounces) of butter
20 grams (about 2/3 of an ounce) of brewer's yeast
less than 1 deciliter (about 2/5 of a cup) of milk or heavy cream,
 so that the mixture comes out firm
3 egg yolks
1 teaspoon of sugar
a generous pinch of salt

Place the yeast in a cup with a spoonful of the flour, moisten it with a little of the lukewarm milk, and set it aside to rise in a warm place. Then put the butter in a bowl (in winter, melt the butter in *bainmarie*) and soften it with a wooden spoon, then adding the egg yolks one at a time. Add the rest of the flour and the yeast mixture after it has doubled in size; then pour in the remaining milk a little at a time, and finally add the salt and sugar. Work this mixture with one hand until it no longer sticks to the sides of the bowl. Then sift a thin layer of ordinary flour over the mixture and set it aside to rise in a warm place. When it has risen, pour it onto a floured pastry board and roll it out gently with a rolling pin until it is about half a finger thick. Then, using the pastry cutter in recipe 7, cut it into 24 disks, on half of which you will place a walnut size amount of some fruit preserves or confectioners' custard. Moisten the disks all around with a finger dipped in milk, then cover with the other 12 disks of dough and press them together. When they have risen, fry them in a generous amount of oil or lard; sprinkle with confectioners' sugar when they have cooled a little, and serve. If you need to make double the amount, 30 grams (about 1 ounce) of yeast should suffice.

5 6 3 . SAVARIN

Perhaps such a name was given to this cake in honor of Brillat-Savarin.[94] Let us therefore content ourselves with calling it by its French name, and with recommending it, for its flavor and elegant shape. To obtain the typical shape of a *Savarin* you need a round mold that holds twice the amount of the mixture you shall put into it.

180 grams (about 6-1/3 ounces) of Hungarian or other very fine flour
60 grams (about 2 ounces) of butter
40 grams (about 1-1/3 ounces) of sugar
40 grams (about 1-1/3 ounces) of sweet almonds
2 deciliters (about 4/5 of a cup) of milk
2 egg yolks
1 egg white
a pinch of salt
brewer's yeast, a ball the size of a small egg

Grease the mold with cold butter, dust with ordinary flour mixed with confectioners' sugar, and sprinkle the peeled, slivered almonds in the bottom of the mold. The almonds taste and look better if you toast them.

    Moisten the yeast with a drop of the warm milk and a generous pinch of the Hungarian flour to make a small loaf that you will set aside to rise as in the recipe for baba, 565. Place the rest of the flour and all the other ingredients, except the milk, in a bowl. The milk should be added little by little. Begin to blend with a wooden spoon, then add the yeast loaf. Work the dough until it no longer sticks to the sides of the bowl, and then pour it into the circular mold on top of the slivered almonds. Now let it rise in a lukewarm place that is well protected from drafts; I warn you that it will take four or five

94 See the note in Artusi's introduction to the section on sauces.

hours for the dough to rise again. Bake in an ordinary oven or a Dutch oven and in the meantime prepare the following mixture. Boil 30 grams (about 1 ounce) of sugar in two fingers of water. When it has become a dense syrup, remove it from the fire, and when it has cooled completely add a teaspoon of vanilla sugar[95] and two tablespoons of rum or kirsch. Then remove the savarin from the mold, and while it is still hot brush it all over with this syrup, until all of the syrup has been used up. Serve hot or cold, as you prefer.

Although this recipe uses small amounts, it serves five to six people. If you see that the dough is becoming too liquid, use less milk. You can also make savarin without the almonds.

564. GATEAU À LA NOISETTE (HAZELNUT CAKE)

Let's give this cake a pompous French name, which is not wholly undeserved.

125 grams (about 4-1/2 ounces) of rice flour
170 grams (about 6 ounces) of sugar
100 grams (about 3-1/2 ounces) of butter
50 grams (about 1-2/3 ounces) of sweet almonds
50 grams (about 1-2/3 ounces) of shelled hazelnuts
4 eggs
a dash of vanilla

Blanch the shelled hazelnuts (or filberts) and almonds in hot water to remove the skins, and dry both well in the sun or over the fire. Then, after grinding them to a very fine powder, mix with the rice flour and two tablespoons of the sugar. Blend the eggs well with the rest of the sugar, and then stir in the nut mixture, whisking vigorously. Finally, add the melted butter and blend once again. Pour into a smooth, round mold rather narrow in diameter so that the mixture is four or five fingers deep, and bake in a moderate oven. Serve cold.

This recipe serves six to seven people.

---

95 This sugar is made by keeping a whole vanilla bean closed up in a canister of confectioners' sugar.

565. BABÀ (BABA AU RHUM)

This is a sweet that stands up to you; that is, to come out well it requires patience and care on the part of the cook. Here are the amounts:

200 grams (about 7 ounces) of Hungarian or other very fine flour
70 grams (about 2-1/3 ounces) of butter
50 grams (about 1-2/3 ounces) of powdered sugar
50 grams (about 1-2/3 ounces) of sultanas or dried currants
30 grams (about 1 ounce) of Malaga grapes, dried and seeded
30 grams (about 1 ounce) of brewer's yeast
about 1 deciliter (about 2/5 of a cup) of milk, or better, heavy
    cream
2 whole eggs
1 egg yolk
1 tablespoon of Marsala
1 tablespoon of rum or cognac
10 grams (about 1/3 of an ounce) of candied fruit, cut into small
    strips
a pinch of salt
a dash of vanilla

Mix the brewer's yeast with one-fourth of the flour and a little of the lukewarm milk to form a small loaf of the right consistency. Make a cross in the loaf with a knife, in this case (as in all the others) not to ward off witches, but so that you can tell when it has risen sufficiently. Place it in a covered bowl coated with a little milk near a very moderately heated oven and let rise. While the loaf is rising, which will take about half an hour, break the eggs into a bowl and beat them with the sugar; then add the rest of the flour, the risen loaf, the melted butter (which should be lukewarm), the Marsala and the rum. If the dough should come out too firm, soften it with some lukewarm milk. Blend well with a wooden spoon until the dough no longer sticks to the sides of the bowl, and finally add the sultanas and the candied fruit and set aside to rise. When it has risen, stir it a little and pour into a mold greased with butter and dusted with confectioners' sugar mixed with flour.

The best mold for this sweet is a ribbed copper mold; but be sure that the mold can hold double the amount of the dough. Cover the mold with a lid to keep the air out, and place to rise in a barely warm warming oven or Dutch oven; this may take more than two hours. If it rises perfectly, the dough will double in size; that is, it will reach the top of the mold. Then bake, making sure not to expose it to drafts in the meantime. Test for doneness by inserting a straw, which should come out dry, and even then leave the baba in the oven at a moderate heat for a while longer to dry it out completely; this is necessary because of the thickness of the cake. When removed from the mold, if it is well cooked it should be the color of bread crust. Sprinkle with confectioners' sugar.

Serve cold.

566. SFOGLIATA DI MARZAPANE (MARZIPAN PUFF PASTRY)

Make a puff pastry using the ingredients and amounts in recipe 154. Roll it out and cut into two rounds the size of an ordinary plate, and make large scallops on the edges. Spread the marzipan mixture given in recipe 579 onto one of the rounds of dough, leaving a little border; the mixture should be about a centimeter (about half an inch) thick. Then place the other round of dough on top, pressing the two rounds together at the edges with your finger, which you have dipped in water.

Gild the surface of the pastry with the egg yolk, bake in the oven or in a Dutch oven, and afterwards sprinkle it with confectioners' sugar. This recipe serves seven to eight people, and it will be highly praised for its delicacy.

567. BUDINO DI NOCCIUOLE O AVELLANE (HAZELNUT PUDDING)

7 deciliters (about 1 pint) of milk
6 eggs
200 grams (about 7 ounces) of shelled hazelnuts
180 grams (about 6-1/3 ounces) of sugar

150 grams (about 5-1/4 ounces) of ladyfingers
20 grams (about 2/3 of an ounce) of butter
a dash of vanilla

Blanch the shelled hazelnuts in hot water to remove the skins and dry them well in the sun or over the fire. Then grind them very finely in a mortar, adding the sugar a little at a time.

Put the milk on the fire and when it starts to boil, crumble the ladyfingers into it and boil for five minutes, adding the butter. Pass this mixture through a strainer and put it back on the fire with the crushed hazelnuts and sugar until the latter melts. Let cool, add the egg yolks and then the egg whites, beaten until stiff. Pour into a mold greased with butter and dusted with bread crumbs, but do not fill the mold up to the brim. Bake in an oven or a Dutch oven until done and serve cold.

This recipe serves nine to ten people.

568. BISCOTTI CROCCANTI I
(CRUNCHY COOKIES I)

500 grams (about 1 pound) of flour
220 grams (about 7-3/4 ounces) of powdered sugar
120 grams (about 4-1/4 ounces) of whole sweet blanched almonds,
*   mixed with some pine nuts*
30 grams (about 1 ounce) of butter
a pinch of aniseed
5 eggs
a pinch of salt

Leave aside the almonds and pine nuts to add later, and blend all the other ingredients with four eggs (you only need to use the fifth egg if necessary) to make a rather soft dough. Add the almonds and pine nuts, and then make four loaves of dough about as thick as a finger and as long as the palm of your hand; arrange them in a baking pan greased with butter and dusted with flour, and gild with egg yolk.

Do not bake the loaves too long, so that you can slice them. This is better done the next day, because the crust has time to soften. Put the slices back in the oven and toast lightly on both sides, and there you have your crunchy cookies.

569. BISCOTTI CROCCANTI II
(CRUNCHY COOKIES II)

400 grams (about 14 ounces) of flour
200 grams (about 7 ounces) of sugar
80 grams (about 2-2/3 ounces) of butter
40 grams (about 1-1/3 ounces) of almonds
30 grams (about 1 ounce) of sultanas
20 grams (about 2/3 of an ounce) of pine nuts
20 grams (about 2/3 of an ounce) of candied citron or candied
    pumpkin
a pinch of aniseed
2 tablespoons of reduced wine
a scant teaspoon baking soda
1 whole egg
3 egg yolks

These cookies are more refined than the ones in the preceding recipe; and I think they leave nothing to be desired. Shell the almonds and pine nuts, remove the skins and leave whole. Cut the candied fruit into tiny pieces. Make a hole in the mound of flour and place the eggs, sugar, butter, wine, and baking soda in it. Blend the mixture without working it too much; then open it up and spread it out so you can add the other ingredients. Form a rather compact narrow cylinder, about 1 meter long (3 feet), which you will divide into four or five parts so that it fits in the baking pan. Gild with egg yolk and bake. When it is cooked, slice into cookies a little more than 1 centimeter (about half an inch) thick, and toast lightly on each side.

570. BASTONCELLI CROCCANTI
(CRUNCHY STICKS)

150 grams (about 5-1/4 ounces) of flour
60 grams (about 2 ounces) of butter
60 grams (about 2 ounces) of confectioners' sugar
1 egg
lemon zest

Make a dough but do not knead it too much; then roll it out to make two dozen little sticks 10 centimeters (about 4 inches long), which you will bake in a pan, with no further preparation. These cookies go well with a cup of tea or a glass of wine.

571. BISCOTTI TENERI
(SOFT COOKIES)

For these cookies, you should have a tin pan 10 centimeters (about 4 inches) wide and a little shorter than the diameter of your Dutch oven, if you are obliged to use that instead of a regular oven. This way the cookies will have crusts on both sides and when cut a centimeter and a half wide (about half an inch), they will be the right size.

40 grams (about 1-1/3 ounces) of wheat flour
30 grams (about 1 ounce) of potato flour
90 grams (about 3 ounces) of sugar
40 grams (about 1-1/3 ounces) of sweet almonds
20 grams (about 2/3 of an ounce) of candied citron or orange
20 grams (about 2/3 of an ounce) of fruit preserves
3 eggs

Blanch the almonds, cut them in half crosswise, and dry in the sun or on the fire. Confectioners usually leave the skin on the almonds, but it is not advisable because the skin often sticks to your palate and is difficult to digest. Dice the candied fruit and the preserves, which can be quince or some other fruit, as long as it is firm.

Beat the egg yolks, sugar, and a little of the flour for a good while—more than half an hour; then fold in the egg whites, beaten until very stiff, and, after the whites have been absorbed, add the rest of the flour, sifting it onto the mixture. Blend gently, as you drop in the almonds, candied fruit, and preserves. Grease the loaf pan with butter and dust it with flour; then bake. Slice the cookies the next day and then toast them on both sides if you like.

572. BISCOTTI DA FAMIGLIA
(FAMILY-STYLE COOKIES)

These cookies are inexpensive, easy to make, and not without their merits because they can be served with tea or any other beverage— they are marvelous for dunking.

250 grams (about 8-4/5 ounces) of flour
50 grams (about 1-2/3 ounces) of butter
50 grams (about 1-2/3 ounces) of confectioners' sugar
5 grams baking powder
a pinch of salt
a dash of vanilla sugar
about 1 deciliter (about 2/5 of a cup) of lukewarm milk

Make a hole in the mound of flour; place all of the other ingredients in it except the milk, which you will use to moisten the dough. The dough should be soft, and must be worked thoroughly until it is smooth. Then roll it out to the thickness of a large coin, dust with flour if necessary, and finally run a ribbed rolling pin over it or use a grater or a fork to make some decorations on it. If you do not want to cut the dough into strips a little longer than a finger and 2 centimeters (about 1 inch) wide, as I do, cut the cookies into whatever shape you like. Place them in a copper baking pan with no further preparation, and bake in an oven or a Dutch oven.

573. BISCOTTI DELLA SALUTE
(HEALTH COOKIES)

Cheer up, for if you eat these cookies you will never die, or you will live as long as Methuselah. I eat them often, in fact, and when some indiscreet person sees me more sprightly than is becoming to my venerable age and asks me how old I am, I answer that I am as old as Methuselah, son of Enoch.

350 grams (about 12-1/3 ounces) of flour
100 grams (about 3-1/2 ounces) of brown sugar
50 grams (about 1-2/3 ounces) of butter
10 grams (about 1/3 of an ounce) of cream of tartar

5 grams (about 1/5 of an ounce) of baking soda
2 eggs
a dash of vanilla sugar
milk, as needed

Mix the flour with the sugar and make a mound with a hole in the middle where you will drop the rest of the ingredients, adding a little milk to obtain a rather soft dough. Shape the dough in a slightly flattened cylinder about half a meter long. Grease a baking pan with butter, and divide the loaf into two parts so that it will fit in the pan. Make sure that the two parts are well separated, because they swell a great deal when baked. Bake in an oven or a Dutch oven. The next day, cut the loaves into cookies, which should number about thirty or so, and toast in the oven.

574. BISCOTTO ALLA SULTANA (SULTAN CAKE)

The name is pretentious, but not wholly unmerited.

150 grams (about 5-1/4 ounces) of powdered sugar
100 grams (about 3 1/2 ounces) wheat flour
50 grams (about 1-2/3 ounces) of potato flour
80 grams (about 2-2/3 ounces) of sultanas
20 grams (about 2/3 of an ounce) of candied fruit
5 eggs
a dash of lemon zest
2 tablespoons rum or cognac

First put on the fire the candied fruit, chopped into pieces the size of watermelon seeds, and the sultanas with enough cognac or rum to cover them. When the liquid boils, light it with a match and let it burn, away from the fire, until all the liquor is evaporated. Then remove the sultanas and candied fruit and place them to dry between the folds of a table napkin. This done, blend the egg yolks in which you have dropped the lemon zest with the sugar, stirring the mixture vigorously with a wooden spoon for half an hour. Beat the egg whites with a whisk until stiff, and fold into the mixture; then add the wheat flour and the potato flour by sifting them over the mixture, stirring slowly and gently until completely blended. Finally, add the sultanas, candied fruit, and two tablespoons of rum or cognac, and pour into a smooth mold or baking dish that will give the cake a high, round shape. Grease the mold with butter and dust with confectioners' sugar and flour. Make sure to put the mold in the oven immediately after pouring the dough into it, so that the sultanas and candied fruit do not sink to the bottom. If this does happen, the next time you make the recipe leave out one of the egg whites. Serve cold.

575. BRIOCHES[96]

300 grams (about 10-1/2 ounces) of Hungarian flour
150 grams (about 5-1/4 ounces) of butter
30 grams (about 1 ounce) of brewer's yeast
20 grams (about 2/3 of an ounce) of sugar
5 grams (about 1/5 of an ounce) of salt
6 eggs

Dissolve the yeast in warm water and a quarter of the flour. Knead until it's just the right consistency, and then shape into a small round loaf. Cut a cross onto the top of the loaf; place in a small baking pan with a film of flour on the bottom, and set aside to rise in a warm place.

Take the rest of the flour, make a hole in the middle, and put the sugar, salt, and egg in the hole. Using your fingers, mix all of this together, and then add the butter, cut into small pieces, and begin to work the dough, using first the blade of a knife and then your hands. Put the dough in a bowl so that you can work it better. When the little loaf that you set aside has become twice its original size, add it to the dough in the bowl and knead thoroughly. Add the remaining eggs one at a time. Then put the bowl in a warm, unventilated place, and when the dough has risen, divide it into pieces big enough to fill twenty small tin fluted molds halfway to the top. Before filling the molds, grease them with melted butter or lard and dust with flour mixed with confectioners' sugar.

Let the dough rise again, gild with egg yolk, and bake in the oven or in a Dutch oven.

96 This is an old Norman term dating back to 1404, from *brier* (*broyer*), "to break apart."

576. PASTA MARGHERITA (SPONGE CAKE)

One day my dear departed friend Antonio Mattei from the town of Prato (of whom I will have occasion to speak again) tasted this pastry at my house and asked for the recipe. Being an industrious man, it didn't take him long to refine and perfect the recipe and begin to sell it in his shop. Later he told me that the success of this sweet was so great that hardly a dinner was given in Prato without it being ordered. People wishing to make their way in the world are quick to grasp any opportunity to seduce Lady Fortune, who—though capricious in how she dispenses her favors—is never a friend to the idle and lazy.

120 grams (about 4-1/4 ounces) of potato flour
120 grams (about 4-1/4 ounces) of powdered sugar
4 eggs
the juice of one lemon

First, thoroughly beat the egg yolks and the sugar. Add the flour and lemon juice and work for more than half an hour. Lastly, beat the egg whites and fold them into the rest of the ingredients; but do so gently, so that they don't go flat. Pour the mixture into a smooth round mold or an appropriately sized baking pan, greased with butter and dusted with confectioners' sugar mixed with flour, and place immediately in the oven. Let cool, then remove from the mold and sprinkle with vanilla confectioners' sugar.

577. TORTA MANTOVANA (MANTUAN CAKE)

170 grams (about 6 ounces) of flour
170 grams (about 6 ounces) of sugar
150 grams (about 5-1/4 ounces) of butter
50 grams (about 1-2/3 ounces) of sweet almonds and pine nuts
1 whole egg
4 egg yolks
lemon zest

Using a wooden spoon, thoroughly beat the eggs with the sugar in a bowl. Then add the flour a little bit at a time, continuing to stir. Lastly, add the butter, which you have melted over a *bain-marie*. Put the mixture in a baking pan greased with butter and dusted with confectioners' sugar mixed with flour or bread crumbs. Garnish with the almonds and pine nuts.

Cut the pine nuts crosswise in two, and after blanching the almonds in hot water, split them in two lengthwise and then cut them crosswise into four or five pieces. Make sure that the cake isn't more than a finger and a half high; otherwise it won't dry properly in the oven, which should be kept at a moderate temperature.

Let the cake cool and sprinkle with confectioners' sugar before serving. It will be greatly enjoyed.

578. TORTA RICCIOLINA I (ALMOND CAKE I)

I'm going to give you two different recipes for almond cake, because after I saw a professional chef make the first one, I decided to modify the recipe to make a better looking, more delicate cake.

120 grams (about 4-1/4 ounces) sweet almonds with a few bitter
*   almonds, blanched*
170 grams (about 6 ounces) powdered sugar
70 grams (about 2-1/3 ounces) candied fruit
60 grams (about 2 ounces) butter
lemon zest

Make some dough with two eggs and some flour, and cut it into strips the same width as the noodles you would use in soup.

In a corner of the pastry board, make a pile with the almonds, sugar, scraped lemon zest, and candied fruit, cut into small pieces. Using a mezzaluna and a rolling pin, chop and crush all of these ingredients until they have been reduced to the size of grains of wheat. Then take a copper baking pan and, without greasing it or adding anything else, place a layer of strips of dough in the middle (if the baking pan is big) and cover them with the above ingredients. Then make another layer of strips and cover. Repeat until you've used up all the ingredients and have a round cake that's at least two fingers high. Once this is done, pour melted butter over the cake, using a brush to cover the surface thoroughly and to ensure that the butter penetrates the whole cake evenly.

Bake in the oven or in a Dutch oven. Actually, if you want to save on coal, you can use just the lid of the Dutch oven. Sprinkle generously with confectioners' sugar while still hot. Let cool before serving.

579. TORTA RICCIOLINA II (ALMOND CAKE II)

Make a shortcrust pastry[97] dough with the following ingredients:

170 grams (about 6 ounces) of flour
70 grams (about 2-1/3 ounces) of sugar
60 grams (about 2 ounces) of butter
25 grams (about 4/5 of an ounce) of lard
1 egg

Use some of the shortcrust pastry dough to make a layer the thickness of a coin on the bottom of a copper baking pan 20 or 21 (about 7-3/4 or 8-1/4 inches) centimeters in diameter (grease the pan with butter first). On top of the layer of pastry, pour a marzipan made with the following ingredients:

120 grams (about 4-1/4 ounces) of sweet almonds and three bitter
    almonds, blanched
100 grams (about 3-1/2 ounces) of sugar
15 grams (about 1/2 an ounce) of butter
15 grams (about 1/2 an ounce) of candied orange
1 egg yolk

Crush the almonds with the sugar in a mortar. Add the candied orange cut into small pieces, and blend in the butter, egg yolk, and a tablespoon of water. Using the rest of the shortcrust pastry, make a circle of dough. Dip your finger in water, and attach the circle of pastry all around the edges of the baking pan. Spread the marzipan evenly in the baking pan and cover it with a layer half a finger high of small strips of dough. The strips should be thin so that they look like decoration, not like the bottom of the cake. Using a brush, cover the strips of dough with 20 grams of melted butter. Bake in the oven at a moderate temperature. Cut ten grams of candied citron into small

97 *Pasta frolla*, a short pastry made with butter and/or lard and eggs.

pieces and sprinkle over the cake after it's done; then sprinkle the cake with vanilla confectioners' sugar. Serve a day or two after cooking, because the cake gets softer and more delicate with time.

Use one egg and the appropriate amount of flour to make the dough for the strips, though you will actually use only half of the strips this amount of dough will yield.

580. TORTA FRANGIPANE[98] (FRANGIPANE CAKE)

This tasty, delicate pastry cake was recommended to me by a man from Venice, a true gentleman.

120 grams (about 4-1/4 ounces) of potato flour
120 grams (about 4-1/4 ounces) of confectioners' sugar
4 eggs
5 grams (about 1/5 of an ounce) of cream of tartar
3 grams (about 1/10 of an ounce) of baking soda
lemon zest

First mix the egg yolk with the sugar, add the potato flour, and blend with a wooden spoon. Then pour in the melted butter, and lastly the beaten egg whites and the other dry ingredients. Use a baking pan small enough so that the cake will be two fingers high. Grease the pan with butter and dust with flour mixed with sugar. You can bake it at home in a Dutch oven.

581. TORTA ALLA MARENGO (CAKE À LA MARENGO)

Make a shortcrust pastry dough using half of the ingredients from recipe 589 A.

Make a custard with the following ingredients:

4 deciliters (about 1-2/3 cups) of milk
60 grams (about 2 ounces) of sugar
3 egg yolks
a dash of vanilla

98 *Frangipane* is a pastry cream that takes its name from the Marquis Muzio Frangipani, a sixteenth-century nobleman living in Paris who invented a perfume based on bitter almonds.

Take 100 grams of sponge cake and cut it into slices half a centimeter thick. Grease a medium-sized copper baking pan with butter and cover the bottom with a layer of the shortcrust pastry dough. Cover this layer all around the edges with a border of the same dough, one finger wide and two fingers high. Dip your finger in water and moisten the pastry around the edges to make it stick better.

After you've finished lining the pan, cover the dough on the bottom with half of the slices of sponge cake, which you've sprinkled with citron cordial.[99] Now use a whisk to beat two of the three egg whites left over from the custard; when they've become stiff, add 130 grams of confectioners' sugar a little at a time and blend gently to make the meringue to cover the surface of the cake. Leave the border of dough uncovered and gild it with egg yolk. Bake in the oven or in a Dutch oven, and when the meringue has become firm, cover it with a sheet of paper so that it doesn't become discolored.

Remove the cake from the pan after it has cooled, and sprinkle lightly with confectioners' sugar. People who don't object to very sweet things will find this cake delicious.

582. TORTA COI PINOLI
(CAKE WITH PINE NUTS)

These cakes are so popular that some pastry shops can't make them fast enough. To those unfamiliar with such things, this cake will appear to have been invented by a professor from the Sorbonne. Here is my exact re-creation of it:

half a liter (about 1/2 pint) of milk
100 grams (about) of medium-sized semolina[100]
65 grams (about 2-1/3 ounces) sugar
50 grams (about 1-2/3 ounces) of pine nuts
10 grams (about 1/3 of an ounce) of butter
2 eggs
a pinch of salt
a dash of vanilla

99 A sugar-based liqueur; see recipe 747.
100 Made by coarsely grinding durum wheat.

The amount of semolina doesn't have to be exact, but make sure to use enough so that the cake will be firm. Chop the pine nuts with a mezzaluna until they're half the size of a grain of rice.

Once the semolina has cooked in the milk, add all the other ingredients and lastly the eggs, quickly blending everything together.

Make a shortcrust pastry dough with the following ingredients:

200 grams (about 7 ounces) of flour
100 grams (about 3-1/2 ounces) of butter
100 grams 2-1/3 ounces sugar
1 egg

If this doesn't moisten the flour sufficiently, add a drop of white wine or Marsala.

Use a baking pan in which the cake won't turn out more than two fingers high. Grease the pan with butter and cover the bottom with a thin layer of pastry. Pour in the mixture and use strips of the dough to make a lozenge-shaped grid on top. Gild with egg yolk, and bake. Let cool before serving, sprinkled with confectioners' sugar.

583. TORTA SVIZZERA
(SWISS CAKE)

Whether or not this cake really comes from Switzerland, that's what I'm calling it. You'll see that it's not bad.

Make a dough of the proper consistency, using the following ingredients:

300 grams (about 10-1/2 ounces) of flour
100 grams (about 3-1/2 ounces) of butter
salt, to taste
a dash of lemon zest
enough milk to moisten the dough, and some to put aside

Take a medium-sized baking pan, grease it with butter, and cover the bottom with a layer of dough as thick as two five-*lire* coins. Use the rest of the dough to make an edge all around, and place in the middle 500 grams of reinette apples or any other tender apples, peeled and cut into sections the size of walnuts. Sprinkle 100 grams (about

3-1/2 ounces) of sugar mixed with two pinches of cinnamon powder and pour 20 grams (about 2/3 of an ounce) of melted butter over the apples.

Bake in the oven, and serve hot or cold. Serves seven or eight people.

The cinnamon, lemon zest, and melted butter poured over the apples are my own additions, but strictly speaking they aren't necessary.

584. BOCCA DI DAMA I (LADY CAKE I)

Those who care to do so can also make this cake without flour—but I think the flour is necessary to give it the right consistency.

250 grams (about 8-4/5 ounces) of powdered sugar
150 grams (about 5-1/4 ounces) of Hungarian flour or extra-fine
*   flour*
50 grams (about 1-2/3 ounces) of sweet almonds mixed with a
*   few bitter almonds*
6 whole eggs and 3 egg yolks
lemon zest

Once you've blanched and thoroughly dried the almonds, crush them in a mortar with a tablespoon of the powdered sugar. Mix with the flour until there are no lumps. Put the rest of the sugar in a bowl with the egg yolks and lemon zest. Blend with a wooden spoon for a quarter of an hour. Add the flour and mix for another half hour. Using a whisk, beat the egg whites in a different bowl. When they have become stiff enough so that a silver two-*lire* piece stands up in them, fold the egg whites into the other bowl and blend everything together very gently.

To bake, pour into a copper baking pan greased with butter and dusted with confectioners' sugar and flour. Or you can use a strainer with a wooden ring, and cover the bottom with a sheet of paper.

585. BOCCA DI DAMA II (LADY CAKE II)

250 grams (about 8-4/5 ounces) of sugar
100 grams (about 3-1/2 ounces) of extra-fine flour
50 grams (about 1-2/3 ounces) of sweet almonds, with three bitter
*   almonds*
9 eggs
lemon zest

Blanch the almonds and dry thoroughly in the sun or on the fire. Crush with a tablespoon of sugar until very fine, and then mix with the flour.

    Put the remaining sugar and the egg yolks together in a copper or brass bowl. Put the bowl over a low flame, and beat the sugar and egg yolks with a whisk for more than a quarter of an hour. Remove from the flame and pour in the flour that has been prepared with the almonds and the lemon zest. After you have mixed all of this together for a while, add the egg whites, thoroughly beaten, and blend it all together gently. Put the mixture in a baking pan greased with butter and dusted with flour mixed with confectioners' sugar, and bake.

586. DOLCE ALLA NAPOLETANA
(NEAPOLITAN CAKE)

This is a lovely-looking, very refined cake.

120 grams (about 4-1/4 ounces) of sugar
120 grams (about 4-1/4 ounces) of Hungarian flour
100 grams (about 3-1/2 ounces) of sweet almonds
4 eggs

Blanch the almonds and dry in the sun or on the fire. Take a third of the larger almonds and divide them in half at their two natural lobes. Cut the other almonds into slivers. Using a whisk, beat the eggs and the sugar in a copper or brass bowl on the fire at 20 degrees Celsius (a little less than 70 degrees Fahrenheit) for a quarter of an hour. Remove this mixture from the fire and add the flour, blending gently. Pour into a smooth mold (it doesn't matter whether it's round or oval) greased with butter and dusted with a teaspoon of confectioners' sugar and a teaspoon of flour mixed together. It would be best to use a mold of such a size that the cake turns out roughly four fingers high when done. Bake in the over or in a Dutch oven at a moderate temperature. When it has completely cooled, slice it into layers about a centimeter (about 1/2 inch) thick.

Make a custard with:

2 egg yolks
3 deciliters (about 1-1/4 cups) of milk
60 grams (about 2 ounces) of sugar
15 grams (about 1/2 ounce) of flour
10 grams (about 1/3 ounce) of butter
a dash of vanilla

Once the custard comes to a boil, spread it on one side of each slice of the cake and then reconstruct the cake by placing one slice on top of the other.

The custard will turn out better if you first put the butter with the flour on the fire, cooking it without letting it brown. Then, when it has cooled to tepid, add the egg yolks, milk, and sugar and put it back on the fire.

Now it's time to frost the whole outside of the cake with a glaze or icing. Using a small saucepan, boil 230 grams (about 8 ounces) of sugar in a deciliter (about 2/5 of a cup) of water until it becomes a little sticky between your fingers, but doesn't form a thread. Another way you'll be able to tell that it's done is when it stops steaming and begins to form rather large bubbles. Remove from the flame, and when it begins to cool add the juice of a quarter of a lemon and blend thoroughly with a wooden spoon until it becomes as white as snow. Should it start to become too firm, just add a little bit of water to make it the consistency of a dense cream. Once this glaze has been prepared, toss in the sliced almonds, blend well, and ice the cake with it. Use the almonds that you split in half to decorate the top, sticking them in straight up.

You can use a fruit filling instead of a custard, but with the custard the cake comes out quite delicious, so I recommend that you try it this way.

587. DOLCE TEDESCO (GERMAN CAKE)

250 grams (about 8-4/5 ounces) of Hungarian flour
100 grams (about 3-1/2 ounces) of butter
100 grams (about 3-1/2 ounces) of powdered sugar
4 eggs
4 tablespoons milk
a dash of vanilla sugar

Blend the butter, sugar, and egg yolks together for half an hour. Add the flour and milk and blend thoroughly.

In order to get this and similar cakes to rise, you can use an odorless white powder[101] that's made in Germany and England. Mix 10 grams (about 1/3 of an ounce) of this powder with the beaten egg whites. If you cannot find this powder where you live, you can substitute 5 grams (about 1/5 of an ounce) of baking soda and 5 grams of cream of tartar mixed together. Pour the cake batter into a large, smooth mold that you have greased with butter, and bake in the oven or Dutch oven. Let cool before serving.

588. PASTA GENOVESE
(GENOESE CAKE)

200 grams (about 7 ounces) of sugar
150 grams (about 5-1/4 ounces) of butter
170 grams (about 6 ounces) of potato flour
110 grams (about 3-4/5 ounces) of wheat flour
12 egg yolks
7 egg whites
lemon zest

First blend the egg yolks, butter, and sugar thoroughly in a bowl. Then add both types of flour and after you've worked the mixture for about half an hour, add the beaten egg whites. Put the batter in the oven in a copper baking pan greased with a little butter and dusted with flour as usual. Keep the height of the cake at about one finger. When it is done, cut into wedges and sprinkle with powdered sugar.

101 Artusi is talking about baking powder.

589. PASTA FROLLA
(SHORTCRUST PASTRY DOUGH)

Here are three different recipes for shortcrust pastry dough or short pastry. You can choose the one that best suits your needs, but I recommend the third recipe as the most refined, especially for pies.

Recipe A

500 grams (about 1 pound) of flour
220 grams (about 7-3/4 ounces) of white sugar
180 grams (about 6-1/3 ounces) of butter
70 grams (about 2-1/3 ounces) of lard
2 whole eggs and one egg yolk

Recipe B

250 grams (about 8-4/5 ounces) of flour
125 grams (about 4-1/2 ounces) of butter
110 grams (about 3-4/5 ounces) of white sugar
1 whole egg and one yolk

Recipe C

270 grams (about 9-1/2 ounces) of flour
115 grams (about 4 ounces) of sugar
90 grams (about 3 ounces) of butter
45 grams (about 1-1/2 ounces) of lard
4 egg yolks
orange zest

If you want to make short pastry without losing your mind, grind the sugar very fine (I use confectioners' sugar) and mix it with the flour. If the butter is still hard, work it beforehand with wet hands on the pastry board until it becomes soft. Make sure that the lard isn't rancid. Blend everything to form a dough, but try to handle it as little as possible or it will "burn," as the chefs say. For this reason it's better to use the blade of a knife to blend the ingredients at the beginning. When convenient, you can make the dough the day before, because raw dough doesn't go bad, and the more time it sits, the more tender it will be when baked. When using the dough for pasticci, pies, cakes, etc., first roll it out with a smooth rolling pin, and then for a nicer appearance, use a ridged rolling pin to roll the part that will go on top, and then gild with egg yolk. If you use confectioners' sugar, the dough will roll out better. In order to work the dough less, you can mix the leftover pieces with white wine or Marsala, which will also help to make it more tender.

590. PASTA DI FARINA GIALLA I
(CORNMEAL PASTRY I)

200 grams (about 7 ounces) of cornmeal
150 grams (about 5-1/4 ounces) of wheat flour
150 grams (about 5-1/4 ounces) of powdered sugar
100 grams (about 3-1/2 ounces) of butter
50 grams (about 1-2/3 ounces) of lard
10 grams (about 1/3 of an ounce) of aniseed
1 egg

Blend the two kinds of flour, the sugar, and the aniseed, and then add the butter, lard, and egg, using as much as you can; make a little loaf and set aside. Mix the remaining dough with a little white wine and a little water and make another loaf. Then mix the two loaves together, but try to handle them as little as possible so that the dough comes out rather soft. Roll it out with a rolling pin until it's half a finger thick. Dust with a mixture of the two kinds of flour so that it doesn't stick to the pastry board, and cut it, using tin cutters of different shapes and sizes. Grease a pan with lard, dust it with flour, and place the pastries on it. Gild with egg, bake in the oven, and sprinkle with powdered sugar.

591. PASTA DI FARINA GIALLA II
(CORNMEAL PASTRY II)

These pastries are much more refined than the preceding ones.

200 grams (about 7 ounces) of cornmeal
100 grams (about 3-1/2 ounces) of butter
80 grams (about 2-2/3 ounces) of confectioners' sugar

413

10 grams (about 1/3 of an ounce) of dried elder flowers
2 egg yolks

If you find the dough to be too firm as you are kneading it, soften it with a drop of water. Roll it out with a rolling pin until it's the thickness of a coin. Cut the dough into small disks as in recipe 634, because these pastries can also be served with tea. To give them a nicer look, you can score them with the tines of a fork or with a grater.

The flowers and leaves of the elder tree, which are sold by herborists, have diuretic and diaphoretic properties; that is to say— all modesty aside, so that everyone understands—they make you urinate and perspire.

592. GIALLETTI (CORNMEAL CAKES I)

Dear Mothers, treat your children to these little cakes, but beware not to taste them yourselves, unless you want your little ones to cry because there will be less for them to eat.

300 grams (about 10-1/2 ounces) of cornmeal
100 grams (about 3-1/2 ounces) of flour
100 grams (about 3-1/2 ounces) of zibibbo

5 9 3 . GIALLETTI II (CORNMEAL CAKES II)

If you don't mind spending the money, the following is a more refined recipe for cornmeal cakes, and it calls for no yeast or water to make the dough.

300 grams (about 10-1/2 ounces) of cornmeal
150 grams (about 5-1/4 ounces) of wheat flour
150 grams (about 5-1/4 ounces) of butter
70 grams (about 2-1/3 ounces) of lard
100 grams (about 3-1/2 ounces) of zibibbo raisins
2 eggs
lemon zest

If you make them the size of half your finger, you should be able to make about twenty little cakes. But you can make them any shape you prefer, and if you keep them small you can make forty instead of twenty. Bake as in the preceding recipe, and treat the dough as you would short pastry.

5 9 4 . ROSCHETTI

200 grams (about 7 ounces) of flour
100 grams (about 3-1/2 ounces) of confectioners' sugar
100 grams (about 3-1/2 ounces) sweet almonds
80 grams(about 2-2/3 ounces) of butter
20 grams (about 2/3 of an ounce) of lard
one whole egg and one yolk

Blanch the almonds, dry in the sun or on the fire, toast until they turn hazelnut-brown, and chop into pieces half the size of a grain of rice. Mix the chopped almonds with the sugar and the flour. Make a hole in the middle of this mixture for the rest of the ingredients, and blend, working the dough as little as possible. Form a round loaf and let it rest for a few hours. Lightly flour the pastry board and roll out the dough, first with a smooth rolling pin and then with a ridged one, until it is just under a centimeter thick. If you use the same pastry cutter as in recipe 162 or a similar one, you'll get about 50 of these pastries, which you can bake in a Dutch oven after placing them in a baking pan lightly greased with cold butter.

595. CENCI
("RAGS")

240 grams (about 8-1/2 ounces) of flour
20 grams (about 2/3 of an ounce) of butter
20 grams (about 2/3 of an ounce) of powdered sugar
2 eggs
1 tablespoon brandy
a pinch of salt

Use these ingredients to make a rather firm dough, working it thoroughly with your hands. Let it rest a little, flour it, and wrap it in a cloth. If the dough comes out too tender for you to handle it, add some more flour. Roll out into a sheet the thickness of a coin, and, using a pastry cutter with a scalloped edge, cut into strips about as wide as your palm and two or three fingers long. Make some incisions in the strips so that they can be folded, twisted, or curled into strange shapes when they go into the pan (which should be bubbling with oil or lard). Remove from the oil, and when they're no longer sizzling, sprinkle with confectioners' sugar. This recipe is enough to make a large plate full of cenci. If the dough should become hard on the outside after being left to rest, knead it again.

596. STIACCIATA CON SICCIOLI
(FLAT CAKE WITH CRACKLINGS)

We ought to respect everyone in the world, and not disdain anyone, however lowly he might be. For if you really think about it, even this humble person may be endowed with some redeeming quality.

This is the general maxim; but to get down to specifics, and even though the comparison doesn't hold up and this is such a humble thing, I will tell you that I am indebted to an uncouth maidservant for this flat cake, which she could make to perfection.

650 grams (about 1-1/2 pounds) of leaven dough
200 grams (about 7 ounces) powdered sugar
100 grams (about 3-1/2 ounces) of cracklings
40 grams (about 1-1/3 ounces) of butter

40 grams (about 1-1/3 ounces) of lard
5 eggs
orange or lemon zest

By leaven dough here I mean dough that is used to make bread.

Prepare the dough the night before. First knead the leaven dough on a pastry board without the seasonings, then in a bowl for more than a half hour with one hand, adding the other ingredients a little at a time, and then the eggs. Then cover well and put in a warm place to rise overnight. The next morning, knead it again and then pour it into a copper baking pan greased with butter and dusted with flour. It shouldn't be more than two fingers high. Once this is done, put the dough in a warming oven so that it can rise again, and then in the oven. You can also do the whole operation in your home and then bake it in a Dutch oven. But I should warn you that this cake is rather difficult to make well, especially during the cold seasons. All the better to wait for warm weather to make it. But don't give up after the first try.

In the unfortunate event that the dough has risen too little or not at all by morning, add some brewer's yeast (a little more than the size of a walnut). Mix the yeast beforehand with a pinch of flour and some lukewarm water.

597. STIACCIATA UNTA
(GREASED FLAT CAKE)

We'll call this flat cake "greased" to distinguish it from the one in the preceding recipe. While the former is better tasting, this one has the advantage of being easier to make.

The portions for this cake and for the Mantuan cake were recommended to me by that good man, the late Antonio Mattei of Prato, whom I've already mentioned earlier. I say "good" because he was a genius in his art and was an honest, very industrious man. But this dear friend of mine, who always reminded me of Boccaccio's character Cisti the baker,[103] died in the year 1885, leaving me deeply grieved.

103 *Decameron* V, 2.

Letters and science aren't always necessary to win public esteem; even a very humble art, accompanied by a kind heart and practiced with skill and decorum, can make us worthy of the respect and love of our fellow men.

> *Beneath rough manners and humble exteriors*
> *often lie noble hearts and pure souls;*
> *we should be wary of men who are too genteel,*
> *for they are like marble: shiny, smooth, and hard.*[104]

But let's get to the point:

700 grams (about 1-1/2 pounds) of leaven dough
120 grams (about 4-1/4 ounces) of lard
100 grams (about 3-1/2 ounces) of sugar
60 grams (about 2 ounces) of cracklings
4 egg yolks
a pinch of salt
orange or lemon zest

Knead the dough gently so that it doesn't lose its elasticity. If you make it in the evening and set it aside in a warm place, it will rise by itself; if you make it in the morning, it will need three hours in an earthenware warming oven.

If you want to make it without cracklings, add two more egg yolks and 30 more grams of lard.

Half of this recipe will serve five or six people.

598. STIACCIATA ALLA LIVORNESE
(LIVORNO-STYLE FLAT CAKE)

Livorno-style flat cake is usually made at Easter time, perhaps because the mildness of the season helps the dough to rise, and because eggs are abundant during that season. It requires a long period to make, perhaps even four days, because it needs to rise several times. Here are the ingredients needed to make three medium-sized cakes, or four small ones:

104 An epigram from Filippo Panati's *Works in Verse and Prose* (Florence, 1824).

12 eggs
1.8 kilograms (about 4 pounds) of extra-fine flour
600 grams (about 1-1/3 pounds) of sugar
200 grams (about 7 ounces) of super-fine oil
70 grams (about 2-1/3 ounces) of butter
30 grams (about 1 ounce) of brewer's yeast
20 grams (about 2/3 of an ounce) of aniseed
1-1/2 deciliters (about 3/5 of a cup) of vin santo[101]
1/2 deciliter (about 1/5 of a cup) of Marsala
1 deciliter (about 2/5 of a cup) of orange-flower water

Mix the two kinds of wine; thoroughly wash the aniseed, and put it to soak in some of this liquid.

You can begin in the late evening:

Step 1: Mix the brewer's yeast with half a glass of lukewarm water, letting it absorb enough flour to make a loaf of the right consistency. Place the loaf on a mound of flour in a bowl, and cover it with a layer of the same flour. Keep the bowl, protected from drafts, in the kitchen, if you don't have any place warmer in your house.

Step 2: The next morning, when the loaf has risen well, place it on a pastry board, spread it out, and mix it again with an egg, a tablespoon of oil, a tablespoon of sugar, a tablespoon of wine, and enough flour to make a larger loaf; blend everything together well without kneading it too much. Put it back on the mound of flour and cover it as you did with the smaller loaf.

Step 3: After six or seven hours (it will take that long for the loaf to rise again), add three eggs, three tablespoons of oil, three of sugar, three of wine, and enough flour to form another loaf and let it rise again, just as you did the other loaves. To gauge the right point of fermentation, calculate that the loaf should grow to about three times its original size.

Step 4: Add five eggs, five tablespoons of sugar, five of oil, five of wine, and the necessary amount of flour.

Step 5, the last step: Add the three remaining eggs and all of the remaining ingredients. Melt the butter and blend well to obtain a smooth dough. If the dough should turn out somewhat soft, which isn't likely, add some more flour to give it the right consistency.

105 A concentrated, highly aromatic golden-colored wine, usually sweet but sometimes dry. It gets its name from the fact that it is used for the celebration of the eucharist during mass.

Divide and shape the dough into three or four balls, and put each one in a baking pan on a sheet of paper greased with butter; the paper should extend well beyond the edge of the pan. Since the fermentation becomes slower as you add more and more of the ingredients, you can speed it up the last time by putting the balls of pastry to rise in a warming oven. When they are nicely puffed up and quivering, use a brush to coat them first with orange-flower water and then with egg yolk. Bake in the oven at a moderate temperature. Remember that this last step is the most important and the most difficult. Since the balls of dough are large, too much heat might quickly cook the surface, leaving the inside raw.

If you carefully follow this recipe for homemade Livorno-style flat cakes, they may not be as light as the ones from Burchi's in Pisa, but to make up for it they'll be more flavorful.

599. PAN DI SPAGNA
(SPONGE CAKE)

6 eggs
170 grams (about 6 ounces) of fine powdered sugar
170 grams (about 6 ounces) of Hungarian flour or extra-fine flour
lemon zest (optional)

First beat the egg yolks with the sugar, then add the flour (dried on the fire or in the sun), and after working the dough for about half an hour, pour in two tablespoons of beaten egg whites to soften the mixture. Then add the rest of the ingredients, blending slowly.

You could also beat the eggs on the fire as in recipe 584, Neapolitan Cake. Bake in the oven.

600. BISCOTTO (UNLEAVENED CAKE)

6 eggs
250 grams (about 8-4/5 ounces) of confectioners' sugar
100 grams (about 3-1/2 ounces) of wheat flour
50 grams (about 1-/2/3 ounces) of potato flour
30 grams (about 1 ounce) of butter
lemon zest

Using a wooden spoon, mix the egg yolks, sugar, and a tablespoon of both kinds of flour for at least half an hour. Beat the egg whites until firm and add to the mixture. Stir slowly, and when the whites are thoroughly blended, use a sieve to sift in the two types of flour, which you have dried in the sun or on the fire. Bake in the oven or in a Dutch oven in a baking pan that makes the cake come out three fingers high, but first grease the pan with cold butter and dust with confectioners' sugar mixed with flour. You can also use the following method to prepare cakes like this that are made with beaten egg whites: first beat the egg yolks with the sugar, then toss in the flour, and after thoroughly working the mixture, beat the egg whites until firm and pour in two tablespoons to soften the mixture. Then add the rest of the beaten egg whites and blend very slowly.

601. BISCOTTO DI CIOCCOLATA
(UNLEAVENED CHOCOLATE CAKE)

6 eggs
200 grams (about 7 ounces) of powdered sugar
150 grams (about 5-1/4 ounces) of flour
50 grams (about 1-2/3 ounces) of vanilla-flavored chocolate

Grate the chocolate and put it in a bowl with the sugar and the egg yolks and stir with a wooden spoon; then add the flour and work the mixture for more than half an hour. Lastly, beat the egg whites, add, and mix gently. Bake as in the preceding recipe.

602. FOCACCIA COI SICCIOLI
(FLATBREAD WITH CRACKLINGS)

500 grams (about 1 pound) of flour
200 grams (about 7 ounces) of fine powdered sugar
160 grams (about 5-2/3 ounces) of butter
150 grams (about 5-1/4 ounces) of cracklings
60 grams (about 2 ounces) of lard
4 tablespoons Marsala or white wine
two whole eggs and two yolks
lemon zest

Once you've made the dough, working it as little as possible, add the cracklings, minced. Grease a copper baking pan with lard and pour in the dough, pressing it down with your knuckles to even it out (though the surface will not be smooth). But don't let it be more than a finger high.

If you want to serve the cake in pieces, cut it into squares with the tip of a knife before you put it in the oven. Repeat this operation when the cake is halfway done, because the cuts close up easily. When it's done, sprinkle with powdered sugar.

603. FOCACCIA ALLA TEDESCA
(GERMAN-STYLE FLATBREAD)

120 grams (about 4-1/4 ounces) of sugar
30 grams (about 1 ounce) of candied fruit, in very small pieces
120 grams (about 4-1/4 ounces) of fine bread crumbs
30 grams (about 1 ounce) of sultanas
lemon zest

First blend the egg yolks with the sugar until they become almost white; add the bread crumbs, then the candied fruit and the sultanas, and lastly the egg whites, beaten until firm. Blend gently so that the egg whites don't go flat, and when the mixture is thoroughly blended, pour into a baking pan greased with butter and dusted with flour or bread crumbs; the batter should be about two fingers high. Bake in the oven. After you've baked and sprinkled it with powdered sugar, this cake will look like a sponge cake.

To serve ten or twelve people, double the ingredients.

604. PANETTONE MARIETTA
(MARIETTA'S PANETTONE)

My Marietta[106] is a good cook, and such a good-hearted, honest woman that she deserves to have this cake named after her, especially since she taught me how to make it.

106 Marietta Sabatini, Artusi's cook.

300 grams (about 10-1/2 ounces) of extra-fine flour
100 grams (about 3-1/2 ounces) of butter
80 grams (about 2-2/3 ounces) of sugar
80 grams (about 2-2/3 ounces) of sultanas
one whole egg and two yolks
a pinch of salt
10 grams (about 1/3 of an ounce) of cream of tartar
a teaspoon or 5 scant grams (about 1/5 of an ounce) of baking soda
20 grams (about 2/3 of an ounce) of candied fruit, in tiny pieces
lemon zest
about 2 deciliters (about 4/5 of a cup) of milk

In wintertime, soften the butter in *bain-marie* and then blend it with the eggs. Add the flour and milk a little at a time, then the rest of the ingredients except the sultanas, cream of tartar, and baking soda, which you should keep for the last. But before adding them, work the mixture for at least half an hour and dilute it with the milk until it's the right consistency—not too liquid, and not too firm. Pour into a mold twice as large as the amount of batter, deeper than it is wide, so that when it rises it doesn't overflow, and it will come out in the shape of a round loaf. Grease the sides of the mold with butter, dust with powdered sugar mixed with flour, and bake in the oven. If it turns out right, it should rise a great deal, and have a puffed-up, dome-shaped top with cracks in it. This panettone is worth trying, because it's much better than the Milanese-style panettone that's sold commercially, and isn't much trouble to make.

605. PANE BOLOGNESE (BOLOGNESE SWEET BREAD)

This is a sweet bread that will do honor to classic Bolognese cooking because it's tasty eaten by itself, and can also be served for dunking in any liquid.

500 grams (about 1 pound) of flour
180 grams (about 6-1/3 ounces) of sugar
180 grams (about 6-1/3 ounces) of butter
70 grams (about 2-1/3 ounces) of zibibbo raisins
50 grams (about 1-2/3) coarsely chopped pine nuts

30 grams (about 1 ounce) of candied citron, in small slivers
8 grams (about 1/3 of an ounce) of cream of tartar
4 grams (about 1/6 of an ounce) of baking soda
2 eggs
a deciliter (about 2/5 of a cup) of milk

Mix the sugar with the flour and form a mound on the pastry board. Make a hole in the middle of the mound, where you will put the butter, eggs, and milk; the milk should be lukewarm, mixed with the cream of tartar and baking soda, which you'll see will have already begun to ferment. Knead it all together, and when the dough is thoroughly mixed, open it and add the pine nuts, candied citron, and rasisins.

Knead the dough again so that all of the ingredients are thoroughly blended, and then make two oblong loaves just over a finger high. Gild with egg yolk, and put immediately in the oven or Dutch oven.

606. CIAMBELLE O BUCCELLATI I
(RING CAKES I)

1.7 kilograms (about 3-3/4 pounds) of extra-fine flour
300 grams (about 10-1/2 ounces) of sugar
200 grams (about 7 ounces) of leaven dough
150 grams (about 5-1/4 ounces) of butter
50 grams (about 1-2/3 ounces) of lard
4 deciliters (about 1-2/3 cups) of milk
2 deciliters (about 4/5 of a cup) of Marsala
2 tablespoons rum
6 eggs
1 teaspoon of baking soda
a pinch of salt
lemon zest

If you use the exact amounts indicated above, the flour should be just right to obtain a dough that's the proper consistency.

As I've said before, by leaven dough I mean pre-prepared dough used to make bread rise.

The lemon for the zest should be freshly picked.

Combine the leaven dough in a bowl with half of the milk. Leave it surrounded by a finger-deep layer of flour. Put the bowl in a warm place, protected from drafts, and when it has risen (depending on the season, this will take eight to ten hours), reshape it and make it bigger by using the rest of the milk and as much flour as you need. Wait until it has risen again and is thoroughly puffed up (this will also take eight to ten hours). Then put it on a pastry board and knead it with the rest of the flour and all of the other ingredients. But knead it vigorously until the dough becomes tender and all of the ingredients are thoroughly blended.

Prepare some iron or tin-plated copper pans, greased with lard and dusted with flour. Make the pastry rings any size you like, and arrange them in the pans, but make sure that they're not too close together. Let them rise in the kitchen or any other warm place, and when they are thoroughly puffed up, make long incisions on the top of each one with the tip of a knife. Gild with egg and sprinkle with coarsely ground crystal sugar.

Bake in the oven at a moderate temperature.

In the wintertime, it would be wise to mix the leaven with luke-warm milk and then let the cakes rise in a warming oven. Using half the ingredients, you should be able to make four nice ring cakes weighing about 350 grams each, unless you prefer to make them smaller.

607. CIAMBELLE O BUCCELLATI II
(RING CAKES II)

These family-style ring cakes are easier to make than the ones in the preceding recipe.

500 grams (about 1 pound) of Hungarian flour
180 grams (about 6-1/3 ounces) of sugar
90 grams (about 3 ounces) of butter
15 grams (about 1/2 an ounce) of cream of tartar
5 grams (about 1/5 of an ounce) of baking soda
2 eggs
lemon zest or aniseed or small pieces of candied citron

Melt the butter and pour it, along with the eggs and the sugar, into a hole that you've made in the mound of flour. Blend the flour with these ingredients and enough milk to give the dough the right consistency, and then knead thoroughly. Lastly, add the cream of tartar, baking soda, and lemon zest or other flavoring.

Instead of making a single cake, you can make two; make the hole larger, because they'll come out quite thick. Make a few incisions on the surface, gild with egg yolk, grease the pan with butter or lard, and bake in the oven or in a Dutch oven. Even with half of the ingredients, you can make a fair-sized ring cake.

608. PASTA MADDALENA
(MADELEINE DOUGH)

130 grams (about 4-1/2 ounces) of sugar
80 grams (about 2-2/3 ounces) of fine flour
30 grams (about 1 ounce) of butter
4 egg yolks
3 egg whites
a pinch of baking soda
lemon zest

First mix the egg yolks with the sugar, and when they have become whitish, add the flour and work the mixture for another quarter of an hour. Add the butter (melted if it's wintertime) to the mixture, and lastly the egg whites, beaten.

Dry the flour on the fire, or in the sun if it's summertime.

You can give these pastries many different shapes, as long as they are thin and small. Many people use small pastry molds greased with butter and floured, or else a baking pan a little less than a finger deep, and cut the pastry into lozenge shapes and then sprinkle it with confectioners' sugar. You can also make it half a finger deep and stick the lozenge-shaped pieces of pastry together two by two with fruit preserves.

609. PIZZA ALLA NAPOLETANA
(NEAPOLITAN-STYLE SWEET PIZZA)

Use half the ingredients in recipe 589 A to make a shortcrust pastry or short pastry dough, or use the full amounts in recipe B.

150 grams (about 5-1/4 ounces) of ricotta cheese
70 grams (about 2-1/3 ounces) of sweet almonds and three bitter
  almonds
50 grams (about 1-2/3 ounces) of sugar
20 grams (about 2/3 of an ounce) of flour
1 egg and one egg yolk
a dash of lemon zest or vanilla
half a glass of milk

Make a custard with the milk, sugar, flour, and the whole egg, and when it's ready and still boiling, add the egg yolk and lemon zest or vanilla. Then add the ricotta and the almonds, blanched and finely ground. Blend it all together and then use this mixture to fill the shortcrust pastry as you would a cake, that is, between two layers, decorated on top and gilded with egg yolk. It goes without saying that it should be baked in the oven and served cold, sprinkled with confectioners' sugar.

In my opinion, this makes a delicious-tasting dessert.

610. PIZZA GRAVIDA ("PREGNANT" PIZZA)

Use the following mixture as you would a custard, as a filling for the dough:

a quarter of a liter (about 1 cup) of milk
60 grams (about 2 ounces) of sugar
30 grams (about 1 ounce) of starch[107]
2 egg yolks
any flavoring you like

When you remove the mixture from the fire, add:

30 grams (about 1 ounce) of whole pine nuts
80 grams (about 2-2/3 ounces) of raisins

107 I.e., a thickening agent such as cornstarch.

Use this mixture to fill a shortcrust pastry crust as you did for Neapolitan-Style Sweet Pizza, and bake as in the preceding recipe.

611. QUATTRO QUARTI ALL'INGLESE
(FOUR QUARTERS, ENGLISH STYLE)

5 eggs
sugar and flour, equal in weight to the eggs with their shells
200 grams (about 7 ounces) of raisins
200 grams (about 7 ounces) of butter
30 grams (about 1 ounce) of candied fruit, in small pieces
a teaspoon of baking soda

First blend the eggs with the sugar, add the flour and continue to work the mixture with a wooden spoon for about half an hour. Let sit for an hour or two, and then add the butter (melted over a *bain-marie*), baking soda, raisins, and candied fruit. Pour into a baking pan or smooth mold greased with butter and dusted with confectioners' sugar mixed with flour. Bake in the oven.

Wash the raisins beforehand to clean them of the grit that they usually contain, and then dry them.

Now is a good time to say a few words about the proverbial indolence of Italians, who usually turn to foreign countries for things they have right in their own back yard. In Lower Romagna they grow a tiny, seedless red grape, which they call *uva romanina*. I have sometimes used this grape in my home, because when it's dried you can't tell it from ordinary raisins except that it's of better quality and free from any grit. To dry the grapes, spread them out on a rack, keep them in a warming oven for seven or eight days, and after they've dried, remove the stems.

612. QUATTRO QUARTI ALL'ITALIANA
(FOUR QUARTERS, ITALIAN STYLE)

This sweet is made the same way as the last one, except you substitute lemon zest for the candied fruit and 100 grams (about 3-1/2 ounces) of sweet almonds with a few bitter almonds for the raisins. If you also use baking soda, it will turn out lighter. After blanching the almonds, dry them in the sun or on the fire. Crush very fine with two tablespoons of the sugar from the recipe, and mix with the flour before tossing into the mixture. If you don't do this, the almonds might all stick together. The dough in this recipe needs to be worked a great deal, both before and after you add the butter. Through experimentation, my cook has found that it helps to keep the mixing bowl immersed in warm water while you're working the dough; this also holds true for other similar kinds of dough. If made carefully, this will be deemed a delicious sweet.

613. DOLCE DI MANDORLE
(ALMOND CAKE)

3 eggs
sugar equal in weight to the eggs
125 grams (about 4-1/2 ounces) of potato flour
125 grams (about 4-1/2 ounces) of butter
125 grams (about 4-1/2 ounces) of sweet almonds, with 3 bitter
  almonds
lemon zest

Blanch the almonds, dry them in the sun or on the fire, and crush very fine in a mortar with a third of the sugar. Using a wooden spoon, blend the three egg yolks with the remaining sugar and the lemon zest until they have become whitish. Then add the potato flour, crushed almonds, and butter (melted), as you continue to work the mixture. Lastly, add the egg whites, beaten, and when all of the ingredients are well blended, bake in a Dutch oven. When it has cooled, sprinkle the cake with confectioners' sugar.

If you use a baking pan with a diameter of about 22 centimeters (about 8-2/3 inches), the cake will turn out just the right height. You can use some of the butter to grease the pan, which, as you know, should be dusted with confectioners' sugar mixed with flour. This is a delicate-tasting cake that serves eight people.

614. OFFELLE DI MARMELLATA (SCALLOPED SWEET PASTRIES WITH FRUIT FILLING)

The word "offella," in this context, comes from the dialect of Romagna, and, if I'm not mistaken, it is used in the Lombard dialect as well. It probably derives from the ancient word *offa*, which means a flat cake or bread made with spelt[108] and various other ingredients.

Dar l'offa al cerbero, "to give Cerberus[109] a sop," is a rather timely expression, since there are so many people these days who seek out public office so that they can gorge themselves on public funds. But we'd better get back to offelle.

500 grams (about 1 pound) of red apples
125 grams (about 4-1/2 ounces) of powdered sugar
30 grams (about 1 ounce) of candied fruit
two teaspoons cinnamon powder

Cut the apples into four sections, peel, and core. Slice the sections as thin as possible and put in a saucepan on the fire with two glasses of water; break apart with a wooden spoon. Since these apples have firm flesh, they need to be cooked in water; if they start to dry out while you're cooking them, just add some more water. Wait until the apples have become mushy before adding the sugar, and then taste to see if they're sweet enough, since fruit in general can be more or less acid, depending upon how ripe it is. Lastly, add the candied fruit, chopped into small pieces, and the cinnamon.

Use the shortcrust pastry dough from recipe 589 A. Spread it out with a rolling pin until it's the thickness of a coin. Then cut it with a round pastry cutter with a scalloped edge like the one indicated on the following page. With one disk of dough underneath and one on top (the latter rolled with a ridged rolling pin), put the cooked apple mixture in the middle and moisten the edges so that the two disks of dough stick together. Gild with egg yolk, and bake. Afterward, sprinkle with confectioners' sugar.

---

108 *Farro*, an ancient variety of wheat with small brown grains.
109 In classical mythology, Cerberus is the three-headed dog that guards the entrance to the infernal regions.

PASTRY CUTTER FOR SCALLOPED
SWEET PASTRIES WITH FRUIT FILLING

615. OFFELLE DI MARZAPANE
(SCALLOPED SWEET PASTRIES WITH MARZIPAN)

Use the same shortcrust pastry dough as in the last recipe, but for the filling use the marzipan described in recipe 579 instead of a fruit mixture. If you don't have any candied orange, use fresh orange peel, which is very pleasant. You can give these pastries a different shape to distinguish them from the ones in the preceding recipe. I use the pastry cutter indicated below,

PASTRY CUTTER FOR SCALLOPED
SWEET PASTRIES WITH MARZIPAN

and then fold the pastry in two to form a scalloped half moon.

616. CROSTATE (TARTS)

By crostate I mean tarts made with shortcrust pastry dough, filled with fruit preserves or pastry cream.

Use recipe 589 B, or half the amounts in recipe 589 A. In either case, use one whole egg and one yolk, as indicated. But before adding the eggs to the dough, beat them, setting a little aside to use later when you gild the top of the tart. It's a good idea to use some flavoring for this kind of pastry dough, such as lemon zest or orange-flower water. The best would be just to use recipe 589 C.

Using a smooth rolling pin, roll out half the dough into a round sheet the thickness of a coin, and put it into a baking pan greased with butter. Spread the fruit preserves or pastry cream (or even both, as long as you keep them separate) over the sheet of dough. If the fruit is too firm, soften it over the flame with a tablespoon of water. Now roll out another sheet of dough with a ridged rolling pin. Cut into strips just under a finger wide, and lay them over the fruit, crisscrossed, with the same distance between the strips so that they form a lattice. Then cover the ends of the strips of dough with the remaining dough, forming an edge all around the tart; moisten the dough first with water so that it will stick better. Gild the top of the tart with the egg you set aside earlier, and bake in the oven or Dutch oven. It gets better after a day or two.

617. CROCCANTE (ALMOND BRITTLE)

120 grams (about 4-1/4 ounces) of sweet almonds
100 grams (about 3-1/2 ounces) of powdered sugar

Blanch the almonds, separate the lobes (in other words, the two parts where they are naturally joined), and cut into slivers lengthwise or crosswise, whichever you prefer. Put these slivered almonds on the fire and dry them until they turn yellowish, but don't toast them. In the meantime, put the sugar on the fire in a saucepan (avoid using a tin-plated pan if possible), and when it's completely liquefied, add the almonds (still nice and hot), and mix. Be sure at this point to throw a shovelful of ashes on the coals so that the almond brittle doesn't turn out bitter because it's been overcooked. You can tell that it's done when it becomes cinnamon colored. Then pour a little at a time into any kind of mold greased with butter or oil, and use a lemon to press it against the sides, forming a layer as thin as possible. When it has cooled, remove from the mold, and should it be difficult to do so, immerse the mold in boiling water. Some people dry the almonds in the sun, chop them very fine with a mezzaluna, and add a bit of butter after adding them to the sugar.

618. SALAME INGLESE (SWEET ENGLISH "SALAMI")

This cake, which could more properly be called sponge cake with filling, makes a handsome sight in the windows of confectioners' shops. To those untrained in the art of baking, it might seem to be a very fancy dish, but it really isn't at all difficult to make.

Make a sponge cake using the following ingredients and bake in a large baking pan (rectangular if possible) greased with butter and dusted with flour. The cake should be half a finger high.

200 grams (about 7 ounces) of powdered sugar
170 grams (about 6 ounces) of very fine flour
6 eggs

In this and similar cases, some cookbooks suggest drying the flour in the sun or on the fire before using it, perhaps to make it lighter.

Work the egg yolks with the sugar for about half an hour and then add the egg whites, beaten thoroughly. When you have gently folded in the whites, sift the flour onto this mixture, or use the method described in recipe 588. Remove from the oven, and while the cake is still hot cut it into a sufficient number of strips two centimeters wide and as long as the remaining piece of sponge cake, for which they will be used as filling. But to give these strips a nice appearance, they should be different colors. So sprinkle some of them with white rosolio,[110] and they'll turn yellow; others with alkermes,[111] and they will turn red; dye the last ones black with white rosolio marinated

---

110 A cordial flavored with rose petals, cloves, cinnamon, etc.
111 A liqueur that derives its red color from the kermes insect. It is made with spices and scented with rose, jasmine, and iris.

with chocolate. Arrange the dyed strips of sponge cake in alternating colors one on top of the other in the middle of the remaining piece of cake, which you have spread with fruit preserves. Spread the fruit preserves on the strips of cake as well, so that they'll stay in place. Pull the edges of the large piece of sponge cake over the strips of cake to form a compact roll. When the roll is sliced, you'll see the multicolored checkerboard filling.

You can make a simpler version of this cake for your family in the following manner; even half of the ingredients will be sufficient for a large baking pan.

Spread the sponge cake with rosolio and fruit preserves—it doesn't matter whether you use quince, apricot, or peach. Arrange thin strips of candied fruit on top of this, and then roll the whole piece of cake up on itself.

Either way you make it, it's a good idea to decorate the top of the cake with either a lacework of sugar or with chocolate icing, as the confectioners do. But those gentlemen have certain secrets for making such things to perfection—secrets that they don't willingly share. But it just so happens that I know one of their special processes, which you will find described in recipe 789.

In the meantime, you'll just have to content yourself with the following method, which is simpler, if not quite perfect:

Mix some confectioners' sugar with egg whites until very firm, and then spread over the cake evenly or put the mixture in a piping bag and squeeze until it comes out of the small hole at the bottom. Pipe the icing all over the top of the cake, making any design you like. If you want dark icing, take 60 grams (about 2 ounces) of powdered sugar and 30 grams (about 1 ounce) of powdered chocolate, mix, blend thoroughly with beaten egg whites, and spread over the cake. If it doesn't harden by itself, expose it to moderate heat.

619. CAVALLUCCI DI SIENA
(SIENESE "LITTLE HORSES")

The specialty sweets of Siena are panforte, ricciarelli, cavallucci, and cupate. Cavallucci are little pastries shaped liked mostaccioli, as shown in the following diagram. You can see that they have nothing to do with horses, and I don't think that they even know why they're called that in Siena, a city, as the saying goes, *where three things abound: towers, bells, and quintains.*[112]

CAVALLUCCI

In this recipe I want to give you a close, but not exact imitation of Sienese cavallucci—we've got the flavor just about right, but the consistency leaves something to be desired, which is only natural. When something is made in large quantities and with methods that are kept secret from the uninitiated, any imitation is bound to falter.

300 grams (about 10-1/2 ounces) of flour
300 grams (about 10-1/2 ounces) of blond sugar
100 grams (about 3-1/2 ounces) of shelled walnuts
50 grams (about 1-2/3 ounces) of candied orange
15 grams (about 1/2 of an ounce) of aniseed
5 grams (about 1/5 of an ounce) of spices and cinnamon powder

Chop the walnuts into pieces about the size of beans. Dice the candied orange. Put the sugar on the fire with a third of its weight in water, and when it has reached the point where it threads from the spoon, add all of the other ingredients and blend. Pour the hot mixture over the flour on a pastry board—but to do this, you'll see that you'll need more flour to give the dough the right consistency. Then form the cavallucci, of which, with these amounts, you should get more than 40. Since the dough is quite sticky on account of the sugar, dust the cookies all over with flour. Place in a baking pan and

112 Quintains are tilting posts (used in the medieval sport of tilting), and, by extension, frivolous pastimes.

bake them plain, at moderate heat. Be very careful when you cook the sugar, because it will turn dark if it cooks too much. Pick up a drop between your thumb and index finger, and if it starts to form a thread, it's cooked enough for this recipe.

620. RICCIARELLI DI SIENA
(SIENESE ALMOND COOKIES)

220 grams (about 7-3/4 ounces) of fine white sugar
200 grams (about 7 ounces) of sweet almonds
20 grams (about 2/3 of an ounce) of bitter almonds
2 egg whites
orange zest

Blanch the almonds, dry them in the sun or on the fire, and crush very fine in a mortar with two tablespoons of the sugar, added a little at a time. Then add the rest of the sugar and mix thoroughly.

Beat the egg whites in any type of bowl and pour in the crushed almonds and the orange rind, grated. Mix again with a wooden spoon and pour the mixture onto a pastry board over a thin layer of flour, just enough so that only the very little bit of flour necessary to roll out of a soft, flat sheet of dough half a finger thick sticks to it. Then cut out the cookies in the shape indicated below, and you'll get between 16 and 19 cookies. Bake in the following manner:

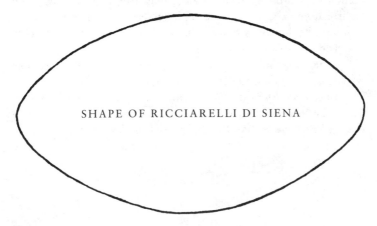

SHAPE OF RICCIARELLI DI SIENA

Take a baking pan, make a layer of bran as thick as a coin, and cover it entirely with wafers, on which you will place the ricciarelli. Bake in the oven at moderate heat so that they stay tender. If you don't have an oven, which it the best way to bake them, use a Dutch oven.

When they're done, cut off the excess wafer around the edges of each cookie, which will turn out of quite high quality.

621. CIALDONI (SWEET WAFERS)

Put in a saucepan:

80 grams (about 2-2/3 ounces) of flour
30 grams (about one ounce) of blond sugar
20 grams (about 2/3 of an ounce) of virgin lard, barely tepid
seven tablespoons cold water

First dissolve the flour and sugar in the water, then add the lard.

Put a waffle iron over a hot burner, and when it's nice and hot open it and pour in half a tablespoon of the batter at a time. Press the two sides of the iron together, hold over the fire first on one side and then on the other, use a knife to remove the excess batter that has oozed out, and open the iron when you know that the wafer has become light brown. Loosen it a bit on one side with a knife, and then, using a little rod or just your hands, roll it up right away, on the iron itself or on a cloth spread out on the hearth. This last operation must be done very quickly, because once the wafer has cooled you won't be able to roll it up.

If the wafers stick to the waffle iron, grease it from time to time with lard, and if they don't come out whole, add a little more flour.

You already know that sweet wafers can be served by themselves; but it's better to accompany them with whipped cream or even with milk *brûlé* (recipe 692) or Portuguese-style milk (recipe 693).

622. FAVE ALLA ROMANA O DEI MORTI (ROMAN-STYLE SWEET FAVA BEANS, OR DEAD MEN'S BEANS)

These sweets are usually made for the Day of the Dead, and they take the place of the *baggiana*, the garden-variety fava bean, which is typically cooked in water with a ham bone for this occasion. This custom must have originated in antiquity, since the fava bean was used as an offering to the Fates, Pluto, and Persephone, and was famous for the superstitious ceremonies in which it was used. The ancient Egyptians abstained from eating the fava; they didn't plant it, nor did they touch it with their hands. Their priests wouldn't even dare to look upon it, deeming it a vile thing. Fava beans, especially black favas, were used as a funeral offering because it was believed that they contained the souls of the dead, and were similar to the gates of Hell.

During the feasts of the *Lemures*,[113] people would spit out black fava beans while beating a copper pot, to chase out of their homes the spirits of their ancestors, the souls of the departed, and the infernal deities.

Festus[114] claimed that there was a funereal sign on the flowers of this legume; and they say that that the custom of offering fava beans to the dead was one of the reasons that Pythagoras ordered his students to abstain from eating them; another reason was to prevent them from getting involved in government affairs, since fava beans were used for balloting in elections.

There are several ways to make sweet favas. Here are three different recipes: the first two are family style; the third is more refined.

First recipe

200 grams (about 7 ounces) of flour
100 grams (about 3-1/2 ounces) of sugar

113 Shades, ghosts of the departed.
114 Pompeius Festus, a Roman grammarian of the fourth century A.D.

100 grams (about 3-1/2 ounces) of sweet almonds
30 grams (about one ounce) of butter
1 egg
a dash of lemon zest, or cinnamon, or orange-flower water

Second recipe

200 grams (about 7 ounces) of sweet almonds
100 grams (about 3-1/2 ounces) of flour
100 grams (about 3-1/2 ounces) of sugar
30 grams (about 1 ounce) of butter
1 egg
flavoring, as above

Third recipe

200 grams (about 7 ounces) of sweet almonds
200 grams (about 7 ounces) of confectioners' sugar
2 egg whites
lemon zest or other flavoring

For the first two recipes, blanch the almonds and crush them with the sugar until they are half as big as a grain of rice. Put them in the middle of the flour along with the other ingredients, and make a soft dough using as much rosolio or brandy as necessary. Then make the dough into small pastries shaped like large fava bean; you should get 60 or 70 for each recipe. Arrange in a baking pan greased with lard or butter and dusted with flour; gild with egg yolk. Bake in the oven or Dutch oven. Remember that since they are so small, they bake very quickly. For the third recipe, dry the almonds in the sun or on the fire and crush them very fine in a mortar, adding the egg whites a little at a time. Lastly, add the sugar and, using your hand, mix together. Pour the dough onto a pastry board over a thin layer of flour. Shape into a long roll and cut it into forty or more pieces. Shape like fava beans and bake as in the preceding recipes.

623. COTOGNATA
(QUINCE JELLY)

3 kilos (about 6 pounds) of quinces
2 kilos (about 4 pounds) of fine white sugar

Cover the quinces with water and put them on the fire; when they begin to shrivel, remove from the fire, peel, and grate them as best you can to remove all the pulp, which you will then strain through a sieve. Put back on the fire with the sugar, and stir constantly so that it doesn't stick. Seven or eight minutes cooking time should be sufficient, but the moment it starts to fall in threads from a wooden spoon, remove it from the fire. If you put it in jars, you can use it as a jam; that way it will stay whiter than it does in the way I'll describe to you in recipe 741, but it will be less fragrant because some of the fruit's aroma is lost when you cook it in water.

To turn it into jelly, take a board and spread the quince paste on it to about the thickness of a coin and dry it in the sun; but cover it with a thin cloth, because flies and wasps just love it. When it's dry on top, cut it into the shape of little chocolate bars, and then use a knife to loosen them from the board and turn them over.

Should you want to give them unusual shapes, get some tin pastry cutters that are open on both sides, fill them with the quince paste, smooth them out, and carefully remove the excess from the edges of the pastry cutters; place them on a board and dry them as above.

You can also glaze them, if you wish. Boil 100 grams (about 3-1/2 ounces) of white sugar with two tablespoons of water, and when it has cooked enough to form a thread when you take a drop between two fingers, use a brush to spread each piece with this icing. If the sugar starts to thicken on you while you're icing the pieces (which it's good to do when it's not a humid day), put it back on the fire with another drop of water and bring it to a boil again. When the sugar glaze has dried on the sides and top, turn over the pieces and glaze the other side.

624. TORTELLI DI CECI
(CHICKPEA FRITTERS)

Here's a dish that's usually made during Lent.

Take 300 grams (about 10-1/2 ounces) of dried chickpeas (I specify dried, because in Tuscany they're sold softened in the water from salt cod).

Soak the chickpeas overnight in cool water, and the next morning add 7 or 8 dried chestnuts; put on the fire in an earthenware pan with cool water and 3 grams (about 1/10 of an ounce) of baking soda tied in a piece of cheesecloth. This is what people call "the secret trick," and it makes cooking chickpeas easier. Instead of baking soda, you can also use lye water: the evening before, put the chickpeas in any type of jar, and cover the mouth of the jar with a cloth on which you've placed a shovelful of ashes; pour boiling water through the cloth until the chickpeas are covered. The next morning, remove the chickpeas from the lye water and rinse thoroughly with cool water before you put them on the fire.

When the chickpeas are cooked, remove them from the water and strain them through a sieve while they're still piping hot, along with the chestnuts. If in spite of the "secret trick" with the baking soda or the lye water they're still too hard, crush them in a mortar. After you've strained them, season with a pinch of salt, enough cooked must[115] to soften the mixture, half a jar of Savignano mostarda[116] (or the relish described in recipe 788), 40 grams (about 1/3 of an ounce) of candied fruit in small pieces, a little sugar if the must hasn't sweetened the chickpeas enough, and two teaspoons of ground cinnamon.

If you don't have a horse, you try to get your donkey to trot: and in this case, if you have neither cooked must nor mostarda (for my tastes, the best mostarda is the one from the town of Savignano in the Romagna region), you can substitute 80 grams (about 2-2/3 ounces) of sugar for the former and 7 grams (less than 1/3 of an ounce) of powdered mustard dissolved in the hot water in which you cooked the chickpeas for the latter.

---

111 *Saba*, filtered, unfermented wine must, boiled down to a third of its original volume; see note to recipe 458.

112 A sweet relish somewhat similar to chutney. "Mostarda" should not be confused (as Italians themselves sometimes do) with mustard ("senape" in Italian).

Now we'll go on to the dough in which you'll put the filling. You can half the recipe for cenci, no. 595, or else use the following ingredients:

270 grams (about 9-1/2 ounces) of flour
20 grams (about 2/3 of an ounce) of butter
15 grams (about 1/2 of an ounce) of sugar
1 egg
about 3 tablespoons of white wine or Marsala
a pinch of salt

Roll out a sheet of dough about the thickness of half a coin and cut with the round, scalloped pastry cutter shown in recipe 614. Put plenty of filling in the disks of pastry, fold and press the edges together, and shape each one like a crescent moon. Fry in lard or oil, and when they're done, sprinkle with confectioners' sugar.

You can use the water from the chickpeas to make soup or to cook store-bought pasta, as they do in Tuscany.

These fritters are so good that nobody will guess that they're made with chickpeas.

625. FOCACCIA ALLA PORTOGHESE (PORTUGUESE-STYLE FLAT CAKE)

Here's a very delicate, dainty cake.

150 grams (about 5-1/4 ounces) of sweet almonds
150 grams (about 5-1/4 ounces) of sugar
50 grams (about 1-2/3 ounces) of potato flour
3 eggs
1-1/2 oranges

First beat the egg yolks with the sugar, add the flour and then the almonds, blanched and crushed fine and mixed with a tablespoon of the sugar. Squeeze the juice from the oranges and scrape the outer peel from only one of them, and add. Lastly, fold in the egg whites, beaten. Pour into a paper box a finger and a half deep greased with butter, and bake in the oven at a moderate temperature. After it's done, cover with a white icing as in recipe 789.

626. AMARETTI I (MACAROONS I)

250 grams (about 8-4/5 ounces) of white powdered sugar
100 grams (about 3-1/2 ounces) of sweet almonds
50 grams (about 1-2/3 ounces) of bitter almonds
2 egg whites

Blanch the almonds and dry in the sun or on the fire. Then chop very fine with a mezzaluna. Using a wooden spoon, beat the sugar and the egg whites for at least half an hour. Add the crushed almonds and work the mixture into a firm dough, with which you can form little balls the size of a small walnut. If the dough is too soft, add some more sugar, and if it's too hard, add some more egg white, beaten. If you'd like to give the macaroons a brownish color, stir a little burnt sugar into the mixture.

As you form the balls, which you'll flatten to a thickness of one centimeter (about half an inch), place them on wafers, or else on little pieces of paper, or in a baking pan greased with butter and dusted with a mixture of one part flour and one part confectioners' sugar. But be sure to keep the balls a good distance from each other, because they spread out quite a bit and puff up, remaining empty inside.

Bake in the oven at moderate heat.

627. AMARETTI II (MACAROONS II)

Here's another recipe for macaroons that I think are better than the ones in the preceding recipe, and they're easier to make.

300 grams (about 10-1/2 ounces) of confectioners' sugar
180 grams (about 6-1/3 ounces) of sweet almonds
20 grams (about 2/3 of an ounce) of bitter almonds
2 egg whites

Blanch the almonds and dry in the sun or on the fire; then crush fine in a mortar with one egg white, added a little at a time. Once this is done, mix in half the sugar, and crumble the mixture with one hand. Then pour it into a bowl, and continuing to work it with your hand so that it blends well, add half an egg white, then the other half of the sugar, and then the last half egg white.

In this way you'll get a smooth mixture that's just the right consistency, which you can shape into a roll and slice into equal pieces. Pick them up one by one (moisten your hands so that they don't stick) and form little balls about the size of walnuts. Flatten the balls until they're a centimeter (about half an inch) thick and then proceed as in the last recipe, but sprinkle lightly with confectioners' sugar before you put them in a hot oven. I say oven and not Dutch oven, which wouldn't do for this dough.

You should get about thirty macaroons with this recipe.

628. PASTICCINI DI MARZAPANE (MARZIPAN PASTRIES)

Make a shortcrust pastry dough with recipe 589 C.

Make a marzipan like the one in recipe 579, with the following proportions:

180 grams (about 6-1/3 ounces) of blanched sweet almonds and 3 bitter almonds
150 grams (about 5-1/4 ounces) of sugar
25 grams (about 4/5 of an ounce) of butter
25 grams (about 4/5 of an ounce) of candied orange
an egg yolk
several tablespoons of water

Use little molds like the ones for individual brioches, or somewhat smaller, which would be better. Grease the molds with butter, line with a layer of the shortcrust pastry about as thick as a coin, fill will the marzipan, fold the edges of the pastry dough over, moisten the edges with water, cover with more pastry dough, gild the top, bake in the oven or Dutch oven and afterwards sprinkle with confectioners' sugar.

With these amounts you will be able to make between 16 and 18 pastries.

629. PASTICCINI DI SEMOLINO
(SEMOLINA PASTRIES)

180 grams (about 6-1/3 ounces) of semolina
100 grams (about 3-1/2 ounces) of sugar
50 grams (about 1-2/3 ounces) of pine nuts
20 grams (about 2/3 of an ounce) of butter
8 deciliters (about 3-1/3 cups) of milk
4 eggs
a pinch of salt
lemon zest

Cook the semolina in the milk, and when it begins to thicken, pour in the pine nuts after crushing them in a mortar with the sugar. Then add the butter and the other ingredients, except for the eggs, which you'll keep for last when the mixture has cooled. From this point on, proceed as for the rice pastries in recipe 630.

With these amounts you can make 18 to 20 pastries.

Before serving, sprinkle with confectioners' sugar.

630. PASTICCINI DI RISO (RICE PASTRIES)

150 grams (about 5-1/4 ounces) of rice
70 grams (about 2-1/3 ounces) of sugar
30 grams (about 1 ounce) of butter
30 grams (about 1 ounce) of candied fruit
8 deciliters (about 3-1/3 cups) of milk
3 eggs
2 tablespoons of rum
a pinch of salt

Cook the rice thoroughly in the milk, stirring often so that it doesn't stick. When the rice is two-thirds cooked, pour in the sugar, butter, salt, and candied fruit, in tiny pieces. When the rice is done, let it cool and then add the rum, then the egg yolks, and lastly the egg whites, beaten.

Take little molds like the ones for individual brioches, grease well with butter, dust with bread crumbs, fill with the rice mixture and bake in a Dutch oven. They're better warm than cold.

You can make 12 to 14 pastries with these amounts.

631. PASTICCINI DI PASTA BEIGNET
(BEIGNET PASTRIES)

150 grams (about 5-1/4 ounces) of water
100 grams (about 3-1/2 ounces) of flour
10 grams (about 1/3 of an ounce) of butter
3 whole eggs and one yolk
salt, to taste

Once the water is boiling, pour all the flour in at once and begin stirring immediately. Add the butter, and keep over the flame for 10 minutes, stirring continuously. The dough should come out firm; stretch it out to the thickness of a finger and grind in a mortar with an egg to soften it somewhat. Once this is done, put it in a bowl and work it with a wooden spoon. Add the other eggs one at a time, beating until the whites are stiff. Don't stop mixing until it is the consistency of a smooth paste. Let sit for a couple of hours, and then drop by tablespoonfuls (there should be between ten and twelve) onto a baking pan greased with butter. Beat an egg yolk with a little bit of the white to make it more liquid and brush this on the beignets (this last step isn't really necessary), and then put in a nice hot oven. When they're done, use a pen knife to make a slit on one side, or a half circle on the bottom, so that you can fill them with pastry cream or fruit preserves; sprinkle with confectioners' sugar, and serve.

Remember that when you're mixing doughs that are supposed to puff up when baked, you should move the wooden spoon up and down rather than stirring in circles.

632. BRIGIDINI[117]
(BRIGETTINE COOKIES)

This is a sweet, or rather an amusing treat local to Tuscany, where it can be found at all the country fairs and festivals. You can see it being cooked in the open air in waffle irons.

2 eggs
120 grams (about 4-1/4 ounces) of sugar
10 grams (about 1 ounce) of aniseed
a pinch of salt
flour, as much as needed

Prepare a rather firm dough, kneading it on a pastry board, and shape into nut-sized nuggets which you will place in a waffle iron at an appropriate distance from one another. Turn the iron this way and that over a wood fire, and remove when brown.

633. DOLCE DI CHIARE D'UOVO (MERINGUE CAKE)

Should you ever have some leftover egg whites, you can use them to make the following dessert, which generally turns out well.

8 or 9 egg whites
300 grams (about 10-1/2 ounces) of Hungarian flour
150 grams (about 5-1/4 ounces) of confectioners' sugar
150 grams (about 5-1/4 ounces) of butter
100 grams (about 3-1/2 ounces) of small sultanas
10 grams (about 1/3 of an ounce) of cream of tartar
5 grams (about 1/5 of an ounce) of baking soda
a dash of vanilla sugar

Beat the egg whites until stiff, and then fold in the flour and the sugar; mix and then add the melted butter. When the mixture is thoroughly blended, add the cream of tartar and the baking powder, and lastly the sultanas.

　　Pour the mixture into a baking pan greased with butter and

117 First made in the convent of Santa Brigida in Pistoia; hence their name.

dusted with confectioners' sugar and flour. The cake should rise to a height of at least two fingers. Bake in the oven or a Dutch oven, and serve cold.

634. PASTINE PEL THE
(TEA COOKIES)

Mistress Wood, an amiable English lady, offered me tea with cookies she had made with her own hands, and had the courtesy, rarely found in pretentious chefs, of giving me the recipe for them. I shall now describe it for you, having first tested it personally.

440 grams (about 15-1/2 ounces) of Hungarian or extra fine flour
160 grams (about 5-2/3 ounces) of potato flour
160 grams (about 5-2/3 ounces) of confectioners' sugar
160 grams (about 5-2/3 ounces) of butter
2 egg whites
lukewarm milk, as needed

Mix the two types of flour and the sugar, and place the mixture in a mound on the pastry board. Make a hole in the middle of the mound, and drop in it the egg whites and butter (in small pats). Then first with a knife blade and later with your hands, blend the ingredients until you have a rather soft dough. Roll out the dough with the rolling pin in a sheet as thick as a large coin. Cut into disks like the ones described in recipe 7, poke little holes in them with a fork, and bake in a baking pan greased in butter in the oven or a Dutch oven.
　　Even half this recipe will yield a good number of cookies.

635. LINGUE DI GATTO (CAT TONGUES)

These tea cookies are taken from a Parisian recipe.

100 grams (about 3-1/2 ounces) of butter
100 grams (about 3-1/2 ounces) of white confectioners' sugar
100 grams (about 3-1/2 ounces) of Hungarian flour
1 egg white

Put the butter as is into a bowl, and begin to soften it with a wooden spoon. Then add the sugar, next the flour, and lastly the egg white, stirring all the while to blend the ingredients into a smooth dough. Place it in a pastry tube with an attachment having a 1 centimeter (about 1/2 an inch) round or square opening at the narrow end. Now squeeze out the dough onto a baking pan lightly greased with butter, forming finger-length segments. Keep them well apart, because they spread out as they melt. Bake in a Dutch oven at a moderate temperature. This recipe should yield about fifty cookies.

636. PANE DI SABBIA
(SAND CAKE)

Sand cake is another German sweet, and it sports this name because it crumbles like sand in the mouth. Consequently, it is generally served with tea, which makes it taste better.

Don't panic when you learn that it takes two hours of uninterrupted labor to make this pastry, and that you must make sure to work in a draft-free area of the kitchen and to turn the mixing spoon always in the same direction. Women, who are naturally patient, particularly those who take pleasure in whipping up desserts, are not put off by this, particularly if they have a second person's stout arms to assist them.

> 185 grams (about 6-1/2 ounces) of fresh butter
> 185 grams (about 6-1/2 ounces) of confectioners' sugar
> 125 grams (about 4-1/2 ounces) of rice flour
> 125 grams (about 4-1/2 ounces) of starch flour
> 60 grams (about 2 ounces) of potato flour
> 4 eggs
> the juice of 1/4 lemon
> 1 tablespoon of cognac
> 1 teaspoon of baking soda
> a dash of vanilla

Starch flour is simply ordinary starch ground up into a fine powder.

First beat the butter by itself, then add the egg yolks one at a time, stirring always in the same direction. Now mix in the sugar, then the cognac and the lemon juice, next the flours, and lastly the baking soda and the egg whites (beaten stiff). But add two table-spoons of the latter first to soften the dough, then slowly fold in the remainder. Put the mixture into an adequate-sized baking pan greased with butter and dusted with confectioners' sugar and flour. Bake in an oven or Dutch oven at a moderate heat for an hour or until done.

CAKES AND SPOON DESSERTS

Not to boast unduly, but to amuse the reader and satisfy the wish of an anonymous admirer, I here publish the following letter, which reached me on July 14, 1906 from Portoferraio, as I was correcting the galley proofs of the 10th edition of this cookbook.

Esteemed Mr. Artusi,

A poet gave me as a gift your lovely book *La scienza in cucina*, adding a few lines of verse, which I transcribe below. Perhaps they may be of use if you print another edition, which I hope you will do in the very near future.

> *Della salute è questo il breviario,*
> *L'apoteosi è qui della papilla:*
> *L'uom mercé sua può viver centenario*
> *Centellando la vita a stilla a stilla.*
> *Il solo gaudio uman (gli altri son giuochi)*
> *Dio lo commmise alla virtù de' cuochi;*
> *Onde sè stesso ogni infelice accusi*
> *Che non ha in casa il libro dell'Artusi;*
> *E dieci volte un asino si chiami*
> *Se a mente non ne sa tutti i dettami.*
> *Un ammiratore*

(This little manual is about health and well-being,
a true apotheosis of the taste buds,
Thanks to which a man can live a hundred years
Sipping life to the fullest drop by drop.

The only joy people have (the rest are a mockery)
God entrusted to the talent of cooks;
So that you have only yourself to blame
If you do not have *Artusi* on your shelves;
And you should call yourself an ass ten times over
If you have not learnt his precepts by heart.

An Admirer)

637. TORTA DI NOCI (WALNUT CAKE)

140 grams (about 5 ounces) of shelled walnuts
140 grams (about 5 ounces) of confectioners' sugar
140 grams (about 5 ounces) of chocolate, powdered or grated
20 grams (about 2/3 of an ounce) of candied citron
4 eggs
a dash of vanilla sugar

Grind the nuts and the sugar in a mortar until fine, then put in a bowl and mix in the chocolate, vanilla sugar, and eggs, first adding the yolks and the whites, beaten until stiff. Lastly stir in the candied citron, chopped up very fine.

Take a baking pan large enough for the finished dessert to be no more than two fingers high, grease it with butter, and coat with bread crumbs. Bake in the oven or a Dutch oven at moderate temperature. My dinner guests have found this cake to be delicious.

638. TORTA DI RISO (RICE CAKE)

1 liter (about 1 quart) of milk
200 grams (about 7 ounces) of rice
150 grams (about 5-1/4 ounces) of sugar
100 grams (about 3-1/2 ounces) of sweet almonds and 4 bitter
    almonds
30 grams (about 1 ounce) of candied citron
3 whole eggs
5 egg yolks
lemon zest
a pinch of salt

Blanch the almonds and grind them in a mortar with two table-spoons of the sugar.

Dice the candied citron very small.

Cook the rice in milk, leaving it rather firm, and then add the flavorings. When cooled, fold in the eggs. Place the mixture in a baking pan greased with butter and dusted with bread crumbs. Cook until firm in a warm oven or in a Dutch oven with fire above and below. The next day cut the cake into lozenge shapes, and only when you are about to serve it sprinkle confectioners' sugar on top.

639. TORTA DI RICOTTA
(RICOTTA CHEESECAKE)

This cake will turn out very similar in taste to the ricotta pudding described in recipe 663, but much more refined. It is the cake tra-ditionally served at peasant weddings in Romagna, and is superior to many of the prettified desserts prepared by professional pastry chefs.

500 grams (about 1 pound) of ricotta cheese
150 grams (about 5-1/4 ounces) of sugar
150 grams (about 5-1/4 ounces) of sweet almonds
4 or 5 bitter almonds
4 whole eggs
4 egg yolks
a dash of vanilla

This dessert is prepared like the pudding described in recipe 663. But it is a good idea to pass through a wire strainer the mixture you have made by grinding the almonds with an egg white in a mortar. Gener-ously grease a baking dish with lard and line it with a sheet of "crazy dough" (recipe 153). Then pour in the mixture, making a layer one and a half fingers deep, and bake in the oven or in a Dutch oven with fire above and below. I recommend very moderate heat, and the addi-tional safeguard of covering the mixture with a sheet of paper greased with butter: the beauty of the cake depends on its turning out white when baked. Once completely cooled, cut it into lozenge shapes in such a way that under every piece there is a wafer of crazy dough, which may be eaten or not, according to taste, as the crazy dough is used here simply as an embellishment and for tidiness' sake.

This recipe serves twelve or more people.

640. TORTA DI ZUCCA GIALLA
(PUMPKIN CAKE)

This cake is made in autumn or winter, when greengrocers have pumpkins for sale.

1 kilogram (about 2 pounds) of pumpkin
100 grams (about 3-1/2 ounces) of sweet almonds
100 grams (about 3-1/2 ounces) of sugar
30 grams (about 1 ounce) of butter
30 grams (about 1 ounce) of bread crumbs
1/2 liter (about 1/2 a quart) of milk
3 eggs
a pinch of salt
a dash of ground cinnamon

Peel the pumpkin, remove the tough filaments on the surface and grate over a kitchen towel. Pick up the towel by the four corners and squeeze tightly until you have removed most of the water in the pumpkin. The kilogram of pumpkin should be reduced to about 300 grams (about 10-1/2 ounces) in weight. Empty the contents into a pot and boil in the milk until done. This should take about 25 to 40 minutes, depending on the type of pumpkin you are using. In the meantime, crush the almonds (blanched) in a mortar together with the sugar until very fine. When the pumpkin is cooked, combine all the ingredients, except the eggs, which you will add later when the mixture has thoroughly cooled. As for the rest, follow the instructions for the ricotta cake described in the preceding recipe.

641. TORTA DI PATATE (POTATO CAKE)

Although we are dealing with the humble potato here, do not scoff at this cake, which is worth making. And if your dinner guests cannot detect the plebeian origins of this cake when they taste it, conceal it from them, for they would only scoff.

Many people eat more with their imagination than with their palate. Accordingly, never mention, at least until your guests have finished eating and digesting what you have served them, foods that are considered inferior for the sole reason that they are inexpensive or because they evoke associations that some people might find distasteful. Yet these very foods, when used well and handled correctly, make for good, tasty dishes. Let me now tell you a story on the subject. Once I found myself invited to dine with some close friends. Our host, to impress us, made a little joke about the roast he was serving, for he remarked: "None of you can complain about the way I am treating you today: we have three different varieties of roast meat: milk-fed veal, chicken and rabbit." At the word "rabbit" some of the guests turned up their noses, others seemed dumbfounded, and someone, a close friend of the family, said: "What on earth did you decide to feed us! At least you could have kept quiet. You've made me lose my appetite."

At another dinner party, when by chance the conversation turned to "porchetta"—a suckling pig of 50 to 60 kilograms (about 110 to 132 pounds), stuffed with spices and roasted whole on a spit—one lady cried out, "If I were offered such filth to eat, I could not possibly do it!" The host, stung by the aspersion she had cast on a dish that was held in high esteem in his part of the country, invited the woman a second time to his house, when he prepared a lovely cut of lean porchetta. She not only ate it but, believing it was milk-fed veal, thought that the roast tasted delicious. I could tell you many similar tales; but I cannot pass over in silence the case of a certain gentleman who, finding a particular pie quite delicious, ate enough for two days. But when he discovered that the pie was made of pumpkin, not only did he never eat it again, but he would also give it such a sinister look you would have thought the pie had seriously offended him.

Now here is the recipe for potato cake.

700 grams (about 1-1/2 pounds) of big starchy potatoes
150 grams (about 5-1/4 ounces) of sugar
70 grams (about 2-1/3 ounces) of sweet almonds and 3 bitter
*   almonds*
5 eggs
30 grams (about 1 ounce) of butter
a pinch of salt
a dash of lemon peel

Boil the potatoes (or better yet, steam them). Peel and purée, passing them through a strainer while they are still hot. Blanch the almonds and crush in a mortar together with the sugar, until you have a very fine paste. Then add this mixture and all the other ingredients to the potatoes, stirring everything with a wooden spoon for a whole hour, breaking in the eggs one at a time, and then pouring in the melted butter. Place the mixture in a baking pan greased with butter or lard and dusted with bread crumbs. Bake in the oven and serve cold.

642. TORTA ALLA MILANESE
(MILANESE PIE)

Due to the strange combination of ingredients in this pie, for a long time I was uncertain as to whether I should offer this recipe to the public, for it is not of sufficient caliber to appear at distinguished tables, and it is a little too expensive for family-style meals. In other respects, it is really not to be sneered at, and since some people may find it to their taste—I know that a family I am well acquainted with likes it because they make it very often—I shall describe it for you.

200 grams (about 7 ounces) of completely lean meat, stewed or
*   roasted, either beef or veal, free of membranes and gristle*
100 grams (about 3-1/2 ounces) of chocolate
100 grams (about 3-1/2 ounces) of sugar
50 grams (about 1-2/3 ounces) of butter
50 grams (about 1-2/3 ounces) of pine nuts
50 grams (about 1-2/3 ounces) of sultanas
25 grams (about 4/5 of an ounce) of candied citron, finely chopped

Mince the meat very finely with a mezzaluna. Roast the pine nuts. Soak the sultanas in Marsala and strain when you are about to use them.

Sauté the meat in the butter, stirring all the while so that it does not stick to the skillet. When it has turned a reddish color, remove from the fire and allow to cool.

Heat the chocolate, grated or finely chopped, in 3 tablespoons of water until it melts. Then add the sugar and pour the liquid over the meat, adding the pine nuts, the sultanas, and the candied citron, stirring well.

Now make a pie shell of shortcrust pastry, with the following ingredients:

170 grams (about 6 ounces) of wheat flour
80 grams (about 2-2/3 ounces) of corn flour
80 grams (about 2-2/3 ounces) of confectioners' sugar
70 grams (about 2-1/3 ounces) of butter
25 grams (about 4/5 of an ounce) of virgin lard
1 egg
white wine or Marsala, enough to blend the dough

Take an appropriately sized baking pan, so the mixture won't be more than a finger deep. Grease the pan with butter or lard and line it with a thin sheet of dough, pour in the mixture, then cover with another sheet of dough rolled out with a ridged rolling pin.

Gild the surface with egg yolk, bake in the oven or a Dutch oven, and serve cold.

643. TORTA DI SEMOLINO (SEMOLINA CAKE)

1 liter (about 1 quart) of milk
130 grams (about 4-1/2 ounces) of fine-grain semolina
130 grams (about 4-1/2 ounces) of sugar
100 grams (about 3-1/2 ounces) of sweet almonds and 3 bitter almonds
20 grams (about 2/3 of an ounce) of butter
4 eggs
scrapings from 1 lemon
a pinch of salt

Blanch the almonds in hot water and then crush them very fine in a mortar with all the sugar, added a tablespoon at a time.

Cook the semolina in the milk. Before removing it from the fire, add the butter and almonds which, having been crushed with the sugar, will quickly dissolve. Then salt the mixture and wait until it has cooled to lukewarm before folding in the eggs, beaten separately. Place the mixture in a baking pan greased with butter and dusted with bread crumbs. Note that the baking pan should be of such a size that the cake will be one and a half fingers deep, or two at the most. Bake in the oven or a Dutch oven. Remove from the pan when cool and serve whole or cut into lozenge shapes.

644. TORTA DI PANE BRUNO ALLA TEDESCA (GERMAN-STYLE BROWN BREAD CAKE)

This is a cake well worth the effort. I advise you try it.

125 grams (about 4-1/2 ounces) of sweet almonds
125 grams (about 4-1/2 ounces) of sugar
4 tablespoons of cognac
3 heaping tablespoons of grated rye bread crust
5 eggs

First mix the sugar and two of the eggs, whole, then add the almonds, which you have blanched and crushed very fine in a mortar with a tablespoon of the sugar. Stir the mixture, then add the rye bread crumbs, three egg yolks, and lastly the cognac. Beat the three remaining egg whites until stiff and fold them in. Prepare a baking pan of the appropriate size, grease it with butter and dust it with confectioners' sugar and flour. Pour the mixture in the baking pan and bake in the oven or a Dutch oven. When done, cover with a thin icing prepared like the one described in recipe 645, or with a chocolate frosting prepared as follows.

Put on the fire 30 grams (about 1 ounce) of butter and 100 grams (about 3-1/2 ounces) of finely chopped chocolate. When nicely dissolved, add 30 grams (about 1 ounce) of confectioners' sugar. Allow the mixture to cool a little, and then spread evenly over the cake.

If I were not afraid of annoying the reader, here would be an opportune moment for another digression on German cooking.[118]

As long as I live, I will never forget the array of foods spread out on a big hotel's buffet at the spa town of Levico.[119] From the fried foods and the boiled dishes, all the way to the roasts, all swam in gallons of the same sauce, that always tasted and smelled alike, with what delight to the stomach you can just imagine. And just to add to the torture, very often these dishes were served accompanied by a timbale[120] of angel hair pasta—angel hair, you understand, the thinnest pasta on the planet!—which when prepared in this way must suffer a doubly long cooking time: a bloody mess.

How utterly at odds with our Italian way of doing things! My cook has standing orders to remove angel hair from the water when it has barely begun to boil, and I am already waiting at the table.

Italian cuisine can rival the French, and in some respects actually surpasses it. However, due to the hordes of invading foreigners who bring us, apparently, about 300 million lire annually and, according to rough calculations, an extra 200 million lire in gold during the Jubilee Year of 1900, our cuisine is slowly beginning to lose its special character in the swirl of wandering nations. These unfortunate changes to our diet have already begun to appear, particularly in the large cities and in those areas heavily frequented by foreigners. I recently became convinced of this on a trip to Pompeii, where my traveling companion and I were preceded into a restaurant by a group of German tourists, both male and female, and were served in the same fashion as they were. When the proprietor later came up and courteously asked how we liked our dinners, I took the liberty of commenting on the

118 See recipes 560 and 645.

119 Levico is a resort town in the Alto Adige, a northern region that includes the South Tyrol and where many Austrian traditions persist.

120 A timbale is a small drum-shaped metal mold, which is filled with pasta along with cheese, chicken, fish, meat, etc., and then is either steamed or boiled for a considerable time. See recipe 279.

nauseating slop of seasonings we had just been served. He replied, "Our cooking has to please these foreigners, since this is how we make our living." Perhaps this is the same reason Bolognese cuisine has begun to change, as I have heard, and no longer deserves the reputation it once had.

645. TORTA TEDESCA (GERMAN CAKE)

Here is another cake from Germany, as tasty as the one described in the preceding recipe; indeed, it's excellent.

Our grandfathers used to tell how toward the end of the 1700s, when the Germans invaded our country, there was still something uncivilized in their customs. For example, they used to provoke everyone's horror by preparing broth with tallow candles that they plunged in a pot of boiling water, then squeezing out the wicks. But when, unfortunately, they descended on us again in 1849, they appeared much more civilized. Then tallow could only be seen on Croat militiamen's long mustachios, which were smeared with it so that they could be twisted and their tips rolled to finger length points that stood up straight and stiff. Nonetheless, from what visitors to that country tell me, tallow has kept a place in German cooking, a cuisine which Italians find in the worst possible taste and positively nauseating, as it uses all manner of fat and makes slop-like soups utterly lacking in flavor.

On the other hand, however, everybody agrees Germans can make delicious desserts. You personally, dear reader, may judge for yourself the truth of this assertion, both from the cake I am about to describe, as well as from some of the other desserts born in Germany that I have offered you in this treatise of mine.

250 grams (about 8-4/5 ounces) of sugar
125 grams (about 4-1/2 ounces) of flour
125 grams (about 4-1/2 ounces) of sweet almonds
100 grams (about 3-1/2 ounces) of butter
15 grams (about 1/2 an ounce) of cream of tartar
5 grams (about 1/5 of an ounce) of baking soda
8 egg yolks

5 egg whites
a dash of vanilla

Blanch the almonds, dry them well in the sun or on the fire, and then crush in a mortar until very fine, adding one of the egg whites. Beat the butter alone with a wooden spoon; in wintertime soften it a little first in *bain-marie*. Add the egg yolks one at a time, then the sugar and blend everything well for at least half an hour. Then add the almonds to the mixture and stir some more. Then fold in the four egg whites (beaten until stiff) and the flour, which you will sift on top of the mixture, stirring gently. Add the cream of tartar and the baking soda at the last, as they will make the cake lighter and softer. Bake in a baking pan well greased with cold butter and lightly dusted with confectioners' sugar and flour. The pan should not be too full.

The only way to blend the almonds satisfactorily into the mixture is to pour a portion of the mixture into the mortar over the almonds and then crush with the pestle.

Now that you have made the cloak, it is time to fashion the hood, which is a light icing that you spread on top of the cake. Here is what you will need:

100 grams (about 3-1/2 ounces) of butter
100 grams (about 3-1/2 ounces) of confectioners' sugar
30 grams (about 1 ounce) of finely ground coffee

Bring the ground coffee to a boil in very little water until you get just two or three tablespoons of clear but very strong coffee. Beat the butter for half an hour (in wintertime softening it first in *bain-marie*), turning the spoon always in the same direction. Add the sugar and stir some more. Finally mix in the coffee a little at a time, in half teaspoons. Stop when you the can clearly taste the coffee flavor. Pour this mixture over the cake after it has cooled, and spread it out evenly with a table knife. To make it uniform and smooth, pass a hot spatula just above the icing.

Normally, this very delicately flavored icing should have the color of *café-au-lait*. If you like, instead of coffee you can use melted chocolate, as described in the preceding recipe for German-style brown bread cake.

646. TORTA DI MANDORLE E CIOCCOLATA
(CHOCOLATE ALMOND CAKE)

For chocolate lovers, this is a delicious cake.

150 grams (about 5-1/4 ounces) of almonds
150 grams (about 5-1/4 ounces) of sugar
100 grams (about 3-1/2 ounces) of chocolate
60 grams (about 2 ounces) of potato flour
50 grams (about 1-2/3 ounces) of butter
3 deciliters (about 1-1/4 cups) of milk
4 eggs
a dash of vanilla sugar

Blanch the almonds, dry well in the sun or over the fire, and then crush them very finely in a mortar with a third of the sugar. Put on the fire and mix the butter, the potato flour, and the milk added a little at a time. When this mixture has acquired the right consistency, add the chocolate (grated), the remaining sugar and, when these two ingredients have been absorbed, the crushed almonds, stirring constantly. Finally, when all the mixture is thoroughly blended stir in the vanilla sugar. Allow to cool before folding in the eggs, beaten separately.

Using 100 grams (about 3-1/2 ounces) of flour, prepare the "crazy dough" described in recipe 153, and then follow recipe 639 for ricotta cheesecake, ensuring that the mixture is about one finger deep when poured in the baking pan. Bake in a Dutch oven and, like the ricotta cake, cut in lozenge shapes when it has cooled.

647. PASTICCINI DI PASTA BEIGNET COPERTI DI
CIOCCOLATA (CHOCOLATE-COVERED BEIGNET PASTRIES)

Follow recipe 631, but keep the pastries smaller so that you will get between 20 and 23 of them. Fill them with custard or pastry cream (recipe 685), whipped cream, or fruit preserves.

Put the following ingredients in a pot to make chocolate and whisk them together over the fire:

120 grams (about 4-1/4 ounces) of chocolate
50 grams (about 1-2/3 ounces) of powdered sugar
1 deciliter (about 2/5 of a cup) of water

When the mixture is nice and fluffy, like hot chocolate to be served in a cup, pour it boiling hot over the pastries layer by layer. Then arrange them in a pretty little pile on a platter.

It is wise to make this dish the same day you intend to serve it, because otherwise the pastries will get hard.

This recipe serves six people.

648. DOLCE ROMA (ROME CAKE)

A gentleman whom I do not have the pleasure of knowing personally kindly sent me this recipe from Rome, and I am very grateful to him for it for two reasons: first because this is a dessert of very elegant appearance and flavor, and second because he described it in such a way that I had no difficulty at all testing the recipe. One thing was missing, however, and that was a name for it, since it had none. Thus, considering the nobility of its provenance, I felt it my duty to associate this dessert with Turin Cake and Florence Cake, naming it after the city that one day will be as famous in the world as it once was in Antiquity.

Select quality apples, not too ripe and of average size. Weigh out 600 grams (about 1-1/3 of a pound), which should amount to no more than five or six apples. Remove the cores with a hollow tin corer, and peel. Then cook in 2 deciliters (about 4/5 of a cup) of white wine and 130 grams (about 4-1/2 ounces) of sugar, taking care not to break the apples when you turn them as they cook, and not to overcook them. When done, remove them from the pot and arrange them upright in a platter nice enough to use for serving but ovenproof as well. Pour over them a custard made of the following ingredients:

4 deciliters (about 1-2/3 cups) of milk
3 egg yolks
70 grams (about 2-1/3 ounces) of sugar
20 grams (about 2/3 of an ounce) of flour
a dash of vanilla sugar

Now whisk the three remaining egg whites. When they are quite stiff, add 20 grams (about 2/3 of an ounce) of confectioners' sugar and cover the custard with it. Then place the cake in a Dutch oven or on the stove under the lid of the Dutch oven, with fire above and a low fire below, to brown the surface of the cake. Before serving, dab the cake with the thick syrup left over from cooking the apples, using a baker's brush.

This recipe serves seven to eight people.

649. DOLCE TORINO (TURIN CAKE)

Prepare this dessert on a tray or platter and shape it into a square.

100 grams (about 3-1/2 ounce) of ladyfingers
100 grams (about 3-1/2 ounce) of chocolate
100 grams (about 3-1/2 ounce) of fresh butter
70 grams (about 2-1/3 ounces) of confectioners' sugar
1 egg yolk
2 tablespoons of milk
a dash of vanilla sugar

Cut the ladyfingers in half lengthwise and soak in rosolio, or, better yet, soak one half of the biscuit in rosolio and the other in alkermes,[121] so that you will be able to arrange them in alternating color bands, which will make for a more handsome display.

Beat together the butter, the sugar, and the egg yolk; then heat the chocolate (grated or chopped) in milk. When it has melted, pour the hot liquid over the softened butter mixture, then add the vanilla sugar, stirring constantly to blend all the ingredients well and obtain a nice smooth mixture.

Arrange on a platter the first layer of the ladyfingers and coat them lightly with the mixture. Then place another layer over the first and coat them once again with the mixture; add a third layer, repeating the procedure. Then pour the remaining mixture on top and all along the sides, making this last layer as even and uniform as you can. The next day, before serving, smooth out the surface of the

---

121 See recipe 618 and note.

cake with the blade of a knife heated over the fire. Next, if you wish, you can make a garnish of pistachios or lightly roasted hazelnuts, chopped as fine as possible, which you will sprinkle over the cake.

40 grams (about 1-1/3 ounces) of hazelnuts weighed with their shells or 15 grams (about 1/2 an ounce) of pistachios will suffice. You should already know that these nuts must be blanched in hot water.

This recipe serves six to seven people.

650. DOLCE FIRENZE (FLORENCE CAKE)

I discovered this dessert in the ancient and beautiful city of flowers, but as no one has taken the trouble to give it a name, I will venture to call it Florence Cake. If, due to its humble nature, it does not bring sufficient honor to such an illustrious city, it will ask your pardon, saying: "Adopt me as a dish for your family and I will sweeten your palates at little cost."

100 grams (about 3-1/2 ounces) of sugar
60 grams (about 2 ounces) of extra fine bread
40 grams (about 1-1/3 ounces) of small sultanas
3 eggs
butter, as needed
1/2 liter (about 1/2 a quart) of milk
lemon zest

Slice the bread thin, toast lightly, butter both sides while still hot, and place in a bowl decent enough to take to the table. Sprinkle the sultanas and the grated lemon peel over the sliced bread. Whisk the eggs in a saucepan together with the sugar and then combine with the milk. Pour this mixture over the ingredients already in the bowl—do not stir. To cook, place on the stove with little heat below and cover with the lid of the Dutch oven, with fire above. Serve hot.

This recipe serves five people.

651. SFORMATO COGLI AMARETTI
COPERTO DI ZABAIONE
(MACAROON PUDDING COVERED WITH ZABAIONE)

100 grams (about 3-1/2 ounces) of macaroons
100 grams (about 3-1/2 ounces) of sugar
80 grams (about 2-2/3 ounces) of potato flour
1/2 liter (about 1/2 a quart) of milk
3 eggs

Put the sugar and the potato flour in a saucepan and pour in the cold milk, a little at a time.

Crush the macaroons in a mortar, reducing them to a powder. If, because of their consistency, this is not possible, moisten them with a little milk, pass through a strainer and then combine with the rest of the mixture, which you will cook over the fire until firm. Remove from the fire and wait for it to cool somewhat, then add the eggs, first the yolks and then the whites, beaten until stiff. Grease a metal mold with a hole in the middle with cold butter, pour the mixture inside, and bake in a Dutch oven. When done, fill the middle and cover it with the zabaione described in recipe 684, and send to the table.

652. SFORMATO DI FARINA DOLCE
(CHESTNUT FLOUR PUDDING)

A gentleman of distinguished lineage from Barga—whom I do not have the pleasure of knowing personally, but who has taken a fancy (as he is so kind to say) to this book of mine—wishing to show his appreciation, sent me the present recipe, which I believe worthy of being published and even lauded.

200 grams (about 7 ounces) of chestnut flour
50 grams (about 1-2/3 ounces) of chocolate
30 grams (about 1 ounce) of sugar
25 grams (about 4/5 of an ounce) of butter
20 grams (about 2/3 of an ounce) of candied citron
12 sweet almonds and a few pistachios

1/2 liter (about 1/2 a quart) of milk
3 eggs
150 grams (about 5-1/4 ounces) of whipped cream with a dash of
vanilla

First blanch the almonds and the pistachios, cut the latter in half, and the former into little strips or chunks and then toast them. Mince the candied fruit into small pieces.

Melt the chocolate in 1 deciliter (about 2/5 of a cup) of the milk, then add the sugar and the butter, and set aside. Place the flour in a baking pan and add the rest of the milk a little at a time, stirring all the while to prevent lumps. Then add the chocolate and cook over the fire. When done, allow to cool before adding the eggs (first the yolks, then the whites, beaten until stiff), and lastly the almonds, the pistachios and the candied citron. Now take a metal mold with a hole in the middle, grease it with cold butter, and pour in the mixture. Bake in *bain-marie* until the pudding has firmed up. Before removing from the mold, place cracked ice mixed with salt all around the mold to chill the pudding, then send to the table filled with the vanilla flavored whipped cream.

This recipe serves seven to eight people.

653. DOLCE DI MARRONI
CON PANNA MONTATA
(CHESTNUT CAKE WITH WHIPPED CREAM)

500 grams (about 1 pound) or about 30 large whole chestnuts
130 grams (about 4-1/2 ounces) of confectioners' sugar
60 grams (about 2 ounces) of chocolate
3 tablespoons of citron cordial

Cook the chestnuts in water, just as you would normally do when making boiled chestnuts. When done, peel and purée them while still hot. Reduce the chocolate to a powder, then combine all the ingredients and make a paste. Take a large round decent-looking platter and place a small coffee saucer upside down in the middle of it. Place a strainer with a soft mesh on top of the saucer and pass the mixture through it, rotating the platter from time to time, so that the mixture is distributed evenly. When you have completed this

vin Santo

J. Meltzer   2002

procedure, carefully remove the saucer and fill the empty space left in the middle of the platter with 300 grams (about 10-1/2 ounces) of whipped cream.

This recipe serves eight people.

654. BISCOTTI PUERPERALI
(COOKIES FOR BIRTHING MOTHERS)

Those of the sex that is rightly called gentle, not so much because of the gentleness of their manners as for the refined moral instinct that by nature inclines them to do whatever it takes to uplift and console suffering humanity, have contributed greatly to making my catalogue of recipes rich and varied.

A lady from Conegliano writes to me to express her surprise at not finding in my book the "pinza dell'Epifania" (Epiphany Sweetbread) and—don't laugh—"biscottini puerperali" (Cookies for Birthing Mothers), two items which according to her are of some importance. This good woman states that on the eve of the feast of the Epiphany, peasant families in the hills and throughout the countryside around her lovely town of Conegliano set huge bonfires and make merry through the night in their farmyards and recite prayers designed to invoke the powers of fructifying Heaven to assure the success of the next harvest. Then they go into their homes delighted with themselves, where "la pinza sotto il camin annaffiata con del buon vin" ("sweetbread by the fireplace, washed down with good wine") awaits them.[122]

122 Neither Artusi nor his informant seem to be aware of this holiday's real significance. In fact what they are describing is the famous Twelfth Night Fires, kindled 12 days after Christmas to herald the sun's return following the Winter Solstice. And very typically, the fires are accompanied by the sort of festivities and prayers mentioned here. In reality this so-called Feast of the Epiphany was stolen or rather "appropriated" by the Christians, as was so much of their myth and ritual, from the Old Religion, here specifically from the Celtic worship of *Sol Invictus* (The Invincible Sun); this holiday has been discussed at length in James Frazer's *Golden Bough*. The Veneto region in Northeastern Italy (where the town of Conegliano is located) was part of ancient Cisalpine Gaul, and it would seem, in light of Artusi's report, that Celtic rituals still survived in the region which is also, and without contradiction, one of the most fervently Catholic parts of the country. We might add that eggs, as seeds of future life, are fare appropriately eaten during a festival intended to honor the agricultural cycle.

While the good country folk are eating their sweetbread—which I will not describe here because it is a dish suitable only to those folk and to the climate of they live in—I shall now return, as the lady demands, to the "Biscuits for Birthing Mothers," which she considers nourishing and delicate, just the thing for restoring the strength of women who have grown weak bringing a baby into the world.

8 egg yolks
150 grams (about 5-1/4 ounces) of confectioners' sugar
40 grams (about 1-1/3 ounces) of powdered cocoa
40 grams (about 1-1/3 ounces) of butter
a dash of vanilla sugar

Place these ingredients in a bowl, and then stir with a wooden spoon for more than fifteen minutes. Then distribute the mixture equally into four paper boxes, each 8 centimeters long (about 3-1/4 inches) and 6 centimeters (about 2-2/5 inches) wide. Place these in a covered copper baking pan with very little heat above and below, so that the mixture solidifies without forming a crust, because you are supposed to eat this sweet with a spoon. For this reason, the name "cookies" is quite inappropriate.

655. RIBES ALL'INGLESE
(CURRANTS ENGLISH STYLE)

300 grams (about 10-1/2 ounces) of red currants
120 grams (about 4-1/4 ounces) of sugar
2 deciliters (about 4/5 of a cup) of water

Remove the stems from the currants and put them on the fire in the water. When they start to boil, add the sugar. Two minutes boiling time is enough, because the currants must remain whole. Place in a compote dish and serve cold like stewed fruit. The seeds, if you do not wish to swallow them, should be sucked and spat out.

Using the same method of preparation, you may also prepare maraschino cherries without removing the pit, boiling them with a little piece of cinnamon.

656. PRUGNE GIULEBBATE
(PRUNES IN AROMATIC SYRUP)

Use Bosnian prunes, which are large, long and pulpy, unlike the small round and lean Marseille prunes, which are covered with a white fuzz the Florentines call "flower" and are unsuited to this dish.

Wash and soak 500 grams (about 1 pound) of Bosnian prunes for two hours in cold water, then strain and put on the fire with the following ingredients:

4 deciliters (about 1-2/3 cups) of good red wine
2 deciliter (about 4/5 of a cup) of water
1 small glass of Marsala
100 grams (about 3-1/2 ounces) of white sugar
a little piece of cinnamon

Allow to simmer for half an hour in a covered saucepan. That should be long enough. But before removing from the fire, check to see if the prunes are sufficiently soft, because the length of cooking time will depend on the quality of the fruit you use.

Strain the prunes and place in the bowl you want to serve them in. The remaining syrup should be returned to the fire for approximately 8 to 10 minutes more, in an uncovered saucepan until it thickens. Then pour it over the prunes. For the cinnamon, which seems to me the spice best suited to this dish, you may substitute a dash of vanilla, or citron or orange peel.

This is a dessert that keeps for a long time and has a delicate flavor that will especially delight the ladies. At the risk of sounding like a grumbler, I should like to touch upon the subject of Italian industry once again, and point out that Bosnian prunes cost 1.5 lire per kilogram, whereas I am certain that here in Italy we could cultivate the kind of plum that best lends itself to being dried and sold for such uses as this.

657. BUDINO DI SEMOLINO
(SEMOLINA PUDDING)

8 deciliters (about 3-1/3 cups) of milk
150 grams (about 5-1/4 ounces) of semolina
100 grams (about 3-1/2 ounces) of sugar
4 eggs
3 tablespoons of rum
a pinch of salt
lemon zest

Some people add pieces of candied fruit, but an excess of flavorings sometimes spoils the result. After mixing everything together and removing from the fire, place in a smooth or decorated mold greased with butter and dusted with bread crumbs. Then bake as follows.

If you don't have an oven or Dutch oven, puddings can be cooked on the hearth.

Serve this pudding hot.

658. BUDINO DI SEMOLINO E CONSERVE
(SEMOLINA AND FRUIT PRESERVE PUDDING)

1/2 liter (about 1/2 a quart) of milk
130 grams (about 4-1/2 ounces) of semolina
15 grams (about 1/2 an ounce) of butter
2 eggs
a pinch of salt
lemon zest
different fruit preserves

Cook the semolina in the milk, add the sugar and the butter when it starts to boil, and, when you remove it from the fire, add the lemon zest and the salt. Fold in the eggs while the mixture is still warm and mix thoroughly. Prepare a smooth or decorated mold, greasing it with butter and dusting it with bread crumbs. Then pour in the mixture (after it has cooled) a little at a time, adding in between the layers the fruit preserves, either chopped in small pieces or in small spoonfuls, depending on whether they are firm or runny. However, make sure that the fruit preserves don't touch the sides of the mold because otherwise they will stick to the metal. And don't use too much, or the pudding will be sickeningly sweet. Place the mold in a Dutch oven in your hearth to bake, then serve hot.

The preserves that to my taste are best here are raspberry and quince, but you can also use apricot, currant and peach.

If you are serving eight to ten people, double the quantities.

659. BUDINO DI FARINA DI RISO
(RICE FLOUR PUDDING)

This very simple dessert possesses, in my opinion, a very delicate flavor, and although almost everyone has tried it at one time or another, it would not hurt to learn the exact ingredients and quantities, which I think should not be increased or decreased.

1 liter (about 1 quart) of milk
200 grams (about 7 ounces) of rice flour
120 grams (about 4-1/4 ounces) of sugar
20 grams (about 2/3 of an ounce) of butter
6 eggs
a pinch of salt
a dash of vanilla

First, dissolve the rice flour in a fourth of the cold milk; then put on the fire. When the mixture starts to boil, add a little more warm milk, and finally pour in the rest of the milk when it is at a full boil. This is to prevent lumps from forming. When cooked, add the sugar, the butter and the salt. Remove from the fire and wait until lukewarm before folding in the eggs and the vanilla. Now bake the pudding as in the previous recipe.

This recipe, which in all likelihood is not very old, makes me think that dishes, too, are subject to fashions, and that tastes change in accordance with progress and civilization. Now we prize light cuisine and dishes that are pleasing to the eye, and perhaps there will come a time when many of the dishes I consider good will be replaced by others even better. The sweet, heavy wines of an earlier era have given way to the dry, full-bodied vintages of today; the baked goose stuffed with garlic and quinces, regarded as a delicacy in 1300, has been replaced by turkey fattened domestically and stuffed with truffles, and by capon in galantine.[123] In the olden days, on great occasions they used to serve boiled or roasted peacock, still arrayed in all its plumage, which was removed before preparing the bird and replaced after the bird was cooked. Then the peacock was served surrounded by aspics of various shapes, colored with mineral powders injurious to the health, and flavored with such spices as cumin and scented red clay ("bucchero")[124A]—about which I will tell you shortly.

In Florence, sweet pastries and baked goods remained rather primitive and simple until the late 16th century, when a company of Lombards arrived and set about baking pies, little cakes, puffy turnovers and other pastries made with eggs, butter, milk, sugar, and honey. But before that, ancient records mention only the donkey-meat pies Malatesta gave as gifts to his friends during the siege of Florence, when shortages of every kind of food, particularly meats, were acute.[124B]

As for bucchero, there was a time when Spain was the fashion trendsetter, just as France is today, and all nations tried to imitate its style of cuisine and flavoring. Thus, at the end of the 17th century and the beginning of the 18th, Spanish-style fragrances and aromas became extremely popular. Above all fragrances, however, bucchero turned everyone's head, and so widespread was its use that ultimately spice merchants[125] and stewards started putting it in tablets and foodstuffs, just as is done with vanilla today. From what fabulous substance was bucchero extracted and what did it taste like? You will be stunned

123 See Artusi's recipe for this dish (366).
124A The Italian "bucchero" derives from Spanish *bucaro* (Portuguese *pucaro*). Imported from the Indies and Portugal, it consisted of scented bole clay, came in various hues, and was used for making fine chinaware. The rage for bucchero spread to Italy in the late 1600s.
124B Artusi is referring to the famous siege of Florence by the imperial army of Charles V in the Spring of 1530, when Malatesta Baglione was commander of the Florence forces.
125 In Artusi's day, "speziali" could fulfill the role of grocer and pharmacist as well.

when you hear. Now judge for yourself the extravagant folly of tastes and people! Bucchero consisted of powdered shards of pottery, and its odor resembled that which the earth scorched by the summer sun exhales when rains fall. It is the same smell of earth that is given off by those dark-red, thin and brittle vases called buccheri, which perhaps gave their name to a dark red color,[126] although the most prized were a glossy black. Vases of this material were first imported into Europe from South America by the Portuguese, who used them as drinking vessels and to boil perfumes and colognes; later, the fragments were used in the manner I just described.

In Homer's *Odyssey* (XVIII, 43-49), Antinous says:

> Gentlemen, quiet! One more thing:
> here are goat stomachs ready on the fire
> to stuff with blood and fat, good supper pudding.
> The man who wins this gallant bout
> may step up here and take the one he likes.
> And let him feast with us from this day on:
> no other beggar will be admitted here
> when we are at our wine.
> (trans. Robert Fitzgerald)

In volume 6 of the *Florentine Observer*, we find the following description of a unique dinner that deserves to be quoted in part:

"Among the most sumptuous dishes there was also peacock, stewed with its feathers, and colored gelatin, molded in various shapes. A man in Siena, who was preparing a supper for a courtier of Pope Pius II named Goro (around 1450), was given such bad advice regarding these two items, that he became the butt of jokes all over Siena. Particularly amusing was the fact that, unable to find peacocks, he substituted wild geese, removing their feet and bills.

When the beakless peacocks were served, the command was given

---

126 It seems that bucchero ultimately derives from Greek *boukaros*, which means dark-red clay and/or the pottery made from it.

to begin carving them up. But the person in charge did not know how to do it, and though he struggled with the birds for a long time he only succeeded in filling with feathers the banquet hall and the table, as well as the eyes, mouth, nose and ears of Messer Goro and everyone else . . .

When that accursed bird was removed from the table, many other roasts prepared with a great deal of cumin were served. Nonetheless, everything still might have been forgiven, had not the master of the house and his misguided advisers decided to further honor their guests with a platter of aspic which they ordered custom made for the occasion. Inside the aspic they had the cooks place, as is sometimes done in Florence and elsewhere, replicas of the papal coat of arms, as well as of Messer Goro's crest and additional heraldic figures. So they used orpiment,[127] white lead, cinnabar, verdigris and other absurdities to make these fantastic patterns inside the aspic. Then they set it before Messer Goro as a festive dish and something new and wonderful. He and all his company ate it happily enough, as a way to get rid of all the bitter flavors left in their mouths by the excessive cumin and the other strange dishes.

And it was a miracle that some of the guests did not die during the night, and first among them Messer Goro, who had a horrible headache and stomachache, and very likely vomited a small bouquet of wild feathers. After these infernal and deadly courses, a great many sweets were served, and the dinner came to an end."

660. BUDINO ALLA TEDESCA
(PUDDING GERMAN STYLE)

140 grams (about 5 ounces) of extra fine crustless bread
100 grams (about 3-1/2 ounces) of butter
80 grams (about 2-2/3 ounces) of sugar

---

127 Orpiment is a lemon-yellow crystalline powder (containing arsenic) used as a pigment and a dyestuff.

4 eggs
a dash of lemon zest
a pinch of salt

The best type of bread for this dish is mold-baked English-style bread; use it if you can find it. Crumble or slice the crustless bread and soak it in cold milk. When well drenched, wring it out in a kitchen towel, and then pass it through a strainer. In wintertime, soften the butter in *bain-marie*, then, using a wooden spoon, beat it with the egg yolks until well blended. Fold in the whites, the bread purée and the sugar, and keep stirring. Pour the mixture into a mold well greased with butter and dusted with bread crumbs. Then bake it as you would any other pudding: that is, in a Dutch oven. If you have prepared it carefully, it will turn out as pleasing to the eye as it is to the taste. Serve hot.

661. BUDINO DI PATATE (POTATO PUDDING)

The potato is a tuberous plant of the *Solanaceae* family that originated in South America, and from there it was introduced in Europe toward the end of the 16th century. However, it was not cultivated on a large scale until the beginning of the 18th century because of the stubborn opposition raised against it by the common folk, who always dislike whatever is strange and new. Gradually it won greater acceptance until it appeared regularly on the rough-hewn tables of the poor as well as in the banquet halls of the wealthy. However, although the potato is delicious, eases hunger, and may readily be prepared in a wide variety of ways, it has the same disadvantage of rice: it is a food that fattens and fills the belly but provides little nourishment. Both rice and potatoes supply no albumen, no phosphorus fats for the brain, no fibrin to the muscles.

700 grams (about 1-1/2 pounds) of starchy mealy potatoes
150 grams (about 5-1/4 ounces) of sugar
40 grams (about 1-1/3 ounces) of butter
20 grams (about 2/3 of an ounce) of wheat flour
2 deciliters (about 4/5 of a cup) of milk
6 eggs

a pinch of salt
a dash of cinnamon or lemon zest

Boil or steam the potatoes, peel and purée by passing them hot through a strainer. Put the purée back on the burner along with the butter, the flour and the milk, added a little at a time, stirring all the while with a wooden spoon. Then add the sugar, the salt, and the cinnamon or the lemon peel, and keep cooking it until everything is thoroughly blended.

Remove from the fire, and when the mixture is lukewarm or cool, add the egg yolks and then the whites, whisked until stiff.

Now prepare as you would any other pudding: that is, in a Dutch oven or in an oven proper, and serve hot.

662. BUDINO DI RISO (RICE PUDDING)

1 liter (about 1 quart) of milk
160 grams (about 5-2/3 ounces) of rice
100 grams (about 3-1/2 ounces) of sugar
80 grams (about 2-2/3 ounces) of sultanas
30 grams (about 1 ounce) of candied fruit
2 whole eggs
2 egg yolks
1 small glass of rum or cognac
a dash of vanilla

Cook the rice thoroughly in the milk, and when half done add the sugar, the sultanas, the candied fruit minced fine, a pinch of salt, and a small egg-sized lump of butter. Once completely cooked, remove from the fire and while still hot but no longer bubbling, fold in the eggs, the rum or cognac and the vanilla, blending everything well. Then pour the mixture into a pudding mold greased with butter and dusted with bread crumbs. Bake in the oven or at home in a Dutch oven. Serve hot.

Keep a third of the milk in reserve and add it to the pudding if necessary, as the rice starts to firm up.

Serves eight people.

663. BUDINO DI RICOTTA (RICOTTA PUDDING)

300 grams (about 10-1/2 ounces) of ricotta cheese
100 grams (about 3-1/2 ounces) of powdered sugar
100 grams (about 3-1/2 ounces) of sweet almonds and 3 or 4
   bitter almonds
5 eggs
a dash of lemon zest

Blanch the almonds in hot water and then crush them as finely as possible in a mortar along with one of the egg whites. Pass the ricotta through a strainer if it is hard or lumpy, and then mix thoroughly with the almonds. Beat the rest of the eggs separately and then fold into the mixture along with the sugar. Now pour the mixture into a pudding mold greased with butter and dusted with bread crumbs. Bake in an oven or in a Dutch oven, and serve cold.

   This recipe serves six to seven people.

664. BUDINO ALLA NAPOLETANA (NEAPOLITAN PUDDING)

Cook some semolina in three glasses of milk, making sure it does not turn out too firm. Remove from the fire and add sugar, a pinch of salt and some lemon zest. When the mixture has cooled down somewhat, add three egg yolks and two whites, stirring until thoroughly blended. Take a medium-sized copper baking pan, grease it with butter or lard, and line it with a sheet of shortcrust pastry dough as thick as a large coin (use half the amounts indicated in recipe 589 A). Pour in a third of the semolina and sprinkle on top, at some distance from each other, small chunks or little spoonfuls of different fruit preserves, such as raspberry, quince, apricot, etc. Over this layer spread a second layer of the semolina, then add more fruit preserves in the same way as before. Repeat the procedure a third and final time, using the last third of the semolina. Now cover the top of the pudding with a sheet of the same dough. Moisten the edges of the dough all around with a finger dipped in water and then seal them. Decorate the top of the pudding with some ornamental designs and gild with egg yolk. Bake in the oven. After you remove the pudding from the mold, sprinkle confectioners' sugar on top and serve cold.

You can substitute small sultanas and finely minced candied fruit for the fruit preserves.

665. BUDINO NERO
(BLACK PUDDING)

This pudding is sometimes made to use up leftover egg whites, and should not be scoffed at.

6 egg whites
170 grams (about 6 ounces) of sweet almonds
170 grams (about 6 ounces) of powdered sugar

Blanch the almonds and dry well in the sun or on the fire; then mince them with a mezzaluna and put them on the fire in a saucepan where the sugar has already melted. Once the mixture has turned the color of a brittle, that is of almond skins, pour it in a mortar, and after it has cooled, crush it to a fine powder. Add the powder to the six egg whites, beaten until stiff. Then pour the mixture into a mold greased only with cool butter, and cook in *bain-marie*. Serve cold.

666. BUDINO DI LIMONE
(LEMON PUDDING)

1 large garden lemon
170 grams (about 6 ounces) of sugar
170 grams (about 6 ounces) of sweet almonds and 3 bitter almonds
6 eggs
1 teaspoon of rum or cognac

Boil the lemon for two hours in water. Strain and then purée by passing it through a strainer. But before doing so, taste it, because if the lemon is still too bitter, you should soak it in cold water until it loses its unpleasant flavor. Then add to it the sugar, the almonds blanched and crushed very fine, the yolks of the six eggs, and the rum. Blend everything together well. Now beat the six whites until stiff and then fold them into the mixture. Pour it into a mold and bake in a Dutch oven or in an oven. It may be served either hot or cold.

667. BUDINO DI CIOCCOLATA
(CHOCOLATE PUDDING)

8 deciliters (about 3-1/3 cups) of milk
80 grams (about 2-2/3 ounces) of sugar
60 grams (about 2 ounces) of chocolate
60 grams (about 2 ounces) of ladyfingers
3 eggs
a dash of vanilla

Grate the chocolate, combine it with the milk and when the latter begins to boil, add the sugar and the ladyfingers, which you will have crumbled with your fingers. Stir the mixture occasionally so it does not stick to the bottom of the pan. After it has boiled for half an hour, pass it through a strainer. When cooled, fold in the eggs (beaten) and the vanilla. Pour into a smooth mold, the bottom of which should be coated with melted sugar, then cook in *bain-marie*.

50 grams (about 1-2/3 ounces) of sugar are enough to glaze the bottom of the mold. Serve cold.

668. DOLCE DI CIOCCOLATA
(CHOCOLATE CAKE)

100 grams (about 3-1/2 ounces) of sponge cake
100 grams (about 3-1/2 ounces) of chocolate
50 grams (about 1-2/3 ounces) of butter
30 grams (about 1 ounce) of sugar
rosolio, as much as needed

Thinly slice the sponge cake. Grate the chocolate. Melt the butter in *bain-marie*, then add the sugar and the chocolate, stirring the mixture with a wooden spoon until it is thoroughly blended. Coat the mold in rosolio (so later you can better remove the dessert from the mold) and layer it with the chocolate mixture and the slices of sponge cake, which should be soaked in rosolio. In summer, keep the mold in ice so that the mixture will firm up more easily.

This recipes serves six people.

669. BUDINO DI MANDORLE TOSTATE (TOASTED ALMOND PUDDING)

8 deciliters (about 3-1/3 cups) of milk, which is the equivalent of
    800 grams (about 1-3/4 pounds)
100 grams (about 31/2 ounces) of sugar
60 grams (about 2 ounces) of ladyfingers
60 grams (about 2 ounces) of sweet almonds
3 eggs

First prepare the almonds: that is, blanch them in hot water, and then toast them on a stone slab or metal sheet placed over the fire. Then crush the almonds in a mortar until they form an extremely fine powder. Then put on the fire the ladyfingers, the milk and the sugar together with the powdered almonds. After this mixture has cooked a short while, pass it through a sieve. Now fold in the eggs, beaten, and allow the mixture to firm up in *bain-marie*, remembering to coat the bottom of the mold with melted sugar. No spices or flavorings are needed. The toasted almonds will give this pudding an ashen color and a flavor so delicious it will win the applause of men and even more the acclaim of the ladies with their delicate taste.

This pudding, as well as the chocolate pudding, may be chilled before serving. And, to give it a more attractive appearance, it may be dressed with whipped cream or with a custard decorated with colored comfits.

670. BUDINO GABINETTO (CABINET PUDDING)

This pudding tastes of diplomacy: this is clear from its name, the laborious preparations it requires, and its complex flavor. I therefore dedicate it to the greatest of ministers, to the cynosure of the hour. The world, as is well known, continually needs an idol to adore; if it does not have one, it will create one, trumpeting his merits to the heavens. I, on the other hand, who am skeptical by nature and in part from experience, agree with the man who said: "Bring him to me dead, then we will talk about it." How many idols, how many stars brightly shining in the firmament have we seen in our time, who soon declined or fell ignominiously! When I was writing out this recipe, one such star, admired by all, was shining radiantly. Now he has plunged into oblivion.

1 liter (about 1 quart) of milk
100 grams (about 3-1/2 ounces) of sugar
100 grams (about 3-1/2 ounces) of ladyfingers
80 grams (about 2-2/3 ounces) of Malaga raisins
50 grams (about 1-2/3 ounces) of sultanas
50 grams (about 1-2/3 ounces) of apricot preserves
50 grams (about 1-2/3 ounces) of quince preserves
20 grams (about 2/3 of an ounce) of candied fruit
1/2 deciliter of kirsch
6 egg yolks
4 whites
2 tablespoons of rum

Simmer the milk and sugar together for half an hour. Remove the seeds from the Malaga raisins; dice the candied fruit and the preserves, if the latter are hard, which in this case would be desirable.

Flambé the grapes and the candied fruit in the rum, as for the sultan cake described in recipe 574.

After the milk has been scalded, let it cool, then add the eggs, beaten, and the kirsch. Take a smooth cylindrical mold, grease it thoroughly with cold butter and fill in the following manner. Cover the bottom of it with a layer of the fruit and over this spread a second layer of ladyfingers, then a third layer of more candied fruit and preserves, then a fourth layer of ladyfingers, and so on, until you run out of ingredients. Finally, over the last layer slowly pour the milk, which has been prepared in the manner explained above. Cook in *bain-marie*, and serve hot.

Some people maintain that this pudding, if it is to live up to its rightful name of cabinet, should appear on the dinner table under wraps: that is, with the filling kept absolutely confidential like state secrets. To accomplish this, take 140 grams (about 5 ounces) of ladyfingers and cover the bottom, sides, surface and all inner partitions, so that the fruit stays utterly hidden from sight.[128]

I must also warn you that when milk is used in preparing a dish, it is unfortunately not always possible to give precise instructions. Milk, by its very nature, is very often the despair of cooks.

Serves ten people.

671. PUDDING CESARINO

I consider this Cesarino a good boy, and I shall sell his pudding to you under the same strange name it bore when I bought it from a young and rather lovely woman, upright and religious, the sort who, without intending to, can by her flirtatious nature compromise anyone in her immediate vicinity.

200 grams (about 7 ounces) of extra fine crustless bread
250 grams (about 8-4/5 ounces) of sugar
approximately 100 grams (about 3-1/2 ounces) of additional sugar,
    for use in the mold
125 grams (about 4-1/2 ounces) of Malaga raisins
125 grams (about 4-1/2 ounces) of sultanas
1/2 liter (about 1/2 a quart) of milk
3 tablespoons in total of Marsala wine and rum
5 eggs

Cut the crustless bread into thin slices, and soak it in the milk. Meanwhile, clean the sultanas, remove the seeds from the Malaga raisins and prepare the mold for cooking. Use a copper mold intended for puddings. Put about 100 grams (about 3-1/2 ounces) of the sugar into a saucepan and, once it has turned nut brown, pour it into the mold, coating it thoroughly. After the mold has cooled, grease the sugar glaze with cold butter.

Combine the milk-soaked bread with the other 250 grams (about

---

128 At the time Artusi was writing, Italy was governed by kings from the House of Savoy, in whose honor "savoiardi" (ladyfingers) were created. There is therefore an element of wry political satire in Artusi's description of this dish.

8-4/5 ounces) of sugar, the egg yolks and the liquors. Blend everything thoroughly. Finally, add the raisins and fold in the egg whites,
beaten until stiff. Place the mixture in the mold prepared as described
above, then put the mold in *bain-marie*, and cook for three whole
hours; but heat from above only for the last hour. Serve hot as a
flambé, sprinkling rum generously over the pudding and setting it
ablaze with a tablespoonful of lit spirits.

These amounts should be enough for ten to twelve people.

672. PLUM-PUDDING[129]

The English name denotes a pudding made of plums; however, no
plums are used in preparing this dish.

Make a mixture in which for each egg you use as binder, you
use the exact amount of the following ingredients:

30 grams (about 1 ounce) of powdered sugar
30 grams (about 1 ounce) of zibibbo raisins
30 grams (about 1 ounce) of sultanas
30 grams (about 1 ounce) of extra fine crustless bread
30 grams (about 1 ounce) of mutton kidney fat
15 grams (about 1/2 an ounce) of candied citron
15 grams (about 1/2 an ounce) of candied orange
1 tablespoon of rum

Remove the seeds from the raisins. Chop the candied fruit into short
thin slivers. If you do not have mutton kidney fat, use calf's kidney
fat instead. Remove all membranes from the fat and dice it, as well
as the bread, as finely as possible.

First beat the eggs separately, then mix all the ingredients
together, and allow to stand for a few hours. Then place the mixture
in the middle of a cloth napkin. Gather the four corners and tie
tightly with twine so that it forms a ball. Heat some water in a pan,
and when it boils, immerse the ball in it in such a way that it does
touch the bottom of the pan. Allow to simmer for as many hours as
eggs used: i.e., one egg, one hour; two eggs, two hours, etc. Then

---

129 In English in the original.

carefully remove the mixture from the napkin, make a small depression on top, and pour into it one or two small glassfuls of cognac or rum, letting it spill all over the whole pudding. Send it to the table flambé. When the flames have subsided, cut into slices and eat.

With three eggs you will make enough pudding for six people.

673. PLUM-CAKE

This is a dessert from the same family as the preceding one; it, too, bears a mendacious name.

250 grams (about 8-4/5 ounces) of sugar
250 grams (about 8-4/5 ounces) of butter
250 grams (about 8-4/5 ounces) of extra fine flour
80 grams (about 2-2/3 ounces) of candied fruit
80 grams (about 2-2/3 ounces) of Malaga raisins
80 grams (about 2-2/3 ounces) of sultanas
80 grams (about 2-2/3 ounces) of raisins
5 whole eggs
4 egg yolks
1 scant deciliter (about 2/5 of a cup) or 5 tablespoons of rum
a dash of lemon zest or vanilla

Cut the candied fruit into thin slivers and remove the seeds from the Malaga raisins.

First beat the butter by itself with a wooden spoon, softening it over the fire if necessary. Then, add the sugar and continue beating until the mixture turns white. Crack the eggs and fold them in one at a time, stirring constantly; then mix in the flour and finally the remaining ingredients. Take a smooth mold, and line it with paper greased on the inside with butter; then pour the mixture over it and bake in the oven.

You may serve this dish hot with confectioners' sugar sprinkled on top, or also cold. It is delicious either way.

The paper prevents the raisins from sticking to the mold. This recipe serves twelve people.

674. BAVARESE LOMBARDA
(LOMBARD BAVARIAN)

This dish, which has many different names, could also be called "dessert of the day," since many families like it and make it often.

180 grams (about 6-1/3 ounces) of fresh, quality butter
180 grams (about 6-1/3 ounces) of confectioners' sugar
approximately 150 grams (about 5-1/4 ounces) of long ladyfin-
*   gers or sponge cake*
6 hard-boiled egg yolks
enough vanilla sugar for flavor
enough rosolio to lightly moisten the ladyfingers

Boil the eggs for seven minutes only, then remove the yolks. Blend them with the butter and pass through a strainer. Then add the confectioners' sugar and the vanilla sugar, stirring the mixture vigorously with a wooden spoon until smooth.

Take a mold, a ribbed one if possible. Brush it with rosolio. Cut the ladyfingers in half lengthwise, dip them lightly in rosolio, or dip half in rosolio and the other half in alkermes. Line the bottom of the mold with half of the ladyfingers, alternating the colors. Now pour in the mixture and cover with more ladyfingers similarly placed in alternating strips of color. Allow to stand for at least three hours in ice and then serve. If more convenient, it may be prepared a day in advance.

These amounts serve eight people. This is an excellent dessert.

675. ZUPPA INGLESE
(ENGLISH TRIFLE)

In Tuscany, due to the region's climate and also because the stomach of its inhabitants has become accustomed to this manner of cooking, the emphasis is on making dishes that turn out light and, whenever possible, rather runny. Thus, the custard there is silky smooth, made without starch or flour, and customarily served in little cups. Yet while it is true that a custard prepared in this fashion is more delicate to the taste, it does not lend itself to English trifle, which is prepared in a mold, nor is it particularly impressive in appearance.

Here are the ingredients and amounts to be used to create confectioners' custard, as chefs call it, to distinguish it from custard made without flour:

5 deciliters (about 2 cups) of milk
85 grams (about 3 ounces) of sugar
40 grams (about 1-1/3 ounces) of flour or preferably powdered
    starch
4 egg yolks
a dash of vanilla

First beat the egg yolks and the sugar together, then add the flour, and lastly the milk, a little at a time. You can begin cooking it over a high flame, stirring constantly, but when you see that the mixture starts to steam, throw a small scoop of ashes over the fire or else move the pot to a cooler corner of the hearth, if you do not want lumps to start forming. After it has firmed up, keep the pot on the fire for another eight to ten minutes, then let it cool.

Take a fluted mold, grease thoroughly with cold butter and begin filling it as follows: if you have good fruit preserves such as apricot, peach or quince, line the bottom of the mold with this, pour a custard layer on top, followed by a layer of ladyfingers dipped in white rosolio. In addition, if, for example, there are 18 flutes in the mold, dip 9 ladyfingers in alkermes and 9 in white rosolio and then fill the flutes with alternating colors. Pour more custard on top, then add another layer of ladyfingers dipped in rosolio over the custard. Repeat the procedure until the mold is full.

Make sure you do not soak the biscuits too long in the rosolio; otherwise the excess liquid will ooze out and spoil the custard. If the liqueur you are using is too sweet, lace it with rum or cognac. If the fruit preserves have hardened over time, soften over the fire with a little water (though, actually, you can make this dessert without it). Make sure the preserves are cold when you pour them into the mold.

This recipe serves seven to eight people.

In summertime you can keep this dish on ice; to remove the

contents from the mold, immerse it for an instant in hot water, so that the butter melts.

You will probably need between 120 and 130 grams (between about 4-1/4 and 4-1/2 ounces) of ladyfingers.

676. ZUPPA TARTARA
(TARTAR CUSTARD)

Take 200 grams (about 7 ounces) of ricotta cheese, soften it somewhat in milk, and sweeten it with 30 grams (about 1 ounce) of confectioners' sugar and two pinches of ground cinnamon, mixing thoroughly.

Take a fancy mold and coat the inside with rosolio or grease with butter. Dip some ladyfingers in rosolio or alkermes. Now, using either the ladyfingers or a fruit preserve that is not too runny, cover the bottom of the mold. Then fill the mold in alternating layers, first with the ricotta, then with the ladyfingers, and then with the fruit preserves, which can be either apricot or peach. After several hours remove the dessert from the mold, and if you have prepared it carefully, it will be both delicious and dazzle your dinner guests with its handsome appearance.

The ricotta may be softened with citron rosolio instead of milk. But in that case, you will not need any cinnamon.

This is a dessert guaranteed to please.

677. DOLCE DI CILIEGE
(CHERRY DELIGHT)

As a family dessert, it is first rate and worth the effort.

200 grams (about 7 ounces) of black cherries, raw, whole and
without the stems
100 grams (about 3-1/2 ounces) of confectioners' sugar
50 grams (about 1-2/3 ounces) of rye bread crumbs
40 grams (about 1-1/3 ounces) of sweet almonds
4 eggs
2 tablespoons of rosolio
a dash of vanilla or lemon zest

If you do not have rye bread, use ordinary bread.

Blanch the almonds, dry and mince finely until each piece is half the size of a grain of rice.

Beat the egg yolks with the sugar until they become fluffy. Add the bread crumbs, the rosolio, the vanilla or the lemon zest, and continue mixing for a while longer. Then fold in gently the egg whites, beaten until quite stiff. Pour the mixture into a smooth mold greased with cold butter and lined with the minced almonds (the almond layer should be thicker on the bottom of the mold). Lastly, add the cherries, but to make sure that they don't sink to the bottom because of their weight, fold any leftover almonds into the mixture.

Bake in the oven or a Dutch oven and serve hot or cold to four or five people.

678. ZUPPA DI VISCIOLE (SOUR CHERRY DELIGHT)

This dessert may be made with either thin, toasted slices of fine bread, or with sponge cake or ladyfingers.

Remove the pits from the quantity of sour cherries you deem sufficient, and put them on the fire in very little water with a little piece of cinnamon, which you will later discard. When the cherries start to boil, add as much sugar as necessary, mixing slowly so as not to squash the cherries. When they start to make a syrup, taste to see if you have added enough sugar. Remove from the fire when you notice that the cherries begin to shrivel and are cooked through. Lightly dip the thin bread slices or the ladyfingers in rosolio and then stack them in alternating layers with the cherries on a platter or in a bowl, so that they fill it up nicely. You may also give this dessert a more regular shape by arranging it in a smooth mold and then putting the mold in ice for some time before taking the cake out, since in cherry season people are already beginning to enjoy chilled dishes. A third of the gross weight in relation to the cherries should be a sufficient amount of sugar.

679. ZUPPA DI LIMONE
(LEMON CUSTARD)

This dessert, which I suspect comes to us from France, is not one of which I am terribly fond. This notwithstanding, let me describe it to you in case you do not have a better one in your repertoire and you have some egg whites on hand.

135 grams (about 4-3/4 ounces) of sugar
2 egg yolks
5 egg whites
the juice of 1 large lemon
1/2 glass of water
1 scant teaspoon of flour

Dissolve the flour in the water, whisking well, then pour into a saucepan and add the remaining ingredients. Mix thoroughly and put on the fire, stirring constantly with a wooden spoon as if you were preparing a custard. When the mixture has thickened, pass it through a strainer, if necessary, then pour half of it into a bowl and cover with ladyfingers or sponge cake; then pour in the remaining mixture. Serve cold.

This recipe serves four to five people.

680. SFORMATO DI CONSERVE
(FRUIT PRESERVE PUDDING)

Take a ribbed or fluted pudding mold, grease thoroughly with cold butter and fill with ladyfingers or sponge cake soaked in rosolio and with fruit preserves. For everything else, follow recipe 675, but do not use any custard. After a few hours, which are required for the ingredients to amalgamate, remove it from the mold. But first plunge the mold into boiling water for an instant, so that the butter melts.

681. BIANCO MANGIARE
(BLANCMANGE OR WHITE ALMOND PUDDING)

150 grams (about 5-1/4 ounces) of sweet almonds and 3 bitter
*   almonds*
150 grams (about 5-1/4 ounces) of powdered sugar
20 grams (about 2/3 of an ounce) of isinglass in sheets
a good 1/2 glass of heavy cream
1 1/2 glasses of water
2 tablespoons of orange-flower water

First prepare the isinglass, and that is easily done. Press it with your fingers to the bottom of a glass, cover it with water and allow to soak so that it has time to soften. When you are ready to use it, discard the water, and rinse it thoroughly. Blanch the almonds and crush them in a mortar, moistening them now and then with a little water. When they are reduced to a very fine paste, dilute with the one and a half glasses of water. Now pass them through a strong, loosely woven kitchen towel, making sure to force as much of the almond paste as you can through the cloth. Now prepare a mold of adequate size and grease it with butter. Next, put in a saucepan on the fire the milky almond mixture, the heavy cream, the sugar, the isinglass, and the orange-flower water. Blend everything thoroughly and allow to boil for a few minutes. Remove from the fire and, when the mixture has cooled, pour it into the mold, which should then be immersed in cold water or covered with ice. To unmold this pudding, all you need to do is wipe the sides of the mold with a kitchen towel soaked in boiling water.

It is necessary to boil the pudding mixture to make sure that the isinglass totally bonds with the other ingredients. Otherwise it might sink to the bottom of the mold.

682. SGONFIOTTO DI FARINA GIALLA
(POLENTA SOUFFLÉ)

This dish:

> I francesi lo chiaman *soufflet*
> E lo notano come *entremet*,
> Io "sgonfiotto," se date il permesso,
> Che servire potrà di tramesso.

> (What the French call soufflé
> And use as an *entremets*,
> By your leave I call "sgonfiotto"
> And serve as a "tramesso.")

1/2 liter (about 1/2 a quart) of milk
170 grams (about 6 ounces) of corn flour
30 grams (about 1 ounce) of butter
6 egg whites
3 egg yolks
a pinch of salt

Prepare a porridge, that is, pour the corn flour into the milk as it boils, or preferably, if you wish to prevent clumps from forming, first soak the corn flour in a little cold milk and then add it to the boiling milk, stirring constantly. Allow to boil for a short while. Remove from the fire, and mix in the butter, the sugar, and the salt. When sufficiently cool, blend in the egg yolks and lastly the egg whites, beaten until quite stiff. Blend gently and pour the mixture into a smooth mold or a saucepan greased with butter and dusted with wheat flour, or into a pan similarly buttered and dusted. Bake in a Dutch iven with fire above and below. When the soufflé has risen, serve immediately, if possible, so that it stays puffed up and fluffy, and does not fall. In my opinion, the best way to handle this dish is to bake it in an ovenproof bowl you serve it in, so that you do not need to transfer it.

This recipe serves six people.

683. BISCOTTO DA SERVIRSI CON LO ZABAIONE (UNLEAVENED CAKE SERVED WITH ZABAIONE)

50 grams (about 1-2/3 ounces) of potato flour
20 grams (about 2/3 of an ounce) of wheat flour
90 grams (about 3 ounces) of powdered sugar
3 eggs
a dash of lemon peel

Beat the egg yolks and sugar together for about half an hour, then fold in the whites (beaten until quite stiff). Now sift both flours over the mixture and blend gently so that it stays light and fluffy. Pour into a mold with a hole in the middle that you have first greased with butter and dusted with flour mixed with confectioners' sugar. Bake immediately in the oven or a Dutch oven. Remove from the mold when it has cooled, and pour into the hole in the middle a zabaione prepared according to recipe 684. Send to the table without further ado.

These amounts serve five to six people.

684. SFORMATO DI SAVOIARDI CON LO ZABAIONE (LADYFINGER PUDDING WITH ZABAIONE)

100 grams (about 3-1/2 ounces) of ladyfingers
70 grams (about 2-1/3 ounces) of Malaga raisins
50 grams (about 1-2/3 ounces) of sultanas
30 grams (about 1 ounce) of candied citron
Marsala wine, as needed

Remove the seeds from the Malaga raisins. Chop the candied citron into tiny pieces. Take a mold with a hole in the middle and grease it with cold butter. Dip the ladyfingers lightly and only on the surface in the Marsala wine. Now fill the mold first with a layer of the ladyfingers and then with a layer of the raisins and the candied citron.

Prepare a custard with the following ingredients:

2 deciliters (about 4/5 of a cup) of milk
2 whole eggs

50 grams (about 1-2/3 ounces) of sugar
a dash of vanilla

Combine all the above items without first cooking them and pour the mixture into the mold over the ladyfingers. Cook the pudding in *bain-marie*. Remove hot from the mold and before serving, fill the hole in the middle with a zabaione until it overflows, covering the whole pudding.

Prepare the zabaione with the following ingredients:

2 whole eggs
1-1/2 deciliters (about 2/3 of a cup) of Marsala
50 grams (about 1-2/3 ounces) of sugar

Beat the zabaione with a whisk in a metal bowl held over the fire. For the raisins you may substitute fruits in syrup, or a mixture of both, even a combination of candied citron and candied orange.

This recipe serves six people. This is a dessert sure to please.

685. CREMA (CUSTARD)

1 liter (about 1 quart) of milk
200 grams (about 7 ounces) of sugar
8 egg yolks
a dash of vanilla

First beat the egg yolks with the sugar and then pour in the milk a little at a time. To hasten the cooking process, you can put the mixture over a high flame, but the moment it begins to smoke reduce the heat to prevent curdling. If it does curdle, pass the mixture though a strainer. Stir constantly; you can tell that the custard is cooked when it sticks to the wooden spoon. Add the vanilla shortly before removing from the fire.

With the above proportions, this custard, which contains no flour or other thickening agent, lends itself admirably to creamy ice creams—so much so that you would be hard pressed to find a comparable ice cream in any café. It can also be used for a runny English trifle: once it has cooled, add some slices of sponge cake or ladyfingers lightly dipped in rosolio. If you want to make it taste even better, add some finely minced candied fruit.

686. LE TAZZINE (CUSTARD CUPS)

This is a very delicate dessert that is offered, like all other desserts, toward the end of a meal. It is served in cups smaller than the ones used for coffee, one per person, which is why it is called "le tazzine" ("little cups").

To serve ten people:

300 grams (about 10-1/2 ounces) of sugar
60 grams (about 2 ounces) of sweet almonds
10 egg yolks
1 deciliter (about 2/5 of a cup) of water
a dash of orange-flower water
ground cinnamon, to taste

Blanch the almonds, toast to a light brown, grind very fine and set aside.

Boil the sugar in the water for a minute or two, taking care that it does not turn brown. Allow it to cool and when it is lukewarm, begin to add the egg yolks, one or two at a time, stirring constantly in the same direction over very moderate heat. When the mixture becomes dense enough so that there is no more danger of it curdling, you can beat it with a whisk with a bottom-to-top motion which will make the cream more fluffy. Work the mixture in this way until the yolks have lost their reddish color and the mixture resembles a thick custard. Then add the orange-flower water and the almonds, mixing well. Pour the mixture into the cups and put a pinch of ground cinnamon in the middle of each one. When mixed in by each guest, this gives the dessert more aroma.

This is a dessert that can be prepared a few days in advance, without adverse consequences. If you want, you can use the leftover egg whites to make black pudding in the proportions described in recipe 665, or the meringue cake in recipe 633.

687. PALLOTTOLE DI MANDORLE
(ALMOND BALLS)

140 grams (about 5 ounces) of sweet almonds
140 grams (about 5 ounces) confectioners' sugar
about 40 grams (about 1-1/3 ounces) of grated or powdered chocolate
4 tablespoons maraschino liqueur

Blanch the almonds, dry them in the sun or on the fire, and crush very fine with two tablespoons of the sugar. Pour them from the mortar into a bowl, add the rest of the sugar, and blend with the maraschino liqueur.

Dust a pastry board with the chocolate. Shape the mixture into little balls somewhat larger than hazelnuts—you should get more than thirty. Coat the balls thoroughly with the chocolate. They will keep for a long time.

688. CREMA ALLA FRANCESE
(FRENCH-STYLE CUSTARD)

It was the time of year when the gray mullet of the Comacchio Valley are excellent grilled, seasoned with pomegranate juice, and when, as the poet would say, the variously colored songbirds are driven by the first frosts to our fields in search of gentler climes, and the poor innocent little creatures get caught in one of the many snares and then threaded on a skewer.

> . . . ed io sol uno
> M'apparecchiava a sostenere la guerra
> Sì del cammino e sì della pietate,
> Che ritrarrà la mente che non erra.[130]
> (. . . and I alone
> was preparing myself to endure
> both the journey and the compassion
> that unerring memory shall relate.)

130 Dante, *Inferno* II, 3-6.

The journey I had to endure was a 200-kilometer trip to spend a holiday at a friend's home on a very pleasant hill; and my compassion was for those charming little animals, for my heart ached every time I would see them, from the little house overlooking the field, get caught in the traitorous nets of the snares. But—since I don't belong to the Pythagorean sect, and hold the firm conviction that when there is no remedy for a particular evil, one must make the best of it either by love or by force, and if possible profit from it—I tried to get on my host's cook's good side by teaching him how to prepare game more elegantly than he had been used to, and to season and cook it in such a way as to make it more pleasing to the taste; and in exchange for that and for some other culinary precepts, during my stay he made this and the next two desserts I am going to describe to you.

Game birds and game in general, in case you don't know, are an aromatic, nutritious, mildly stimulating food. I know of a reputable doctor whose cook has orders to chose game, when he can find it, over any other meat. And as far as gray mullet goes, I will tell you that when I was at that wonderful age when one can digest even nails, our maidservant would serve this fish with an accompaniment of white onions, halved and roasted on the grill, seasoned, as the fish was, with olive oil, salt, pepper, and pomegranate juice.

The season for gray mullet in the Comacchio Valley runs from October to the end of February. And while I am on the subject of this fishing spot, I should add (as an amazing thing that is worth knowing) that up to the first of November of the year 1905, the catch in those valleys was the following:

eel	487,653 kg
gray mullet	59,451 kg
smelt	105,580 kg

So, after that prelude I will preach the sermon, and tell you how to make this so-called French-style custard.

1/2 liter (about 1/2 a quart) of milk
150 grams (about 5-1/4 ounces) of sugar
1 whole egg
4 egg yolks
2 sheets of isinglass[131]
a dash of vanilla or lemon zest

Blend the sugar and the eggs well, add the milk a little at a time, and lastly the isinglass. Put the pan on the fire, stirring continuously in the same direction. When the custard starts to thicken and stick to the spoon, remove the pan from the fire. Take a smooth mold with a hole in the middle, of a size that the custard will fill; coat the bottom of the mold with a thin layer of butter or rosolio, and pour in the custard. In the summertime, place the mold on ice, and in the wintertime, in cold water. Unmold the custard on a kitchen towel folded over a tray.

If you don't trust the quality of the milk, boil it for at least a quarter of an hour before you make the custard, or else increase the amount of isinglass by one sheet.

689. CREMA MONTATA IN GELO
(CHILLED WHIPPED CUSTARD)

6 egg yolks
70 grams (about 2-1/3 ounces) of powdered sugar
15 grams (about 1/2 an ounce) of isinglass, equal to 6 or 7 sheets
3/4 of a glass of water
3 whole cherry laurel leaves or any other flavoring you like

Beat the egg yolks with the sugar in a saucepan; add the water and the laurel leaves, and put on the fire, stirring until done, which, as I have already told you, you can tell when the mixture thickens and coats the spoon. Then pour the mixture into a bowl, and while it is still hot, beat it vigorously with a whisk until it is fluffy and stiff. Remove the laurel leaves and add the isinglass a little at a time, continuing to beat with the whisk.

---

131 A pure, transparent form of gelatin obtained from the air bladders of certain fish. See recipe 479.

Take a decorated mold, grease it with oil, put ice all around it and pour in the whipped custard. If you like, you can add in the middle of the custard a layer of ladyfingers dipped in rosolio or spread with fruit preserves. Leave it in the ice for more than an hour; if it is difficult to remove the custard from the mold, wipe the outside of the mold with a cloth soaked in hot water.

Prepare the isinglass ahead of time as follows: first soak it, and then put it on the fire with two fingers of water. Cook down the mixture until it forms a rather thick liquid that sticks to your fingers. While it is still boiling hot, pour it into the custard, which you can flavor with alkermes,[132] coffee, or chocolate.

This recipe serves five or six people.

690. CROCCANTE A BAGNO-MARIA
(BAIN-MARIE ALMOND BRITTLE)

150 grams (about 5-1/4 ounces) of sugar
85 grams (about 3 ounces) of sweet almonds
5 egg yolks
4 deciliters (about 1-2/3 cups) of milk

Blanch the almonds, and use a mezzaluna to chop them to about the size of grains of wheat. Put 110 grams (about 3-4/5 ounces) of the sugar on the fire, and when it has melted, pour in the almonds, stirring constantly with a wooden spoon until the mixture turns cinnamon-brown. Then transfer the mixture to a baking pan greased with butter, and when it has cooled, crush it in a mortar with the remaining 40 grams (about 1-1/3 ounces) of sugar until very fine.

Add the egg yolks and then the milk, mix well, and then pour into a mold with a hole in the middle; grease the mold first with butter. Cook in *bain-marie* and afterward, in summertime, keep the mold on ice.

If you are serving this dessert to more than six people, double the amounts, and if you are not sure about the quality of the milk, boil it first by itself for at least a quarter of an hour.

132 See note to recipe 618.

691. UOVA DI NEVE (FLOATING ISLANDS)

1 liter (about 1 quart) of milk
150 grams (about 5-1/4 ounces) of sugar
6 eggs
confectioners' sugar, as needed
a dash of vanilla

Put a wide saucepan on the fire with the milk. As the milk is warm-ing up, use a whisk to beat the egg whites, which you have separated from the yolks; add a pinch of salt to the whites, which helps make them stiffer. When the egg whites are nice and stiff, sprinkle on them enough confectioners' sugar from the perforated jar where it is usu-ally kept, to make the whites quite sweet. About 20 to 30 grams (about 2/3 to 1 ounce) of sugar should be enough, but it is better to taste them. This done, take a tablespoon of the egg white, shape it like an egg and toss it into the boiling milk. Turn these "eggs" so that they cook on all sides, and when you see them firming up, re-move them from the milk with a slotted spoon and place them in a colander to drain. Stain the milk and when it has cooled, use it along with the yolks to make a custard like the one described in recipe 685. Flavor the custard with a dash of vanilla. Then arrange on a platter the "eggs" you have just made, making a nice pile over which you will pour the custard. Serve cold.

These amounts serve eight to ten people.

692. LATTE BRÛLÉ (MILK BRÛLÉ)

1 liter (about 1 quart) of milk
180 grams (about 6-1/3 ounces) of sugar
8 egg yolks
2 egg whites

Put the milk on the fire with 100 grams (about 3-1/2 ounces) of the sugar. Allow to boil for a full hour, then remove it from the fire and let it cool. Dissolve in a separate saucepan the remaining 80 grams (about 2-2/3 ounces) of sugar and when it has thoroughly melted, use enough of it to coat the bottom of a smooth mold. Keep the excess in the saucepan and cook it until it turns quite black. Then pour in a ladleful of water: this will stop it from burning further and you will hear it sizzle as it clumps up. But keep the saucepan on the fire and keep stirring, and you will have a thick dark liquid, which you will set aside. Beat in a pot the eggs and then mix in all the other ingredients, namely: the milk, the eggs, and the burned sugar. Taste the mixture to ensure that it is sweet enough; then strain it in a tin colander with fairly large holes, and pour it in the mold you have prepared. Cook in *bain-marie* with fire from above, and when the surface begins to brown, put a buttered piece of paper under the lid of the Dutch oven. Test for readiness with a thin broom-twig: if it comes out clean and dry when you prick the pudding, that means it is ready to be removed from the fire. Allow it to cool thoroughly and before unmolding it onto a tray (over a napkin if you like) pass a thin knife blade around the sides. In summer, you may want to put the mold in ice for a while before unmolding the pudding.

If possible, use an oval-shaped mold for this recipe. Ideally, the mold should have a finger-wide rim which prevents water from spattering into it as it is cooking.

These amounts serve ten people.

693. LATTE ALLA PORTOGHESE
(MILK PORTUGUESE STYLE)

This recipe is identical to the previous one, except for the burned sugar. Therefore the ingredients are:

1 liter (about 1 quart) of milk
100 grams (about 3-1/2 ounces) of sugar
8 egg yolks
2 egg whites

Suitable flavorings for this recipe are a dash of vanilla, or coriander, or coffee. If you choose coffee, grind several toasted coffee beans; if you like coriander or vanilla, both of which go well with this dish, pound a pinch of either and put it to boil in the milk, which you will then strain. If the milk is a little thin, boil it for up to an hour and a quarter.

Don't forget to coat the mold with a thin layer of melted sugar.

694. LATTERUOLO (MILK PUDDING)

This is a very delicate dessert that peasants in certain parts of Romagna (and perhaps elsewhere in Italy) take to the landowner as a gift on the feast of Corpus Christi.

(about 1 quart) of milk
100 grams (about 3-1/2 ounces) of sugar
8 egg yolks
2 egg whites
a dash of vanilla or coriander

Boil the milk with the sugar for an hour and, if you are not sure about the milk's quality, even an hour and a quarter. If you use coriander use it as indicated in the previous recipe. Remember to stir the milk from time to time, to break the skin that forms as it boils. To be sure that it has no lumps, strain the milk, allow it to cool, and then mix in the eggs which you will have beaten in advance.

Line a baking dish with "crazy" dough (recipe 153), arranging it as for the Romagna blood pudding (recipe 702). Pour in the mixture, cook it with heat above and below at a moderate temperature, covering it with a buttered piece of paper so that it will not turn brown on top. Wait until it has thoroughly cooled before cutting it, like the blood pudding, into lozenges with a bottom crust.

695. LATTERUOLO SEMPLICE
(SIMPLE MILK PUDDING)

This recipe is less delicate than the preceding one, but it is an excellent family dessert, and very nutritious, especially for children.

1 liter (about 1 quart) of milk
100 grams (about 3-1/2 ounces) of powdered sugar
6 eggs
lemon rind

Since the essences of citrus fruits reside in the volatile oil trapped in the surface cells of the rind, just slice off with a penknife a very thin palm-length strip of peel and put it to boil in the liquid you want to flavor.

With a penknife slice off from the surface of a lemon a thin strip of peel of some length, and put it to boil in the milk, which you will let boil for half an hour with the sugar. When the milk has cooled, remove the lemon peel and stir in the beaten eggs. Cook as in the preceding recipe or, if you prefer, without a crust, but then you must generously grease the baking dish with cold butter to ensure that the mixture will not stick to it.

696. MELE IN GELATINA (JELLIED APPLES)

Take reinette apples or some other high-quality apples, not too ripe or large. Core them with a tin corer, peel, and then drop them immediately one by one in cool water into which you have squeezed the juice of half a lemon. Assuming that they weigh between 650 and 700 grams, dissolve over a flame 120 grams (about 4-1/4 ounces) of sugar in 1/2 a liter (about 1/2 a quart) of water to which a spoonful of kirsch has been added. Pour this mixture over the apples, which you have arranged evenly in a saucepan. As they cook, make sure that they remain whole. Once done, strain the apples and arrange them on a fruit tray. When they have cooled fill the cored centers with red currant jelly (recipe 739) which, being red, makes a nice color contrast with the white of the apples. Cook down the liquid remaining in the saucepan until it thickens to a syrupy consistency, then strain it through a wet cloth. Add to it another spoonful of kirsch and pour this mixture around the apples which you have arranged as described above. Serve cold.

If you are out of kirsch, use rosolio. And if you don't have red currant jelly, use fruit preserves.

697. PESCHE RIPIENE (STUFFED PEACHES)

6 large peaches, barely ripe
4 small ladyfingers
80 grams (about 2-2/3 ounces) of powdered sugar
50 grams (about 1-2/3 ounces) of sweet almonds, with three peach stones
10 grams (about 1/3 of an ounce) of candied citrus or orange
a scant 1/2 glass of good white wine

Slice the peaches in half. Remove the stones and, with the tip of a knife, enlarge the resulting cavities somewhat. Mix the pulp you have removed with the almonds, blanched in advance, and grind the mixture very finely in a mortar with 50 grams (about 1-2/3 ounces) of powdered sugar. Then add the ladyfingers (crumbled) and, lastly, the candied fruit, diced very small. This is the stuffing which you will use to generously fill the twelve half peaches. Arrange the peaches evenly face up in a copper baking dish and pour the wine and the remaining 30 grams of sugar over them. Cook with heat above and below.

You may serve the peaches either cold or hot as you wish, with the sauce around them. If they turn out well, they will look beautiful on a platter, and the thin crinkled crust that forms on the filling will make them resemble little pastries.

698. FRITTATA A SGONFIOTTO OSSIA MONTATA (OMELETTE SOUFFLÉ)

The French call this dish an *omelette soufflée* and it can serve as an expedient dessert, if you have nothing better and you have leftover egg whites.

100 grams (about 3-1/2 ounces) of powdered sugar
3 egg yolks
6 egg whites
a dash of lemon zest

First, beat the egg yolks with the sugar for several minutes, then beat the egg whites until stiff. Fold the yolks gently into the white. Grease an ovenproof bowl with cold butter and pour in the mixture, making sure it fills the bowl to the brim. Place it immediately in a hot Dutch oven.

After it has been in the oven for five minutes, cut some slits into it with a knife and dust it with powdered sugar. Then finish cooking, which should take ten to twelve minutes in all. Be careful not to burn the top, and send it to the table immediately. In order to help it rise better, some people add a little lemon juice to the mixture.

699. GNOCCHI DI LATTE
(MILK DUMPLINGS)

To serve six people:

1 liter (about 1 quart) of milk
240 grams (about 8-1/2 ounces) of sugar
120 grams (about 4-1/4 ounces) of powdered starch
8 egg yolks
a dash of vanilla

Mix all the ingredients together as you would for a custard, and put over the fire in a saucepan, stirring constantly. When the mixture has thickened, keep it on the fire for a few more minutes and then pour it into a baking dish or plate where it should form a layer 1-1/2 fingers deep. After it has cooled, cut it into almond-shaped pieces. Arrange these pieces symmetrically one on top of the other in a copper or ovenproof porcelain dish, interspersing pats of butter. Brown for awhile in a Dutch oven and serve hot.

700. CIARLOTTA
(CHARLOTTE)

Make a custard with:

2 deciliters (about 4/5 of a cup) of milk
30 grams (about 1 ounce) of sugar
1/2 tablespoon of flour
1 egg
a dash of lemon zest

Make a syrup with:

2 deciliters (about 4/5 of a cup) of water
50 grams (about 1-2/3 ounces) of sugar

Boil the sugar and the water for ten minutes; when the syrup has cooled squeeze the juice of a lemon into it.

Fill a nicely decorated pudding mold with 300 grams (about 10-1/2 ounces) of sliced sponge cake, fruit preserves and the above-mentioned custard. Lastly, pour in the syrup to soak the sponge cake or, if you prefer, the ladyfingers. Allow it to set for several hours before taking it out of the mold and serving.

This recipe serves eight people.

701. CIARLOTTA DI MELE
(APPLE CHARLOTTE)

500 grams (about 1 pound) of reinette apples
125 grams (about 4-1/2 ounces) of powdered sugar
crustless stale bread, as needed
high-quality fresh butter, as needed
1 cinnamon stick
1/2 a lemon

Reinette apples are preferable because they are soft and fragrant. If they are not available, use apples of a similar variety. If this jam-like filling is to be preserved for a long time, you should use twice as much sugar; but if you use it right away, sugar in the amount of one-fourth of the weight of the apples is enough.

Peel and quarter the apples, remove the seeds and seed compartments, and toss them in cool water to which lemon juice has been added. Then drain the apple quarters, and cut them crosswise into thin slices. Next, place them in a saucepan over the fire with a cinnamon stick and no water. When they begin to dissolve, add the sugar and stir frequently until they are cooked, which is easy to tell. Then remove the cinnamon stick and proceed as follows.

Melt the butter and when it bubbles, that is when it is quite hot, dip in as many slices of crustless bread as needed. Prepare these slices ahead of time, taking care that they are not more than 1 centimeter (about 1/2 an inch) wide. Use the bread to line the bottom and sides of a smooth round mold, making sure you leave no gaps. Pour in the filling and cover it with more buttered bread slices. Cook it like a pudding with fire from above, keeping in mind that all you need to do is to brown the bread. Serve it hot.

You might try more varied and elaborate versions of this dessert. For example you can make a hole in the middle of the preparation and fill it with apricot or some other preserves, or you can arrange the filling in layers with the bread slices.

This apple filling would also do nicely in a short pastry crust.

702. MIGLIACCIO DI ROMAGNA
(ROMAGNA BLOOD PUDDING)

Se il maiale volasse
Non ci saria danar che lo pagasse.

(If pigs had wings to fly on,
you couldn't afford to buy one.)

This is what someone once said; and someone else replied: "A pig, with all the cuts of meat it provides, and all the various manipulations these cuts can be subjected to, lets you taste as many flavors as there are days in a year." I let the reader decide which of these two silly sayings comes closer to the mark. As for myself, I will be happy to evoke that the so-called "pig's wedding,"[133] for even this filthy animal can be amusing, but, just like the miser, only on the day of his death.

In Romagna, well-to-do families and peasants slaughter pigs at home, which is an occasion to make merry and for the children to romp. This is also a great opportunity to remember friends, relatives and other people towards whom you may have some obligation by making a gift of three or four loin chops to one, a slab of liver to another, while sending to yet a third a good plate of blood pudding. The families receiving these things will of course do the same in return. "One gives bread in exchange for flour," one might say. But regardless, these are customs that help maintain goodwill and friendships among families.

Coming at last to the point, after this preamble, here is the recipe for Romagna blood pudding. On account of its nobility this blood pudding would not even deign to recognize as kin the sweet-flour blood pudding you can find on any street corner in Florence:

7 deciliters (2 4/5 cups) of milk
330 grams (about 11-2/3 ounces) of pig's blood

133 A euphemism for a pig's slaughter.

200 grams (about 7 ounces) of concentrated must,[134] or refined
   honey
100 grams (about 3-1/2 ounces) of shelled sweet almonds
100 grams (about 3-1/2 ounces) of sugar
80 grams (about 2-2/3 ounces) of very fine bread crumbs
50 grams (about 1-2/3 ounces) of minced candied fruit
50 grams (about 1-2/3 ounces) of butter
2 teaspoons allspice
100 grams (about 3-1/2 ounces) of chocolate
1 teaspoon nutmeg
a strip of lemon peel

Crush the almonds in a mortar together with the candied fruit, which you have first diced, moistening the mixture now and then with a few teaspoons of milk. Then pass through a sieve. Boil the milk with the lemon peel for ten minutes, then remove the lemon peel, add the grated chocolate and stir until melted. Remove the milk from the fire and let it cool a little. Then pour into the same bowl the blood, which you have already passed through a sieve, and all the other ingredients, adding the bread crumbs last, so that if you have too much you can leave some of it aside.

Cook the mixture in *bain-marie*, stirring often so as not let it stick to the bowl. You will know that the mixture has achieved the right consistency and is done when the mixing spoon remains upright, if you stand it in the center of the mixture. If this does not happen eventually, add the rest of the bread crumbs, if you have not already used all of them. For the rest, follow the directions for ricotta cake (recipe 639), that is, pour the mixture into a baking pan lined with crazy dough (recipe 153), and when it has cooled completely, cut it into almond shaped pieces. Cook the dough as little as possible, so that it is easier to slice, and do not let the pudding dry out over the fire, but rather remove it from the hearth as soon as the broom-twig with which you are pricking it to test for doneness comes out clean.

If you are using honey instead of the concentrated must, taste it before adding the sugar to avoid making it too sweet, and keep in mind that one of the beauties of this dish lies in a creamy consistency.

134 See note to recipe 458.

My fear of not being understood by everyone often leads me to provide too many details, which I would gladly spare the reader. Still, some people never seem to be satisfied. For instance, a cook from a town in Romagna wrote to me: "I prepared the blood pudding described in your highly esteemed cookbook for my employers. It was very well liked, except that I didn't quite understand how to pass the almonds and the candied fruit through the sieve. Would you be good enough to tell me how to do this?"

Delighted by the question, I answered her: "I am not sure if you know that you can find sieves made especially for this purpose. One type is strong and widely spaced, and is made with horsehair. Another is made of very fine wire. With these, a good mortar and *elbow-grease*, you can purée even the most difficult things."

703. SOUFFLET DI CIOCCOLATA
(CHOCOLATE SOUFFLÉ)

120 grams (about 4-1/4 ounces) of sugar
80 grams (about 2-2/3 ounces) of potato flour
80 grams (about 2 2/3 ounces) of chocolate
30 grams (about 1 ounce) of butter
4 deciliters (about 1-2/3 cups) of milk
3 eggs
1 tablespoon of rum

Melt the butter over the fire, then add the grated chocolate. When this too has melted, pour in the potato flour and then the hot milk a little at a time. Keep stirring briskly as you add the sugar. When the mixture is blended and the flour is cooked, allow the preparation to cool. Lastly, add the rum and the eggs, first the yolks and then the whites beaten until stiff. If you use more than three whites this dessert will come out even better.

Grease an overproof bowl with butter, pour in the mixture, place it in a Dutch oven or simply on a burner with fire above and below. Serve hot as soon as it has risen.

These amounts serve six people.

704. SOUFFLET DI LUISETTA (LUISETTA'S SOUFFLÉ)

Try this because it's worth it—in fact it will be pronounced delicious.

1/2 liter (about 1/2 a quart) of milk
80 grams (about 2-2/3 ounces) of sugar
70 grams (about 2-1/3 ounces) of flour
50 grams (about 1-2/3 ounces) of butter
30 grams (about 1 ounce) of sweet almonds
3 eggs
a dash of vanilla sugar

Blanch the almonds, dry them, and crush them in a mortar until very fine with a spoonful of the sugar.

Make a béchamel with the butter, flour, and hot milk. Before removing it from the fire stir in the crushed almonds, the sugar, and the vanilla sugar. Once it has cooled, add the eggs, first the yolks and then the whites, beaten until stiff. Grease an ovenproof bowl with butter, pour in the mixture and bake in a Dutch oven.

This recipe serves five to six people.

705. SOUFFLET DI FARINA DI PATATE (POTATO FLOUR SOUFFLÉ)

100 grams (about 3-1/2 ounces) of sugar
80 grams (about 2-2/3 ounces) of potato flour
1/2 liter (about 1/2 a quart) of milk
3 whole eggs
2 or 3 egg whites
a dash of vanilla or lemon zest

Put the sugar and the flour in a saucepan and stir in the cold milk a little at a time. Put the mixture to thicken over the fire; keep stirring with the mixing spoon and don't worry if it comes to a boil. Add the vanilla or lemon zest.

Allow the mixture to cool and when it is lukewarm, mix in the three egg yolks, then beat the whites and fold them in gently. Pour the mixture into a metal bowl and place it on a burner, covering it with the lid of a Dutch oven, with fire above and below. Wait until it rises and turns lightly brown; sprinkle confectioners' sugar on it and send it to the table right away. It will be praised for its delicacy and, if there is any left, you will find it is also quite good cold.

This recipe serves five people.

706. SOUFFLET DI RISO (RICE SOUFFLÉ)

100 grams (about 3-1/2 ounces) of rice
80 grams (about 2-2/3 ounces) of sugar
6 deciliters (about 2-2/5 cups) of milk
3 eggs
a small piece of butter
1 tablespoon of rum
a dash of vanilla

Boil the rice in the milk, but unless you cook it for a very long time nothing good will come of it. When it is half done, add the butter and the sugar, including vanilla sugar for flavor, and, when it is done and has cooled, mix in the egg yolks, the rum and the egg whites, beaten until stiff.

As to the rest, follow the directions for the potato flour soufflé.

This recipe serves four people.

707. SOUFFLET DI CASTAGNE
(CHESTNUT SOUFFLÉ)

150 grams (about 5-1/4 ounces) of chestnuts, the largest available
90 grams (about 3 ounces) of sugar
40 grams (about 1-1/3 ounces) of butter
5 eggs
2 deciliters (about 4/5 of a cup) of milk
2 tablespoons Maraschino liqueur
a dash of vanilla

Boil the chestnuts in water for only five minutes because that is all it takes to be able to shell them and remove the inner skin. Then cook them in the milk and pass them through a sieve. Then add the sugar, melted butter, Maraschino, and vanilla. Stir in the eggs at the end, first the yolks and then the whites, beaten until good and stiff.

Grease an ovenproof bowl with butter, pour in the mixture, and bake it in a Dutch oven. Before sending it to the table, dust with confectioners' sugar.

This recipe serves five people.

708. ALBICOCCHE IN COMPOSTA
(APRICOT COMPOTE)

600 grams (about 1-1/3 pounds) of apricots, barely ripe
100 grams (about 3-1/2 ounces) of powdered sugar
1 glass of water

Make a small incision in the apricots to remove the stone, carefully so as not to spoil their appearance, and put them in the water to cook. When the water begins to boil, add the sugar. Shake the saucepan now and then as the apricots are cooking. When they have become soft and quite wrinkled, remove them one by one from the saucepan with a spoon and place them in a compote dish; drain them, and reduce the juice that has remained in the saucepan to the consistency of a syrup. Then pour it over the apricots. Serve cold.

709. PERE IN COMPOSTA I
(PEAR COMPOTE I)

600 grams (about 1-1/3 pounds) of pears
100 grams (about 3-1/2 ounces) of fine powdered sugar
2 glasses of water
half a lemon

If the pears are very small, keep them whole with their stems; if they are large, cut them into wedges. In either case, as you peel them toss them in the water, to which you have added the juice of half a lemon. This keeps the fruit white. Strain the water through a colander, then cook the pears in it, adding the sugar when the water begins to boil.

For the rest proceed as with the apricots in the preceding recipe. Serve cold.

710. PERE IN COMPOSTA II
(PEAR COMPOTE II)

This second way of preparing pear compote is not very different in its result from the preceding recipe, but the pears are handled with a bit more care.

600 grams (about 1/3 pounds) of small pears, barely ripe
120 grams (about 4-1/4 ounces) of sugar
2 glasses of water
half a lemon

Squeeze the lemon into the water and set aside.

Put the pears on the fire, with water to cover them, and let them boil for four to five minutes; then toss them into cool water, peel them, trim half their stems, and put them into the lemon water as you go along. This done, take the same water, strain it through a colander, and put it on the fire. When it begins to boil, add the sugar and let simmer for some time. Then, toss the pears back in to cook, making sure they do not begin to dissolve. Then strain the pears and arrange them in a compote dish. Reduce the water in which they have boiled to the consistency of a syrup and pour it over the pears, straining the liquid once more through the colander.

If the pears are very large, cut them into wedges after the first boiling. They are also quite good cooked with red wine, sugar, and a piece of cinnamon stick, as is commonly done in many households. Serve cold.

711. COMPOSTA DI COTOGNE
(QUINCE COMPOTE)

Peel the quinces, cut them into fairly small wedges making sure to remove the part in the middle that formed the core. Supposing you have 500 grams (about 1 pound) of quinces, put them on the fire in a saucepan with a glass and a half of water. Boil covered for a quarter of an hour and then add 180 grams (about 6-1/3 ounces) of fine sugar. As soon as they are cooked, strain and arrange them in the dish you are sending to the table. Reduce the remaining juice to a syrup, then pour it over the quinces. Serve cold.

712. RISO IN COMPOSTA
(RICE COMPOTE)

If you don't think that rice compote is an appropriate name for this dessert, you might prefer to call it compote in rice.

7 deciliters (about 2-4/5 cups) of milk
100 grams (about 3-1/2 ounces) of rice
50 grams (about 1-2/3 ounces) of sugar
20 grams (about 2/3 of an ounce) of butter
a pinch salt
a dash of lemon zest

Cook the rice in 6 deciliters (about 2-2/5 cups) of the milk and, when it is half cooked, pour all the other ingredients into it. Stir frequently with a wooden spoon because it sticks easily. When the milk has been absorbed, remove the rice from the flame and add the remaining deciliter of milk. Take a smooth mold with a hole in the middle. The size of the mold must be such that the mixture will form a layer at least two fingers deep. Coat the bottom and sides of the mold with sugar that has been melted over the fire to a light chestnut color. Pour the rice mixture into the mold, which you will put back on the fire in *bain-marie* so that the rice continues to firm up and the sugar is melted on the bottom. Allow it to cool before taking out of the mold.

The time has come now to fill the hole in the rice pudding with a fruit compote of your choice. Let us suppose it to be of apples or prunes.

If you are using apples, choose the red ones, which are firm and fragrant—200 grams (about 7 ounces) should suffice. Peel them, and cut them into wedges, discarding the core. To keep the pulp white, toss them as you go along in cool water to which you have added some lemon juice. Put the apples in a saucepan with enough water to barely cover them. When they reach a boil, add 70 grams (about 2-1/3 ounces) of sugar and a spoonful of kirsch. Once done, strain them. Reduce the remaining liquid to a syrup to which you will add, when it has cooled, another spoonful of kirsch. Pour the syrup over the apples. Fill the hole in the rice pudding and with this preparation before sending it to the table.

If you choose prunes, use 100 grams (about 3-1/2 ounces) of fruit, and 60 grams (about 2 ounces) of sugar will be enough. Soak the prunes in water for five or six hours before putting them on the fire to boil. As to the rest, prepare them as you did the apples, and don't forget the kirsch.

Double the amounts if you are serving ten to twelve people. Serve cold.

713. PASTICCIO A SORPRESA
(SURPRISE PIE)

1 liter (about 1 quart) of milk
200 grams (about 7 ounces) of rice flour
120 grams (about 4-1/4 ounces) of sugar
20 grams (about 2/3 of an ounce) of butter
6 eggs
a pinch of salt
a dash of vanilla

Take a saucepan and combine in it a little at a time the eggs, sugar, flour, and milk, stirring all the while to prevent lumps; but leave out some of the milk to be added later if necessary. Put the saucepan on the fire to cook, stirring constantly with a wooden spoon as you do when you make a custard. Before taking it off the fire, add the butter, vanilla, and salt. Allow it to cool, then pour it into a metal pie plate or an ovenproof earthenware pie pan, filling it up to the brim.

Cover it with shortcrust pastry dough (recipe 589 B or C), which you will decorate, gild with egg yolk and bake in the oven. Serve hot after sprinkling with confectioners' sugar.

714. GELATINA DI ARANCIO IN GELO
(CHILLED ORANGE GELATIN)

150 grams (about 5-1/4 ounces) of sugar
20 grams (about 2/3 of an ounce) of isinglass
4 deciliters (about 1-2/3 cups) of water
4 tablespoons of alkermes
2 tablespoons of rum
1 large sweet orange
1 lemon

Soak the isinglass for one or two hours, changing the water once.

Boil the sugar in half of the water for ten minutes and strain it through a cheesecloth.

Squeeze the juice of the orange and lemon, strain it through the same cheesecloth and then add to the syrup.

Remove the isinglass, which has now softened, and bring it to a boil in the remaining two deciliters of water. Then pour this into the syrup, adding to it the alkermes and the rum. Mix everything well and, when it begins to cool, pour it into the mold which you will keep on ice in summer and in cold water in winter.

The molds for this type of dessert are made of copper. They are intricately decorated with fancy ridges, and some have a hole in the middle, while others do not. In sum, they are designed to produce fancy shapes that will make an impressive presentation at the table. To remove this dessert from the mold properly, lightly grease the mold with oil before pouring in the mixture and then dip it in hot water for a moment or wipe it with a very hot cloth.

Isinglass is harmless, but it does have the disadvantage of sitting rather heavily on the stomach.

715. GELATINA DI FRAGOLE IN GELO
(CHILLED STRAWBERRY GELATIN)

300 grams (about 10-1/2 ounces) of very red, ripe strawberries
200 grams (about 7 ounces) of sugar
20 grams (about 2/3 of an ounce) of isinglass
3 deciliters (about 2-1/5 cups) of water

3 tablespoons of rum
the juice of a lemon

Squeeze the strawberries in a cheesecloth to extract all of their juice. Boil the sugar for ten minutes in 2 deciliters (about 4/5 of a cup) of the water and then add this syrup to the strawberry juice; mix in the lemon juice and strain everything through a tightly-woven cloth. Soak the isinglass as in the preceding recipe, and then bring it to a boil in the remaining 1 deciliter (about 2/5 of a cup) of water. Pour it, scalding hot, into the mixture; then add the rum, mix well, and pour the mixture into a mold to be chilled.

This gelatin will be well received by the ladies.

716. GELATINA DI MARASCHE O DI VISCIOLE IN GELO (CHILLED MORELLO OR BITTER CHERRY GELATIN)

400 grams (about 14 ounces) of morello or bitter cherries
200 grams (about 7 ounces) of sugar
20 grams (about 2/3 of an ounce) of isinglass
3 deciliters (about 1-1/5 cups) of water
3 tablespoons of rum
a cinnamon stick

Remove the stems and crush the cherries by hand, adding just a few ground cherrystones. Let them rest for a few hours and then strain the juice through a cheesecloth, squeezing well. Allow the juice to rest yet again and then strain it more than once through either paper or cotton, so that it becomes clear. Boil the sugar for ten minutes in 2 deciliters (about 4/5 of a cup) of the water with the cinnamon. Then strain this also through the cheesecloth and mix with the cherry juice. Add the isinglass, which you will have dissolved in the remaining 1 deciliter (about 2/5 of a cup) of water. Lastly add the rum, and then proceed as in the preceding gelatin recipes.

717. GELATINA DI RIBES IN GELO
(CHILLED RED CURRANT GELATIN)

300 grams (about 10-1/2 ounces) of red currants
130 grams (about 4-1/2 ounces) of sugar
20 grams (about 2/3 of an ounce) of isinglass
2 deciliters (about 4/5 of a cup) of water
4 tablespoons of Marsala wine
a dash of vanilla

Make this recipe just like the preceding recipe for morello cherry gelatin.

Ordinarily, foods are flavored with vanilla by means of vanilla sugar; but in this and similar cases it is better to use the natural bean or pod of that plant, by boiling a small piece of it in water together with sugar. As a rule of thumb, when buying vanilla beans make sure they are plump and not dried out. Store them tightly sealed mixed in with blond sugar to which they will transfer their flavor, so that in turn this sugar can be used for flavoring.

A native of the tropical forests of America, vanilla is a climbing plant like ivy and belongs to the orchid family. Its pollen is viscous and, since it cannot be carried by the wind, is carried by insects. This phenomenon was discovered only in the first decades of the last century, and now man performs this function himself and pollinates the plants grown in greenhouses. These plants produced no fruit until 1837, when the first fruits were produced in Belgium.

718. GELATINA DI LAMPONE IN GELO
(CHILLED RASPBERRY GELATIN)

If you have raspberry syrup (see recipe 723) you can make a nice dessert gelatin. Dissolve 20 grams (about 2/3 of an ounce) of isinglass over a flame in 3 deciliters (about 1 1/5 cups) of water and mix into it:

2 deciliters (about 4/5 of a cup) of syrup
1 deciliter (about 2/5 of a cup) of Marsala wine
1 tablespoon of rum

You do not need any sugar. If you must, use very little of it since the syrup is already very sweet. In all other respects proceed as in the previous gelatin recipes.

If you use fresh raspberries instead of syrup, use the same proportions and follow the same directions for strawberry gelatin (see recipe 715).

719. UN UOVO PER UN BAMBINO
(AN EGG FOR A CHILD)

Would you like to know how to quiet a child who is crying for a morning treat? All you need is a fresh egg. Beat the yolk with two or three teaspoons of powdered sugar in a shallow bowl. Beat the egg white until stiff and carefully fold it into the yolk. Place the bowl before the child with slices of bread which he can dip in the egg, and with which he can make himself a yellow mustache—he'll be in heaven.

Would that all children's meals were as harmless as this, for there would be far fewer hysterical and convulsive children in this world! I am talking about foods that irritate people's nerves, such as coffee, tea, wine and other products, tobacco among them, which become part of household routines much more quickly than they should.

720. BUDINO DI PANE E CIOCCOLATA
(BREAD-AND-CHOCOLATE PUDDING)

This is a family pudding—do not expect anything exquisite.

100 grams (about 3-1/2 ounces) of good, ordinary bread
70 grams (about 2-1/3 ounces) of sugar
40 grams (about 1-1/3 ounces) of chocolate
20 grams (about 2/3 of an ounce) of butter
4 deciliters (about 1-2/3 cups) of milk
3 eggs

Pour boiling milk over the bread, cut into thin slices. After allowing it to soak for approximately two hours, pass the mixture through a strainer to obtain a smooth cream; put it then on the fire, adding the sugar, butter, and chocolate, which you have grated. Stir the mixture often and boil it for some time. Then let it cool. Next add the eggs, first the yolks and then the whites, beaten until stiff. Cook in *bain-marie* in a smooth mold greased with butter and serve cold. To give it a more attractive appearance, it would not be a bad idea to cover the pudding with a custard after removing it from the mold.

These amounts serve five people.

721. MELE ALL'INGLESE (ENGLISH APPLES)

This dish could be called "apple pie" which would not be an improper term.

Core and peel red apples or some other kind of firm apples and cut them into thin, round slices. Place them on the fire with enough water to cook them and a cinnamon stick. When the apples are half-cooked, add enough sugar to make them sweet and some bits of candied fruit.

Pour the apples into a copper pie plate or an ovenproof porcelain dish, cover them with shortcrust pastry dough, bake in an oven or a Dutch oven, and serve hot as a dessert.

722. ZABAIONE

3 egg yolks
30 grams (about 1 ounce) of powdered sugar
1-1/2 deciliters (about 3/5 of a cup) equal to approximately nine
*   tablespoons of Cyprus, Marsala or Madeira wine*

Double these amounts to serve eight people. If you prefer it more "spirited," add a tablespoon of rum; adding one teaspoon of ground cinnamon wouldn't be a bad idea either.

With a wooden spoon beat the yolks with the sugar until they turn almost white, then add the liquid, mix well and put over a high flame, whisking constantly and taking care not to let the mixture boil, because in that case it would curdle. Remove the zabaione from the flame the moment it begins to turn light and fluffy. In my opinion, it is best to use a chocolate pot.

SYRUPS

Dissolved in cold or iced water, syrups made with tart fruits are pleasant, refreshing drinks, most fitting for the heat of a summer's day. However, it is better to consume them only after digestion is complete, since that natural process might be disturbed by the sugar they contain, which makes them sit rather heavily on the stomach.

723. SIROPPO DI LAMPONE
(RASPBERRY SYRUP)

The delicate flavor of this fruit (*framboise*, as the French call it) makes this the king of syrups. After crushing the fruit by hand, proceed as in recipe 725, with the same proportions of sugar and citric acid. Since raspberries are less glutinous than red currants, the fermentation time is shorter. If you are curious to know why these syrups require so much sugar I will tell you that it is necessary to preserve them. The citric acid counteracts the excessive sweetness.

724. ACETOSA DI LAMPONE
(TART RASPBERRY SYRUP)

This tart drink flavoring is made by replacing the citric acid with high-quality wine vinegar which you will add upon removing the raspberry syrup from the fire. The amount of vinegar is according to taste; therefore start with very little, and taste a drop of the syrup diluted in two fingers of water before adding more vinegar if you deem it necessary. This drink will be more refreshing and just as pleasant as the other syrups.

725. SIROPPO DI RIBES
(RED CURRANT SYRUP)

As it is very glutinous, this fruit requires a long fermentation; so much so that if you were to dissolve the sugar in freshly-squeezed red currant juice and put it on the fire the result would be not a syrup but a jelly. Crush the red currants while still on the stem, as you would with grapes to make must, and leave in an earthenware or wooden container in a cool place. When fermentation begins (it might take three to four days) push to the bottom any matter that has risen to the top, and stir twice a day with a large wooden spoon. Continue this procedure until the surface of the liquid remains clear, then strain through a kitchen towel a little at a time, squeezing by hand if you do not have a press. Then filter the juice two or three times, or even more if necessary, to obtain a very clear liquid. Place on the fire, and when it begins to boil pour in the sugar and the citric acid in the following proportions:

3 kilograms (about 3 quarts) of liquid
4 kilograms (about 8 pounds) of very white powdered sugar
30 grams (about 1 ounce) of citric acid

Stir constantly with a wooden spoon so that the sugar does not stick. Boil briskly for two or three minutes, and taste to see if more citric acid needs to be added. When it has cooled, bottle it and keep it in the cellar. Let me remind you that the beauty of these syrups lies in their clarity, which is the result of thorough fermentation.

726. SIROPPO DI CEDRO
(CITRON SYRUP)

3 garden lemons
600 grams (about 1-1/3 pounds) of fine white sugar
a table glass (about 3 deciliters or 1-1/5 cups) of water

Without squeezing it, cut out the pulp of the lemons, removing all seeds and peeling off the white rind. Put the water on the fire with the peel of one of the lemons cut into thin strips with a penknife. When the water begins to boil, pour in the sugar. Let it boil for a while, then remove the peel and add the lemon pulp. Keep boiling until the syrup is reduced and cooked to just the right consistency, that is when the bubbles acquire a pearl-like appearance and the liquid becomes the color of white wine. If possible, store it in a glass container, so that it can be taken out by the spoonful and dissolved in cold water. You will have an excellent, refreshing drink whose absence from the list of drinks served in cafés in several Italian provinces astounds me.

727. MARENA (SOUR CHERRY SYRUP)

Take true morello cherries, which even when ripe should be very sour. Remove the stems and crush them as you do grapes to make wine. Set aside a handful of cherrystones (the use of which I will tell you later on), and place the cherries together with a large cinnamon stick in an earthenware jar in a cool place. Allow them to ferment for at least forty-eight hours. However, the moment the pulp from the cherries begin to rise, push it down into the liquid, stirring every now and then. Now you should use a press to extract the juice; if you don't have a press, use your hands, squeezing the mixture a little at a time through loosely woven cloth.

The beauty of these syrups, as I have said, is their clarity; therefore, when the juice has rested a while, decant the clear portion and strain the remaining liquid several times through a woolen filter. Once all impurities have been removed from the liquid in this way, put it on the fire in the following proportions with the cinnamon stick.

6 kilograms (about 6 quarts) of filtered juice
8 kilograms (about 16 pounds) of very white sugar
50 grams (about 1-2/3 ounces) of citric acid

Wait until the liquid is quite hot before pouring in the sugar and the citric acid. Stir frequently so that the sugar does not sink to the bottom, where it would begin to burn. Boil as little as possible: four or five minutes is enough to dissolve the sugar into the liquid. Boiling the liquid too long would cause the fruit to lose much of its aroma, while boiling it too little would cause the sugar to settle at the bottom over time. When you remove the cherry syrup from the fire, pour it into an earthenware container to cool, then bottle it. Cork the bottles without any paraffin and store in the cellar where this and other syrups can be kept for some years.

Lastly, I will explain how to use the cherrystones mentioned above. Dry them in the sun, crush them, and remove up to 30 grams (about 1 ounce) worth of the kernels inside. These you will pound very fine in a mortar and mix in with the cherries before fermentation. The pleasant bitterness of these kernels makes the syrup even more tasty.

728. MARENA DA TRASTULLARSI
(CHERRIES FOR A JOLLY DIVERSION)

The most refined way to prepare morello cherries is the one I have described in the previous recipe. However, if you would like to eat as well as drink the fruit, as they do in some places, mix into the preceding syrup some cherries which have been prepared as follows:

1-1/2 kilograms (about 3 pounds) of morello cherries
2 kilograms (about 4 pounds) of very fine powdered sugar

Remove the stems and keep the cherries in the sun for five to six hours. Then put them on the fire with a small piece of cinnamon. When they have lost some of their liquid, add the sugar, stirring carefully so as not to damage the fruit. When they become wrinkled and turn brown, remove them from the fire and use them as I've just suggested.

729. ORZATA
(ALMOND SYRUP)

200 grams (about 7 ounces) of sweet almonds with 10 or 12 bitter
  almonds
600 grams (about 2-2/5 cups) of water
800 grams (about 1-3/4 pounds) of fine white sugar
2 tablespoons orange-flower water

Blanch and crush the almonds in a mortar, moistening them every now and then with the orange-flower water. When they have been reduced to a very fine paste, dissolve them in a third of the water and strain the juice through a cloth, squeezing well. Return to the mortar the dried paste remaining in the cloth and pound again with the pestle. Dilute again with another third of the water and strain the juice. Repeat the procedure a third time. Place all of the liquid thus obtained on the fire, and when it is very hot pour in the sugar. Stir and boil for about twenty minutes. When it has cooled, bottle it and keep it in a cool place. If made in this way, this orange-flavored syrup will not ferment and will keep for quite a while, but not as long as fruit syrups. Moreover its consistency is such that a very small amount of it diluted in a glass of water is enough for an excellent, refreshing drink. It comes out even more delicate made with melon seeds.

730. CLARET CUP

You need good red wine to make this drink, which deserves to be included here both for its taste and its ease of preparation. You can use Bordeaux, Chianti, Sangiovese and similar wines.

5 deciliters (about 2 cups) of wine
5 deciliters (about 2 cups) of water
5 lemons
500 grams (about 1 pound) of white sugar

Boil the sugar in the water for five minutes. Remove from the fire and squeeze into the syrup the juice of the lemons, then pour in the wine. Strain through a cheesecloth. Put it back on the fire and let simmer for twenty-five minutes. Bottle it after it has cooled. Serve it diluted with water and on ice in the summer. For long preservation, store in the cellar.

7 3 1 . SAPA (GRAPE SYRUP)

Must[135] is really nothing more than a grape syrup. In the kitchen it can be used in a variety of ways because its special flavor goes well with certain dishes. Children are especially fond of it and in winter they mix it with freshly fallen snow to create instant sherbet.

Press some good quality very ripe freshly harvested white grapes. After a fermentation of approximately twenty-four hours, collect the must and strain it through a cheesecloth. Put the must on the fire and boil for many hours until it reaches a syrupy consistency. Bottle it for storage.

135 See note to recipe 458.

PRESERVES

Preserves and fruit jellies are good to have on hand as they are often ingredients in the preparation of sweet dishes. They are enjoyed by the ladies as a finishing touch to a morning meal, and, spread on a slice of bread, they make an excellent snack for children, healthy and nutritious.

732. CONSERVA DI POMODORO SENZA SALE
(SALTLESS TOMATO PRESERVES)

If this precious fruit of the solanaceae family (*Solanum Lycopersicum*), originally from South America, were more rare, it would be as costly as truffles, and maybe more so. Its juice goes well with so many dishes and keeps these such excellent company, that good tomato preserves are worth all the effort they require. There are many ways to make tomato preserves and everyone has his own. I will describe for you the recipe that I use and have been following for many years because I am happy with it.

Take field tomatoes, as those from the garden are too watery, and choose small ones over large ones. Crush them whole and put them over a wood fire in a copper kettle that is not tin-plated. Don't be afraid: the acid in the tomatoes will only attack the copper if the sauce is removed from the fire and loses heat. If it weren't so, I would have experienced the symptoms of poisoning at least a hundred times. When they have cooked enough to dissolve, pour them into a finely-woven draining bag, and when the water has drained off, pass the pulp through a sieve to separate the flesh from the seeds and skin; be sure to press down hard.

Wash the kettle carefully and return the puréed tomatoes to the fire to reduce them as much as necessary. To determine the precise consistency the preserves should have—and herein lies the difficulty— pour a few drops onto a plate and if they do not run nor form a watery ring, then you know that they are done. Bottle the preserves; here you will have further evidence of their sufficient density if you see that they take a while to go through the funnel.

Salicylic acid in the proportion of 3 grams (about 1/10 of an ounce) for every 2-1/3 liters (about 2-1/3 quarts) of preserves is used to preserve a fruit that has cooked less than I have described, and therefore is more liquid and natural. It is said to be harmless, but up until now I have refrained from using it because I know that the Government, as a matter of public health, has prohibited the sale of it. If you use the preserves on a daily basis it is better not to use the acid.

Choose small bottles that will be used up quickly. However, once opened, they keep for 12 or 13 days without harm to the preserves. I use those clear glass bottles in which Recoaro water is sold or, lacking these, the dark half bottles used for beer. Cork them by hand, but be sure that they are well sealed, and tie the corks with a string. Be sure to allow a little air between the cork and the liquid. Here the operation would appear to be complete, but there is an addendum which, however brief, is nevertheless necessary. Place the bottles in a large kettle with straw, rags or something similar packed around them so that they fit snugly. Pour enough water into the kettle to reach the neck of the bottles and light the fire underneath. Keep an eye on the bottles and when they get to the point where the cork would pop out had they not been properly tied, put out the fire, for now the operation is truly complete. Remove the bottles when the water has cooled or even sooner, press down the corks securely with your fingers and store the bottles in the cellar. There is no need to seal them, because well-made preserves will not ferment; but if they do ferment and the bottles should explode, you could safely assume that too much water was left in them and that is due to undercooking.

I have heard that if you heat the empty bottles in a stove and fill them when they are very hot, there is no need to boil the preserves once they are bottled; but I myself have not tested this procedure.

I highly recommend tomato preserves made in this manner, for they are very useful in the kitchen. However, even better than this is the procedure known as vacuum packing, in which you preserve fresh whole tomatoes in tin cans. I wished success to this little industry, which began in the town of Forlì and seemed poised to do well; alas, difficulties arose; the Treasury immediately slapped a tax on them and the poor owner told me that he was thinking of closing down.

733. CONSERVA DOLCE DI POMODORO
(SWEET TOMATO PRESERVES)

It would seem from the name that this is one of the strangest preserves, but upon testing, I found it no less worthy than many others.

Every plant is known by its seed, says Dante; however, if there remains no seed to betray the secret, no one would guess what these preserves are made of.

1 kilogram (about 2 pounds) of tomatoes
300 grams (about 10-1/2 ounces) of white sugar
the juice of one lemon
a dash of vanilla and lemon zest

The tomatoes used for this recipe should be very ripe, meaty, and, if possible, round. Scald them in hot water, which makes them easy to peel. Once peeled, cut them in half and remove the seeds with the handle of a teaspoon. Dissolve the sugar over the fire in 2 fingers of water, then toss in the tomatoes, the lemon juice and a little grated lemon peel. Boil slowly, uncovered, stirring frequently and removing any seeds that remain. Lastly add a little vanilla sugar, and remove the mixture from the fire when it reaches the right consistency for preserves.

It is difficult to determine the amount of sugar for these preserves since it depends on the amount of water in the tomatoes. Make a double batch, since the tomatoes reduce significantly.

734. CONSERVA DI ALBICOCCHE
(APRICOT PRESERVES)

If plum preserves are the worst of all, apricot preserves are among the most delicate and therefore most people like them.

Take very ripe, good-quality apricots, as it is an error to believe that with inferior fruit you can achieve the same result; remove the stones, put them on the fire without water and while they are cooking crush them with the spoon to make a mush. When they have boiled for about a half hour, pass them through a sieve to separate the pulp from the skins and fibers. Return the apricots to the fire and add fine white powdered sugar, in the amount of 800 grams (about 1-3/4 pounds) of sugar for every kilogram (about 2 pounds) of puréed apricots. Stir frequently until the mixture reaches the consistency of preserves, which you can check by pouring a small spoonful on a plate; if the mixture runs slowly down the plate it is done. Pour the hot preserves into jars, and when they are cool, place wax paper directly on the preserves and cap the jar with thick paper tied with string.

Peach preserves are made in the same way, using very ripe peaches.

735. CONSERVA DI SUSINE (PLUM PRESERVES)

Even though plum preserves are one of the least liked, it would not be a bad idea to explain how to make them since many people nevertheless use them.

Any variety would do but it is preferable to use ripe greengage plums. Remove the stone and after a few minutes of boiling, pass them through a sieve. Return the plums to the heat with white powdered sugar, 60 grams (about 2 ounces) of sugar for every 100 grams (about 3-1/2 ounces) of whole plums, weighed as they are right off the tree.

If after some time the preserves begin to get moldy, it is a sign of undercooking. You can remedy this problem by reheating them. I keep them sometimes for four or five years and they suffer not at all or very little.

7 3 6. CONSERVA DI MORE
(BLACKBERRY PRESERVES)

These preserves are known to soothe a sore throat, as well as being good to eat.

1 kilogram (about 2 pounds) of blackberries
200 grams (about 7 ounces) of white sugar

Use your hands to crush the blackberries, and then boil them for about ten minutes. Pass through a sieve and put back on the fire with the sugar. Cook until reduced to the consistency of fruit preserves.

7 3 7. CONSERVE DI RIBES E DI LAMPONE
(RED CURRANT AND RASPBERRY PRESERVES)

For red currant preserves you can use recipe 739 for red currant jelly. For raspberry preserves, boil the unfermented fruit for twenty minutes and then pass through a sieve. Weigh the fruit without the seeds and return it to the fire, adding an equal weight of powdered sugar. Boil the mixture until it is reaches the consistency of preserves, which by now you should know how to recognize.

Raspberry preserves, used in small quantity, seem to me more suitable than any other as a filling for puff pastries.

7 3 8. GELATINA DI COTOGNE (QUINCE JELLY)

Take yellow quinces, which are riper than green ones, core and cut them into slices half a finger thick. Cover with water and boil without stirring in a covered saucepan until well cooked. Pour them into a very fine-meshed sieve over a basin to catch all the water without squeezing them. Weigh this water and return it to the fire adding an equal weight of fine white sugar. Boil uncovered, skimming off the foam, until the liquid thickens sufficiently, which you will know either because the bubbles begin to form little pearls in the syrup, or because a drop of syrup poured on a plate does't run.

zucchero
1   2   3
pera   prugna
composta

G. Mele 2001

With the remaining quinces you can make preserves as in recipe 742, using as much sugar as the weight of the quinces once you have passed them through a sieve. I warn you, however, that they turn out to have little flavor or aroma.

Fruit jellies look best in little glass jars so that their color can be better appreciated, like this one, for instance, which turns a beautiful garnet red.

739. GELATINA DI RIBES (RED CURRANT JELLY)

As we said in recipe 725 for red currant syrup, this fruit contains a great deal of gluten. Squeeze the juice through a kitchen towel and put it on the fire without fermenting it, along with 80 parts of white sugar for every 100 parts of juice. You will obtain a jelly even without much boiling. This jelly can be stored in jars like preserves, and is good for garnishing various desserts. It is a light and healthy food for convalescents.

740. CONSERVA DI AZZERUOLE
(AZAROLE PRESERVES)

Azaroles, which in some places are called royal apples, are a fruit that ripens toward the end of September; they can be red or white. To make preserves, choose the white ones, the largest and ripest you can find, that is those that have lost their greenish color.

1 kilogram (about 2 pounds) of azarole
80 grams (about 2-2/3 ounces) of white sugar
7 deciliters (about 2-4/5 cups) of water

Toss the azaroles in boiling water with their stems still attached; boil for ten minutes. While still hot, use the point of a small knife to remove the stones from the flower side, and if any of the fruit loses its shape, put it back together with your fingers, then peel without removing the stem. Dissolve the sugar in the 7 deciliters (about 2-4/5 cups) of water—you can even use the water in which you boiled the fruit. Add the azaroles, and when the liquid becomes a syrup, that is, when it begins to fall in threads from the spoon, remove from the fire and store the fruit with the liquid in jars. They look as if they werer candied, and are very good.

741. CONSERVA SODA DI COTOGNE
(THICK QUINCE PRESERVES)

Spread on bread slices, fruit preserves are a good way of satisfying children's hunger once in a while. For this reason alone, if for nothing else, prudent mothers should keep them on hand.

Some people recommend that quinces be cooked unpeeled so that they retain more of their aroma. But this seems unnecessary to me, since this fruit has plenty of aroma and by cooking as explained below you are saved the trouble of passing them through a sieve.

800 grams (about 1-3/4 pounds) of quinces, peeled and cored
500 grams (about 1 pound) of fine white sugar

Dissolve the sugar on the fire in half a glass of water, boil for a short while and then set aside.

Cut the quinces into very thin slices and put them on the fire in a copper saucepan with a cup of water. Keep them covered but stir often, using the spoon to break and crush them. When they have become tender, pour in the sugar syrup you have prepared. Stir often and allow the mixture to boil in an uncovered saucepan until it reaches the right consistency, which you can recognize when it falls in thin sheets from the spoon.

742. CONSERVA LIQUIDA DI COTOGNE
(SMOOTH QUINCE PRESERVES)

Made in the following manner you can keep it thin enough to be spread on bread.

Cut the quinces into sections, core them, leave the peel, weigh them, then cover them with water and put on the fire.

When the quinces are well cooked, pass them through a sieve.

Put them back on the fire in their water and as much powdered sugar as the weight of the raw quinces. But only add the sugar after the mixture has come to a boil. Stir often and when you see that they are not too thin (test by pouring a few drops on a plate), remove them from the heat.

743. CONSERVA DI ARANCI
(ORANGE PRESERVES)

12 oranges
1 garden lemon
the weight of the oranges in fine white sugar
1/2 the weight of the oranges in water
4 tablespoons of genuine rum

Prick the oranges all over with a fork, then soak them for 3 days, changing the water morning and night. On the fourth day, cut the oranges in half, and then each half into half-centimeter sections (about 1/4 of an inch), discarding the seeds. Weigh the oranges and only then determine how much sugar and water you will need according to the above proportions. First boil the oranges in the water for ten minutes, then add the lemon cut in half, and immediately thereafter pour in the sugar, stirring constantly until the mixture returns to a fast boil—this will prevent the sugar from settling at the bottom and sticking to the saucepan.

In order to determine when they are done, every now and then pour a drop onto a plate, blow on it and when it does not run easily, immediately remove the mixture from the heat. Wait until the preserves are lukewarm to add the rum, and then store in jars like all other fruit preserves. Keep in mind that these have the added virtue of aiding digestion.

You can also do without the lemon.

744. CONSERVA DI ARANCI FORTI
(BITTER ORANGE PRESERVES)

Let's see if I can also satisfy those who would like to know how to make preserves with bitter oranges.

Boil the bitter oranges in water until a twig will pass easily through them. Transfer the oranges to cold water and let them soak for two days, changing the water often. Then cut them as in the preceding recipe, discarding the seeds and the white filaments that you find on the inside. Then weigh them and put them on the fire without water with 150 grams (about 5-1/4 ounces) of fine white sugar for every 100 grams (about 3-1/2 ounces) of fruit. Simmer and make sure that the syrup does not become too thick, which will cause the oranges to become hard.

745. CONSERVA DI ROSE (ROSE PRESERVES)

I did not know that the rose, the queen of flowers whose splendid palace is in the Orient, counts among its many merits that singular quality of transforming itself into a good-tasting, fragrant preserve.

Out of all its species and varieties, the one that I prize and admire above all is the moss rose[136] since, when its blossoms begin to open and I observe them closely, they reawaken in me, as they likely do in others, the symbolic idea of virginal chastity. And perhaps it was these blossoms that inspired Ariosto to write these beautiful octaves:

> *La verginella è simile alla rosa*
> *Ch'in bel giardin sulla nativa spina*
> *Mentre sola a sicura si riposa,*
> *Né gregge né pastor se le avvicina:*
> *L'aura soave e l'alba rugiadosa,*
> *L'acqua, la terra al suo favor s'inchina;*
> *Giovani vaghi e donne innamorate*
> *Amano averne e seni e tempie ornate.*
>
> *Ma non sì tosto dal materno stelo*
> *Rimossa viene, e dal suo ceppo verde,*

136 A variety of cabbage rose, with a mossy calyx.

che quanto avea dagli uomini e dal cielo
Favor, grazia e belleza, tutto perde.
La vergine che 'l fior, di che più zelo
Che de' begli occhi e della vita aver de',
Lascia altrui corre, il pregio ch'avea innanti
Perde nel cor di tutti gli altri amanti.

(The virgin has her image in the rose
Sheltered in garden on its native stock,
Which there in solitude and safe repose,
Blooms unapproached by shepherd or by flock.
For this earth teems, and freshening water flows,
And breeze and dewy dawn their sweets unlock:
With such the wishful youth his bosom dresses,
With such the enamored damsel braids her tresses.

But wanton hands no sooner this displace
From the maternal stem, where it was grown,
Than all is withered; whatsoever grace
It found with man or heaven; bloom, beauty, gone.
The damsel who should hold in higher place
Than light or life the flower which is her own,
Suffering the Spoiler's hand to crop the prize,
Forfeits her worth in every other's eyes.)[137]

A kind elderly lady, whose memory I carry etched in my heart, cultivated this species of rose in her garden as her favorite, and knowing
my predilection for those lovely, poetic flowers, gave me some every
year in the month of May.

The best time to make this preserve is when the roses are in full
bloom from the 15th of May to the 10th of June. Use the so-called
"May" roses, which are pink and very fragrant. Remove the petal
from the flowers and cut away the yellow part found at the base of
the petal; the most time-saving way to do this is to take the entire
blossom in your left hand, or better, the corolla of the rose, and with

137 *Orlando Furioso*, vol. 1, stanzas 42-43, by Ludovico Ariosto, translation by William
Stewart Rose, in *Ariosto's Orlando Furioso*, Vol. I (London: John Murray Albemarle-Street, 1823).

your right hand, armed with scissors, cut it all the way around just above the base of the calyx. Here is the recipe:

600 grams (about 1-1/3 pounds) of fine white sugar
200 grams (about 7 ounces) rose petals
6 deciliters (2-2/5 cups) of water
1/2 a lemon
1 teaspoon breton for coloring

Place the petals in a metal bowl with 200 grams (about 7 ounces) of sugar and the juice of the half lemon. Mash the petals with your hands, tearing them and reducing them as best you can to a paste. Dissolve the rest of the sugar in the water and then add the petals: boil until thickened to the consistency of a syrup (test by taking a drop between your fingers to see if it is sticky but be careful not to wait until it forms a thread). Before removing it from the fire, add color with the *breton,* which is optional if you don't care about the color. *Breton* is a harmless red vegetable liquid, named as such by its inventor, which is used to color any sort of sweet.

What I have just described is the simplest way to make rose preserves, and the way I prefer, but the petals do get a little tough. If you would like more tender petals, first boil them for five minutes in water, strain, squeeze to remove the excess water and then crush them in a mortar as much as possible with the 200 grams (about 7 ounces) of sugar and the lemon juice. Next dissolve the remaining sugar in the same water and then add the rose paste. From here proceed as already explained.

When the preserves have cooled, can and store them as you would other fruit preserves.

LIQUEURS

746. ROSOLIO DI PORTOGALLO
(PORTUGUESE LIQUEUR)

650 grams (about 1-1/2 pounds) of very fine white sugar
360 grams (about 12-2/3 ounces) of water
250 grams (about 1 cup) of 36-proof wine spirits
a pinch of saffron
1 orange

Remove the outermost part of the orange peel with a penknife and
place it in a jar, pouring over it the spirits mixed with the saffron.
Cover the jar with perforated paper and let sit for three days. In
another jar, combine the sugar and the water. Shake the jar every
now and then so that the sugar dissolves completely. On the fourth
day mix the two liquids together and let them rest for another eight
days. Now strain the rosolio through a cloth, then filter it through
paper or cotton, and finally bottle it.

747. ROSOLIO DI CEDRO (CITRON LIQUEUR)

800 grams (about 1-3/4 pounds) of fine white powdered sugar
1 liter (about 1 quart) of rain or spring water
8 deciliters (about 3-1/3 cups) of strong spirits
3 garden lemons, still somewhat green

Combine the sugar and water in a jar which you will shake every
day until the sugar is completely dissolved.

In the meantime, grate the lemon peels and steep them in 2

deciliters (about 4/5 of a cup) of the spirits for eight days. For the first three or four days, shake the jar often, and in the winter keep in a warm place. After eight days, strain the infusion of lemon peels through a wet cloth, squeezing well. Mix the extracted liquid with the remaining 6 deciliters (about 2-2/5 of a cup) of spirits and allow it to rest for twenty-four hours. The next day mix the lemon water with the syrup and then pour the liquid into a flask, which you should shake every now and then. After fifteen days, strain the liquid through paper or several times through cotton. Place the cotton in the narrow end of a funnel and insert a broom twig with a few branches in it to facilitate the passage of the liquid.

748. ROSOLIO DI ANACI
(ANISETTE)

This is made in the same way described in the preceding recipe. However, instead of making an infusion of lemon peels, use 50 grams (about 1-2/3 ounces) of Romagnol aniseed, and I specify Romagnol because this aniseed, on account of its pleasant flavor and strong fragrance, is without exaggeration the best in the world. However, before using the seeds, wash them in water to remove the soil that has most likely been mixed in with them deliberately to adulterate the product. It must have been sixty years ago by now when some honest men pointed out to me the villain who had begun this disgraceful practice. Those who follow in his footsteps, and there are many, use a clay soil similar in color to aniseed. They dry it in the oven, then sift it to reduce it to the same size as the aniseed, into which it is mixed in a ratio of ten or even twenty percent.

Some earboxing would be in order for those who make an ill-gotten profit by adulterating the products of their own land. They don't consider the harm that they do, which most of the time comes back to haunt them. They do not think about the discredit they do to their own merchandise, the mistrust that ensues, and the danger of alienating their customers. I have always heard it said that honesty is the heart of business, and Benjamin Franklin said that if rascals knew all the advantages that come from being honest they would be gentlemen purely on the basis of selfish interest.

My long experience in life has shown me that honesty, in business and in industry, is the best policy if you want to be successful in this world.

A soldier of the first empire told me that he had read on a pharmacy canister in Moscow: *Aniseed from Forlì*. I do not know if it is known by this name outside of Italy; but this plant of the umbelliferous family is exclusively cultivated in the countryside around Meldola, Bertinoro and Faenza, near Brisighella.

749. ROSOLIO TEDESCO
(GERMAN LIQUEUR)

Don't be put off by the strange way to prepare this liqueur, for it is easier than it seems, and the liqueur will turn out clear as water and delightful to the taste.

500 grams (about 17-2/3 fluid ounces) of the best wine spirits
500 grams (about 1 pound) of white confectioners' sugar
1/2 a liter (about 1/2 a quart) of milk
1 garden lemon
1/2 of a vanilla bean

Mince the whole lemon, removing the seeds and adding the peel, which you have grated in advance. Break the vanilla bean into tiny pieces, and combine everything together in a glass jar; the milk will curdle immediately. Shake the jar once a day; after eight days, strain the liquid through a cloth and then filter through paper.

750. NOCINO (WALNUT LIQUEUR)

Nocino is a liqueur that should be made toward the middle of June, when the walnuts have not yet fully ripened. It has a pleasant taste, aids digestion, and has a tonic effect.

30 walnuts (with the husk)
1-1/2 liters (about 1-1/2 quarts) of spirits
750 grams (about 1-2/3 pounds) of powdered sugar
2 grams (about 1/10 of an ounce) of minced "queen" cinnamon

10 whole cloves
4 deciliters (about 1-2/3 cups) of water
the peel of 1 garden lemon, cut into small pieces

Cut the walnuts into four sections and infuse them with the other ingredients in a demijohn or a 4- to 5-liter (4 to 5 quarts) flask. Seal it tightly and keep in a warm place for forty days, shaking it every now and then.

After the forty days have gone by, strain the liquid through a cloth and then, to clarify it completely, filter it through cotton or paper. Make sure to taste it a day or two in advance, however, to see if it is too strong, in which case you can add a cup of water.

751. ELISIR DI CHINA
(CINCHONA ELIXIR)

I do not offer to the public every recipe that I test; many I omit because they do not seem worthwhile. However, I will describe this elixir which I found very satisfying.

50 grams (about 1-2/3 ounces) of bruised Peruvian cinchona bark
5 grams (about 1/6 of an ounce) of bruised dried bitter orange
*   peel*
700 grams (about 24-2/3 fluid ounces) of wine spirits
700 grams (about 24-2/3 fluid ounces) of water
700 grams (about 1 1/2 pounds) of white sugar

First combine 250 grams (about 8-4/5 fluid ounces) of spirits with 150 grams (about 5-1/4 fluid ounces) of water, and with this mixture make an infusion of the cinchona bark and orange peel, keeping it in a warm place for ten days, and shaking the jar at least once a day. Then strain it through a cloth, squeezing hard to get all the essences out, and then filter through paper. Next dissolve the sugar on the fire in the remaining 550 grams (about 19-1/3 fluid ounces) of water without bringing it to a boil. Then pass the syrup through a sieve, or better through a cloth, to remove any possible impurity. Add the remaining 450 grams (about 15-4/5 fluid ounces) of spirits and mix everything together. Your elixir is done. Before filtering it, taste it and, if it seems too strong, add more water.

752. PONCE DI ARANCIO
(ORANGE PUNCH)

1-1/2 liters (about 1-1/2 quarts) of rum
1 liter (about 1 quart) of spirits
1 liter (about 1 quart) of water
1 kilogram (about 2 pounds) of fine white sugar
the juice of 3 oranges
the grated peel of one garden lemon, steeped in 1 deciliter (about
*   3-1/2 fluid ounces) of the spirits for 3 days*

Combine the water and the sugar and boil for five or six minutes. After it has cooled, add the rum, the orange juice and the spirits, including the infusion which you have first passed through a cloth.

Filter it as for other liqueurs and then bottle the punch. Serve it *flambé* in liqueur glasses.

ICE CREAMS

I read in an Italian newspaper that the art of making ice cream belongs preeminently to Italy, that the origin of ice cream is ancient, and that the first ice creams in Paris were served to Catherine de' Medici in 1533. This article added that the Florentine pastry makers, chefs, and icers of the royal palace would not share knowledge of their art. As a result the secret recipe for making ice cream remained within the confines of the Louvre, and Parisians had to wait another century to taste ice cream.

All my research to verify this story has been in vain. One thing that is sure on the subject of ice cream is this: the use of snow and stored ice to produce iced drinks is of oriental origin and goes all the way back to remote antiquity. Ice creams came into fashion in France around 1660, when a certain Procopio Coltelli from Palermo opened a shop in Paris under his own name: *Café Procope*. The establishment was across from the *Comédie Française*, which was then the meeting place of all the Parisian *beaux esprits*. The immediate success of this place, which was the first to serve ice cream in the shape of an egg in stemmed cups, drove the vendors of lemonade and other drinks to imitate it. Among these should be remembered Tortoni, whose delicious ice creams were so in vogue that his café acquired a European reputation, and made him his fortune.

According to Atheneus and Seneca, the ancients built ice boxes to store snow and ice using a technique not so different from ours today, namely: digging deep into the earth and, after compacting the ice and snow, covering them with oak branches and straw. But the ancients did not yet know the properties of salt, which when added to ice accelerates the freezing process, making it much easier to make sherbet with liqueurs of every kind.

You will almost surely please all your dinner guests, especially in the summer, if at the end of the meal you offer them sherbet or ice cream. These desserts, in addition to satisfying one's palate, also aid digestion by recalling heat to the stomach. And today, thanks to the American ice cream makers, which have triple action and need no spatula, making ice cream has become so much easier and faster that it would be a shame not to enjoy much more frequently the sensual pleasure of this delicious food.

To save money you can re-use the salt by drying it out on the fire, thus evaporating the water that had resulted from the freezing process.

753. PEZZO IN GELO (BISCUIT)
(ICE CREAM MOLD)

Make a custard with:

140 grams (about 5 fluid ounces) of water
50 grams (about 1-2/3 ounces) of sugar
4 egg yolks
a dash of vanilla

Put the custard on the fire, stirring constantly, and when it begins to coat the spoon, remove it from the flame and whip it with a whisk. If it takes too long to fluff up, put the basin on ice, then pour in little by little two sheets of isinglass dissolved on the fire in a little of water. Once it has fluffed up, fold in 150 grams (about 5-1/4 ounces) of whipped cream and pour the mixture into a mold made especially for ice cream or in a saucepan or a copper bowl, provided that it has a lid. Freeze for at least three hours between thick layers of ice and salt. This recipe serves seven to eight people and is a dessert sure to please.

754. GELATO DI LIMONE (LEMON ICE)

300 grams (about 10-1/2 ounces) of fine white sugar
1/2 a liter (about 1/2 a quart) of water
3 lemons

If possible, it is better to use garden lemons because they are more fragrant and better tasting than imported lemons, which often taste a little off.

Put the sugar and some pieces of lemon peel in the water, and boil for ten minutes in an uncovered saucepan. When the syrup has cooled, squeeze in the lemons, one at a time, tasting the mixture to be sure that it is not too sour; strain it and pour it into the ice cream maker.

This recipe serves six people.

755. GELATO DI FRAGOLE (STRAWBERRY ICE)

300 grams (about 10-1/2 ounces) of very ripe strawberries
300 grams (about 10-1/2 ounces) of fine white sugar
1/2 a liter (about 1/2 a quart) of water
1 large garden lemon
1 orange

Boil the sugar in the water for ten minutes in an uncovered saucepan. Pass the strawberries through a sieve, and strain the lemon juice and the orange juice. Strain the syrup as well, and then add it to the other ingredients. Blend everything together and pour the mixture into the ice cream maker.

This recipe serves eight people.

756. GELATO DI LAMPONE
(RASPBERRY ICE)

Except for their unique flavor, raspberries are almost identical to strawberries; therefore prepare according to the strawberry ice recipe, but omit the orange juice.

757. GELATO DI PESCHE (PEACH ICE)

400 grams (about 14 ounces) of very ripe soft peaches, weighed
with the stones
250 grams (about 8-4/5 ounces) of sugar
1/2 a liter (about 1/2 a quart) of water
1 garden lemon
3 lemon seed kernels

Crush the seed kernels with the sugar and boil the mixture in water for ten minutes. Purée the peach pulp, squeeze in the lemon and after mixing everything together, pass the mixture through a very fine sieve.

This recipe serves six people.

758. GELATO DI ALBICOCCHE
(APRICOT ICE)

300 grams (about 10-1/2 ounces) of very ripe, flavorful apricots,
weighed with their stones
200 grams (about 7 ounces) of fine white sugar
1/2 a liter (about 1/2 a quart) of water
1 garden lemon

Boil the sugar in the water for ten minutes. When it has cooled, add the apricots, which you have passed through a sieve, and the juice from the lemon. Pass the mixture through a sieve once again before pouring it into the ice cream maker.

These amounts make four generous servings.

759. GELATO DI CREMA (CUSTARD ICE CREAM)

Follow recipe 685 to make a custard with:

1 liter (about 1 quart) of milk
200 grams (about 7 ounces) of sugar
8 egg yolks
a dash of vanilla

You will have a delicious ice cream, creamy and firm, if you know how to make it correctly.

This recipe serves ten people.

Instead of vanilla you can use coriander or toasted coffee or toasted almonds. If you use the coriander see recipe 693 for milk Portuguese style; if you use coffee, boil several ground coffee beans in the milk separately. If you use toasted almonds, make a little almond brittle as described in recipe 617 (cooking it a bit longer) with 100 grams (about 3-1/2 ounces) of almonds and 80 grams (about 2-2/3 ounces) of sugar; crush it finely, boil it separately in a little milk, pass it through a sieve and add it to the custard.

760. GELATO DI AMARETTI
(MACAROON ICE CREAM)

1 liter (about 1 quart) of milk
200 grams (about 7 ounces) of sugar
100 grams (about 3-1/2 ounces) of macaroons
6 egg yolks
a dash of vanilla sugar

Crush the macaroons very fine in a mortar and then place them in a saucepan, adding the sugar, the yolks and the vanilla sugar; mix well, then pour in the milk a little at a time. Place the milk on the fire to thicken the mixture, as you would for custard, then pour it into the ice cream maker to freeze it.

You will have a delicious ice cream that makes eight generous servings.

Half these amounts make four to five servings.

761. GELATO DI CIOCCOLATA
(CHOCOLATE ICE CREAM)

1 liter (about 1 quart) of milk
200 grams (about 7 ounces) of fine chocolate
100 grams (about 3 1/2 ounces) of sugar

Grate the chocolate and put it on the fire with the sugar and 4 deciliters (about 1-2/3 cups) of the milk in a small saucepan. Boil the
mixture for a few minutes, whisking all the while so that it is smooth.
Remove it from the fire, add the remaining milk and then pour the
mixture into the ice cream maker.

This recipe serves ten people.

If you prefer this ice cream even richer, increase the sugar to
120 grams (about 4-1/4 ounces) and add 2 egg yolks once you have
removed the chocolate from the fire and when it is no longer boiling. Blend, return it to the fire for a few more minutes and then add
the rest of the milk.

762. GELATO DI CILIEGE VISCIOLE
(SOUR CHERRY ICE)

1 kilogram (about 2 pounds) of sour cherries
250 grams (about 8-4/5 ounces) of sugar
2 deciliters (about 4/5 of a cup) of water
cinnamon

Remove the stones from 150 grams (about 5-1/4 ounces) of the cherries, damaging them as little as possible, and put them on the fire
with 50 grams (about 1-2/3 ounces) of the sugar and a piece of cinnamon stick, which you will later discard. When the cherries become
syrupy and wrinkled, put them aside. Crush the remaining 850 grams
(about 1-4/5 pounds) of cherries by hand, then crush a handful of
the stones in a mortar and add them to the cherries. Strain them a
handful at a time through a cloth, squeezing the crushed cherries
firmly to extract all the juice. Place solid bits of cherry that are left
on the fire with the 2 deciliters (about 4/5 of a cup) of water to get
all the remaining juice out: boil for four to five minutes, then strain

the liquid through the same cloth, and add it to the juice from the first straining. Put all of the liquid on the fire with two pinches of ground cinnamon; when it is just about to boil, pour in the remaining 200 grams (about 7 ounces) of sugar. Stir, boil for two minutes and then pass through a sieve.

Put the juice into the ice cream maker. When it is completely frozen mix in the syrupy cherries, distributing them evenly throughout. Serve in small glasses, and you will see that it will be enjoyed by all.

This recipe serves eight people.

763. GELATO DI ARANCI (ORANGE ICE)

4 large oranges
1 garden lemon
6 deciliters (about 2-2/5 cups) of water
300 grams (about 10-1/2 ounces) of sugar

Squeeze the oranges and the lemon, and strain the juice.

Boil the sugar in the water for ten minutes, pour in the juice, strain the mixture once again and put it into the ice cream maker. Serve in mounds in small dessert cups or in a single piece.

This recipe serves eight people.

764. GELATO DI RIBES
(RED CURRANT ICE)

I offer you this recipe though this ice cream is nothing exceptional.

500 grams (about 1 pound) of red currants
300 grams (about 10-1/2 ounces) of sugar
150 grams (about 5-1/4 ounces) of black cherries
1/2 a liter (about 1/2 a quart) of water
1 large garden lemon

Crush the red currants and cherries by hand, add the lemon juice, and pass the whole mixture through a sieve, squeezing well.

Make the syrup by boiling the sugar in the water for ten minutes in an uncovered saucepan. When it has cooled, add the red currant and cherry mixture, and then pour into the ice cream maker.

This recipe serves seven to eight people. Send to the table in little stemmed glasses. In addition to their special flavor, the cherries lend a prettier color to the ice.

765. GELATO DI TUTTI I FRUTTI
(TUTTI FRUTTI ICE)

While this ice is called "all fruits," three different kinds of fruit are enough, as you can see from the following recipe, which serves four people.

200 grams (about 7 ounces) of sugar
100 grams (about 3-1/2 ounces) of very ripe apricots, weighed
*   with the stones*
100 grams (about 3-1/2 ounces) raspberries
100 grams (about 3-1/2 ounces) red currants
20 grams (about 2/3 of an ounce) of candied citron
1/2 a liter (about 1/2 a quart) of water

Boil the sugar in the water for ten minutes; next pass the fruit pulp through a sieve and add to the syrup, then add the candied citron, finely chopped.

Soft peaches can be substituted for the apricots and strawberries for the red currants.

766. GELATO DI BANANE (BANANA ICE)

The banana tree, Linnaeus's *musa paradisiaca*, is popularly called *Adam's Fig* or *Tree of Paradise* in his country because it is commonly believed that this is the famous forbidden fruit, and that its ample leaves were used to cover Adam and Eve's nakedness after the sin of disobedience.

It grows in the Indies and its fruit is in the form of a large pod whose appearance resembles a green cucumber, but it is smooth,

triangular and curved. Its pulp has a delicate flavor but can be somewhat bitter if not completely ripe; when making ice, choose very yellow fruits to be sure the bananas are ripe.

The following amounts serve six people.

4 peeled bananas, equaling 240 grams (about 8-1/2 ounces)
200 grams (about 7 ounces) of white sugar
1 garden lemon
1/2 a liter (about 1/2 a quart) of water

Pass the pulp of the bananas through a sieve and then add the lemon
juice. Boil the sugar in the water for five minutes in an uncovered
saucepan; combine all ingredients and pour the mixture into the ice
cream maker. Do not skimp on the salt and ice.

767. GELATO DI PISTACCHIO (PISTACHIO ICE CREAM)

8 deciliters (about 3-1/3 cups) of milk
150 grams (about 5-1/4 ounces) of sugar
50 grams (about 1-2/3 ounces) of pistachios
6 egg yolks

Blanch the pistachios in hot water and crush them very fine in a
mortar with a tablespoon of the sugar; then put them in a saucepan
with the egg yolks and the remaining sugar, stirring until thoroughly
blended. Add the milk and place the mixture on the fire, stirring
constantly. When the mixture has thickened to the consistency of a
custard, allow it to cool, and then pour it into the ice cream maker.

This recipe serves eight people.

Some people toast the pistachios but I do not, because they lose
their distinct flavor when toasted.

They say that to deepen the green color of the pistachios, you
can add some Swiss chard, boiled and puréed.

768. GELATO DI TORRONE (NOUGAT ICE CREAM)

1 liter (about 1 quart) of milk
250 grams (about 8-4/5 ounces) of sugar
40 grams (about 1-1/3 ounces) of candied pumpkin
40 grams (about 1-1/3 ounces) of candied citron
30 grams (about 1 ounce) of almonds
20 grams (about 2/3 of an ounce) of pistachios
4 egg yolks
a dash of vanilla

Make a custard with the milk, sugar and egg yolks; add the vanilla and pour the mixture into the ice cream maker. When it is frozen, add the other ingredients. Blanch the pistachios and the almonds in hot water. Divide the pistachios in three parts. Chop the almonds into pieces the size of vetch seeds and then then toast them. Cut the citron into slivers and the pumpkin into largish cubes, which give a nice color to the ice cream.

Boil the milk for half an hour with the sugar. If the milk is of good quality you can make the ice cream without the egg yolks, but it will not be as flavorful.

In this case and in similar cases, almonds are best toasted in the following manner. Blanch and chop them, and then put them on the fire with a tablespoon of sugar and a drop of water. Stir constantly and when they have browned, halt the cooking process with another drop of water. Then pour the almonds in a colander on top of the remaining sugar and they are ready to use.

769. GELATO DI CASTAGNE (CHESTNUT ICE CREAM)

This is an ordinary ice cream, but many like it, since almost everyone likes the flavor of chestnuts. And here is the recipe.

200 grams (about 7 ounces) of chestnuts
150 grams (about 5-1/4 ounces) of sugar
1/2 a liter (about 1/2 a quart) of milk
a dash of vanilla

Cook the chestnuts in water as if you were preparing them boiled. Once they are well cooked, remove the shell and skin, and then pass through a strainer. Put the puréed pulp on the fire with the milk and sugar, and simmer in an uncovered saucepan for a quarter of an hour. Add the vanilla sugar and pour the mixture into the ice cream maker. Serve in a single piece. If you are serving nine to ten people, double the amounts.

770. PONCE ALLA ROMANA (ROMAN PUNCH)

This recipe serves six people.

Lately, this kind of ice cream has become popular at fancy dinner parties. It is usually served before the roasted meat course, because it aids digestion and prepares the stomach to receive the remaining courses.

450 grams (about 1 pound) of sugar
5 deciliters (about 2 cups) of water
2 oranges
2 lemons
2 egg whites
1 small glass of rum
a dash of vanilla

Boil 250 grams (about 8-4/5 ounces) of the sugar in 4 deciliters (about 1-2/3 cups) of water with a little lemon and orange peel. Remove from the fire and squeeze the juice of the oranges and lemons into the syrup. Strain the mixture through a cloth, and pour it into the ice cream maker to freeze.

Put the remaining 200 grams (about 7 ounces) of sugar in the remaining 1 deciliter (about 2/5 of a cup) of water, add the vanilla, and boil until a drop does not run when poured onto a plate or makes a thread when tested between two fingers. By now you will have beaten the egg whites quite stiff, and you are ready to pour the syrup over them while it is still very hot. Then beat well to obtain a smooth consistency. After this mixture has cooled, combine it with the ice cream and blend well. Add the rum just before sending to the table in stemmed glasses.

771. SPUMONE DI THE (TEA SPUMONE)

250 grams (about 8-4/5 ounces) of whipped cream, the kind that
you find at the dairy
200 grams (about 7 fluid ounces) of water
100 grams (about 3-1/2 ounces) of sugar
15 grams (about 1/2 an ounce) of the best quality tea
3 egg whites
3 sheets isinglass

Boil the water and pour it over the tea, steeping nearly at a boil for forty minutes. Strain it through a cloth, squeezing well to extract all of the flavor; the liquid should be as black as coffee.

Next, prepare a custard as in recipe 753 with the tea, the egg yolks and the sugar; add in the isinglass as you do in that recipe, then gently fold in the whipped cream. Pour the mixture into an ice cream mold and surround the mold with layers of ice and salt as in recipe 753.

This recipe serves eight people.

772. MACEDONIA (MIXED FRUIT ICE CREAM)

And now we bid welcome to Madam Macedonia, to whom I would rather give the simpler name of "Mixed Fruit Ice Cream," a dessert that will be especially welcome in the scorching months of July and August.

For this dessert, if you do not have an ice cream mold, you can use a tin-plated metal container (shaped like a mess tin or a small saucepan) with a lid that can be hermetically sealed.

Take many varieties of fruit in season, ripe and of good quality, for example: red currants, strawberries, raspberries, cherries, plums, apricots, a peach and a pear. Starting with the cherries, peel all the fruit and chop to the size of pumpkin seeds, discarding the cores and stones. Use only a very small amount of red currants because their seeds are too big and too hard. Some fragrant melon would make a nice addition.

Weigh the fruit once you have prepared it in this manner; let's say you have 500 grams (about 1 pound) of fruit, then sprinkle 100 grams (about 3-1/2 ounces) of confectioners' sugar on top, and add the juice of 1 garden lemon. Blend well and let sit for half an hour.

Use a piece of paper to line the bottom of the metal container, then pour in the fruit, packing it well. Cover the container and place it in a tub filled with ice and salt. Leave it to freeze for several hours. If it will not unmold easily, wet the sides of the container with warm water. It will make an attractive display as a frozen, marbled block of ice cream.

These amounts serve four to five people.

773. GELATO DI LATTE DI MANDORLE
(ALMOND MILK ICE CREAM)

I describe the following dish especially for you, ladies of delicate, refined taste, for I am sure that you will find it delightful; and since I often think of you when I create these dishes, which, I hope, take into account and satisfy your taste, I must take advantage of this opportunity to say that I hope you long preserve the enviable qualities of blooming health and beauty.

200 grams (about 7 ounces) of sugar
150 grams (about 5-1/4 ounces) of sweet almonds, and 4 or 5
*   bitter almonds*
8 deciliters (about 3-1/3 cups) of water
2 deciliters (about 4/5 of a cup) of heavy cream
a dash of orange-flower water or coriander seeds

Boil the sugar in the water for ten minutes together with the coriander seeds, if you are using the coriander or comfits for flavor, as described in recipe 693 for Portuguese-style milk. Blanch the almonds and crush them very fine in a mortar along with a few tablespoons of the syrup, then stir them into the syrup. Strain the mixture through a loosely woven cloth, squeezing well to extract as much of the flavor as possible; crush the almonds in the mortar with some syrup a few more times if necessary. Add the cream to the extracted liquid and then freeze in the ice cream maker. Once it has hardened, serve it in stemmed glasses.

This recipe serves nine to ten people.

774. ZORAMA
(MARBLED ICE CREAM)

If you would like to make a black and white marbled ice cream, here's how to do it:

First of all, soak three sheets of isinglass in cold water and in the meantime, prepare the following custard:

100 grams (about 3-1/2 ounces) of sugar
80 grams (about 2-2/3 ounces) of powdered chocolate
3 egg yolks
3 deciliters (about 1-1/5 cups) of milk

Once the custard has cooled, add in 3 beaten egg whites and then 150 grams (about 5-1/4 ounces) of whipped cream, the kind that you can find at the dairy. Make sure to fold in the egg whites and cream so that the color is not uniform but instead forms a marbled effect with the chocolate. Next put the isinglass on the fire in a little water to dissolve it, and while it is still hot blend it into the mixture. Then pour it into an ice cream mold or some other container that can be hermetically sealed, and which you will have coated with rosolio. Keep for three or four hours in a large amount of ice mixed with salt.

This recipe serves eight people.

775. GELATO DI CAFFÈ-LATTE
(CAFFÈ-LATTE ICE CREAM)

On hot summer days you can enjoy an ice cream made with espresso and milk. Use the following amounts:

1 liter (about 1 quart) of milk
1/2 a liter (about-1/2 a quart) of espresso
300 grams (about 10-1/2 ounces) of sugar

Put the milk on the fire with the sugar just long enough for the latter to melt. Stir in the espresso and then pour the mixture into the ice cream maker, as you would for any other ice cream. When it has hardened, serve in cups or stemmed glasses.

776. CAFFÈ (COFFEE)

There are those who believe that coffee originated in Persia, others maintain that it comes from Ethiopia, and still others who believe it was first grown in *Arabia Felix*. But in spite of their differences, all agree that it is an oriental plant: an evergreen bush the stalk of which grows four to five meters high, and five to eight centimeters in diameter. The best coffee is always from Mocha, which could confirm the opinion that this is truly its native soil.[138] They say that a Muslim priest in Yemen, having observed that the goats that ate the berries from a local plant were more festive and lively than other goats, toasted the seeds from this plant, then ground and steeped them in water, thus discovering the coffee that we drink today.

This precious beverage that spreads a joyful excitement throughout the entire body was called the beverage of intellectuals, the friend of literati, scientists and poets because, as it strikes the nerves, it helps clarify ideas, renders the imagination more active and accelerates thinking processes.

It is difficult to judge the quality of coffee beans without tasting the coffee, and their green color, which many prize, is often artificially added.

The process of roasting coffee deserves special attention since, the

138 Mocha is a seaport in what is now Yemen; it was a major center for the export of coffee.

quality of the coffee aside, it is roasting that determines how good coffee will taste. It is better to heat it gradually and, since a wood fire is easier to control, it is preferable to use wood instead of coal as fuel. When the coffee begins to crackle and smoke, shake the toaster often and take care to remove it from the fire as soon as the coffee turns a chestnut brown and before it begins to sweat oil. Accordingly, I do not disapprove of the Florentine method, for in that city, in order to halt the roasting immediately, they expose the coffee to the air, whereas I disapprove of the practice of placing coffee between two plates as soon as it is toasted, for in this way the beans give off their essential oil and lose flavor. Coffee loses twenty percent of its weight during roasting, so 500 grams become 400 grams.

Just as different qualities of meat make the best broth, so different qualities of coffee, roasted separately, yield a more pleasing flavor. To me the best combination for a most pleasing drink is 250 grams (about 8-4/5 ounces) of Puerto Rican beans, 100 grams (about 3-1/2 ounce) of Santo Domingo beans and 150 grams (about 5-1/4 ounces) of Mocha beans. 300 grams (about 10-1/2 ounces) of Puerto Rican with 200 grams (about 7 ounces) of Mocha also give excellent results. 15 grams (about 1/2 an ounce) of ground coffee yields one generous cup; but when making many cups at a time, 10 grams (about 1/3 of an ounce) per person should be enough for the usual small cup. Roast the coffee in small quantities and keep it in a well-sealed metal container, grinding only what you need each time, since ground coffee easily loses its aroma.

If coffee causes too much agitation and insomnia, it is better to abstain from it or use it in moderation; you can also temper its effect by mixing it with a little chicory or toasted barley. Regular use may neutralize the effect, but it can also be harmful if one's sensitivity to stimulants is too strong to be corrected, and in this regard a doctor told me about a peasant who, on those rare occasions when he drank coffee, displayed all the symptoms of someone who had been poisoned. Children should be absolutely forbidden to drink coffee.

Coffee seems to cause less agitation in humid, damp places and perhaps this is the reason the European countries where the consumption of coffee is highest are Belgium and Holland. In the Orient, the custom is to grind coffee to a very fine powder, make it the old-fashioned way, and drink it as a dense, cloudy liquid. In the private homes of that part of the world, the coffee pot is always on the fire.

As for what Professor Mantegazza says, that is, that coffee does not in any way aid in digestion,[139] I believe that it is necessary to make a distinction. He perhaps would say that this is true for those whose nervous system is indifferent to coffee; but for those whose nervous system (including the pneumogastric nerve) is affected by this beverage, it is undeniable that they digest better after drinking it, and the prevailing custom of having a good cup of coffee after a rich meal confirms this. It also appears that coffee, when drunk in the morning on an empty stomach, rids the organism of the residue of an imperfect digestion and prepares it to receive a more appetizing breakfast. I, for one, when my stomach is upset, find there is no better way to encourage digestion than to slowly sip some coffee, lightly sweetened and diluted with water, and to abstain from breakfast.

> E se noiosa ipocondria t'opprime
> O troppo intorno alle vezzose membra
> Adipe cresce, de' tuoi labbri onora
> La nettarea bevanda ove abbronzato
> Fuma ed arde il legume a te d'Aleppo
> Giunto, e da Moka che di mille navi
> Popolata mai sempre insuperbisce.[140]
> (Should hypochondria's torments thee oppress,
> Or thy fair form to corpulence incline,
> Then honour with thy lips the nectar flowing,
> Steaming and fragrant, from the roasted bean
> That far Aleppo sent, or Mocha proud
> Forever busy with a thousand ships.)

139 Artusi is debating with Paolo Mantegazza (1831–1910), a noted physician and anthropologist. See Lorenza de' Medici's Introduction, page xxxix.
140 From *Il Giorno* (*The Day*), "Morning," by Giuseppe Parini (1729–1799).

Because it traded with the Orient, Venice was the first city in Italy where coffee was drunk, perhaps beginning in the sixteenth century; but the first coffee shops were opened there in 1645; next in London and then soon after in Paris, where a pound of coffee could cost up to 40 crowns.

The use of coffee began to spread and grow until the immense consumption of today; but two centuries ago, Redi, in his dithyramb,[141] wrote:

> Beverei prima il veleno
> Che un bicchier che fosse pieno
> Dell'amaro e reo caffè.
> (I would rather drink poison
> Than a glassful of
> Bitter, evil coffee.)

And a century ago, it seemed that its use in Italy was still rare, since in Florence they did not yet use the word "caffettiere" (coffee vendor) but "acquacedrataio" (citron water vendor) for someone who sold hot chocolate, coffee and other beverages.

Carlo Goldoni, in his comedy *La sposa persiana* (*The Persian Bride*), has the character Curcuma, a slave, say:

> Ecco il caffè, signore, caffè in Arabia nato
> E dalle carovane in Ispaan portato.
> L'arabo certamente sempre è il caffè migliore;
> Mentre spunta da un lato, mette dall'altro il fiore.
> Nasce in pingue terreno, vuol ombra, o poco sole,
> Piantare ogni tre anni l'arboscel si suole.
> Il frutto non è vero, ch'esser debba piccino,
> Anzi dev'esser grosso, basta sia verdolino,
> Usarlo indi conviene di fresco macinato,
> In luogo caldo e asciutto con gelosia guardato.
> . . . A farlo vi vuol poco;
> Mettervi la sua dose e non versarla al fuoco.

---

141 Francesco Redi (1626–1698), a physician, naturalist, and man of letters. The poem Artusi quotes is *Bacco in Toscana* (*Bacchus in Tuscany*).

Far sollevar la spuma, poi abbassarla a un tratto
Sei, sette volte almeno, il caffè presto è fatto.
(Here is the coffee, Sir, coffee born in Arabia,
And carried by the caravans into Spain.
Arab coffee is surely the best;
While it sends out sprouts on one side,
It sends out a flower on the other.
It is born in fertile soil, and needs shade, or little sun.
The bush is planted every three years.
It is not true that the fruit should be small,
Rather, it should be fat, and at least a little green,
It is best to use it freshly ground,
Kept in a warm dry place, and jealously guarded.
. . . It takes little to make it;
Put in the amount of coffee, and do not spill it on the fire.
Allow the foam to rise, then lower it all at once,
six, seven times at least, and soon the coffee is done.)[142]

777. THE (TEA)

Tea is cultivated almost exclusively in China and Japan, and is one of the chief exports of those countries. Teas from Java, the Indies and Brazil are considered of much inferior quality.

Its small leaves, rolled up and dried to be sold, are produced by an evergreen shrub with many branches, which does not grow higher than two meters. The leaves are harvested three times a year: first in April, then at the beginning of the summer and finally towards the middle of autumn.

The first harvest yields leaves that are small and very delicate, because they have just sprouted a few days earlier. With these *imperial tea* is produced, which is not exported but stays in the country for use by the highest echelons of the local aristocracy; the third harvest

142 Act IV, scene iv.

yields leaves which, having grown to their fullest extent, are of an inferior quality.

All of the tea that is in circulation can be divided into two main categories: green or black. These two categories can then be subdivided into many types: but the most commonly used are *pearl*, *souchong*, and *white tail pekoe*, whose fragrance is the most aromatic and pleasing. Green tea, which is obtained by a more rapid drying process that prevents fermentation, is the most rich in essential oil, and thus more stimulating; therefore it is better to abstain from it or use it in small doses mixed with black tea.

In China, the use of tea dates back to many centuries before the Christian Era; but in Europe it was introduced by the Holland Company of the East Indies at the beginning of the sixteenth century. Alexandre Dumas *père* maintains that it was in 1666, under the reign of Louis XIV, that tea, after an opposition no less strenuous than that against coffee, was introduced in France.

Tea is made by steeping and is best when made in English metal teapots. A heaping teaspoon is more than enough for a regular cup. Put the tea into a teapot which has been first warmed with boiling water and then pour in just enough boiling water to cover the leaves; after five or six minutes, sufficient time for the leaves to unfold, add the rest of the boiling water, stir, and after a few minutes the infusion is done. If you leave it too long, it becomes dark and bitter because with time the leaves give off tannic acid, which is an astringent. If for the first five or six minutes you can keep the teapot over the steam of boiling water, you will get the best flavor. And if it seems too strong, you can dilute it with boiling water.

The use of tea in some Italian provinces, especially in small towns, is still rare. Not many years ago I sent one of my young servants to the spa town of Porretta in the province of Bologna to see if he could learn something from the capable mastery of Bolognese cooks. If what he told me is true, some foreigners happened by and asked for tea; since they had everything there but tea, it was immediately ordered from Bologna. The tea arrived but the foreigners complained that the infusion had no taste. Can you guess why? They had made tea without steeping it and by merely pouring boiling water over the leaves in a colander. The young servant, who had prepared tea many times in my house, corrected the error and it was found to be done right.

Tea, like coffee, excites the nerves and causes insomnia; but its effect, in most cases, is less powerful than coffee's. I would also say that its effect is less poetical, since it seems to me that tea depresses and coffee excites. However, the Chinese leaf has this advantage over the Aleppo[143] bean: it opens the skin's pores, and helps one to endure the cold in harsh winters. For this reason, those who can go without wine with their midday meal, might find that tea, alone or with milk, is a most delightful beverage. I use a blend of leaves: half Souchong and half Pekoe.

778. CIOCCOLATA
(HOT CHOCOLATE)

It is not easy to satisfy everyone, much less on the subject of food and cooking, so many and varied are people's tastes. I could not have supposed that a gentleman would have noticed in this book of mine a lacuna that tormented him. "How can you"—he said—"waste so many words of praise on coffee and tea and not mention the 'food of the gods,' chocolate, which is my passion, my favorite drink?" I will say to that gentleman that I had not talked about it first of all because if I had to recount its history, as well as the many ways in which this product is adulterated by manufacturers, I would have gone on too

---

143 A city in what is now modern Syria; a major center of transportation and commerce, including that of coffee.

long; and secondly, because everyone knows how to make hot chocolate more or less well.

The cocoa tree *(Theobroma cacao)* grows naturally in South America, especially in Mexico, where its fruit has been used for food and beverages from time immemorial, and where the Spanish tasted it the first time they landed there.

The two most valued varieties are Caracas and Marignone cocoa which, mixed together in the right proportions, make the best chocolate. To guarantee the best quality it is best to avoid the lowest prices and give preference to the most trustworthy manufacturers. For a generous cup use no less than 60 grams (about 2 ounces) of chocolate, dissolved in 2 deciliters (about 4/5 of a cup) of water; but you can also use 50 grams (about 1-2/3 ounces) if you prefer it light, or as much as 80 grams (about 2-2/3 ounces) if you prefer it very thick.

Toss the chocolate, in small pieces, into the water in the chocolate pot and when it begins to get hot, stir it so that it does not stick and melts completely. As soon as it begins to boil, remove it from the fire and whisk it for five minutes. Then bring it back to a boil and serve.

Like other foods that stimulate the nervous system, chocolate also excites the intellectual faculties and enhances sensitivity; but, as it is rich in albumin and fat (cocoa butter), chocolate is also very nourishing, acts as an aphrodisiac, and is not easily digested, and for this last reason it is flavored with cinnamon or vanilla. For those who have the stomach to tolerate it, "chocolate is good"—says Professor Mantegazza[144]—"for the elderly, for weak, emaciated youths, and for persons prostrated by a long illness and the abuses of life." For those who are engaged in intellectual work and want to avoid tiring their stomach early in the morning with a rich breakfast, chocolate offers an excellent morning food.

144 See note to recipe 776.

779. FRUTTA IN GUAZZO
(FRUITS PRESERVED IN SPIRITS)

Those who enjoy fruit preserved in spirits may find that they like this way of preparing it.

Begin with the first fruits of the season: strawberries, red currants, and raspberries. Place in a container, using 50 or 100 grams (about 1-2/3 or 3-1/2 ounces) of each kind; add half their weight in sugar and enough brandy or cognac to cover them completely. Then prepare cherries, plums, apricots, and peaches. Remove the stones, cut all the fruit (except the cherries) into slices, and cover with the appropriate amount of sugar and brandy.

You can also use gooseberry and salamanna[144] grapes and some nice pears; but taste the liquid, and add sugar or brandy to obtain the flavor you like.

Once the container has been filled, set it aside for a few months before serving.

780. PESCHE NELLO SPIRITO
(PEACHES IN SPIRITS)

1 kilogram (about 2 pounds) of clingstone peaches, not too ripe
440 grams (about 15-1/2 ounces) of white sugar
1 liter (about 1 quart) of water
a finger-length piece of cinnamon
a few cloves
wine spirits, as needed

Clingstone peaches are red-yellow or simply yellow, with the flesh attached to the stone. Wipe the peaches with a cloth to remove the fuzz, and prick them four or five times with a toothpick.

Boil the sugar in the water for twenty minutes in an uncovered saucepan, then add the whole peaches, stirring them frequently if the syrup does not cover them. Bring the liquid back to a boil and boil the peaches for twenty minutes, then strain them from the syrup using a slotted spoon.

Once the syrup and the peaches have cooled, or preferably the

144 A white grape, first grown by a man named Alamanno Salviati.

next day, place them in a glass jar or, better yet, in a new glass-lined earthenware jar, pouring the syrup over the peaches along with enough wine spirits or cognac to cover them completely. Add the spices and see to it that the peaches remain covered in liquid, adding some more spirits if necessary.

Keep the jar hermetically sealed and do not eat them before one month's time.

781. PESCHE DI GHIACCIO (ICED PEACHES)

This is the only recipe in this collection that I hadn't tried because, when an English lady spontaneously offered it to me, peach season had already passed and the publishing date of this reprint was imminent. However, the lady recommended it and assured me that in her country it was quite well liked and thus I hazard to publish it.

Take freestone peaches, ripe and in good condition, and place them two at a time in boiling water for one minute; remove them from the water and peel them, leaving the flesh intact. Roll them thoroughly in white powdered sugar and place them in a deep, attractive bowl. Then take as many sugar cubes as there are peaches and rub them against the peel of a ripe garden lemon until the cubes are saturated with lemon essence, and then nestle them among the peaches. Leave them like this for at least two hours (longer won't hurt). Keep the jar sealed, surrounded with a good amount of ice, for two to three hours before serving.

Once peaches came back in season I quickly put this recipe to the test and I can tell you straight off that it is worthwhile. I used a metal container, a generous amount of confectioners' sugar, and I mixed salt with the ice.

782. CILIEGE VISCIOLE IN GUAZZO (FERMENTED SOUR CHERRIES)

When these cherries are prepared like this they do not need spirits, for they make their own.

1 kilogram (about 2 pounds) of sour cherries

300 grams (about 10-1/2 ounces) of white sugar
1 small piece cinnamon

Separate out 200 grams (about 7 ounces) of the cherries, choosing the ones that are the most crushed or unattractive looking. Crush them, extract the juice and strain it. Remove the stems from the rest of the cherries and layer them in a crystal jar, alternating one layer of cherries and one of sugar, then pour in the juice. Remove the kernels from some of the stones of the crushed cherries and add these and the cinnamon to the jar, which you will then seal and set aside for at least two months. You will see that little by little the sugar will dissolve and the cherries will begin to float. Then, as the liquid converts to alcohol, the cherries will sink and this will be a sign that they are ready to be eaten.

783. RIBES ALLA FRANCESE
(FRENCH-STYLE RED CURRANTS)

Dissolve some powdered gum Arabic[145] in water. Take some fresh red currants and, holding a bunch between your fingers, dip it in the liquid, then sprinkle with powdered sugar. Arrange the little clusters on a platter where the sparkling red currants will make a beautiful display among the fruit served at a fancy dinner, and will delight the ladies.

You can also alternate red currant with white currant clusters.

784. PONCE ALLA PARIGINA
(PUNCH PARISIAN STYLE)

This is an invigorating punch, which may come in handy when you need to calm your stomach between meals.

Take a cup that holds about 2 deciliters (about 4/5 of a cup) of liquid. Whisk in it an egg yolk with two teaspoons of sugar. Keep stirring until the egg turns almost white. Then add two or three tablespoons (according to taste) of cognac, rum or some other spirit you like. Then fill the cup with boiling water, which you will add a little at a time, whisking constantly to make a nice foam.

145 A gummy substance obtained from the Acacia tree, used as an emulsifier.

785. MANDORLE TOSTATE
(TOASTED ALMONDS)

200 grams (about 7 ounces) of sweet almonds
200 grams (about 7 ounces) of sugar

Rub the almonds with a kitchen towel. Put the sugar on the fire in an untinned saucepan with two fingers of water. When the sugar has melted, pour in the almonds, stirring constantly. When the almonds begin to crackle, move the saucepan away from the fire and place it at the edge of the hearth. You will note that the sugar begins to crystallize, acquiring the consistency of sand. Then remove the pan from the hearth altogether, and separate out the almonds. Put half of the sugar back on the fire with another two fingers of water, and when it turns to caramel (you will know by the distinctive smell), pour in the almonds, stir and remove from the fire as soon as they have soaked up the sugar. Then put on the fire the other half of the sugar, with yet another two fingers of water, and repeat the operation for the third and last time. Pour the almonds onto a platter and separate the ones that have become stuck together.

They are delicious even without any flavoring, but if you like you can use vanilla sugar to add the aroma of vanilla, or 30 grams (about 1 ounce) of grated chocolate. But either flavoring is best added at the very last moment.

786. OLIVE IN SALAMOIA
(BRINE-CURED OLIVES)

There may be more modern and better recipes for making pickled olives, but the one I am about to give you comes from Romagna and is used there with excellent results.

Here are the amounts for each kilogram (about 2 pounds) of olives:

1 kilogram (about 2 pounds) of ashes
80 grams (about 2-2/3 ounces) of quicklime
80 grams (about 2-2/3 ounces) of salt
8 deciliters (about 3-1/3 cups) of water for pickling

Lime is called "quick" when adding water to it triggers a chemical reaction that produces heat, smoke, and bubbles that burst and fall into dust. It is once the reaction is over that you must use it, mixing it with the ashes. Then add water to make a mud-like mixture, which you will keep neither too thick nor too runny. Soak the olives in this mixture, using a weight to keep them submerged. Keep them like this for twelve to fourteen hours, that is until they become quite tender. Watch them closely and test their consistency frequently. Some people wait until the flesh pulls away from the pit, but this is not always a reliable guide.

Remove the olives from the mixture, wash them thoroughly and then keep them soaking in fresh water for four or five days, changing the water three times a day, until they no longer cloud the water and lose their bitterness. At this point, put on the fire the 8 deciliters (about 3-1/3 cups) of water with the salt, and add several pieces of thick stalks of wild fennel, which you will boil for a few minutes. Once this brine has cooled completely, pour it over the olives, storing them in a glass jar or a glass-lined earthenware container.

The best way to wet the lime is to dip it with one hand for a moment (five or six seconds are enough) in water and then place it on a sheet of paper.

787. FUNGHI SOTTOLIO
(MUSHROOMS PRESERVED IN OIL)

Choose porcini mushrooms, also called "morecci," the smallest you can find, and if some are the size of walnuts, slice these in half. Clean and wash the mushrooms, then boil them in white vinegar for twenty-five minutes; if the vinegar seems too strong you can dilute it with a little water. Remove the mushrooms from the fire, dry them well with a kitchen towel, and then leave them exposed to the air until the next day. Then place them in a glass jar or glass-lined earthenware container, covering them with oil and any herbs or flavoring you like. Some people use a clove or two of peeled garlic, others use cloves, and still others use bay leaves, which you can boil with the vinegar.

They are usually eaten with boiled meats.

788. MOSTARDA ALL'USO TOSCANO
(CHUTNEY TUSCAN STYLE)

For this recipe you need 2 kilograms (about 4 pounds) of sweet grapes, 1/3 red and 2/3 white grapes, or all white.

Press the grapes as if you were making wine, and after a day or two, when the dregs have come to the surface, drain off the must.[146]

1 kilogram (about 2 pounds) of red or reinette apples
2 large pears
240 grams (about 1 cup) of white wine or better vin santo[147]
120 grams (about 4-1/4 ounces) of candied citron
40 grams (about 1-1/3 ounces) of white mustard powder

Peel the apples and the pears, slice them thinly, then put on the fire in the wine and, when they have absorbed it completely, pour in the must. Stir often and when the mixture has reached a firmer consistency than for fruit preserves, let it cool and add the powdered mustard, which you will have dissolved in advance in a little hot wine, and the candied fruit, diced in tiny pieces. Keep in small jars covered with a thin film of ground cinnamon.

Mustard can also be used at the table to stimulate the appetite and facilitate digestion.

789. CROSTA E MODO DI CROSTARE
(GLAZE AND GLAZING TECHNIQUE)

I take the liberty to translate in this way the two gallicisms commonly used in Italian, namely, "glassa" and "glassare," leaving to others the task to find more technical and appropriate Italian terms. I am talking about that white, black or otherwise colored glaze used on several of the cakes described in the preceding pages, such as the Lady Cake (recipes 584 and 585), sweet English salami (recipe 618), and the German cakes.

To make a black glaze, use 50 grams (about 1-2/3 ounces) of chocolate and 100 grams (about 3-1/2 ounces) of powdered sugar.

---

146 See notes to recipes 458 and 624.
147 See note to recipe 598.

Grate the chocolate and put it on the fire in a small saucepan with three tablespoons of water. Once the chocolate has melted, add the sugar and simmer, stirring often. The key to the whole operation is to cook the glaze just right. The way to know when you have reached this exact point is to test the mixture between your thumb and index finger: if the mixture makes a thread, it is done. But don't wait until you can make a thread longer than 1 centimeter (about 1/2 an inch), otherwise you will overcook it. Then remove the saucepan from the fire and put it in cool water. Keep stirring and when you see that the surface of the liquid tends to cloud over as if it were forming a veil, spread it on the pastry. Then put the pastry back in the oven or under an iron lid, with fire above. After two or three minutes you will find that the glaze becomes smooth, shiny and hard.

To make a white glaze, use egg whites, confectioners' sugar, lemon juice and rosolio. If you want a pink glaze use alkermes rather than rosolio. The following are the approximate amounts for the desserts described earlier.

One egg white, 130 grams (about 4-1/2 ounces) of sugar, a quarter of a lemon, 1 tablespoon of rosolio or enough alkermes to obtain the color you want. Beat all the ingredients together well and when the mixture is nice and firm, though it still runs a little, spread it over the dessert. It will dry on its own, and there is no need to bake it.

If instead of spreading the white glaze in a single sheet, you would like to decorate the dessert with some pattern, you should go to one of those shops that sell what you need to make this type of decoration and buy those tiny tin attachments for a pastry tube or a pastry bag; these are the kind of cooking tools we must import from France, much to our shame. Lacking these implements, you can try to make do with paper funnels, which you can put together yourself. Put in the mixture and then squeeze it out of the small hole at the bottom, forming a thin thread. If the glaze is too runny, add sugar.

Recipe 586 for Neapolitan cake describes a white glaze that can be used as an alternative. Also see the dessert recipes 644 and 645.

790. SPEZIE FINI
(ALLSPICE)

If you really want to use fine good quality spices in your cooking, here is the recipe.

2 nutmeg kernels
50 grams (about 1-2/3 ounces) of Ceylon cinnamon, also known
*   as "queen" cinnamon*
30 grams (about 1 ounce) of clove-flavored pepper
20 grams (about 2/3 of an ounce) of cloves
20 grams (about 2/3 of an ounce) of sweet almonds

You will not improve on this mixture by adding other spices (except for mace, which is the ground outer covering of the nutmeg seed, and is excellent). Also, do not imitate the grocers who use cinnamon from Goa instead of Ceylon cinnamon and throw in handfuls of coriander seeds to increase the volume with a cheap ingredient.

Crush everything together in a bronze mortar, pass the spices through a small strainer with a very fine silk mesh and keep them in a glass jar with a scalloped cap, or in a small bottle with a cork. In this way they keep for years and remain as fragrant as when you first prepared them.

Spices are stimulants, but used in moderation they aid digestion.

APPENDIX

FOODS FOR WEAK STOMACHS

Nowadays you often hear talk of foods for weak stomachs. It seems that this type of cooking has come into fashion.

It is necessary therefore to say a few words on this subject without claiming that with my principles I can strengthen or satisfy these paper stomachs. It is not easy to identify with scientific precision which foods are more suitable to an individual weakened by the passing of years, illnesses, excesses, or weak by nature, since the stomach is a fickle, unpredictable organ; moreover, there are those who digest easily what is indigestible to others.

Nevertheless, I will try to point out those foods which, in my opinion, are more suitable to a weak stomach that finds digestion difficult, beginning with the first and only food that nature administers to newborn mammals: milk. I believe that you can use and abuse milk as much as you want, and as long as it does not cause you any gastric disturbance.

Next I will mention broth, which should be de-fatted, the most suitable being broths of chicken, mutton, and veal; but before mentioning the most suitable solid foods, I might remind you what I said about chewing in my opening comments on health. Chewing well stimulates salivation, which makes food easier to digest and assimilate; those who chew quickly and swallow foods that are poorly minced, force the stomach to do more work, and thus digestion becomes more difficult and laborious.

It also helps to set regular hours for breakfast and lunch. The most healthy time to have lunch is noon or one o'clock, because then you have the opportunity to take a walk and a little nap in the summer, a season during which food should be lighter and less rich than in winter. I would also warn against snacking during the day, and advise the ladies not to weaken their stomachs with a constant diet of sweets. In fact, one should eat only when the stomach begs for food, which is more likely to happen after physical exercise. Indeed, exercise and temperance are the two pillars upon which good health rests.

FIRST COURSES

As for firsts courses, let's begin with angel hair or tiny pasta. Never use those that have been dyed yellow artificially; rather, use only pastas made with durum wheat which do not need dyes since they naturally possess a wax-yellow color. They hold up better when cooked and retain a pleasantly firm consistency when done.

Perhaps a weak stomach can also tolerate egg noodles, taglierini for example, since they are very fine, and bread crumb dumplings. Make simple soups or use vegetables; tapioca (which I hate on account of its gelatinous consistency), rice bound with egg yolks and Parmesan cheese.

Spanish soup (recipe 40), pumpkin soup (recipe 34), sorrel soup (recipe 37), egg-bread soup (recipe 41), the queen of soups (recipe 39), soup with meat stuffing (recipe 32), healthy soup (recipe 36), bread soup (recipe 11), bread crumb soup (recipe 12), thin semolina noodles (recipe 13), semolina soup (recipes 15 and 16), paradise soup (recipe 18), puréed meat soup (recipe 19), soup with semolina dumplings (recipe 23), thousand foot soldiers soup (recipe 26), passatelli noodles made with semolina (recipe 48), passatelli noodle soup (recipe 20), where you can replace the crustless bread with 20 grams (about 2/3 of an ounce) of butter.

For meatless soups I can only recommend those with angel hair or extra-thin capellini seasoned with cheese and butter or with sauce, rice cooked in milk, and porridge made with yellow cornmeal flour in milk, as long it does not give you acid, two fish soups (recipe 65 and 66), frog soup (recipe 64) but without the eggs, which make a mess.

All spices must also be banished when cooking in this way, (keeping at best a few traces here and there), since they are not appreciated by our delicate ladies or by those whose palate is too sensitive.

APPETIZERS

Sandwiches (recipe 114). Canapés with butter and anchovies (recipe 113), canapés with chicken livers and anchovies (recipe 115), fancy canapés (recipe 117). Cooked ham and Nantes sardines served with butter.

SAUCES

Sauce *maître d'hôtel* style (recipe 123), white sauce (recipe 124), mayonnaise (recipe 126), tangy sauce I (recipe 127), yellow sauce for poached fish (recipe 129), Hollandaise sauce (recipe 130), sauce for grilled fish (recipe 131).

EGGS

Fresh eggs are nutritious and are easily digested if eaten neither raw nor overcooked. If you serve omelettes, choose those mixed with vegetables and kept thin, and do not turn them so that they remain soft. The asparagus omelette (recipe 145) is also quite healthy, as are egg-yolk canapés (recipe 142).

FRIED FOODS

Some people find fried foods rather heavy on the stomach on account of the grease that these dishes absorb in the pan; nevertheless, the most tolerable fried foods are brains, sweetbreads, saddles, semolina fritters, milk-fed veal liver, lamb giblets, and plain liver. In addition, golden chicken I (recipe 205), chicken breasts with salted tongue (recipe 207), testicles (recipe 174), rice fritters II (recipe 179), tube pastries and pastry puffs (recipe 183), stuffed cutlets (recipe 220), milk-fed veal chops little bird style (recipe 221), stuffed bread morsels (recipe 223), kidney for lunch (recipe 292), sweetbread croquettes (recipe 197), basic rice croquettes (recipe 198), mixed fry Bolognese style (recipe 175), veal chops Roman style (recipe 222), and several similar dishes you'll find listed under fried foods.

BOILED MEATS

Boiled meats can be served with impunity when cooking for someone with a weak stomach. They can be accompanied by spinach cooked in butter or in a sauce, as long as they are chopped extremely fine. The healthiest greens are cardoons, zucchini, turnip greens, and asparagus. Green beans, if they are small, can also be part of the a convalescent's diet. Boiled chicken or capon with rice as a side dish (recipe 245) are also appropriate, and do not forget boiled mutton, which is eminently suitable.

VEGETABLES

In addition to the vegetables mentioned in the previous paragraph, you can serve artichokes cooked straight up (recipe 418); artichoke cutlets (recipe 187); cardoon, spinach, artichoke and fennel molds (recipes 389, 390, 391 and 392); fried and stewed eggplant (recipes 400 and 401); celery as a side dish (recipe 413); and artichokes in sauce (recipe 416).

ENTREMETS

Here you can serve semolina dumplings (recipe 230); Roman-style dumplings (recipe 231); pan-cooked artichokes (recipe 246).

COLD DISHES

The following dishes are suitable: capon galantine (recipe 366); capon cooked in a bladder (recipe 367); roasted saddle of pork (recipe 369); corned tongue (recipe 360); and liver loaf (recipe 374).

STEWS

The healthiest and most delicate stews are, in my opinion, the following: *fricassée* (recipe 256); chicken giblets *fricassée* (recipe 257); chicken soufflé (recipe 259); sautéed or pan-broiled beef cutlets (recipe 262); stuffed loin of mutton (recipe 296); chicken in egg sauce (recipe 266); sautéed chicken breasts (recipe 269) with lemon juice; braised top round of beef (recipe 299); "drowned" rump roast (recipe 301); veal chops Livorno style (recipe 302); milk-fed veal cutlets in egg sauce (recipe 311); cutlets with prosciutto (recipe 313); French-style dumplings (recipe 317); milk-fed veal stew (recipe 325); fillet with Marsala wine (recipe 340); fillet Parisian style (recipe 341); Signora Adele's gruyère mold (recipe 346); stew in a shell (recipe 350); chicken or capon galantine (recipe 366); and finally, as a most appetizing dish, veal in tuna sauce (recipe 363).

FISH

The most digestible ordinary fish are hake and cod, particularly if grilled or boiled and seasoned only with oil and lemon juice. Also suitable are sole, turbot, sturgeon, umber, weever, sea bream, gilt head, dogfish (see recipe 464 for dogfish rounds in sauce), and also fried or grilled mullet. But do not serve any blue fish, since those are the least digestible varieties.[148]

ROASTED MEATS

Being an analogous substance to the human body, meats can generally be easily assimilated if roasted, as long as they are not tough and fibrous. Poultry is the preferable meat in this context, especially Guinea hen (recipe 546), and milk-fed veal. Steak Florentine style (recipe 556) may also be suitable, especially the fillet cut; as well as pan-fried steak (recipe 557); sautéed or pan-broiled beef cutlets (recipe 262) or roast beef (recipes 521 and 522). You can also serve milk-fed veal cutlet Milanese style (recipe 538), and mutton chops, which are excellent. Also suitable are roast of milk-fed veal (recipe 524); roasted milk-fed veal chops with sage (recipe 327); roast leg of mutton (recipe 530); or leg of kid on a spit or pot roast (recipe 526), quail (recipe 536), chicken Rudinì (recipe 544); and turkey prepared like Guinea hen (recipe 546). Braised pot roast (recipe 526) is excellent with a side dish of peas, as long as they do not upset your stomach. Squab meat, the meat of full-grown turkey, and of birds in general are considered very nutritious but high in calories; therefore, serve them sparingly until a more opportune time.

SALADS

There are few salads that I can identify as being healthy, but if I were you I would favor the following: cooked radicchio mixed with beets

148 See note to recipe 481.

which you will bake in the oven if they are large or boil if small; asparagus (recipe 450), zucchini (recipes 376, 377 and 378) and very young green beans (recipe 380).

DESSERTS

As far as desserts are concerned, I will leave the choice up to you and you can, with a little common sense, judge which ones are suitable. However, I will warn you that shortcrust pastry and puff pastry doughs are difficult to digest, as are all doughs made without yeast. If you suffer from constipation, I recommend cooked apples and pears, stewed prunes, apricots and pear compote, and, as long as milk does not bother you, you can have milk *brûlé* (recipe 692), milk Portuguese style (recipe 693), as well as milk pudding (recipes 694 and 695).

FRUIT

Use only fruit that is in good condition, ripe and in season. In the winter, avoid dried fruits, and eat dates, oranges and mandarins; and don't forget the prickly pear which, when accompanied by a piece of cheese of your choice (as long as your stomach will tolerate it) is, as everyone knows, an appetizing morsel. In other seasons you can have a few varieties of grapes (the excellent white "salamanna," muscatel and the red "aleatico"); spadona pears, which are very juicy, green-gage plums, butter peaches, black cherries, apricots, and apples if they are tender. However, sacrifice gluttony a little, and do without straw-berries, which can cause trouble on account of their many little seeds; large strawberries may be less dangerous but are also less flavorful.

ICE CREAM

You can have ice cream, especially fruit ices, at the end of a meal or once digestion is complete.

WINES AND LIQUEURS

I think that dry white wine is the most suitable for the table of someone with a weak stomach, and I consider Orvieto wine to be excellent on account of its pleasant taste and because it is very digestible. This wine can also be served with dessert, which you can also accompany with vin santo, Asti spumante, and Malaga wine, as well as other similar wines you can find on the market—but can one trust those products? As far as liqueurs are concerned, you would do well to exclude them from your diet, because use can turn into abuse and this could be fatal. The only exception is cognac, without abusing it, however, and only that which costs more than 6 or 7 lire a bottle.

And in conclusion, I'll echo the poet:

I've set the board: henceforth 'tis yours to eat.[149]

---

149 Dante, *The Divine Comedy*, Paradiso X, 25. Bickersmith translation.

SUGGESTED DINNER MENUS

Since it often happens that having to prepare a dinner, one cannot decide what to serve, I thought it might be useful to describe for you in this appendix a number of menus, two for each month of the year, and an additional ten for the main holidays. For the holidays, the choice of fruit is better dictated by what is in season than by me. Even if you do not follow my suggestions to the letter, this will at least provide you with some ideas that will make your choices easier.

JANUARY

I.

Soup: tortellini Bolognese style (recipe 9).
Boiled course: capon with rice as a side dish (recipe 245).
Fried dish: tube pastries (recipe 183); sweetbread croquettes (recipe 197).
Entremets: zampone or cotechino with potato pie (recipes 446 or 447).
Vegetables: side dish of celery (recipe 412).
Roast: thrushes (recipe 528) and green salad.
Dessert: almond cake (recipe 579), Cesarino pudding (recipe 671).
Fruit and cheese: pears, apples, oranges and dried fruits.

II.

Soup: soup with semolina dumplings (recipe 23), soup with potato fritters (recipe 29).
Boiled course: poached fish (recipe 459) with a side dish.
Stew: sweet-and-sour wild boar or hare (recipe 285).

Entremets: puff pastries with meat stuffing (recipe 161).

Roast: roast beef with potatoes and green salad (recipe 521 or 522).

Dessert: sponge cake (recipe 576), blancmange or white almond pudding (recipe 681).

Fruit and cheese: pears, apples, mandarin oranges and a selection of dried fruits.

FEBRUARY

I.

Soup: tortellini Italian style (recipe 8).

Boiled course: chicken and veal with side dish of spinach (recipe 448).

Cold dish: hare loaf (recipe 373).

Entremets: clams in egg sauce (recipes 498).

Stew: milk-fed veal cutlets with truffles Bolognese style (recipe 312).

Roast: birds and woodcocks (recipe 528) and green salad.

Dessert: Savarin (recipe 563); French-style custard (recipe 688).

Fruit and cheese: pears, apples, and a selection of dried fruits.

II.

Soup: soup with meat stuffing (recipe 32).

Appetizers: a variety of canapés (recipe 113).

Boiled course: pullet with mashed potatoes (recipe 443), side dish of Savoy cabbage (recipe 453).

Stew: meat and macaroni pie (recipe 349).

Roast: Guinea hen (recipe 546) and squab.

Dessert: sweet pizza Neapolitan style (recipe 609), ice cream mold (recipe 753).

Fruit and cheese: pears, apples, mandarin oranges and dried fruits.

MARCH

I.

Meatless Dinner

Soup: frog soup (recipe 64), soup Carthusian style (recipe 66).

Appetizers: canapés with caviar and anchovies (recipe 113).

Entremets: seafood pie (recipe 502).
Vegetables: spinach mold (recipe 390).
Roast: grilled fish with sauce (recipe 131).
Dessert: chick-pea fritters (recipe 624), chilled whipped custard (recipe 689).
Fruit: pears, apples, oranges and dried fruits.

II.
Soup: passatelli noodle soup (recipe 20).
Boiled course: a large fish with mayonnaise (recipe 126).
Stew: mutton chops and veal fillet with *financière* sauce (recipe 338).
Entremets: canapés with capers (recipe 108).
Roast: roasted stuffed rib steak (recipe 537).
Dessert: Mantuan cake (recipe 577), custard ice cream (recipe 759), nougat ice cream (recipe 768).
Fruit and cheese: a variety of fruits and soft cookies (recipe 571).

APRIL
I.
Soup: soup with little bricks of ricotta cheese (recipe 25).
Boiled course: veal with asparagus in white sauce (recipe 124).
Entremets: stuffed rolls (recipe 239).
Vegetables: artichoke mold (recipe 391).
Roast: milk-fed veal with green salad.
Dessert: Marietta's fluffy fruit cake (recipe 604), milk *brulé* (recipe 692) with sweet wafers (recipe 621).
Fruit: green fava beans, green almonds in the shell, sponge cake (recipe 608).

II.
Soup: bread soup (recipe 11).
Fried dish: *Krapfen* (recipe 182).
Stew: stuffed boneless chicken (recipe 258) with peas.
Entremets: Roman-style dumplings (recipe 231).
Roast: Easter lamb with green salad and hard-boiled eggs.
Dessert: Neapolitan cake (recipe 586), chocolate ice cream (recipe 761).
Fruit: seasonal fresh fruits, flat cake Livorno style (recipe 598).

MAY

I.

Soup: Spanish-style soup (recipe 40).
Appetizers: chicken liver canapés (recipe 110).
Stew: stew in a shell (recipe 350).
Vegetables: peas French style (recipes 424 or 425).
Roast: roasted stuffed rib steak (recipe 537), baby new potatoes and green salad.
Dessert: Marengo cake (recipe 581), lemon ice (recipe 754).
Fruit and cheese: a variety of fruits, strawberries sprinkled with Chianti or another red wine and seasoned with confectioners' sugar and Marsala.

II.

Soup: healthy soup (recipe 36).
Fried dish: mixed fry Bolognese style (recipe 175), fried artichokes (recipe 186), fried zucchini (recipe 188).
Stew: squab timbale (recipe 279).
Vegetables: asparagus with butter (recipe 450).
Roast: milk-fed veal with a side dish of artichokes cooked straight up (recipe 418).
Dessert: flat cake made with marzipan (recipe 615), strawberry ice (recipe 755).
Fruit and cheese: seasonal fruits, macaroons (recipes 626 or 627).

JUNE

I.

Soup: strichetti noodles Bolognese style (recipe 51).
Fried dish: mushrooms with milk-fed calf's liver, sweetbreads, and brain.
Stew: squab with peas (recipe 354).
Entremets: zucchini with meat filling (recipe 377).
Vegetables: side dish of celery (recipe 412).
Roast: cockerels and green salad.
Dessert: lady cake (recipe 585), sour cherry ice (recipe 762).
Fruit and cheese: seasonal fruits, beignet pastries (recipe 631).

II.

Soup: pea soup with meat broth (recipe 35).

Fried dish: milk-fed veal cutlets, fried custard (recipe 214), fried zucchini (recipe 188).

Boiled course: twice-cooked meat (recipe 355) with mushrooms as a side dish.

Vegetables: green-bean mold (recipe 386).

Roast: cockerels with mayonnaise salad (recipe 251).

Dessert: egg, raisin, butter and fruit cake Italian style (recipe 612), sour cherry delight (recipe 678).

Fruit and cheese: fresh seasonal fruits.

JULY

I.

Soup: soup with flour fritters (recipe 24).

Boiled course: stuffed pullet (recipe 160).

Stew: puréed zucchini mold (recipe 451) filled with giblets and milk-fed veal chops.

Entremets: Louisetta's soufflé (recipe 704).

Roast: milk-fed veal with Russian salad (recipe 454).

Dessert: Sultan cake (recipe 574), chilled raspberry gelatin (recipe 718).

Fruit and cheese: peaches, apricots and other seasonal fruits.

II.

Soup: puréed meat soup (recipe 19).

Appetizers: prosciutto with figs.

Stew: stuffed boneless chicken (recipe 258).

Cold dish: veal in tuna sauce (recipe 363).

Entremets: liver loaf (recipe 374).

Roast: squab and cockerels with mayonnaise salad (recipe 251).

Dessert: plum cake (recipe 673), *bain-marie* almond brittle (recipe 690)

Fruit and cheese: a selection of seasonal fruits.

AUGUST
I.

Soup: taglierini noodles.

Appetizers: prosciutto with melon, accompanied with a generous quantity of wine, because, as the proverb says:

Quando sole est in leone
Pone muliem in cantone
Bibe vinum cum sifone.

(When the sun is in Leo
Put your wife in a corner
And drink wine with a siphon.)

Boiled course: Veal with black-eyed beans Arezzo style (recipe 383), or with green beans with béchamel sauce (recipe 381).

Entremets: *vols-au-vent* with meat stuffing (recipe 161).

Stew: milk-fed veal cutlets with prosciutto (recipe 313).

Roast: turkey pullet (recipe 549) with green salad.

Dessert: pear compote (recipe 709), chilled whipped custard (recipe 689), Lombard cake with custard (recipe 674).

Fruit and cheese: a selection of seasonal fruits.

II.

Soup: the queen of soups (recipe 39).

Boiled course: lobster with mayonnaise (recipe 476).

Stew: sautéed chicken breasts (recipe 269).

Vegetables: puréed zucchini mold (recipe 451).

Roast: domestic duck, squab and green salad.

Dessert: stuffed peaches (recipe 697), raspberry ice (recipe 756).

Fruit and cheese: melon, figs, and other seasonal fruits.

SEPTEMBER

I.

Soup: royal agaric mushroom soup (recipe 33).

Appetizers: prosciutto with figs and salted anchovies.

Fried dish: bread morsels (recipe 223) stuffed with sweetbreads and brain.

Entremets: mushrooms mold (recipe 452) stuffed with giblets.

Roast: turkey pullet (recipe 548) with green salad, or chicken Rudinì (recipe 544).

Dessert: babà (recipe 565), almond milk ice cream (recipe 773), marbled ice cream (recipe 774).

Fruit and cheese: peaches, grapes, and other seasonal fruits.

II.

Soup: semolina soup (recipe 15 or 16).

Fried dish: sole, flying squid, and fried mushrooms.

Stew: domestic duck with pappardelle noodles Arezzo style (recipe 91).

Roast: roast beef on a spit with potatoes (recipe 521) and salad.

Dessert: fruit tart (recipe 616), toasted almond pudding (recipe 669).

Fruit and cheese: a selection of seasonal fruits, sweet wafers (recipe 621).

OCTOBER

I.

Soup: dumplings (recipe 14).

Boiled course: capon with spinach.

Cold dish: corned tongue (recipe 360) with aspic (recipe 3).

Entremets: puff pastries with meat stuffing (recipe 161).

Roast: thrushes with toasted bread rounds (recipe 528) and salad.

Dessert: pumpkin cake (recipe 640), fruit preserve pudding (recipe 680).

Fruit and cheese: A variety of fruit including mandarin oranges.

II.

Soup: soup with rice fritters (recipe 30).

Fried dish: dressed lamb chops (recipe 236).

Entremets: red mullet with prosciutto (recipe 468).

Stew: birds in wine sauce (recipe 283).

Roast: Guinea hen (recipe 546) and squab.

Dessert: tartar custard (recipe 676), strudel (recipe 559), or Neapolitan cake (recipe 586).

Fruit: pears, apples, medlars, sorb apples,[150] grapes.

NOVEMBER

I.

First course: macaroni French style (recipe 84) or soup with meat sauce (recipe 38).

Stew: mallard or wild duck with a side dish of lentils or red cabbage (recipe 270).

Entremets: hare loaf (recipe 373).

Vegetables: cauliflower with béchamel sauce (recipe 431), or cauliflower mold (recipe 387).

Roast: truffled beef loin (recipe 523).

Dessert: ladyfinger pudding with zabaione (recipe 684), chilled orange gelatin (recipe 714).

Fruit: pears, apples, oranges and dried fruits.

II.

Soup: tortellini stuffed with squab (recipe 10), or pumpkin soup (recipe 34).

Appetizers: truffle canapés (recipe 109).

Boiled course: stuffed pullet (recipe 160).

Stew: spiced pork sausage or cotechino boiled in a wrap (recipe 322).

Vegetables: spinach mold (recipe 390), or fennel mold (recipe 392).

Roast: roast pork loin (recipe 552) and birds (recipe 528).

Dessert: *presnitz* (recipe 560), surprise pie (recipe 713), ladyfinger pudding with zabaione (recipe 684).

Fruit and cheese: pears, apples, mandarin oranges and dried fruits.

150 The fruit of the service tree, resembling small pears.

DECEMBER

I.

Meatless Dinner

First course: stuffed dumplings (recipe 55) or rice with clams (recipe 72).

Appetizers: canapés with caviar, anchovies, oil and lemon juice (recipe 113).

Fried dish: sole, squid, and red mullet.

Vegetables: cardoons with béchamel sauce (recipe 407), or spinach fritters (recipe 195).

Roast: eel or some other fish.

Dessert: almond brittle (recipe 617), jellied apples (recipe 696), sliced oranges flavored with confectioners' sugar and alkermes.

Fruit and cheese: pears, apples, and dried fruit.

II.

First course: cappelletti Romagna style (recipe 7).

Stew: Signora Adele's Gruyère mold (recipe 346).

Cold dish: capon galantine (recipe 366), or boned thrushes in aspic (recipe 368).

Roast: hare (recipe 531), or woodcock (recipe 112) and green salad.

Dessert: "panforte" from Siena, brown bread cake German style (recipe 644), plum pudding (recipe 672).

Fruit and cheese: pears, apples, mandarin oranges and dates.

NEW YEAR'S DAY

Soup: the stuffing described in recipe 7 for cappelletti Romagna style, but without enclosing it in dough.

Fried dish: stuffed cutlets (recipe 220).

Stew: braised beef (recipe 298), with carrots, or milk-fed veal cutlets with truffles Bolognese style (recipe 312).

Cold dish: cold game pie (recipe 370).

Roast: domestic duck and squabs (recipe 528) with green salad.

Dessert: hazelnut cake (recipe 564), Turin cake (recipe 649).

EPIPHANY

Soup: Spanish-style soup (recipe 40).

Fried dish: sweetbreads or brain mixed with a Garisenda fry (recipe 224).

Boiled course: capon with side dish of celery (recipe 412).

Stew: rice pudding with giblet sauce (recipe 345).

Roast: thrushes (recipe 528), or woodcock canapés (recipe 112).

Dessert: marzipan puff pastry (recipe 566), chocolate covered puff pastries (recipe 647), Rome cake (recipe 648).

FAT THURSDAY[151]

First course: pappardelle noodles with hare (recipe 95), or macaroni Bolognese style (recipe 87).

Appetizers: truffle canapés (recipe 109).

Stew: pudding Genoese style (recipe 347).

Entremets: Ferrara fresh salami (recipe 238) with sauerkraut (recipe 433).

Roast: capon with green salad, or truffled capon (recipe 540).

Dessert: Turin cake (recipe 649), orange ice (recipe 764).

LENTEN DINNER

Soup: soup with mullet broth (recipe 65), or soup Carthusian style (recipe 66).

Appetizers: salted codfish Montblanc style (recipe 118), and caviar canapés (recipe 113).

Boiled course: poached fish with Genoese sauce (recipe 134).

Entremets: Roman-style dumplings (recipe 231).

Stew: fish fillets (recipe 461).

Roast: eel (recipe 491).

Dessert: marzipan pastries (recipe 628), pistachio ice cream (recipe 767).

---

151 The holiday Artusi mentions here is Berlingaccio, the last Thursday before Lent.

EASTER

Soup: bread soup (recipe 11), or paradise soup (recipe 18).
Fried dish: artichoke, sweetbreads, and stuffed bread morsels (recipe 223).
Stew: squab delight (recipe 278).
Entremets: potato flour soufflé (recipe 705), or Roman-style dumplings (recipe 231).
Roast: lamb and green salad.
Dessert: Portuguese-style milk (recipe 693), flat cake Livorno style (recipe 598).

PENTECOST

Soup: semolina soup (recipe 16), or puréed meat soup (recipe 19).
Boiled course: fattened pullet with asparagus in white sauce (recipe 124).
Stew: milk-fed veal (recipe 325) with zucchini with meat filling (recipe 377), or stew in a shell (recipe 350).
Entremets: green-bean mold (recipe 386).
Roast: quail (recipe 536) with mayonnaise salad (recipe 251).
Dessert: English trifle Italian style (recipe 675), mixed fruit ice cream (recipe 772).

UNIFICATION DAY[152]

Soup: passatelli noodles made with semolina (recipe 48).
Fried dish: golden chicken (recipes 205 or 206) with little rice "pears" (recipe 202).
Stew: squab timbale (recipe 279).
Vegetables: green beans in béchamel sauce (recipe 381).
Roast: milk-fed veal (recipe 524) with potatoes and green salad.
Dessert: Marengo cake (recipe 581), red currant ice (recipe 764).

---

152 On May 5, 1861, i.e., soon after the unification of Italy under the rule of the House of Savoy, the first Sunday in June of each year was declared to be a national holiday to commemorate the unification of the country and the establishment of the kingdom.

15TH OF AUGUST[153]

Soup: quail in rice (recipe 44), or semolina soup (recipe 16).
Fried dish: tube pastries (recipe 183); Roman-style fry (recipe 176).
Stew: beef à la mode (recipe 297) with zucchini pie (recipe 445).
Entremets: chicken in tuna sauce (recipe 365).
Roast: young cockerels and green salad.
Dessert: babà (recipe 565), or Neapolitan cake (recipe 586), tea
   spumone (recipe 771), or chocolate ice cream (recipe 761).

8TH OF SEPTEMBER[154]

Soup: rice Milanese style III (recipe 80).
Fried dish: sole, flying squid, mushrooms.
Stew: milk-fed veal fricassée (recipe 256).
Entremets: canapés with capers (recipe 108), or potato flour soufflé
   (recipe 705).
Roast: leg of mutton (recipe 530).
Dessert: cake with pine nuts (recipe 582), cake served with zabaione
   (recipe 683), or chocolate pudding (recipe 667) covered with
   whipped cream.

CHRISTMAS

Soup: cappelletti Romagna style (recipe 7).
Appetizers: chicken-liver canapés (recipe 110).
Boiled meat: capon with green rice mold as a side dish (recipe 245).
Cold dish: hare pie (recipe 372).
Roast: Guinea hen (recipe 546) and birds.
Dessert: panforte from Siena, "certosino" bread from Bologna,
   toasted almond ice cream (recipe 759).

153 August 15 is the feast of the Assumption of the Virgin Mary.
154 This holiday celebrates the birth of the Virgin Mary.

LUNCHEONS

Someone asked me what principles should be kept in mind when pre-paring a midday meal. If the lunch is a simple affair, as is usually the case when you eat at an inn or a café, the answer is easily given.

The main course is always a hot meat dish (a generous portion) accompanied by a side dish. But you must start with a first course or an appetizer. If you serve a first course, you have all the rice and pasta recipes to choose from. As an appetizer, on the other hand, you can serve omelettes, eggs in butter, poached eggs with some tangy sauce, as well as cold dishes with aspic. Cured meats, caviar and Nantes sar-dines, served with butter, are also appropriate, as is fried fish.

The last course should be fruits and cheeses. If you serve fruit pre-serves or gelatins, you will especially please the ladies. And finally, good coffee, which prepares the stomach for the coming evening's dinner.

LIST OF RECIPES

INDEX I
NAMES OF DISHES IN ITALIAN

INDEX II
NAMES OF DISHES IN ENGLISH

INDEX I – NAMES OF DISHES IN ITALIAN

INDEX II – NAMES OF DISHES IN ENGLISH